THE COMPLETE ESSAYS OF MARK TWAIN

Books by Charles Neider

FICTION

THE LEFT EYE CRIES FIRST
OVERFLIGHT
A VISIT TO YAZOO
MOZART AND THE ARCHBOOBY
NAKED EYE
THE AUTHENTIC DEATH OF HENDRY JONES
THE WHITE CITADEL

NONFICTION

BEYOND CAPE HORN: TRAVELS IN THE ANTARCTIC
EDGE OF THE WORLD: ROSS ISLAND, ANTARCTICA
SUSY: A CHILDHOOD
MARK TWAIN
THE FROZEN SEA: A STUDY OF FRANZ KAFKA

Some Books Edited by Charles Neider

THE COMPLETE TALES OF WASHINGTON IRVING
THE COMPLETE SHORT STORIES OF ROBERT LOUIS STEVENSON
THE COMPLETE HUMOROUS SKETCHES AND TALES OF MARK TWAIN
THE AUTOBIOGRAPHY OF MARK TWAIN
THE COMPLETE SHORT STORIES OF MARK TWAIN
SHORT NOVELS OF THE MASTERS
GREAT SHORT STORIES FROM THE WORLD'S LITERATURE
THE GREAT WEST: A TREASURY OF FIRSTHAND ACCOUNTS
THE COMPLETE ESSAYS OF MARK TWAIN
GEORGE WASHINGTON: A BIOGRAPHY BY WASHINGTON IRVING
MAN AGAINST NATURE: TALES OF ADVENTURE AND EXPLORATION

The Complete Essays
of
Mark Twain

Edited and with an introduction by

Charles Neider

Drawings by Mark Twain

DA CAPO PRESS

Is Shakespeare Dead? © 1909 by The Mark Twain Co.; *Mark Twain's Speeches*, 1910 edition © 1910 by Harper & Brothers; *Mark Twain's Speeches*, 1923 edition © 1923 by The Mark Twain Co.; *What Is Man?* © 1917 by The Mark Twain Co.; *Europe and Elsewhere* © 1923 by The Mark Twain Co.; "Marjorie Fleming, the Wonder Child" © 1909 by Harper & Brothers; "The New Planet" © 1909 by Harper & Brothers; "The Death of Jean" © 1910 by Harper & Brothers; "How to Make History Dates Stick" © 1914 by Harper & Brothers; "A Scrap of Curious History" © 1914 by Harper & Brothers; "Letter from the Recording Angel" © 1946 by The Mark Twain Co.

Cataloging in Publication data is available from the Library of Congress.

ISBN 0-306-80957-5

First Da Capo Press Edition 2000

Published by Da Capo Press
A Member of the Perseus Books Group
http://www.dacapopress.com

1 2 3 4 5 6 7 8 9 10——04 03 02 01 00

TO MY OLD FRIEND
CARL FAITH

CONTENTS

Editor's Note

The present volume contains sixty-eight essays. With two exceptions the text is that of the Stormfield Edition of Mark Twain's works, published in 1929 by Harper & Brothers in thirty-seven volumes. The exceptions are "Letter from the Recording Angel," which was first published in 1946, and "The Sandwich Islands," the text of which is from the *New York Tribune* of 1873 (this essay was not included in the Stormfield Edition). I have also included nine speeches which possess the characteristic style of Clemens's essays. Mark Twain usually wrote his speeches out with care, memorized them and then delivered them with conscious art, shrewdly giving the effect of casualness. Many of his speeches look and read like speeches. That is, they wind about, are padded and too often strive to be "cute"; also in their countless and improvised personal allusions they retain a good deal of the flavor of the banquet hall or dining club. Such speeches have no place in the present volume but the nine speeches do, for they are really orally delivered essays.

This volume contains all of Mark Twain's essays to be found in his collected works. Clemens was never a purist in the matter of genre and sometimes a work of his can be classified under more than one heading. Thus I included "Fenimore Cooper's Literary Offenses" in my volume of sketches and am not reprinting it here. In dealing with Mark Twain's works certain decisions seem inevitably personal and arbitrary and one tries to make one's peace with this fact. I have not attempted to include here those essays which remained uncollected in Mark Twain's lifetime or in that of his chief literary executor, Albert Bigelow Paine, having recently (1961) issued a large volume, *Life As I Find It*, which gathered such essays together. Examples are "The Curious Republic of Gondour" and "King Leopold's Soliloquy."

The contents of the present volume, like those of its two predecessors, are arranged chronologically according to the years of first publication, and alphabetically within a given year whenever more than one item was published in that year. A much better chronological arrangement would be according to the years of composition, but unfortunately these are often unknown. In some instances, luckily, the date of first publication followed hard upon the date of composition. The present volume, however, contains many items which first saw publication posthumously, in such books as *What Is Man?* (1917) and *Europe and Elsewhere* (1923). The chronological arrangement of these items is therefore a purely formal matter.

C.N.

Introduction
by
CHARLES NEIDER

Mark Twain's characteristics as an essayist may perhaps best be gauged by comparing him with other essayists, particularly with those who did not make their reputations chiefly as essayists but who rather wrote essays as part of a broader, motley career. These I think of as amateur essayists. Clemens was certainly an amateur in the essay form, in the best sense of the word, as he was also an amateur in almost every other literary form he used, with the exception of humor. Like the great pendulum in San Francisco, which visually proves that the earth rotates (and confounds one's attempts to understand it), his genius, pervading his essays, tries to prove that it is human, while often crippling one's hopes of comprehending it.

Humor, like quicksilver, is elusive. It is like the snaky tumble-polished agate shedding its skin with the light's every refraction. It is an Apache tear, now transparent, now opaque, now almost black, now an emerging, lighthearted tea color. It seems to reside in the very center of the human drama and perhaps for this reason to surpass our understanding. How rare the best kind is, which Clemens was apparently inexhaustible in, may be seen in a survey of modern world literature. His humor performs the subtlest of functions; it humanizes. It leavens; it anoints; it lulls dissension; through the sound of our common laughter it hints to us of our origin and destiny, our brotherhood, our vale of tears.

Many years ago I edited a college textbook called *Essays of the Masters*. It did not focus on the history or the development or the "form" of the essay and didn't concentrate on the professional essayists at all—and by "professional" I mean those writers like Lamb and de Quincey and, in modern times, Mencken and E. B. White, who find their best and fullest expression in the essay medium. What it did instead was to show how the large creative minds, which produced the novels, plays, and poems of the past century and a half, put the essay to their use. Professional essayists commonly project their personalities directly onto paper. The flavor of their personalities is an important stock of their trade. Whereas in their major works the writers of my textbook generally project their personalities in disguised forms. For example, Clemens projected his through the voice and character of Huck Finn. You are left to make out what you can about the authors when you read novels like *The Magic Mountain* or *The Counterfeiters* or *The Castle*, and although in the long run the impression of personality is overwhelming, still it is tantalizingly indirect. Curiosity being what it is, we want a more direct view and a more intimate sampling. The hope to satisfy this desire was one of the chief inspirations for the making of the textbook. Leafing through the book helps me to differentiate Mark Twain's qualities as an essayist.

Here is Henry James on Turgenev, displaying a cultivated mind and sensibility, with subtlety of insight and phrase, beauty and rightness of tone, and sound personal and literary judgments. There is no humor and only a little wit, but the sparkle of good will, good mind, and enthusiasm is very winning. Here is Somerset Maugham in *A Summing Up*, a piece dry, shrewd, intelligent, frank, written with precision and without flourish or humor; the interest is in the sharpness of insight and language. Here is Tolstoy's "On Art," without humor, didactic, stubborn, dogmatic. A little humor could lighten the discussion, endow it with perspective, relieve it of its close air, make it more palatable. But this is Tolstoy in his later phase, and humor would probably seem frivolous to him. Mark Twain also had a later and dogmatic period but it was not without humor except in the avowedly didactic pieces like "What Is Man?"

Here is Thomas Hardy with "The Profitable Reading of Fiction," sometimes dull, prosaic, sometimes heavily hifalutin, as when he writes "efficacious for renovation" when he means "beneficial." He could have learned something from Clemens. Here is Shaw's witty, persuasive, expansive, brilliant review of Chesterton's book on Shaw. Here is Dickens on "New York," with an exuberant piece of observation, full of dry humor or a tone just suggestive of humor, and full of vitality and felicity, colorful, pungent, manly, greatly gifted, and greatly sustained. And here is Heine's "London and the English," an energetic essay, its independence and perception, its clarity of mind and lively fancy evidencing a great spirit and sounding quite modern.

Which reminds one that Mark Twain's language dates so much less than that of most of his English and American contemporaries. He is so vital in his idiom. His texture, however, seems rather coarse when compared with Shaw's or Hawthorne's or James's. This is at least partly due to his colloquial tone, the very thing which makes his language live. Many of his essays sound like dictated utterances.

Clemens as an essayist? A man of strong opinions. Self-educated and surprisingly well-read, especially in history. His journalistic apprenticeship often shows in his work. Bold, direct, impatient, restless. A traveler who claims to loathe travel, yet who endures a great deal of it and gives the impression of enjoying it. Like James fascinated by the innocent and ignorant American among the tradition-encrusted Europeans. An optimist by physiology and a pessimist by sustained observation of "the damned human race." Like Voltaire, a self-appointed correction officer for the species. (Some of Voltaire's *Philosophical Dictionary* sounds as if it had been written by Mark Twain, especially the section on "fatalism": determinism or a variant of it.)

A haloed clown. A dogmatic, saddened, weary tragedian. A night-watch man patrolling with his torch the dark streets of sham, cant, and oppression. A bloodhound sniffing out injustice. A Bessemer oven blasting at it. A knight-errant cantering to the aid of unfranchised holocausting damsels in distress. A lynx-eyed observer of his own foibles, also of the foibles of the race. A competent journalist who like every professional enjoys the exercise of his skill. An amateur literary man in every sense, including love of the vocation. A dogged researcher into the Case of Adam and Eve. A stout defender of Satan on the ground that Satan is the original underdog. ("I have no special regard for Satan; but I can at least claim that I have no prejudice against him. It may even be that I lean a little his way, on account of his not having a fair show. All religions issue bibles against him, and say the most injurious things about him, but we never hear his side.")

The man with the unruly mop and the assassin's drawl telling the nations how to behave. The printer's devil from Hannibal sounding off to the globe and, like Ambrose Bierce, finding it, in the end, mostly rotten, inherited as it is by man. No ivory tower man, occasionally no humor-for-humor's-sake man. At times a deliberate censor of his work, withholding it from public view through paying too much homage to the power of public opinion. Sometimes, extending himself beyond the sphere of his competence, as in the Shakespeare essay: very human, which is to say very foolish.

A man of moods and whims. He detests the French, derides the Italians, adores the English, and covertly respects the Germans and the Austrians while overtly ridiculing their language and certain of their institutions, such as student dueling. He deplores dueling yet uses sarcasm on the French because they don't duel bloodily enough, not as bloodily as the Austrians. A republican, he waxes warm through contact with the English nobility and the Viennese court, enough to neutralize some of the acid of his thought and prose and to set down statements, as in "The Memorable Assassination," which show his perspective to have blown away in the winds of monarchial excitement. In short he is masculine, personal, sarcastic, tender, and nostalgic. He is also sometimes funny.

So much for a long view. Close-ups show more interesting features. "Two Mark Twain Editorials," for example, is an early witness of both his strong and weak sides. The first editorial is wry, clever, in a sound vein. The second is bombastic, flowery, emotional, the big bass drum effect. It is a pulpit style, and all that is missing is the acknowledgment that the orator knew the deceased, a fact which for some reason Clemens is reticent about, perhaps because he considers it too personal for a newspaper. Yet his having known Burlingame and having been generously helped by him at a crucial moment in his career (see "My Debut as a Literary Person") have a bearing on the emotional style of the eulogy. That he is a beautifully descriptive writer, fertile and energetic, and essentially a noble writer despite his fondness for jokes, pranks, hoaxes, tall tales, and guffaws, is made clear by "Queen Victoria's Jubilee." In "War Prayer" he speaks with the mind and tongue of one of the old prophets, only he includes himself among the sinners and has compassion for them. The essays which I like best are those that are outrageously funny, like "Letters to Satan," and those that are outraged—by politics, human stupidity, human cruelty, vested interest.

For deep thinking in an orderly, intellectual way I don't go to Twain, nor for closely reasoned textual or biographical analysis in the way of James or Thomas Mann. As for intellectual consistency, Clemens is often without it. There are passages in "Saint Joan of Arc" which can be used to confute the chief arguments in "What Is Man?"—that influence is merely external, that there is no free choice, that motives boil down to selfishness. Even an early and minor piece, "Disgraceful Persecution of a Boy," illuminates him clearly, showing how ferocious, deadly, inspired his sarcasms can be, and evidencing the fertility of his mind, his humanitarianism, and his extraordinary tendency to identify with all kinds of people.

I have been flitting about in an effort to call his full figure to mind, not merely the image of a man writing at a desk but of one who like Dickens went out and met his large public and enthralled them. His public did not simply read him, they saw him and they felt they knew him as a friend. In few instances in modern literature has there been so little "distance" between an author and his audience. This fact profoundly influenced his writing. If one wishes to read the essays as his contemporaries read them one ought to keep in mind the vitality of his public image. He was an extraordinary figure, impressive not only to his countrymen but to many people abroad, and not only as a novelist and sage but as a platform figure as well. The following contemporary account (signed "R.C.B.," it appeared in *The Critic* of April 25, 1896) affords a striking view of him on the Australian lecture circuit that time when he was circling the globe in a determined and finally successful effort to pay off his debts. It is well worth reviving here.

As a lecturer—or rather, story-teller, for the author objects to being called a lecturer—Mark Twain is, and has proved himself to be, in his opening Australian "At Homes," a decided success. Like Charles Dickens, he relies entirely on his old books for the pabulum of his discourses, but, unlike the author of Pickwick, he does not read long extracts from the books. He takes some of his best stories—"The Jumping Frog," *Huck Finn*, the difficulties of the German language, *par exemple*—and re-tells them, with many subtle additions of humor and some fresh observations, in the most irresistibly amusing manner. He is in no sense a disappointment as a humorist. He starts his audience laughing in the very first sentence he utters, and for two hours keeps them in a continual roar. The only serious moments occur when, with the unutterable pathos of which the true humorist alone is capable, he interpolates a few pathetic touches which almost make the tears mingle with the smiles. Every story he tells serves the purpose of illustrating a moral, and, although, for the most part, he talks in low, slow, conversational tones, at times he rises to real bursts of eloquence— not the polished, grandiloquent eloquence of the average American speaker, but the eloquence conveyed in simple words and phrases, and prompted by some deep and sincerely felt sentiment. The author has the power of seeming to jest at his serious side, just as in his books; but there is no mistaking the seriousness with which, for example, he is moved by the remembrance of the iniquities perpetrated on liberty in the old slavery days amid which Huck Finn and Jim the slave lived. He makes the most unexpected anecdotes point the most unexpected morals, but it is the recital of the old, familiar stories without any moral attaching to them which pleases most, coming as they do warm from the brain of the man who invented them.

Mark Twain steals unobtrusively on to the platform, dressed in the regulation evening-clothes, with the trouser-pockets cut high up, into which he occasionally dives both hands. He bows with a quiet dignity to the roaring cheers which greet him at every "At Home." Then, with natural, unaffected gesture, and with scarcely any prelude, he gets under way with his first story. He is a picturesque figure on the stage. His long, shaggy, white hair surmounts a face full of intellectual fire. The eyes, arched with bushy brows, and which seemed to be closed most of the time while he is speaking, flash out now and then from their deep sockets with a genial, kindly, pathetic look, and the face is deeply drawn with the furrows accumulated during an existence of sixty years. He talks in short sentences, with a peculiar smack of the lips at the end of each. His language is just that of his books, full of the quaintest Americanisms, and showing an utter disregard for the polished diction of most lecturers. "It was not" is always "'twarn't" with Mark Twain, and "mighty fine" and "my kingdom" and "they done it" and "catched," and various other purely trans-atlantic words and phrases, crop up profusely during his talk. He speaks slowly, lazily, and wearily, as a man dropping off to sleep, rarely raising his voice above a conversational tone; but it has that characteristic nasal sound which penetrates to the back of the largest building. His figure is rather slight, not above middle height, and the whole man suggests an utter lack of physical energy. As a matter of fact, Mark Twain detests exercise, and the attraction must be very strong to induce him to go very far out of doors. With the exception of an occasional curious trot, as when recounting his buck-jumping experiences, Mark Twain stands perfectly still in one place during the whole of the time he is talking to the audience. He rarely moves his arms, unless it is to adjust his spectacles or to show by action how a certain thing was done. His characteristic attitude is to stand quite still, with the right arm across the abdomen and the left resting on it and supporting his chin. In this way he talks on for nearly two hours; and, while the audience is laughing uproariously, he never by any chance relapses into a smile. To have read Mark Twain is a delight, but to have seen and heard him is a joy not readily to be forgotten.

"The Sandwich Islands" letters appeared in the New York *Tribune* of January 6 and 9, 1873. They were dated January 3 and 6 from Hartford and were occasioned by the death of King Kamehameha, with the consequent renewed interest in the fate of the islands, which were subsequently renamed the Hawaiian Islands. I located the letters by a fluke, after several vain attempts. Knowing from experience the unreliability of Twain's bibliographer, Merle Johnson, I had about assumed he was again in error regarding dates and perhaps even the name of the newspaper. There was no sign of the letters in the two issues of the *Tribune* which he listed as source. Then one day, while working at the New-York Historical Society, I requested the issues again, and to my surprise received a bound volume I had not seen before. It was a variant edition of the run of those two days and contained the letters. Johnson had probably seen scrapbook copies of them. The letters were shortly afterward reprinted in an edition of the weekly *Tribune,* from the same type, and in 1920, according to Johnson, were included in *The Sandwich Islands,* a volume of thirty-nine pages, the edition being "strictly limited to thirty copies." I suffered remorse for having murdered Johnson several times in my daydreams.

"A Memorable Midnight Experience" is part of an aborted book on the English people and their institutions. Clemens sailed alone for England in August 1872 with the intention of collecting material for the book. The warm welcome he received, together with a good deal of socializing, ended note-taking for the project, and the project was abandoned. The idea had been to strike a satirical or at least an ironic note but Clemens was disinclined to sustain the attempt. The essay was written in 1872 and first appeared in *Sketches, No. 1* in 1874. Vivid, it is permeated by his love affair with the romantic past, which was later to find fictional expression in such works as *Huckleberry Finn, A Connecticut Yankee,* and *Joan of Arc.* He writes: "It was a derisive reminder that we were a part of this present sordid, plodding, commonplace time, and not august relics of a bygone age. . . ."

Clemens abandoned another projected book in 1891. In the spring of that year he closed his manorial Hartford house and went with this family to Europe in the hope of finding a quieter and less expensive life. He was suffering from rheumatism of his right arm, the Paige typesetter bubble was threatening to burst, and his publishing company was in serious financial trouble. Not long afterward he announced to his business manager that he intended to write another travel book and would take a year or two to collect materials for it. He had agreed to write six letters for the New York *Sun,* which he proceeded to do. One, "Playing Courier," which was the third in the series, I included among his complete short stories, for it is far and away too fanciful to be considered nonfiction. The five, in the order of their appearance in the *Sun*, are "Aix, the Paradise of the Rheumatics," "At the Shrine of St. Wagner," "Marienbad, a Health Factory," "Switzerland, the Cradle of Liberty," and "The German Chicago." The first letter appeared in the *Sun* of November 8, 1891, and the last in the issue of April 3, 1892. The letters also appeared in the *Illustrated London News*, sometimes with minor variations in the text.

Clemens at first believed that the six letters could make a small book, then thought better of the idea and embarked on a trip down the Rhone, minus the family, in the hope of turning the journey into literature and thus filling out the desired book. The Rhone journey was made in September. It resulted in "Down the Rhone," which was published posthumously. Clemens filled 174 pages of notes before the pleasure of the trip made note-taking seem beside the point. Small wonder—he had spent three months in travel and sightseeing, and what with the worrisome matters occurring back home in the States, he had every justification for dreaming, smoking, forgetting. Besides, the journey lacked incidents and colorful characters. For an experienced journalist there was not enough copy. After ten days of it Clemens rejoined his family.

Clemens was a masterful writer of travel pieces—vivid, precise, breathing his curiosity, vitality, play, and opinions into many of the places and people he encountered. He had a wonderful copiousness of thought and language and was one of the most natural writers we have had. His "voice" was always his own, easily, gracefully reflecting ideas and feelings. He was also an uneven writer. The "Aix" piece is well controlled but the "Marienbad" one wanders—there is a good deal of landscape, a few anecdotes, a Goethe poem, and little of the feeling of the health resort. Still, the letters as a group are excellent, and very fresh from a tired man of fifty-six, who often sounds as enthusiastic and as playful as in those halcyon days of *Innocents Abroad*. The "Switzerland" essay witnesses his continuing delight in portraying his countryman in Europe as a thick-head, a democratic shover of men, atwitter with the aspects of life. "The Cholera Epidemic in Hamburg," written in 1892, according to A. B. Paine, Clemens's biographer, for some reason was not published during the author's lifetime.

One of Clemens's favorite roles is that of Mark the Dragon-Killer. In the Harriet Shelley episode the unfortunate dragon is Edward Dowden, Irish Shakespeare scholar, also the official biographer of Shelley under the patronage of Lady Shelley, Mary Godwin's daughter-in-law and detractor and suppressor of Harriet. Louise Schutz Boas, author of *Harriet Shelley* (1962), asserts that Dowden's Victorian mortality

compelled him to disparage Harriet in order to make a purer portrait
of Shelley. She also states, "The letters between these two gentlemen
[Dowden and Richard Garnett, Lady Shelley's coadjutor] trying to be
gentlemanly in their denigration of Harriet make an amusing study
in self-justification, Victorian smugness, and determined prejudice."
Clemens read the Dowden biography, concluded that it was a character assassination of Harriet, and proceeded, in three issues of the
North American Review of 1894, to assassinate Dowden in every possible department—style, logic, innuendo, guesswork, evidence, scholar-
ship, decency, sanity: the whole spectrum of the Dragon's armor.

He had the will, the motive, and the genius to make an astounding
performance of it. Clemens was rarely in danger of verbal constipation,
but now his literary sluices were wide open. Not, however, at the
expense of organization, logic, or cool-headedness. He did not stammer
or go blind with rage or slam into dead ends. Instead, he proceeded
with forensic skill and the passion of a knight-errant. The flow of
energy, the tenaciousness of mind, the untiring stream of language are
amazing. He is writing about people long dead, yet he is as excited
and angered as if Bysshe and Harriet are still alive, or as if Harriet is
a dead relative, or perhaps a girl he once loved. Fortifying his anger
is his Victorian idealization of woman, family, and the home. Bysshe
had promised to be a husband to Harriet and had turned out to be
something of a rake, at least in Twain's view. Therefore he is a scoundrel. Clemens is too worked up to stop to consider Shelley's views on
marriage and to attempt to see the institution with the poet's eyes.
Having stern notions of his own, he is not averse to roundly condemning
the young poet for failing to live up to them. Clemens was no ethical
relativist. He was deadly on the subject of the French because of their
different approach to the world of sex. One wonders what Dowden's
reaction was to this shower of brimstone.

Another Dragon was Paul Bourget, French man of letters. Bourget's
mistake was that he published *Outre-Mer*, a critical journal of his visit
to the United States in 1893. As Paine has well said, "Clemens could
criticize his own nation freely enough, but he could hardly be patient
under the strictures of a Frenchman, especially upon American women."
Once again there is hell to pay. This moralizing humorist, who early
was known as "the moralist of the Main," is sometimes a cramped
American moralist, a Protestant, even a Presbyterian, moralist, and
nothing gives him more refined pleasure than taking digs at the French.

A countryman of Bourget's, Max O'Rell (nom de plume of Paul
Blouet), offered a clumsy defense of Bourget in the pages of the

North American Review, in which the attack had occurred. Whereupon Clemens belabored O'Rell with a shillelagh. Clemens's rejoinder is not successful. It is coy and unclear in its pretense that O'Rell's reply is by Bourget, and this device guts much of its strength.

"Concerning the Jews" was first published in *Harper's Magazine* in September 1899. Clemens wrote to his friend H. H. Rogers, the financier, "The Jew article is my 'gem of the ocean.' I have taken a world of pleasure in writing it & doctoring it & fussing at it. Neither Jew nor Christian will approve of it, but people who are neither Jews nor Christians will, for they are in a condition to know the truth when they see it." Clemens was a great admirer of the Jews. He once wrote to his friend and pastor, Joseph Twichell, "The difference between the brain of the average Christian and that of the average Jew—certainly in Europe—is about the difference between a tadpole's and an archbishop's. It is a marvelous race; by long odds the most marvelous race the world has produced, I suppose."

The essay elicited an interesting reply from M. S. Levy, a rabbi, which appeared in the *Overland Monthly*. Responding to Twain's statement, "In the United States he [the Jew] was created free in the beginning—he did not need to help, of course," which implied that the Jew in America did not help in the struggle against England, Levy listed names of Jews who had fought in the war. He also mentioned those who had given large sums to the cause, among them Haym Salomon ($300,000, "an immense fortune for those days") and Manuel Mordecai Noah (£20,000). He went on to cite Jewish patriots of the Civil War. Mark Twain wrote in his essay, "The Jew is a money-getter," and spoke of "all his fat wealth." To which Levy retorted, "Money-getters? The Vanderbilts, the Goulds, Astors, Havemeyers, Rockefellers, Mackays, Huntington, Armours, Carnegies, Sloanes, Whitneys, are not Jews, and yet they control and possess more than twenty-five per cent of all the circulated wealth of the United States. They seem to be all right as 'money-getters,' and little have they done for humanity. Baron de Hirsh was a 'money-getter,' and 'fat in wealth,' but he gave his millions to suffering human kind irrespective of creed. Nathan Strauss, of New York, saved infant mortality by twenty-five per cent by his sterilized milk societies. Baroness de Hirsh, a Jewess, gives fifty millions to charity in her lifetime." Possibly Clemens added the postscript to his essay partly as a result of the Levy reply. The statistics of the postscript, however, are not taken from the Levy article.

"What Is Man?" is the ultimate, the perfect, expression of the least attractive side of Mark Twain—his dreary penchant for determinism, which he seized upon with the fanaticism of one who believes he has at last found the light. How is it that this noteworthy product of the freetrading, freewheeling Mississippi and the western frontier took to his mind with such ardor a system of thought which denies the possibility of individual choice, which asserts that all is predestined, that man is a machine, and that we are all slaves of the great chain of circumstance? To these views Clemens added others—that God is indifferent to man's fate if not hostile to it; that man is the butt of nature's practical joke; that his fate is to be born of woman and to suffer evil, sin, and disease until a blessed death releases him from bondage—and he fictionalized all of them with great skill in "The Mysterious Stranger," a long short story. In the present essay, however, as also in "The Turning-point of My Life," he tries to sledgehammer them into the reader's head.

The best thing about this side of Twain is that he himself had serious doubts about it underneath the burning faith, which is why he couldn't speak suavely, cooly, gracefully, and humorously on the subject. His style is strident with italics, his language dull when he touches upon this awful wisdom, this fixed idea. Fortunately, there is a distinction to be made between his preachment and his practice. He condemned the Italian anarchist who assassinated the Empress of Austria, yet did not excuse the crime on the ground that its perpetrator had no choice but to commit it. It is interesting to speculate how he would have reacted to twentieth-century science, in which the principle of indeterminacy of quantum physics has lent support to the doctrine of free will the opposite of his favorite doctrine.

Another quixotic aspect of Clemens is his belief in the Baconian authorship of the Shakespeare works. As strict argument, "Is Shakespeare Dead?" is often difficult to take seriously, it wanders so from the point, with its claimants, recollections of Ealer and the river, its remarks on Satan, and so on. Its main "evidence" is the statements by the several lawyers on the legal knowledge in the plays. It is curious that Clemens doesn't see that all the arguments in favor of a great, systematic legal knowledge prove nothing about the so-called legal training of the author of the plays—that it is surmising of the very sort that he, Clemens, objects to. A skilled dialectician, using the kind of "evidence" that Clemens here finds acceptable, could no doubt prove that Clemens could not have written most of his books, having been too uneducated, too etcetera, to have done so. He could probably prove they were written by William Dean Howells, whose natural modesty prevented him from owning up to the authorship of so vast an array of works.

Clemens's seventieth-birthday speech is possibly the finest he ever made. It exemplifies an uncanny knack which in him was developed to the point of genius. A thing sounds absurdly exaggerated, then as an afterthought you see sound reality in it, and finally wisdom. His humor often seems to spring from a sense of the incongruity of life, of man's estate, and to rise from the depths as if certain that the bottom is a great joke, or a laugh, or a sarcasm. At other times it is the humor of the surface, inspired slapstick. One is aware in this speech of the breadth of his experience. He seemed to have a genius for partaking of the world and for being allowed to partake of it. Franz Kafka, the Jew, the alien, sensed his time in an altogether different way; he felt the moral discontinuity of it and had to flesh out his visions with fantastic, incoherent shapes. Clemens, like Tolstoy and Balzac, had the breadth of popular experience to rely on.

"The Memorable Assassination" has as its subject Amelie Eugenie Elizabeth, consort of Francis Joseph, emperor of Austria and king of Hungary. She was stabbed in Geneva on September 10, 1898, and died within a few hours. Mark Twain was living near Vienna when he received the news from Countess Wydenbouck-Esterhazy. He went to the capital and watched the funeral ceremonies from the new Krantz Hotel, which faced the Capuchin church where the royal dead lay buried. He sent the essay to H. H. Rogers to offer to the magazines, then recalled it for reasons not clear. It was not published until posthumously. It is not one of his perceptive pieces. Some of it is excited chatter, making him seem like a court-dazzled American. The stir of the moment and of his surroundings have engulfed his better judgment. He writes about the funeral crowd being dispersed by soldiers: "It was all so swift, noiseless, exact—like a beautifully ordered machine." Yes, and deadly when one thinks of the repressions of the Empire. Kafka could have enlightened Clemens, although he was only fifteen at the time. Clemens relates the rumor that the assassin may have been prompted by "the criminal militarism which is impoverishing Europe and driving the starving poor mad" (a militarism which was to find fruit in the First World War), yet fails to see the irony of the square's being filled exclusively by the military. Clemens writes, "Dull clothes would have marred the radiant spectacle." Would they? Ought there to be a radiant spectacle at a time of national mourning? Or a spectacle of men at arms? The spectacle was pure barbarism, a pluming of males on the occasion of the killing of a woman. Clemens misses much, although he is cool enough to use field glasses the better to collect material. Perhaps he saw the essay's shortcomings afterward and for this reason didn't publish it.

Long ago my daughter Susy, four and a half, a blonde with explosive brown eyes, hearing I was going to the library, asked, "Are you going to meet Mark Twain?"

"Well, not exactly."

"Is he nice?"

"Very."

"Why does he have a mustache?"

"To warm his nose."

"Really really?"

"No, he really has it to hide his upper lip."

"Why?"

"He likes his upper lip to be like a garden, with grass growing all over it and partly covering his mouth. That way everything's toasty."

"Are you and Mark Twain writing a book?"

"I'm writing a book."

"Why?"

"Because he's lazy."

"You mean he doesn't help?"

"Well . . . I guess he helps—a little."

Two Mark Twain Editorials[1]

I

"SALUTATORY"

Being a stranger, it would be immodest and unbecoming in me to suddenly and violently assume the associate editorship of the *Buffalo Express* without a single explanatory word of comfort or encouragement to the unoffending patrons of the paper, who are about to be exposed to constant attacks of my wisdom and learning. But this explanatory word shall be as brief as possible. I only wish to assure parties having a friendly interest in the prosperity of the journal, that I am not going to hurt the paper deliberately and intentionally at any time. I am not going to introduce any startling reforms, or in any way attempt to make trouble. I am simply going to do my plain, unpretending duty, when I cannot get out of it; I shall work diligently and honestly and faithfully at all times and upon all occasions, when privation and want shall compel me to do it; in writing, I shall always confine myself strictly to the truth, except when it is attended with inconvenience; I shall witheringly rebuke all forms of crime and misconduct, except when committed by the party inhabiting my own vest; I shall not make use of slang or vulgarity upon any occasion or under any circumstances, and shall never use profanity except in discussing house rent and taxes. Indeed, upon second thought, I will not even use it then, for it is unchristian, inelegant, and degrading—though to speak truly I do not see how house rent and taxes are going to be discussed worth a cent without it. I shall not often meddle with politics, because we have a political editor who is already excellent, and only needs to serve a term in the penitentiary in order to be perfect. I shall not write any poetry, unless I conceive a spite against the subscribers.

Such is my platform. I do not see any earthly use in it, but custom is law, and custom must be obeyed, no matter how much

---

[1] These first appeared in the *Buffalo Express* at a time when Clemens owned a third-interest in the paper. They were included by Paine in *Europe and Elsewhere* (1923).—C.N.

violence it may do to one's feelings. And this custom which I am slavishly following now is surely one of the least necessary that ever came into vogue. In private life a man does not go and trumpet his crime before he commits it, but your new editor is such an important personage that he feels called upon to write a "salutatory" at once, and he puts into it all that he knows, and all that he don't know, and some things he thinks he knows but isn't certain of and he parades his list of wonders which he is going to perform; of reforms which he is going to introduce, and public evils which he is going to exterminate; and public blessings which he is going to create; and public nuisances which he is going to abate. He spreads this all out with oppressive solemnity over a column and a half of large print, and feels that the country is saved. His satisfaction over it, something enormous. He then settles down to his miracles and inflicts profound platitudes and impenetrable wisdom upon a helpless public as long as they can stand it, and then they send him off consul to some savage island in the Pacific in the vague hope that the cannibals will like him well enough to eat him. And with an inhumanity which is but a fitting climax to his career of persecution, instead of packing his trunk at once he lingers to inflict upon his benefactors a "valedictory." If there is anything more uncalled for than a "salutatory," it is one of those tearful, blubbering, long-winded "valedictories"—wherein a man who has been annoying the public for ten years cannot take leave of them without sitting down to cry a column and a half. Still, it is the custom to write valedictories, and custom should be respected. In my secret heart I admire my predecessor for declining to print a valedictory, though in public I say and shall continue to say sternly, it is custom and he ought to have printed one. People never read them any more than they do the "salutatories," but nevertheless he ought to have honored the old fossil—he ought to have printed a valedictory. I said as much to him, and he replied:

"I have resigned my place—I have departed this life—I am journalistically dead, at present, ain't I?"

"Yes."

"Well, wouldn't you consider it disgraceful in a corpse to sit up and comment on the funeral?"

I record it here, and preserve it from oblivion, as the briefest and best "valedictory" that has yet come under my notice.

MARK TWAIN

P.S.—I am grateful for the kindly way in which the press of the land have taken notice of my irruption into regular journalistic life, telegraphically or editorially, and am happy in this place to express the feeling.

1869

II

A TRIBUTE TO ANSON BURLINGAME

On Wednesday, in St. Petersburg, Mr. Burlingame died after a short illness. It is not easy to comprehend, at an instant's warning, the exceeding magnitude of the loss which mankind sustains in this death—the loss which all nations and all peoples sustain in it. For he had outgrown the narrow citizenship of a state and become a citizen of the world; and his charity was large enough and his great heart warm enough to feel for all its races and to labor for them. He was a true man, a brave man, an earnest man, a liberal man, a just man, a generous man, in all his ways and by all his instincts a noble man; he was a man of education and culture, a finished conversationalist, a ready, able, and graceful speaker, a man of great brain, a broad and deep and weighty thinker. He was a great man—a very, very great man. He was imperially endowed by nature; he was faithfully befriended by circumstances, and he wrought gallantly always, in whatever station he found himself.

He was a large, handsome man, with such a face as children instinctively trust in, and homeless and friendless creatures appeal to without fear. He was courteous at all times and to all people, and he had the rare and winning faculty of being always *interested* in whatever a man had to say—a faculty which he possessed simply because nothing was trivial to him which any man or woman or child had at heart. When others said harsh things about even unconscionable and intrusive bores after they had retired from his presence, Mr. Burlingame often said a generous word in their favor, but never an unkind one.

A chivalrous generosity was his most marked characteristic—a large charity, a noble kindliness that could not comprehend narrowness or meanness. It is this that shows out in his fervent abolitionism, manifested at a time when it was neither very creditable nor very safe to hold such a creed; it was this that prompted him to hurl his famous Brooks-and-Sumner speech in the face of an astonished South at a time when all the North was smarting under the sneers and taunts and material aggressions of admired and applauded Southerners. It was this that made him so warmly espouse the cause of Italian liberty—an espousal so pointed and so vigorous as to attract the attention of Austria, which empire afterward declined to receive him when he was appointed Austrian envoy by Mr. Lincoln. It was this trait which prompted him to punish Americans in China when they imposed upon the Chinese. It was this trait which moved him, in framing treaties, to frame them in the broad interest of the world, instead of selfishly seeking to acquire advantages for his own country alone and at the expense of the other party to the treaty, as had always before been the recognized "diplomacy." It was this trait which was and is the soul of the crowning achievements of his career, the treaties with America and England in behalf of China. In every labor of this man's life there was present a good and noble motive; and in nothing that he ever did or said was there anything small or base. In real greatness, ability, grandeur of character, and achievement, he stood head and shoulders above all the Americans of to-day, save one or two.

Without any noise, or any show, or any flourish, Mr. Burlingame did a score of things of shining mark during his official residence in China. They were hardly heard of away here in America. When he first went to China, he found that with all their kingly powers, American envoys were still not of much consequence in the eyes of their countrymen of either civil or official position. But he was a man who was always "posted." He knew all about the state of things he would find in China before he sailed from America. And so he took care to demand and receive additional powers before he turned his back upon Washington. When the customary consular irregularities placidly continued and he notified those officials that such irregularities must instantly cease, and they inquired with insolent flippancy what the consequence might be in case they did not cease, he answered blandly that he would *dismiss* them, from the highest to the lowest! (He had quietly come armed with absolute authority over their official lives.) The consular irregularities ceased. A far healthier condition of American commercial interests ensued there.

To punish a foreigner in China was an unheard-of thing. There was no way of accomplishing it. Each Embassy had its own private district or grounds, forced from the imperial government, and into that sacred district Chinese law officers could not intrude. All foreigners guilty of offenses against Chinamen were tried by their own countrymen, in these holy places, and as no Chinese testimony was admitted, the culprit almost always went free. One of the very first things Mr. Burlingame did was to make a Chinaman's oath as good as a foreigner's; and in his ministerial court, through Chinese and American testimony combined, he very shortly convicted a noted American ruffian of murdering a Chinaman. And now a community accustomed to light sentences were naturally startled when, under Mr. Burlingame's hand, and bearing the broad seal of the American Embassy, came an order to take him out and hang him!

Mr. Burlingame broke up the "extra-territorial" privileges (as they were called), as far as our country was concerned, and made justice as free to all and as untrammeled in the metes and bounds of its jurisdiction, in China, as ever it was in any land.

Mr. Burlingame was the leading spirit in the co-operative policy. He got the Imperial College established. He procured permission for an American to open the coal mines of China. Through his efforts China was the first country to close her ports against the war vessels of the Southern Confederacy; and Prince Kung's order, in this matter, was singularly energetic, comprehensive, and in earnest. The ports were closed then, and never opened to a Southern warship afterward.

Mr. Burlingame "construed" the treaties existing between China and the other nations. For many years the ablest diplomatists had vainly tried to come to a satisfactory understanding of certain obscure clauses of these treaties, and more than once powder had been burned in consequences of failure to come to such understandings. But the clear and comprehensive intellect of the American envoy reduced the wordy tangle of diplomatic phrases to a plain and honest handful of paragraphs, and these were unanimously and thankfully accepted by the other foreign envoys, and officially declared by them to be a thorough and satisfactory elucidation of all the uncertain clauses in the treaties.

Mr. Burlingame did a mighty work, and made official intercourse with China lucid, simple, and systematic, thenceforth for all time, when he persuaded that government to adopt and accept the code of international law by which the civilized nations of the earth are guided and controlled.

It is not possible to specify all the acts by which Mr. Burlingame made himself largely useful to the world during his official residence in China. At least it would not be possible to do it without making this sketch too lengthy and pretentious for a newspaper article.

Mr. Burlingame's short history—for he was only forty-seven—reads like a fairy tale. Its successes, its surprises, its happy situations, occur all along, and each new episode is always an improvement upon the one which went before it.

He begins life an assistant in a surveying party away out on the Western frontier; then enters a branch of a Western college; then passes through Harvard with the honors; becomes a Boston lawyer and looks back complacently from his high perch upon the old days when he was a surveyor nobody in the woods; becomes a state senator, and makes laws; still advancing, goes to the Constitutional Convention and makes regulations wherewith to rule the makers of laws; enters Congress and smiles back upon the Legislature and the Boston lawyer, and from these smiles still back upon the country surveyor, recognizes that he is known to fame in Massachusetts; challenges Brooks and is known to the nation; next, with a long stride upward, he is clothed with ministerial dignity and journeys to the under side of the world to represent the youngest in the court of the oldest of the nations; and finally, after years go by, we see him moving serenely among the crowned heads of the Old World, a magnate with secretaries and undersecretaries about him, a retinue of quaint, outlandish Orientals in his wake, and a long following of servants—and the world is aware that his salary is unbelievably enormous, not to say imperial, and likewise knows that he is invested with power to make treaties with all the chief nations of the earth, and that he bears the stately title of Ambassador, and in his person represents the mysterious and awful grandeur of that vague colossus, the Emperor of China, his mighty empire and his four hundred millions of subjects! Down what a dreamy vista his backward glance must stretch, now, to reach the insignificant surveyor in the Western woods!

He was a good man, and a very, very great man. America lost a son, and all the world a servant, when he died.

1870

Disgraceful Persecution of a Boy[1]

In San Francisco, the other day, "A well-dressed boy, on his way to Sunday-school, was arrested and thrown into the city prison for stoning Chinamen."

What a commentary is this upon human justice! What sad prominence it gives to our human disposition to tyrannize over the weak! San Francisco has little right to take credit to herself for her treatment of this poor boy. What had the child's education been? How should he suppose it was wrong to stone a Chinaman? Before we side against him, along with outraged San Francisco, let us give him a chance— let us hear the testimony for the defense.

He was a "well-dressed" boy, and a Sunday-school scholar, and therefore the chances are that his parents were intelligent, well-to-do people, with just enough natural villainy in their composition to make them yearn after the daily papers, and enjoy them; and so this boy had opportunities to learn all through the week how to do right, as well as on Sunday.

It was in this way that he found out that the great commonwealth of California imposes an unlawful mining-tax upon John the foreigner, and allows Patrick the foreigner to dig gold for nothing—probably because the degraded Mongol is at no expense for whisky, and the refined Celt cannot exist without it.

It was in this way that he found out that a respectable number of the tax-gatherers—it would be unkind to say all of them—collect the tax twice, instead of once; and that, inasmuch as they do it solely to discourage Chinese immigration into the mines, it is a thing that is much applauded, and likewise regarded as being singularly facetious.

It was in this way that he found out that when a white man robs a sluice-box (by the term white man is meant Spaniards, Mexicans, Portuguese, Irish, Hondurans, Peruvians, Chileans, etc., etc.), they make him leave the camp; and when a Chinaman does that thing, they hang him.

[1] First published in *The Galaxy*, May 1870. Mark Twain's indignation at the mistreatment of the Chinese in California also found a fictional outlet: "Goldsmith's Friend Abroad Again" (see *Mark Twain: Life As I Find It*, pp. 75–89).— C.N.

It was in this way that he found out that in many districts of the vast Pacific coast, so strong is the wild, free love of justice in the hearts of the people, that whenever any secret and mysterious crime is committed, they say, "Let justice be done, though the heavens fall," and go straightway and swing a Chinaman.

It was in this way that he found out that by studying one half of each day's "local items," it would appear that the police of San Francisco were either asleep or dead, and by studying the other half it would seem that the reporters were gone mad with admiration of the energy, the virtue, the high effectiveness, and the dare-devil intrepidity of that very police—making exultant mention of how "the Argus-eyed officer So-and-so" captured a wretched knave of a Chinaman who was stealing chickens, and brought him gloriously to the city prison; and how "the gallant officer Such-and-such-a-one" quietly kept an eye on the movements of an "unsuspecting, almond-eyed son of Confucius" (your reporter is nothing if not facetious), following him around with that far-off look of vacancy and unconsciousness always so finely affected by that inscrutable being, the forty-dollar policeman, during a waking interval, and captured him at last in the very act of placing his hands in a suspicious manner upon a paper of tacks, left by the owner in an exposed situation; and how one officer performed this prodigious thing, and another officer that, and another the other—and pretty much every one of these performances having for a dazzling central incident a Chinaman guilty of a shilling's worth of crime, an unfortunate, whose misdemeanor must be hurrahed into something enormous in order to keep the public from noticing how many really important rascals went uncaptured in the mean time, and how overrated those glorified policemen actually are.

It was in this way that the boy found out that the legislature, being aware that the Constitution has made America an asylum for the poor and the oppressed of all nations, and that, therefore, the poor and oppressed who fly to our shelter must not be charged a disabling admission fee, made a law that every Chinaman, upon landing, must be *vaccinated* upon the wharf, and pay to the state's appointed officer *ten dollars* for the service, when there are plenty of doctors in San Francisco who would be glad enough to do it for him for fifty cents.

It was in this way that the boy found out that a Chinaman had no rights that any man was bound to respect; that he had no sorrows that any man was bound to pity; that neither his life nor his liberty was worth the purchase of a penny when a white man needed a scapegoat;

that nobody loved Chinamen, nobody befriended them, nobody spared them suffering when it was convenient to inflict it; everybody, individuals, communities, the majesty of the state itself, joined in hating, abusing, and persecuting these humble strangers.

And, therefore, what *could* have been more natural than for this sunny-hearted boy, tripping along to Sunday-school, with his mind teeming with freshly learned incentives to high and virtuous action, to say to himself:

"Ah, there goes a Chinaman! God will not love me if I do not stone him."

And for this he was arrested and put in the city jail.

Everything conspired to teach him that it was a high and holy thing to stone a Chinaman, and yet he no sooner attempts to do his duty than he is punished for it—he, poor chap, who has been aware all his life that one of the principal recreations of the police, out toward the Gold Refinery, is to look on with tranquil enjoyment while the butchers of Brannan Street set their dogs on unoffending Chinamen, and make them flee for their lives."[2]

Keeping in mind the tuition in the humanities which the entire "Pacific coast" gives its youth, there is a very sublimity of incongruity in the virtuous flourish with which the good city fathers of San Francisco proclaim (as they have lately done) that "The police are positively ordered to arrest all boys, of every description and wherever found, who engage in assaulting Chinamen."

Still, let us be truly glad they have made the order, notwithstanding its inconsistency; and let us rest perfectly confident the police are glad, too. Because there is no personal peril in arresting boys, provided they be of the small kind, and the reporters will have to laud their performances just as loyally as ever, or go without items.

The new form for local items in San Francisco will now be: "The ever-vigilant and efficient officer So-and-so succeeded, yesterday afternoon, in arresting Master Tommy Jones, after a determined resistance," etc., etc., followed by the customary statistics and final hurrah, with

---

[2] I have many such memories in my mind, but am thinking just at present of one particular one, where the Brannan Street butchers set their dogs on a Chinaman who was quietly passing with a basket of clothes on his head; and while the dogs mutilated his flesh, a butcher increased the hilarity of the occasion by knocking some of the Chinaman's teeth down his throat with half a brick. This incident sticks in my memory with a more malevolent tenacity, perhaps, on account of the fact that I was in the employ of a San Francisco journal at the time, and was not allowed to publish it because it might offend some of the peculiar element that subscribed for the paper.—M.T.

its unconscious sarcasm: "We are happy in being able to state that this is the forty-seventh boy arrested by this gallant officer since the new ordinance went into effect. The most extraordinary activity prevails in the police department. Nothing like it has been seen since we can remember."

1870

License of the Press

A talk before the Monday Evening Club, Hartford, 1873.

(First paragraph missing)

. . . It (the press) has scoffed at religion till it has made scoffing popular. It has defended official criminals, on party pretexts, until it has created a United States Senate whose members are incapable of determining what crime against law and the dignity of their own body *is*, they are so morally blind, and it has made light of dishonesty till we have as a result a Congress which contracts to work for a certain sum and then deliberately steals additional wages out of the public pocket and is pained and surprised that anybody should worry about a little thing like that.

I am putting all this odious state of things upon the newspaper, and I believe it belongs there—chiefly, at any rate. It is a free press—a press that is more than free—a press which is licensed to say any infamous thing it chooses about a private or a public man, or advocate any outrageous doctrine it pleases. It is tied in *no* way. The public opinion which *should* hold it in bounds it has itself degraded to its own level. There are laws to protect the freedom of the press's speech, but none that are worth anything to protect the people from the press. A libel suit simply brings the plaintiff before a vast newspaper court to be tried before the law tries him, and reviled and ridiculed without mercy. The touchy Charles Reade can sue English newspapers and get verdicts; he would soon change his tactics here; the papers (backed by a public well taught by themselves) would soon teach him that it is better to suffer any amount of misrepresentation than go into our courts with a libel suit and make himself the laughing stock of the community.

It seems to me that just in the ratio that our newspapers increase, our morals decay. The more newspapers the worse morals. Where we have one newspaper that does good, I think we have fifty that do harm. We *ought* to look upon the establishment of a newspaper of the average pattern in a virtuous village as a calamity.

The difference between the tone and conduct of newspapers to-day and those of thirty or forty years ago is *very* noteworthy and very sad —I mean the average newspaper (for they had bad ones then, too). In those days the average newspaper was the champion of right and morals, and it dealt conscientiously in the truth. It is not the case now. The other day a reputable New York daily had an editorial defending the salary steal and justifying it on the ground that Congressmen were not paid enough—as if that were an all-sufficient excuse for stealing. That editorial put the matter in a new and perfectly satisfactory light with many a leather-headed reader, without a doubt. It has become a sarcastic proverb that a thing must be true if you saw it in a newspaper. That is the opinion intelligent people have of that lying vehicle in a nutshell. But the trouble is that the stupid people—who constitute the grand overwhelming majority of this and all other nations—*do* believe and *are* moulded and convinced by what they get out of a newspaper, and there is where the harm lies.

Among us, the newspaper is a tremendous power. It can make or mar any man's reputation. It has perfect freedom to call the best man in the land a fraud and a thief, and he is destroyed beyond help. Whether Mr. Colfax is a liar or not can never be ascertained now— but he will rank as one till the day of his death—for the newspapers have so doomed him. Our newspapers—*all* of them, without exception —glorify the "Black Crook" and make it an opulent success—they could have killed it dead with one broadside of contemptuous silence if they had wanted to. *Days Doings* and *Police Gazettes* flourish in the land unmolested by the law, because the *virtuous* newspapers long ago nurtured up a public laxity that loves indecency and never cares whether laws are administered or not.

In the newspapers of the West you can use the *editorial voice* in the editorial columns to defend any wretched and injurious dogma you please by paying a dollar a line for it.

Nearly all newspapers foster Rozensweigs and kindred criminals and send victims to them by opening their columns to their advertisements. You all know that.

In the Foster murder case[1] the New York papers made a weak pretense of upholding the hands of the Governor and urging the people to sustain him in standing firmly by the law; but they printed a whole page of sickly, maudlin appeals to his clemency as a paid advertisement. And I suppose they would have published enough pages of abuse of the Governor to destroy his efficiency as a public official to the end of his term if anybody had come forward and paid them for it—as an advertisement. The newspaper that obstructs the law on a trivial pretext, for money's sake, is a dangerous enemy to the public weal.

That awful power, the public opinion of a nation, is created in America by a horde of ignorant, self-complacent simpletons who failed at ditching and shoemaking and fetched up in journalism on their way to the poorhouse. I am personally acquainted with hundreds of journalists, and the opinion of the majority of them would not be worth tuppence in private, but when they speak in print it is the *newspaper* that is talking (the pygmy scribe is not visible) and *then* their utterances shake the community like the thunders of prophecy.

I know from personal experience the proneness of journalists to lie. I once started a peculiar and picturesque fashion of lying myself on the Pacific coast, and it is not dead there to this day. Whenever I hear of a shower of blood and frogs combined, in California, or a sea serpent found in some desert, there, or a cave frescoed with diamonds and emeralds (*always* found by an Injun who died before he could finish telling where it was), I say to myself I am the father of this child—I have got to answer for this lie. And habit is everything—to this day I am liable to lie if I don't watch all the time.

The license of the press has scorched every individual of us in our time, I make no doubt. Poor Stanley[2] was a very god, in England, his praises in every man's mouth. But nobody said anything about his lectures—they were charitably quiet on that head, and were content to praise his higher virtues. But our papers tore the poor creature limb from limb and scattered the fragments from Maine to California— merely because he couldn't lecture well. His prodigious achievement in Africa goes for naught—the man is pulled down and utterly destroyed—but *still* the persecution follows him as relentlessly from city to city and from village to village as if he had committed some bloody

---

[1] For Mark Twain's letter to the editor of the *New York Tribune* on the Foster case, see *Mark Twain: Life As I Find It*, pp. 166-7.—C.N.

[2] Henry Morton Stanley.—C.N.

and detestable crime. Bret Harte was suddenly snatched out of obscurity by our papers and throned in the clouds—all the editors in the land stood out in the inclement weather and adored him through their telescopes and swung their hats till they wore them out and then borrowed more; and the first time his family fell sick, and in his trouble and harassment he ground out a rather flat article in place of another heathen Chinee, that hurrahing host said, "Why, this man's a fraud," and then they began to reach up there for him. And they got him, too, and fetched him down, and walked over him, and rolled him in the mud, and tarred and feathered him, and then set him up for a target and have been heaving dirt at him ever since. The result is that the man has had only just nineteen engagements to lecture this year, and the audience have been so scattering, too, that he has never discharged a sentence yet that hit two people at the same time. The man is ruined—never can get up again. And yet he is a person who had great capabilities, and might have accomplished great things for our literature and for himself if he had had a happier chance. And he made the mistake, too, of doing a pecuniary kindness for a starving beggar of our guild—one of the journalistic shoemaker class—and that beggar made it his business as soon as he got back to San Francisco to publish four columns of exposures of crimes committed by his benefactor, the least of which ought to make any decent man blush. The press that admitted that stuff to its columns had too much license.

In a town in Michigan I declined to dine with an editor who was drunk, and he said, in his paper, that my lecture was profane, indecent, and calculated to encourage intemperance. And yet that man never heard it. It might have reformed him if he had.

A Detroit paper once said that I was in the constant habit of beating my wife and that I still kept this recreation up, although I had crippled her for life and she was no longer able to keep out of my way when I came home in my usual frantic frame of mind. Now scarcely the half of that was true. Perhaps I ought to have sued that man for libel—but I knew better. All the papers in America—with a few creditable exceptions—would have found out then, to *their* satisfaction, that I was a wife beater, and they would have given it a pretty general airing, too.

Why *I* have published vicious libels upon people *myself*—and ought to have been hanged before my time for it, too—if I *do* say it myself, that shouldn't.

But I will not continue these remarks. I have a sort of vague general idea that there is too much liberty of the press in this country, and that through the absence of all wholesome restraint the newspaper has become in a large degree a national *curse*, and will probably damn the Republic yet.

There *are* some excellent virtues in newspapers, some powers that wield vast influences for good; and I could have told all about these things, and glorified them exhaustively—but that would have left you gentlemen nothing to say.

1873

The Sandwich Islands[1]

I

Sir: When you do me the honor to suggest that I write an article about the Sandwich Islands, just now when the death of the King has turned something of the public attention in that direction, you unkennel a man whose modesty would have kept him in hiding otherwise. I could fill you full of statistics, but most human beings like gossip better and so you will not blame me if I proceed after the largest audience and leave other people to worry the minority with arithmetic.

I spent several months in the Sandwich Islands, six years ago, and if I could have my way about it, I would go back there and remain the rest of my days. It is paradise for an indolent man. If a man is rich he can live expensively, and his grandeur will be respected as in other parts of the earth; if he is poor he can herd with the natives, and live on next to nothing; he can sun himself all day long under the palm trees, and be no more troubled by his conscience than a butterfly would.

When you are in that blessed retreat, you are safe from the turmoil of life; you drowse your days away in a long deep dream of peace;

---

[1] Clemens on at least two other occasions reminisced about the Islands. See chapters XXII–XXXVI of *Roughing It* and the lecture on the Islands reprinted in *Mark Twain: Life As I Find It* (pp. 183–188). The present two letters are brilliant. In the second Clemens really gets going. It's a privilege to be able to resurrect this typical product of his genius.—C.N.

the past is a forgotten thing, the present is heaven, the future you leave to take care of itself. You are in the center of the Pacific Ocean; you are two thousand miles from any continent; you are millions of miles from the world; as far as you can see, on any hand, the crested billows wall the horizon, and beyond this barrier the wide universe is but a foreign land to you, and barren of interest.

The climate is simply delicious—never cold at the sea level, and never really too warm, for you are at the half-way house—that is, twenty degrees above the equator. But then you may order your own climate for this reason: the eight inhabited islands are merely mountains that lift themselves out of the sea—a group of bells, if you please, with some (but not very much) "flare" at their bases. You get the idea. Well, you take a thermometer, and mark on it where you want the mercury to stand permanently forever (with not more than 12 degrees variation) Winter and Summer. If 82 in the shade is your figure (with the privilege of going down or up 5 or 6 degrees at long intervals), you build your house down on the "flare"—the sloping or level ground by the sea-shore—and you have the deadest surest thing in the world on that temperature. And such is the climate of Honolulu, the capital of the kingdom. If you mark 70 as your mean temperature, you build your house on any mountain side, 400 or 500 feet above sea level. If you mark 55 or 60, go 1,500 feet higher. If you mark for Wintry weather, go on climbing and watching your mercury. If you want snow and ice forever and ever, and zero and below, build on the summit of Mauna Kea, 16,000 feet[2] up in the air. If you must have hot weather, you should build at Lahaina, where they do not hang the thermometer on a nail because the solder might melt and the instrument get broken; or you should build in the crater of Kilauea, which would be the same as going home before your time. You cannot find as much climate bunched together anywhere in the world as you can in the Sandwich Islands. You may stand on the summit of Mauna Kea, in the midst of snow-banks that were there before Capt. Cook was born, maybe, and while you shiver in your furs you may cast your eye down the sweep of the mountain side and tell exactly where the frigid zone ends and vegetable life begins; a stunted and tormented growth of trees shades down into a taller and freer species, and that in turn, into the full foliage and varied tints of the temperate zone; further down, the mere ordinary green tone of a forest washes over

---

[2] This is an exaggeration by a couple of thousand feet.—C.N.

the edges of a broad bar of orange trees that embraces the mountain like a belt, and is so deep and dark a green that distance makes it black; and still further down, your eye rests upon the levels of the sea-shore, where the sugar-cane is scorching in the sun, and the feathery cocoa-palm glassing itself in the tropical waves, and where you know the sinful natives are toiling about in utter nakedness and never know-ing or caring that you and your snow and your chattering teeth are so close by. So you perceive, you can look down upon all the climates of the earth, and note the kinds of colors of all the vegetations, just with a glance of the eye—and this glance only travels over about three miles as the bird flies, too.

The natives of the islands number only about 50,000, and the whites about 3,000, chiefly Americans. According to Capt. Cook, the natives numbered 400,000 less than a hundred years ago. But the traders brought labor and fancy diseases—in other words, long, deliberate, infallible destruction; and the missionaires brought the means of grace and got them ready. So the two forces are working along harmoniously, and anybody who knows anything about figures can tell you exactly when the last Kanaka will be in Abraham's bosom and his islands in the hands of the whites. It is the same as calculating an eclipse—if you get started right, you cannot miss it. For nearly a century the natives have been keeping up a ratio of about three births to five deaths, and you can see what that must result in. No doubt in fifty years a Kanaka will be a curiosity in his own land, and as an investment will be superior to a circus.

I am truly sorry that these people are dying out, for they are about the most interesting savages there are. Their language is soft and musical, it has not a hissing sound in it, and *all* their words end with a vowel. They would call Jim Fisk *Jimmy Fikki*, for they will even do violence to a proper name if it grates too harshly in its natural state. The Italian is raspy and disagreeable compared to the Hawaiian tongue.

These people used to go naked, but the missionaries broke that up; in towns the men wear clothing now, and in the country a plug hat and a breech-clout; or if they have company they put on a shirt collar and a vest. Nothing but religion and education could have wrought these admirable changes. The women wear a single loose calico gown, that falls without a break from neck to heels.

In the old times, to speak plainly, there was absolutely no bar to the commerce of the sexes. To refuse the solicitations of a stranger was regarded as a contemptible thing for a girl or a woman to do; but the missionaries have so bitterly fought this thing that they have succeeded at least in driving it out of sight—and now it exists only in reality, not in name.

These natives are the simplest, the kindest-hearted, the most un-selfish creatures that bear the image of the Maker. Where white in-fluence has not changed them, they will make any chance stranger welcome, and divide their all with him—a trait which has never existed among any other people, perhaps. They live only for to-day; to-morrow is a thing which does not enter into their calculations. I had a native youth in my employ in Honolulu, a graduate of a missionary college, and he divided his time between translating the Greek Testament and taking care of a piece of property of mine which I considered a horse. Whenever this boy could collect his wages, he would go and lay out the entire amount, all the way up from fifty cents to a dollar, in *poi* (which is a paste made of the taro root, and is the national dish), and call in all the native ragamuffins that came along to help him eat it. And there, in the rich grass, under the tamarind trees, the gentle savages would sit and gorge till all was gone. My boy would go hungry and content for a day or two, and then some Kanaka he probably had never seen before would invite him to a similar feast, and give him a fresh start.

The ancient religion was only a jumble of curious superstitions. The shark seems to have been the god they chiefly worshipped—or rather sought to propitiate. Then there was Pele, a goddess who pre-sided over the terrible fires of Kilauea; minor gods were not scarce. The natives are all Christians, now—every one of them; they all belong to the church, and are fonder of theology than they are of pie; they will sweat out a sermon as long as the Declaration of Independence; the duller it is the more it infatuates them; they would sit there and stew and stew in a trance of enjoyment till they floated away in their own grease if the ministers would stand watch-and-watch, and see them through. Sunday-schools are a favorite dissipation with them, and they never get enough. If there was physical as well as mental intoxication in this limb of the service, they would never draw a sober breath. Religion is drink and meat to the native. He can read his neatly printed Bible (in the native tongue—every solitary man, woman, and little child in the islands can), and he reads it over and over again. And he reads a whole world of moral tales, built on the good old Sunday-school book pattern exaggerated, and he worships their heroes—heroes who walk the world with their mouths full of butter, and who are simply impossibly chuckle-headed and pious. And he knows all the hymns you ever heard in your life, and he sings them in a soft, pleasant voice, to native words that make "On Jordan's stormy banks I stand" sound as grotesquely and sweetly foreign to you as if it were a dictionary grinding wrong end first through a sugar-mill. Now you see how these natives, great and small, old and young, are saturated with religion—at least the poetry and the music of it. But as to the practice of it, they vary. Some of the nobler precepts of Christianity they have always practiced naturally, and they always will. Some of the minor precepts they as naturally do not practice, and as naturally they never will. The white man has taught them to lie, and they take to it pleasantly and without sin—for there cannot be much sin in a thing which they cannot be made to comprehend is a sin. Adultery they look upon as poetically wrong but practically proper.

These people are sentimentally religious—perhaps that describes it. They pray and sing and moralize in fair weather, but when they get into trouble, that is "business"—and then they are tolerably apt to drop poetry and call on the Great Shark God of their fathers to give them a lift. Their ancient superstitions are in their blood and bones, and they keep cropping out now and then in the most natural and pardonable way.

I am one who regards missionary work as slow and discouraging labor, and not immediately satisfactory in its results. But I am very far from considering such work either hopeless or useless. I believe that such seed, sown in savage ground, will produce wholesome fruit in the third generation, and certainly that result is worth striving for. But I do not think much can reasonably be expected of the first and second generations. It is against nature. It takes long and patient cultivation to turn the bitter almond into the peach. But we do not refrain from the effort on that account, for, after all, it pays.

The natives make excellent seamen, and the whalers would rather have them than any other race. They are so tractable, docile and willing, and withal so faithful, that they rank first in sugar-planters' esteem as laborers. Do not these facts speak well for our poor, brown Sunday-school children of the far islands!

There is a small property tax, and any native who has an income of $50 a year can vote.

The 3,000 whites in the islands handle all the money and carry on all the commerce and agriculture—and superintend the religion. Americans are largely in the majority. These whites are sugar-planters, merchants, whale-ship officers, and missionaries. The missionaries are sorry the most of the other whites are there, and these latter are sorry the missionaries don't migrate. The most of the belt of sloping land that borders the sea and rises toward the bases of the mountains, is rich and fertile. There are only 200,000 acres of this productive soil, but only think of its capabilities! In Louisiana, 200,000 acres of sugar land would only yield 50,000 tuns of sugar per annum, and possibly not so much; but in the Sandwich Islands, you could get at least 400,000 tuns out of it. This is a good, strong statement, but it is true, nevertheless. Two and a half tuns to the acre is a common yield in the islands; three and a half tuns is by no means unusual; five tuns is frequent; and I can name the man who took fifty tuns of sugar from seven acres of ground, one season. This cane was on the mountain-side, 2,500 feet above sea level, and it took it three years to mature. Address your inquiries to Capt. McKee, Island of Mani, S.I. Few plantations are stuck up in the air like that, and so twelve months is ample time for the maturing of cane down there. And I would like to call attention to two or three exceedingly noteworthy facts. For instance, there you do not hurry up and cut your cane when it blossoms, but you just let it alone and cut it when you choose—no harm will come of it. And you do not have to keep an army of hands to plant in the planting season, grind in the grinding season, and rush in frantically and cut down the crop when a frost threatens. Not at all. There is no hurry. You run a large plantation with but a few hands, because you plant pretty much when you please, and you cut your cane and grind it when it suits your convenience. There is no frost, and the longer the cane stands the better it grows. Sometimes—often, in fact—part of your gang are planting a field, another part are cutting the crop from an adjoining field, and the rest are grinding at the mill. You only plant once in three years, and you take off two ratoon crops without replanting. You may keep on taking off ratoon crops about as long as you please, indeed; every year the bulk of the cane will be smaller, but the juice will grow regularly denser and richer, and so you are all right. I know of one lazy man who took off sixteen ratoon crops without replanting!

What fortunes those planters made during our war, when sugar went up into the twenties! It had cost them about ten or eleven cents a pound, delivered in San Francisco, and all charges paid. Now if any one desires to know why these planters would probably like to be under our flag, the answer is simple: We make them pay us a duty of four cents a pound on refined sugars at present; brokerage, freights and handling (two or three times), costs three cents more; rearing the cane, and making the sugar, is an item of five cents more— total, 12 cents a pound, or within a cent of it, anyhow. And to-day refined sugar is only worth about 12½ cents (wholesale) in our markets. Profit—none worth mentioning. But if we were to annex the islands and do away with that crushing duty of four cents a pound, some of those heavy planters who can hardly keep their heads above water now, would clear $75,000 a year and upward. Two such years would pay for their plantations, and all their stock and machinery. It is so long since I was in the islands that I feel doubtful about swearing that the United States duty on their sugars was four cents a pound, but I can swear it was not under three.

I would like to say a word about the late King Kamehameha V. and the system of government, but I will wait a day. Also, I would like to know why your correspondents so calmly ignore the true heir to the Sandwich Islands throne, as if he had no existence and no chances; and I would like to heave in a word for him. I refer to our stanch American sympathizer, Prince William Lunalilo, descendant of eleven generations of sceptered savages—a splendid fellow, with talent, genius, education, gentlemanly manners, generous instincts, and an intellect that shines as radiantly through floods of whisky as if that fluid but fed a calcium light in his head. All people in the islands know that William—or "Prince Bill," as they call him, more in affection than otherwise—stands next to the throne; and so why is he ignored?

II

SIR: Having explained who the 3,000 whites are, and what sort of people the 50,000 natives are, I will now shovel in some information as to how this toy realm, with its toy population, is governed. By a constable and six policemen? By a justice of the peace and a jury? By a mayor and a board of aldermen? Oh, no. But by a King—and a Parliament—and a Ministry—and a Privy Council—and a standing army (200 soldiers)—and a navy (steam ferry-boat and a raft)—and a grand bench of supreme justices—and a lord high sheriff on each island. That is the way it is done. It is like propelling a sardine dish with the Great Eastern's machinery.

Something over 50 years ago the natives, by a sudden impulse which they could not understand themselves, burned all their idols and overthrew the ancient religion of the land. Curiously enough, our first invoice of missionaries were sailing around the Horn at the time, and they arrived just in season to furnish the people a new and much better means of grace. They baptized men, women, and children at once and by wholesale, and proceeded to instruct them in the tenets of the new religion immediately afterward. They built enormous churches, and received into communion as many as 5,000 people in a single day. The fame of it went abroad in the earth, and everywhere the nations rejoiced; the unworldly called it a "great awakening," and even the unregenerated were touched, and spoke of it with admiration. The missionaries learned the language, translated the Bible and other books into it, established schools, and even very complete colleges, and taught the whole nation to read and write; the princes and nobles acquired collegiate educations, and became familiar with half a dozen dead and living languages. Then, some twenty years later, the missionaries framed a constitution which became the law of the land. It lifted woman up to a level with her lord; placed the tenant less at the mercy of his landlord; it established a just and equable system of taxation; it introduced the ballot and universal suffrage; it defined and secured to king, chiefs, and people their several rights and privileges; and it instituted a parliament in which all the estates of the realm were to be represented, and, if I remember rightly, it gave this parliament power to pass laws over the King's veto.

Things went on swimmingly for several years, and especially under the reign of the late King's brother, an enlightened and liberal-minded prince; but when he died and Kamehameha V. ascended the throne, matters took a different turn. He was one of your swell "grace of God" Kings, and not the "figure-head" some have said he was; indeed, he was the biggest power in the Islands all his days, and his royal will was sufficient to create a law any time or overturn one.

He was master in the beginning, and at the middle, and to the end. The Parliament was the "figure-head," and it never was much else in his time. One of his very first acts was to fly into a splendid passion (when his Parliament voted down some measure of his), and tear the beautiful Constitution into shreds, and stamp on them with his royal No. 18s! And his next act was to violently prorogue the Parliament and send the members about their business. He hated Parliaments, as being a rasping and useless incumbrance upon a king, but he allowed them to exist because as an obstruction they were more ornamental than real. He hated universal suffrage and he destroyed it—at least, he took the insides out of it and left the harmless figure. He said he would not have beggars voting industrious people's money away, and so he compelled the adoption of a cash qualification to vote. He surrounded himself with an obsequious royal Cabinet of American and other foreigners, and he dictated his measures to them and, through them, to his Parliament; and the latter institution opposed them respectfully, not to say apologetically, and passed them.

This is but a sad kind of royal "figure-head." He was not a fool. He was a wise sovereign; he had seen something of the world; he was educated and accomplished, and he tried hard to do well by his people, and succeeded. There was no trivial royal nonsense about him; he dressed plainly, poked about Honolulu, night or day, on his old horse, unattended; he was popular, greatly respected, and even beloved. Perhaps the only man who never feared him was "Prince Bill," whom I have mentioned heretofore. Perhaps the only man who ever ventured to speak his whole mind about the King, in Parliament and on the hustings, was the present true heir to the throne—if Prince Bill is still alive, and I have not heard that he is dead. This go-ahead young fellow used to handle His Majesty without gloves, and wholly indifferent to consequences; and being a shade more popular with the native masses than the King himself, perhaps, his opposition amounted to something. The foregoing was the common talk of Honolulu six years ago, and I set the statements down here because I believe them to be true, and not because I know them to be true.

Prince William is about 35 years of age, now, I should think. There is no blood relationship between him and the house of the Kamehamehas. He comes of an older and prouder race; a race of imperious chiefs and princes of the Island of Maui, who held undisputed sway there during several hundred years. He is the eleventh prince in direct descent, and the natives always paid a peculiar homage to his venerable nobility, which they never vouchsafed to the mushroom Kamehamehas. He is considered the true heir to the Hawaiian throne, for this reason, viz.: A dying or retiring king can name his own successor, by the law of the land—he can name any child of his he pleases, or he can name his brother or any other member of the royal family. The late king has passed away without leaving son, daughter, brother, uncle, nephew, or father (his father never was king—he died a year or two ago), and without appointing a successor. The Parliament has power now to elect a king, and this king can be chosen from any one of the twelve chief families. This has been my understanding of the matter, and I am very sure I am right. In rank, Prince William overtops any chief in the Islands about as an English royal duke overtops a mere earl. He is the only Hawaiian, outside of the royal family, who is entitled to bear and transmit the title of Prince; and he is so popular that if the scepter were put to a popular vote he would "walk over the track."

He used to be a very handsome fellow, with a truly princely deportment, drunk or sober; but I merely speak figuratively—he never was drunk; he did not hold enough. All his features were fine, and he had a Roman nose that was a model of beauty and grandeur. He was brim full of spirit, pluck and enterprise; his head was full of brains, and his speech was facile and all alive with point and vigor; there was nothing underhanded or two-faced about him, but he always went straight at everything he undertook, without caring who saw his hand or understood his game. He was a potent friend of America and Americans. Such is the true heir to the vacant throne—if he is not dead, as I said before.

I have suggested that William drinks. That is not an objection to a Sandwich Islander. Whisky cannot hurt them; it can seldom even tangle the legs or befog the brains of a practiced native. It is only water with a flavor to it, to Prince Bill; it is what cider is to us. *Poi* is the all-powerful agent that protects the lover of whisky. Whoever eats it habitually may imbibe habitually without serious harm. The late king and his late sister Victoria both drank unlimited whisky, and so would the rest of the natives if they could get it. The native beverage, *awa*, is so terrific that mere whisky is foolishness to it. It turns a man's skin to white fish-scales that are so tough a dog might bite him, and he would not know it till he read about it in the papers. It is made of a root of some kind. The "quality" drink this to some extent, but the Excise law has placed it almost beyond the reach of the plebeians. After *awa*, what is whisky?

Many years ago the late King and his brother visited California, and some Sacramento folks thought it would be fun to get them drunk. So they gathered together the most responsible soakers in the town and began to fill up royalty and themselves with strong brandy punches. At the end of two or three hours the citizens were all lying torpid under the table and the two princes were sitting disconsolate and saying what a lonely, dry country it was! I tell it to you as it was told to me in Sacramento.

The Hawaiian Parliament consists of half a dozen chiefs, a few whites, and perhaps thirty or forty common Kanakas. The King's ministers (half a dozen whites) sit with them and ride over all opposition to the King's wishes. There are always two people speaking at once—the member and the public translator. The little legislature is as proud of itself as any parliament could be, and puts on no end of airs. The wisdom of a Kanaka legislature is as profound as that of our ordinary run of State legislatures, but no more so. Perhaps God makes all legislatures alike in that respect. I remember one Kanaka bill that struck me: it proposed to connect the islands of Oahu and Hawaii with a suspension bridge, because the sea voyage between these points was attended with so much sea-sickness that the natives were greatly discommoded by it. This suspension bridge would have been 150 miles long!

I can imagine what is going on in Honolulu now, during this month of mourning, for I was there when the late King's sister, Victoria, died. David Kalakaua (a chief), Commander-in-Chief of the Household Troops (how is that, for a title?) is no doubt standing guard now over the closed entrances to the "palace" grounds, keeping out all whites but officers of State; and within, the Christianized heathen are howling and dancing and wailing and carrying on in the same old savage fashion that obtained before Cook discovered the country. I lived three blocks from the wooden two-story palace when Victoria was being lamented, and for thirty nights in succession the morning pow-wow defied sleep. All that time the Christianized but morally unclean Princess lay in state in the palace. I got into the grounds one night and saw some hundreds of half-naked savages of both sexes beating their dismal tom-toms, and wailing and caterwauling in the weird glare of innumerable torches; and while a great band of women swayed and jiggered their pliant bodies through the intricate movements of a lascivious dance called the hula-hula, they chanted an accompaniment in native words. I asked the son of a missionary what the words meant. He said they celebrated certain admired gifts and physical excellencies of the dead princess. I inquired further, but he said the words were too foul for translation; that the bodily excellencies were unmentionable; that the capabilities so lauded and so glorified had better be left to the imagination. He said the King was doubtless sitting where he could hear these ghastly praises and enjoy them. That is, the late King—the educated, cultivated Kamehameha V. And mind you, one of his titles was "the Head of the Church;" for, although he was brought up in the religion of the missionaries, and educated in their schools and colleges, he early learned to despise their plebeian form of worship, and had imported the English system and an English bishop, and bossed the works himself. You can imagine the saturnalia that is making the night hideous in the palace grounds now, where His Majesty is lying in state.

The late King was frequently on hand in the royal pew in the Royal Hawaiian Reformed Catholic Church, on Sundays; but whenever he got into trouble he did not fly to the cross for help—he flew to the heathen gods of his ancestors. Now this was a man who would write you a beautiful letter, in a faultless hand, and word it in faultless English; and perhaps throw in a few graceful classic allusions; and perhaps a few happy references to science, international law, or the world's political history; or he would array himself in elegant evening dress and entertain you at his board in princely style, and converse like a born Christian gentleman; and day after day he would work like a beaver in affairs of State, and on occasion exchange autograph letters with the kings and emperors of the old world. And the very next week, business being over, he would retire to a cluster of dismal little straw-thatched native huts by the sea-shore, and there for a fortnight he would turn himself into a heathen whom you could not tell from his savage grandfather. He would reduce his dress to a breech-clout, fill himself daily full of whisky, and sit with certain of his concubines while others danced the peculiar hula-hula. And if oppressed by great responsibilities he would summon one of his familiars, an ancient witch, and ask her to tell him the opinion and the commands of the heathen gods, and these commands he would obey. He was so superstitious that he would not step over a line drawn across a road, but would walk around it. These matters were common talk in the Islands. I never saw this King but once, and then he was not on his periodical debauch. He was in evening dress attending the funeral of his sister, and had a yard of crape depending from his stovepipe hat.

If you will be so good as to remember that the population of the islands is but a little over 50,000 souls, and that over that little handful of people roosts a monarchy with its coat-tails fringed with as many mighty-titled dignitaries as would suffice to run the Russian Empire, you will wonder how, the offices all being filled, there can be anybody left to govern. And the truth is, that it is one of the oddest things in the world to stumble on a man there who has no title. I felt so lonesome, as being about the only unofficial person in Honolulu, that I had to leave the country to find company.

After all this exhibition of imperial grandeur, it is humiliating to have to say that the entire exports of the kingdom are not as much as $1,500,000, the imports in the neighborhood of that figure, and the revenues, say $500,000. And yet they pay the King $36,000 a year, and the other officials from $3,000 to $8,000—and heaven knows there are enough of them.

The National Debt was $150,000 when I was there—and there was nothing in the country they were so proud of. They wouldn't have taken any money for it. With what an air His Excellency the Minister of Finance lugged in his Annual Budget and read off the impressive items and flourished the stately total!

The "Royal Ministers" are natural curiosities. They are white men of various nationalities, who have wandered thither in times gone by. I will give you a specimen—but not the most favorable. Harris, for instance. Harris is an American—a long-legged, vain, light-weight village lawyer from New Hampshire. If he had brains in proportion to his legs, he would make Solomon seem a failure; if his modesty equaled his ignorance, he would make a violet seem stuck-up; if his learning equaled his· vanity, he would make von Humboldt seem as unlettered as the backside of a tombstone; if his stature were proportioned to his conscience, he would be a gem for the microscope; if his ideas were as large as his words, it would take a man three months to walk around one of them; if an audience were to contract to listen as long as he would talk, that audience would die of old age; and if he were to talk until he said something, he would still be on his hind legs when the last trump sounded. And he would have cheek enough to wait till the disturbance was over, and go on again.

Such is (or was) His Excellency Mr. Harris, his late Majesty's Minister of This, That, and The Other—for he was a little of everything; and particularly and always he was the King's most obedient humble servant and loving worshiper, and his chief champion and mouthpiece in the parliamentary branch of ministers. And when a question came up (it didn't make any difference what it was), how he would rise up and saw the air with his bony flails, and storm and cavort and hurl sounding emptiness which he thought was eloquence, and discharge bile which he fancied was satire, and issue dreary rubbish which he took for humor, and accompany it with contortions of his undertaker countenance which he believed to be comic expression!

He began in the islands as a little, obscure lawyer, and rose (?) to be such a many-sided official grandee that sarcastic folk dubbed him, "the wheels of the Government." He became a great man in a pigmy land—he was of the caliber that other countries construct constables and coroners of. I do not wish to seem prejudiced against Harris, and I hope that nothing I have said will convey such an impression. I

must be an honest historian, and to do this in the present case I have
to reveal the fact that this stately figure, which looks so like a Washington monument in the distance, is nothing but a thirty-dollar windmill when you get close to him.

Harris loves to proclaim that he is no longer an American, and is
proud of it; that he is a Hawaiian through and through, and is proud
of that, too; and that he is a willing subject and servant of his lord
and master, the King, and is proud and grateful that it is so.

Now, let us annex the islands. Think how we could build up that
whaling trade! [Though under our courts and judges it might soon
be as impossible for whaleships to rendezvous there without being
fleeced and "pulled" by sailors and pettifoggers as it now is in San
Francisco—a place the skippers shun as they would rocks and shoals.]
Let us annex. We could make sugar enough there to supply all America, perhaps, and the prices would be very easy with the duties removed. And then we would have such a fine half-way house for our
Pacific-plying ships; and such a convenient supply depot and such a
commanding sentry-box for an armed squadron; and we could raise
cotton and coffee there and make it pay pretty well, with the duties off
and capital easier to get at. And then we would own the mightiest
volcano on earth—Kilauea! Barnum could run it—he understands fires
now. Let us annex, by all means. We could pacify Prince Bill and
other nobles easily enough—put them on a reservation. Nothing pleases
a savage like a reservation—a reservation where he has his annual hoes,
and Bibles and blankets to trade for powder and whisky—a sweet Ar-
cadian retreat fenced in with soldiers. By annexing, we would get all
those 50,000 natives cheap as dirt, with their morals and other diseases
thrown in. No expense for education—they are already educated; no
need to convert them—they are already converted; no expense to
clothe them—for obvious reasons.

We *must* annex those people. We can afflict them with our wise
and beneficent government. We can introduce the novelty of thieves,
all the way up from street-car pickpockets to municipal robbers and
Government defaulters, and show them how amusing it is to arrest
them and try them and then turn them loose—some for cash and
some for "political influence." We can make them ashamed of their
simple and primitive justice. We can do away with their occasional
hangings for murder, and let them have Judge Pratt to teach them how
to save imperiled Avery-assassins to society. We can give them some
Barnards to keep their money corporations out of difficulties. We
can give them juries composed entirely of the most simple and charm-

ing leatherheads. We can give them railway corporations who will buy their Legislatures like old clothes, and run over their best citizens and complain of the corpses for smearing their unpleasant juices on the track. In place of harmless and vaporing Harris, we can give them Tweed. We can let them have Connolly; we can loan them Sweeny; we can furnish them some Jay Goulds who will do away with their old-time notion that stealing is not respectable. We can confer Woodhull and Claflin on them. And George Francis Train. We can give them lecturers! I will go myself.

We can make that little bunch of sleepy islands the hottest corner on earth, and array it in the moral splendor of our high and holy civilization. Annexation is what the poor islanders need. "Shall we to men benighted, the lamp of life deny?"

1873

A Memorable Midnight Experience[1]

"Come along—and hurry. Few people have got originality enough to think of the expedition I have been planning, and still fewer could carry it out, maybe, even if they *did* think of it. Hurry, now. Cab at the door."

It was past eleven o'clock and I was just going to bed. But this friend of mine was as reliable as he was eccentric, and so there was not a not a doubt in my mind that his "expedition" had merit in it. I put on my coat and boots again, and we drove away.

"Where is it? Where are we going?"

"Don't worry. You'll see."

He was not inclined to talk. So I thought this must be a weighty matter. My curiosity grew with the minutes, but I kept it manfully under the surface. I watched the lamps, the signs, the numbers, as we thundered down the long streets, but it was of no use—I am always lost in London, day or night. It was very chilly—almost bleak. People leaned against the gusty blasts as if it were the dead of winter. The crowds grew thinner and thinner and the noises waxed faint and

[1] For other fragments of the aborted book about the English see *Letters from the Earth* (1962), pp. 171–180.—C.N.

seemed far away. The sky was overcast and threatening. We drove on, and still on, till I wondered if we were ever going to stop. At last we passed by a spacious bridge and a vast building with a lighted clock tower, and presently entered a gateway, passed through a sort of tunnel, and stopped in a court surrounded by the black outlines of a great edifice. Then we alighted, walked a dozen steps or so, and waited. In a little while footsteps were heard and a man emerged from the darkness and we dropped into his wake without saying anything. He led us under an archway of masonry, and from that into a roomy tunnel, through a tall iron gate, which he locked behind us. We followed him down this tunnel, guided more by his footsteps on the stone flagging than by anything we could very distinctly see. At the end of it we came to another iron gate, and our conductor stopped there and lit a little bull's-eye lantern. Then he unlocked the gate—and I wished he had oiled it first, it grated so dismally. The gate swung open and we stood on the threshold of what seemed a limitless domed and pillared cavern carved out of the solid darkness. The conductor and my friend took off their hats reverently, and I did likewise. For the moment that we stood thus there was not a sound, and the silence seemed to add to the solemnity of the gloom. I *looked* my inquiry!

"It is the tomb of the great dead of England—*Westminster Abbey*."

(One cannot express a start—in words.) Down among the columns—ever so far away, it seemed—a light revealed itself like a star, and a voice came echoing through the spacious emptiness:

"Who goes there!"

"Wright!"

The star disappeared and the footsteps that accompanied it clanked out of hearing in the distance. Mr. Wright held up his lantern and the vague vastness took something of form to itself—the stately columns developed stronger outlines, and a dim pallor here and there marked the places of lofty windows. We were among the tombs; and on every hand dull shapes of men, sitting, standing or stooping, inspected us curiously out of the darkness—reached out their hands toward us—some appealing, some beckoning, some warning us away. Effigies, they were—statues over the graves; but they looked human and natural in the murky shadows. Now a little half-grown black-and-white cat squeezed herself through the bars of the iron gate and came purring lovingly about us, unawed by the time or the place—unimpressed by the marble pomp that sepulchers a line

of mighty dead that ends with a great author of yesterday and
began with a sceptered monarch away back in the dawn of history
more than twelve hundred years ago. And she followed us about
and never left us while we pursued our work. We wandered hither
and thither, uncovered, speaking in low voices, and stepping softly
by instinct, for any little noise rang and echoed there in a way
to make one shudder. Mr. Wright flashed his lantern first upon
this object and then upon that, and kept up a running commentary
that showed that there was nothing about the venerable Abbey
that was trivial in his eyes or void of interest. He is a man in
authority—being superintendent of the works—and his daily business
keeps him familiar with every nook and corner of the great pile.
Casting a luminous ray now here, now yonder, he would say:

"Observe the height of the Abbey—one hundred and three feet
to the base of the roof—I measured it myself the other day. Notice
the base of this column—old, very old—hundreds and hundreds of
years; and how well they knew how to build in those old days.
Notice it—every stone is laid horizontally—that is to say, just as
nature laid it originally in the quarry—not set up edgewise; in our
day some people set them on edge, and then wonder why they
split and flake. Architects cannot teach nature anything. Let me remove this matting—it is put there to preserve the pavement; now,
there is a bit of pavement that is seven hundred years old; you
can see by these scattering clusters of colored mosaics how beautiful it was before time and sacrilegious idlers marred it. Now there,
in the border, was an inscription once; see, follow the circle—you
can trace it by the ornaments that have been pulled out—here is
an A, and there is an O, and yonder another A—all beautiful old
English capitals—there is no telling what the inscription was—no record left, now. Now move along in this direction, if you please.
Yonder is where old King Sebert the Saxon, lies—his monument
is the oldest one in the Abbey; Sebert died in 616, and that's
as much as twelve hundred and fifty years ago—think of it!—twelve
hundred and fifty years. Now yonder is the last one—Charles Dickens—there on the floor with the brass letters on the slab—and to
this day the people come and put flowers on it. Why, along at
first they almost had to *cart* the flowers out, there were so many.
Could not *leave* them there, you know, because it's where everybody walks—and a body wouldn't want them trampled on, anyway. All this place about here, now, is the Poet's Corner. There

is Garrick's monument, and Addison's, and Thackeray's bust—and Macaulay lies there. And here, close to Dickens and Garrick, lie Sheridan and Doctor Johnson—and here is old Parr—Thomas Parr— you can read the inscription:"

> Tho: Par of Y Covny of Sallop Borne A :1483. He
> Lived in Y Reignes of Ten Princes, viz: K. Edw. 4
> K. Ed. 5. K. Rich 3. K. Hen. 7. K. Hen. 8. Edw. 6. QVV. Ma.
> Q. Eliz. K. IA. and K. Charles, Ages 152 Yeares, And
> Was Buryed Here Novemb 15. 1635.

"Very old man indeed, and saw a deal of life. (Come off the grave, Kitty, poor thing; she keeps the rats away from the office, and there's no harm in her—her and her mother.) And here—this is Shakespeare's statue"—leaning on his elbow and pointing with his finger at the lines on the scroll:

> The cloud-capt towers, the gorgeous palaces,
> The solemn temples, the great globe itself,
> Yea, all which it inherit shall dissolve,
> And, like the baseless fabric of a vision,
> Leave not a wrack behind.

"That stone there covers Campbell the poet. Here are names you know pretty well—Milton, and Gray who wrote the 'Elegy,' and Butler who wrote 'Hudibras,' and Edmund Spencer, and Ben Jonson—there are three tablets to him scattered about the Abbey, and all got 'O Rare Ben Jonson' cut on them—you were standing on one of them just now—he is buried standing up. There used to be a tradition here that explains it. The story goes that he did not dare ask to be buried in the Abbey, so he asked King James if he would make him a present of eighteen inches of English ground, and the king said yes, and asked him where he would have it, and he said in Westminster Abbey. Well, the king wouldn't go back on his word, and so there he is sure enough—stood up on end. Years ago, in Dean Buckland's time—before my day—they were digging a grave close to Jonson and they uncovered him and his head fell off. Toward night the clerk of the works hid the head to keep it from being stolen, as the ground was to remain open till next day. Presently the dean's son came along and he found a head, and hid it away for Jonson's. And by and by along comes a stranger, and *he* found a head, too, and walked off with it under his cloak, and a month or so afterward he was heard to boast that he had Ben Jonson's head. Then there was a deal of correspondence about it, in the *Times,* and everybody distressed. But Mr. Frank Buckland came out and comforted everybody by telling how he saved the true head, and so the stranger must have got one that wasn't of any consequence. And then up speaks the clerk of the works and tells how *he* saved the right head, and so *Dean Buckland* must have got a wrong one. Well, it was all settled satisfactorily at last, because the clerk of the works *proved* his head. And then I believe they got that head from the stranger—so now we have three. But it shows you what regiments of people you are walking over—been collecting here for twelve hundred years— in some places, no doubt, the bones are fairly matted together.

"And here are some unfortunates. Under this place lies Anne, queen of Richard III, and daughter of the Kingmaker, the great Earl of Warwick—murdered she was—poisoned by her husband. And here is a slab which you see has once had the figure of a man in armor on it, in brass or copper, let into the stone. You can see the shape of it—but it is all worn away now by people's feet; the man has been dead five hundred years that lies under it. He was a knight in Richard II's time. His enemies pressed him close and he fled and took sanctuary here in the Abbey. Generally a man was safe when he took sanctuary in those days, but this man was not. The captain of the Tower and a band of men pursued him and his friends and they had a bloody fight here on this floor; but this poor fellow did not stand much of a chance, and they butchered him right before the altar."

We wandered over to another part of the Abbey, and came to a place where the pavement was being repaired. Every paving stone has an inscription on it and covers a grave. Mr. Wright continued:

"Now, you are standing on William Pitt's grave—you can read the name, though it is a good deal worn—and you, sir, are standing on the grave of Charles James Fox. I found a very good place here the other day—nobody suspected it—been curiously overlooked, somehow—but—it is a very nice place indeed, and very comfortable" (holding his bull's eye to the pavement and searching around). "Ah, here it is—this is the stone—nothing under here—nothing at all—a very nice place indeed—and very comfortable."

Mr. Wright spoke in a professional way, of course, and after the manner of a man who takes an interest in his business and is gratified at any piece of good luck that fortune favors him with; and yet with all that silence and gloom and solemnity about me, there was something about his idea of a nice, comfortable place that made the cold chills creep up my back. Presently we began to come upon little chamberlike chapels, with solemn figures ranged around the sides, lying apparently asleep, in sumptuous marble beds, with their hands placed together above their breasts—the figures and all their surroundings black with age. Some were dukes and earls, some were kings and queens, some were ancient abbots whose effigies had lain there so many centuries and suffered such disfigurement that their faces were almost as smooth and featureless as the stony pillows their heads reposed upon. At one time while I stood looking at a distant part of the pavement, admiring the delicate tracery which the now flooding moonlight was casting upon it through a lofty window, the party moved on and I lost them. The first step I made in the dark, holding my hands before me, as one does under such circumstances, I touched a cold object, and stopped to feel its shape. I made out a thumb, and then delicate fingers. It was the clasped, appealing hands of one of those reposing images—a lady, a queen. I touched the face—by accident, not design—and shuddered inwardly, if not outwardly; and then something rubbed against my leg, and I shuddered outwardly and inwardly both. It was the cat. The friendly creature meant well, but, as the English say, she gave me "such a turn." I took her in my arms for company and wandered among the grim sleepers till I caught the glimmer of the lantern again. Presently, in a little chapel, we were looking at the sarcophagus, let into the wall, which contains the bones of the infant princes who were smothered in the Tower. Behind us was the stately monument of Queen Elizabeth, with her effigy dressed in the royal robes, lying as if at rest. When we turned around, the cat, with stupendous simplicity, was coiled up and sound asleep upon the feet of the Great Queen! Truly this was reaching far toward the millennium when the lion and the lamb shall lie down together. The murderer of Mary and Essex, the conqueror of the Armada, the imperious ruler of a turbulent empire, become a couch, at last, for a tired kitten! It was the most eloquent sermon upon the vanity of human pride and human grandeur that inspired Westminster preached to us that night.

We would have turned puss out of the Abbey, but for the fact that her small body made light of railed gates and she would have come straight back again. We walked up a flight of half a dozen steps and, stopping upon a pavement laid down in 1260, stood in the core of English history, as it were—upon the holiest ground in the British Empire, if profusion of kingly bones and kingly names of old renown make holy ground. For here in this little space were the ashes, the monuments and gilded effigies, of ten of the most illustrious personages who have worn crowns and borne scepters in this realm. This royal dust was the slow accumulation of hundreds of years. The latest comer entered into his rest four hundred years ago, and since the earliest was sepulchered, more than eight centuries have drifted by. Edward the Confessor, Henry the Fifth, Edward the First, Edward the Third, Richard the Second, Henry the Third, Eleanor, Philippa, Margaret Woodville—it was like bringing the collossal myths of history out of the forgotten ages and speaking to them face to face. The gilded effigies were scarcely marred—the faces were comely and majestic, old Edward the First looked the king—one had no impulse to be familiar with him. While we were contemplating the figure of Queen Eleanor lying in state, and calling to mind how like an ordinary human being the great king mourned for her six hundred years ago, we saw the vast illuminated clock face of the Parliament House tower glowering at us through a window of the Abbey and pointing with both hands to midnight. It was a derisive reminder that we were a part of this present sordid, plodding, commonplace time, and not august relics of a bygone age and the comrades of kings—and then the booming of the great bell tolled twelve, and with the last stroke the mocking clock face vanished in sudden darkness and left us with the past and its grandeurs again.

We descended, and entered the nave of the splendid Chapel of Henry VII. Mr. Wright said:

"Here is where the order of knighthood was conferred for centuries; the candidates sat in these seats; these brasses bear their coats of arms; these are their banners overhead, torn and dusty, poor old things, for they have hung there many and many a long year. In the floor you see inscriptions—kings and queens that lie in the vault below. When this vault was opened in our time they found them lying there in beautiful order—all quiet and comfortable— the red velvet on the coffins hardly faded any. And the bodies were sound—I saw them myself. They were embalmed, and looked natural, although they had been there such an awful time. Now in this place here, which is called the chantry, is a curious old group of statuary—the figures are mourning over George Villiers, Duke of Buckingham, who was assassinated by Felton in Charles I's time.

Yonder, Cromwell and his family used to lie. Now we come to the south aisle and this is the grand monument to Mary Queen of Scots, and her effigy—you easily see they get all the portraits from this effigy. Here in the wall of the aisle is a bit of a curiosity pretty roughly carved:"

Wm. WEST TOOME
SHOWER
1698

"William West, tomb shower, 1698. That fellow carved his name around in several places about the Abbey."

This was a sort of revelation to me. I had been wandering through the Abbey, never imagining but that its shows were created only for us—the people of the nineteenth century. But here is a man (become a show himself now, and a curiosity) to whom all these things were sights and wonders a hundred and seventy-five years ago. When curious idlers from the country and from foreign lands came here to look, he showed them old Sebert's tomb and those of the other old worthies I have been speaking of, and called them ancient and venerable; and he showed them Charles II's tomb as the newest and latest novelty he had; and he was doubtless present at the funeral. Three hundred years before his time some ancestor of his, perchance, used to point out the ancient marvels, in the immemorial way and then say: "This, gentlemen, is the tomb of his late Majesty Edward the Third—and I wish I could see him alive and hearty again, as I saw him twenty years ago; yonder is the tomb of Sebert the Saxon king—he has been lying there well on to eight hundred years, they say." And three hundred years before *this* party, Westminster was still a show, and Edward the Confessor's grave was a novelty of some thirty years' standing—but old "Sebert" was hoary and ancient still, and people who spoke of Alfred the Great as a comparatively recent man pondered over Sebert's grave and tried to take in all the tremendous meaning of it when the "toome shower" said, "This man has lain here well nigh five hundred years." It does seem as if all the generations that have lived and died since the world was created have visited Westminster to stare and wonder— and still found ancient things there. And some day a curiously clad company may arrive here in a balloon ship from some remote corner of the globe, and as they follow the verger among the monuments they may hear him say: "This is the tomb of Victoria the Good

Queen; battered and uncouth as it looks, it once was a wonder of
magnificence—but twelve hundred years work a deal of damage to
these things."

As we turned toward the door the moonlight was beaming in
at the windows, and it gave to the sacred place such an air
of restfulness and peace that Westminster was no longer a grisly
museum of moldering vanities, but her better and worthier self—
the deathless mentor of a great nation, the guide and encourager
of right ambitions, the preserver of just fame, and the home and
refuge for the nation's best and bravest when their work is done.

1874

English As She Is Taught

In the appendix to Croker's Boswell's *Johnson* one finds this anecdote:

Cato's Soliloquy.—One day Mrs. Gastrel set a little girl to repeat to
him [Dr. Samuel Johnson] Cato's Soliloquy, which she went through very
correctly. The Doctor, after a pause, asked the child:

"What was to bring Cato to an end?"

She said it was a knife.

"No, my dear, it was not so."

"My aunt Polly said it was a knife."

"Why, Aunt Polly's knife *may do,* but it was a *dagger,* my dear."

He then asked her the meaning of "bane and antidote," which she was
unable to give. Mrs. Gastrel said:

"You cannot expect so young a child to know the meaning of such
words."

He then said:

"My dear, how many pence are there in *sixpence?*"

"I cannot tell, sir," was the half-terrified reply.

On this, addressing himself to Mrs. Gastrel, he said:

"Now, my dear lady, can anything be more ridiculous than to teach a
child Cato's Soliloquy, who does not know how many pence there are in
sixpence?"

In a lecture before the Royal Geographical Society Professor Ravenstein quoted the following list of frantic questions, and said that
they had been asked in an examination:

Mention all the names of places in the world derived from Julius Caesar or Augustus Caesar.

Where are the following rivers: Pisuerga, Sakaria, Guadalete, Jalon, Mulde?

All you know of the following: Machacha, Pilmo, Schebulos, Crivoscia, Basecs, Mancikert, Taxhem, Citeaux, Meloria, Zutphen.

The highest peaks of the Karakorum range.

The number of universities in Prussia.

Why are the tops of mountains continually covered with snow [sic]?

Name the length and breadth of the streams of lava which issued from the Skaptar Jokul in the eruption of 1783.

That list would oversize nearly anybody's geographical knowledge. Isn't it reasonably possible that in our schools many of the questions in all studies are several miles ahead of where the pupil is?—that he is set to struggle with things that are ludicrously beyond his present reach, hopelessly beyond his present strength? This remark in passing, and by way of text; now I come to what I was going to say.

I have just now fallen upon a darling literary curiosity. It is a little book, a manuscript compilation, and the compiler sent it to me with the request that I say whether I think it ought to be published or not. I said, Yes; but as I slowly grow wise I briskly grow cautious; and so, now that the publication is imminent, it has seemed to me that I should feel more comfortable if I could divide up this responsibility with the public by adding them to the court. Therefore I will print some extracts from the book, in the hope that they may make converts to my judgment that the volume has merit which entitles it to publication.

As to its character. Every one has sampled "English as She Is Spoke" and "English as She Is Wrote"; this little volume furnishes us an instructive array of examples of "English as She Is Taught"—in the public schools of—well, this country. The collection is made by a teacher in those schools, and all the examples in it are genuine; none of them have been tampered with, or doctored in any way. From time to time, during several years, whenever a pupil has delivered himself of anything peculiarly quaint or toothsome in the course of his recitations, this teacher and her associates have privately set that thing down in a memorandum-book; strictly following the original, as to grammar, construction, spelling, and all; and the result is this literary curiosity.

The contents of the book consist mainly of answers given by the boys and girls to questions, said answers being given sometimes verbally, sometimes in writing. The subjects touched upon are fifteen in number: I. Etymology; II. Grammar; III. Mathematics; IV. Geography; V. "Original"; VI. Analysis; VII. History; VIII. "Intellectual"; IX. Philosophy; X. Physiology; XI. Astronomy; XII. Politics; XIII. Music; XIV. Oratory; XV. Metaphysics.

You perceive that the poor little young idea has taken a shot at a good many kinds of game in the course of the book. Now as to results. Here are some quaint definitions of words. It will be noticed that in all of these instances the sound of the word, or the look of it on paper, has misled the child:

Aborigines, a system of mountains.
Alias, a good man in the Bible.
Amenable, anything that is mean.
Ammonia, the food of the gods.
Assiduity, state of being an acid.
Auriferous, pertaining to an orifice.
Capillary, a little caterpillar.
Corniferous, rocks in which fossil corn is found.
Emolument, a headstone to a grave.
Equestrian, one who asks questions.
Eucharist, one who plays euchre.
Franchise, anything belonging to the French.
Idolater, a very idol person.
Ipecac, a man who likes a good dinner.
Irrigate, to make fun of.
Mendacious, what can be mended.
Mercenary, one who feels for another.
Parasite, a kind of umbrella.
Parasite, the murder of an infant.
Publican, a man who does his prayers in public.
Tenacious, ten acres of land.

Here is one where the phrase "publicans and sinners" has got mixed up in the child's mind with politics, and the result is a definition which takes one in a sudden and unexpected way:

Republican, a sinner mentioned in the Bible.

Also in Democratic newspapers now and then. Here are two where the mistake has resulted from sound assisted by remote fact:

Plagiarist, a writer of plays.
Demagogue, a vessel containing beer and other liquids.

I cannot quite make out what it was that misled the pupil in the following instances; it would not seem to have been the sound of the word, nor the look of it in print:

Asphyxia, a grumbling, fussy temper.
Quarternions, a bird with a flat beak and no bill, living in New Zealand.
Quarternions, the name given to a style of art practiced by the Phoenicians.
Quarternions, a religious convention held every hundred years.
Sibilant, the state of being idiotic.
Crosier, a staff carried by the Deity.

In the following sentences the pupil's ear has been deceiving him again:

The marriage was illegible.
He was totally dismasted with the whole performance.
He enjoys riding on a philosopher.
She was very quick at repertoire.
He prayed for the waters to subsidize.
The leopard is watching his sheep.
They had a strawberry vestibule.

Here is one which—well, now, how often we do slam right into the truth without ever suspecting it:

The men employed by the Gas Company go around and speculate the meter.

Indeed they do, dear; and when you grow up, many and many's the time you will notice it in the gas bill. In the following sentences the little people have some information to convey, every time; but in my case they fail to connect: the light always went out on the keystone word:

The coercion of some things is remarkable; as bread and molasses.
Her hat is contiguous because she wears it on one side.
He preached to an egregious congregation.
The captain eliminated a bullet through the man's heart.
You should take caution and be precarious.
The supercilious girl acted with vicissitude when the perennial time came.

That last is a curiously plausible sentence; one seems to know what it means, and yet he knows all the time that he doesn't. Here is an odd (but entirely proper) use of a word, and a most sudden descent from a lofty philosophical altitude to a very practical and homely illustration:

We should endeavor to avoid extremes—like those of wasps and bees.

And here—with "zoological" and "geological" in his mind, but not ready to his tongue—the small scholar has innocently gone and let out a couple of secrets which ought never to have been divulged in any circumstances:

There are a good many donkeys in theological gardens.
Some of the best fossils are found in theological cabinets.

Under the head of "Grammar" the little scholars furnish the following information:

Gender is the distinguishing nouns without regard to sex.
A verb is something to eat.
Adverbs should always be used as adjectives and adjectives as adverbs.
Every sentence and name of God must begin with a caterpillar.

"Caterpillar" is well enough, but capital letter would have been stricter. The following is a brave attempt at a solution, but it failed to liquify:

When they are going to say some prose or poetry before they say the poetry or prose they must put a semicolon just after the introduction of the prose or poetry.

The chapter on "Mathematics" is full of fruit. From it I take a few samples—mainly in an unripe state.

A straight line is any distance between two places.
Parallel lines are lines that can never meet until they run together.
A circle is a round straight line with a hole in the middle.
Things which are equal to each other are equal to anything else.
To find the number of square feet in a room you multiply the room by the number of the feet. The product is the result.

Right you are. In the matter of geography this little book is unspeakably rich. The questions do not appear to have applied the microscope to the subject, as did those quoted by Professor Ravenstein; still, they proved plenty difficult enough without that. These pupils did not hunt with a microscope, they hunted with a shotgun; this is shown by the crippled condition of the game they brought in:

America is divided into the Passiffic slope and the Mississippi valey.

North America is separated by Spain.

America consists from north to south about five hundred miles.

The United States is quite a small country compared with some other countrys, but is about as industrious.

The capital of the United States is Long Island.

The five seaports of the U. S. are Newfunlan and Sanfrancisco.

The principal products of the U. S. is earthquakes and volcanoes.

The Alaginnies are mountains in Philadelphia.

The Rocky Mountains are on the western side of Philadelphia.

Cape Hateras is a vast body of water surrounded by land and flowing into the Gulf of Mexico.

Mason and Dixon's line is the Equater.

One of the leading industries of the United States is mollasses, bookcovers, numbers, gas, teaching, lumber, manufacturers, paper-making, publishers, coal.

In Austria the principal occupation is gathering Austrich feathers.

Gibraltar is an island built on a rock.

Russia is very cold and tyrannical.

Sicily is one of the Sandwich Islands.

Hindoostan flows through the Ganges and empties into the Mediterranean Sea.

Ireland is called the Emigrant Isle because it is so beautiful and green.

The width of the different zones Europe lies in depend upon the surrounding country.

The imports of a country are the things that are paid for, the exports are the things that are not.

Climate lasts all the time and weather only a few days.

The two most famous volcanoes of Europe are Sodom and Gomorrah.

The chapter headed "Analysis" shows us that the pupils in our public schools are not merely loaded up with those showy facts about geography, mathematics, and so on, and left in that incomplete state; no, there's machinery for clarifying and expanding their minds. They are required to take poems and analyze them, dig out their common sense, reduce them to statistics, and reproduce them in a luminous prose translation which shall tell you at a glance what the poet was trying to get at. One sample will do. Here is a stanza from "The Lady of the Lake," followed by the pupil's impressive explanation of it:

Alone, but with unbated zeal,
The horseman plied with scourge and steel;
For jaded now and spent with toil,
Embossed with foam and dark with soil,
While every gasp with sobs he drew,
The laboring stag strained full in view.

The man who rode on the horse performed the whip and an instrument made of steel alone with strong ardor not diminishing, for, being tired from the time passed with hard labor overworked with anger and ignorant with weariness, while every breath for labor he drew with cries full of sorrow, the young deer made imperfect who worked hard filtered in sight.

I see, now, that I never understood that poem before. I have had glimpses of its meaning, in moments when I was not as ignorant with weariness as usual, but this is the first time the whole spacious idea of it ever filtered in sight. If I were a public-school pupil I would put those other studies aside and stick to analysis; for, after all, it is the thing to spread your mind.

We come now to historical matters, historical remains, one might say. As one turns the pages he is impressed with the depth to which one date has been driven into the American child's head— 1492. The date is there, and it is there to stay. And it is always at hand, always deliverable at a moment's notice. But the Fact that belongs with it? That is quite another matter. Only the date itself is familiar and sure: its vast Fact has failed of lodgment. It would appear that whenever you ask a public-school pupil when a thing— anything, no matter what—happened, and he is in doubt, he always rips out his 1492. He applies it to everything, from the landing of the ark to the introduction of the horse-car. Well, after all, it is our first date, and so it is right enough to honor it, and pay the public schools to teach our children to honor it:

George Washington was born in 1492.
Washington wrote the Declareation of Independence in 1492.
St. Bartholemew was massacred in 1492.
The Brittains were the Saxons who entered England in 1492 under Julius Caesar.
The earth is 1492 miles in circumference.

To proceed with "History"

Christopher Columbus was called the Father of his Country.
Queen Isabella of Spain sold her watch and chain and other millinery so that Columbus could discover America.

The Indian wars were very desecrating to the country.

The Indians pursued their warfare by hiding in the bushes and then scalping them.

Captain John Smith has been styled the father of his country. His life was saved by his daughter Pochahantas.

The Puritans found an insane asylum in the wilds of America.

The Stamp Act was to make everybody stamp all materials so they should be null and void.

Washington died in Spain almost broken-hearted. His remains were taken to the cathedral in Havana.

Gorilla warfare was where men rode on gorillas.

John Brown was a very good insane man who tried to get fugitives slaves into Virginia. He captured all the inhabitants, but was finally conquered and condemned to his death. The Confederasy was formed by the fugitive slaves.

Alfred the Great reigned 872 years. He was distinguished for letting some buckwheat cakes burn, and the lady scolded him.

Henry Eight was famous for being a great widower haveing lost several wives.

Lady Jane Grey studied Greek and Latin and was beheaded after a few days.

John Bright is noted for an incurable disease.

Lord James Gordon Bennett instigated the Gordon Riots.

The Middle Ages come in between antiquity and posterity.

Luther introduced Christianity into England a good many thousand years ago. His birthday was November 1883. He was once a Pope. He lived at the time of the Rebellion of Worms.

Julius Casar is noted for his famous telegram dispatch I came I saw I conquered.

Julius Caesar was really a very great man. He was a very great soldier and wrote a book for beginners in the Latin.

Cleopatra was caused by the death of an asp which she dissolved in a wine cup.

The only form of government in Greece was a limited monkey.

The Persian war lasted about 500 years.

Greece had only 7 wise men.

Socrates . . . destroyed some statues and had to drink Shamrock.

Here is a fact correctly stated; and yet it is phrased with such ingenious infelicity that it can be depended upon to convey misinformation every time it is uncarefully read:

By the Salic law no woman or descendant of a woman could occupy the throne.

To show how far a child can travel in history with judicious and diligent boosting in the public school, we select the following mosaic:

Abraham Lincoln was born in Wales in 1599.

In the chapter headed "Intellectual" I find a great number of most interesting statements. A sample or two may be found not amiss:

Bracebridge Hall was written by Henry Irving.
Snow Bound was written by Peter Cooper.
The House of the Seven Gables was written by Lord Bryant.
Edgar A. Poe was a very curdling writer.
Cotton Mather was a writer who invented the cotten gin and wrote histories.
Beowulf wrote the Scriptures.
Ben Johnson survived Shakespeare in some respects.
In the Canterbury Tale it gives account of King Alfred on his way to the shrine of Thomas Bucket.
Chaucer was the father of English pottery.
Chaucer was a bland verse writer of the third century.
Chaucer was succeeded by H. Wads. Longfellow an American Writer. His writings were chiefly prose and nearly one hundred years elapsed.
Shakspeare translated the Scriptures and it was called St. James because he did it.

In the middle of the chapter I find many pages of information concerning Shakespeare's plays, Milton's works, and those of Bacon, Addison, Samuel Johnson, Fielding, Richardson, Sterne, Smollett, De Foe, Locke, Pope, Swift, Goldsmith, Burns, Cowper, Wordsworth, Gibbon, Byron, Coleridge, Hood, Scott, Macaulay, George Eliot, Dickens, Bulwer, Thackeray, Browning, Mrs. Browning, Tennyson, and Disraeli—a fact which shows that into the restricted stomach of the public-school pupil is shoveled every year the blood, bone, and viscera of a gigantic literature, and the same is there digested and disposed of in a most successful and characteristic and gratifying public-school way. I have space for but a trifling few of the results:

Lord Byron was the son of an heiress and a drunken man.
Wm. Wordsworth wrote the Barefoot Boy and Imitations on Immortality.
Gibbon wrote a history of his travels in Italy. This was original.
George Eliot left a wife and children who mourned greatly for his genius.

George Eliot Miss Mary Evans Mrs. Cross Mrs. Lewis was the greatest female poet unless George Sands is made an exception of.

Bulwell is considered a good writer.

Sir Walter Scott Charles Bronte Alfred the Great and Johnson were the first great novelists.

Thomas Babington Makorlay graduated at Harvard and then studied law, he was raised to the peerage as baron in 1557 and died in 1776.

Here are two or three miscellaneous facts that may be of value, if taken in moderation:

Homer's writings are Homer's Essays Virgil the Aneid and Paradise lost some people say that these poems were not written by Homer but by another man of the same name.

A sort of sadness kind of shone in Bryant's poems.

Holmes is a very profligate and amusing writer.

When the public-school pupil wrestles with the political features of the Great Republic, they throw him sometimes:

A bill becomes a law when the President vetoes it.

The three departments of the government is the President rules the world, the governor rules the State, the mayor rules the city.

The first conscientious Congress met in Philadelphia.

The Constitution of the United States was established to ensure domestic hostility.

Truth crushed to earth will rise again. As follows:

The Constitution of the United States is that part of the book at the end which nobody reads.

And here she rises once more and untimely. There should be a limit to public-school instruction; it cannot be wise or well to let the young find out everything:

Congress is divided into civilized half civilized and savage.

Here are some results of study in music and oratory:

An interval in music is the distance on the keyboard from one piano to the next.

A rest means you are not to sing it.

Emphasis is putting more distress on one word than another.

The chapter on "Physiology" contains much that ought not to be lost to science:

Physillogigy is to study about your bones stummick and vertebry.

Occupations which are injurious to health are cabolic acid gas which is impure blood.

We have an upper and a lower skin. The lower skin moves all the time and the upper skin moves when we do.

The body is mostly composed of water and about one half is avaricious tissue.

The stomach is a small pear-shaped bone situated in the body.

The gastric juice keeps the bones from creaking.

The Chyle flows up the middle of the backbone and reaches the heart where it meets the oxygen and is purified.

The salivary glands are used to salivate the body.

In the stomach starch is changed to cane sugar and cane sugar to sugar cane.

The olfactory nerve enters the cavity of the orbit and is developed into the special sense of hearing.

The growth of a tooth begins in the back of the mouth and extends to the stomach.

If we were on a railroad track and a train was coming the train would deafen our ears so that we couldn't see to get off the track.

If, up to this point, none of my quotations have added flavor to the Johnsonian anecdote at the head of this article, let us make another attempt:

The theory that intuitive truths are discovered by the light of nature originated from St. John's interpretation of a passage in the Gospel of Plato.

The weight of the earth is found by comparing a mass of known lead with that of a mass of unknown lead.

To find the weight of the earth take the length of a degree on a meridian and multiply by 62½ pounds.

The spheres are to each other as the squares of their homologous sides.

A body will go just as far in the first second as the body will go plus the force of gravity and that's equal to twice what the body will go.

Specific gravity is the weight to be compared weight of an equal volume of or that is the weight of a body compared with the weight of an equal volume.

The law of fluid pressure divide the different forms of organized bodies by the form of attraction and the number increased will be the form.

Inertia is that property of bodies by virtue of which it cannot change its own condition of rest or motion. In other words it is the negative quality of passiveness either in recoverable latency or insipient latescence.

If a laugh is fair here, not the struggling child, nor the unintelligent teacher—or rather the unintelligent Boards, Committees, and Trustees—

are the proper target for it. All through this little book one detects the signs of a certain probable fact—that a large part of the pupil's "instruction" consists in cramming him with obscure and wordy "rules" which he does not understand and has no time to understand. It would be as useful to cram him with brickbats; they would at least stay. In a town in the interior of New York, a few years ago, a gentleman set forth a mathematical problem and proposed to give a prize to every public-school pupil who should furnish the correct solution of it. Twenty-two of the brightest boys in the public schools entered the contest. The problem was not a very difficult one for pupils of their mathematical rank and standing, yet they all failed—by a hair—through one trifling mistake or another. Some searching questions were asked, when it turned out that these lads were as glib as parrots with the "rules," but could not reason out a single rule or explain the principle underlying it. Their memories had been stocked, but not their understandings. It was a case of brickbat culture, pure and simple.

There are several curious "compositions" in the little book, and we must make room for one. It is full of naïveté, brutal truth, and unembarrassed directness, and is the funniest (genuine) boy's composition I think I have ever seen:

ON GIRLS

Girls are very stuck up and dignefied in their maner and be have your. They think more of dress than anything and like to play with dowls and rags. They cry if they see a cow in a far distance and are afraid of guns. They stay at home all the time and go to church on Sunday. They are al-ways sick. They are al-ways funy and making fun of boy's hands and they say how dirty. They cant play marbels. I pity them poor things. They make fun of boys and then turn round and love them. I dont beleave they ever kiled a cat or anything. They look out every nite and say oh ant the moon lovely. Thir is one thing I have not told and that is they al-ways now their lessons bettern boys.

From Mr. Edward Channing's recent article in *Science:*

The marked difference between the books now being produced by French, English, and American travelers, on the one hand, and German explorers, on the other, is too great to escape attention. That difference is due entirely to the fact that in school and university the German is taught, in the first place to see, and in the second place to understand what he does see.

1887

Aix, the Paradise of the Rheumatics

Aix-les-Bains. Certainly this is an enchanting place. It is a strong word, but I think the facts justify it. True, there is a rabble of nobilities, big and little, here all the time, and often a king or two; but as these behave quite nicely and also keep mainly to themselves, they are little or no annoyance. And then a king makes the best advertisement there is, and the cheapest. All he costs is a reception at the station by the mayor and the police in their Sunday uniforms, shop-front decorations along the route from station to hotel, brass band at the hotel, fireworks in the evening, free bath in the morning. This is the whole expense; and in return for it he goes away from here with the broad of his back metaphorically stenciled over with display ads., which shout to all nations of the world, assisted by the telegraph:

Rheumatism routed at Aix-les-Bains!
Gout admonished, Nerves braced up!
All diseases welcomed, and satisfaction given or the money returned at the door!

We leave nature's noble cliffs and crags undefiled and uninsulted by the advertiser's paint brush. We use the back of a king, which is better and properer and more effective, too, for the cliffs stay still and few see it, but the king moves across the fields of the world and is visible from all points, like a constellation. We are out for kings this week, but one will be along soon—possibly His Satanic Majesty of Russia. There's a colossus for you! A mysterious and terrible form that towers up into unsearchable space and casts a shadow across the universe like a planet in eclipse. There will be but one absorbing spectacle in this world when we stencil him and start him out.

This is an old valley, this of Aix, both in the history of man and in the geological records of its rocks. Its little lake of Bourget carries the human history back to the lake dwellers, furnishing seven groups of their habitations, and Dr. William Wakefield says in his interesting local guide that the mountains round about furnish "Geographically, a veritable epitome of the globe." The stratified chapters of the earth's history are clearly and permanently written on the sides of the roaring bulk of the Dent du Chat, but many of the layers of race, religion, and government which in turn have flourished and perished here between the lake dweller of several thousand years ago and the French republican of to-day, are ill defined and uninforming by comparison. There are several varieties of pagans. They went their way, one after the other, down into night and oblivion, leaving no account of themselves, no memorials. The Romans arrived 2,300 years ago, other parts of France are rich with remembrances of their eight centuries of occupation, but not many are here. Other pagans followed the Romans. By and by Christianity arrived, some 400 years after the time of Christ. The long procession of races, languages, religions, and dynasties demolished one another's records—it is man's way always.

As a result, nothing is left of the handiwork of the remoter inhabitants of the region except the constructions of the lake dwellers and some Roman odds and ends. There is part of a small Roman temple, there is part of a Roman bath, there is a graceful and battered Roman arch. It stands on a turfy level over the way from the present great bath house, is surrounded by magnolia trees, and is both a picturesque and suggestive object. It has stood there some 1,600 years. Its nearest neighbor, not twenty steps away, is a Catholic church. They are symbols of the two chief eras in the history of Aix. Yes, and of the European world. I judge that the venerable arch is held in reverent esteem by everybody, and that this esteem is its sufficient protection from insult, for it is the only public structure I have yet seen in France which lacks the sign, "It is forbidden to post bills here." Its neighbor the church has that sign on more than one of its sides, and other signs, too, forbidding certain other sorts of desecration.

The arch's nearest neighbor—just at its elbow, like the church—is the telegraph office. So there you have the three great eras bunched together—the era of War, the era of Theology, the era of Business. You pass under the arch, and the buried Caesars seem to rise from the dust of the centuries and flit before you; you pass by that old battered church, and are in touch with the Middle Ages, and with another step you can put down ten francs and shake hands with Oshkosh under the Atlantic.

It is curious to think what changes the last of the three symbols stand for; changes in men's ways and thoughts, changes in material civilization, changes in the Deity—or in men's conception of the Deity, if that is an exacter way of putting it. The second of the symbols arrived in the earth at a time when the Deity's possessions consisted of a small sky freckled with mustard-seed stars, and under it a patch of landed estate not so big as the holdings of the Tsar to-day, and all His time was taken up in trying to keep a handful of Jews in some sort of order—exactly the same number of them that the Tsar has lately been dealing with in a more abrupt and far less loving and long-suffering way. At a later time—a time within all old men's memories—the Deity was otherwise engaged. He was dreaming His eternities away on His Great White Throne, steeped in the soft bliss of hymns of praise wafted aloft without ceasing from choirs of ransomed souls, Presbyterians and the rest. This was a Deity proper enough to the size and conditions of things, no doubt a provincial Deity with provincial tastes. The change since has been inconceivably vast. His empire has been unimaginably enlarged. To-day He is a Master of a universe made up of myriads upon myriads of gigantic suns, and among them, lost in that limitless sea of light, floats that atom. His earth, which once seemed so good and satisfactory and cost so many days of patient labor to build, is a mere cork adrift in the waters of a shoreless Atlantic. This is a business era, and no doubt he is governing His huge empire now, not by dreaming the time away in the buzz of hymning choirs, with occasional explosions of arbitary power disproportioned to the size of the annoyance, but by applying laws of a sort proper and necessary to the sane and successful management of a complex and prodigious establishment, and by seeing to it that the exact and constant operation of these laws is not interfered with for the accommodation of any individual or political or religious faction or nation.

Mighty has been the advance of the nations and the liberalization of thought. A result of it is a changed Deity, a Deity of a dignity and sublimity proportioned to the majesty of His office and the magnitude of His empire, a Deity who has been freed from a hundred fretting chains and will in time be freed from the rest by the several ecclesiastical bodies who have these matters in charge. It was, without doubt, a mistake and a step backward when the Presbyterian Synods of America lately decided, by vote, to leave Him still embarrassed with the dogma of infant damnation. Situated as we are, we cannot at present know with how much of anxiety

He watched the balloting, nor with how much of grieved disappointment He observed the result.

Well, all these eras above spoken of are modern, they are of last week, they are of yesterday, they are of this morning, so to speak. The springs, the healing waters that gush up from under this hillside village, indeed are ancient. They, indeed, are a genuine antiquity; they antedate all those fresh human matters by processions of centuries; they were born with the fossils of the Dent du Chat, and they have been always abundant. They furnished a million gallons a day to wash the lake dwellers with, the same to wash the Cæsars with, no less to wash Balzac with, and have not diminished on my account. A million gallons a day for how many days? Figures cannot set forth the number. The delivery, in the aggregate, has amounted to an Atlantic. And there is still an Atlantic down in there. By Doctor Wakefield's calculation the Atlantic is three-quarters of a mile down in the earth. The calculation is based upon the temperature of the water, which is 114 degrees to 117 degrees Fahrenheit, the natural law being that below a certain depth heat augments at the rate of one degree for every sixty feet of descent.

Aix is handsome, and is handsomely situated, too, on its hill slope, with its stately prospect of mountain range and plain spread out before it and about it. The streets are mainly narrow, and steep and crooked and interesting, and offer considerable variety in the way of names; on the corner of one of them you read this: "Rue du Puits d'Enfer" ("Pit of Hell Street"). Some of the sidewalks are only eighteen inches wide; they are for the cats, probably. There is a pleasant park, and there are spacious and beautiful grounds connected with the two great pleasure resorts, the Cercle and the Villa des Fleurs. The town consists of big hotels, little hotels, and *pensions*. The season lasts about six months, beginning with May. When it is at its height there are thousands of visitors here, and in the course of the season as many as 20,000 in the aggregate come and go.

These are not all here for the baths; some come for the gambling facilities and some for the climate. It is a climate where the field strawberry flourishes through the spring, summer, and fall. It is hot in the summer, and hot in earnest; but this is only in the daytime; it is not hot at night. The English season is May and June; they get a good deal of rain then, and they like that. The Americans take July, and the French take August. By the 1st of July the open-air music and the evening concerts and operas and plays are fairly

under way, and from that time onward the rush of pleasure has a
steadily increasing boom. It is said that in August the great grounds
and the gambling rooms are crowded all the time and no end of
ostensible fun going on.

It is a good place for rest and sleep and general recuperation
of forces. The book of Doctor Wakefield says there is something
about this atmosphere which is the deadly enemy of insomnia, and
I think this must be true, for if I am any judge, this town
is at times the noisiest one in Europe, and yet a body gets more
sleep here than he would at home, I don't care where his home
is. Now, we are living at a most comfortable and satisfactory *pension*,
with a garden of shade trees and flowers and shrubs, and a convincing air of quiet and repose. But just across the narrow street
is the little market square, and at the corner of that is the church
that is neighbor to the Roman arch, and that narrow street, and
that billiard table of a market place, and that church are able,
on a bet, to turn out more noise to a cubic yard at the wrong time
than any other similar combination in the earth or out of it. In the
street you have the skull-bursting thunder of the passing hack, a
volume of sound not producible by six hacks anywhere else; on
the hack is a lunatic with a whip which he cracks to notify the
public to get out of his way. This crack is as keen and sharp and
penetrating and ear-splitting as a pistol shot at close range, and
the lunatic delivers it in volleys, not single shots. You think you will
not be able to live till he gets by, and when he does get by he
leaves only a vacancy for the bandit who sells *Le Petit Journal*
to fill with his strange and awful yell. He arrives with the early
morning and the market people, and there is a dog that arrives
at about the same time and barks steadily at nothing till he dies, and
they fetch another dog just like him. The bark of this breed is the
twin of the whip volley, and stabs like a knife. By and by, what
is left of you the church bell gets. There are many bells, and apparently six or seven thousand town clocks, and as they are all five
minutes apart—probably by law—there are no intervals. Some of
them are striking all the time—at least, after you go to bed they are.
There is one clock that strikes the hour and then strikes it over
again to see if it was right. Then for evenings and Sundays there
is a chime—a chime that starts in pleasantly and musically, then
suddenly breaks into a frantic roar, and boom, and crash of warring
sounds that makes you think Paris is up and the Revolution come
again. And yet, as I have said, one sleeps here—sleeps like the

dead. Once he gets his grip on his sleep, neither hack, nor whip, nor news fiend, nor dog, nor bell cyclone, nor all of them together, can wrench it loose or mar its deep and tranquil continuity. Yes, there is indeed something in this air that is death to insomnia.

The buildings of the Cercle and the Villa des Fleurs are huge in size, and each has a theater in it, and a great restaurant, also conveniences for gambling and general and variegated entertainment.

They stand in ornamental grounds of great extent and beauty. The multitudes of fashionable folk sit at refreshment tables in the open air, afternoons, and listen to the music, and it is there that they mainly go to break the Sabbath.

To get the privilege of entering these grounds and buildings you buy a ticket for a few francs, which is good for the whole season. You are then free to go and come at all hours, attend the plays and concerts free, except on special occasions, gamble, buy refreshments, and make yourself symmetrically comfortable.

Nothing could be handier than those two little theaters. The curtain doesn't rise until 8.30; then between the acts one can idle for half an hour in the other departments of the building, damaging his appetite in the restaurants or his pocketbook in the baccarat room. The singers and actors are from Paris, and their performance is beyond praise.

I was never in a fashionable gambling hell until I came here. I had read several millions of descriptions of such places, but the reality was new to me. I very much wanted to see this animal, especially the new historic game of baccarat, and this was a good place, for Aix ranks next to Monte Carlo for high play and plenty of it. But the result was what I might have expected—the interest of the looker-on perishes with the novelty of the spectacle; that is to say, in a few minutes. A permanent and intense interest is acquirable in baccarat, or in any other game, but you have to buy it. You don't get it by standing around and looking on.

The baccarat table is covered with green cloth and is marked off in divisions with chalk or something. The banker sits in the middle, the croupier opposite. The customers fill all the chairs at the table, and the rest of the crowd are massed at their back and leaning over them to deposit chips or gold coins. Constantly money and chips are flung upon the table, and the game seems to consist in the croupier's reaching for these things with a flexible sculling oar, and raking them home. It appeared to be a rational enough game for him, and if I could have borrowed his oar I would have stayed, but I didn't

see where the entertainment of the others came in. This was because
I saw without perceiving, and observed without understanding. For
the widow and the orphan and the others do win money there. Once
an old gray mother in Israel or elsewhere pulled out, and I heard her
say to her daughter or her granddaughter as they passed me, "There,
I've won six louis, and I'm going to quit while I'm ahead." Also there
was this statistic. A friend pointed to a young man with the dead
stub of a cigar in his mouth, which he kept munching nervously all
the time and pitching hundred-dollar chips on the board while two
sweet young girls reached down over his shoulders to deposit modest
little gold pieces, and said: "He's only funning, now; wasting a few
hundred to pass the time—waiting for the gold room to open, you
know, which won't be till after midnight—then you'll see him bet! He
won £14,000 there last night. They don't bet anything there but big
money."

The thing I chiefly missed was the haggard people with the intense
eye, the hunted look, the desperate mien, candidates for suicide and
the pauper's grave. They are in the description, as a rule, but they
were off duty that night. All the gamblers, male and female, old
and young, looked abnormally cheerful and prosperous.

However, all the nations were there, clothed richly and speaking all
the languages. Some of the women were painted, and were evidently
shaky as to character. These items tallied with the descriptions well
enough.

The etiquette of the place was difficult to master. In the brilliant
and populous halls and corridors you don't smoke, and you wear your
hat, no matter how many ladies are in the thick throng of drifting
humanity, but the moment you cross the sacred threshold and enter
the gambling hell, off the hat must come, and everybody lights his
cigar and goes to suffocating the ladies.

But what I came here for five weeks ago was the baths. My right
arm was disabled with rheumatism. To sit at home in America and
guess out the European bath best fitted for a particular ailment or
combination of ailments, it is not possible, and it would not be a good
idea to experiment in that way, anyhow. There are a great many
curative baths on the Continent, and some are good for one disease
and bad for another. So it is necessary to let your physician name a
bath for you. As a rule, Americans go to Europe to get this advice,
and South Americans go to Paris for it. Now and then an economist
chooses his bath himself and does a thousand miles of railroading to
get to it, and then the local physicians tell him he has come to the

wrong place. He sees that he has lost time and money and strength, and almost the minute he realizes this he loses his temper. I had the rheumatism and was advised to go to Aix, not so much because I had that disease as because I had the promise of certain others. What they were was not explained to me, but they are either in the following menu or I have been sent to the wrong place. Doctor Wakefield's book says:

We know that the class of maladies benefited by the water and baths at Aix are those due to defect of nourishment, debility of the nervous system, or to a gouty, rheumatic, herpetic, or scrofulous diathesis—all diseases extremely debilitating, and requiring a tonic, and not depressing action of the remedy. This it seems to find here, as recorded experience and daily action can testify. According to the line of treatment followed particularly with due regard to the temperature, the action of the Aix waters can be made sedative, exciting, derivative, or alterative and tonic.

The "Establishment" is the property of France, and all the officers and servants are employees of the French government. The bathhouse is a huge and massive pile of white marble masonry, and looks more like a temple than anything else. It has several floors and each is full of bath cabinets. There is every kind of bath—for the nose, the ears, the throat, vapor baths, swimming baths, and all people's favorite, the douche. It is a good building to get lost in, when you are not familiar with it. From early morning until nearly noon people are streaming in and streaming out without halt. The majority come afoot, but great numbers are brought in sedan chairs, a sufficiently ugly contrivance whose cover is a steep little tent made of striped canvas. You see nothing of the patient in this diving bell as the bearers tramp along, except a glimpse of his ankles bound together and swathed around with blankets or towels to that generous degree that the result suggests a sore piano leg. By attention and practice the pallbearers have got so that they can keep out of step all the time—and they do it. As a consequence their veiled churn goes rocking, tilting, swaying along like a bell buoy in a ground swell. It makes the oldest sailor homesick to look at that spectacle.

The "course" is usually fifteen douche baths and five tub baths. You take the douche three days in succession, then knock off and take a tub. You keep up this distribution through the course. If one course does not cure you, you take another one after an interval. You seek a local physician and he examines your case and prescribes the kind of bath required for it, with various other particulars; then you buy your course tickets and pay for them in advance—nine dollars.

With the tickets you get a memorandum book with your dates and hours all set down on it. The doctor takes you into the bath the first morning and gives some instructions to the two *doucheurs* who are to handle you through the course. The *pourboires* are about ten cents to each of the men for each bath, payable at the end of the course. Also at the end of the course you pay three or four francs to the superintendent of your department of the bathhouse. These are useful particulars to know, and are not to be found in the books. A servant of your hotel carries your towels and sheet to the bath daily and brings them away again. They are the property of the hotel; the French government doesn't furnish these things.

You meet all kinds of people at a place like this, and if you give them a chance they will submerge you under their circumstances, for they are either very glad or very sorry they came, and they want to spread their feelings out and enjoy them. One of these said to me:

"It's great, these baths. I didn't come here for my health; I only came to find out if there was anything the matter with me. The doctor told me if there was the symptoms would soon appear. After the first douche I had sharp pains in all my muscles. The doctor said it was different varieties of rheumatism, and the best varieties there were, too. After my second bath I had aches in my bones, and skull and around. The doctor said it was different varieties of neuralgia, and the best in the market, anybody would tell me so. I got many new kinds of pains out of my third douche. These were in my joints. The doctor said it was gout, complicated with heart disease, and encouraged me to go on. Then we had the fourth douche, and I came out on a stretcher that time, and fetched with me one vast, diversified undulating continental kind of pain, with horizons to it, and zones, and parallels of latitude, and meridians of longitude, and isothermal belts, and variations of the compass—oh, everything tidy, and right up to the latest developments, you know. The doctor said it was inflammation of the soul, and just the very thing. Well, I went right on gathering them in, toothache, liver complaint, softening of the brain, nostalgia, bronchitis, osteology, fits, Coleoptera, hydrangea, Cyclopædia Britannica, delirium tremens, and a lot of other things that I've got down on my list that I'll show you, and you can keep it if you like and tally off the bric-à-brac as you lay it in.

"The doctor said I was a grand proof of what these baths could do; said I had come here as innocent of disease as a grindstone, and inside of three weeks these baths had sluiced out of me every important ailment known to medical science, along with considerable more that were entirely new and patentable. Why, he wanted to exhibit me in his bay window!"

There seem to be a good many liars this year. I began to take the baths and found them most enjoyable; so enjoyable that if I hadn't had a disease I would have borrowed one, just to have a pretext for going on. They took me into a stone-floored basin about fourteen feet square, which had enough strange-looking pipes and things in it to make it look like a torture chamber. The two half-naked men seated me on a pine stool and kept a couple of warm-water jets as thick as one's wrist playing upon me while they kneaded me, stroked me, twisted me, and applied all the other details of the scientific massage to me for seven or eight minutes. Then they stood me up and played a powerful jet upon me all around for another minute. The cool shower bath came next, and the thing was over. I came out of the bathhouse a few minutes later feeling younger and fresher and finer than I have felt since I was a boy. The spring and cheer and delight of this exaltation lasted three hours, and the same uplifting effect has followed the twenty douches which I have taken since.

After my first douche I went to the chemist's on the corner, as per instructions, and asked for half a glass of Challe water. It comes from a spring sixteen miles from here. It was furnished to me, but, perceiving that there was something the matter with it, I offered to wait till they could get some that was fresh, but they said it always smelled that way. They said the reason that this was so much ranker than the sulphur water of the bath was that this contained thirty-two times as much sulphur as that. It is true, but in my opinion that water comes from a cemetery, and not a fresh cemetery, either. History says that one of the early Roman generals lost an army down there somewhere. If he could come back now I think this water would help him find it again. However, I drank the Challe, and have drunk it once or twice every day since. I suppose it is all right, but I wish I knew what was the matter with those Romans.

My first baths developed plenty of pain, but the subsequent ones removed almost all of it. I have got back the use of my arm these last few days, and I am going away now.

There are many beautiful drives about Aix, many interesting places to visit, and much pleasure to be found in paddling around the little Lake Bourget on the small steamers, but the excursion which satisfied me best was a trip to Annecy and its neighborhood. You go to Annecy in an hour by rail, through a garden land that has not had its equal for beauty perhaps since Eden; and certainly not Eden was cultivated

as this garden is. The charm and loveliness of the whole region are
bewildering. Picturesque rocks, forest-clothed hills, slopes richly bright
in the cleanest and greenest grass, fields of grain without freck or
flaw, dainty of color and as shiny and shimmery as silk, old gray
mansions and towers, half buried in foliage and sunny eminences, deep
chasms with precipitous walls, and a swift stream of pale-blue water
between, with now and then a tumbling cascade, and always noble
mountains in view, with vagrant white clouds curling about their
summits.

Then at the end of an hour you come to Annecy and rattle through
its old crooked lanes, built solidly up with curious old houses that are
a dream of the Middle Ages, and presently you come to the main
object of your trip—Lake Annecy. It is a revelation; it is a miracle.
It brings the tears to a body's eyes, it affects you just as all things
that you instantly recognize as perfect affect you—perfect music, perfect eloquence, perfect art, perfect joy, perfect grief. It stretches itself
out there in a caressing sunlight, and away toward its border of majestic mountains, a crisped and radiant plain of water of the divinest blue
that can be imagined. All the blues are there, from the faintest shoal-
water suggestion of the color, detectable only in the shadow of some
overhanging object, all the way through, a little blue and a little
bluer still, and again a shade bluer, till you strike the deep, rich
Mediterranean splendor which breaks the heart in your bosom, it is
so beautiful.

And the mountains, as you skim along on the steamboat, how stately
their forms, how noble their proportions, how green their velvet
slopes, how soft the mottlings of the sun and shadow that play about
the rocky ramparts that crown them, how opaline the vast upheavals
of snow banked against the sky in the remotenesses beyond—Mont
Blanc and the others—how shall anybody describe? Why, not even the
painter can quite do it, and the most the pen can do is to suggest.

Up the lake there is an old abbey—Tallories—relic of the Middle
Ages. We stopped there; stepped from the sparkling water and the
rush and boom and fret and fever of the nineteenth century into
the solemnity and the silence and the soft gloom and the brooding
mystery of a remote antiquity. The stone step at the water's edge
had the traces of a worn-out inscription on it; the wide flight of stone
steps that led up to the front door was polished smooth by the passing
feet of forgotten centuries, and there was not an unbroken stone
among them all. Within the pile was the old square cloister with
covered arcade all around it where the monks of the ancient times

used to sit and meditate, and now and then welcome to their hospitalities the wandering knight with his tin breeches on, and in the
middle of the square court (open to the sky) was a stone well
curb, cracked and slick with age and use, and all about it were weeds,
and among the weeds moldy brickbats that the Crusaders used to
throw at one another. A passage at the further side of the cloister led
to another weedy and roofless little inclosure beyond where there was
a ruined wall clothed to the top with masses of ivy, and flanking it
was a battered and picturesque arch. All over the building there
were comfortable rooms and comfortable beds and clean plank floors
with no carpets on them. In one room upstairs were half a dozen
portraits, dimming relics of the vanished centuries—portraits of abbots
who used to be as grand as princes in their old day, and very rich,
and much worshiped and very bold; and in the next room there were
a howling chromo and an electric bell. Downstairs there was an
ancient wood carving with a Latin word commanding silence, and
there was a spang-new piano close by. Two elderly French women,
with the kindest and honestest and sincerest faces, have the abbey
now, and they board and lodge people who are tired of the roar
of cities and want to be where the dead silence and serenity and
peace of this old nest will heal their blistered spirits and patch up
their ragged minds. They fed us well, they slept us well, and I wish
I could have stayed there a few years and got a solid rest.

1891

At the Shrine of St. Wagner

BAYREUTH, Aug. 2d, 1891.

It was at Nuremberg that we struck the inundation of music-mad
strangers that was rolling down upon Bayreuth. It had been long
since we had seen such multitudes of excited and struggling people.
It took a good half-hour to pack them and pair them into the train—
and it was the longest train we have yet seen in Europe. Nuremberg
had been witnessing this sort of experience a couple of times a day for
about two weeks. It gives one an impressive sense of the magnitude of
this biennial pilgrimage. For a pilgrimage is what it is. The devotees

come from the very ends of the earth to worship their prophet in his own Kaaba in his own Mecca.

If you are living in New York or San Francisco or Chicago or any-where else in America, and you conclude, by the middle of May, that you would like to attend the Bayreuth opera two months and a half later, you must use the cable and get about it immediately or you will get no seats, and you must cable for lodgings, too. Then if you are lucky you will get seats in the last row and lodgings in the fringe of the town. If you stop to write you will get nothing. There were plenty of people in Nuremberg when we passed through who had come on pilgrimage without first securing seats and lodgings. They had found neither in Bayreuth; they had walked Bayreuth streets a while in sorrow, then had gone to Nuremberg and found neither beds nor standing room, and had walked those quaint streets all night, waiting for the hotels to open and empty their guests into the trains, and so make room for these, their defeated brethren and sisters in the faith. They had endured from thirty to forty hours' railroading on the continent of Europe—with all which that implies of worry, fatigue, and financial impoverishment—and all they had got and all they were to get for it was handiness and accuracy in kicking themselves, ac-quired by practice in the back streets of the two towns when other people were in bed; for back they must go over that unspeakable journey with their pious mission unfulfilled. These humiliated outcasts had the frowsy and unbrushed and apologetic look of wet cats, and their eyes were glazed with drowsiness, their bodies were adroop from crown to sole, and all kind-hearted people refrained from asking them if they had been to Bayreuth and failed to connect, as knowing they would lie.

We reached here (Bayreuth) about mid-afternoon of a rainy Sat-urday. We were of the wise, and had secured lodgings and opera seats months in advance.

I am not a musical critic, and did not come here to write essays about the operas and deliver judgment upon their merits. The little children of Bayreuth could do that with a finer sympathy and a broader in-telligence than I. I only care to bring four or five pilgrims to the operas, pilgrims able to appreciate them and enjoy them. What I write about the performance to put in my odd time would be offered to the public as merely a cat's view of a king, and not of didactic value.

Next day, which was Sunday, we left for the opera-house—that is to say, the Wagner temple—a little after the middle of the afternoon.

The great building stands all by itself, grand and lonely, on a high ground outside the town. We were warned that if we arrived after four o'clock we should be obliged to pay two dollars and a half apiece extra by way of fine. We saved that; and it may be remarked here that this is the only opportunity that Europe offers of saving money. There was a big crowd in the grounds about the building, and the ladies' dresses took the sun with fine effect. I do not mean to intimate that ladies were in full dress, for that was not so. The dresses were pretty, but neither sex was in evening dress.

The interior of the building is simple—severely so; but there is no occasion for color and decoration, since the people sit in the dark. The auditorium has the shape of a keystone, with the stage at the narrow end. There is an aisle on each side, but no aisle in the body of the house. Each row of seats extends in an unbroken curve from one side of the house to the other. There are seven entrance doors on each side of the theater and four at the butt, eighteen doors to admit and emit 1,650 persons. The number of the particular door by which you are to enter the house or leave it is printed on your ticket, and you can use no door but that one. Thus, crowding and confusion are impossible. Not so many as a hundred people use any one door. This is better than having the usual (and useless) elaborate fireproof arrangements. It is the model theater of the world. It can be emptied while the second hand of a watch makes its circuit. It would be entirely safe, even if it were built of lucifer matches.

If your seat is near the center of a row and you enter late you must work your way along a rank of about twenty-five ladies and gentlemen to get to it. Yet this causes no trouble, for everybody stands up until all the seats are full, and the filling is accomplished in a very few minutes. Then all sit down, and you have a solid mass of fifteen hundred heads, making a steep cellar-door slant from the rear of the house down to the stage.

All the lights were turned low, so low that the congregation sat in deep and solemn gloom. The funereal rustling of dresses and the low buzz of conversation began to die swiftly down, and presently not the ghost of a sound was left. This profound and increasingly impressive stillness endured for some time—the best preparation for music, spectacle, or speech conceivable. I should think our show people would have invented or imported that simple and impressive device for securing and solidifying the attention of an audience long ago; instead of which they continue to this day to open a performance against a deadly competition in the form of noise, confusion, and a scattered interest.

Finally, out of darkness and distance and mystery soft rich notes rose upon the stillness, and from his grave the dead magician began to weave his spells about his disciples and steep their souls in his enchantment. There was something strangely impressive in the fancy which kept intruding itself that the composer was conscious in his grave of what was going on here, and that these divine sounds were the clothing of thoughts which were at this moment passing through his brain, and not recognized and familiar ones which had issued from it at some former time.

The entire overture, long as it was, was played to a dark house with the curtain down. It was exquisite; it was delicious. But straightway thereafter, of course, came the singing, and it does seem to me that nothing can make a Wagner opera absolutely perfect and satisfactory to the untutored but to leave out the vocal parts. I wish I could see a Wagner opera done in pantomime once. Then one would have the lovely orchestration unvexed to listen to and bathe his spirit in, and the bewildering beautiful scenery to intoxicate his eyes with, and the dumb acting couldn't mar these pleasures, because there isn't often anything in the Wagner opera that one would call by such a violent name as acting; as a rule all you would see would be a couple of silent people, one of them standing still, the other catching flies. Of course I do not really mean that he would be catching flies; I only mean that the usual operatic gestures which consist in reaching first one hand out into the air and then the other might suggest the sport I speak of if the operator attended strictly to business and uttered no sound.

This present opera was "Parsifal." Madame Wagner does not permit its representation anywhere but in Bayreuth. The first act of the three occupied two hours, and I enjoyed that in spite of the singing.

I trust that I know as well as anybody that singing is one of the most entrancing and bewitching and moving and eloquent of all the vehicles invented by man for the conveying of feeling; but it seems to me that the chief virtue in song is melody, air, tune, rhythm, or what you please to call it, and that when this feature is absent what remains is a picture with the color left out. I was not able to detect in the vocal parts of "Parisifal" anything that might with confidence be called rhythm or tune or melody; one person performed at a time—and a long time, too—often in a noble, and always in a high-toned, voice; but he only pulled out long notes, then some short ones, then another long one, then a sharp, quick, peremptory bark or two—and so on and so on; and when he was done you saw that the information which he had conveyed had not compensated for the disturbance. Not always, but pretty often. If two of them would but put in a duet occasionally and blend the voices; but no, they don't do that. The great master, who knew so well how to make a hundred instruments rejoice in unison and pour out their souls in mingled and melodious tides of delicious sound, deals only in barren solos when he puts in the vocal parts. It may be that he was deep, and only added the singing to his operas for the sake of the contrast it would make with the music. Singing! It does seem the wrong name to apply to it. Strictly described, it is a practising of difficult and unpleasant intervals, mainly. An ignorant person gets tired of listening to gymnastic intervals in the long run, no matter how pleasant they may be. In "Parsifal" there is a hermit named Gurnemanz who stands on the stage in one spot and practises by the hour, while first one and then another character of the cast endures what he can of it and then retires to die.

During the evening there was an intermission of three-quarters of an hour after the first act and one an hour long after the second. In both instances the theater was totally emptied. People who had previously engaged tables in the one sole eating-house were able to put in their time very satisfactorily; the other thousand went hungry. The opera was concluded at ten in the evening or a little later. When we reached home we had been gone more than seven hours. Seven hours at five dollars a ticket is almost too much for the money.

While browsing about the front yard among the crowd between the acts I encountered twelve or fifteen friends from different parts of America, and those of them who were most familiar with Wagner said that "Parsifal" seldom pleased at first, but that after one had heard it several times it was almost sure to become a favorite. It seemed impossible, but it was true, for the statement came from people whose word was not to be doubted.

And I gathered some further information. On the ground I found part of a German musical magazine, and in it a letter written by Uhlic thirty-three years ago, in which he defends the scorned and abused Wagner against people like me, who found fault with the comprehensive absence of what our kind regards as singing. Uhlic says Wagner despised "*Jene plapperude musik*," and therefore "runs, trills, and *schnorkel* are discarded by him." I don't know what a *schnorkel* is, but now that I know it has been left out of these operas I never have missed so much in my life. And Uhlic further says that Wagner's song is true: that it is "simply emphasized intoned speech." That certainly describes it—in "Parsifal" and some of the other operas; and if I understand Uhlic's elaborate German he apologizes for the beautiful airs in "Tannhäuser." Very well; now that Wagner and I understand each other, perhaps we shall get along better, and I shall stop calling him Waggner, on the American plan, and thereafter call him Wagner as per German custom, for I feel entirely friendly now. The minute we get reconciled to a person, how willing we are to throw aside little needless punctilios and pronounce his name right!

Of course I came home wondering why people should come from all corners of America to hear these operas, when we have lately had a season or two of them in New York with these same singers in the several parts, and possibly this same orchestra. I resolved to think that out at all hazards.

Tuesday.—Yesterday they played the only operatic favorite I have ever had—an opera which has always driven me mad with ignorant delight whenever I have heard it—"Tannhäuser." I heard it first when I was a youth; I heard it last in the last German season in New York. I was busy yesterday and I did not intend to go, knowing I should have another "Tannhäuser" opportunity in a few days; but after five o'clock I found myself free and walked out to the opera-house and arrived about the beginning of the second act. My opera ticket admitted me to the grounds in front, past the policeman and the chain, and I thought I would take a rest on a bench for an hour or two and wait for the third act.

In a moment or so the first bugles blew, and the multitude began to crumble apart and melt into the theater. I will explain this bugle-call is one of the pretty features here. You see, the theater is empty, and hundreds of the audience are a good way off in the feeding-house; the first bugle-call is blown about a quarter of an hour before time for the curtain to rise. This company of buglers, in uniform, march out with military step and send out over the landscape a few bars of the theme of the approaching act, piercing the distances with the gracious notes; then they march to the other entrance and repeat. Presently they do this over again. Yesterday only about two hundred people were still left in front of the house when the second call was blown; in another half-minute they would have been in the house, but then a thing happened which delayed them—the one solitary thing in this world which could be relied on with certainty to accomplish it, I suppose— an imperial princess appeared in the balcony above them. They stopped dead in their tracks and began to gaze in a stupor of gratitude and satisfaction. The lady presently saw that she must disappear or the doors would be closed upon these worshipers, so she returned to her box. This daughter-in-law of an emperor was pretty; she had a kind face; she was without airs; she is known to be full of common human sympathies. There are many kinds of princesses, but this kind is the most harmful of all, for wherever they go they reconcile people to monarchy and set back the clock of progress. The valuable princes, the desirable princes, are the czars and their sort. By their mere dumb presence in the world they cover with derision every argument that can be invented in favor of royalty by the most ingenious casuist. In his time the husband of this princess was valuable. He led a degraded life, he ended it with his own hand in circumstances and surroundings of a hideous sort, and was buried like a god.

In the opera-house there is a long loft back of the audience, a kind of open gallery, in which princes are displayed. It is sacred to them; it is the holy of holies. As soon as the filling of the house is about complete the standing multitude turn and fix their eyes upon the princely layout and gaze mutely and longingly and adoringly and regretfully like sinners looking into heaven. They become rapt, unconscious, steeped in worship. There is no spectacle anywhere that is more pathetic than this. It is worth crossing many oceans to see. It is somehow not the same gaze that people rivet upon a Victor Hugo, or Niagara, or the bones of the mastodon, or the guillotine of the Revolution, or the great pyramid, or distant Vesuvius smoking in the sky, or any man long celebrated to you by his genius and achievements, or thing long celebrated to you by the praises of books and pictures— no, that gaze is only the gaze of intense curiosity, interest, wonder, engaged in drinking delicious deep draughts that taste good all the way down and appease and satisfy the thirst of a lifetime. Satisfy it— that is the word. Hugo and the mastodon will still have a degree of intense interest thereafter when encountered, but never anything approaching the ecstasy of that first view. The interest of a prince is different. It may be envy, it may be worship, doubtless it is a mixture of both—and it does not satisfy its thirst with one view, or even noticeably diminish it. Perhaps the essence of the thing is the value which men attach to a valuable something which has come by luck and not been earned. A dollar picked up in the road is more satisfaction to you than the ninety-and-nine which you had to work for, and money won at faro or in stocks snuggles into your heart in the same way. A prince picks up grandeur, power, and a permanent holiday and gratis support by a pure accident, the accident of birth, and he stands always before the grieved eye of poverty and obscurity a monumental representative of luck. And then—supremest value of all—his is the only high fortune on the earth which is secure. The commercial millionaire may become a beggar; the illustrious states-man can make a vital mistake and be dropped and forgotten; the illustrious general can lose a decisive battle and with it the consider-ation of men; but once a prince always a prince—that is to say, an imitation god, and neither hard fortune nor an infamous character nor an addled brain nor the speech of an ass can undeify him. By common consent of all the nations and all the ages the most valuable thing in this world is the homage of men, whether deserved or unde-served. It follows without doubt or question, then, that the most desirable position possible is that of a prince. And I think it also follows that the so-called usurpations with which history is littered are the most excusable misdemeanors which men have committed. To usurp a usurpation—that is all it amounts to, isn't it?

A prince is not to us what he is to a European, of course. We have not been taught to regard him as a god, and so one good look at him is likely to so nearly appease our curiosity as to make him an object of no greater interest the next time. We want a fresh one. But it is not so with the European. I am quite sure of it. The same old one will answer; he never stales. Eighteen years ago I was in London and I called at an Englishman's house on a bleak and foggy and dismal December afternoon to visit his wife and married daughter by appoint-ment. I waited half an hour and then they arrived, frozen. They ex-plained that they had been delayed by an unlooked-for circumstance: while passing in the neighborhood of Marlborough House they saw a crowd gathering and were told that the Prince of Wales was about to drive out, so they stopped to get a sight of him. They had waited half an hour on the sidewalk, freezing with the crowd, but were disappointed at last—the Prince had changed his mind. I said, with a good deal of surprise, "Is it possible that you two have lived in London all your lives and have never seen the Prince of Wales?"

Apparently it was their turn to be surprised, for they exclaimed: "What an idea! Why, we have seen him hundreds of times."

They had seen him hundreds of times, yet they had waited half an hour in the gloom and the bitter cold, in the midst of a jam of patients from the same asylum, on the chance of seeing him again. It was a stupefying statement, but one is obliged to believe the English,

even when they say a thing like that. I fumbled around for a remark,
and got out this one:

"I can't understand it at all. If I had never seen General Grant I
doubt if I would do that even to get a sight of him." With a slight
emphasis on the last word.

Their blank faces showed that they wondered where the parallel
came in. Then they said, blankly: "Of course not. He is only a
President."

It is doubtless a fact that a prince is a permanent interest, an interest
not subject to deterioration. The general who was never defeated, the
general who never held a council of war, the only general who ever
commanded a connected battle-front twelve hundred miles long, the
smith who welded together the broken parts of a great republic
and re-established it where it is quite likely to outlast all the monarchies present and to come, was really a person of no serious consequence to these people. To them, with their training, my General
was only a man, after all, while their Prince was clearly much more
than that—a being of a wholly unsimilar construction and constitution,
and being of no more blood and kinship with men than are the serene
eternal lights of the firmament with the poor dull tallow candles of
commerce that sputter and die and leave nothing behind but a pinch
of ashes and a stink.

I saw the last act of "Tannhäuser." I sat in the gloom and the deep
stillness, waiting—one minute, two minutes, I do not know exactly
how long—then the soft music of the hidden orchestra began to breathe
its rich, long sighs out from under the distant stage, and by and by the
drop-curtain parted in the middle and was drawn softly aside, disclos-
ing the twilighted wood and a wayside shrine, with a white-robed
girl praying and a man standing near. Presently that noble chorus
of men's voices was heard approaching, and from that moment until
the closing of the curtain it was music, just music—music to make
one drunk with pleasure, music to make one take scrip and staff and
beg his way round the globe to hear it.

To such as are intending to come here in the Wagner season next
year I wish to say, bring your dinner-pail with you. If you do, you
will never cease to be thankful. If you do not, you will find it a hard
fight to save yourself from famishing in Bayreuth. Bayreuth is merely
a large village, and has no very large hotels or eating-houses. The
principal inns are the Golden Anchor and the Sun. At either of these
places you can get an excellent meal—no, I mean you can go there and
see other people get it. There is no charge for this. The town is

littered with restaurants, but they are small and bad, and they are over-driven with custom. You must secure a table hours beforehand, and often when you arrive you will find somebody occupying it. We have had this experience. We have had a daily scramble for life; and when I say we, I include shoals of people. I have the impression that the only people who do not have to scramble are the veterans—the disciples who have been here before and know the ropes. I think they arrive about a week before the first opera, and engage all the tables for the season. My tribe have tried all kinds of places—some outside of the town, a mile or two—and have captured only nibblings and odds and ends, never in any instance a complete and satisfying meal. Digestible? No, the reverse. These odds and ends are going to serve as souvenirs of Bayreuth, and in that regard their value is not to be over-estimated. Photographs fade, bric-à-brac gets lost, busts of Wagner get broken, but once you absorb a Bayreuth-restaurant meal it is your possession and your property until the time comes to embalm the rest of you. Some of these pilgrims here become, in effect, cabinets; cabinets of souvenirs of Bayreuth. It is believed among scientists that you could examine the crop of a dead Bayreuth pilgrim anywhere in the earth and tell where he came from. But I like this ballast. I think a "Hermitage" scrape-up at eight in the evening, when all the famine-breeders have been there and laid in their mementoes and gone, is the quietest thing you can lay on your keelson except gravel.

Thursday.—They keep two teams of singers in stock for the chief rôles, and one of these is composed of the most renowned artists in the world, with Materna and Alvary in the lead. I suppose a double team is necessary; doubtless a single team would die of exhaustion in a week, for all the plays last from four in the afternoon till ten at night. Nearly all the labor falls upon the half-dozen head singers, and apparently they are required to furnish all the noise they can for the money. If they feel a soft, whispery, mysterious feeling they are required to open out and let the public know it. Operas are given only on Sundays, Mondays, Wednesdays, and Thursdays, with three days of ostensible rest per week, and two teams to do the four operas; but the ostensible rest is devoted largely to rehearsing. It is said that the off days are devoted to rehearsing from some time in the morning till ten at night. Are there two orchestras also? It is quite likely, since there are one hundred and ten names in the orchestra list

Yesterday the opera was "Tristan and Isolde." I have seen all sorts of audiences—at theaters, operas, concerts, lectures, sermons, funerals —but none which was twin to the Wagner audience of Bayreuth for

fixed and reverential attention. Absolute attention and petrified reten-
tion to the end of an act of the attitude assumed at the beginning of it.
You detect no movement in the solid mass of heads and shoulders. You
seem to sit with the dead in the gloom of a tomb. You know that they
are being stirred to their profoundest depths; that there are times
when they want to rise and wave handkerchiefs and shout their
approbation, and times when tears are running down their faces, and
it would be a relief to free their pent emotions in sobs or screams;
yet you hear not one utterance till the curtain swings together and the
closing strains have slowly faded out and died; then the dead rise with
one impulse and shake the building with their applause. Every seat is
full in the first act; there is not a vacant one in the last. If a man
would be conspicuous, let him come here and retire from the house
in the midst of an act. It would make him celebrated.

This audience reminds me of nothing I have ever seen and of
nothing I have read about except the city in the Arabian tale where
all the inhabitants have been turned to brass and the traveler finds
them after centuries mute, motionless, and still retaining the attitudes
which they last knew in life. Here the Wagner audience dress as they
please, and sit in the dark and worship in silence. At the Metropolitan
in New York they sit in a glare, and wear their showiest harness; they
hum airs, they squeak fans, they titter, and they gabble all the time.
In some of the boxes the conversation and laughter are so loud as
to divide the attention of the house with the stage. In large measure
the Metropolitan is a show-case for rich fashionables who are not
trained in Wagnerian music and have no reverence for it, but who
like to promote art and show their clothes.

Can that be an agreeable atmosphere to persons in whom this
music produces a sort of divine ecstasy and to whom its creator is a
very deity, his stage a temple, the works of his brain and hands
consecrated things, and the partaking of them with eye and ear a
sacred solemnity? Manifestly, no. Then, perhaps the temporary ex-
patriation, the tedious traversing of seas and continents, the pilgrimage to Bayreuth stands explained. These devotees would worship
in an atmosphere of devotion. It is only here that they can find it
without fleck or blemish or any worldly pollution. In this remote
village there are no sights to see, there is no newspaper to intrude
the worries of the distant world, there is nothing going on, it is always
Sunday. The pilgrim wends to his temple out of town, sits out his
moving service, returns to his bed with his heart and soul and his
body exhausted by long hours of tremendous emotion, and he is in

no fit condition to do anything but to lie torpid and slowly gather back life and strength for the next service. This opera of "Tristan and Isolde" last night broke the hearts of all witnesses who were of the faith, and I know of some who have heard of many who could not sleep after it, but cried the night away. I feel strongly out of place here. Sometimes I feel like the sane person in a community of the mad; sometimes I feel like the one blind man where all others see; the one groping savage in the college of the learned, and always, during service, I feel like a heretic in heaven.

But by no means do I ever overlook or minify the fact that this is one of the most extraordinary experiences of my life. I have never seen anything like this before. I have never seen anything so great and fine and real as this devotion.

Friday.—Yesterday's opera was "Parsifal" again. The others went and they show marked advance in appreciation; but I went hunting for relics and reminders of the Margravine Wilhelmina, she of the imperishable "Memoirs." I am properly grateful to her for her (unconscious) satire upon monarchy and nobility, and therefore nothing which her hand touched or her eye looked upon is indifferent to me. I am her pilgrim; the rest of this multitude here are Wagner's.

Tuesday.—I have seen my last two operas; my season is ended, and we cross over into Bohemia this afternoon. I was supposing that my musical regeneration was accomplished and perfected, because I enjoyed both of these operas, singing and all, and, moreover, one of them was "Parsifal," but the experts have disenchanted me. They say:

"Singing! That wasn't singing; that was the wailing, screeching of third-rate obscurities, palmed off on us in the interest of economy."

Well, I ought to have recognized the sign—the old, sure sign that has never failed me in matters of art. Whenever I enjoy anything in art it means that it is mighty poor. The private knowledge of this fact has saved me from going to pieces with enthusiasm in front of many and many a chromo. However, my base instinct does bring me profit sometimes; I was the only man out of thirty-two hundred who got his money back on those two operas.

1891

Mental Telegraphy

NOTE TO THE EDITOR.[1]—By glancing over the inclosed bundle of rusty old manuscript, you will perceive that I once made a great discovery: the discovery that certain sorts of thing which, from the beginning of the world, had always been regarded as merely "curious coincidences"—that is to say, accidents—were no more accidental than is the sending and receiving of a telegram an accident. I made this discovery sixteen or seventeen years ago, and gave it a name—"Mental Telegraphy." It is the same thing around the outer edges of which the Psychical Society of England began to group (and play with) four or five years ago, and which they named "Telepathy." Within the last two or three years they have penetrated toward the heart of the matter, however, and have found out that mind can act upon mind in a quite detailed and elaborate way over vast stretches of land and water. And they have succeeded in doing, by their great credit and influence, what I could never have done—they have convinced the world that mental telegraphy is not a jest, but a fact, and that it is a thing not rare, but exceedingly common. They have done our age a service —and a very great service, I think.

In this old manuscript you will find mention of an extraordinary experience of mine in the mental telegraphic line, of date about the year 1874 or 1875—the one concerning the Great Bonanza book. It was this experience that called my attention to the matter under consideration. I began to keep a record, after that, of such experiences of mine as seemed explicable by the theory that minds telegraph thoughts to each other. In 1878 I went to Germany and began to write the book called *A Tramp Abroad*. The bulk of this old batch of manuscript was written at that time and for that book. But I removed it when I came to revise the volume for the press; for I feared that the public would treat the thing as a joke and throw it aside, whereas I was in earnest.

At home, eight or ten years ago, I tried to creep in under shelter of an authority grave enough to protect the article from ridicule—*The North American Review*. But Mr Metcalf was too wary for me. He said that to treat these mere "coincidences" seriously was a thing which the *Review* couldn't dare to do; that I must put either my name or my *nom de plume* to the article, and thus save the *Review* from harm. But I couldn't consent to that; it would be the surest possible way to defeat my desire that the

[1] The editor of *Harper's Magazine*, in which this essay was first published.—C.N.

public should receive the thing seriously, and be willing to stop and give it some fair degree of attention. So I pigeonholed the MS., because I could not get it published anonymously.

Now see how the world has moved since then. These small experiences of mine, which were too formidable at that time for admission to a grave magazine—if the magazine must allow them to appear as something above and beyond "accidents" and "coincidences"—are trifling and commonplace now, since the flood of light recently cast upon mental telegraphy by the intelligent labors of the Psychical Society. But I think they are worth publishing, just to show what harmless and ordinary matters were considered dangerous and incredible eight or ten years ago.

As I have said, the bulk of this old manuscript was written in 1878; a later part was written from time to time two, three, and four years afterward. The "Postscript" I add to-day.

MAY, '78.—Another of those apparently trifling things has happened to me which puzzle and perplex all men every now and then, keep them thinking an hour or two, and leave their minds barren of explanation or solution at last. Here it is—and it looks inconsequential enough, I am obliged to say. A few days ago I said: "It must be that Frank Millet doesn't know we are in Germany, or he would have written long before this. I have been on the point of dropping him a line at least a dozen times during the past six weeks, but I always decided to wait a day or two longer, and see if we shouldn't hear from him. But now I *will* write." And so I did. I directed the letter to Paris, and thought, "*Now* we shall hear from him before this letter is fifty miles from Heidelberg—it always happens so."

True enough; but *why* should it? That is the puzzling part of it. We are always talking about letters "crossing" each other, for that is one of the very commonest accidents of this life. We call it "accident," but perhaps we misname it. We have the instinct a dozen times a year that the letter we are writing is going to "cross" the other person's letter; and if the reader will rack his memory a little he will recall the fact that this presentiment had strength enough to it to make him cut his letter down to a decided briefness, because it would be a waste of time to write a letter which was going to "cross," and hence be a useless letter. I think that in my experience this instinct has generally come to me in cases where I had put off my letter a good while in the hope that the other person would write.

Yes, as I was saying, I had waited five or six weeks; then I wrote but three lines, because I felt and seemed to know that a letter from Millet would cross mine. And so it did. He wrote the same day that

I wrote. The letters crossed each other. His letter went to Berlin, care of the American minister, who sent it to me. In this letter Millet said he had been trying for six weeks to stumble upon somebody who knew my German address, and at last the idea had occured to him that a letter sent to the care of the embassy at Berlin might possibly find me. Maybe it was an "accident" that he finally determined to write me at the same moment that I finally determined to write him, but I think not.

With me the most irritating thing has been to wait a tedious time in a purely business matter, hoping that the other party will do the writing, and then sit down and do it myself, perfectly satisfied that that other man is sitting down at the same moment to write a letter which will "cross" mine. And yet one must go on writing, just the same; because if you get up from your table and postpone, that other man will do the same thing, exactly as if you two were harnessed together like the Siamese twins, and must duplicate each other's movements.

Several months before I left home a New York firm did some work about the house for me, and did not make a success of it, as it seemed to me. When the bill came, I wrote and said I wanted the work perfected before I paid. They replied that they were very busy, but that as soon as they could spare the proper man the thing should be done. I waited more than two months, enduring as patiently as possible the companionship of bells which would fire away of their own accord sometimes when nobody was touching them, and at other times wouldn't ring though you struck the button with a sledge-hammer. Many a time I got ready to write and then postponed it; but at last I sat down one evening and poured out my grief to the extent of a page or so, and then cut my letter suddenly short, because a strong instinct told me that the firm had begun to move in the matter. When I came down to breakfast next morning the postman had not yet taken my letter away, but the electrical man had been there, done his work, and was gone again! He had received his orders the previous evening from his employers, and had come up by the night train.

If that was an "accident," it took about three months to get it up in good shape.

One evening last summer I arrived in Washington, registered at the Arlington Hotel, and went to my room. I read and smoked until ten o'clock; then, finding I was not yet sleepy, I thought I would take a breath of fresh air. So I went forth in the rain, and tramped through one street after another in an aimless and enjoyable way. I knew that Mr. O——, a friend of mine, was in town, and I wished I might run across him; but I did not propose to hunt for him at midnight, especially as I did not know where he was stopping. Toward twelve o'clock the streets had become so deserted that I felt lonesome; so I stepped into a cigar shop far up the avenue, and remained there fifteen minutes, listening to some bummers discussing national politics. Suddenly the spirit of prophecy came upon me, and I said to myself, "Now I will go out at this door, turn to the left, walk ten steps, and meet Mr. O—— face to face." I did it, too! I could not see his face, because he had an umbrella before it, and it was pretty dark anyhow, but he interrupted the man he was walking and talking with, and I recognized his voice and stopped him.

That I should step out there and stumble upon Mr. O—— was nothing, but that I should know beforehand that I was going to do it was a good deal. It is a very curious thing when you come to look at it. I stood far within the cigar shop when I delivered my prophecy; I walked about five steps to the door, opened it, closed it after me, walked down a flight of three steps to the sidewalk, then turned to the left and walked four or five more, and found my man. I repeat that in itself the thing was nothing; but to know it would happen so *beforehand,* wasn't that really curious?

I have criticized absent people so often, and then discovered, to my humiliation, that I was talking with their relatives, that I have grown superstitious about that sort of thing and dropped it. How like an idiot one feels after a blunder like that!

We are always mentioning people, and in that very instant they appear before us. We laugh, and say, "Speak of the devil," and so forth, and there we drop it, considering it an "accident." It is a cheap and convenient way of disposing of a grave and very puzzling mystery. The fact is, it does seem to happen too often to be an accident.

Now I come to the oddest thing that ever happened to me. Two or three years ago I was lying in bed, idly musing, one morning— it was the 2d of March—when suddenly a red-hot new idea came whistling down into my camp, and exploded with such comprehensive effectiveness as to sweep the vicinity clean of rubbishy reflections and fill the air with their dust and flying fragments. This idea, stated in simple phrase, was that the time was ripe and the market ready for a certain book; a book which ought to be written at once; a book which must command attention and be of peculiar interest —to wit, a book about the Nevada silver-mines. The "Great Bonanza" was a new wonder then, and everybody was talking about it. It seemed to me that the person best qualified to write this book was Mr. William H. Wright,[2] a journalist of Virginia, Nevada, by whose side I had scribbled many months when I was a reporter there ten or twelve years before. He might be alive still; he might be dead; I could not tell; but I would write him, anyway. I began by merely and modestly suggesting that he make such a book; but my interest grew as I went on, and I ventured to map out what I thought ought to be the plan of the work, he being an old friend, and not given to taking good intentions for ill. I even dealt with details, and suggested the order and sequence which they should follow. I was about to put the manuscript in an envelope, when the thought occurred to me that if this book should be written at my suggestion, and then no publisher happened to want it, I should feel uncomfortable; so I concluded to keep my letter back until I should have secured a publisher. I pigeonholed my document, and dropped a note to my own publisher, asking him to name a day for a business consultation. He was out of town on a far journey.

My note remained unanswered, and at the end of three or four days the whole matter had passed out of my mind. On the 9th of March the postman brought three or four letters, and among them a thick one whose superscription was in a hand which seemed dimly familiar to me. I could not "place" it at first, but presently I succeeded. Then I said to a visiting relative who was present:

"Now I will do a miracle. I will tell you everything this letter contains—date, signature, and all—without breaking the seal. It is from a Mr. Wright, of Virginia, Nevada, and is dated the 2d of March—seven days ago. Mr. Wright proposes to make a book about the silver-mines and the Great Bonanza, and asks what I, as a friend, think of the idea. He says his subjects are to be so and so, their order and sequence so and so, and he will close with a history of the chief feature of the book, the Great Bonanza."

I opened the letter, and showed that I had stated the date and the contents correctly. Mr. Wright's letter simply contained, what my own letter, written on the same date, contained, and mine still lay in its pigeonhole, where it had been lying during the seven days since it was written.

There was no clairvoyance about this, if I rightly comprehend what clairvoyance is. I think the clairvoyant professes to actually *see* concealed writing, and read it off word for word. This was not my case.

[2] Wright's pseudonym was Dan de Quille.—C.N.

I only seemed to know, and to know absolutely, the contents of the letter in detail and due order, but I had to *word* them myself. I translated them, so to speak, out of Wright's language into my own.

Wright's letter and the one which I had written to him but never sent were in substance the same.

Necessarily this could not come by accident; such elaborate accidents cannot happen. Chance might have duplicated one or two of the details, but she would have broken down on the rest. I could not doubt—there was no tenable reason for doubting—that Mr. Wright's mind and mine had been in close and crystal-clear communication with each other across three thousand miles of mountain and desert on the morning of the 2d of March. I did not consider that both minds *originated* that succession of ideas, but that one mind originated it, and simply telegraphed it to the other. I was curious to know which brain was the telegrapher and which the receiver, so I wrote and asked for particulars. Mr. Wright's reply showed that his mind had done the originating and telegraphing, and mine the receiving. Mark that significant thing now; consider for a moment how many a splendid "original" idea has been unconsciously stolen from a man three thousand miles away! If one should question that this is so, let him look into the cyclopedia and con once more that curious thing in the history of inventions which has puzzled every one so much—that is, the frequency with which the same machine or other contrivance has been invented at the same time by several persons in different quarters of the globe. The world was without an electric telegraph for several thousand years; then Professor Henry, the American, Wheatstone in England, Morse on the sea, and a German in Munich, all invented it at the same time. The discovery of certain ways of applying steam was made in two or three countries in the same year. Is it not possible that inventors are constantly and unwittingly stealing each other's ideas whilst they stand thousands of miles asunder?

Last spring a literary friend of mine,[3] who lived a hundred miles away, paid me a visit, and in the course of our talk he said he had made a discovery—conceived an entirely new idea—one which certainly had never been used in literature. He told me what it was. I handed him a manuscript, and said he would find substantially the same idea in that—a manuscript which I had written a week before. The idea had been in my mind since the previous November; it had only entered his while I was putting it on paper, a week gone by. He

[3] W. D. Howells.—M.T.

had not yet written his; so he left it unwritten, and gracefully made over all his right and title in the idea to me.

The following statement, which I have clipped from a newspaper, is true. I had the facts from Mr. Howell's lips when the episode was new:

A remarkable story of a literary coincidence is told of Mr. Howells's *Atlantic Monthly* serial, "Dr. Breen's Practice." A lady of Rochester, New York, contributed to the magazine after "Dr. Breen's Practice" was in type, a short story which so much resembled Mr. Howells's that he felt it necessary to call upon her and explain the situation of affairs in order that no charge of plagiarism might be preferred against him. He showed her the proof-sheets of his story, and satisfied her that the similarity between her work and his was one of those strange coincidences which have from time to time occurred in the literary world.

I had read portions of Mr. Howells's story, both in MS. and in proof, before the lady offered her contribution to the magazine.

Here is another case. I clip it from a newspaper:

The republication of Miss Alcott's novel *Moods* recalls to a writer in the Boston *Post* a singular coincidence which was brought to light before the book was first published: "Miss Anna M. Crane, of Baltimore, published *Emily Chester*, a novel which was pronounced a very striking and strong story. A comparison of this book with *Moods* showed that the two writers, though entire strangers to each other, and living hundreds of miles apart, had both chosen the same subject for their novels, had followed almost the same line of treatment up to a certain point, where the parallel ceased, and the dénouements were entirely opposite. And even more curious, the leading characters in both books had identically the same names, so that the names in Miss Alcott's novel had to be changed. Then the book was published by Loring."

Four or five times within my recollection there has been a lively newspaper war in this country over poems whose authorship was claimed by two or three different people at the same time. There was a war of this kind over "Nothing to Wear," "Beautiful Snow," "Rock me to Sleep, Mother," and also over one of Mr. Will Carleton's early ballads, I think. These were all blameless cases of unintentional and unwitting mental telegraphy, I judge.

A word more as to Mr. Wright. He had had his book in mind some time; consequently he, and not I, had originated the idea of it. The subject was entirely foreign to my thoughts; I was wholly absorbed in other things. Yet this friend, whom I had not seen and had hardly thought of for eleven years, was able to shoot his thoughts at me across three thousand miles of country, and fill my head with them, to the exclusion of every other interest, in a single moment. He had begun his letter after finishing his work on the morning paper—a little after three o'clock, he said. When it was three in the morning in Nevada it was about six in Hartford, where I lay awake thinking about nothing in particular; and just about that time his ideas came pouring into my head from across the continent, and I got up and put them on paper, under the impression that they were my own original thoughts.

I have never seen any mesmeric or clairvoyant performances or spiritual manifestations which were in the least degree convincing—a fact which is not of consequence, since my opportunities have been meager; but I am forced to believe that one human mind (still inhabiting the flesh) can communicate with another, over any sort of a distance, and without any *artificial* preparation of "sympathetic conditions" to act as a transmitting agent. I suppose that when the sympathetic conditions happen to exist the two minds communicate with each other, and that otherwise they don't; and I suppose that if the sympathetic conditions could be kept up right along, the two minds would continue to correspond without limit as to time.

Now there is that curious thing which happens to everybody: suddenly a succession of thoughts or sensations flocks in upon you, which startles you with the weird idea that you have ages ago experienced just this succession of thoughts or sensations in a previous existence. The previous existence is possible, no doubt, but I am persuaded that the solution of this hoary mystery lies not there, but in the fact that some far-off stranger has been telegraphing his thoughts and sensations into your consciousness, and that he stopped because some counter-current or other obstruction intruded and broke the line of communication. Perhaps they seem repetitions to you because they *are* repetitions, got at second hand from the other man. Possibly Mr. Brown, the "mind-reader," reads other people's minds, possibly he does not; but I know of a surety that I have read another man's mind, and therefore I do not see why Mr. Brown shouldn't do the like also.

I wrote the foregoing about three years ago, in Heidelberg, and laid the manuscript aside, purposing to add to it instances of mind-telegraphing from time to time as they should fall under my experience. Meantime the "crossing" of letters has been so frequent as to become monotonous. However, I have managed to get something useful out of this hint; for now, when I get tired of waiting upon a man whom I very much wish to hear from, I sit down and *compel* him to write, whether he wants to or not; that is to say, I sit down and write him, and then tear my letter up, satisfied that my act has forced him to write me at the same moment. I do not need to mail my letter—the writing it is the only essential thing.

Of course I have grown superstitious about this letter-crossing business—this was natural. We stayed awhile in Venice after leaving Heidelberg. One day I was going down the Grand Canal in a gondola, when I heard a shout behind me, and looked around to see what the matter was; a gondola was rapidly following, and the gondolier was making signs to me to stop. I did so, and the pursuing boat ranged up alongside. There was an American lady in it—a resident of Venice. She was in a good deal of distress. She said:

"There's a New York gentleman and his wife at the Hotel Britannia who arrived a week ago, expecting to find news of their son, whom they have heard nothing about during eight months. There was no news. The lady is down sick with despair; the gentleman can't sleep or eat. Their son arrived at San Francisco eight months ago, and announced the fact in a letter to his parents the same day. That is the last trace of him. The parents have been in Europe ever since; but their trip has been spoiled, for they have occupied their time simply in drifting restlessly from place to place, and writing letters everywhere and to everybody, begging for news of their son; but the mystery remains as dense as ever. Now the gentleman wants to stop writing and go calling. He wants to cable San Francisco. He has never done it before, because he is afraid of—of he doesn't know what— death of his son, no doubt. But he wants somebody to *advise* him to cable; wants me to do it. Now I simply can't; for if no news came, that mother yonder would die. So I have chased you up in order to get you to support me in urging him to be patient, and put the thing off a week or two longer; it may be the saving of this lady. Come along; let's not lose any time."

So I went along, but I had a program of my own. When I was introduced to the gentleman I said: "I have some superstitions, but they are worthy of respect. If you will cable San Francisco immediately, you will hear news of your son inside of twenty-four hours. I don't know that you will get the news from San Francisco, but you will get it from somewhere. The only necessary thing is to *cable* —that is all. The news will come within twenty-four hours. Cable Peking, if you prefer; there is no choice in this matter. This delay is

all occasioned by your not cabling long ago, when you were first moved
to do it."

It seems absurd that this gentleman should have been cheered up by
this nonsense, but he was; he brightened up at once, and sent his
cablegram; and next day, at noon, when a long letter arrived from his
lost son, the man was as grateful to me as if I had really had
something to do with the hurrying up of that letter. The son had
shipped from San Francisco in a sailing-vessel, and his letter was
written from the first port he touched at, months afterward.

This incident argues nothing, and is valueless. I insert it only to
show how strong is the superstition which "letter-crossing" has bred
in me. I was so sure that a cablegram sent to any place, no matter
where, would defeat itself by "crossing" the incoming news, that
my confidence was able to raise up a hopeless man and make him
cheery and hopeful.

But here are two or three incidents which come strictly under the
head of mind-telegraphing. One Monday morning, about a year ago,
the mail came in, and I picked up one of the letters and said to a
friend: "Without opening this letter I will tell you what it says. It is
from Mrs. ——, and, she says she was in New York last Saturday, and
was purposing to run up here in the afternoon train and surprise us,
but at the last moment changed her mind and returned westward to
her home."

I was right; my details were exactly correct. Yet we had had no
suspicion that Mrs. —— was coming to New York, or that she had even
a remote intention of visiting us.

I smoke a good deal—that is to say, all the time—so, during seven
years, I have tried to keep a box of matches handy, behind a picture on
the mantelpiece; but I have had to take it out in trying, because
George (colored), who makes the fires and lights the gas, always
uses my matches and never replaces them. Commands and persuasions
have gone for nothing with him all these seven years. One day last
summer, when our family had been away from home several months,
I said to a member of the household:

"Now, with all this long holiday, and nothing in the way to inter-
rupt—"

"I can finish the sentence for you," said the member of the household.

"Do it, then," said I.

"George ought to be able, by practising, to learn to let those matches
alone."

It was correctly done. That was what I was going to say. Yet until that moment George and the matches had not been in my mind for three months, and it is plain that the part of the sentence which I uttered offers not the least cue or suggestion of what I was purposing to follow it with.

My mother[4] is descended from the younger of two English brothers named Lambton, who settled in this country a few generations ago. The tradition goes that the elder of the two eventually fell heir to a certain estate in England (now an earldom), and died right away. This has always been the way with our family. They always die when they could make anything by not doing it. The two Lambtons left plenty of Lambtons behind them; and when at last, about fifty years ago, the English baronetcy was exalted to an earldom, the great tribe of American Lambtons began to bestir themselves—that is, those descended from the elder branch. Ever since that day one or another of these has been fretting his life uselessly away with schemes to get at his "rights." The present "rightful earl"—I mean the American one—used to write me occasionally, and try to interest me in his projected raids upon the title and estates by offering me a share in the latter portion of the spoil; but I have always managed to resist his temptations.

Well, one day last summer I was lying under a tree, thinking about nothing in particular, when an absurd idea flashed into my head, and I said to a member of the household, "Suppose I should live to be ninety-two, and dumb and blind and toothless, and just as I was gasping out what was left of me on my death-bed—"

"Wait, I will finish the sentence," said a member of the household.

"Go on," said I.

"Somebody should rush in with a document, and say, 'All the other heirs are dead, and you are the Earl of Durham!'"

That is truly what I was going to say. Yet until that moment the subject had not entered my mind or been referred to in my hearing for months before. A few years ago this thing would have astounded me, but the like could not much surprise me now, though it happened every week; for I think I *know* now that mind can communicate accurately with mind without the aid of the slow and clumsy vehicle of speech.

This age does seem to have exhausted invention nearly; still, it has one important contract on its hands yet—the invention of the *phreno-phone*; that is to say, a method whereby the communicating of mind

[4] She was still living when this was written.—M.T.

with mind may be brought under command and reduced to certainty and system. The telegraph and the telephone are going to become too slow and wordy for our needs. We must have the *thought* itself shot into our minds from a distance; then, if we need to put it into words, we can do that tedious work at our leisure. Doubtless the something which conveys our thoughts through the air from brain to brain is a finer and subtler form of electricity, and all we need do is to find out how to capture it and how to force it to do its work, as we have had to do in the case of the electric currents. Before the day of telegraphs neither one of these marvels would have seemed any easier to achieve than the other.

While I am writing this, doubtless somebody on the other side of the globe is writing it, too. The question is, am I inspiring him or is he inspiring me? I cannot answer that; but that these thoughts have been passing through somebody else's mind all the time I have been setting them down I have no sort of doubt.

I will close this paper with a remark which I found some time ago in Boswell's *Johnson:*

"Voltaire's *Candide* is wonderfully similar in its plan and conduct to Johnson's *Rasselas;* insomuch that I have heard Johnson say that if they had not been published so closely one after the other that there was not time for imitation, *it would have been in vain to deny that the scheme of that which came latest was taken from the other.*"

The two men were widely separated from each other at the time, and the sea lay between them.

POSTSCRIPT

In the *Atlantic* for June, 1882, Mr. John Fiske refers to the often-quoted Darwin-and-Wallace "coincidence":

I alluded, just now, to the "unforeseen circumstance" which led Mr. Darwin in 1859 to break his long silence, and to write and publish the *Origin of Species.* This circumstance served, no less than the extraordinary success of his book, to show how ripe the minds of men had become for entertaining such views as those which Mr. Darwin propounded. In 1858 Mr. Wallace, who was then engaged in studying the natural history of the Malay Archipelago, sent to Mr. Darwin (as the man most likely to understand him) a paper in which he sketched the outlines of a theory identical with that upon which Mr. Darwin had so long been at work. The same sequence of observed facts and inferences that had led Mr. Darwin to the discovery of natural selection and its consequences had led Mr. Wallace to the very threshold of the same discovery; but in Mr. Wallace's mind the theory had by no means been wrought out to the same degree of completeness to which it had been wrought in the mind of Mr. Darwin. In the preface to his charming book on Natural Selection, Mr. Wallace, with rare modesty and candor, acknowledges that whatever value his speculations may have had, they have been utterly surpassed in richness and cogency of proof by those of Mr. Darwin. This is no doubt true, and Mr. Wallace has done such good work in further illustration of the theory that he can well afford to rest content with the second place in the first announcement of it.

The coincidence, however, between Mr. Wallace's conclusions and those of Mr. Darwin was very remarkable. But, after all, coincidences of this sort have not been uncommon in the history of scientific inquiry. Nor is it at all surprising that they should occur now and then, when we remember that a great and pregnant discovery must always be concerned with some question which many of the foremost minds in the world are busy thinking about. It was so with the discovery of the differential calculus, and again with the discovery of the planet Neptune. It was so with the interpretation of the Egyptian hieroglyphics, and with the establishment of the undulatory theory of light. It was so, to a considerable extent, with the introduction of the new chemistry, with the discovery of the mechanical equivalent of heat, and the whole doctrine of the correlation of forces. It was so with the invention of the electric telegraph and with the discovery of spectrum analysis. And it is not at all strange that it should have been so with the doctrine of the origin of species through natural selection.

He thinks these "coincidences" were apt to happen because the matters from which they sprang were matters which many of the foremost minds in the world were busy thinking about. But perhaps *one* man in each case did the telegraphing to the others. The aberrations which gave Leverrier the idea that there must be a planet of such and such mass and such and such orbit hidden from sight out yonder in the remote abysses of space were not new; they had been noticed by astronomers for generations. Then why should it happen to occur to three people, widely separated—Leverrier, Mrs. Somerville, and Adams—to suddenly go to worrying about those aberrations all at the same time, and set themselves to work to find out what caused them, and to measure and weigh an invisible planet, and calculate its orbit, and hunt it down and catch it?—a strange project which nobody but they had ever thought of before. If one astronomer had invented that odd and happy project fifty years before, don't you think he would have telegraphed it to several others without knowing it?

But now I come to a puzzler. How is it that *inanimate* objects are able to affect the mind? They seem to do that. However, I wish to throw in a parenthesis first—just a reference to a thing everybody is familiar with—the experience of receiving a clear and particular *answer* to your telegram before your telegram has reached the sender of the answer. That is a case where your telegram has gone straight from your brain to the man it was meant for, far outstripping the wire's slow electricity, and it is an exercise of mental telegraphy which is as common as dining. To return to the influence of inanimate things. In the cases of non-professional clairvoyance examined by the Psychical Society the clairvoyant has usually been blindfolded, then some object which has been touched or worn by a person is placed in his hand; the clairvoyant immediately describes that person, and goes on and gives a history of some event with which the text object has been connected. If the inanimate object is able to affect and inform the clairvoyant's mind, maybe it can do the same when it is working in the interest of mental telegraphy. Once a lady in the West wrote me that her son was coming to New York to remain three weeks, and would pay me a visit if invited, and she gave me his address. I mislaid the letter, and forgot all about the matter till the three weeks were about up. Then a sudden and fiery irruption of remorse burst up in my brain that illuminated all the region round about, and I sat down at once and wrote to the lady and asked for that lost address. But, upon reflection, I judged that the stirring up of my recollection had not been an accident, so I added a postscript to say, never mind, I should get a letter from her son before night. And I did get it; for the letter was already in the town, although not delivered yet. It had influenced me somehow. I have had so many experiences of this sort—a dozen of them at least —that I am nearly persuaded that inanimate objects do not confine their activities to helping the clairvoyant, but do every now and then give the mental telegraphist a lift.

The case of mental telegraphy which I am coming to now comes under I don't exactly know what head. I clipped it from one of our local papers six or eight years ago. I know the details to be right and true, for the story was told to me in the same form by one of the two persons concerned (a clergyman of Hartford) at the time that the curious thing happened:

A REMARKABLE COINCIDENCE.—Strange coincidences make the most interesting of stories and most curious of studies. Nobody can quite say how they come about, but everybody appreciates the fact when they do come, and it is seldom that any more complete and curious coincidence is recorded of minor importance than the following, which is absolutely true and occurred in this city.

At the time of the building of one of the finest residences of Hartford, which is still a very new house, a local firm supplied the wall-paper for certain rooms, contracting both to furnish and to put on the paper. It happened that they did not calculate the size of one room exactly right, and the paper of the design selected for it fell short just half a roll. They asked for delay enough to send on to the manufacturers for what was needed, and were told that there was no especial hurry. It happened that the manufacturers had none on hand, and had destroyed the blocks from which it was printed. They wrote that they had a full list of the dealers to whom they had sold that paper, and that they would write to each of these and get from some of them a roll. It might involve a delay of a couple of weeks, but they would surely get it.

In the course of time came a letter saying that, to their great surprise, they could not find a single roll. Such a thing was very unusual, but in this case it had so happened. Accordingly the local firm asked for further time, saying they would write to their own customers who had bought of that pattern, and would get the piece from them. But to their surprise, this effort also failed. A long time had now elapsed, and there was no use of delaying any longer. They had contracted to paper the room, and their only course was to take off that which was insufficient and put on some other of which there was enough to go around. Accordingly at length a man was sent out to remove the paper. He got his apparatus ready, and was about to begin to work, under the direction of the owner of the building, when the latter was for the moment called away. The house was large and very interesting, and so many people had rambled about it that finally admission had been refused by a sign at the door. On the occasion, however, when a gentleman had knocked and asked for leave to look about, the owner, being on the premises, had been sent for to reply to the request in person. That was the call that for the moment delayed the final preparations. The gentleman went to the door and admitted the stranger, saying he would show him about the house, but first must return for a moment to that room to finish his directions there, and he told the curious story about the paper as they went on. They entered the room together, and the first thing the stranger, who lived fifty miles away, said on looking about was, "Why, I have that very paper on a room in my house, and I have an extra roll of it laid away, which is at your service." In a few days the wall was papered according to the original contract. Had not the owner been at the house, the stranger would not have been admitted; had he called a day later, it would have been too late; had not the facts been almost accidentally told to him, he would probably have said nothing of the paper, and so on. The exact fitting of all the circumstances is something very remarkable, and makes one of those stories that seem hardly accidental in their nature.

Something that happened the other day brought my hoary MS. to mind, and that is how I came to dig it out from its dusty pigeon-hole grave for publication. The thing that happened was a question. A lady asked: "Have you ever had a vision—when awake?" I was about to answer promptly when the last two words of the question began to grow and spread and swell, and presently they attained to vast dimensions. She did not know that they were important; and I did not at first, but I soon saw that they were putting me on the track of the solution of a mystery which had perplexed me a good deal. You will see what I mean when I get down to it. Ever since the English Society for Psychical Research began its investigations of ghost stories, haunted houses, and apparitions of the living and the dead, I have read their pamphlets with avidity as fast as they arrived. Now one of their commonest inquiries of a dreamer or a vision-seer is, "Are you sure you were awake at the time?" If the man can't say he is sure he was awake, a doubt falls upon his tale right there. But if he is positive he was awake, and offers reasonable evidence to substantiate it, the fact counts largely for the credibility of his story. It does with the society, and it did with me until that lady asked me the above question the other day.

The question set me to considering, and brought me to the conclusion that you can be asleep—at least, wholly unconscious—for a time, and not suspect that it has happened, and not have any way to prove that it *has* happened. A memorable case was in my mind. About a year ago I was standing on the porch one day, when I saw a man coming up the walk. He was a stranger, and I hoped he would ring and carry his business into the house without stopping to argue with me; he would have to pass the front door to get to me, and I hoped he wouldn't take the trouble; to help, I tried to look like a stranger myself—it often works. I was looking straight at that man; he had got to within ten feet of the door and within twenty-five feet of me—and suddenly he disappeared. It was as astounding as if a church should vanish from before your face and leave nothing behind it but a vacant lot. I was unspeakably de-lighted. I had seen an apparition at last, with my own eyes, in broad daylight. I made up my mind to write an account of it to the society. I ran to where the specter had been, to make sure he was playing fair, then I ran to the other end of the porch, scanning the open grounds as I went. No, everything was perfect; he couldn't have escaped with-out my seeing him; he was an apparition, without the slightest doubt, and I would write him up before he was cold. I ran, hot with excite-

ment, and let myself in with a latch-key. When I stepped into the hall
my lungs collapsed and my heart stood still. For there sat that same
apparition in a chair all alone, and as quiet and reposeful as if he
had come to stay a year! The shock kept me dumb for a moment or
two then I said, "Did you come in at that door?"

"Yes."

"Did *you* open it, or did you ring?"

"I rang, and the colored man opened it."

I said to myself: "This is astonishing. It takes George all of two
minutes to answer the doorbell when he is in a hurry, and I have never
seen him in a hurry. How *did* this man stand two minutes at that
door, within five steps of me, and I did not see him?"

I should have gone to my grave puzzling over that riddle but for that
lady's chance question last week: "Have you ever had a vision—when
awake?" It stands explained now. During at least sixty seconds that day
I was asleep, or at least totally unconscious, without suspecting it. In
that interval the man came to my immediate vicinity, rang, stood there
and waited, then entered and closed the door, and I did not see him
and did not hear the door slam.

If he had slipped around the house in that interval and gone
into the cellar—he had time enough—I should have written him
up for the society, and magnified him, and gloated over him,
and hurrahed about him, and thirty yoke of oxen could not have
pulled the belief out of me that I was of the favored ones of
the earth, and had seen a vision—while wide awake.

Now how are you to tell when you are awake? What are you
to go by? People bite their fingers to find out. Why, you can do that
in a dream.

1891

The German Chicago

I feel lost in Berlin. It has no resemblance to the city I had
supposed it was. There was once a Berlin which I would have known,
from descriptions in books—the Berlin of the last century and the
beginning of the present one: a dingy city in a marsh, with rough

streets, muddy and lantern-lighted, dividing straight rows of ugly
houses all alike, compacted into blocks as square and plain and uniform and monotonous and serious as so many dry-goods boxes. But
that Berlin has disappeared. It seems to have disappeared totally,
and left no sign. The bulk of the Berlin of to-day has about it no
suggestion of a former period. The site it stands on has traditions
and a history, but the city itself has no traditions and no history.
It is a new city; the newest I have ever seen. Chicago would seem
venerable beside it; for there are many old-looking districts in
Chicago, but not many in Berlin. The main mass of the city looks
as if it had been built last week, the rest of it has a just per-
ceptibly graver tone, and looks as if it might be six or even eight
months old.

The next feature that strikes one is the spaciousness, the roominess
of the city. There is no other city, in any country, whose streets are
so generally wide. Berlin is not merely *a* city of wide streets, it
is *the* city of wide streets. As a wide-street city it has never had
its equal, in any age of the world. "Unter den Linden" is three
streets in one; the Potsdamerstrasse is bordered on both sides by
sidewalks which are themselves wider than some of the historic
thoroughfares of the old European capitals; there seem to be no
lanes or alleys; there are no short cuts; here and there, where several
important streets empty into a common center, that center's circumference is of a magnitude calculated to bring that word spaciousness into your mind again. The park in the middle of the city
is so huge that it calls up that expression once more.

The next feature that strikes one is the straightness of the streets.
The short ones haven't so much as a waver in them; the long ones
stretch out to prodigious distances and then tilt a little to the right
or left, then stretch out on another immense reach as straight as
a ray of light. A result of this arrangement is, that at night Berlin
is an inspiring sight to see. Gas and the electric light are employed
with a wasteful liberality, and so, wherever one goes, he has always
double ranks of brilliant lights stretching far down into the night
on every hand, with here and there a wide and splendid constellation
of them spread out over an intervening "Platz"; and between the
interminable double procession of street lamps one has the swarming
and darting cab lamps, a lively and pretty addition to the fine
spectacle, for they counterfeit the rush and confusion and sparkle
of an invasion of fireflies.

There is one other noticeable feature—the absolutely level surface

of the site of Berlin. Berlin—to recapitulate—is newer to the eye
than is any other city, and also blonder of complexion and tidier;
no other city has such an air of roominess, freedom from crowding;
no other city has so many straight streets; and with Chicago it
contests the chromo for flatness of surface and for phenomenal swiftness of growth. Berlin is the European Chicago. The two cities have
about the same population—say a million and a half. I cannot speak
in exact terms, because I only know what Chicago's population was
week before last; but at that time it was about a million and a half.
Fifteen years ago Berlin and Chicago were large cities, of course,
but neither of them was the giant it now is.

But now the parallels fail. Only parts of Chicago are stately and
beautiful, whereas all of Berlin is stately and substantial, and it is
not merely in parts but uniformly beautiful. There are buildings in
Chicago that are architecturally finer than any in Berlin, I think,
but what I have just said above is still true. These two flat cities
would lead the world for phenomenal good health if London were
out of the way. As it is, London leads by a point or two. Berlin's
death rate is only nineteen in the thousand. Fourteen years ago
the rate was a third higher.

Berlin is a surprise in a great many ways—in a multitude of ways,
to speak strongly and be exact. It seems to be the most governed
city in the world, but one must admit that it also seems to be the
best governed. Method and system are observable on every hand—in
great things, in little things, in all details, of whatsoever size. And
it is not method and system on paper, and there an end—it is method
and system in practice. It has a rule for everything, and puts the
rule in force; puts it in force against the poor and powerful alike, without favor or prejudice. It deals with great matters and minute particulars with equal faithfulness, and with a plodding and painstaking
diligence and persistency which compel admiration—and sometimes
regret. There are several taxes, and they are collected quarterly. Collected is the word; they are not merely levied, they are collected—
every time. This makes light taxes. It is in cities and countries where
a considerable part of the community shirk payment that taxes
have to be lifted to a burdensome rate. Here the police keep coming,
calmly and patiently, until you pay your tax. They charge you five or
ten cents per visit after the first call. By experiment you will find
that they will presently collect that money.

In one respect the million and a half of Berlin's population are
like a family: the head of this large family knows the names of

its several members, and where the said members are located, and when and where they were born, and what they do for a living, and what their religious brand is. Whoever comes to Berlin must furnish these particulars to the police immediately; moreover, if he knows how long he is going to stay, he must say so. If he take a house he will be taxed on the rent and taxed also on his income. He will not be asked what his income is, and so he may save some lies for home consumption. The police will estimate his income from the house-rent he pays, and tax him on that basis.

Duties on imported articles are collected with inflexible fidelity, be the sum large or little; but the methods are gentle, prompt, and full of the spirit of accommodation. The postman attends to the whole matter for you, in cases where the article comes by mail, and you have no trouble and suffer no inconvenience. The other day a friend of mine was informed that there was a package in the post-office for him, containing a lady's silk belt with gold clasp, and a gold chain to hang a bunch of keys on. In his first agitation he was going to try to bribe the postman to chalk it through, but acted upon his sober second thought and allowed the matter to take its proper and regular course. In a little while the post-man brought the package and made these several collections: duty on the silk belt, 7½ cents; duty on the gold chain, 10 cents; charge for fetching the package, 5 cents. These devastating imposts are exacted for the protection of German home industries.

The calm, quiet, courteous, cussed persistence of the police is the most admirable thing I have encountered on this side. They undertook to persuade me to send and get a passport for a Swiss maid whom we had brought with us, and at the end of six weeks of patient, tranquil, angelic daily effort they succeeded. I was not intending to give them trouble, but I was lazy and I thought they would get tired. Meanwhile they probably thought I would be the one. It turned out just so.

One is not allowed to build unstable, unsafe, or unsightly houses in Berlin; the result is this comely and conspicuously stately city, with its security from conflagrations and breakdowns. It is built of architectural Gibraltars. The building commissioners inspect while the building is going up. It has been found that this is better than to wait till it falls down. These people are full of whims.

One is not allowed to cram poor folk into cramped and dirty tene-ment houses. Each individual must have just so many cubic feet of room-space, and sanitary inspections are systematic and frequent.

Everything is orderly. The fire brigade march in rank, curiously uniformed, and so grave is their demeanor that they look like a Salvation Army under conviction of sin. People tell me that when a fire alarm is sounded, the firemen assemble calmly, answer to their names when the roll is called, then proceed to the fire. There they are ranked up, military fashion, and told off in detachments by the chief, who parcels out to the detachments the several parts of the work which they are to undertake in putting out that fire. This is all done with low-voiced propriety, and strangers think these people are working a funeral. As a rule, the fire is confined to a single floor in these great masses of bricks and masonry, and consequently there is little or no interest attaching to a fire here for the rest of the occupants of the house.

There is abundance of newspapers in Berlin, and there was also a newsboy, but he died. At intervals of half a mile on the thoroughfares there are booths, and it is at these that you buy your papers. There are plenty of theaters, but they do not advertise in a loud way. There are no big posters of any kind, and the display of vast type and of pictures of actors and performance framed on a big scale and done in rainbow colors is a thing unknown. If the big show-bills existed there would be no place to exhibit them; for there are no poster-fences, and one would not be allowed to disfigure dead walls with them. Unsightly things are forbidden here; Berlin is a rest to the eye.

And yet the saunterer can easily find out what is going on at the theaters. All over the city, at short distances apart, there are neat round pillars eighteen feet high and about as thick as a hogshead, and on these the little black and white theater bills and other notices are posted. One generally finds a group around each pillar reading these things. There are plenty of things in Berlin worth importing to America. It is these that I have particularly wished to make a note of. When Buffalo Bill was here his biggest poster was probably not larger than the top of an ordinary trunk.

There is a multiplicity of clean and comfortable horse-cars, but whenever you think you know where a car is going to you would better stop ashore, because that car is not going to that place at all. The car routes are marvelously intricate, and often the drivers get lost and are not heard of for years. The signs on the cars furnish no details as to the course of the journey; they name the end of it, and then experiment around to see how much territory they can cover before they get there. The conductor will collect your fare over again every few miles, and give you a ticket which he hasn't apparently kept any record of, and you keep it till an inspector comes aboard by and by and tears a corner off it (which he does not keep), then you throw the ticket away and get ready to buy another. Brains are of no value when you are trying to navigate Berlin in a horse-car. When the ablest of Brooklyn's editors was here on a visit he took a horse-car in the early morning, and wore it out trying to go to a point in the center of the city. He was on board all day and spent many dollars in fares, and then did not arrive at the place which he had started to go to. This is the most thorough way to see Berlin, but it is also the most expensive.

But there are excellent features about the car system, nevertheless. The car will not stop for you to get on or off, except at certain places a block or two apart where there is a sign to indicate that that is a halting station. This system saves many bones. There are twenty places inside the car; when these seats are filled, no more can enter. Four or five persons may stand on each platform—the law decrees the number—and when these standing-places are all occupied the next applicant is refused. As there is no crowding, and as no rowdyism is allowed, women stand on the platforms as well as the men; they often stand there when there are vacant seats inside, for these places are comfortable, there being little or no jolting. A native tells me that when the first car was put on, thirty or forty years ago, the public had such a terror of it that they didn't feel safe inside of it, or outside either. They made the company keep a man at every crossing with a red flag in his hand. Nobody would travel in the car except convicts on the way to the gallows. This made business in only one direction, and the car had to go back light. To save the company, the city government transferred the convict cemetery to the other end of the line. This made traffic in both directions and kept the company from going under. This sounds like some of the information which traveling foreigners are furnished with in America. To my mind it has a doubtful ring about it.

The first-class cab is neat and trim, and has leather-cushion seats and a swift horse. The second-class cab is an ugly and lubberly vehicle, and is always old. It seems a strange thing that they have never built any new ones. Still, if such a thing were done everybody that had time to flock would flock to see it, and that would make a crowd, and the police do not like crowds and disorder here. If there were an earthquake in Berlin the police would take charge of it and conduct it in that sort of orderly way that would make you think it was a prayer-meeting. That is what an earthquake generally ends in, but this one would be different from those others; it would be kind of soft and self-contained, like a republican praying for a mugwump.

For a course (a quarter of an hour or less), one pays twenty-five cents in a first-class cab, and fifteen cents in a second-class. The first-class will take you along faster, for the second-class horse is old—always old—as old as his cab, some authorities say—and ill-fed and weak. He has been a first-class once, but has been degraded to second class for long and faithful service.

Still, he must take you as *far* for fifteen cents as the other horse takes you for twenty-five. If he can't do his fifteen-minute distance in fifteen minutes, he must still do the distance for the fifteen cents.

Any stranger can check the distance off—by means of the most curious map I am acquainted with. It is issued by the city government and can be bought in any shop for a trifle. In it every street is sectioned off like a string of long beads of different colors. Each long bead represents a minute's travel, and when you have covered fifteen of the beads you have got your money's worth. This map of Berlin is a gay-colored maze, and looks like pictures of the circulation of the blood.

The streets are very clean. They are kept so—not by prayer and talk and the other New York methods, but by daily and hourly work with scrapers and brooms; and when an asphalted street has been tidily scraped after a rain or a light snowfall, they scatter clean sand over it. This saves some of the horses from falling down. In fact, this is a city government which seems to stop at no expense where the convenience, comfort, and health are concerned—except in one detail. That is the naming of the streets and the numbering of the houses. Sometimes the name of a street will change in the middle of a block. You will not find it out till you get to the next corner and discover the new name on the wall, and of course you don't know just when the change happened.

The names are plainly marked on the corners—on all the corners—there are no exceptions. But the numbering of the houses—there has never been anything like it since original chaos. It is not possible that it was done by this wise city government. At first one thinks it was done by an idiot; but there is too much variety about it for that; an idiot could not think of so many different ways of making confusion and propagating blasphemy. The numbers run up one side the street and down the other. That is endurable, but the rest isn't. They often use one number for three or four houses—and sometimes they put the number on only one of the houses and let you guess at the others. Sometimes they put a number on a house—4, for instance—then put 4*a*, 4*b*, 4*c*, on the succeeding houses, and one becomes old and decrepit before he finally arrives at 5. A result of this systemless system is that when you are at No. 1 in a street you haven't any idea how far it may be to No. 150; it may be only six or eight blocks, it may be a couple of miles. Frederick Street is long, and is one of the great thoroughfares. The other day a man put up his money behind the assertion that there were more refreshment places in that street than numbers on the houses—and he won. There were 254 numbers and 257 refreshment places. Yet as I have said, it is a long street.

But the worst feature of all this complex business is that in Berlin the numbers do not travel in any one direction; no, they travel along until they get to 50 or 60, perhaps, then suddenly you find yourself up in the hundreds—140, maybe; the next will be 139—then you perceive by that sign that the numbers are now traveling toward you from the opposite direction. They will keep that sort of insanity up as long as you travel that street; every now and then the numbers will turn and run the other way. As a rule, there is an arrow under the number, to show by the direction of its flight which way the numbers are proceeding. There are a good many suicides in Berlin; I have seen six reported in a single day. There is always a deal of learned and laborious arguing and ciphering going on as to the cause of this state of things. If they will set to work and number their houses in a rational way perhaps they will find out what was the matter.

More than a month ago Berlin began to prepare to celebrate Professor Virchow's seventieth birthday. When the birthday arrived, the middle of October, it seemed to me that all the world of science arrived with it; deputation after deputation came, bringing the homage and reverence of far cities and centers of learning, and during the whole of a long day the hero of it sat and received such witness of his greatness as has seldom been vouchsafed to any man in any walk of life in any time, ancient or modern. These demonstrations were continued in one form or another day after day, and were presently merged in similar demonstrations to his twin in science and achievement, Professor Helmholtz, whose seventieth birthday is separated from Virchow's by only about three weeks; so nearly as this did these two extraordinary men come to being

born together. Two such births have seldom signalized a single year
in human history.

But perhaps the final and closing demonstration was peculiarly
grateful to them. This was a Commers given in their honor the
other night by 1,000 students. It was held in a huge hall, very
long and very lofty, which had five galleries, far above everybody's
head, which were crowded with ladies—four or five hundred, I judged.

It was beautifully decorated with clustered flags and various ornamental devices, and was brilliantly lighted. On the spacious floor
of this place were ranged, in files, innumerable tables, seating twenty-
four persons each, extending from one end of the great hall clear
to the other, and with narrow aisles between the files. In the center
on one side was a high and tastefully decorated platform twenty
or thirty feet long, with a long table on it behind which sat the
half-dozen chiefs of the givers of the Commers in the rich medieval
costumes of as many different college corps. Behind these youths
a band of musicians was concealed. On the floor directly in front
of this platform were half a dozen tables which were distinguished
from the outlying continent of tables by being covered instead of
left naked. Of these the central table was reserved for the two
heroes of the occasion and twenty particularly eminent professors
of the Berlin University, and the other covered tables were for
the occupancy of a hundred less distinguished professors.

I was glad to be honored with a place at the table of the two
heroes of the occasion, although I was not really learned enough
to deserve it. Indeed, there was a pleasant strangeness in being
in such company; to be thus associated with twenty-three men who
forget more every day than I ever knew. Yet there was nothing
embarrassing about it, because loaded men and empty ones look
about alike, and I knew that to that multitude there I was a professor. It required but little art to catch the ways and attitude
of those men and imitate them, and I had no difficulty in looking
as much like a professor as anybody there.

We arrived early; so early that only Professors Virchow and
Helmholtz and a dozen guests of the special tables were ahead of us,
and three hundred or four hundred students. But people were arriving in floods now, and within fifteen minutes all but the special
tables were occupied, and the great house was crammed, the aisles
included. It was said that there were four thousand men present. It
was a most animated scene, there is no doubt about that; it was
a stupendous beehive. At each end of each table stood a corps student

in the uniform of his corps. These quaint costumes are of brilliant colored silks and velvets, with sometimes a high plumed hat, sometimes a broad Scotch cap, with a great plume wound about it, sometimes—oftenest—a little shallow silk cap on the tip of the crown, like an inverted saucer; sometimes the pantaloons are snow-white, sometimes of other colors; the boots in all cases come up well above the knee; and in all cases also white gauntlets are worn; the sword is a rapier with a bowl-shaped guard for the hand, painted in several colors. Each corps has a uniform of its own, and all are of rich material brilliant in color, and exceedingly picturesque; for they are survivals of the vanished costumes of the Middle Ages, and they reproduce for us the time when men were beautiful to look at. The student who stood guard at our end of the table was of grave countenance and great frame and grace of form, and he was doubtless an accurate reproduction, clothes and all, of some ancestor of his of two or three centuries ago—a reproduction as far as the outside, the animal man, goes, I mean.

As I say, the place was now crowded. The nearest aisle was packed with students standing up, and they made a fence which shut off the rest of the house from view. As far down this fence as you could see all these wholesome young faces were turned in one direction, all these intent and worshiping eyes were centered upon one spot—the place where Virchow and Helmholtz sat. The boys seemed lost to everything, unconscious of their own existence; they devoured these two intellectual giants with their eyes, they feasted upon them, and the worship that was in their hearts shone in their faces. It seemed to me that I would rather be flooded with a glory like that, instinct with sincerity, innocent of self-seeking, than win a hundred battles and break a million hearts.

There was a big mug of beer in front of each of us, and more to come when wanted. There was also a quarto pamphlet containing the words of the songs to be sung. After the names of the officers of the feast were these words in large type:

"*Während des Kommerses herrscht allgemeiner Burgfriede.*"

I was not able to translate this to my satisfaction, but a professor helped me out. This was his explanation: The students in uniform belong to different college corps; not all students belong to corps; none join the corps except those who enjoy fighting. The corps students fight duels with swords every week, one corps challenging another corps to furnish a certain number of duelists for the occasion, and it is only on this battle-field that students of different corps exchange courtesies. In common life they do not drink with each other or speak. The above line now translates itself: there is truce during the Commers, war is laid aside and fellowship takes its place.

Now the performance began. The concealed band played a piece of martial music; then there was a pause. The students on the platform rose to their feet, the middle one gave a toast to the Emperor, then all the house rose, mugs in hand. At the call "One—two—three!" all glasses were drained and then brought down with a slam on the tables in unison. The result was as good an imitation of thunder as I have ever heard. From now on, during an hour, there was singing, in mighty chorus. During each interval between songs a number of the special guests—the professors—arrived. There seemed to be some signal whereby the students on the platform were made aware that a professor had arrived at the remote door of entrance; for you would see them suddenly rise to their feet, strike an erect military attitude, then draw their swords; the swords of all their brethren standing guard at the innumerable tables would flash from their scabbards and be held aloft—a handsome spectacle! Three clear bugle notes would ring out, then all these swords would come down with a crash, twice repeated, on the tables, and be uplifted and held aloft again; then in the distance you would see the gay uniforms and uplifted swords of a guard of honor clearing the way and conducting the guest down to his place. The songs were stirring, the immense outpour from young life and young lungs, the crash of swords and the thunder of the beer-mugs gradually worked a body up to what seemed the last possible summit of excitement. It surely seemed to me that I had reached that summit, that I had reached my limit, and that there was no higher lift desirable for me. When apparently the last eminent guest had long ago taken his place, again those three bugle blasts rang out and once more the swords leaped from their scabbards. Who might this late comer be? Nobody was interested to inquire. Still, indolent eyes were turned toward the distant entrance; we saw the silken gleam and the lifted swords of a guard of honor plowing through the remote crowds. Then we saw that end of the house rising to its feet; saw it rise abreast the advancing guard all along, like a wave. This supreme honor had been offered to no one before. Then there was an excited whisper at our table—"MOMMSEN!" and the whole house rose. Rose and shouted and stamped and clapped, and banged the beer-mugs.

Just simply a storm! Then the little man with his long hair and Emersonian face edged his way past us and took his seat. I could have touched him with my hand—Mommsen!—think of it!

This was one of those immense surprises that can happen only a few times in one's life. I was not dreaming of him, he was to me only a giant myth, a world-shadowing specter, not a reality. The surprise of it all can be only comparable to a man's suddenly coming upon Mont Blanc, with its awful form towering into the sky, when he didn't suspect he was in its neighborhood. I would have walked a great many miles to get a sight of him, and here he was, without trouble or tramp or cost of any kind. Here he was, clothed in a Titanic deceptive modesty which made him look like other men. Here he was, carrying the Roman world and all the Cæsars in his hospitable skull, and doing it as easily as that other luminous vault, the skull of the universe, carries the Milky Way and the constellations.

One of the professors said that once upon a time an American young lady was introduced to Mommsen, and found herself badly scared and speechless. She dreaded to see his mouth unclose, for she was expecting him to choose a subject several miles above her comprehension, and didn't suppose he *could* get down to the world that other people lived in; but when his remark came, her terrors disappeared: "Well, how do you do? Have you read Howells's last book? *I* think it's his best."

The active ceremonies of the evening closed with the speeches of welcome delivered by two students and the replies made by Professors Virchow and Helmholtz.

Virchow has long been a member of the city government of Berlin. He works as hard for the city as does any other Berlin alderman, and gets the same pay—nothing. I don't know that we in America could venture to ask our most illustrious citizen to serve in a board of aldermen, and if we might venture it I am not positively sure that we could elect him. But here the municipal system is such that the best men in the city consider it an honor to serve gratis as aldermen, and the people have the good sense to prefer these men and to elect them year after year. As a result Berlin is a thoroughly well-governed city. It is a free city; its affairs are not meddled with by the state; they are managed by its own citizens, and after methods of their own devising.

1892

Marienbad, a Health Factory[1]

This place is the village of Marienbad, Bohemia. It seems no very great distance from Annecy, in Haute-Savoie, to this place—you make it in less than thirty hours by these continental express trains—but the changes in the scenery are great; they are quite out of proportion to the distance covered. From Annecy by Aix to Geneva, you have blue lakes, with bold mountains springing from their borders, and far glimpses of snowy wastes lifted against the horizon beyond, while all about you is a garden cultivated to the last possibility of grace and beauty—a cultivation which doesn't stop with the handy lower levels, but is carried right up the sheer steeps and propped there with ribs of masonry, and made to stay there in spite of Newton's law. Beyond Geneva—beyond Lausanne, at any rate—you have for a while a country which noticeably resembles New England, and seems out of place and like an intruder—an intruder who is wearing his every-day clothes at a fancy-dress ball. But presently on your right, huge green mountain ramparts rise up, and after that for hours you are absorbed in watching the rich shadow effects which they furnish, and are only dully aware that New England is gone and that you are flying past quaint and unspeakable old towns and towers. Next day you have the lake of Zurich, and presently the Rhine is swinging by you. How clean it is! How clear it is! How blue it is! How green it is! How swift and rollicking and insolent are its gait and style! How vivid and splendid its colors—beautiful wreck and chaos of all the soap bubbles in the universe! A person born on the Rhine must worship it.

I saw the blue Rhine sweep along; I heard, or seemed to hear,
The German songs we used to sing in chorus sweet and clear.

[1] This essay first appeared in book form (and was first reprinted) in *Europe and Elsewhere* (1923), edited by Paine. Checking Paine's text against that of the *New York Sun* of February 7, 1892 (p. 190) I found that Paine omitted a section without warning, probably because he thought it was not in the best of taste. Paine was obsessed with notions of "good" taste, and was not a sound judge of taste. I have restored the suppressed section and have marked it with a footnote.—C.N.

Yes, that is where his heart would be, that is where his last thoughts would be, the "soldier of the legion" who "lay dying in Algiers."

And by and by you are in a German region, which you discover to be quite different from the recent Swiss lands behind you. You have a sea before you, that is to say; the green land goes rolling away, in ocean swells, to the horizon. And there is another new feature. Here and there at wide intervals you have islands, hills two hundred and three hundred feet high, of a haystack form, that rise abruptly out of the green plain, and are wooded solidly to the top. On the top there is just room for a ruined castle, and there it is, every time; above the summit you see the crumbling arches and broken towers projecting.

Beyond Stuttgart, next day, you find other changes still. By and by, approaching and leaving Nuremberg and down by Newhaus, your landscape is humped everywhere with scattered knobs of rock, unsociable crags of a rude, towerlike look, and thatched with grass and vines and bushes. And now and then you have gorges, too, of a modest pattern as to size, with precipice walls curiously carved and honeycombed by—I don't know what—but water, no doubt.

The changes are not done yet, for the instant the country finds it is out of Württemberg and into Bavaria it discards one more thickness of soil to go with previous disrobings, and then nothing remains over the bones but the shift. There may be a poorer soil somewhere, but it is not likely.

A couple of hours from Bayreuth you cross into Bohemia, and before long you reach this Marienbad, and recognize another sharp change, the change from the long ago to to-day; that is to say from the very old to the spick and span new; from an architecture totally without shapeliness or ornament to an architecture attractively equipped with both; from universal dismalness as to color to universal brightness and beauty as to tint; from a town which seems made up of prisons to a town which is made up of gracious and graceful mansions proper to the light of heart and crimeless. It is like jumping out of Jerusalem into Chicago.

The more I think of these many changes, the more surprising the thing seems. I have never made so picturesque a journey before, and there cannot be another trip of like length in the world that can furnish so much variety and of so charming and interesting a sort.

There are only two or three streets here in this snug pocket in the hemlock hills, but they are handsome. When you stand at the foot of a street and look up at the slant of it you see only block fronts of graceful pattern, with happily broken lines and the pleasant accent of bay projections and balconies in orderly disorder and harmonious confusion, and always the color is fresh and cheery, various shades of cream, with softly contrasting trimmings of white, and now and then a touch of dim red. These blocks are all thick walled, solid, massive, tall for this Europe; but it is the brightest and newest looking town on the Continent, and as pretty as anybody could require. The steep hills spring high aloft from their very back doors and are clothed densely to their tops with hemlocks.

In Bavaria everybody is in uniform, and you wonder where the private citizens are, but here in Bohemia the uniforms are very rare. Occasionally one catches a glimpse of an Austrian officer, but it is only occasionally. Uniforms are so scarce that we seem to be in a republic. Almost the only striking figure is the Polish Jew. He is very frequent. He is tall and of grave countenance and wears a coat that reaches to his ankle bones, and he has a little wee curl or two in front of each ear. He has a prosperous look, and seems to be as much respected as anybody.

The crowds that drift along the promenade at music time twice a day are fashionably dressed after the Parisian pattern, and they look a good deal alike, but they speak a lot of languages which you have not encountered before, and no ignorant person can spell their names, and they can't pronounce them themselves.

Marienbad—Mary's Bath. The Mary is the Virgin. She is the patroness of these curative springs. They try to cure everything—gout, rheumatism, leanness, fatness, dyspepsia, and all the rest. The whole thing is the property of a convent, and has been for six or seven hundred years. However, there was never a boom here until a quarter of a century ago.

If a person has the gout, this is what they do with him: they have him out at 5.30 in the morning, and give him an egg and let him look at a cup of tea. At six he must be at his particular spring, with his tumbler hanging at his belt—and he will have plenty of company there. At the first note of the orchestra he must lift his tumbler and begin to sip his dreadful water with the rest. He must sip slowly and be a long time at it. Then he must tramp about the hills for an hour or so, and get all the exercise and fresh air possible. Then he takes his tub or wallows in his mud, if mud baths are his sort. By noon he has a fine appetite, and the rules allow

him to turn himself loose and satisfy it, so long as he is careful
and eats only such things as he doesn't want. He puts in the afternoon
walking the hills and filling up with fresh air. At night he is allowed
to take three ounces of any kind of food he doesn't like and drink
one glass of any kind of liquor that he has a prejudice against;
he may also smoke one pipe if he isn't used to it. At half past nine sharp
he must be in bed and his candle out. Repeat the whole thing
the next day. I don't see any advantage in this over having the
gout.

In the case of most diseases that is about what one is required to
undergo, and if you have any pleasant habit that you value, they
want that. They want that the first thing. They make you drop
everything that gives an interest to life. Their idea is to reverse
your whole system of existence and make a regenerating revolution.
If you are a Republican, they make you talk free trade. If you are
a Democrat they make you talk protection; if you are a Prohibitionist, you have got to go to bed drunk every night till you get
well. They spare nothing, they spare nobody. Reform, reform, that
is the whole song. If a person is an orator, they gag him; if he
likes to read, they won't let him; if he wants to sing, they make
him whistle. They say they can cure any ailment, and they do
seem to do it; but why should a patient come all the way here?
Why shouldn't he do these things at home and save the money?
No disease would stay with a person who treated it like that.

I didn't come here to take baths, I only came to look around.
But first one person, then another began to throw out hints, and
pretty soon I was a good deal concerned about myself. One of these
goutees here said I had a gouty look about the eye; next a person
who has catarrh of the intestines asked me if I didn't notice a
dim sort of stomach ache when I sneezed. I hadn't before, but I
seem to notice it then. A man that's here for heart disease said he
wouldn't come downstairs so fast if he had my build and aspect.
A person with an old-gold complexion said a man died here in the
mud bath last week that had a petrified liver—good deal such a
looking man as I am, and the same initials, and so on, and so on.

Of course, there was nothing to be uneasy about, and I wasn't what
you may call really uneasy; but I was not feeling very well—that
is, not brisk—and I went to bed. I suppose that that was not a good
idea, because then they had me. I started in at the supper end
of the mill and went through. I am said to be all right now,
and free from disease, but this does not surprise me. What I have

been through in these two weeks would free a person of pretty much everything in him that wasn't nailed there—any loose thing, any unattached fragment of bone, or meat or morals, or disease or propensities or accomplishments, or what not. And I don't say but that I feel well enough, I feel better than I would if I was dead, I reckon. And, besides, they say I am going to build up now and come right along and be all right. I am not saying anything, but I wish I had enough of my diseases back to make me aware of myself, and enough of my habits to make it worth while to live. To have nothing the matter with you and no habits is pretty tame, pretty colorless. It is just the way a saint feels, I reckon; it is at least the way he looks. I never could stand a saint. That reminds me that you see very few priests around here, and yet, as I have already said, this whole big enterprise is owned and managed by a convent. The few priests one does see here are dressed like human beings, and so there may be more of them than I imagine. Fifteen priests dressed like these could not attract as much of your attention as would one priest at Aix-les-Bains. Your cannot pull your eye loose from the French priest as long as he is in sight, his dress is so fascinatingly ugly. I seem to be wandering from the subject, but I am not. This is about the coldest place I ever saw, and the wettest, too. This August seems like an English November to me. Rain? Why, it seems to like to rain here. It seems to rain every time there is a chance. You are strictly required to be out airing and exercising whenever the sun is shining, so I hate to see the sun shining because I hate air and exercise—duty air and duty exercise taken for medicine. It seems ungenuine, out of season, degraded to sordid utilities, a subtle spiritual something gone from it which one can't describe in words, but—don't you understand? With that gone what is left but canned air, canned exercise, and you don't want it.

When the sun does shine for a few moments or a few hours these people swarm out and flock through the streets and over the hills and through the pine woods, and make the most of the chance, and I have flocked out, too, on some of these occasions, but as a rule I stay in and try to get warm.

And what is there for means, besides heavy clothing and rugs, and the polished white tomb that stands lofty and heartless in the corner and thinks it is a stove? Of all the creations of human insanity this thing is the most forbidding. Whether it is heating the room or isn't, the impression is the same—cold indifference. You can't tell which it is doing without going and putting your hand on it. They burn little handfuls of kindlings in it, no substantial wood, and no coal.

The fire burns out every fifteen minutes, and there is no way to tell when this has happened. On these dismal days, with the rain steadily falling, it is no better company than a corpse. A roaring hickory fire, with the cordial flames leaping up the chimney— But I must not think of such things, they make a person homesick. This is a most strange place to come to get rid of disease.

That is what you think most of the time. But in the intervals, when the sun shines and you are tramping the hills and are comparatively warm, you get to be neutral, maybe even friendly. I went up to the Aussichtthurm the other day. This is a tower which stands on the summit of a steep hemlock mountain here; a tower which there isn't the least use for, because the view is as good at the base of it as it is at the top of it. But Germanic people are just mad for views—they never get enough of a view—if they owned Mount Blanc, they would build a tower on top of it.

The roads up that mountain through that hemlock forest are hard packed and smooth, and the grades are easy and comfortable. They are for walkers, not for carriages. You move through steep silence and twilight, and you seem to be in a million-columned temple; whether you look up the hill or down it you catch glimpses of distant figures flitting without sound, appearing and disappearing in the dim distances, among the stems of the trees, and it is all very spectral, and solemn and impressive. Now and then the gloom is accented and sized up to your comprehension in a striking way; a ray of sunshine finds its way down through and suddenly calls your attention, for where it falls, far up the hillslope in the brown duskiness, it lays a stripe that has a glare like lightning. The utter stillness of the forest depths, the soundless hush, the total absence of stir or motion of any kind in leaf or branch, are things which we have no experience of at home, and consequently no name for in our language. At home there would be the plaint of insects and the twittering of birds and vagrant breezes would quiver the foliage. Here it is the stillness of death. This is what the Germans are forever talking about, dreaming about, and despairingly trying to catch and imprison in a poem, or a picture, or a song—they adored Waldeinsamkeit, loneliness of the woods. But how catch it? It has not a body; it is a spirit. We don't talk about it in America, or dream of it, or sing about it, because we haven't it. Certainly there is something wonderfully alluring about it, beguiling, dreamy, unworldly. Where the gloom is softest and richest, and the peace and stillness deepest, far up on the side of that hemlock mountain, a spot where Goethe used to sit and dream, is marked by a granite obelisk, and on its side is carved this famous poem, which is the master's idea of Waldeinsamkeit:

> Ueber allen Wipfeln ist Ruh,
> In allen Wipfeln spürest du
> Kaum einen Hauch:
> Die Vögelein schweigen im Walde,
> Warte nur—balde
> Ruhest du auch.

It is raining again now. However, it was doing that before. I have been over to the establishment and had a tub bath with two kinds of pine juice in it. These fill the room with a pungent and most pleasant perfume; they also turn the water to a color of ink and cover it with a snowy suds, two or three inches deep. The bath is cool—about 75° or 80° F., and there is a cooler shower bath after it. While waiting in the reception room all by myself two men came in and began to talk. Politics, literature, religion? No, their ailments. There is no other subject here, apparently. Wherever two or three of these people are gathered together, there you have it, every time. The first that can get his mouth open contributes his disease and the condition of it, and the others follow with theirs. The two men just referred to were acquaintances, and they followed the custom. One of them was built like a gasometer and is here to reduce his girth; the other was built like a derrick and is here to fat up, as they express it, at this resort. They were well satisfied with the progress they were making. The gasometer had lost a quarter of a ton in ten days, and showed the record on his belt with pride, and he walked briskly across the room, smiling in a vast and luminous way, like a harvest moon, and said he couldn't have done that when he arrived here. He buttoned his coat around his equator and showed how loose it was. It was pretty to see his happiness, it was so childlike and honest. He set his feet together and leaned out over his person and proved that he could see them. He said he hadn't seen them from that point before for fifteen years. He had a hand like a boxing glove. And on one of his fingers he had just found a diamond ring which he had missed eleven years ago.

The minute the derrick got a chance he broke in and began

to tell how he was piling on blubber right along—three-quarters of an ounce every four days; and he was still piping away when I was sent for. I left the fat man standing there panting and blowing, and swelling and collapsing like a balloon, his next speech all ready and urgent for delivery.

The patients are always at that sort of thing, trying to talk one another to death. The fat ones and the lean ones are nearly the worse at it, but not quite; the dyspeptics are the worst. They are at it all day and all night, and all along. They have more symptoms than all the others put together and so there is more variety of experience, more change of condition, more adventure, and consequently more play for the imagination, more scope for lying, and in every way a bigger field to talk. Go where you will, hide where you may, you cannot escape that word liver; you overhear it constantly—in the street, in the shop, in the theater, in the music grounds. Wherever you see two or a dozen people of ordinary bulk talking together, you know they are talking about their livers. When you first arrive here your new acquaintances seem sad and hard to talk to, but pretty soon you get the lay of the land and the hand of things, and after that you haven't any more trouble. You look into the dreary dull eye and softly say:

"Well, how's your liver?"

You will see that dim eye flash up with a grateful flame, and you will see that jaw begin to work, and you will recognize that nothing is required of you from this out but to listen as long as you remain conscious. After a few days you will begin to notice that out of these people's talk a gospel is framing itself and next you will find yourself believing it. It is this—that a man is not what his rearing, his schooling, his beliefs, his principles make him, he is what his liver makes him; that with a healthy liver he will have the clear-seeing eye, the honest heart, the sincere mind, the loving spirit, the loyal soul, the truth and trust and faith that are based as Gibraltar is based, and that with an unhealthy liver he must and will have the opposite of all these, he will see nothing as it really is, he cannot trust anybody, or believe in anything, his moral foundations are gone from under him. Now, isn't that interesting? I think it is.[2]

Two days ago, perceiving that there was something unusual the

[2] Here follows the part which Paine suppressed. It concludes with "and I consider that I am a judge."—C.N.

matter with me, I went around from doctor to doctor, but without avail; they said they had never seen this kind of symptoms before— at least, not all of them. They had seen some of them, but differently arranged. It was a new disease, as far as they could see. Apparently it was scrofulous, but a new kind. That was as much as they felt able to say. Then they made a stethoscopic examination, and decided that if anything would dislodge it, a mud bath was the thing. It was a very ingenious idea. I took the mud bath, and it did dislodge it. Here it is—A Love Song:

I ask not, "Is thy heart still sure,
Thy love still warm, thy faith secure?"
I ask not, "Dream'st thou still of me?—
Long'st alway to fly to me?"
    Ah no—but as the sun includeth all
        The good gifts of the Giver,
    I sum all these in asking thee,
        "O sweetheart, how's your liver?"
For if thy liver worketh right,
Thy faith stands sure, thy hope is bright,
Their dreams are sweet and I their god,
Doubt threats in vain—thou scorn'st his rod.
    Keep only thy digestion clear.
    No other foe my love doth fear.

But indigestion hath the power
To mar the soul's serenest hour—
To crumble adamantine trust
And turn its certainties to dust,
To dim the eye with nameless grief,
To chill the heart with unbelief,
To banish hope, and faith, and love,
Place heaven below and hell above.
    Then list—details are naught to me
        So thou'st the sum-gift of the Giver—
    I ask thee all in asking thee,
        "O darling, how's your liver?"

Yes, it is easy to say it is scrofulous, but I don't see the signs of it. In my opinion it is as good poetry as I have ever written. Experts say it isn't poetry at all, because it lacks the element of fiction, but that is the voice of envy, I reckon. I call it good medical poetry, and I consider that I am a judge.

One of the most curious things in these countries is the street manners of the men and women. In meeting you they come straight on without swerving a hair's breadth from the direct line and wholly ignoring your right to any part of the road. At the last moment you must yield up your share of it and step aside, or there will be a collision. I noticed this strange barbarism first in Geneva twelve years ago.

In Aix-les-Bains, where sidewalks are scarce and everybody walks in the streets, there is plenty of room, but that is no matter; you are always escaping collisions by mere quarter inches. A man or woman who is headed in such a way as to cross your course presently without a collision will actually alter his direction shade by shade and compel a collision unless at the last instant you jump out of the way. Those folks are not dressed as ladies and gentlemen. And they do not seem to be consciously crowding you out of the road; they seem to be innocently and stupidly unaware that they are doing it. But not so in Geneva. There this class, especially the men, crowd out men, women, and girls of all rank and raiment consciously and intentionally—crowd them off the sidewalk and into the gutter.

There was nothing of this sort in Bayreuth. But here—well, here the thing is astonishing. Collisions are unavoidable unless you do all the yielding yourself. Another odd thing—here this savagery is confined to the folk who wear the fine clothes; the others are courteous and considerate. A big burly Comanche, with all the signs about him of wealth and education, will tranquilly force young ladies to step off into the gutter to avoid being run down by him. It is a mistake that there is no bath that will cure people's manners. But drowning would help.

However, perhaps one can't look for any real showy amount of delicacy of feeling in a country where a person is brought up to contemplate without a shudder the spectacle of women harnessed up with dogs and hauling carts. The woman is on one side of the pole, the dog on the other, and they bend to the work and tug and pant and strain—and the man tramps leisurely alongside and smokes his pipe. Often the woman is old and gray, and the man is her grandson. The Austrian national ornithological device ought to be replaced by a grandmother harnessed to a slush cart with a dog. This merely in the interest of fact. Heraldic fancy has been a little too much overworked in these countries, anyway.

Lately one of those curious things happened here which justify the felicitous extravagances of the stage and help us to accept them. A despondent man, bankrupt, friendless, and desperate, dropped a dose of strychnia into a bottle of whisky and went out in the dusk to find a handy place for his purpose, which was suicide. In a lonely spot he was stopped by a tramp, who said he would kill him if he didn't give up his money. Instead of jumping at the chance of getting himself killed and thus saving himself the impropriety and annoyance of suicide, he forgot all about his late project and attacked the tramp in a most sturdy and valiant fashion. He made a good fight, but failed to win. The night passed, the morning came, and he woke out of unconsciousness to find that he had been clubbed half to death and left to perish at his leisure. Then he reached for his bottle to add the finishing touch, but it was gone. He pulled himself together and went limping away, and presently came upon the tramp stretched out stone dead with the empty bottle beside him. He had drunk the whisky and committed suicide innocently. Now, while the man who had been cheated out of his suicide stood there bemoaning his hard luck and wondering how he might manage to raise money enough to buy some more whisky and poison, some people of the neighborhood came by and he told them about his curious adventure. They said that this tramp had been the scourge of the neighborhood and the dread of the constabulary. The inquest passed off quietly and to everybody's satisfaction, and then the people, to testify their gratitude to the hero of the occasion, put him on the police, on a good-enough salary, and he is all right now and is not meditating suicide any more. Here are all the elements of the naïvest Arabian tale; a man who resists robbery when he hasn't anything to be robbed of does the very best to save his life when he has come out purposely to throw it away; and finally is victorious in defeat, killing his adversary in an effectual and poetic fashion after being already *hors du combat* himself. Now if you let him rise in the service and marry the chief of police's daughter it has the requisite elements of the Oriental romance, lacking not a detail so far as I can see.

1892

Switzerland, the Cradle of Liberty

It is a good many years since I was in Switzerland last. In that remote time there was only one ladder railway in the country. That state of things is all changed. There isn't a mountain in Switzerland now that hasn't a ladder railroad or two up its back like suspenders; indeed, some mountains are latticed with them, and two years hence all will be. In that day the peasant of the high altitudes will have to carry a lantern when he goes visting in the night to keep from stumbling over railroads that have been built since his last round. And also in that day, if there shall remain a high-altitude peasant whose potato-patch hasn't a railroad through it, it will make him as conspicuous as William Tell.

However, there are only two best ways to travel through Switzerland. The first best is afloat. The second best is by open two-horse carriage. One can come from Lucerne to Interlaken over the Brunig by ladder railroad in an hour or so now, but you can glide smoothly in a carriage in ten, and have two hours for luncheon at noon—for luncheon, not for rest. There is no fatigue connected with the trip. One arrives fresh in spirit and in person in the evening—no fret in his heart, no grime on his face, no grit in his hair, not a cinder in his eye. This is the right condition of mind and body, the right and due preparation for the solemn event which closed the day—stepping with metaphorically uncovered head into the presence of the most impressive mountain mass that the globe can show—the Jungfrau. The stranger's first feeling, when suddenly confronted by that towering and awful apparition wrapped in its shroud of snow, is breathtaking astonishment. It is as if heaven's gates had swung open and exposed the throne.

It is peaceful here and pleasant at Interlaken. Nothing going on—at least nothing but brilliant life-giving sunshine. There are floods and floods of that. One may properly speak of it as "going on," for it is full of the suggestion of activity; the light pours down with energy, with visible enthusiasm. This is a good atmosphere to be in, morally as well as physically. After trying the political atmosphere of the

neighboring monarchies, it is healing and refreshing to breathe
in air that has known no taint of slavery for six hundred years,
and to come among a people whose political history is great and
fine, and worthy to be taught in all schools and studied by all
races and peoples. For the struggle here throughout the centuries
has not been in the interest of any private family, or any church,
but in the interest of the whole body of the nation, and for shelter
and protection of all forms of belief. This fact is colossal. If one
would realize how colossal it is, and of what dignity and majesty,
let him contrast it with the purposes and objects of the Crusades,
the siege of York, the War of the Roses, and other historic comedies
of that sort and size.

Last week I was beating around the Lake of Four Cantons, and
I saw Rutli and Altorf. Rutli is a remote little patch of a meadow,
but I do not know how any piece of ground could be holier or
better worth crossing oceans and continents to see, since it was there
that the great trinity of Switzerland joined hands six centuries ago
and swore the oath which set their enslaved and insulted country
forever free; and Altorf is also honorable ground and worshipful,
since it was there that William, surnamed Tell (which interpreted
means "The foolish talker"—that is to say, the too-daring talker), refused to bow to Gessler's hat. Of late years the prying student
of history has been delighting himself beyond measure over a wonderful find which he has made—to wit, that Tell did not shoot
the apple from his son's head. To hear the students jubilate, one
would suppose that the question of whether Tell shot the apple
or didn't was an important matter; whereas it ranks in importance
exactly with the question of whether Washington chopped down the
cherry-tree or didn't. The deeds of Washington, the patriot, are the
essential thing; the cherry-tree incident is of no consequence. To prove
that Tell did shoot the apple from his son's head would merely prove
that he had better nerve than most men and was as skilful with
a bow as a million others who preceded and followed him, but not
one whit more so. But Tell was more and better than a mere marks-
man, more and better than a mere cool head; he was a type; he
stands for Swiss patriotism; in his person was represented a whole
people; his spirit was their spirit—the spirit which would bow to
none but God, the spirit which said this in words and confirmed
it with deeds. There have always been Tells in Switzerland—people
who would not bow. There was a sufficiency of them at Rutli; there
were plenty of them at Murten; plenty at Grandson; there are plenty

to-day. And the first of them all—the very first, earliest banner-bearer of human freedom in this world—was not a man, but a woman—Stauffacher's wife. There she looms dim and great, through the haze of the centuries, delivering into her husband's ear that gospel of revolt which was to bear fruit in the conspiracy of Rutli and the birth of the first free government the world had ever seen.

From this Victoria Hotel one looks straight across a flat of trifling width to a lofty mountain barrier, which has a gateway in it shaped like an inverted pyramid. Beyond this gateway arises the vast bulk of the Jungfrau, a spotless mass of gleaming snow, into the sky. The gateway, in the dark-colored barrier, makes a strong frame for the great picture. The somber frame and the glowing snow-pile are startlingly contrasted. It is this frame which concentrates and emphasizes the glory of the Jungfrau and makes it the most engaging and beguiling and fascinating spectacle that exists on the earth. There are many mountains of snow that are as lofty as the Jungfrau and as nobly proportioned, but they lack the fame. They stand at large; they are intruded upon and elbowed by neighboring domes and summits, and their grandeur is diminished and fails of effect.

It is a good name, Jungfrau—Virgin. Nothing could be whiter; nothing could be purer; nothing could be saintlier of aspect. At six yesterday evening the great intervening barrier seen through a faint bluish haze seemed made of air and substanceless, so soft and rich it was, so shimmering where the wandering lights touched it and so dim where the shadows lay. Apparently it was a dream stuff, a work of the imagination, nothing real about it. The tint was green, slightly varying shades of it, but mainly very dark. The sun was down—as far as that barrier was concerned, but not for the Jungfrau, towering into the heavens beyond the gateway. She was a roaring conflagration of blinding white.

It is said that Fridolin (the old Fridolin), a new saint, but formerly a missionary, gave the mountain its gracious name. He was an Irishman, son of an Irish king—there were thirty thousand kings reigning in County Cork alone in his time, fifteen hundred years ago. It got so that they could not make a living, there was so much competition and wages got cut so. Some of them were out of work months at a time, with wife and little children to feed, and not a crust in the place. At last a particularly severe winter fell upon the country, and hundreds of them were reduced to mendicancy and were to be seen day after day in the bitterest weather, standing barefoot in the snow, holding out their crowns for alms. Indeed, they would have been obliged to emigrate or starve but for a fortunate idea of Prince Fridolin's, who started a labor-union, the first one in history, and got the great bulk of them to join it. He thus won the general gratitude, and they wanted to make him emperor—emperor over them all—emperor of County Cork, but he said, No, walking delegate was good enough for him. For, behold! he was modest beyond his years, and keen as a whip. To this day in Germany and Switzerland, where St. Fridolin is revered and honored, the peasantry speak of him affectionately as the first walking delegate.

The first walk he took was into France and Germany, missionary-ing—for missionarying was a better thing in those days than it is in ours. All you had to do was to cure the head savage's sick daughter by a "miracle"—a miracle like the miracle of Lourdes in our day, for instance—and immediately that head savage was your convert, and filled to the eyes with a new convert's enthusiasm. You could sit down and make yourself easy, now. He would take the ax and convert the rest of the nation himself. Charlemagne was that kind of a walking delegate.

Yes, there were great missionaries in those days, for the methods were sure and the rewards great. We have no such missionaries now, and no such methods.

But to continue the history of the first walking delegate, if you are interested. I am interested myself because I have seen his relics at Sackingen, and also the very spot where he worked his great miracle—the one which won him his saintship in the papal court a few centuries later. To have seen these things makes me feel very near to him, almost like a member of the family, in fact. While wandering about the Continent he arrived at the spot on the Rhine which is now occupied by Sackingen, and proposed to settle there, but the people warned him off. He appealed to the king of the Franks, who made him a present of the whole region, people and all. He built a great cloister there for women and pro-ceeded to teach in it and accumulate more land. There were two wealthy brothers in the neighborhood, Urso and Landulph. Urso died and Fridolin claimed his estates. Landulph asked for documents and papers. Fridolin had none to show. He said the bequest had been made to him by word of mouth. Landulph suggested that he produce a witness and said it in a way which he thought was very witty, very sarcastic. This shows that he did not know the walking delegate. Fridolin was not disturbed. He said:

"Appoint your court. I will bring a witness."

The court thus created consisted of fifteen counts and barons. A day was appointed for the trial of the case. On that day the judges took their seats in state, and proclamation was made that the court was ready for business. Five minutes, ten minutes, fifteen minutes passed, and yet no Fridolin appeared. Landulph rose, and was in the act of claiming judgment by default when a strange clacking sound was heard coming up the stairs. In another moment Fridolin entered at the door and came walking in a deep hush down the middle aisle, with a tall skeleton stalking in his rear.

Amazement and terror sat upon every countenance, for everybody suspected that the skeleton was Urso's. It stopped before the chief judge and raised its bony arm aloft and began to speak, while all the assembly shuddered, for they could see the words leak out between its ribs. It said:

"Brother, why dost thou disturb my blessed rest and withhold by robbery the gift which I gave thee for the honor of God?"

It seems a strange thing and most irregular, but the verdict was actually given against Landulph on the testimony of this wandering rack-heap of unidentified bones. In our day a skeleton would not be allowed to testify at all, for a skeleton has no moral responsibility, and its word could not be rationally trusted. Most skeletons are not to be believed on oath, and this was probably one of them. However, the incident is valuable as preserving to us a curious sample of the quaint laws of evidence of that remote time—a time so remote, so far back toward the beginning of original idiocy, that the difference between a bench of judges and a basket of vegetables was as yet so slight that we may say with all confidence that it didn't really exist.

During several afternoons I have been engaged in an interesting, maybe useful, piece of work—that is to say, I have been trying to make the mighty Jungfrau earn her living—earn it in a most humble sphere, but on a prodigious scale, on a prodigious scale of necessity, for she couldn't do anything in a small way with her size and style. I have been trying to make her do service on a stupendous dial and check off the hours as they glide along her pallid face up there against the sky, and tell the time of day to the populations lying within fifty miles of her and to the people in the moon, if they have a good telescope there.

Until late in the afternoon the Jungfrau's aspect is that of a spotless desert of snow set upon edge against the sky. But by mid-afternoon some elevations which rise out of the western border of the desert, whose presence you perhaps had not detected or suspected up to that time, begin to cast black shadows eastward across the gleaming surface. At first there is only one shadow; later there are two. Toward 4 P.M. the other day I was gazing and worshiping as usual when I chanced to notice that shadow No. 1 was beginning to take itself something of the shape of the human profile. By four the back of the head was good, the military cap was pretty good, the nose was bold and strong, the upper lip sharp, but not pretty, and there was a great goatee that shot straight aggressively forward from the chin.

At four-thirty the nose had changed its shape considerably, and the altered slant of the sun had revealed and made conspicuous a huge buttress or barrier of naked rock which was so located as to answer very well for a shoulder or coat-collar to this swarthy and indiscreet sweetheart who had stolen out there right before everybody to pillow his head on the Virgin's white breast and whisper soft sentimentalities to her to the sensuous music of crashing ice-domes and the boom and thunder of the passing avalanche—music very familiar to his ear, for he has heard it every afternoon at this hour since the day he first came courting this child of the earth, who lives in the sky, and that day is far, yes—for he was at this pleasant sport before the Middle Ages drifted by him in the valley; before the Romans marched past, and before the antique and record-less barbarians fished and hunted here and wondered who he might be, and were probably afraid of him; and before primeval man himself, just emerged from his four-footed estate, stepped out upon this plain, first sample of his race, a thousand centuries ago, and cast a glad eye up there, judging he had found a brother human being and consequently something to kill; and before the big saurians wallowed here, still some eons earlier. Oh yes, a day so far back that the eternal son was present to see that first visit; a day so far back that neither tradition nor history was born yet and a whole weary eternity must come and go before the restless little creature, of whose face this stupendous Shadow Face was the prophecy, would arrive in the earth and begin his shabby career and think it a big thing.

Oh, indeed yes; when you talk about your poor Roman and Egyptian day-before-yesterday antiquities, you should choose a time when the hoary Shadow Face of the Jungfrau is not by. It antedates all antiquities known or imaginable; for it was here the world itself created the theater of future antiquities. And it is the only witness with a human face that was there to see the marvel, and remains to us a memorial of it.

By 4.40 P.M. the nose of the shadow is perfect and is beautiful. It is black and is powerfully marked against the upright canvas of glowing snow, and covers hundreds of acres of that resplendent surface.

Meantime shadow No. 2 has been creeping out well to the rear of the face west of it—and at five o'clock has assumed a shape that has rather a poor and rude semblance of a shoe.

Meantime, also, the great Shadow Face has been gradually changing for twenty minutes, and now, 5 P.M., it is becoming a quite fair portrait of Roscoe Conkling. The likeness is there, and is unmistakable. The goatee is shortened, now, and has an end; formerly it hadn't any, but ran off eastward and arrived nowhere.

By 6 P.M. the face has dissolved and gone, and the goatee has become what looks like the shadow of a tower with a pointed roof, and the shoe had turned into what the printers call a "fist" with a finger pointing.

If I were now imprisoned on a mountain summit a hundred miles northward of this point, and was denied a timepiece, I could get along well enough from four till six on clear days, for I could keep trace of the time by the changing shapes of these mighty shadows on the Virgin's front, the most stupendous dial I am acquainted with, the oldest clock in the world by a couple of million years.

I suppose I should not have noticed the forms of the shadows if I hadn't the habit of hunting for faces in the clouds and in mountain crags—a sort of amusement which is very entertaining even when you don't find any, and brilliantly satisfying when you do. I have searched through several bushels of photographs of the Jungfrau here, but found only one with the Face in it, and in this case it was not strictly recognizable as a face, which was evidence that the picture was taken before four o'clock in the afternoon, and also evidence that all the photographers have persistently overlooked one of the most fascinating features of the Jungfrau show. I say fascinating, because if you once detect a human face produced on a great plan by unconscious nature, you never get tired of watching it. At first you can't make another person see it at all, but after he has made it out once he can't see anything else afterward.

The King of Greece is a man who goes around quietly enough when off duty. One day this summer he was traveling in an ordinary first-class compartment, just in his other suit, the one which he works the realm in when he is at home, and so he was not looking like anybody in particular, but a good deal like everybody in general. By and by a hearty and healthy German-American got in and opened up a frank and interesting and sympathetic conversation with him, and asked him a couple of thousand questions about himself, which the king answered good-naturedly, but in a more or less indefinite way as to private particulars.

"Where do you live when you are at home?"

"In Greece."

"Greece! Well, now, that is just astonishing! Born there?"

"No."

"Do you speak Greek?"

"Yes."

"Now, ain't that strange! I never expected to live to see that. What is your trade? I mean how do you get your living? What is your line of business?"

"Well, I hardly know how to answer. I am only a kind of foreman, on a salary; and the business—well, is a very general kind of business."

"Yes, I understand—general jobbing—little of everything—anything that there's money in."

"That's about it, yes."

"Are you traveling for the house now?"

"Well, partly; but not entirely. Of course I do a stroke of business if it falls in the way—"

"Good! I like that in you! That's me every time. Go on."

"I was only going to say I am off on my vacation now."

"Well, that's all right. No harm in that. A man works all the better for a little let-up now and then. Not that I've been used to having it myself; for I haven't. I reckon this is my first. I was born in Germany, and when I was a couple of weeks old shipped for America, and I've been there ever since, and that's sixty-four years by the watch. I'm an American in principle and a German at heart, and it's the boss combination. Well, how do you get along, as a rule—pretty fair?"

"I've a rather large family—"

"There, that's it—big family and trying to raise them on a salary. Now, what did you go to do that for?"

"Well, I thought—"

"Of course you did. You were young and confident and thought you could branch out and make things go with a whirl, and here you are, you see! But never mind about that. I'm not trying to discourage you. Dear me! I've been just where you are myself! You've got good grit; there's good stuff in you, I can see that. You got a wrong start, that's the whole trouble. But you hold your grip, and we'll see what can be done. Your case ain't half as bad as it might be. You are going to come out all right—I'm bail for that. Boys and girls?"

"My family? Yes, some of them are boys—"

"And the rest girls. It's just as I expected. But that's all right, and it's better so, anyway. What are the boys doing—learning a trade?"

"Well, no—I thought—"

"It's a great mistake. It's the biggest mistake you ever made. You see that in your own case. A man ought always to have a trade to fall back on. Now, I was harness-maker at first. Did that prevent me from becoming one of the biggest brewers in America? Oh no. I always had the harness trick to fall back on in rough weather. Now, if you had learned how to make harness— However, it's too late now; too late. But it's no good plan to cry over spilt milk. But as to the boys, you see— what's to become of them if anything happens to you?"

"It has been my idea to let the eldest one succeed me—"

"Oh, come! Suppose the firm don't want him?"

"I hadn't thought of that, but—"

"Now, look here; you want to get right down to business and stop dreaming. You are capable of immense things—man. You can make a perfect success in life. All you want is somebody to steady you and boost you along on the right road. Do you own anything in the business?"

"No—not exactly; but if I continue to give satisfaction, I suppose I can keep my—"

"Keep your place—yes. Well, don't you depend on anything of the kind. They'll bounce you the minute you get a little old and worked out; they'll do it sure. Can't you manage somehow to get into the firm? That's the great thing, you know."

"I think it is doubtful; very doubtful."

"Um—that's bad—yes, and unfair, too. Do you suppose that if I should go there and have a talk with your people— Look here—do you think you could run a brewery?"

"I have never tried, but I think I could do it after I got a little familiarity with the business."

The German was silent for some time. He did a good deal of thinking, and the king waited with curiosity to see what the result was going to be. Finally the German said:

"My mind's made up. You leave that crowd—you'll never amount to anything there. In these old countries they never give a fellow a show. Yes, you come over to America—come to my place in Rochester; bring the family along. You shall have a show in the business and the foremanship, besides. George—you said your name was George?—I'll make a man of you. I give you my word. You've never had a chance here, but that's all going to change. By gracious! I'll give you a lift that'll make your hair curl!"

1892

In Defense of Harriet Shelley

I

I have committed sins, of course; but I have not committed enough of them to entitle me to the punishment of reduction to the bread and water of ordinary literature during six years when I might have been living on the fat diet spread for the righteous in Professor Dowden's *Life of Shelley*, if I had been justly dealt with.

During these six years I have been living a life of peaceful ignorance. I was not aware that Shelley's first wife was unfaithful to him, and that that was why he deserted her and wiped the stain from his sensitive honor by entering into soiled relations with Godwin's young daughter. This was all new to me when I heard it lately, and was told that the proofs of it were in this book, and that this book's verdict is accepted in the girls' colleges of America and its view taught in their literary classes.

In each of these six years multitudes of young people in our country have arrived at the Shelley-reading age. Are these six multitudes unacquainted with this life of Shelley? Perhaps they are; indeed, one may feel pretty sure that the great bulk of them are. To these, then, I address myself, in the hope that some account of this romantic historical fable and the fabulist's manner of constructing and adorning it may interest them.

First, as to its literary style. Our negroes in America have several ways of entertaining themselves which are not found among the whites anywhere. Among these inventions of theirs is one which is particularly popular with them. It is a competition in elegant deportment. They hire a hall and bank the spectators' seats in rising tiers along the two sides, leaving all the middle stretch of the floor free. A cake is provided as a prize for the winner in the competition, and a bench of experts in deportment is appointed to award it. Sometimes there are as many as fifty contestants, male and female, and five hundred spectators. One at a time the contestants enter, clothed regardless of expense in what each considers the perfection of style and taste, and walk down the vacant central space and back again with that multitude of critical eyes on them. All that the competitor knows of fine airs and graces he throws into his carriage, all that he knows of seductive expression he throws into his countenance. He may use all the helps he can devise: watch-chain to twirl with his fingers, cane to do graceful things with, snowy handkerchief to flourish and get artful effects out of, shiny new stovepipe hat to assist in his courtly bows; and the colored lady may have a fan to work up *her* effects with, and smile over and blush behind, and she may add other helps, according to her judgment. When the review by individual detail is over, a grand review of all the contestants in procession follows, with all the airs and graces and all the bowings and smirkings on exhibition at once, and this enables the bench of experts to make the necessary comparisons and arrive at a verdict. The successful competitor gets the prize which I have before mentioned, and an abundance of applause and envy along with it. The negroes have a name for this grave deportment tournament; a name taken from the prize contended for. They call it a Cake-Walk.

The Shelley biography is a literary cake-walk. The ordinary forms of speech are absent from it. All the pages, all the paragraphs, walk by sedately, elegantly, not to say mincingly, in their Sunday-best, shiny and sleek, perfumed, and with *boutonnières* in their buttonholes; it is rare to find even a chance sentence that has forgotten to dress. If the book wishes to tell us that Mary Godwin, child of sixteen, had known afflictions, the fact saunters forth in this nobby outfit: "Mary was herself not unlearned in the lore of pain"—meaning by that that she had not always traveled on asphalt; or, as some authorities would frame it, that she had "been there herself," a form which, while preferable to the book's form, is still not to be recommended. If the book wishes to tell us that Harriet Shelley hired a wet-nurse, that commonplace fact gets turned into a dancing-master, who does his professional bow before us in pumps and knee-breeches, with his fiddle under one arm and his crush-hat under the other, thus: "The beauty of Harriet's motherly relation to her babe was marred in Shelley's eyes by the introduction into his house of a hireling nurse to whom was delegated the mother's tenderest office."

This is perhaps the strangest book that has seen the light since Frankenstein. Indeed, it is a Frankenstein itself; a Frankenstein with the original infirmity supplemented by a new one; a Frankenstein with the reasoning faculty wanting. Yet it believes it can reason, and is always trying. It is not content to leave a mountain of fact standing in the clear sunshine, where the simplest reader can perceive its form, its details, and its relation to the rest of the landscape, but thinks it must help him examine it and understand it; so its drifting mind settles upon it with that intent, but always with one and the same result: there is a change of temperature and the mountain is hid in a fog. Every time it sets up a premise and starts to reason from it, there is a surprise in store for the reader. It is strangely nearsighted, cross-eyed, and purblind. Sometimes when a mastodon walks across the field of its vision it takes it for a rat; at other times it does not see it at all.

The materials of this biographical fable are facts, rumors, and poetry. They are connected together and harmonized by the help of suggestion, conjecture, innuendo, perversion, and semi-suppression.

The fable has a distinct object in view, but this object is not acknowledged in set words. Percy Bysshe Shelley has done something which in the case of other men is called a grave crime; it must be shown that in his case it is not that, because he does not think as other men do about these things.

Ought not that to be enough, if the fabulist is serious? Having proved that a crime is not a crime, was it worth while to go on and fasten the responsibility of a crime which was not a crime upon somebody else? What is the use of hunting down and holding to bitter account people who are responsible for other people's innocent acts?

Still, the fabulist thinks it a good idea to do that. In his view Shelley's first wife, Harriet, free of all offense as far as we have historical facts for guidance, must be held unforgivably responsible for her husband's innocent act in deserting her and taking up with another woman.

Any one will suspect that this task has its difficulties. Any one will divine that nice work is necessary here, cautious work, wily work, and that there is entertainment to be had in watching the magician do it. There is indeed entertainment in watching him. He arranges his facts, his rumors, and his poems on his table in full view of the house, and shows you that everything is there—no deception, everything fair and aboveboard. And this is apparently true, yet there is a defect, for some of his best stock is hid in an appendix-basket behind the door, and you do not come upon it until the exhibition is over and the enchantment of your mind accomplished—as the magician thinks.

There is an insistent atmosphere of candor and fairness about this book which is engaging at first, then a little burdensome, then a trifle fatiguing, then progressively suspicious, annoying, irritating, and oppressive. It takes one some little time to find out that phrases which seem intended to guide the reader aright are there to mislead him; that phrases which seem intended to throw light are there to throw darkness; that phrases which seem intended to interpret a fact are there to misinterpret it; that phrases which seem intended to forestall prejudice are there to create it; that phrases which seem antidotes are poisons in disguise. The naked facts arrayed in the book establish Shelley's guilt in that one episode which disfigures his otherwise superlatively lofty and beautiful life; but the historian's careful and methodical misinterpretation of them transfers the responsibility to the wife's shoulders—as he persuades himself. The few meager facts of Harriet Shelley's life, as furnished by the book, acquit her of offense; but by calling in the forbidden helps of rumor, gossip, conjecture, insinuation, and innuendo he destroys her character and rehabilitates Shelley's—as he believes. And in truth his unheroic work has not been barren of the results he aimed at; as witness the assertion made to me that girls in the colleges of America are taught that Harriet Shelley put a stain upon her husband's honor, and that that was what stung him into repurifying himself by deserting her and his child and entering into scandalous relations with a school-girl acquaintance of his.

If that assertion is true, they probably use a reduction of this work in those colleges, maybe only a sketch outlined from it. Such a thing as that could be harmful and misleading. They ought to cast it out and put the whole book in its place. It would not deceive. It would not deceive the janitor.

All of this book is interesting on account of the sorcerer's methods and the attractiveness of some of his characters and the repulsiveness of the rest, but no part of it is so much so as are the chapters wherein he tries to think he thinks he sets forth the causes which led to Shelley's desertion of his wife in 1814.

Harriet Westbrook was a school-girl sixteen years old. Shelley was teeming with advanced thought. He believed that Christianity was a degrading and selfish superstition, and he had a deep and sincere desire to rescue one of his sisters from it. Harriet was impressed by his various philosophies and looked upon him as an intellectual wonder—which indeed he was. He had an idea that she could give him valuable help in his scheme regarding his sister; therefore he asked her to correspond with him. She was quite willing. Shelley was not thinking of love, for he was just getting over a passion for his cousin, Harriet Grove, and just getting well steeped in one for Miss Hitchener, a school-teacher. What might happen to Harriet Westbrook before the letter-writing was ended did not enter his mind. Yet an older person could have made a good guess at it, for in person Shelley was as beautiful as an angel, he was frank, sweet, winning, unassuming, and so rich in unselfishness, generosities, and magnanimities that he made his whole generation seem poor in these great qualities by comparison. Besides, he was in distress. His college had expelled him for writing an atheistical pamphlet and afflicting the reverend heads of the university with it, his rich father and grandfather had closed their purses against him, his friends were cold. Necessarily, Harriet fell in love with him; and so deeply, indeed, that there was no way for Shelley to save her from suicide but to marry her. He believed himself to blame for this state of things, so the marriage took place. He was pretty fairly in love with Harriet, although he loved Miss Hitchener better. He wrote and explained the case to Miss Hitchener after the wedding, and he could not have been franker or more naïve and less stirred up about the circumstance if the matter in issue had been a commercial transaction involving thirty-five dollars.

Shelley was nineteen. He was not a youth, but a man. He had never had any youth. He was an erratic and fantastic child during eighteen years, then he stepped into manhood, as one steps over a doorsill. He was curiously mature at nineteen in his ability to do independent thinking on the deep questions of life and to arrive at sharply definite decisions regarding them, and stick to them—stick to them and stand by them at cost of bread, friendships, esteem, respect, and approbation.

For the sake of his opinions he was willing to sacrifice all these valuable things, and did sacrifice them; and went on doing it, too, when he could at any moment have made himself rich and supplied himself with friends and esteem by compromising with his father, at the moderate expense of throwing overboard one or two indifferent details of his cargo of principles.

He and Harriet eloped to Scotland and got married. They took lodgings in Edinburgh of a sort answerable to their purse, which was about empty, and there their life was a happy one and grew daily more so. They had only themselves for company, but they needed no additions to it. They were as cozy and contented as birds in a nest. Harriet sang evenings or read aloud; also she studied and tried to improve her mind, her husband instructing her in Latin. She was very beautiful, she was modest, quiet, genuine, and, according to her husband's testimony, she had no fine-lady airs or aspirations about her. In Matthew Arnold's judgment, she was "a pleasing figure."

The pair remained five weeks in Edinburgh, and then took lodgings in York, where Shelley's college-mate, Hogg, lived. Shelley presently ran down to London, and Hogg took this opportunity to make love to the young wife. She repulsed him, and reported the fact to her husband when he got back. It seems a pity that Shelley did not copy this creditable conduct of hers some time or other when under temptation, so that we might have seen the author of his biography hang the miracle in the skies and squirt rainbows at it.

At the end of the first year of marriage—the most trying year for any young couple, for then the mutual failings are coming one by one to light, and the necessary adjustments are being made in pain and tribulation—Shelley was able to recognize that his marriage venture had been a safe one. As we have seen, his love for his wife had begun in a rather shallow way and with not much force, but now it was become deep and strong, which entitles his wife to a broad credit mark, one may admit. He addresses a long and loving poem to her, in which both passion and worship appear:

Exhibit A

O thou
Whose dear love gleamed upon the gloomy path
Which this lone spirit travelled,

.   .   .   .

. . . wilt thou not turn
Those spirit-beaming eyes and look on me,
Until I be assured that Earth is Heaven
And Heaven is Earth?

.   .   .   .

Harriet! let death all mortal ties dissolve,
But ours shall not be mortal.

Shelley also wrote a sonnet to her in August of this same year in celebration of her birthday:

Exhibit B

Ever as now with Love and Virtue's glow
  May thy unwithering soul not cease to burn,
Still may thine heart with those pure thoughts o'erflow
  Which force from mine such quick and warm return.

Was the girl of seventeen glad and proud and happy? We may conjecture that she was.

That was the year 1812. Another year passed—still happily, still successfully—a child was born in June, 1813, and in September, three months later, Shelley addresses a poem to this child, Ianthe, in which he points out just when the little creature is most particularly dear to him:

Exhibit C

Dearest when most thy tender traits express
The image of thy mother's loveliness.

Up to this point the fabulist counsel for Shelley and prosecutor of his young wife has had easy sailing, but now his trouble begins, for Shelley is getting ready to make some unpleasant history for himself, and it will.be necessary to put the blame of it on the wife.

Shelley had made the acquaintance of a charming gray-haired, young-hearted Mrs. Boinville, whose face "retained a certain youthful beauty"; she lived at Bracknell, and had a young daughter named Cornelia Turner, who was equipped with many fascinations. Apparently these people were sufficiently sentimental. Hogg says of Mrs. Boinville:

"The greater part of her associates were odious. I generally found there two or three sentimental young butchers, an eminently philosophical tinker, and several very unsophisticated medical practitioners or medical students, all of low origin and vulgar and offensive manners. They sighed, turned up their eyes, retailed philosophy, such as it was," etc.

Shelley moved to Bracknell, July 27th (this is still 1813) purposely to be near this unwholesome prairie-dogs' nest. The fabulist says: "It was the entrance into a world more amiable and exquisite than he had yet known."

"In this acquaintance the attraction was mutual"—and presently it grew to be very mutual indeed, between Shelley and Cornelia Turner, when they got to studying the Italian poets together. Shelley, "responding like a tremulous instrument to every breath of passion or of sentiment," had his chance here. It took only four days for Cornelia's attractions to begin to dim Harriet's. Shelley arrived on the 27th of July; on the 31st he wrote a sonnet to Harriet in which "one detects already the little rift in the lover's lute which had seemed to be healed or never to have gaped at all when the later and happier sonnet to Ianthe was written"—in September, we remember:

Exhibit D

EVENING. TO HARRIET

O thou bright Sun! Beneath the dark blue line
Of western distance that sublime descendest,
And, gleaming lovelier as thy beams decline,
Thy million hues to every vapor lendest,
And over cobweb, lawn, and grove, and stream
Sheddest the liquid magic of thy light,
Till calm Earth, with the parting splendor bright,
Shows like the vision of a beauteous dream;
What gazer now with astronomic eye
Could coldly count the spots within thy sphere?
Such were thy lover, Harriet, could he fly
The thoughts of all that makes his passion dear,
And turning senseless from thy warm caress
Pick flaws in our close-woven happiness.

I cannot find the "rift"; still it may be there. What the poem *seems* to say is, that a person would be coldly ungrateful who could consent to count and consider little spots and flaws in such a warm, great, satisfying sun as Harriet is. It is a "little rift which had seemed to be healed, *or* never to have gaped at all." That is, "one *detects*" a little rift which perhaps had never existed. How does one do that? How does one see the invisible? It is the fabulist's secret; he knows how to detect what does not exist, he knows how to see what is not seeable; it is his gift, and he works it many a time to poor dead Harriet Shelley's deep damage.

"As yet, however, if there was a speck upon Shelley's happiness it was no more than a speck"—meaning the one which one detects where "it may never have gaped at all"—"nor had Harriet cause for discontent."

Shelley's Latin instructions to his wife had ceased. "From a teacher he had now become a pupil." Mrs. Boinville and her young married daughter Cornelia were teaching him Italian poetry; a fact which warns one to receive with some caution that other statement that Harriet had no "cause for discontent."

Shelley had stopped instructing Harriet in Latin, as before mentioned. The biographer thinks that the busy life in London some time back, and the intrusion of the baby, account for this. These were hindrances, but were there no others? He is always overlooking a detail here and there that might be valuable in helping us understand a situation. For instance, when a man has been hard at work at the Italian poets with a pretty woman, hour after hour, and responding like a tremulous instrument to every breath of passion or of sentiment in the mean time, that man is dog-tired when he gets home, and he *can't* teach his wife Latin; it would be unreasonable to expect it.

Up to this time we have submitted to having Mrs. Boinville pushed upon us as ostensibly concerned in these Italian lessons, but the biographer drops her now, of his own accord. Cornelia "perhaps" is sole teacher. Hogg says she was a prey to a kind of sweet melancholy, arising from causes purely imaginary; she required consolation, and found it in Petrarch. He also says, "Bysshe entered at once fully into her views and caught the soft infection, breathing the tenderest and sweetest melancholy, as every true poet ought."

Then the author of the book interlards a most stately and fine compliment to Cornelia, furnished by a man of approved judgment who knew her well "in later years." It is a very good compliment indeed, and she no doubt deserved it in her "later years," when she had for generations ceased to be sentimental and lackadaisical, and was no longer engaged in enchanting young husbands and sowing sorrow for young wives. But why is that compliment to that old gentlewoman intruded there? Is it to make the reader believe she was well-chosen and safe society for a young, sentimental husband? The biographer's device was not well planned. That old person was not present—it was her other self that was there, her young, sentimental, melancholy, warm-blooded self, in those early sweet times before antiquity had cooled her off and mossed her back.

"In choosing for friends such women as Mrs. Newton, Mrs. Boinville, and Cornelia Turner, Shelley gave good proof of his insight and discrimination." That is the fabulist's opinion—Harriet Shelley's is not reported.

Early in August, Shelley was in London trying to raise money. In September he wrote the poem to the baby, already quoted from. In

the first week of October Shelley and family went to Warwick, then
to Edinburgh, arriving there about the middle of the month.

"Harriet was happy." Why? The author furnishes a reason, but
hides from us whether it is history or conjecture; it is because *the babe
had borne the journey well.*" It has all the aspect of one of his artful
devices—flung in in his favorite casual way—the way he has when he
wants to draw one's attention away from an obvious thing and amuse
it with some trifle that is less obvious but more useful—in a history
like this. The obvious thing is, that Harriet was happy because there
was much territory between her husband and Cornelia Turner now;
and because the perilous Italian lessons were taking a rest; and because, if there chanced to be any respondings like a tremulous instrument to every breath of passion or of sentiment in stock in these days,
she might hope to get a share of them herself; and because, with her
husband liberated, now, from the fetid fascinations of that sentimental retreat so pitilessly described by Hogg, who also dubbed it
"Shelley's paradise" later, she might hope to persuade him to stay
away from it permanently; and because she might also hope that his
brain would cool, now, and his heart become healthy, and both brain
and heart consider the situation and resolve that it would be a right
and manly thing to stand by this girl wife and her child and see that
they were honorably dealt with, and cherished and protected and
loved by the man that had promised these things, and so be made
happy and kept so. And because, also—may we conjecture this?—
we may hope for the privilege of taking up our cozy Latin lessons
again, that used to be so pleasant, and brought us so near together—so
near, indeed, that often our heads touched, just as heads do over
Italian lessons; and our hands met in casual and unintentional, but
still most delicious and thrilling little contacts and momentary clasps,
just as they inevitably do over Italian lessons. Suppose one should
say to any young wife: "I find that your husband is poring over the
Italian poets and being instructed in the beautiful Italian language by
the lovely Cornelia Robinson"—would that cozy picture fail to rise
before her mind? would its possibilities fail to suggest themselves to
her? would there be a pang in her heart and a blush on her face? or,
on the contrary, would the remark give her pleasure, make her joyous
and gay? Why, one needs only to make the experiment—the result
will not be uncertain.

However, we learn—by authority of deeply reasoned and searching
conjecture—that the baby bore the journey well, and that that was
why the young wife was happy. That accounts for two per cent. of

the happiness, but it was not right to imply that it accounted for the other ninety-eight also.

Peacock, a scholar, poet, and friend of the Shelleys, was of their party when they went away. He used to laugh at the Boinville menagerie, and "was not a favorite." One of the Boinville group, writing to Hogg, said, "The Shelleys have made an addition to their party in the person of a cold scholar, who, I think, has neither taste nor feeling. This, Shelley will perceive sooner or later, for his warm nature craves sympathy." True, and Shelley will fight his way back there to get it—there will be no way to head him off.

Toward the end of November it was necessary for Shelley to pay a business visit to London, and he conceived the project of leaving Harriet and the baby in Edinburgh with Harriet's sister, Eliza Westbrook, a sensible, practical maiden lady about thirty years old, who had spent a great part of her time with the family since the marriage. She was an estimable woman, and Shelley had had reason to like her, and did like her; but along about this time his feeling toward her changed. Part of Shelley's plan, as he wrote Hogg, was to spend his London evenings with the Newtons—members of the Boinville Hysterical Society. But, alas, when he arrived early in December, that pleasant game was partially blocked, for Eliza and the family arrived *with* him. We are left destitute of conjectures at this point by the biographer, and it is my duty to supply one. I chance the conjecture that it was Eliza who interfered with that game. I think she tried to do what she could toward modifying the Boinville connection, in the interest of her young sister's peace and honor.

If it was she who blocked that game, she was not strong enough to block the next one. Before the month and year were out—no date given, let us call it Christmas—Shelly and family were nested in a furnished house in Windsor, "at no great distance from the Boinvilles" —these decoys still residing at Bracknell.

What we need, now, is a misleading conjecture. We get it with characteristic promptness and depravity:

> But Prince Athanase found not the aged Zonoras, the friend of his boyhood, in any wanderings to Windsor. Dr. Lind had died a year since, and with his death Windsor must have lost, for Shelley, its chief attraction.

Still, not to mention Shelley's wife, there was Bracknell, at any rate. Bracknell remains, all solace is not lost. Shelley is represented by this biographer as doing a great many careless things, but to my mind this hiring a furnished house for three months in order to be with a man who has been dead a year, is the carelessest of them all. One feels for him—that is but natural, and does us honor besides—yet one is vexed, for all that. He could have written and asked about the aged Zonoras before taking the house. He may not have had the address, but that is nothing—any postman would know the aged Zonoras; a dead postman would remember a name like that.

And yet, why throw a rag like this to us ravening wolves? Is it seriously supposable that we will stop to chew it and let our prey escape? No, we are getting to expect this kind of device, and to give it merely a sniff for certainty's sake and then walk around it and leave it lying. Shelley was not after the aged Zonoras; he was pointed for Cornelia and the Italian lessons, for his warm nature was craving sympathy.

II

The year 1813 is just ended now, and we step into 1814.

To recapitulate, how much of Cornelia's society has Shelley had, thus far? Portions of August and September, and four days of July. That is to say, he has had opportunity to enjoy it, more or less, during that brief period. Did he want some more of it? We must fall back upon history, and then go to conjecturing.

In the early part of the year 1814, Shelley was a frequent visitor at Bracknell.

"Frequent" is a cautious word, in this author's mouth; the very cautiousness of it, the vagueness of it, provokes suspicion; it makes one suspect that this frequency was more frequent than the mere common every-day kinds of frequency which one is in the habit of averaging up with the unassuming term "frequent." I think so because they fixed up a bedroom for him in the Boinville house. One doesn't need a bedroom if one is only going to run over now and then in a disconnected way to respond like a tremulous instrument to every breath of passion or of sentiment and rub up one's Italian poetry a little.

The young wife was not invited, perhaps. If she was, she most certainly did not come, or she would have straightened the room up; the most ignorant of us knows that a wife would not endure a room in the condition in which Hogg found this one when he occupied it one night. Shelley was away—why, nobody can divine. Clothes were scattered about, there were books on every side: "Wherever a book could be laid was an open book turned down on its face to keep its place." It seems plain that the wife was not invited. No, not that; I think she was invited, but said to herself that she could not bear to go there and see another young woman touching heads with her husband over an Italian book and making thrilling hand-contacts with him accidentally.

As remarked, he was a frequent visitor there, "where he found an easeful resting-place in the house of Mrs. Boinville—the white-haired Maimuna—and of her daughter, Mrs. Turner." The aged Zonoras was deceased, but the white-haired Maimuna was still on deck, as we see. "Three charming ladies entertained the mocker (Hogg) with cups of tea, late hours, Wieland's Agathon, sighs and smiles, and the celestial manna of refined sentiment." "Such," says Hogg, "were the delights of Shelley's paradise in Bracknell."

The white-haired Maimuna presently writes to Hogg:

I will not have you despise home-spun pleasures. Shelley is making a trial of them with us—

A trial of them. It may be called that. It was March 11, and he had been in the house a month. She continues:

Shelley "likes them so well that he is resolved to leave off rambling—"

But he has *already* left it off. He has been there a month.

"And begin a course of them himself."

But he has already begun it. He has been at it a *month*. He likes it so well that he has forgotten all about his wife, as a letter of his reveals.

Seriously, I think his mind and body want rest.

Yet he has been resting both for a month, with Italian, and tea, and manna of sentiment, and late hours, and every restful thing a young husband could need for the refreshment of weary limbs and a sore conscience, and a nagging sense of shabbiness and treachery.

His journeys after what he has never found have racked his purse and his tranquillity. He is resolved to take a little care of the former, in pity to the latter, which I applaud, and shall second with all my might.

But she does not say whether the young wife, a stranger and lonely yonder, wants another woman and her daughter Cornelia to be lavishing so much inflamed interest on her husband or not. That young wife is always silent—we are never allowed to hear from her. She must have opinions about such things, she cannot be indifferent, she must be approving or disapproving, surely she would speak if she were allowed—even to-day and from her grave she would, if she could, I think—but we get only the other side, they keep her silent always.

He has deeply interested us. In the course of your intimacy he must have made you feel what we now feel for him. He is seeking a house close to us—

Ah! he is not close enough yet, it seems—

and if he succeeds we shall have an additional motive to induce you to come among us in the summer.

The reader would puzzle a long time and not guess the biographer's comment upon the above letter. It is this:

These sound like words of a considerate and judicious friend.

That is what he thinks. That is, it is what he thinks he thinks. No, that is not quite it: it is what he thinks he can stupefy a particularly and unspeakably dull reader into thinking it is what he thinks. He makes that comment with the knowledge that Shelley is in love with this woman's daughter, and that it is because of the fascinations of these two that Shelley has deserted his wife—for this month, considering all the circumstances, and his new passion, and his employment of the time, amounted to desertion; that is its rightful name. We cannot know how the wife regarded it and felt about it; but if she could have read the letter which Shelley was writing to Hogg four or five days later, we could guess her thought and how she felt. Hear him:

.   .   .   .

I have been staying with Mrs. Boinville for the last month; I have escaped, in the society of all that philosophy and friendship combine, from the dismaying solitude of myself.

It is fair to conjecture that he was feeling ashamed.

They have revived in my heart the expiring flame of life. I have felt myself translated to a paradise which has nothing of mortality but its transitoriness; my heart sickens at the view of that necessity which will quickly divide me from the delightful tranquillity of this happy home—for it has become my home.

.   .   .   .

Eliza is still with us—not here!—but will be with me when the infinite malice of destiny forces me to depart.

Eliza is she who blocked that game—the game in London—the one where we were purposing to dine every night with one of the "three charming ladies" who fed tea and manna and late hours to Hogg at Bracknell.

Shelley could send Eliza away, of course; could have cleared her out long ago if so minded, just as he had previously done with a predecessor of hers whom he had first worshiped and then turned against; but perhaps she was useful there as a thin excuse for staying away himself.

I am now but little inclined to contest this point. I certainly hate her with all my heart and soul. . . .

It is a sight which awakens an inexpressible sensation of disgust and horror, to see her caress my poor little Ianthe, in whom I may hereafter find the consolation of sympathy. I sometimes feel faint with the fatigue of checking the overflowings of my unbounded abhorrence for this miserable wretch. But she is no more than a blind and loathsome worm, that cannot see to sting.

I have begun to learn Italian again. . . . Cornelia assists me in this language. Did I not once tell you that I thought her cold and reserved? She is the reverse of this, as she is the reverse of everything bad. She inherits all the divinity of her mother. . . . I have sometimes forgotten that I am not an inmate of this delightful home—that a time will come which will cast me again into the boundless ocean of abhorred society.

I have written nothing but one stanza, which has no meaning, and that I have only written in thought:

> Thy dewy looks sink in my breast;
>   Thy gentle words stir poison there;
> Thou hast disturbed the only rest
>   That was the portion of despair.
> Subdued to duty's hard control,
>   I could have borne my wayward lot:
> The chains that bind this ruined soul
>   Had cankered then, but crushed it not.

This is the vision of a delirious and distempered dream, which passes away at the cold clear light of morning. Its surpassing excellence and exquisite perfections have no more reality than the color of an autumnal sunset.

Then it did not refer to his wife. That is plain; otherwise he would have said so. It is well that he explained that it has no meaning, for if he had not done that, the previous soft references to Cornelia and the way he has come to feel about her now would make us think she was the person who had inspired it while teaching him how to read the warm and ruddy Italian poets during a month.

The biography observes that portions of this letter "read like the tired moaning of a wounded creature." Guesses at the nature of the wound are permissible; we will hazard one.

Read by the light of Shelley's previous history, his letter seems to be the cry of a tortured conscience. Until this time it was a conscience that had never felt a pang or known a smirch. It was the conscience of one who, until this time, had never done a dishonorable thing, or an ungenerous, or cruel, or treacherous thing, but was now doing all of these, and was keenly aware of it. Up to this time Shelley had been master of his nature, and it was a nature which was as beautiful and as nearly perfect as any merely human nature may be. But he was drunk now, with a debasing passion, and was not himself. There is nothing in his previous history that is in character with the Shelley of this letter. He had done boyish things, foolish things, even crazy things, but never a thing to be ashamed of. He had done things which one might laugh at, but the privilege of laughing was limited always to the thing itself; you could not laugh at the motive back of it—that was high, that was noble. His most fantastic and quixotic acts had a purpose back of them which made them fine, often great, and made the rising laugh seem profanation and quenched it; quenched it, and changed the impulse to homage. Up to this time he had been loyalty itself, where his obligations lay—treachery was new to him; he had never done an ignoble thing—baseness was new to him; he had never done an unkind thing—that also was new to him.

This was the author of that letter, this was the man who had deserted his young wife and was lamenting, because he must leave another woman's house which had become a "home" to him, and go away. Is he lamenting *mainly* because he must go back to his wife and child? No, the lament is mainly for what he is to leave behind him. The physical comforts of the house? No, in his life he had never attached importance to such things. Then the thing which he grieves to leave is narrowed down to a person—to the person whose "dewy looks" had sunk into his breast, and whose seducing words had "stirred poison there."

He was ashamed of himself, his conscience was upbraiding him.

He was the slave of a degrading love; he was drunk with his passion, the real Shelley was in temporary eclipse. This is the verdict which his previous history must certainly deliver upon this episode, I think.

One must be allowed to assist himself with conjectures like these when trying to find his way through a literary swamp which has so many misleading finger-boards up as this book is furnished with.

We have now arrived at a part of the swamp where the difficulties and perplexities are going to be greater than any we have yet met with—where, indeed, the finger-boards are multitudinous, and the most of them pointing diligently in the wrong direction. We are to be told by the biography why Shelley deserted his wife and child and took up with Cornelia Turner and Italian. It was not on account of Cornelia's sighs and sentimentalities and tea and manna and late hours and soft and sweet and industrious enticements; no, it was because "his happiness in his home had been wounded and bruised almost to death."

It had been wounded and bruised almost to death in this way:

1st. Harriet persuaded him to set up a carriage.

2d. After the intrusion of the baby, Harriet stopped reading aloud and studying.

3d. Harriet's walks with Hogg "commonly conducted us to some fashionable bonnet-shop."

4th. Harriet hired a wet-nurse.

5th. When an operation was being performed upon the baby, "Harriet stood by, narrowly observing all that was done, but, to the astonishment of the operator, betraying not the smallest sign of emotion."

6th. Eliza Westbrook, sister-in-law, was still of the household.

The evidence against Harriet Shelley is all in; there is no more. Upon these six counts she stands indicted of the crime of driving her husband into that sty at Bracknell; and this crime, by these helps, the biographical prosecuting attorney has set himself the task of proving upon her.

Does the biographer *call* himself the attorney for the prosecution? No, only to himself, privately; publicly he is the passionless, disinterested, impartial judge on the bench. He holds up his judicial scales before the world, that all may see; and it all tries to look so fair that a blind person would sometimes fail to see him slip the false weights in.

Shelley's happiness in his home had been wounded and bruised almost to death, first, because Harriet had persuaded him to set up a carriage. I cannot discover that any evidence is offered that she asked him to set up a carriage. Still, if she did, was it a heavy offense? Was it unique? Other young wives had committed it before, others have committed it since. Shelley had dearly loved her in those London days; possibly he set up the carriage gladly to please her; affectionate young husbands do such things. When Shelley ran away with another girl, by and by, this girl persuaded him to pour the price of many carriages and many horses down the bottomless well of her father's debts, but this impartial judge finds no fault with that. Once she appeals to Shelley to raise money—necessarily by borrowing, there was no other way—to pay her father's debts with at a time when Shelley was in danger of being arrested and imprisoned for his own debts; yet the good judge finds no fault with her even for this.

First and last, Shelley emptied into that rapacious mendicant's lap a sum which cost him—for he borrowed it at ruinous rates—from eighty to one hundred thousand dollars. But it was Mary Godwin's papa, the supplications were often sent through Mary, the good judge is Mary's strenuous friend, so Mary gets no censures. On the Continent *Mary rode in her private carriage*, built, as Shelley boasts, "by one of the best makers in Bond Street," yet the good judge makes not even a passing comment on this iniquity. Let us throw out Count No. 1 against Harriet Shelley as being far-fetched and frivolous.

Shelley's happiness in his home had been wounded and bruised almost to death, secondly, because Harriet's studies "had dwindled away to nothing, Bysshe had ceased to express any interest in them." At what time was this? It was when Harriet "had fully recovered from the fatigue of her first effort of maternity, . . . and was now in full force, vigor, and effect." Very well, the baby was born two days before the close of June. It took the mother a month to get back her full force, vigor, and effect; this brings us to July 27th and the deadly Cornelia. If a wife of eighteen is studying with her husband and he gets smitten with another woman, isn't he likely to lose interest in his wife's studies for *that* reason, and is not his wife's interest in her studies likely to languish for the *same* reason? Would not the mere sight of those books of hers sharpen the pain that is in her heart? This sudden breaking down of a mutual intellectual interest of two years' standing is coincident with Shelley's re-encounter with Cornelia; and we are allowed to gather from that time forth for nearly two months he did all his studying in that person's society. We feel at liberty to rule out Count No. 2 from the indictment against Harriet.

Shelley's happiness in his home had been wounded and bruised almost to death, thirdly, because Harriet's walks with Hogg commonly led to some fashionable bonnet-shop. I offer no palliation; I only ask why the dispassionate, impartial judge did not offer one himself— merely, I mean, to offset his leniency in a similar case or two where the girl who ran away with Harriet's husband was the shopper. There are several occasions where she interested herself with shopping—among them being walks which ended at the bonnet-shop—yet in none of these cases does she get a word of blame from the good judge, while in one of them he covers the deed with a justifying remark, she doing the shopping that time to find easement for her mind, her child having died.

Shelley's happiness in his home had been wounded and bruised almost to death, fourthly, by the introduction there of a wet-nurse. The wet-nurse was introduced at the time of the Edinburgh sojourn, immediately after Shelley had been enjoying the two months of study with Cornelia which broke up his wife's studies and destroyed his personal interest in them. Why, by this time, nothing that Shelley's wife could do would have been satisfactory to him, for he was in love with another woman, and was never going to be contented again until he got back to her. If he had been still in love with his wife it is not easily conceivable that he would care much who nursed the baby, provided the baby was well nursed. Harriet's jealousy was assuredly voicing itself now, Shelley's conscience was assuredly nagging him, pestering him, persecuting him. Shelley needed excuses for his altered attitude toward his wife; Providence pitied him and sent the wet-nurse. If Providence had sent him a cotton doughnut it would have answered just as well; all he wanted was something to find fault with.

Shelley's happiness in his home had been wounded and bruised almost to death, fifthly, because Harriet narrowly watched a surgical operation which was being performed upon her child, and, "to the astonishment of the operator," who was watching Harriet instead of attending to his operation, she betrayed "not the smallest sign of emotion." The author of this biography was not ashamed to set down that exultant slander. He was apparently not aware that it was a small business to bring into his court a witness whose name he does not know, and whose character and veracity there is none to vouch for, and allow him to strike this blow at the mother-heart of this friendless girl. The biographer says, "We may not infer from this that Harriet did not feel"—why put it in, then?—"but we learn that

those about her could believe her to be hard and insensible." Who
were those who were about her? Her husband? He hated her now,
because he was in love elsewhere. Her sister? Of course that is not
charged. Peacock? Peacock does not testify. The wet-nurse? She does
not testify. If any others were there we have no mention of them.
"Those about her" are reduced to one person—her husband. Who
reports the circumstance? It is Hogg. Perhaps he was there—we do
not know. But if he was, he still got his information at second hand,
as it was the operator who noticed Harriet's lack of emotion, not
himself. Hogg is not given to saying kind things when Harriet is his
subject. He may have said them the time that he tried to tempt her
to soil her honor, but after that he mentions her usually with a sneer.
"Among those who were about her" was one witness well equipped to
silence all tongues, abolish all doubts, set our minds at rest; one witness, not called, and not callable, whose evidence, if we could but
get it, would outweigh the oaths of whole battalions of hostile Hoggs
and nameless surgeons—the baby. I wish we had the baby's testimony; and yet if we had it it would not do us any good—a furtive
conjecture, a sly insinuation, a pious "if" or two, would be smuggled
in, here and there, with a solemn air of judicial investigation, and
its positiveness would wilt into dubiety.

The biographer says of Harriet, "If words of tender affection and
motherly pride proved the reality of love, then undoubtedly she loved
her first-born child." That is, if mere empty words can prove it, it
stands proved—and in this way, without committing himself, he gives
the reader a chance to infer that there isn't any extant evidence but
words, and that he doesn't take much stock in them. How seldom
he shows his hand! He is always lurking behind a non-committal
"if" or something of that kind; always gliding and dodging around,
distributing colorless poison here and there and everywhere, but always leaving himself in a position to say that his language will be
found innocuous if taken to pieces and examined. He clearly exhibits
a steady and never-relaxing purpose to make Harriet the scapegoat
for her husband's first great sin—but it is in the general view that
this is revealed, not in the details. His insidious literature is like blue
water; you know what it is that makes it blue, but you cannot produce
and verify any detail of the cloud of microscopic dust in it that
does it. Your adversary can dip up a glassful and show you that
it is pure white and you cannot deny it; and he can dip the lake
dry, glass by glass, and show that every glassful is white, and prove

it to any one's eye—and yet that lake *was* blue and you can swear it. This book is blue—with slander in solution.

Let the reader examine, for example, the paragraph of comment which immediately follows the letter containing Shelley's self-exposure which we have been considering. This is it. One should inspect the individual sentences as they go by, then pass them in procession and review the cake-walk as a whole:

> Shelley's happiness in his home, as is evident from this pathetic letter, had been fatally stricken; it is evident, also, that he knew where duty lay; he felt that his part was to take up his burden, silently and sorrowfully, and to bear it henceforth with the quietness of despair. But we can perceive that he scarcely possessed the strength and fortitude needful for success in such an attempt. And clearly Shelley himself was aware how perilous it was to accept that respite of blissful ease which he enjoyed in the Boinville household: for gentle voices and dewy looks and words of sympathy could not fail to remind him of an ideal of tranquillity or of joy which could never be his, and which he must henceforth sternly exclude from his imagination.

That paragraph commits the author in no way. Taken sentence by sentence it *asserts* nothing against anybody or in favor of anybody, pleads for nobody, accuses nobody. Taken detail by detail, it is as innocent as moonshine. And yet, taken as a whole, it is a design against the reader; its intent is to remove the feeling which the letter must leave with him if let alone, and put a different one in its place—to remove a feeling justified by the letter and substitute one not justified by it. The letter itself gives you no uncertain picture—no lecturer is needed to stand by with a stick and point out its details and let on to explain what they mean. The picture is the very clear and remorsefully faithful picture of a fallen and fettered angel who is ashamed of himself; an angel who beats his soiled wings and cries, who complains to the woman who enticed him that he *could* have borne his wayward lot, he *could* have stood by his duty if it had not been for her beguilements; an angel who rails at the "boundless ocean of abhorred society," and rages at his poor judicious sister-in-law. If there is any dignity about this spectacle it will escape most people.

Yet when the paragraph of comment is taken as a whole, the picture is full of dignity and pathos; we have before us a blameless and noble spirit stricken to the earth by malign powers, but not conquered; tempted, but grandly putting the temptation away; enmeshed by subtle coils, but sternly resolved to rend them and march forth victorious, at any peril of life or limb. Curtain—slow music.

Was it the purpose of the paragraph to take the bad taste of Shelley's letter out of the reader's mouth? If that was not it, good ink was wasted; without that, it has no relevancy—the multiplication table would have padded the space as rationally.

We have inspected the six reasons which we are asked to believe drove a man of conspicuous patience, honor, justice, fairness, kindliness, and iron firmness, resolution, and steadfastness, from the wife whom he loved and who loved him, to a refuge in the mephitic paradise of Bracknell. These are six infinitely little reasons; but there were six colossal ones, and these the counsel for the destruction of Harriet Shelley persists in not considering very important.

Moreover, the colossal six preceded the little six, and had done the mischief before they were born. Let us double-column the twelve; then we shall see at a glance that each little reason is in turn answered by a retorting reason of a size to overshadow it and make it insignificant:

1. Harriet sets up carriage.	1. CORNELIA TURNER.
2. Harriet stops studying.	2. CORNELIA TURNER.
3. Harriet goes to bonnet-shop.	3. CORNELIA TURNER.
4. Harriet takes a wet-nurse.	4. CORNELIA TURNER.
5. Harriet has too much nerve.	5. CORNELIA TURNER.
6. Detested sister-in-law.	6. CORNELIA TURNER.

As soon as we comprehend that Cornelia Turner and the Italian lessons happened *before* the little six had been discovered to be grievances, we understand why Shelley's happiness in his home had been wounded and bruised almost to death, and no one can persuade us into laying it on Harriet. Shelley and Cornelia are the responsible persons, and we cannot in honor and decency allow the cruelties which they practised upon the unoffending wife to be pushed aside in order to give us a chance to waste time and tears over six sentimental justifications of an offense which the six can't justify, nor even respectably assist in justifying.

Six? There were seven; but in charity to the biographer the seventh ought not to be exposed. Still, he hung it out himself, and not only hung it out, but thought it was a good point in Shelley's favor. For two years Shelley found sympathy and intellectual food and all that at home; there was enough for spiritual and mental support, but not enough for luxury; and so, at the end of the contented two years, this latter detail justifies him in going bag and baggage over to Cornelia

Turner and supplying the rest of his need in the way of surplus sympathy and intellectual pie unlawfully. By the same reasoning a man in merely comfortable circumstances may rob a bank without sin.

III

It is 1814, it is the 16th of March, Shelley had written his letter, he has been in the Boinville paradise a month, his deserted wife is in her husbandless home. Mischief has been wrought. It is the biographer who concedes this. We greatly need some light on Harriet's side of the case now; we need to know how she enjoyed the month, but there is no way to inform ourselves; there seems to be a strange absence of documents and letters and diaries on that side. Shelley kept a diary, the approaching Mary Godwin kept a diary, her father kept one, her half-sister by marriage, adoption, and the dispensation of God kept one, and the entire tribe and all its friends wrote and received letters, and the letters were kept and are producible when this biography needs them; but there are only three or four scraps of Harriet's writing, and no diary. Harriet wrote plenty of letters to her husband—nobody knows where they are, I suppose; she wrote plenty of letters to other people—apparently they have disappeared, too. Peacock says she wrote good letters, but apparently interested people had sagacity enough to mislay them in time. After all her industry she went down into her grave and lies silent there—silent, when she has so much need to speak. We can only wonder at this mystery, not account for it.

No, there is no way of finding out what Harriet's state of feeling was during the month that Shelley was disporting himself in the Bracknell paradise. We have to fall back upon conjecture, as our fabulist does when he has nothing more substantial to work with. Then we easily conjecture that as the days dragged by Harriet's heart grew heavier and heavier under its two burdens—shame and resentment; the shame of being pointed at and gossiped about as a deserted wife, and resentment against the woman who had beguiled her husband from her and now kept him in a disreputable captivity. Deserted wives—deserted whether for cause or without cause—find small charity among the virtuous and the discreet. We conjecture that one after another the neighbors ceased to call; that one after another they got to being "engaged" when Harriet called; that finally they one after the other cut her dead on the street; that after that she stayed in the house daytimes, and brooded over her sorrows, and nighttimes did the same, there being nothing else to do with the heavy hours and the silence and solitude and the dreary intervals which sleep should have charitably bridged, but didn't.

Yes, mischief had been wrought. The biographer arrives at this conclusion, and it is a most just one. Then, just as you begin to half hope he is going to discover the cause of it and launch hot bolts of wrath at the guilty manufacturers of it, you have to turn away disappointed. You are disappointed, and you sigh. This is what he says— the italics are mine:

> However the mischief may have been wrought—*and at this day no one can wish to heap blame on any buried head—*

So it is poor Harriet, after all. Stern justice must take its course— justice tempered with delicacy, justice tempered with compassion, justice that pities a forlorn dead girl and refuses to strike her. Except in the back. Will not be ignoble and *say* the harsh thing, but only insinuate it. Stern justice knows about the carriage and the wet-nurse and the bonnet-shop and the other dark things that caused this sad mischief, and may not, *must* not blink them; so it delivers judgment where judgment belongs, but softens the blow by not seeming to deliver judgment at all. To resume—the italics are mine:

> However the mischief may have been wrought—and at this day no one can wish to heap blame on any buried head—*it is certain that some cause or causes of deep division between Shelley and his wife were in operation during the early part of the year 1814.*

This shows penetration. No deduction could be more accurate than this. There were indeed some causes of deep division. But next comes another disappointing sentence:

> To guess at the precise nature of these causes, in the absence of definite statement, were useless.

Why, he has already been guessing at them for several pages, and we have been trying to outguess him, and now all of a sudden he is tired of it and won't play any more. It is not quite fair to us. However, he will get over this by and by, when Shelley commits his next indiscretion and has to be guessed out of it at Harriet's expense.

"We may rest content with Shelley's own words"—in a Chancery paper drawn up by him three years later. They were these: "Delicacy forbids me to say more than that we were disunited by incurable dissensions."

As for me, I do not quite see why we should rest content with anything of the sort. It is not a very definite statement. It does not necessarily mean anything more than that he did not wish to go into the tedious details of those family quarrels. Delicacy could quite properly excuse him from saying, "I was in love with Cornelia all that time; my wife kept crying and worrying about it and upbraiding me and begging me to cut myself free from a connection which was wronging her and disgracing us both; and I being stung by these reproaches retorted with fierce and bitter speeches—for it is my nature to do that when I am stirred, especially if the target of them is a person whom I had greatly loved and respected before, as witness my various attitudes toward Miss Hitchener, the Gisbornes, Harriet's sister, and others—and finally I did not improve this state of things when I deserted my wife and spent a whole month with the woman who had infatuated me."

No, he could not go into those details, and we excuse him; but, nevertheless, we do not rest content with this bland proposition to puff away that whole long disreputable episode with a single meaningless remark of Shelley's.

We do admit that "it is certain that some cause or causes of deep division were in operation." We would admit it just the same if the grammar of the statement were as straight as a string, for we drift into pretty indifferent grammar ourselves when we are absorbed in historical work; but we have to decline to admit that we cannot guess those cause or causes.

But guessing is not really necessary. There is evidence attainable—evidence from the batch discredited by the biographer and set out at the back door in his appendix-basket; and yet a court of law would think twice before throwing it out, whereas it would be a hardy person who would venture to offer in such a place a good part of the material which is placed before the readers of this book as "evidence," and so treated by this daring biographer. Among some letters (in the appendix-basket) from Mrs. Godwin, detailing the Godwinian share in the Shelleyan events of 1814, she tells how Harriet Shelley came to her and her husband, agitated and weeping, to implore them to forbid Shelley the house, and prevent his seeing Mary Godwin.

She related that last November he had fallen in love with Mrs. Turner and paid her such marked attentions Mr. Turner, the husband, had carried off his wife to Devonshire.

The biographer finds a technical fault in this: "the Shelleys were in *Edinburgh* in November." What of that? The woman is recalling a conversation which is more than two months old; besides, she was probably more intent upon the central and important fact of it than upon its unimportant date. Harriet's quoted statement has some sense in it; for that reason, if for no other, it ought to have been put in the body of the book. Still, that would not have answered; even the biographer's enemy could not be cruel enough to ask him to let this real grievance, this compact and substantial and picturesque figure, this rawhead-and-bloody-bones, come striding in there among those pale shams, those rickety specters labeled WET-NURSE, BONNET-SHOP, and so on—no, the father of all malice could not ask the biographer to expose his pathetic goblins to a competition like that.

The fabulist finds fault with the statement because it has a technical error in it; and he does this at the moment that he is furnishing us an error himself, and of a graver sort. He says:

If Turner carried off his wife to Devonshire he brought her back, and Shelley was staying with her and her mother on terms of cordial intimacy in March, 1814.

We accept the "cordial intimacy"—it was the very thing Harriet was complaining of—but there is nothing to show that it was Turner who brought his wife back. The statement is thrown in as if it were not only true, but was proof that Turner was not uneasy. Turner's *movements* are proof of nothing. Nothing but a statement from Turner's mouth would have any value here, and he made none.

Six days after writing his letter Shelley and his wife were together again for a moment—to get remarried according to the rites of the English Church.

Within three weeks the new husband and wife were apart again, and the former was back in his odorous paradise. This time it is the wife who does the deserting. She finds Cornelia too strong for her, probably. At any rate, she goes away with her baby and sister, and we have a playful fling at her from good Mrs. Boinville, the "mysterious spinner Maimuna"; she whose "face was as a damsel's face, and yet her hair was gray"; she of whom the biographer has said, "Shelley was indeed caught in an almost invisible thread spun around him, but unconsciously, by this subtle and benignant enchantress." The subtle and benignant enchantress writes to Hogg, April 18: "Shelley is again a widower; his beauteous half went to town on Thursday."

Then Shelley writes a poem—a chant of grief over the hard fate which obliges him now to leave his paradise and take up with his wife again. It seems to intimate that the paradise is cooling toward him; that he is warned off by acclamation; that he must not even venture to tempt with one last tear his friend Cornelia's ungentle mood, for her eye is glazed and cold and dares not entreat her lover to stay:

Exhibit E

Pause not! the time is past! Every voice cries "Away!"
 Tempt not with one last tear thy friend's ungentle mood;
 Thy lover's eye, so glazed and cold, dares not entreat thy stay:
 Duty and dereliction guide thee back to solitude.

Back to the solitude of his now empty home, that is!

Away! away! to thy sad and silent home;
 Pour bitter tears on its desolated hearth.

. . . .

But he will have rest in the grave by and by. Until that time comes, the charms of Bracknell will remain in his memory, along with Mrs. Boinville's voice and Cornelia Turner's smile:

Thou in the grave shalt rest—yet, till the phantoms flee
 Which that house and hearth and garden made dear to thee
 erewhile,
Thy remembrance and repentance and deep musings are not free
 From the music of two voices and the light of one sweet
 smile.

We *cannot* wonder that Harriet could not stand it. Any of us would have left. We would not even stay with a cat that was in this condition. Even the Boinvilles could not endure it; and so, as we have seen, they gave this one notice.

Early in May, Shelley was in London. He did not yet despair of reconciliation with Harriet, nor had he ceased to love her.

Shelley's poems are a good deal of trouble to his biographer. They are constantly inserted as "evidence," and they make much confusion. As soon as one of them has proved one thing, another one follows and proves quite a different thing. The poem just quoted shows that he was in love with Cornelia, but a month later he is in love with Harriet again, and there is a poem to prove it.

In this piteous appeal Shelley declares that he has now no grief but one—the grief of having known and lost his wife's love.

Exhibit F

Thy look of love has power to calm
The stormiest passion of my soul.

But without doubt she had been reserving her looks of love a good part of the time for ten months, now—ever since he began to lavish his own on Cornelia Turner at the end of the previous July. He does really seem to have already forgotten Cornelia's merits in one brief month, for he eulogizes Harriet in a way which rules all competition out:

Thou only virtuous, gentle, kind,
Amid a world of hate.

He complains of her hardness, and begs her to make the concession of a "slight endurance"—of his waywardness, perhaps—for the sake of "a fellow-being's lasting weal." But the main force of his appeal is in his closing stanza, and is strongly worded:

O trust for once no erring guide!
  Bid the remorseless feeling flee;
'Tis malice, 'tis revenge, 'tis pride,
  'Tis anything but thee;
O deign a nobler pride to prove,
And pity if thou canst not love.

This is in May—apparently toward the end of it. Harriet and Shelley were corresponding all the time. Harriet got the poem—a copy exists in her own handwriting; she being the only gentle and kind person amid a world of hate, according to Shelley's own testimony in the poem, we are permitted to think that the daily letters would presently have melted that kind and gentle heart and brought about the reconciliation, if there had been time—but there wasn't; for in a very few days—in fact, before the 8th of June—Shelley was in love with *another* woman.

And so—perhaps while Harriet was walking the floor nights, trying to get *her* poem by heart—her husband was doing a fresh one—for the other girl—Mary Wollstonecraft Godwin—with sentiments like these in it:

Exhibit G

To spend years thus and be rewarded,
As thou, sweet love, requited me
When none were near.
. . . thy lips did meet

> Mine tremblingly; . . .
> Gentle and good and mild thou art,
> Nor can I live if thou appear
> Aught but thyself. . . .

And so on. "Before the close of June it was known and felt by Mary and Shelley that each was inexpressibly dear to the other." Yes, Shelley had found this child of sixteen to his liking, and had wooed and won her in the graveyard. But that is nothing; it was better than wooing her in her nursery, at any rate, where it might have disturbed the other children.

However, she was a child in years only. From the day that she set her masculine grip on Shelley he was to frisk no more. If she had occupied the only kind of gentle Harriet's place in March it would have been a thrilling spectacle to see her invade the Boinville rookery and read the riot act. That holiday of Shelley's would have been of short duration, and Cornelia's hair would have been as gray as her mother's when the services were over.

Hogg went to the Godwin residence in Skinner Street with Shelley on that 8th of June. They passed through Godwin's little debt-factory of a book-shop and went up-stairs hunting for the proprietor. Nobody there. Shelley strode about the room impatiently, making its crazy floor quake under him. Then a door "was partially and softly opened. A thrilling voice called, 'Shelley!' A thrilling voice answered, 'Mary!' And he darted out of the room like an arrow from the bow of the far-shooting King. A very young female, fair and fair-haired, pale, indeed, and with a piercing look, wearing a frock of tartan, an unusual dress in London at that time, had called him out of the room."

This is Mary Godwin, as described by Hogg. The thrill of the voices shows that the love of Shelley and Mary was already upward of a fortnight old; therefore it had been born within the month of May—born while Harriet was still trying to get her poem by heart, we think. I must not be asked how I know so much about that thrill; it is my secret. The biographer and I have private ways of finding out things when it is necessary to find them out and the customary methods fail.

Shelley left London that day, and was gone ten days. The biographer conjectures that he spent this interval with Harriet in Bath. It would be just like him. To the end of his days he liked to be in love with two women at once. He was more in love with Miss Hitchener when he married Harriet than he was with Harriet, and told the lady so with simple and unostentatious candor. He was more in love with Cornelia than he was with Harriet in the end of 1813 and the beginning of 1814, yet he supplied both of them with love poems of an equal temperature meantime; he loved Mary and Harriet in June, and while getting ready to run off with the one, it is conjectured that he put in his odd time trying to get reconciled to the other; by and by, while still in love with Mary, he will make love to her half-sister by marriage, adoption, and the visitation of God, through the medium of clandestine letters, and she will answer with letters that are for no eye but his own.

When Shelley encountered Mary Godwin he was looking around for another paradise. He had tastes of his own, and there were features about the Godwin establishment that strongly recommended it. Godwin was an advanced thinker and an able writer. One of his romances is still read, but his philosophical works, once so esteemed, are out of vogue now; their authority was already declining when Shelley made his acquaintance—that is, it was declining with the public, but not with Shelley. They had been his moral and political Bible, and they were that yet. Shelley the infidel would himself have claimed to be less a work of God than work of Godwin. Godwin's philosophies had formed his mind and interwoven themselves into it and become a part of its texture; he regarded himself as Godwin's spiritual son. Godwin was not without self-appreciation; indeed, it may be conjectured that from his point of view the last syllable of his name was surplusage. He lived serene in his lofty world of philosophy, far above the mean interests that absorbed smaller men, and only came down to the ground at intervals to pass the hat for alms to pay his debts with, and insult the man that relieved him. Several of his principles were out of the ordinary. For example, he was opposed to marriage. He was not aware that his preachings from this text were but theory and wind; he supposed he was in earnest in imploring people to live together without marrying, until Shelley furnished him a working model of his scheme and a practical example to analyze, by applying the principle in his own family; the matter took a different and surprising aspect then. The late Matthew Arnold said that the main defect in Shelley's make-up was that he was destitute of the sense of humor. This episode must have escaped Mr. Arnold's attention.

But we have said enough about the head of the new paradise. Mrs. Godwin is described as being in several ways a terror; and even when her soul was in repose she wore green spectacles. But I suspect that her main unattractiveness was born of the fact that she wrote the letters that are out in the appendix-basket in the back yard—

letters which are an outrage and wholly untrustworthy, for they say
some kind things about poor Harriet and tell some disagreeable truths
about her husband; and these things make the fabulist grit his teeth a
good deal.

Next we have Fanny Godwin—a Godwin by courtesy only; she was
Mrs. Godwin's natural daughter by a former friend. She was a sweet
and winning girl, but she presently wearied of the Godwin paradise,
and poisoned herself.

Last in the list is Jane (or Claire, as she preferred to call herself)
Clairmont, daughter of Mrs. Godwin by a former marriage. She was
very young and pretty and accommodating, and always ready to do
what she could to make things pleasant. After Shelley ran off with
her part-sister Mary, she became the guest of the pair, and contributed
a natural child to their nursery—Allegra. Lord Byron was the father.

We have named the several members and advantages of the new
paradise in Skinner Street, with its crazy book-shop underneath. Shelley
was all right now, this was a better place than the other; more variety
anyway, and more different kinds of fragrance. One could turn out
poetry here without any trouble at all.

The way the new love-match came about was this: Shelley told
Mary all his aggravations and sorrows and griefs, and about the wet-
nurse and the bonnet-shop and the surgeon and the carriage, and the
sister-in-law that blocked the London game, and about Cornelia
and her mamma, and how they had turned him out of the house
after making so much of him; and how he had deserted Harriet and
then Harriet had deserted him, and how the reconciliation was working along and Harriet getting her poem by heart; and still he was
not happy, and Mary pitied him, for she had had trouble herself.
But I am not satisfied with this. It reads too much like statistics.
It lacks smoothness and grace, and is too earthy and business-like.
It has the sordid look of a trades-union procession out on strike. That
is not the right form for it. The book does it better; we will fall
back on the book and have a cake-walk:

> It was easy to divine that some restless grief possessed him; Mary
> herself was not unlearned in the lore of pain. His generous zeal in her
> father's behalf, his spiritual sonship to Godwin, his reverence for her
> mother's memory, were guarantees with Mary of his excellence.[1] The new
> friends could not lack subjects of discourse, and underneath their words

[1] What she was after was guarantees of his excellence. That he stood ready
to desert his wife and child was one of them, apparently.—M.T.

about Mary's mother, and "Political Justice," and "Rights of Woman," were two young hearts, each feeling toward the other, each perhaps unaware, trembling in the direction of the other. The desire to assuage the suffering of one whose happiness has grown precious to us may become a hunger of the spirit as keen as any other, and this hunger now possessed Mary's heart; when her eyes rested unseen on Shelley, it was with a look full of the ardor of a "soothing pity."

Yes, that is better and has more composure. That is just the way it happened. He told her about the wet-nurse, she told him about political justice; he told her about the deadly sister-in-law, she told him about her mother; he told her about the bonnet-shop, she murmured back about the rights of woman; then he assuaged her, then she assuaged him; then he assuaged her some more, next she assuaged him some more; then they both assuaged one another simultaneously; and so they went on by the hour assuaging and assuaging and assuaging, until at last what was the result? They were in love. It will happen so every time.

He had married a woman who, as he now persuaded himself, had never truly loved him, who loved only his fortune and his rank, and who proved her selfishness by deserting him in his misery.

I think that that is not quite fair to Harriet. We have no certainty that she knew Cornelia had turned him out of the house. He went back to Cornelia, and Harriet may have supposed that he was as happy with her as ever. Still, it was judicious to begin to lay on the whitewash, for Shelley is going to need many a coat of it now, and the sooner the reader becomes used to the intrusion of the brush the sooner he will get reconciled to it and stop fretting about it.

After Shelley's (conjectured) visit to Harriet at Bath—8th of June to 18th—"it seems to have been arranged that Shelley should henceforth join the Skinner Street household each day at dinner."

Nothing could be handier than this; things will swim along now.

Although now Shelley was coming to believe that his wedded union with Harriet was a thing of the past, he had not ceased to regard her with affectionate consideration; he wrote to her frequently, and kept her informed of his whereabouts.

We must not get impatient over these curious inharmoniousnesses and irreconcilabilities in Shelley's character. You can see by the biographer's attitude toward them that there is nothing objectionable about them. Shelley was doing his best to make two adoring young creatures happy: he was regarding the one with affectionate consideration by mail, and he was assuaging the other one at home.

Unhappy Harriet, residing at Bath, had perhaps never desired that the breach between herself and her husband should be irreparable and complete.

I find no fault with that sentence except that the "perhaps" is not strictly warranted. It should have been left out. In support—or shall we say extenuation?—of this opinion I submit that there is not sufficient evidence to warrant the uncertainty which it implies. The only "evidence" offered that Harriet was hard and proud and standing out against a reconciliation is a poem—the poem in which Shelley beseeches her to "bid the remorseless feeling flee" and "pity" if she "cannot love." We have just that as "evidence," and out of its meager materials the biographer builds a cobhouse of conjectures as big as the Coliseum; conjectures which convince him, the prosecuting attorney, but ought to fall far short of convincing any fair-minded jury.

Shelley's love poems may be very good evidence, but we know well that they are "good for this day and train only." We are able to believe that they spoke the truth for that one day, but we know by experience that they could not be depended on to speak it the next. The very supplication for a re-warming of Harriet's chilled love was followed so suddenly by the poet's plunge into an adoring passion for Mary Godwin that if it had been a check it would have lost its value before a lazy person could have gotten to the bank with it.

Hardness, stubbornness, pride, vindictiveness—these may sometimes reside in a young wife and mother of nineteen, but they are not charged against Harriet Shelley outside of that poem, and one has no right to insert them into her character on such shadowy "evidence" as that. Peacock knew Harriet well, and she has a flexible and persuadable look, as painted by him:

Her manners were good, and her whole aspect and demeanor such manifest emanations of pure and truthful nature that to be once in her company was to know her thoroughly. She was fond of her husband, and accommodated herself in every way to his tastes. If they mixed in society, she adorned it; if they lived in retirement, she was satisfied; if they traveled, she enjoyed the change of scene.

"Perhaps" she had never desired that the breach should be irreparable and complete. The truth is, we do not even know that there was any breach at all at this time. We know that the husband and

wife went before the altar and took a new oath on the 24th of March
to love and cherish each other until death—and this may be regarded
as a sort of reconciliation itself, and a wiping out of the old grudges.
Then Harriet went away, and the sister-in-law removed herself from
her society. That was in April. Shelley wrote his "appeal" in May,
but the corresponding went right along afterward. We have a right
to doubt that the subject of it was a "reconciliation," or that Harriet
had any suspicion that she needed to be reconciled and that her
husband was trying to persuade her to it—as the biographer has
sought to make us believe, with his Coliseum of conjectures built
out of a waste-basket of poetry. For we have "evidence" now—not
poetry and conjecture. When Shelley had been dining daily in the
Skinner Street paradise fifteen days and continuing the love-match
which was already a fortnight old twenty-five days earlier, he forgot
to write Harriet; forgot it the next day and the next. During four
days Harriet got no letter from him. Then her fright and anxiety rose
to expression-heat, and she wrote a letter to Shelley's publisher which
seems to reveal to us that Shelley's letters to her had been the
customary affectionate letters of husband to wife, and had carried
no appeals for reconciliation and had not needed to:

BATH (postmark July 7, 1814).

MY DEAR SIR,—You will greatly oblige me by giving the inclosed to Mr.
Shelley. I would not trouble you, but it is now four days since I have
heard from him, which to me is an age. Will you write by return of post
and tell me what has become of him? as I always fancy something dreadful has happened if I do not hear from him. If you tell me that he is well
I shall not come to London, but if I do not hear from you or him I shall
certainly come, as I cannot endure this dreadful state of suspense. You are
his friend and you can feel for me.

I remain yours truly,

H. S.

Even without Peacock's testimony that "her whole aspect and
demeanor were manifest emanations of a pure and truthful nature,"
we should hold this to be a truthful letter, a sincere letter, a loving
letter; it bears those marks; I think it is also the letter of a person
accustomed to receiving letters from her husband frequently, and that
they have been of a welcome and satisfactory sort, too, this long time
back—ever since the solemn remarriage and reconciliation at the altar
most likely.

The biographer follows Harriet's letter with a conjecture. He conjectures that she "would now gladly have retraced her steps." Which

means that it is proven that she had steps to retrace—proven by the poem. Well, if the poem is better evidence than the letter, we must let it stand at that.

Then the biographer attacks Harriet Shelley's honor—by authority of random and unverified gossip scavengered from a group of people whose very names make a person shudder: Mary Godwin, mistress of Shelley; her part-sister, discarded mistress of Lord Byron; Godwin, the philosophical tramp, who gathers his share of it from a shadow—that is to say, from a person whom he shirks out of naming. Yet the biographer dignifies this sorry rubbish with the name of "evidence."

Nothing remotely resembling a distinct charge from a named person professing to know is offered among this precious "evidence."

1. "Shelley *believed*" so and so.

2. Byron's discarded mistress says that Shelley told Mary Godwin so and so, and *Mary* told *her*.

3. "Shelley said" so and so—and later "admitted over and over again that he had been in error."

4. The unspeakable Godwin "wrote to Mr. Baxter" that he knew so and so "from unquestionable authority"—name not furnished.

How any man in his right mind could bring himself to defile the grave of a shamefully abused and defenseless girl with these baseless fabrications, this manufactured filth, is inconceivable. How any man, in his right mind or out of it, could sit down and coldly try to persuade anybody to believe it, or listen patiently to it, or, indeed, do anything but scoff at it and deride it, is astonishing.

The charge insinuated by these odious slanders is one of the most difficult of all offenses to prove; it is also one which no man has a right to mention even in a whisper about any woman, living or dead, unless he knows it to be true, and not even then unless he can also *prove* it to be true. There is no justification for the abomination of putting this stuff in the book.

Against Harriet Shelley's good name there is not one scrap of tarnishing evidence, and not even a scrap of evil gossip, that comes from a source that entitles it to a hearing.

On the credit side of the account we have strong opinions from the people who knew her best. Peacock says:

I feel it due to the memory of Harriet to state my most decided conviction that her conduct as a wife was as pure, as true, as absolutely faultless, as that of any who for such conduct are held most in honor.

Thornton Hunt, who had picked and published slight flaws in Harriet's character, says, as regards this alleged large one:

There is not a trace of evidence or a whisper of scandal against her before her voluntary departure from Shelley.

Trelawney says:

I was assured by the evidence of the few friends who knew both Shelley and his wife—Hookham, Hogg, Peacock, and one of the Godwins —that Harriet was perfectly innocent of all offense.

What excuse was there for raking up a parcel of foul rumors from malicious and discredited sources and flinging them at this dead girl's head? Her very defenselessness should have been her protection. The fact that all letters to her or about her, with almost every scrap of her own writing, had been diligently mislaid, leaving her case destitute of a voice, while every pen-stroke which could help her husband's side had been as diligently preserved, should have excused her from being brought to trial. Her witnesses have all disappeared, yet we see her summoned in her grave-clothes to plead for the life of her character, without the help of an advocate, before a disqualified judge and a packed jury.

Harriet Shelley wrote her distressed letter on the 7th of July. On the 28th her husband ran away with Mary Godwin and her part-sister Claire to the Continent. He deserted his wife when her confinement was approaching. She bore him a child at the end of November, his mistress bore him another one something over two months later. The truants were back in London before either of these events occurred.

On one occasion, presently, Shelley was so pressed for money to support his mistress with that he went to his wife and got some money of his that was in her hands—twenty pounds. Yet the mistress was not moved to gratitude; for later, when the wife was troubled to meet her engagements, the mistress makes this entry in her diary:

Harriet sends her creditors here; nasty woman. Now we shall have to change our lodgings.

The deserted wife bore the bitterness and obloquy of her situation two years and a quarter; then she gave up, and drowned herself. A month afterward the body was found in the water. Three weeks later Shelley married his mistress.

I must here be allowed to italicize a remark of the biographer's concerning Harriet Shelley:

That no act of Shelley's during the two years which immediately pre-
ceded her death tended to cause the rash act which brought her life to
its close seems certain.

Yet her husband had deserted her and her children, and was living
with a concubine all that time! Why should a person attempt to write
biography when the simplest facts have no meaning to him? This book
is littered with as crass stupidities as that one—deductions by the
page which bear no discoverable kinship to their premises.

The biographer throws off that extraordinary remark without any
perceptible disturbance to his serenity; for he follows it with a sentimental justification of Shelley's conduct which has not a pang of
conscience in it, but is silky and smooth and undulating and pious—
a cake-walk with all the colored brethren at their best. There may be
people who can read that page and keep their temper, but it is
doubtful.

Shelley's life has the one indelible blot upon it, but is otherwise
worshipfully noble and beautiful. It even stands out indestructibly
gracious and lovely from the ruck of these disastrous pages, in spite
of the fact that they expose and establish his responsibility for
his forsaken wife's pitiful fate—a responsibility which he himself tacitly
admits in a letter to Eliza Westbrook, wherein he refers to his taking
up with Mary Godwin as an act which Eliza "might excusably regard as the cause of her sister's ruin."

1894

How to Tell a Story

I do not claim that I can tell a story as it ought to be told. I only
claim to know how a story ought to be told, for I have been almost
daily in the company of the most expert story-tellers for many years.

There are several kinds of stories, but only one difficult kind—the
humorous. I will talk mainly about that one. The humorous story is
American, the comic story is English, the witty story is French. The
humorous story depends for its effect upon the *manner* of the telling;
the comic story and the witty story upon the *matter*.

The humorous story may be spun out to great length, and may
wander around as much as it pleases, and arrive nowhere in particular;

but the comic and witty stories must be brief and end with a point. The humorous story bubbles gently along, the others burst.

The humorous story is strictly a work of art—high and delicate art— and only an artist can tell it; but no art is necessary in telling the comic and the witty story; anybody can do it. The art of telling a humorous story—understand, I mean by word of mouth, not print— was created in America, and has remained at home.

The humorous story is told gravely; the teller does his best to conceal the fact that he even dimly suspects that there is anything funny about it; but the teller of the comic story tells you beforehand that it is one of the funniest things he has ever heard, then tells it with eager delight, and is the first person to laugh when he gets through. And sometimes, if he has had good success, he is so glad and happy that he will repeat the "nub" of it and glance around from face to face, collecting applause, and then repeat it again. It is a pathetic thing to see.

Very often, of course, the rambling and disjointed humorous story finishes with a nub, point, snapper, or whatever you like to call it. Then the listener must be alert, for in many cases the teller will divert attention from that nub by dropping it in a carefully casual and indifferent way, with the pretense that he does not know it is a nub.

Artemus Ward used that trick a good deal; then when the belated audience presently caught the joke he would look up with innocent surprise, as if wondering what they had found to laugh at. Dan Setchell used it before him, Nye and Riley and others use it to-day.

But the teller of the comic story does not slur the nub; he shouts it at you—every time. And when he prints it, in England, France, Germany, and Italy, he italicizes it, puts some whooping exclamation-points after it, and sometimes explains it in a parenthesis. All of which is very depressing, and makes one want to renounce joking and lead a better life.

Let me set down an instance of the comic method, using an anecdote which has been popular all over the world for twelve or fifteen hundred years. The teller tells it in this way:

THE WOUNDED SOLDIER

In the course of a certain battle a soldier whose leg had been shot off appealed to another soldier who was hurrying by to carry him to the rear, informing him at the same time of the loss which he had sustained; whereupon the generous son of Mars, shouldering the unfortunate, proceeded to carry out his desire. The bullets and cannon-balls were flying in all directions, and presently one of the latter took the wounded man's head off—without, however, his deliverer being aware of it. In no long time he was hailed by an officer, who said:

"Where are you going with that carcass?"

"To the rear, sir—he's lost his leg!"

"His leg, forsooth?" responded the astonished officer, "you mean his head, you booby."

Whereupon the soldier dispossessed himself of his burden, and stood looking down upon it in great perplexity. At length he said:

"It is true, sir, just as you have said." Then after a pause he added, *"But he* TOLD *me* IT WAS HIS LEG! ! ! !"

Here the narrator bursts into explosion after explosion of thunderous horse-laughter, repeating that nub from time to time through his gaspings and shriekings and suffocatings.

It takes only a minute and a half to tell that in its comic-story form; and isn't worth the telling, after all. Put into the humorous-story form it takes ten minutes, and is about the funniest thing I have ever listened to—as James Whitcomb Riley tells it.

He tells it in the character of a dull-witted old farmer who has just heard it for the first time, thinks it is unspeakably funny, and is trying to repeat it to a neighbor. But he can't remember it; so he gets all mixed up and wanders helplessly round and round, putting in tedious details that don't belong in the tale and only retard it; taking them out conscientiously and putting in others that are just as useless; making minor mistakes now and then and stopping to correct them and explain how he came to make them; remembering things which he forgot to put in in their proper place and going back to put them in there; stopping his narrative a good while in order to try to recall the name of the soldier that was hurt, and finally remembering that the soldier's name was not mentioned, and remarking placidly that the name is of no real importance, anyway—better, of course, if one knew it, but not essential, after all—and so on, and so on, and so on.

The teller is innocent and happy and pleased with himself, and has to stop every little while to hold himself in and keep from laughing outright; and does hold in, but his body quakes in a jelly-like way with interior chuckles; and at the end of the ten minutes the audience have laughed until they are exhausted, and the tears are running down their faces.

The simplicity and innocence and sincerity and unconsciousness of the old farmer are perfectly simulated, and the result is a performance which is thoroughly charming and delicious. This is art—and fine and beautiful, and only a master can compass it; but a machine could tell the other story.

To string incongruities and absurdities together in a wandering and sometimes purposeless way, and seem innocently unaware that they are absurdities, is the basis of the American art, if my position is correct. Another feature is the slurring of the point. A third is the dropping of a studied remark apparently without knowing it, as if one were thinking aloud. The fourth and last is the pause.

Artemus Ward dealt in numbers three and four a good deal. He would begin to tell with great animation something which he seemed to think was wonderful; then lose confidence, and after an apparently absent-minded pause add an incongruous remark in a soliloquizing way; and that was the remark intended to explode the mine—and it did.

For instance, he would say eagerly, excitedly, "I once knew a man in New Zealand who hadn't a tooth in his head"—here his animation would die out; a silent, reflective pause would follow, then he would say dreamily, and as if to himself, "and yet that man could beat a drum better than any man I ever saw."

The pause is an exceedingly important feature in any kind of story, and a frequently recurring feature, too. It is a dainty thing, and delicate, and also uncertain and treacherous; for it must be exactly the right length—no more and no less—or it fails of its purpose and makes trouble. If the pause is too short the impressive point is passed, and the audience have had time to divine that a surprise is intended—and then you can't surprise them, of course.

On the platform I used to tell a negro ghost story that had a pause in front of the snapper on the end, and that pause was the most important thing in the whole story. If I got it the right length precisely, I could spring the finishing ejaculation with effect enough to make some impressible girl deliver a startled little yelp and jump out of her seat—and that was what I was after. This story was called "The Golden Arm," and was told in this fashion. You can practise with it yourself—and mind you look out for the pause and get it right.

THE GOLDEN ARM

Once 'pon a time dey wuz a monsus mean man, en he live 'way out in de praire all 'lone by hisself, 'cep'n he had a wife. En bimeby she died, en he tuck en toted her way out dah in de prairie en buried her. Well, she had a golden arm—all solid gold, fum de shoulder down. He wuz pow'ful mean—pow'ful; en dat night he couldn't sleep, caze he want dat golden arm so bad.

When it come midnight he couldn't stan' it no mo'; so he git up, he did, en tuck his lantern en shoved out thoo de storm en dug her up en got de golden arm; en he bent his head down 'gin de win', en plowed en plowed en plowed thoo de snow. Den all on a sudden he stop (make a considerable pause here, and look startled, and take a listening attitude) en say: "My *lan'*, what's dat?"

En he listen—en listen—en de win' say (set your teeth together and imitate the wailing and wheezing singsong of the wind), "Bzzz-z-zzz" —en den, way back yonder whah de grave is, he hear a *voice!*—he hear a voice all mix' up in de win'—can't hardly tell 'em 'part— "Bzzz—zzz—W-h-o—g-o-t—m-y—g-o-l-d-e-n *arm?*" (You must begin to shiver violently now.)

En he begin to shiver en shake, en say, "Oh, my! *Oh*, my lan'!" en de win' blow de lantern out, en de snow en sleet blow in his face en mos' choke him, en he start a-plowin' knee-deep towards home mos' dead, he so sk'yerd—en pooty soon he hear de voice agin, en (pause) it 'us comin' *after* him! "Bzzz—zzz—zzz—W-h-o—g-o-t—m-y —g-o-l-d-e-n—*arm?*"

When he git to de pasture he hear it agin—closter now, en a-*comin'!* —a-comin' back dah in de dark en de storm—(repeat the wind and the voice). When he git to de house he rush up-stairs en jump in de bed en kiver up, head and years, en lay dah shiverin' en shakin'—en den way out dah he hear it *agin!*—en a-*comin'!* En bimeby he hear (pause—awed, listening attitude)—pat—pat—pat—*hit's a-comin' upstairs!* Den he hear de latch, en he *know* it's in de room!

Den pooty soon he know it's a-*stannin' by de bed!* (Pause.) Den— he know it's a-*bendin' down over him*—en he cain't skasely git his breath! Den—den—he seem to feel someth'n' *c-o-l-d*, right down 'most agin his head! (Pause.)

Den de voice say, *right at his year*—"W-h-o—g-o-t—m-y—g-o-l-d-e-n *arm?*" (You must wail it out very plaintively and accusingly; then you stare steadily and impressively into the face of the farthest-gone auditor—a girl, preferably—and let that awe-inspiring pause begin to build itself in the deep hush. When it has reached exactly the right length, jump suddenly at that girl and yell, "*You've* got it!"

If you've got the *pause* right, she'll fetch a dear little yelp and spring right out of her shoes. But you *must* get the pause right; and you will find it the most troublesome and aggravating and uncertain thing you ever undertook.

1895

Mental Telegraphy Again

I have three or four curious incidents to tell about. They seem to come under the head of what I named "Mental Telegraphy" in a paper written seventeen years ago, and published long afterward.

Several years ago I made a campaign on the platform with Mr. George W. Cable. In Montreal we were honored with a reception. It began at two in the afternoon in a long drawing-room in the Windsor Hotel. Mr. Cable and I stood at one end of this room, and the ladies and gentlemen entered it at the other end, crossed it at that end, then came up the long left-hand side, shook hands with us, said a word or two, and passed on, in the usual way. My sight is of the telescopic sort, and I presently recognized a familiar face among the throng of strangers drifting in at the distant door, and I said to myself, with surprise and high gratification, "That is Mrs. R.; I had forgotten that she was a Canadian." She had been a great friend of mine in Carson City, Nevada, in the early days. I had not seen her or heard of her for twenty years; I had not been thinking about her; there was nothing to suggest her to me, nothing to bring her to my mind; in fact, to me she had long ago ceased to exist, and had disappeared from my consciousness. But I knew her instantly; and I saw her so clearly that I was able to note some of the particulars of her dress, and did note them, and they remained in my mind. I was impatient for her to come. In the midst of the hand-shakings I snatched glimpses of her and noted her progress with the slow-moving file across the end of the room; then I saw her start up the side, and this gave me a full front view of her face. I saw her last when she was within twenty-five feet of me. For an hour I kept thinking she must still be in the room somewhere and would come at last, but I was disappointed.

When I arrived in the lecture-hall that evening some one said: "Come into the waiting-room; there's a friend of yours there who wants to see you. You'll not be introduced—you are to do the recognizing without help if you can."

I said to myself: "It is Mrs. R.; I sha'n't have any trouble."

There were perhaps ten ladies present, all seated. In the midst of them was Mrs. R., as I had expected. She was dressed exactly as she was when I had seen her in the afternoon. I went forward and shook hands with her and called her by name, and said:

"I knew you the moment you appeared at the reception this afternoon."

She looked surprised, and said: "But I was not at the reception. I have just arrived from Quebec, and have not been in town an hour."

It was my turn to be surprised now. I said: "I can't help it. I give you my word of honor that it is as I say. I saw you at the reception, and you were dressed precisely as you are now. When they told me a moment ago that I should find a friend in this room, your image rose before me, dress and all, just as I had seen you at the reception."

Those are the facts. She was not at the reception at all, or anywhere near it; but I saw her there nevertheless, and most clearly and unmistakably. To that I could make oath. How is one to explain this? I was not thinking of her at the time; had not thought of her for years. But she had been thinking of me, no doubt; did her thoughts flit through leagues of air to me, and bring with it that clear and pleasant vision of herself? I think so. That was and remains my sole experience in the matter of apparitions—I mean apparitions that come when one is (ostensibly awake. I could have been asleep for a moment; the apparition could have been the creature of a dream. Still, that is nothing to the point; the feature of interest is the happening of the thing just at that time, instead of at an earlier or later time, which is argument that its orgin lay in thought-transference.

My next incident will be set aside by most persons as being merely a "coincidence," I suppose. Years ago I used to think sometimes of making a lecturing trip through the antipodes and the borders of the Orient, but always gave up the idea, partly because of the great length of the journey and partly because my wife could not well manage to go with me. Toward the end of last January that idea, after an interval of years, came suddenly into my head again—forcefully, too, and without any apparent reason. Whence came it? What suggested it? I will touch upon that presently.

I was at that time where I am now—in Paris. I wrote at once to Henry M. Stanley (London), and asked him some questions about his Australian lecture tour, and inquired who had conducted him and what were the terms. After a day or two his answer came. It began:

The lecture agent for Australia and New Zealand is *par excellence* Mr. R. S. Smythe, of Melbourne.

He added his itinerary, terms, sea expenses, and some other matters, and advised me to write Mr. Smythe, which I did—February 3d. I began my letter by saying in substance that, while he did not know me personally, we had a mutual friend in Stanley, and that would answer for an introduction. Then I proposed my trip, and asked if he would give me the same terms which he had given Stanley.

I mailed my letter to Mr. Smythe February 6th, and three days later I got a letter from the selfsame Smythe, dated Melbourne, December 17th. I would as soon have expected to get a letter from the late George Washington. The letter began somewhat as mine to him had begun—with a self-introduction:

DEAR MR. CLEMENS.—It is so long since Archibald Forbes and I spent that pleasant afternoon in your comfortable house at Hartford that you have probably quite forgotten the occasion.

In the course of his letter this occurs:

I am willing to give you [here he named the terms which he had given Stanley] for an antipodean tour to last, say, three months.

Here was the single essential detail of my letter answered three days after I had mailed my inquiry. I might have saved myself the trouble and the postage—and a few years ago I would have done that very thing, for I would have argued that my sudden and strong impulse to write and ask some questions of a stranger on the under side of the globe meant that the impulse came from that stranger, and that he would answer my questions of his own motion if I would let him alone.

Mr. Smythe's letter probably passed under my nose on its way to lose three weeks traveling to America and back, and gave me a whiff of its contents as it went along. Letters often act like that. Instead of the *thought* coming to you in an instant from Australia, the (apparently) unsentient letter imparts it to you as it glides invisibly past your elbow in the mail-bag.

Next incident. In the following month—March—I was in America. I spent a Sunday at Irvington-on-the-Hudson with Mr. John Brisben Walker, of the *Cosmopolitan* magazine. We came into New York next morning, and went to the Century Club for luncheon. He said some praiseful things about the character of the club and the orderly serenity and pleasantness of its quarters, and asked if I had never tried to acquire membership in it. I said I had not, and that New York clubs were a continuous expense to the country members without being of frequent use or benefit to them.

"And now I've got an idea!" said I. "There's the Lotos—the first New York club I was ever a member of—my very earliest love in that line. I have been a member of it for considerably more than twenty years, yet have seldom had a chance to look in and see the boys. They turn gray and grow old while I am not watching. And *my dues go on*. I am going to Hartford this afternoon for a day or two, but as soon as I get back I will go to John Elderkin very privately and say: 'Remember the veteran and confer distinction upon him, for the sake of old times. Make me an honorary member and abolish the tax. If you haven't any such thing as honorary membership, all the better—create it for my honor and glory.' That would be a great thing; I will go to John Elderkin as soon as I get back from Hartford."

I took the fast express that afternoon, first telegraphing Mr. F. G. Whitmore to come and see me next day. When he came he asked:

"Did you get a letter from Mr. John Elderkin, secretary of the Lotos Club, before you left New York?"

"No."

"Then it just missed you. If I had known you were coming I would have kept it. It is beautiful, and will make you proud. The Board of Directors, by unanimous vote, have made you a life member, and *squelched those dues;* and you are to be on hand and receive your distinction on the night of the 30th, which is the twenty-fifth anniversary of the founding of the club, and it will not surprise me if they have some great times there."

What put the honorary membership in my head that day in the Century Club? for I had never thought of it before. I don't know what brought the thought to me at *that* particular time instead of earlier, but I am well satisfied that it originated with the Board of Directors, and had been on its way to my brain through the air ever since the moment that saw their vote recorded.

Another incident. I was in Hartford two or three days as a guest of
the Rev. Joseph H. Twichell. I have held the rank of Honorary Uncle
to his children for a quarter of a century, and I went out with him in
the trolley-car to visit one of my nieces, who is at Miss Porter's famous
school in Farmington. The distance is eight or nine miles. On the way,
talking, I illustrated something with an anecdote. This is the anecdote:

Two years and a half ago I and the family arrived at Milan on our
way to Rome, and stopped at the Continental. After dinner I went
below and took a seat in the stone-paved court, where the customary
lemon trees stand in the customary tubs, and said to myself, "Now *this*
is comfort, comfort and repose, and nobody to disturb it; I do not know
anybody in Milan."

Then a young gentleman stepped up and shook hands, which damaged my theory. He said, in substance:

"You won't remember me, Mr. Clemens, but I remember you very
well. I was a cadet at West Point when you and Rev. Joseph H.
Twichell came there some years ago and talked to us on a Hundredth
Night. I am a lieutenant in the regular army now, and my name is
H. I am in Europe, all alone, for a modest little tour; my regiment is
in Arizona."

We became friendly and sociable, and in the course of the talk he
told me of an adventure which had befallen him—about to this effect:

"I was at Bellagio, stopping at the big hotel there, and ten days ago
I lost my letter of credit. I did not know what in the world to do. I
was a stranger; I knew no one in Europe; I hadn't a penny in my
pocket; I couldn't even send a telegram to London to get my lost letter
replaced; my hotel bill was a week old, and the presentation of it imminent—so imminent that it could happen at any moment now. I was
so frightened that my wits seemed to leave me. I tramped and
tramped, back and forth, like a crazy person. If anybody approached
me I hurried away, for no matter what a person looked like, I took
him for the head waiter with the bill.

"I was at last in such a desperate state that I was ready to do any
wild thing that promised even the shadow of help, and so this is the
insane thing that I did. I saw a family lunching at a small table on the
veranda, and recognized their nationality—Americans—father, mother,
and several young daughters—young, tastefully dressed, and pretty—
the rule with our people. I went straight there in my civilian costume,
named my name, said I was a lieutenant in the army, and told my
story and asked for help.

"What do you suppose the gentleman did? But you would not guess in twenty years. He took out a handful of gold coin and told me to help myself—freely. That is what he did."

The next morning the lieutenant told me his new letter of credit had arrived in the night, so we strolled to Cook's to draw money to pay back the benefactor with. We got it, and then went strolling through the great arcade. Presently he said, "Yonder they are; come and be introduced." I was introduced to the parents and the young ladies; then we separated, and I never saw him or them any m—

"Here we are at Farmington," said Twichell, interrupting.

We left the trolley-car and tramped through the mud a hundred yards or so to the school, talking about the time we and Warner walked out there years ago, and the pleasant time we had.

We had a visit with my niece in the parlor, then started for the trolley again. Outside the house we encountered a double rank of twenty or thirty of Miss Porter's young ladies arriving from a walk, and we stood aside, ostensibly to let them have room to file past, but really to look at them. Presently one of them stepped out of the rank and said:

"You don't know me, Mr. Twichell, but I know your daughter and that gives me the privilege of shaking hands with you."

Then she put out her hand to me, and said:

"And I wish to shake hands with you too, Mr. Clemens. You don't remember me, but you were introduced to me in the arcade in Milan two years and a half ago by Lieutenant H."

What had put that story into my head after all that stretch of time? Was it just the proximity of that young girl, or was it merely an odd accident?

1895

What Paul Bourget[1] Thinks of Us

He reports the American joke correctly. In Boston they ask, How much does he know? in New York, How much is he worth? in Philadelphia, Who were his parents? And when an alien observer turns his telescope upon us—advertisedly in our own special interest—a natural apprehension moves us to ask, What is the diameter of his reflector?

I take a great interest in M. Bourget's chapters, for I know by the newspapers that there are several Americans who are expecting to get a whole education out of them; several who foresaw, and also foretold, that our long night was over, and a light almost divine about to break upon the land.

His utterances concerning us are bound to be weighty and well timed.
He gives us an object-lesson which should be thoughtfully and profitably studied.

These well-considered and important verdicts were of a nature to restore public confidence, which had been disquieted by questionings as to whether so young a teacher would be qualified to take so large a class as seventy million, distributed over so extensive a school-house as America, and pull it through without assistance.

I was even disquieted myself, although I am of a cold, calm temperament, and not easily disturbed. I feared for my country. And I was not wholly tranquilized by the verdicts rendered as above. It seemed to me that there was still room for doubt. In fact, in looking the ground over I became more disturbed than I was before. Many worrying questions came up in my mind. Two were prominent. Where had the teacher gotten his equipment? What was his method?

He had gotten his equipment in France.

Then as to his method! I saw by his own intimations that he was an Observer, and had a System—that used by naturalists and other scientists. The naturalist collects many bugs and reptiles and butterflies and studies their ways a long time patiently. By this means he is presently

---

[1] Paul Bourget (1852–1935), French novelist, critic, poet, journalist. Admitted to the French Academy in 1894.—C.N.

able to group these creatures into families and subdivisions of families by nice shadings of differences observable in their characters. Then he labels all those shaded bugs and things with nicely descriptive group names, and is now happy, for his great work is completed, and as a result he intimately knows every bug and shade of a bug there, inside and out. It may be true, but a person who was not a naturalist would feel safer about it if he had the opinion of the bug. I think it is a pleasant System, but subject to error.

The Observer of Peoples has to be a Classifier, a Grouper, a Deducer, a Generalizer, a Psychologizer; and, first and last, a Thinker. He has to be all these, and when he is at home, observing his own folk, he is often able to prove competency. But history has shown that when he is abroad observing unfamiliar peoples the chances are heavily against him. He is then a naturalist observing a bug, with no more than a naturalist's chance of being able to tell the bug anything new about itself, and no more than a naturalist's chance of being able to teach it any new ways which it will prefer to its own.

To return to that first question. M. Bourget, as teacher, would simply be France teaching America. It seemed to me that the outlook was dark—almost Egyptian, in fact. What would the new teacher, representing France, teach us? Railroading? No. France knows nothing valuable about railroading. Steamshipping? No. France has no superiorities over us in that matter. Steamboating? No. French steamboating is still of Fulton's date—1809. Postal service? No. France is a back number there. Telegraphy? No, we taught her that ourselves. Journalism? No. Magazining? No, that is our own specialty. Government? No; Liberty, Equality, Fraternity, Nobility, Democracy, Adultery—the system is too variegated for our climate. Religion? No, not variegated enough for our climate. Morals? No, we cannot rob the poor to enrich ourselves. Novel-writing? No. M. Bourget and the others know only one plan, and when that is expurgated there is nothing left of the book.

I wish I could think what he is going to teach us. Can it be Deportment? But he experimented in that at Newport and failed to give satisfaction, except to a few. Those few are pleased. They are enjoying their joy as well as they can. They confess their happiness to the interviewer. They feel pretty striped, but they remember with reverent recognition that they had sugar between the cuts. True, sugar with sand in it, but sugar. And true, they had some trouble to tell which was sugar and which was sand, because the sugar itself looked just like the sand, and also had a gravelly taste; still, they knew that the sugar was there, and would have been very good sugar indeed if it had been screened. Yes, they are pleased; not noisily so, but pleased; invaded, or streaked, as one may say, with little recurrent shivers of joy—subdued joy, so to speak, not the overdone kind. And they commune together, these, and massage each other with comforting sayings, in a sweet spirit of resignation and thankfulness, mixing these elements in the same proportions as the sugar and the sand, as a memorial, and saying, the one to the other, and to the interviewer: "It was severe—yes, it was bitterly severe; but oh, how true it was; and it will do us so much good!"

If it isn't Deportment, what is left? It was at this point that I seemed to get on the right track at last. M. Bourget would teach us to know ourselves; that was it: he would reveal us to ourselves. That would be an education. He would explain us to ourselves. Then we should understand ourselves; and after that be able to go on more intelligently.

It seemed a doubtful scheme. He could explain *us* to *himself*—that would be easy. That would be the same as the naturalist explaining the bug to himself. But to explain the bug to the bug—that is quite a different matter. The bug may not know himself perfectly, but he knows himself better than the naturalist can know him, at any rate.

A foreigner can photograph the exteriors of a nation, but I think that that is as far as he can get. I think that no foreigner can report its interior—its soul, its life, its speech, its thought. I think that a knowledge of these things is acquirable in only one way—not two or four or six—*absorption;* years and years of unconscious absorption; years and years of intercourse with the life concerned; of living it, indeed; sharing personally in its shames and prides, its joys and griefs, its loves and hates, its prosperities and reverses, its shows and shabbinesses, its deep patriotism, its whirlwinds of political passion, its adoration—of flag, and heroic dead, and the glory of the national name. Observation? Of what real value is it? One learns peoples through the heart, not the eyes or the intellect.

There is only one expert who is qualified to examine the souls and the life of a people and make a valuable report—the native novelist. This expert is so rare that the most populous country can never have fifteen conspicuously and confessedly competent ones in stock at one time. This native specialist is not qualified to begin work until he has been absorbing during twenty-five years. How much of his competency is derived from conscious "observation"? The amount is so slight that it counts for next to nothing in the equipment. Almost the whole capital of the novelist is the slow accumulation of *unconscious* observation—absorption. The native expert's intentional observation of manners, speech, character, and ways of life can have value, for the native knows what they mean without having to cipher out the meaning. But I should be astonished to see a foreigner get at the right meanings, catch the elusive shades of these subtle things. Even the native novelist becomes a foreigner, with a foreigner's limitations, when he steps from the state whose life is familiar to him into a state whose life he has not lived. Bret Harte got his California and his Californians by unconscious absorption, and put both of them into his tales alive. But when he came from the Pacific to the Atlantic and tried to do Newport life from study—conscious observation—his failure was absolutely monumental. Newport is a disastrous place for the unacclimated observer, evidently.

To return to novel-building. Does the native novelist try to generalize the nation? No, he lays plainly before you the ways and speech and life of a few people grouped in a certain place—his own place—and that is one book. In time he and his brethren will report to you the life and the people of the whole nation—the life of a group in a New England village; in a New York village; in a Texan village; in an Oregon village; in villages in fifty states and territories; then the farm-life in fifty states and territories; a hundred patches of life and groups of people in a dozen widely separated cities. And the Indians will be attended to; and the cowboys; and the gold and silver miners; and the negroes; and the Idiots and Congressmen; and the Irish, the Germans, the Italians, the Swedes, the French, the Chinamen, the Greasers; and the Catholics, the Methodists, the Presbyterians, the Congregationalists, the Baptists, the Spiritualists, the Mormons, the Shakers, the Quakers, the Jews, the Campbellites, the infidels, the Christian Scientists, the Mind-Curists, the Faith-Curists, the train-robbers, the White Caps, the Moonshiners. And when a thousand able novels have been written, *there* you have the soul of the people, the life of the people, the speech of the people; and not anywhere else can these be had. And the shadings of character, manners, feelings, ambitions, will be infinite.

The nature of a people is always of a similar shade in its vices and its virtues, in its frivolities and in its labor. *It is this physiognomy which it is necessary to discover,* and every document is good, from the hall of a casino to the church, from the foibles of a fashionable woman to the suggestions of a revolutionary leader. I am therefore quite sure that this *American soul,* the principal interest and the great object of my voyage, appears behind the records of Newport for those who choose to see it.— *M. Paul Bourget.*

[The italics are mine.] It is a large contract which he has under-
taken. "Records" is a pretty poor word there, but I think the use of it
is due to hasty translation. In the original the word is *fastes*. I think
M. Bourget meant to suggest that he expected to find the great "American soul" secreted behind the *ostentations* of Newport; and that he
was going to get it out and examine it, and generalize it, and psychologize it, and make it reveal to him its hidden vast mystery: "the nature
of the people" of the United States of America. We have been accused
of being a nation addicted to inventing wild schemes. I trust that we
shall be allowed to retire to second place now.

There isn't a single human characteristic that can be safely labeled
"American." There isn't a single human ambition, or religious trend, or
drift of thought, or peculiarity of education, or code of principles, or
breed of folly, or style of conversation, or preference for a particular
subject for discussion, or form of legs or trunk or head or face or expression or complexion, or gait, or dress, or manners, or disposition, or
any other human detail, inside or outside, that can rationally be generalized as "American."

Whenever you have found what seems to be an "American" peculiarity, you have only to cross a frontier or two, or go down or up in
the social scale, and you perceive that it has disappeared. And you
can cross the Atlantic and find it again. There may be a Newport religious drift, or sporting drift, or conversational style or complexion,
or cut of face, but there are entire empires in America, north, south,
east, and west, where you could not find your duplicates. It is the same
with everything else which one might propose to call "American." M.
Bourget thinks he has found the American Coquette. If he had really
found her he would also have found, I am sure, that she was not new,
that she exists in other lands in the same forms, and with the same
frivolous heart and the same ways and impulses. I think this because I
have seen our coquette; I have seen her in life; better still, I have seen
her in our novels, and seen her twin in foreign novels. I wish M. Bourget had seen ours. He thought he saw her. And so he applied his
System to her. She was a Species. So he gathered a number of samples
of what seemed to be her, and put them under his glass, and divided
them into groups which he calls "types," and labeled them in his usual
scientific way with "formulas"—brief, sharp descriptive flashes that
make a person blink, sometimes, they are so sudden and vivid. As a
rule they are pretty far-fetched, but that is not an important matter;
they surprise, they compel admiration, and I notice by some of the
comments which his efforts have called forth that they deceive the

unwary. Here are a few of the coquette variants which he has grouped
and labeled:

THE COLLECTOR.

THE EQUILIBREE.

THE PROFESSIONAL BEAUTY.

THE BLUFFER.

THE GIRL-BOY.

If he had stopped with describing these characters we should have
been obliged to believe that they exist; that they exist, and that he
has seen them and spoken with them. But he did not stop there; he
went further and furnished to us light-throwing samples of their behavior, and also light-throwing samples of their speeches. He entered
those things in his note-book without suspicion, he takes them out and
delivers them to the world with a candor and simplicity which show
that he believed them genuine. They throw altogether too much light.
They reveal to the native the origin of his find. I suppose he knows
how he came to make that novel and captivating discovery, by this
time. If he does not, any American can tell him—any American to
whom he will show his anecdotes. It was "put up" on him, as we say.
It was a jest—to be plain, it was a series of frauds. To my mind it was
a poor sort of jest, witless and contemptible. The players of it have
their reward, such as it is; they have exhibited the fact that whatever
they may be they are not ladies. M. Bourget did not discover a type
of coquette; he merely discovered a type of practical joker. One may
say *the* type of practical joker, for these people are exactly alike all
over the world. Their equipment is always the same: a vulgar mind,
a puerile wit, a cruel disposition as a rule, and always the spirit of
treachery.

In his Chapter IV. M. Bourget has two or three columns gravely
devoted to the collating and examining and psychologizing of these
sorry little frauds. One is not moved to laugh. There is nothing funny
in the situation; it is only pathetic. The stranger gave those people
his confidence, and they dishonorably treated him in return.

But one must be allowed to suspect that M. Bourget was a little
to blame himself. Even a practical joker has some little judgment. He
has to exercise some degree of sagacity in selecting his prey if he would
save himself from getting into trouble. In my time I have seldom seen
such daring things marketed at any price as these conscienceless folk
have worked off at par on this confiding observer. It compels the conviction that there was something about him that bred in those specu-

lators a quite unusual sense of safety, and encouraged them to strain
their powers in his behalf. They seem to have satisfied themselves that
all he wanted was "significant" facts, and that he was not accustomed
to examine the source whence they proceeded. It is plain that there
was a sort of conspiracy against him almost from the start—a conspiracy
to freight him up with all the strange extravagances those people's
decayed brains could invent.

The lengths to which they went are next to incredible. They told
him things which surely would have excited any one else's suspicion,
but they did not excite his. Consider this:

There is not in all the United States an entirely nude statue.

If an angel should come down and say such a thing about heaven,
a reasonably cautious observer would take that angel's number and
inquire a little further before he added it to his catch. What does the
present observer do? Adds it. Adds it at once. Adds it, and labels it
with this innocent comment:

This small fact is strangely significant.

It does seem to me that this kind of observing is defective.

Here is another curiosity which some liberal person made him a
present of. I should think it ought to have disturbed the deep slumber
of his suspicion a little, but it didn't. It was a note from a fog-horn for
strenuousness, it seems to me, but the doomed voyager did not catch
it. If he had but caught it, it would have saved him from several disasters:

*If the American knows that you are traveling to take notes, he is inter-
ested in it, and at the same time rejoices in it, as in a tribute.*

Again, this is defective observation. It is human to like to be praised;
one can even notice it in the French. But it is not human to like to be
ridiculed, even when it comes in the form of a "tribute." I think a little
psychologizing ought to have come in there. Something like this: A
dog does not like to be ridiculed, a redskin does not like to be ridiculed, a negro does not like to be ridiculed, a Chinaman does not like
to be ridiculed; let us deduce from these significant facts this formula:
the American's grade being higher than these, and the chain of argument stretching unbroken all the way up to him, there is room for
suspicion that the person who said the American likes to be ridiculed,
and regards it as a tribute, is not a capable observer.

I feel persuaded that in the matter of psychologizing, a professional is too apt to yield to the fascinations of the loftier regions of that great art, to the neglect of its lowlier walks. Every now and then, at half-hour intervals, M. Bourget collects a hatful of airy inaccuracies and dissolves them in a panful of assorted abstractions, and runs the charge into a mold and turns you out a compact principle which will explain an American girl, or an American woman, or why new people yearn for old things, or any other impossible riddle which a person wants answered.

It seems to be conceded that there are a few human peculiarities that can be generalized and located here and there in the world and named by the name of the nation where they are found. I wonder what they are. Perhaps one of them is temperament. One speaks of French vivacity and German gravity and English stubbornness. There is no American temperament. The nearest that one can come at it is to say there are two—the composed Northern and the impetuous Southern; and both are found in other countries. Morals? Purity of women may fairly be called universal with us, but that is the case in some other countries. We have no monopoly of it; it cannot be named American. I think that there is but a single specialty with us, only one thing that can be called by the wide name "American." That is the national devotion to ice-water. All Germans drink beer, but the British nation drinks beer, too; so neither of those peoples is *the* beer-drinking nation. I suppose we do stand alone in having a drink that nobody likes but ourselves. When we have been a month in Europe we lose our craving for it, and we finally tell the hotel folk that they needn't provide it any more. Yet we hardly touch our native shore again, winter or summer, before we are eager for it. The reasons for this state of things have not been psychologized yet. I drop the hint and say no more.

It is my belief that there are some "national" traits and things scattered about the world that are mere superstitions, frauds that have lived so long that they have the solid look of facts. One of them is the dogma that the French are the only chaste people in the world. Ever since I arrived in France this last time I have been accumulating doubts about that; and before I leave this sunny land again I will gather in a few random statistics and psychologize the plausibilities out of it. If people are to come over to America and find fault with our girls and our women, and psychologize every little thing they do, and try to teach them how to behave, and how to cultivate themselves up to where one cannot tell them from the French model, I intend to find out whether those missionaries are qualified or not. A nation ought always to examine into this detail before engaging the teacher for good. This last one has let fall a remark which renewed those doubts of mine when I read it:

> In our high Parisian existence, for instance, we find applied to arts and luxury, and to debauchery, all the powers and all the weaknesses of the French soul.

You see, it amounts to a trade with the French soul; a profession; a science; the serious business of life, so to speak, in our high Parisian existence. I do not quite like the look of it. I question if it can be taught with profit in our country, except, of course, to those pathetic, neglected minds that are waiting there so yearningly for the education which M. Bourget is going to furnish them from the serene summits of our high Parisian life.

I spoke a moment ago of the existence of some superstitions that have been parading the world as facts this long time. For instance, consider the Dollar. The world seems to think that the love of money is "American"; and that the mad desire to get suddenly rich is "American." I believe that both of these things are merely and broadly human, not American monopolies at all. The love of money is natural to all nations, for money is a good and strong friend. I think that this love has existed everywhere, ever since the Bible called it the root of all evil.

I think that the reason why we Americans seem to be so addicted to trying to get rich suddenly is merely because the *opportunity* to make promising efforts in that direction has offered itself to us with a frequency out of all proportion to the European experience. For eighty years this opportunity has been offering itself in one new town or region after another straight westward, step by step, all the way from the Atlantic coast to the Pacific. When a mechanic could buy ten town lots on tolerably long credit for ten months' savings out of his wages, and reasonably expect to sell them in a couple of years for ten times what he gave for them, it was human for him to try the venture, and he did it no matter what his nationality was. He would have done it in Europe or China if he had had the same chance.

In the flush times in the silver regions a cook or any other humble worker stood a very good chance to get rich out of a trifle of money risked in a stock deal; and that person promptly took that risk, no matter what his or her nationality might be. I was there, and saw it.

But these opportunities have not been plenty in our Southern states; so there you have a prodigious region where the rush for sudden wealth is almost an unknown thing—and has been, from the beginning.

Europe has offered few opportunities for poor Tom, Dick, and Harry; but when she has offered one, there has been no noticeable difference between European eagerness and American. England saw this in the wild days of the Railroad King; France saw it in 1720—time of Law and the Mississippi Bubble. I am sure have never seen in the gold and silver mines any madness, fury, frenzy to get suddenly rich which was even remotely comparable to that which raged in France in the Bubble day. If I had a cyclopedia here I could turn to that memorable case, and satisfy nearly anybody that the hunger for the sudden dollar is no more "American" than it is French. And if I could furnish an American opportunity to staid Germany, I think I could wake her up like a house afire.

But I must return to the Generalizations, Psychologizings, Deductions. When M. Bourget is exploiting these arts, it is then that he is peculiarly and particularly himself. His ways are wholly original when he encounters a trait or a custom which is new to him. Another person would merely examine the find, verify it, estimate its value, and let it go; but that is not sufficient for M. Bourget: he always wants to know *why* that thing exists, he wants to know how it came to happen; and he will not let go of it until he has found out. And in every instance he will find that reason where no one but himself would have thought of looking for it. He does not seem to care for a reason that is not picturesquely located; one might almost say picturesquely and impossibly located.

He found out that in America men do not try to hunt down young married women. At once, as usual, he wanted to know *why*. Any one could have told him. He could have divined it by the lights thrown by the novels of the country. But no, he preferred to find out for himself. He has a trustfulness as regards men and facts which is fine and unusual; he is not particular about the source of a fact, he is not particular about the character and standing of the fact itself; but when it comes to pounding out the reason for the existence of the fact, he will trust no one but himself.

In the present instance here was his fact: American young married women are not pursued by the corrupter; and here was the question: What is it that protects her?

It seems quite unlikely that that problem could have offered difficulties to any but a trained philosopher. Nearly any person would have said to M. Bourget: "Oh, that is very simple. It is very seldom in America that a marriage is made on a commercial basis; our marriages, from the beginning, have been made for love; and where love is there is no room for the corrupter."

Now, it is interesting to see the formidable way in which M. Bourget went at that poor, humble little thing. He moved upon it in column —three columns—and with artillery.

"Two reasons of a very different kind explain"—that fact.

And now that I have got so far, I am almost afraid to say what his two reasons are, lest I be charged with inventing them. But I will not retreat now; I will condense them and print them, giving my word that I am honest and not trying to deceive any one.

1. Young married women are protected from the approaches of the seducer in New England and vicinity by the diluted remains of a prudence created by a Puritan law of two hundred years ago, which for a while punished adultery with death.

2. And young married women of the other forty or fifty states are protected by laws which afford extraordinary facilities for divorce.

If I have not lost my mind I have accurately conveyed those two Vesuvian irruptions of philosophy. But the reader can consult Chapter IV. of *Outre-Mer*, and decide for himself. Let us examine this paralyzing Deduction or Explanation by the light of a few sane facts.

1. This universality of "protection" has existed in our country *from the beginning;* before the death-penalty existed in New England, and during all the generations that have dragged by since it was annulled.

2. Extraordinary facilities for divorce are of such recent creation that any middle-aged American can remember a time when such things had not yet been thought of.

Let us suppose that the first easy divorce law went into effect forty years ago, and got noised around and fairly started in business thirty-five years ago, when we had, say, 25,000,000 of white population. Let us suppose that among 5,000,000 of them the young married women were "protected" by the surviving shudder of that ancient Puritan scare —what is M. Bourget going to do about those who lived among the 20,000,000? They were clean in their morals, they were pure, yet there was no easy divorce law to protect them.

Awhile ago I said that M. Bourget's method of truth-seeking—hunting for it in out-of-the-way places—was new; but that was an error. I remember that when Leverrier discovered the Milky Way, he and the other astronomers began to theorize about it in substantially the same fashion which M. Bourget employs in his reasonings about American social facts and their origin. Leverrier advanced the hypothesis that the Milky Way was caused by gaseous protoplasmic emanations from

WHAT PAUL BOURGET THINKS OF US   177

the field of Waterloo, which, ascending to an altitude determinable by
their own specific gravity, became luminous through the development
and exposure—by the natural processes of animal decay—of the phos-
phorus contained in them.

This theory was warmly complimented by Ptolemy, who, however,
after much thought and research, decided that he could not accept it
as final. His own theory was that the Milky Way was an emigration
of lightning-bugs; and he supported and reinforced this theorem by
the well-known fact that the locusts do like that in Egypt.

Giordano Bruno also was outspoken in his praises of Leverrier's important contribution to astronomical science, and was at first inclined
to regard it as conclusive; but later, conceiving it to be erroneous, he
pronounced against it, and advanced the hypothesis that the Milky
Way was a detachment or corps of stars which became arrested and
held in *suspenso suspensorum* by refraction of gravitation while on the
march to join their several constellations; a proposition for which he
was afterward burned at the stake in Jacksonville, Illinois.

These were all brilliant and picturesque theories, and each was received with enthusiasm by the scientific world; but when a New England farmer, who was not a thinker, but only a plain sort of person who
tried to account for large facts in simple ways, came out with the opinion that the Milky Way was just common, ordinary stars, and was put
where it was because God "wanted to hev it so," the admirable idea fell
perfectly flat.

As a literary artist, M. Bourget is as fresh and striking as he is as a
scientific one. He says, "Above all, I do not believe much in anecdotes."
Why? "In history they are all false"—a sufficiently broad statement—
"in literature all libelous"—also a sufficiently sweeping statement, coming from a critic who notes that we are a people who are peculiarly
extravagant in our language—"and when it is a matter of social life,
almost all biased." It seems to amount to stultification, almost. He has
built two or three breeds of American coquettes out of anecdotes—
mainly "biased" ones, I suppose; and, as they occur "in literature," furnished by his pen, they must be "all libelous." Or did he mean not *in*
literature or anecdotes *about* literature or literary people? I am not
able to answer that. Perhaps the original would be clearer, but I have
only the translation of this instalment by me. I think the remark had
an intention; also that this intention was booked for the trip; but that
either in the hurry of the remark's departure it got left, or in the confusion of changing cars at the translator's frontier it got side-tracked.

"But on the other hand I believe in statistics; and those on divorces appear to me to be most conclusive." And he sets himself the task of explaining—in a couple of columns—the process by which Easy-Divorce conceived, invented, originated, developed, and perfected an empire-embracing condition of sexual purity in the States. *In forty years.* No, he doesn't state the interval. With all his passion for statistics he forgot to ask how long it took to produce this gigantic miracle.

I have followed his pleasant but devious trail through those columns, but I was not able to get hold of his argument and find out what it was. I was not even able to find out where it left off. It seemed to gradually dissolve and flow off into other matters. I followed it with interest, for I was anxious to learn how easy-divorce eradicated adultery in America, but I was disappointed; I have no idea yet how it did it. I only know it didn't. But that is not valuable; I knew it before.

Well, humor is the great thing, the saving thing, after all. The minute it crops up, all our hardnesses yield, all our irritations and resentments flit away, and a sunny spirit takes their place. And so, when M. Bourget said that bright thing about our grandfathers, I broke all up. I remember exploding its American countermine once, under that grand hero, Napoleon. He was only First Consul then, and I was Consul-General—for the United States, of course; but we were very intimate, notwithstanding the difference in rank, for I waived that. One day something offered the opening, and he said:

"Well, General, I suppose life can never get entirely dull to an American, because whenever he can't strike up any other way to put in his time he can always get away with a few years trying to find out who his grandfather was!"

I fairly shouted, for I had never heard it sound better; and then I was back at him as quick as a flash:

"Right, your Excellency! But I reckon a Frenchman's got *his* little stand-by for a dull time, too; because when all other interests fail he can turn in and see if he can't find out who his father was!"

Well, you should have heard him just whoop, and cackle, and carry on! He reached up and hit me one on the shoulder, and says:

"Land, but it's good! It's im-mensely good! I'George, I never heard it said so good in my life before! Say it again."

So I said it again, and he said his again, and I said mine again, and then he did, and then I did, and then he did, and we kept on doing it, and doing it, and I *never* had such a good time, and he said the same. In my opinion there isn't anything that is as killing as one of those dear old ripe pensioners if you know how to snatch it out in a kind of a fresh sort of original way.

But I wish M. Bourget had read more of our novels before he came. It is the only way to thoroughly understand a people. When I found I was coming to Paris, I read *La Terre*.[2]

1895

A Little Note to M. Paul Bourget

[The preceding squib was assailed in *The North American Review* in an article entitled "Mark Twain and Paul Bourget," by Max O'Rell. The following little note is a Rejoinder to that article. It is possible that the position assumed here—that M. Bourget dictated the O'Rell article himself—is untenable.]

You have every right, my dear M. Bourget, to retort upon me by dictation, if you prefer that method to writing at me with your pen; but if I may say it without hurt—and certainly I mean no offense—I believe you would have acquitted yourself better with the pen. With the pen you are at home; it is your natural weapon; you use it with grace, eloquence, charm, persuasiveness, when men are to be convinced, and with formidable effect when they have earned a castigation. But I am sure I see signs in the above article that you are either unaccustomed to dictating or are out of practice. If you will reread it you will notice, yourself, that it lacks definiteness; that it lacks purpose; that it lacks coherence; that it lacks a subject to talk about; that it is loose and wabbly; that it wanders around; that it loses itself early and does not find itself any more. There are some other defects as you will notice, but I think I have named the main ones. I feel sure that they are all due to your lack of practice in dictating.

Inasmuch as you had not signed it I had the impression at first that you had not dictated it. But only for a moment. Certain quite simple and definite facts reminded me that the article *had* to come from you, for the reason that it could not come from any one else without a specific invitation from you or from me. I mean, it could not except as an intrusion, a transgression of the law which forbids strangers to mix into a private dispute between friends, unasked.

[2] A novel by Zola. Bourget wrote a novel called *La Terre promise*.—C.N.

Those simple and definite facts were these: I had published an article in this magazine, with you for my subject; just you yourself; I stuck strictly to that one subject, and did not interlard any other. No one, of course, could call me to account but you alone, or your authorized representative. I asked some questions—asked them of myself. I answered them myself. My article was thirteen pages long, and all devoted to you; devoted to you, and divided up in this way: one page of guesses as to what subjects you would instruct us in, as teacher; one page of doubts as to the effectiveness of your method of examining us and our ways; two or three pages of criticism of your method, and of certain results which it furnished you; two or three pages of attempts to show the justness of these same criticisms; half a dozen pages made up of slight fault-findings with certain minor details of your literary workmanship, of extracts from your *Outre-Mer* and comments upon them; then I closed with an anecdote. I repeat—for certain reasons— that I *closed with an anecdote.*

When I was asked by this magazine if I wished to "answer" a "reply" to that article of mine, I said "yes," and waited in Paris for the proof-sheets of the "reply" to come. I already knew, by the cablegram, that the "reply" would not be signed by you, but upon reflection I knew it would be dictated by you, because no volunteer would feel himself at liberty to assume your championship in a private dispute, unasked, in view of the fact that you are quite well able to take care of your matters of that sort yourself and are not in need of any one's help. No, a volunteer could not make such a venture. It would be too immodest. Also too gratuitously generous. And a shade too self-sufficient. No, he could not venture it. It would look too much like anxiety to get in at a feast where no plate had been provided for him. In fact he could not get in at all, except by the back way, and with a false key; that is to say, a pretext—a pretext invented for the occasion by putting into my mouth words which I did not use, and by wresting sayings of mine from their plain and true meaning. Would he resort to methods like those to get in? No; there are no people of that kind. So then I knew for a certainty that you dictated the Reply yourself. I knew you did it to save yourself manual labor.

And you had the right, as I have already said; and I am content— perfectly content. Yet it would have been little trouble to you, and a great kindness to me, if you had written your Reply all out with your own capable hand.

Because then it would have replied—and that is really what a Reply is for. Broadly speaking, its function is to refute—as you will easily concede. That leaves something for the other person to take hold of: he has a chance to reply to the Reply, he has a chance to refute the refutation. This would have happened if you had written it out instead of dictating. Dictating is nearly sure to unconcentrate the dictator's mind, when he is out of practice, confuse him, and betray him into using one set of literary rules when he ought to use a quite different set. Often it betrays him into employing the RULES FOR CONVERSATION BETWEEN A SHOUTER AND A DEAF PERSON—as in the present case—when he ought to employ the RULES FOR CONDUCTING DISCUSSION WITH A FAULT-FINDER. The great foundation-rule and basic principle of discussion with a fault-finder is relevancy and concentration upon the subject; whereas the great foundation-rule and basic principle governing conversation between a shouter and a deaf person is irrelevancy and persistent desertion of the topic in hand. If I may be allowed to illustrate by quoting example IV., section 7, from chapter ix of "Revised Rules for Conducting Conversation between a Shouter and a Deaf Person," it will assist us in getting a clear idea of the difference between the two sets of rules:

Shouter. Did you say his name is WETHERBY?

Deaf Person. Change? Yes, I think it will. Though if it should clear off I—

Shouter. It's his NAME I want—his NAME.

Deaf Person. Maybe so, maybe so; but it will only be a shower, I think.

Shouter. No, no, *no!*—you have quite misunderSTOOD me. If—

Deaf Person. Ah! GOOD morning; I am sorry you must go. But call again, and let me continue to be of assistance to you in every way I can.

You see it is a perfect kodak of the article you have dictated. It is really curious and interesting when you come to compare it with yours; in detail, with my former article to which it is a Reply in your hand. I talk twelve pages about your American instruction projects, and your doubtful scientific system, and your painstaking classification of non-existent things, and your diligence and zeal and sincerity, and your disloyal attitude toward anecdotes, and your undue reverence for unsafe statistics and for facts that lack a pedigree; and you turn around and come back at me with eight pages of weather.

I do not see how a person can act so. It is good of you to repeat, with change of language, in the bulk of your rejoinder, so much of my own article, and adopt my sentiments, and make them over, and put new buttons on; and I like the compliment, and am frank to say so; but *agreeing* with a person cripples controversy and ought not to be allowed. It is weather; and of almost the worst sort. It pleases me greatly to hear you discourse with such approval and expansiveness upon my text:

"A foreigner can photograph the exteriors of a nation, but I think that is as far as he can get. I think that no foreigner can report its interior";[1] which is a quite clear way of saying that a foreigner's report is only valuable when it restricts itself to *impressions*. It pleases me to have you follow my lead in that glowing way, but it leaves me nothing to combat. You should give me something to deny and refute; I would do as much for you.

It pleases me to have you playfully warn the public against taking one of your books seriously.[2] Because I used to do that cunning thing myself in earlier days. I did it in a prefatory note to a book of mine called *Tom Sawyer*.[3]

NOTICE

Persons attempting to find a motive in this narrative will be prosecuted; persons attempting to find a moral in it will be banished; persons attempting to find a plot in it will be shot.

BY ORDER OF THE AUTHOR,
PER G. G., CHIEF OF ORDNANCE.

The kernel is the same in both prefaces, you see—the public must not take us too seriously. If we remove that kernel we remove the life-principle, and the preface is a corpse. Yes, it pleases me to have you use that idea, for it is a high compliment. But it leaves me nothing to combat; and that is damage to me.

Am I seeming to say that your Reply is not a reply at all, M. Bourget? If so, I must modify that; it is too sweeping. For you have furnished a general answer to my inquiry as to what France—through you—can

[1] And you say: "A man of average intelligence, who has passed six months among a people, cannot express opinions that are worth jotting down, but he can form impressions that are worth repeating. For my part, I think that foreigners' impressions are more interesting than native opinions. After all, such impressions merely mean 'how the country *struck* the foreigner.'"
[2] "When I published *Jonathan and His Continent*, I wrote in a preface addressed to Jonathan: 'If ever you should insist on seeing in this little volume a serious study of your country and of your countrymen, I warn you that your world-wide fame for humor will be exploded.'"
[3] A curious slip. He meant *Huckleberry Finn*.—C.N.

teach us.[4] It is a good answer. It relates to manners, customs, and morals—three things concerning which we can never have exhaustive and determinate statistics, and so the verdicts delivered upon them must always lack conclusiveness and be subject to revision; but you have stated the truth, possibly, as nearly as any one could do it, in the circumstances. But why did you choose a detail of my question which could be answered only with vague hearsay evidence, and go right by one which could have been answered with deadly facts?— facts in everybody's reach, facts which none can dispute. I asked what France could teach us about government. I laid myself pretty wide open, there; and I thought I was handsomely generous, too, when I did it. France can teach us how to levy village and city taxes which distribute the burden with a nearer approach to perfect fairness than is the case in any other land; and she can teach us the wisest and surest system of collecting them that exists. She can teach us how to elect a President in a sane way; and also how to do it without throwing the country into earthquakes and convulsions that cripple and embarrass business, stir up party hatred in the hearts of men, and make peaceful people wish the term extended to thirty years. France can teach us—but enough of that part of the question. And what else can France teach us? She can teach us all the fine arts—and does. She throws open her hospitable art academies, and says to us, "Come"— and we come, troops and troops of our young and gifted; and she sets over us the ablest masters in the world and bearing the greatest names;

[4] " 'What could France teach America?' exclaims Mark Twain. France can teach America all the higher pursuits of life, and there is more artistic feeling and refinement in a street of French workingmen than in many avenues inhabited by American millionaires. She can teach her, not perhaps how to work, but how to rest, how to live, how to be happy. She can teach her that the aim of life is not money-making, but that money-making is only a means to obtain an end. She can teach her that wives are not expensive toys, but useful partners, friends, and confidants, who should always keep men under their wholesome influence by their diplomacy, their tact, their common sense, without bumptiousness. These qualities, added to the highest standard of morality (not angular and morose, but cheerful morality), are conceded to Frenchwomen by whoever knows something of French life outside of the Paris boulevards, and Mark Twain's ill-natured sneer cannot even so much as stain them.
I might tell Mark Twain that in France a man who was seen tipsy in his club would immediately see his name canceled from membership. A man who had settled his fortune on his wife to avoid meeting his creditors would be refused admission into any decent society. Many a Frenchman has blown his brains out rather than declare himself a bankrupt. Now would Mark Twain remark to this: 'An American is not such a fool: when a creditor stands in his way he closes his doors, and reopens them the following day. When he has been a bankrupt three times he can retire from business'?"

and she teaches us all that we are capable of learning, and persuades us and encourages us with prizes and honors, much as if we were somehow children of her own; and when this noble education is finished and we are ready to carry it home and spread its gracious ministries abroad over our nation, and we come with homage and gratitude and ask France for the bill—*there is nothing to pay.* And in return for this imperial generosity, what does America do? She charges a duty on French works of art!

I wish I had your end of this dispute; I should have something worth talking about. If you would only furnish me something to argue, something to refute—but you persistently won't. You leave good chances unutilized and spend your strength in proving and establishing unimportant things. For instance, you have proven and established these eight facts here following—a good score as to number, but not worth while:

Mark Twain is—

1. "Insulting."
2. (Sarcastically speaking) "This refined humorist."
3. Prefers the manure-pile to the violets.
4. Has uttered "an ill-natured sneer."
5. Is "nasty."
6. Needs a "lesson in politeness and good manners."
7. Has published a "nasty article."
8. Has made remarks "unworthy of a gentleman."[5] These are all true, but really they are not valuable; no one cares much for such finds. In our American magazines we recognize this and suppress them. We avoid naming them. American writers never allow themselves to name them. It would look as if they were in a temper, and we hold that exhibitions of temper in public are not good form—except in the very young and inexperienced. And even if we had the disposition to name them, in order to fill up a gap when we were short of ideas and arguments, our magazines would not allow us to do it, because they think

[5] "It is more funny than his [Mark Twain's] anecdote, and would have been less insulting."

A quoted remark of mine "is a gross insult to a nation friendly to America."
"He has read *La Terre*, this refined humorist."
"When Mark Twain visits a garden . . . he goes in the far-away corner where the soil is prepared."
"Mark Twain's ill-natured sneer cannot so much as stain them" (the French women).
"When he [Mark Twain] takes his revenge he is unkind, unfair, bitter, nasty."

that such words sully their pages. This present magazine is particularly strenuous about it. Its note to me announcing the forwarding of your proof-sheets to France closed thus—for your protection:

"It is needless to ask you to avoid anything that he might consider as personal."

It was well enough, as a measure of precaution, but really it was not needed. You can trust me implicitly, M. Bourget; I shall never call you any names in print which I should be ashamed to call you with your unoffending and dearest ones present.

Indeed, we are reserved, and particular in America to a degree which you would consider exaggerated. For instance, we should not write notes like that one of yours to a lady for a small fault—or a large one.[6] We should not think it kind. No matter how much we might have

---

"But not even your nasty article on my country, Mark," etc.

"Mark might certainly have derived from it [M. Bourget's book] a lesson in politeness and good manners."

A quoted remark of mine is "unworthy of a gentleman."

[6] "When M. Paul Bourget indulges in a little chaffing at the expense of the Americans, 'who can always get away with a few years' trying to find out who their grandfathers were,' he merely makes an allusion to an American foible; but, forsooth, what a kind man, what a humorist Mark Twain is when he retorts by calling France a nation of bastards! How the Americans of culture and refinement will admire him for thus speaking in their name!

"Snobbery. . . . I could give Mark Twain an example of the American specimen. It is a piquant story. I never published it because I feared my readers might think that I was giving them a typical illustration of American character instead of a rare exception.

"I was once booked by my manager to give a *causerie* in the drawing-room of a New York millionaire. I accepted with reluctance. I do not like private engagements. At five o'clock on the day the *causerie* was to be given, the lady sent to my manager to say that she would expect me to arrive at nine o'clock and to speak for about an hour. Then she wrote a postscript. Many women are unfortunate there. Their minds are full of afterthoughts, and the most important part of their letters is generally to be found after their signature. This lady's P.S. ran thus: 'I suppose he will not expect to be entertained after the lecture.'

"I fairly shouted, as Mark Twain would say, and then, indulging myself in a bit of snobbishness, I was back at her as quick as a flash—

"'Dear Madam: As a literary man of some reputation, I have many times had the pleasure of being entertained by the members of the old aristocracy of France. I have also many times had the pleasure of being entertained by the members of the old aristocracy of England. If it may interest you, I can even tell you that I have several times had the honor of being entertained by royalty; but my ambition has never been so wild as to expect that one day I might be entertained by the aristocracy of New York. No, I do not expect to be entertained by you, nor do I want you to expect me to entertain you and your friends tonight, for I decline to keep the engagement.'

"Now, I could fill a book on America with reminiscences of this sort, adding a few chapters on bosses and boodlers, on New York *chronique scandaleuse,* on

associated with kings and nobilities, we should not think it right to
crush her with it and make her ashamed of her lowlier walk in life; for
we have a saying, "Who humiliates my mother includes his own."

Do I seriously imagine you to be the author of that strange letter,
M. Bourget? Indeed I do not. I believe it to have been surreptitiously
inserted by your amanuensis when your back was turned. I think he
did it with a good motive, expecting it to add force and piquancy to
your article, but it does not reflect your nature, and I know it will
grieve you when you see it. I also think he interlarded many other
things which you will disapprove of when you see them. I am certain
that all the harsh names discharged at me come from him, not you.
No doubt you could have proved me entitled to them with as little
trouble as it has cost him to do it, but it would have been your disposition to hunt game of a higher quality.

Why, I even doubt if it is you who furnish me all that excellent information about Balzac and those others.[7] All this in simple justice
to you—and to me; for, to gravely accept those interlardings as yours
would be to wrong your head and heart, and at the same time convict
myself of being equipped with a vacancy where my penetration ought
to be lodged.

And now finally I must uncover the secret pain, the wee sore from
which the Reply grew—*the anecdote which closed my recent article*
—and consider how it is that this pimple has spread to these cancerous
dimensions. If any but you had dictated the Reply, M. Bourget, I would
know that that anecdote was twisted around and its intention magnified some hundreds of times, in order that it might be used as a

---

the tenement houses of the large cities, on the gambling-hells of Denver, and
the dens of San Francisco, and what not! But not even your nasty article on
my country, Mark, will make me do it."

[7] "Now the style of M. Bourget and many other French writers is apparently
a closed letter to Mark Twain; but let us leave that alone. Has he read Erck-
mann-Chatrian, Victor Hugo, Lamartine, Edmond About, Cherbuliez, Renan?
Has he read Gustave Droz's *Monsieur, Madame, et Bébé,* and those books which
leave for a long time a perfume about you? Has he read the novels of Alexandre
Dumas, Eugène Sue, George Sand, and Balzac? Has he read Victor Hugo's *Les
Misérables* and *Notre Dame de Paris?* Has he read or heard the plays of Sandeau,
Augier, Dumas, and Sardou, the works of those Titans of modern literature, whose
names will be household words all over the world for hundreds of years to
come? He has read *La Terre*—this kind-hearted, refined humorist! When Mark
Twain visits a garden does he smell the violets, the roses, the jasmine, or the
honeysuckle? No, he goes in the far-away corner where the soil is prepared.
Hear what he says: 'I wish M. Paul Bourget had read more of our novels before
he came. It is the only way to thoroughly understand a people. When I found
I was coming to Paris I read *La Terre.*'"

pretext to creep in the back way. But I accuse you of nothing—nothing but error. When you say that I "retort by calling France a nation of bastards," it is an error. And not a small one, but a large one. I made no such remark, nor anything resembling it. Moreover, the magazine would not have allowed me to use so gross a word as that.

You told an anecdote. A funny one—I admit that. It hit a foible of our American aristocracy, and it stung me—I admit that; it stung me sharply. It was like this: You found some ancient portraits of French kings in the gallery of one of our aristocracy, and you said:

"He has the Grand Monarch, but *where is the portrait of his grandfather?*" That is, the American aristocrat's grandfather.

Now that hits only a few of us, I grant—just the upper crust only—but it hits exceedingly hard.

I wondered if there was any way of getting back at you. In one of your chapters I found this chance:

"In our high Parisian existence, for instance, we find applied to arts and luxury, and to debauchery, all the powers and all the weaknesses of the French soul."

You see? Your "higher Parisian" class—not everybody, not the nation, but only the *top crust* of the nation—*applies to debauchery all the powers of its soul.*

I argued to myself that that energy must produce results. So I built an anecdote out of your remark. In it I make Napoleon Bonaparte say to me—but see for yourself the anecdote (ingeniously clipped and curtailed) in paragraph eleven of your Reply.[8]

[8] "So, I repeat, Mark Twain does not like M. Paul Bourget's book. So long as he makes light fun of the great French writer he is at home, he is pleasant, he is the American humorist we know. When he takes his revenge (and where is the reason for taking a revenge?) he is unkind, unfair, bitter, nasty.
"For example:
"See his answer to a Frenchman who jokingly remarks to him:
" 'I suppose life can never get entirely dull to an American, because whenever he can't strike up any other way to put in his time, he can always get away with a few years trying to find out who his grandfather was.'
"Hear the answer:
" 'I reckon a Frenchman's got *his* little standby for a dull time, too; because when all other interests fail, he can turn in and see if he can't find out who his father was.'
"The first remark is a good-humored bit of chaffing on American snobbery. I may be utterly destitute of humor, but I call the second remark a gratuitous charge of immorality hurled at the French women—a remark unworthy of a man who has the ear of the public, unworthy of a gentleman, a gross insult to a nation friendly to America, a nation that helped Mark Twain's ancestors

Now, then, your anecdote about the grandfathers hurt me. Why? Because it had a *point*. It wouldn't have hurt me if it hadn't had point. You wouldn't have wasted space on it if it hadn't had point.

My anecdote has hurt you. Why? Because it had point, I suppose. It wouldn't have hurt you if it hadn't had point. I judged from your remark about the diligence and industry of the high Parisian upper crust that it would have *some* point, but really I had no idea what a gold-mine I had struck. I never suspected that the point was going to stick into the entire nation; but of course you know your nation better than I do, and if you think it punctures them all, I have to yield to your judgment. But you are to blame, your own self. Your remark misled me. I supposed the industry was confined to that little unnumerous upper layer.

Well, now that the unfortunate thing has been done, let us do what we can to undo it. There must be a way, M. Bourget, and I am willing to do anything that will help; for I am as sorry as you can be yourself.

I will tell you what I think will be the very thing. We will *swap anecdotes*. I will take your anecdote and you take mine. I will say to the dukes and counts and princes of the ancient nobility of France:

"Ha, ha! You must have a pretty hard time trying to find out who your grandfathers were?"

They will merely smile indifferently and not feel hurt, because they can trace their lineage back through centuries.

And you will hurl mine at every individual in the American nation, saying:

"And *you* must have a pretty hard time trying to find out who your *fathers* were." They will merely smile indifferently, and not feel hurt, because they haven't any difficulty in finding their fathers.

Do you get the idea? The whole harm in the anecdotes is in the *point*, you see; and when we swap them around that way, they *haven't* any.

That settles it perfectly and beautifully, and I am glad I thought of it. I am very glad indeed, M. Bourget; for it was just that little wee

---

in their struggle for liberty, a nation where to-day it is enough to say that you are American to see every door open wide to you.

"If Mark Twain was hard up in search of a French 'chestnut,' I might have told him the following little anecdote. It is more funny than his, and would have been less insulting: Two little street boys are abusing each other. 'Ah, hold your tongue,' says one, 'you ain't got no father.'

"'Ain't got no father!' replied the other; 'I've got more fathers than you.'"

thing that caused the whole difficulty and made you dictate the Reply, and your amanuensis call me all those hard names which the magazines dislike so. And I did it all in fun, too, trying to cap your funny anecdote with another one—on the give-and-take principle, you know—which is American. *I* didn't know that with the French it was all give and no take, and you didn't tell me. But now that I have made everything comfortable again, and fixed both anecdotes so they can never have any point any more, I know you will forgive me.

1896

Queen Victoria's Jubilee

So far as I can see, a procession has value in but two ways—as a show and as a symbol; its minor function being to delight the eye, its major one to compel thought, exalt the spirit, stir the heart, and inflame the imagination. As a mere show, and meaningless—like a Mardi-Gras march—a magnificent procession is a sight worth a long journey to see; as a symbol, the most colorless and unpicturesque procession, if it have a moving history back of it, is worth a thousand of it.

After the Civil War ten regiments of bronzed New York veterans marched up Broadway in faded uniforms and bearing faded battle flags that were mere shot-riddled rags—and in each battalion as it swung by, one noted a great gap, an eloquent vacancy where had marched the comrades who had fallen and would march no more! Always, as this procession advanced between the massed multitudes, its approach was welcomed by each block of people with a burst of proud and grateful enthusiasm—then the head of it passed, and suddenly revealed those pathetic gaps, and silence fell upon that block; for every man in it had choked up, and could not get command of his voice and add it to the storm again for many minutes. That was the most moving and tremendous effect that I have ever witnessed—those affecting silences falling between those hurricanes of worshiping enthusiasm.

There was no costumery in that procession, no color, no tinsel, no brilliancy, yet it was the greatest spectacle and the most gracious and exalting and beautiful that has come within my experience. It was because it had history back of it, and because it was a symbol, and stood for something, and because one viewed it with the spiritual vision, not the physical. There was not much for the physical eye to see, but it revealed continental areas, limitless horizons, to the eye of the imagination and the spirit.

A procession, to be valuable, must do one thing or the other—clothe itself in splendors and charm the eye, or symbolize something sublime and uplifting, and so appeal to the imagination. As a mere spectacle to look at, I suppose that the Queen's procession will not be as showy as the Tsar's late pageant; it will probably fall much short of the one in Tannhäuser in the matter of rich and adorable costumery; in the number of renowned personages on view in it, it will probably fall short of some that have been seen in England before this. And yet in its major function, its symbolic function, I think that if all the people in it wore their everyday clothes and marched without flags or music, it would still be incomparably the most memorable and most important procession that ever moved through the streets of London.

For it will stand for English history, English growth, English achievement, the accumulated power and renown and dignity of twenty centuries of strenuous effort. Many things about it will set one to reflecting upon what a large feature of this world England is to-day, and this will in turn move one, even the least imaginative, to cast a glance down her long perspective and note the steps of her progress and the insignificance of her first estate. In this matter London is itself a suggestive object lesson.

I suppose that London has always existed. One cannot easily imagine an England that had no London. No doubt there was a village here 5,000 years ago. It was on the river somewhere west of where the Tower is now; it was built of thatched mud huts close to a couple of limpid brooks, and on every hand for miles and miles stretched rolling plains of fresh green grass, and here and there were groups and groves of trees. The tribes wore skins—sometimes merely their own, sometimes those of other animals. The chief was monarch, and helped out his complexion with blue paint. His industry was the chase; his relaxation was war. Some of the Englishmen who will view the procession to-day are carrying his ancient blood in their veins.

It may be that that village remained about as it began, away down to the Roman occupation, a couple of thousand years ago. It was still not much of a town when Alfred burned the cakes. Even when the Conqueror first saw it, it did not amount to much. I think it must have been short of distinguished architecture or he would not have traveled down into the country to the village of Westminster to get crowned. If you skip down 350 years further you will find a London of some little consequence, but I believe that that is as much as you can say for it. Still, I am interested in that London, for it saw the first of two processions which will live longer than any others in English history, I think; the date of the one is 1415, that of the other is 1897.

The compactly built part of the London of 1415 was a narrow strip not a mile long, which stretched east and west through the middle of what is now called "the City." The houses were densest in the region of Cheapside. South of the strip were scattering residences which stood in turfy lawns which sloped to the river. North of the strip, fields and country homes extended to the walls. Let us represent that London by three checker-board squares placed in a row; then open out a New York newspaper like a book, and the space which it covers will properly represent the London of to-day by comparison. It is the difference between your hand and a blanket. It is possible that that ancient London had 100,000 inhabitants, and that 100,000 outsiders came to town to see the procession. The present London contains five or six million inhabitants, and it has been calculated that the population has jumped to 10,000,000 to-day.

The pageant of 1415 was to celebrate the gigantic victory of Agincourt, then and still the most colossal in England's history.

From that day to this there had been nothing that even approached it but Plassey. It was the third and greatest in the series of monster victories won by the English over the French in the Hundred Years' War—Crecy, Poitiers, Agincourt. At Agincourt, according to history, 15,000 English, under Henry V, defeated and routed an army of 100,000 French. Sometimes history makes it 8,000 English and 60,000 French; but no matter, in both cases the proportions are preserved. Eight thousand of the French nobility were slain and the rest of the order taken prisoners—1,500 in number—among them the Dukes of Orléans and Bourbon and Marshal Boucicaut; and the victory left the whole northern half of France an English possession. This wholesale depletion of the aristocracy made such a stringent scarcity in its ranks that when the young peasant girl, Joan of Arc, came to undo Henry's mighty work fourteen years later she could hardly gather together nobles enough to man her staff.

The battle of Agincourt was fought on the 25th of October, and a few days later the tremendous news was percolating through England. Presently it was sweeping the country like a tidal wave, like a cyclone, like a conflagration. Choose your own figure, there is no metaphor known to the language that can exaggerate the tempest of joy and pride and exultation that burst everywhere along the progress of that great news.

The king came home and brought his soldiers with him—he and they the idols of the nation, now. He brought his 1,500 captive knights and nobles, too—we shall not see any such output of blue blood as that to-day, bond or free. The king rested three weeks in his palace, the Tower of London, while the people made preparations and prepared the welcome due him. On the 22d of December all was ready.

There were no cables, no correspondents, no newspapers then—a regrettable defect, but not irremediable. A young man who would have been a correspondent if he had been born 500 years later was in London at the time, and he remembers the details. He has communicated them to me through a competent spirit medium, phrased in a troublesome mixture of obsolete English and moldy French, and I have thoroughly modernized his story and put it into straight English, and will here record it. I will explain that his Sir John Oldcastle is a person whom we do not know very well by that name, nor much care for; but we know him well and adore him, too, under his other name—Sir John Falstaff. Also, I will remark that two miles of the Queen's progress to-day will be over ground traversed by the procession of Henry V; all solid bricks and mortar, now, but open country in Henry's day, and clothed in that unapproachable beauty which has been the monopoly of sylvan England since the creation. Ah, where now are those long-vanished forms, those unreturning feet! Let us not inquire too closely. Translated, this is the narrative of the spirit-correspondent, who is looking down upon me at this moment from his high home, and admiring to see how the art and mystery of spelling has improved since his time!

NARRATIVE OF THE SPIRIT CORRESPONDENT

I was commanded by my lord the Lord Mayor to make a report for the archives, and was furnished with a fleet horse, and with a paper permitting me to go anywhere at my will, without let or hindrance, even up and down the processional route, though no other person not of the procession itself was allowed this unique privilege during the whole of the 21st and the 22d.

On the morning of the 22d, toward noon, I rode from the Tower into the city, and through it as far as St. Paul's. All the way, on both sides, all the windows, balconies, and roofs were crowded with people, and wherever there was a vacancy it had been built up in high tiers of seats covered with red cloth, and these seats were also filled with people—in all cases in bright holiday attire—the woman of fashion barring the view from all in the rear with those tiresome extinguisher hats, which of late have grown to be a cloth-yard high. From every balcony depended silken stuffs of splendid and various colors, and figured and pictured rich tapestries. It was brisk, sharp weather, but a rare one for sun, and when one looked down this swinging double wall of beautiful fabrics, glowing and flashing and changing color like prisms in the flooding light, it was a most fair sight to see. And there were frequent May poles, garlanded to their tops, and from the tops swung sheaves of silken long ribbons of all bright colors, which in the light breeze writhed and twisted and prettily mingled themselves together.

I rode solitary—in state, as it might be—and was envied, as I could see, and did not escape comment, but had a plenty of it; for the conduits were running gratis wine, and the results were accumulating. I got many ribald compliments on my riding, on my clothes, on my office. Everybody was happy, so it was best to seem so myself, which I did— for those people's aim was better than their eggs.

A place had been reserved for me on a fine and fanciful erection in St. Paul's Churchyard, and there I waited for the procession. It seemed a long time, but at last a dull booming sound arose in the distance, and after a while we saw the banners and the head of the procession come into view, and heard the muffled roar of voices that welcomed it. The roar moved continuously toward us, growing steadily louder and louder, and stronger and stronger, and with it the bray and crash of music; and presently it was right with us, and seemed to roll over us and submerge us, and stun us, and deafen us—and behold, there was the hero of Agincourt passing by!

All the multitude was standing up, red-faced, frantic, bellowing, shouting, the tears running down their faces; and through the storm of waving hats and handkerchiefs one glimpsed the battle banners and the drifting host of marching men as though a dimming flurry of snow.

The king, tall, slender, handsome, rode with his visor up, that all might see his face. He was clad in his silver armor from head to heel, and had his great two-handed sword at his side, his battle-ax at his pommel, his shield upon his arm, and about his helmet waved and tossed a white mass of fluffy plumes. On either side of him rode the captive dukes, plumed like himself, but wearing long crimson satin gowns over their armor; after these came the French marshal similarly

habited; after him followed the fifteen hundred French knights, with
robes of various colors over their armor, and with each two rode two
English knights, sometimes robed in various colors, sometimes in white
with a red cross on the shoulder, these white-clad ones being Knights
Templars. Every man of the three thousand bore his shield upon his
left arm, newly polished and burnished, and on it was his device.

As the king passed the church he bowed his head and lifted his
shield, and by one impulse all the knights did the same; and so as far
down the line as the eye could reach one saw the lifted shields simultaneously catch the sun, and it was like a sudden mile-long shaft of
flashing light; and, Lord! it lit up that dappled sea of color with a glory
like "the golden vortex in the west over the foundered sun"! (The introduction of this quotation is very interesting, for it shows that our
literature of to-day has a circulation in heaven—pirated editions, no
doubt.—M.T.)

The knights were a long time in passing; then came 5,000 Agincourt
men-at-arms, and they were a long time; and at the very end, last of
all, came that intolerable old tun of sack and godless ruffler, Sir John
Oldcastle (now risen from the dead for the third time), fat-faced, purple with the spirit of bygone and lamented drink, smiling his hospitable,
wide smile upon all the world, leering at the women, wallowing about
in his saddle, proclaiming his valorous deeds as fast as he could lie,
taking the whole glory of Agincourt to his single self, measuring off the
miles of his slain and then multiplying them by 5, 7, 10, 15, as inspiration after inspiration came to his help—the most inhuman spectacle in
England, a living, breathing outrage, a slander upon the human race;
and after him came, mumming and blethering, his infamous lieutenants; and after them his "paladins," as he calls them, the mangiest lot
of starvelings and cowards that was ever littered, the disgrace of the
noblest pageant that England has ever seen. God rest their souls in the
place appointed for all such!

There was a moment of prayer at the Temple, the procession moved
down the country road, its way walled on both sides by welcoming
multitudes, and so, by Charing Cross, and at last to the Abbey for the
great ceremonies. It was a grand day, and will remain in men's memories.

That was as much of it as the spirit correspondent could let me
have; he was obliged to stop there because he had an engagement to
sing in the choir, and was already late.

The contrast between that old England and the present England is one of the things which will make the pageant of the present day impressive and thought-breeding. The contrast between the England of the Queen's reign and the England of any previous British reign is also an impressive thing. British history is two thousand years old, and yet in a good many ways the world has moved further ahead since the Queen was born than it moved in all the rest of the two thousand put together. A large part of this progress has been moral, but naturally the material part of it is the most striking and the easiest to measure. Since the Queen first saw the light she has seen invented and brought into use (with the exception of the cotton gin, the spinning frames, and the steamboat) every one of the myriad of strictly modern inventions which, by their united powers, have created the bulk of the modern civilization and made life under it easy and difficult, convenient and awkward, happy and horrible, soothing and irritating, grand and trivial, an indispensable blessing and an unimaginable curse—she has seen all these miracles, these wonders, these marvels piled up in her time, and yet she is but seventy-eight years old. That is to say, she has seen more things invented than any other monarch that ever lived; and more than the oldest old-time English commoner that ever lived, including Old Parr; and more than Methuselah himself—five times over.

Some of the details of the moral advancement which she has seen are also very striking and easily graspable.

She has seen the English criminal laws prodigiously modified, and seen capital crimes swept from the statute book.

She has seen English liberty greatly broadened—the governing and lawmaking powers, formerly the possession of the few, extended to the body of the people, and purchase in the army abolished.

She has seen the public educator—the newspaper—created, and its teachings placed within the reach of the leanest purse. There was nothing properly describable as a newspaper until long after she was born.

She has seen the world's literature set free, through the institution of international copyright.

She has seen America invent arbitration, the eventual substitute for that enslaver of nations, the standing army; and she has seen England pay the first bill under it, and America shirk the second—but only temporarily; of this we may be sure.

She has seen a Hartford American (Doctor Wells) apply anaesthetics in surgery for the first time in history, and for all time banish the terrors of the surgeon's knife; and she has seen the rest of the world ignore the discoverer and a Boston doctor steal the credit of his work.

She has seen medical science and scientific sanitation cut down the

death rate of civilized cities by more than half, and she has seen these
agencies set bounds to the European march of the cholera and imprison
the Black Death in its own home.

She has seen woman freed from the oppression of many burdensome
and unjust laws; colleges established for her; privileged to earn degrees
in men's colleges—but not get them; in some regions rights accorded
to her which lifted her near to political equality with man, and a hundred bread-winning occupations found for her where hardly one existed
before—among them medicine, the law, and professional nursing. The
Queen has herself recognized merit in her sex; of the 501 lordships
which she has conferred in sixty years, one was upon a woman.

The Queen has seen the right to organize trade unions extended to
the workman, after that right had been the monopoly of guilds of masters for six hundred years.

She has seen the workman rise into political notice, then into political force, then (in some parts of the world) into the chief and commanding political force; she has seen the day's labor of twelve, fourteen, and eighteen hours reduced to eight, a reform which has made
labor a means of extending life instead of a means of committing
salaried suicide.

But it is useless to continue the list—it has no end.

There will be complexions in the procession to-day which will suggest the vast distances to which the British dominion has extended
itself around the fat rotundity of the globe since Britain was a remote
unknown back settlement of savages with tin for sale, two or three
thousand years ago; and also how great a part of this extension is comparatively recent; also, how surprisingly speakers of the English tongue
have increased within the Queen's time.

When the Queen was born there were not more than 25,000,000
English-speaking people in the world; there are about 120,000,000 now.
The other long-reign queen, Elizabeth, ruled over a short 100,000
square miles of territory and perhaps 5,000,000 subjects; Victoria reigns
over more territory than any other sovereign in the world's history ever
reigned over; her estate covers a fourth part of the habitable area of the
globe, and her subjects number about 400,000,000.

It is indeed a mighty estate, and I perceive now that the English
are mentioned in the Bible:

"Blessed are the meek, for they shall inherit the earth."

The Long-Reign Pageant will be a memorable thing to see, for it
stands for the grandeur of England, and is full of suggestion as to how

it had its beginning and what have been the forces that have built it up.

I got to my seat in the Strand just in time—five minutes past ten—for a glance around before the show began. The houses opposite, as far as the eye could reach in both directions, suggested boxes in a theater snugly packed. The gentleman next to me likened the groups to beds of flowers, and said he had never seen such a massed and multitudinous array of bright colors and fine clothes.

These displays rose up and up, story by story, all balconies and windows being packed, and also the battlements stretching along the roofs. The sidewalks were filled with standing people, but were not uncomfortably crowded. They were fenced from the roadway by red-coated soldiers, a double stripe of vivid color which extended throughout the six miles which the procession would traverse.

Five minutes later the head of the column came into view and was presently filing by, led by Captain Ames, the tallest man in the British army. And then the cheering began. It took me but a little while to determine that this procession could not be described. There was going to be too much of it, and too much variety in it, so I gave up the idea. It was to be a spectacle for the kodak, not the pen.

Presently the procession was without visible beginning or end, but stretched to the limit of sight in both directions—bodies of soldiery in blue, followed by a block of soldiers in buff, then a block of red, a block of buff, a block of yellow, and so on, an interminable drift of swaying and swinging splotches of strong color sparkling and flashing with shifty light reflected from bayonets, lance heads, brazen helmets, and burnished breastplates. For varied and beautiful uniforms and unceasing surprises in the way of new and unexpected splendors, it much surpassed any pageant that I have ever seen.

I was not dreaming of so stunning a show. All the nations seemed to be filing by. They all seemed to be represented. It was sort of allegorical suggestion of the Last Day, and some who live to see that day will probably recall this one if they are not too much disturbed in mind at the time.

There were five bodies of Oriental soldiers of five different nationalities, with complexions differentiated by five distinct shades of yellow. There were about a dozen bodies of black soldiers from various parts of Africa, whose complexions covered as many shades of black, and some of these were the very blackest people I have ever seen yet.

Then there was an exhaustive exhibition of the hundred separate brown races of India, the most beautiful and satisfying of all the com-

2

plexions that have been vouchsafed to man, and the one which best sets off colored clothes and best harmonizes with all tints.

The Chinese, the Japanese, the Koreans, the Africans, the Indians, the Pacific Islanders—they were all there, and with them samples of all the whites that inhabit the wide reach of the Queen's dominions.

The procession was the human race on exhibition, a spectacle curious and interesting and worth traveling far to see. The most splendid of the costumes were those worn by the Indian princes, and they were also the most beautiful and richest. They were men of stately build and princely carriage, and wherever they passed the applause burst forth.

Soldiers, soldiers, soldiers, and still more and more soldiers and cannon and muskets and lances—there seemed to be no end to this feature. There are 50,000 soldiers in London, and they all seemed to be on hand. I have not seen so many except in the theater, when thirty-five privates and a general march across the stage and behind the scenes and across the front again and keep it up till they have represented 300,000.

In the early part of the procession the colonial premiers drove by, and by and by after a long time there was a grand output of foreign princes, thirty-one in the invoice.

The feature of high romance was not wanting, for among them rode Prince Rupert of Bavaria, who would be Prince of Wales now and future king of England and emperor of India if his Stuart ancestors had conducted their royal affairs more wisely than they did. He came as a peaceful guest to represent his mother, Princess Ludwig, heiress of the house of Stuart, to whom English Jacobites still pay unavailing homage as the rightful queen of England.

The house of Stuart was formally and officially shelved nearly two centuries ago, but the microbe of Jacobite loyalty is a thing which is not exterminable by time, force, or argument.

At last, when the procession had been on view an hour and a half, carriages began to appear. In the first came a detachment of two-horse ones containing ambassadors extraordinary, in one of them Whitelaw Reid, representing the United States; then six containing minor foreign and domestic princes and princesses; then five four-horse carriages freighted with offshoots of the family.

The excitement was growing now; interest was rising toward the boiling point. Finally a landau driven by eight cream-colored horses, most lavishly upholstered in gold stuffs, with postilions and no drivers, and preceded by Lord Wolseley, came bowling along, followed by the Prince of Wales, and all the world rose to its feet and uncovered.

The Queen Empress was come. She was received with great enthusiasm. It was realizable that she was the procession herself; that all the rest of it was mere embroidery; that in her the public saw the British Empire itself. She was a symbol, an allegory of England's grandeur and the might of the British name.

It is over now; the British Empire has marched past under review and inspection. The procession stood for sixty years of progress and accumulation, moral, material, and political. It was made up rather of the beneficiaries of these prosperities than of the creators of them.

As far as mere glory goes, the foreign trade of Great Britain has grown in a wonderful way since the Queen ascended the throne. Last year it reached the enormous figure of £620,000,000, but the capitalist, the manufacturer, the merchant, and the workingmen were not officially in the procession to get their large share of the resulting glory.

Great Britain has added to her real estate an average of 165 miles of territory per day for the past sixty years, which is to say she has added more than the bulk of an England proper per year, or an aggregate of seventy Englands in the sixty years.

But Cecil Rhodes was not in the procession, the Chartered Company was absent from it. Nobody was there to collect his share of the glory due for his formidable contributions to the imperial estate. Even Doctor Jameson was out, and yet he had tried so hard to accumulate territory.

Eleven colonial premiers were in the procession, but the dean of order, the imperial Premier, was not, nor the Lord Chief Justice of England, nor the Speaker of the House. The bulk of the religious strength of England dissent was not officially represented in the religious ceremonials. At the Cathedral that immense new industry, speculative expansion, was not represented unless the pathetic shade of Barnato rode invisible in the pageant.

It was a memorable display and must live in history. It suggested the material glories of the reign finely and adequately. The absence of the chief creators of them was perhaps not a serious disadvantage. One could supply the vacancies by imagination, and thus fill out the procession very effectively. One can enjoy a rainbow without necessarily forgetting the forces that made it.

1897

About Play-Acting

I have a project to suggest. But first I will write a chapter of introduction.

I have just been witnessing a remarkable play, here at the Burg Theater in Vienna. I do not know of any play that much resembles it. In fact, it is such a departure from the common laws of the drama that the name "play" doesn't seem to fit it quite snugly. However, whatever else it may be, it is in any case a great and stately metaphysical poem, and deeply fascinating. "Deeply fascinating" is the right term, for the audience sat four hours and five minutes without thrice breaking into applause, except at the close of each act; sat rapt and silent—fascinated. This piece is "The Master of Palmyra." It is twenty years old; yet I doubt if you have ever heard of it. It is by Wilbrandt, and is his masterpiece and the work which is to make his name permanent in German literature. It has never been played anywhere except in Berlin and in the great Burg Theater in Vienna. Yet whenever it is put on the stage it packs the house, and the free list is suspended. I know people who have seen it ten times; they know the most of it by heart; they do not tire of it; and they say they shall still be quite willing to go and sit under its spell whenever they get the opportunity.

There is a dash of metempsychosis in it—and it is the strength of the piece. The play gave me the sense of the passage of a dimly connected procession of dream-pictures. The scene of it is Palmyra in Roman times. It covers a wide stretch of time—I don't know how many years—and in the course of it the chief actress is reincarnated several times: four times she is a more or less young woman, and once she is a lad. In the first act she is Zoë—a Christian girl who has wandered across the desert from Damascus to try to Christianize the Zeus-worshiping pagans of Palmyra. In this character she is wholly spiritual, a religious enthusiast, a devotee who covets martyrdom—and gets it.

After many years she appears in the second act as Phoebe, a graceful and beautiful young light-o'-love from Rome, whose soul is all for the shows and luxuries and delights of this life—a dainty and capricious featherhead, a creature of shower and sunshine, a spoiled child, but a charming one.

In the third act, after an interval of many years, she reappears as Persida, mother of a daughter in the fresh bloom of youth. She is now a sort of combination of her two earlier selves: in religious loyalty and subjection she is Zoë; in triviality of character and shallowness of judgment—together with a touch of vanity in dress—she is Phoebe.

After a lapse of years she appears in the fourth act as Nymphas, a beautiful boy, in whose character the previous incarnations are engagingly mixed.

And after another stretch of years all these heredities are joined in the Zenobia of the fifth act—a person of gravity, dignity, sweetness, with a heart filled with compassion for all who suffer, and a hand prompt to put into practical form the heart's benignant impulses.

You will easily concede that the actress who proposes to discriminate nicely these five characters, and play them to the satisfaction of a cultivated and exacting audience, has her work cut out for her. Mme. Hohenfels has made these parts her peculiar property; and she is well able to meet all the requirements. You perceive, now, where the chief part of the absorbing fascination of this piece lies; it is in watching this extraordinary artist melt these five characters into each other—grow, shade by shade, out of one and into another through a stretch of four hours and five minutes.

There are a number of curious and interesting features in this piece. For instance, its hero, Apelles, young, handsome, vigorous, in the first act, remains so all through the long flight of years covered by the five acts. Other men, young in the first act, are touched with gray in the second, are old and racked with infirmities in the third, in the fourth, all but one are gone to their long home, and he is a blind and helpless hulk of ninety or a hundred years. It indicates that the stretch of time covered by the piece is seventy years or more. The scenery undergoes decay, too—the decay of age, assisted and perfected by a conflagration. The fine new temples and palaces of the second act are by and by a wreck of crumbled walls and prostrate columns, moldy, grass-grown, and desolate; but their former selves are still recognizable in their ruins. The aging men and the aging scenery together convey a profound illusion of that long lapse of time: they make you live it yourself! You leave the theater with the weight of a century upon you.

Another strong effect: Death, in person, walks about the stage in every act. So far as I could make out, he was supposedly not visible to any excepting two persons—the one he came for and Apelles. He

used various costumes: but there was always more black about them
than any other tint; and so they were always somber. Also they were
always deeply impressive, and indeed awe-inspiring. The face was not
subjected to changes, but remained the same, first and last—a ghastly
white. To me he was always welcome, he seemed so real—the actual
Death, not a play-acting artificiality. He was of a solemn and stately
carriage; he had a deep voice, and used it with a noble dignity. Wherever there was a turmoil of merry-making or fighting or feasting or
chaffing or quarreling, or a gilded pageant, or other manifestation of
our trivial and fleeting life, into it drifted that black figure with the
corpse-face, and looked its fateful look and passed on; leaving its victim
shuddering and smitten. And always its coming made the fussy human
pack seem infinitely pitiful and shabby and hardly worth the attention
of either saving or damning.

In the beginning of the first act the young girl Zoë appears by some
great rocks in the desert, and sits down, exhausted, to rest. Presently
arrive a pauper couple, stricken with age and infirmities; and they
begin to mumble and pray to the Spirit of Life, who is said to
inhabit that spot. The Spirit of Life appears; also Death—uninvited.
They are (supposably) invisible. Death, tall, black-robed, corpse-
faced, stands motionless and waits. The aged couple pray to the Spirit
of Life for a means to prop up their existence and continue it. Their
prayer fails. The Spirit of Life prophesies Zoë's martyrdom: it will take
place before night. Soon Apelles arrives, young and vigorous and
full of enthusiasm; he has led a host against the Persians and won the
battle; he is the pet of fortune, rich, honored, beloved, "Master of
Palmyra." He has heard that whoever stretches himself out on one of
those rocks there, and asks for a deathless life, can have his wish. He
laughs at the tradition, but wants to make the trial anyway. The
invisible Spirit of Life warns him: "Life without end can be regret
without end." But he persists: let him keep his youth, his strength,
and his mental faculties unimpaired, and he will take all the risks. He
has his desire.

From this time forth, act after act, the troubles and sorrows and
misfortunes and humiliations of life beat upon him without pity or res-
pite; but he will not give up, he will not confess his mistake. Whenever
he meets Death he still furiously defies him—but Death patiently waits.
He, the healer of sorrows, is man's best friend: the recognition of this
will come. As the years drag on, and on, and on, the friends of the
Master's youth grow old; and one by one they totter to the grave: he
goes on with his proud fight, and will not yield. At length he is wholly

alone in the world; all his friends are dead; last of all, his darling of
darlings, his son, the lad Nymphas, who dies in his arms. His pride is
broken now; and he would welcome Death, if Death would come, if
Death would hear his prayers and give him peace. The closing act is
fine and pathetic. Apelles meets Zenobia, the helper of all who suffer,
and tells her his story, which moves her to pity. By common report she
is endowed with more than earthly powers; and, since he cannot have
the boon of death, he appeals to her to drown his memory in forgetfulness of his griefs—forgetfulness, "which is death's equivalent." She says
(roughly translated), in an exaltation of compassion:

> Come to me!
> Kneel; and may the power be granted me
> To cool the fires of this poor tortured brain,
> And bring it peace and healing.

He kneels. From her hand, which she lays upon his head, a mysterious influence steals through him; and he sinks into a dreamy tranquillity.

> Oh, if I could but so drift
> Through this soft twilight into the night of peace,
> Never to wake again!
> (Raising his hand, as if in benediction.)
> O mother earth, farewell!
> Gracious thou wert to me. Farewell!
> Apelles goes to rest.

Death appears behind him and incloses the uplifted hand in his.
Apelles shudders, wearily and slowly turns, and recognizes his life-long
adversary. He smiles and puts all his gratitude into one simple and
touching sentence, "Ich danke dir," and dies.

Nothing, I think, could be more moving, more beautiful, than this
close. This piece is just one long, soulful, sardonic laugh at human life.
Its title might properly be "Is Life a Failure?" and leave the five acts
to play with the answer. I am not at all sure that the author meant to
laugh at life. I only notice that he has done it. Without putting into
words any ungracious or discourteous things about life, the episodes
in the piece seem to be saying all the time, inarticulately: "Note what
a silly, poor thing human life is; how childish its ambitions, how ridiculous its pomps, how trivial its dignities, how cheap its heroisms, how
capricious its course, how brief its flight, how stingy in happiness, how
opulent in miseries, how few its prides, how multitudinous its humiliations, how comic its tragedies, how tragic its comedies, how wearisome

and monotonous its repetition of its stupid history through the ages, with never the introduction of a new detail, how hard it has tried, from the Creation down, to play itself upon its possessor as a boon, and has never proved its case in a single instance!"

Take note of some of the details of the piece. Each of the five acts contains an independent tragedy of its own. In each act somebody's edifice of hope, or of ambition, or of happiness, goes down in ruins. Even Apelles's perennial youth is only a long tragedy, and his life a failure. There are two martyrdoms in the piece; and they are curiously and sarcastically contrasted. In the first act the pagans persecute Zoë, the Christian girl, and a pagan mob slaughters her. In the fourth act those same pagans—now very old and zealous—are become Christians, and they persecute the pagans: a mob of them slaughters the pagan youth, Nymphas, who is standing up for the old gods of his fathers. No remark is made about this picturesque failure of civilization; but there it stands, as an unworded suggestion that civilization, even when Christianized, was not able wholly to subdue the natural man in that old day—just as in our day, the spectacle of a shipwrecked French crew clubbing women and children who tried to climb into the life-boats suggests that civilization has not succeeded in entirely obliterating the natural man even yet. Common sailors! A year ago, in Paris, at a fire, the aristocracy of the same nation clubbed girls and women out of the way to save themselves. Civilization tested at top and bottom both, you see. And in still another panic of fright we have this same "tough" civilization saving its honor by condemning an innocent man to multiform death, and hugging and whitewashing the guilty one.

In the second act a grand Roman official is not above trying to blast Apelles's reputation by falsely charging him with misappropriating public moneys. Apelles, who is too proud to endure even the suspicion of irregularity, strips himself to naked poverty to square the unfair account; and *his* troubles begin: the blight which is to continue and spread strikes his life; for the frivolous, pretty creature whom he has brought from Rome has no taste for poverty, and agrees to elope with a more competent candidate. Her presence in the house has previously brought down the pride and broken the heart of Apelles's poor old mother; and *her* life is a failure. Death comes for her, but is willing to trade her for the Roman girl; so the bargain is struck with Apelles, and the mother spared for the present.

No one's life escapes the blight. Timoleus, the gay satirist of the first two acts, who scoffed at the pious hypocrisies and money-grubbing ways of the great Roman lords, is grown old and fat and blear-eyed and racked with disease in the third, has lost his stately purities, and watered the acid of his wit. *His* life has suffered defeat. Unthinkingly he swears by Zeus—from ancient habit—and then quakes with fright; for a fellow-communicant is passing by. Reproached by a pagan friend of his youth for his apostasy, he confesses that principle, when unsupported by an assenting stomach, has to climb down. One must have bread; and "the bread is Christian now." Then the poor old wreck, once so proud of iron rectitude, hobbles away, coughing and barking.

In the same act Apelles gives his sweet young Christian daughter and her fine young pagan lover his consent and blessing, and makes them utterly happy—for five minutes. Then the priest and the mob come, to tear them apart and put the girl in a nunnery; for marriage between the sects is forbidden. Apelles's wife could dissolve the rule; and she wants to do it: but under priestly pressure she wavers; then, fearing that in providing happiness for her child she would be committing a sin dangerous to herself, she goes over to the opposition, throwing the casting vote for the nunnery. The blight has fallen upon the young couple; *their* life is a failure.

In the fourth act, Longinus, who made such a prosperous and enviable start in the first act, is left alone in the desert, sick, blind, helpless, incredibly old, to die: not a friend left in the world—another ruined life. And in that act, also, Apelles's worshiped boy, Nymphas, done to death by the mob, breathes out his last sigh in his father's arms—one more failure. In the fifth act, Apelles himself dies, and is glad to do it; he who so ignorantly rejoiced, only four acts before, over the splendid present of an earthly immortality—the very worst failure of the lot!

II

Now I approach my project. The theater list for Saturday, May 7, 1898, cut from the advertising columns of a New York paper, is given on following page.

Now I arrive at my project, and make my suggestion. From the look of this lightsome feast, I conclude that what you need is a tonic. Send for "The Master of Palmyra." You are trying to make yourself believe that life is a comedy, that its sole business is fun, that there is nothing serious in it. You are ignoring the skeleton in your closet. Send for "The Master of Palmyra." You are neglecting a valuable side of your life; presently it will be atrophied. You are eating too much mental

sugar; you will bring on Bright's disease of the intellect. You need a
tonic; you need it very much. Send for "The Master of Palmyra." You
will not need to translate it: its story is as plain as a procession of
pictures.

I have made my suggestion. Now I wish to put an annex to it. And
that is this: It is right and wholesome to have those light comedies and

entertaining shows; and I shouldn't wish to see them diminished. But
none of us is *always* in the comedy spirit: we have our graver moods;
they come to us all; the lightest of us cannot escape them. These
moods have their appetites—healthy and legitimate appetites—and
there ought to be some way of satisfying them. It seems to me that
New York ought to have one theater devoted to tragedy. With her
three millions of population, and seventy outside millions to draw upon,
she can afford it, she can support it. America devotes more time, labor,

money, and attention to distributing literary and musical culture among the general public than does any other nation, perhaps; yet here you find her neglecting what is possibly the most effective of all the breeders and nurses and disseminators of high literary taste and lofty emotion—the tragic stage. To leave that powerful agency out is to haul the culture-wagon with a crippled team. Nowadays, when a mood comes which only Shakespeare can set to music, what must we do? Read Shakespeare ourselves! Isn't it pitiful? It is playing an organ solo on a jew's-harp. We can't read. None but the Booths can do it.

Thirty years ago Edwin Booth played "Hamlet" a hundred nights in New York. With three times the population, how often is "Hamlet" played now in a year? If Booth were back now in his prime, how often could he play it in New York? Some will say twenty-five nights. I will say three hundred, and say it with confidence. The tragedians are dead, but I think that the taste and intelligence which made their market are not.

What *has* come over us English-speaking people? During the first half of this century tragedies and great tragedians were as common with us as farce and comedy; and it was the same in England. Now we have not a tragedian, I believe; and London, with her fifty shows and theaters, has but three, I think. It is an astonishing thing, when you come to consider it. Vienna remains upon the ancient basis: there has been no change. She sticks to the former proportions: a number of rollicking comedies, admirably played, every night; and also every night at the Burg Theater—that wonder of the world for grace and beauty and richness and splendor and costliness—a majestic drama of depth and seriousness, or a standard old tragedy. It is only within the last dozen years that men have learned to do miracles on the stage in the way of grand and enchanting scenic effects; and it is at such a time as this that we have reduced our scenery mainly to different breeds of parlors and varying aspects of furniture and rugs. I think we must have a Burg in New York, and Burg scenery, and a great company like the Burg company. Then, with a tragedy tonic once or twice a month, we shall enjoy the comedies all the better. Comedy keeps the heart sweet; but we all know that there is wholesome refreshment for both mind and heart in an occasional climb among the pomps of the intellectual snow-summits built by Shakespeare and those others. Do I seem to be preaching? It is out of my line: I only do it because the rest of the clergy seem to be on vacation.

1898

Stirring Times in Austria

Here in Vienna in these closing days of 1897 one's blood gets no chance to stagnate. The atmosphere is brimful of political electricity. All conversation is political; every man is a battery, with brushes over-worn, and gives out blue sparks when you set him going on the common topic. Everybody has an opinion, and lets you have it frank and hot, and out of this multitude of counsel you get merely confusion and despair. For no one really understands this political situation, or can tell you what is going to be the outcome of it.

Things have happened here recently which would set any country but Austria on fire from end to end, and upset the government to a certainty; but no one feels confident that such results will follow here. Here, apparently, one must wait and see what will happen, then he will know, and not before; guessing is idle; guessing cannot help the matter. This is what the wise tell you; they all say it; they say it every day, and it is the sole detail upon which they all agree.

There is some approach to agreement upon another point: that there will be no revolution. Men say: "Look at our history—revolutions have not been in our line; and look at our political map—its construction is unfavorable to an organized uprising, and without unity what could a revolt accomplish? It is *disunion* which has held our empire together for centuries, and what it has done in the past it may continue to do now and in the future."

The most intelligible sketch I have encountered of this unintelligible arrangement of things was contributed to the *Travelers Record* by Mr. Forrest Morgan, of Hartford, three years ago. He says:

The Austro-Hungarian Monarchy is the patchwork quilt, the Midway Plaisance, the national chain-gang of Europe; a state that is not a nation but a collection of nations, some with national memories and aspirations and others without, some occupying distinct provinces almost purely their own, and others mixed with alien races, but each with a different language, and each mostly holding the others foreigners as much as if the link of a common government did not exist. Only one of its races even now comprises so much as *one-fourth* of the whole, and not another so much as *one-sixth;* and each has remained for ages as unchanged in isolation, however mingled together in locality, as globules of oil in water. There is nothing else in the modern world that is nearly like it, though there have been plenty in past ages; it seems unreal and impossible even though we know it is true; it violates all our feeling as to what a country should be in order to have a right to exist; and it seems as though it was too ramshackle to go on holding together any length of time. Yet it has survived, much in its present shape, two centuries of storms that have swept perfectly unified countries from existence and others that have brought it to the verge of ruin, has survived formidable European coalitions to dismember it, and has steadily gained force after each; forever changing in its exact make-up, losing in the West but gaining in the East, the changes leave the structure as firm as ever, like the dropping off and adding on of logs in a raft, its mechanical union of pieces showing all the vitality of genuine national life.

That seems to confirm and justify the prevalent Austrian faith that in this confusion of unrelated and irreconcilable elements, this condition of incurable disunion, there is strength—for the government. Nearly every day some one explains to me that a revolution would not succeed here. "It couldn't, you know. Broadly speaking, all the nations in the empire hate the government—but they all hate each other, too, and with devoted and enthusiastic bitterness; no two of them can combine; the nation that rises must rise alone; then the others would joyfully join the government against her, and she would have just a fly's chance against a combination of spiders. This government is entirely independent. It can go its own road, and do as it pleases; it has nothing to fear. In countries like England and America, where there is one tongue and the public interests are common, the government must take account of public opinion; but in Austria-Hungary there are nineteen public opinions—one for each state. No—two or three for each state, since there are two or three nationalities in each. A government cannot satisfy all these public opinions; it can only go through the motions of trying. This government does that. It goes through the motions, and they do not succeed; but that does not worry the government much."

The next man will give you some further information. "The government has a policy—a wise one—and sticks steadily to it. This policy is—*tranquillity:* keep this hive of excitable nations as quiet as possible; encourage them to amuse themselves with things less inflammatory than politics. To this end it furnishes them an abundance of Catholic priests to teach them to be docile and obedient, and to be diligent in acquiring ignorance about things here below, and knowledge about the kingdom of heaven, to whose historic delights they are going to add the charm of their society by and by; and further—to this same end—it cools off the newspapers every morning at five o'clock, whenever warm events are happening." There is a censor of the press, and apparently he is always on duty and hard at work. A copy of each morning paper is brought to him at five o'clock. His official wagons wait at the doors of the newspaper offices and scud to him with the first copies that come from the press. His company of assistants read every line in these papers, and mark everything which seems to have a dangerous look; then he passes final judgement upon these markings. Two things conspire to give to the results a capricious and unbalanced look: his assistants have diversified notions as to what is dangerous and what isn't; he can't get time to examine their criticisms in much detail; and so sometimes the very same matter which is suppressed in one paper fails to be damned in another one, and gets published in full feather and unmodified. Then the paper in which it was suppressed blandly copies the forbidden matter into its evening edition—provokingly giving credit and detailing all the circumstances in courteous and inoffensive language—and of course the censor cannot say a word.

Sometimes the censor sucks all the blood out of a newspaper and leaves it colorless and inane; sometimes he leaves it undisturbed, and lets it talk out its opinions with a frankness and vigor hardly to be surpassed, I think, in the journals of any country. Apparently the censor sometimes revises his verdicts upon second thought, for several times lately he has suppressed journals after their issue and partial distribution. The distributed copies are then sent for by the censor and destroyed. I have two of these, but at the time they were sent for I could not remember what I had done with them.

If the censor did his work before the morning edition was printed, he would be less of an inconvenience than he is; but of course the papers cannot wait many minutes after five o'clock to get his verdict; they might as well go out of business as do that; so they print, and take the chances. Then, if they get caught by a suppression, they must strike out the condemned matter and print the edition over again. That delays the issue several hours, and is expensive besides. The government gets the suppressed edition for nothing. If it bought it, that would be joyful, and would give great satisfaction. Also, the edition would be larger. Some of the papers do not replace the condemned paragraphs with other matter; they merely snatch them out and leave blanks behind—mourning blanks, marked *"Confiscated."*

The government discourages the dissemination of newspaper information in other ways. For instance, it does not allow newspapers to be sold on the streets; therefore the newsboy is unknown in Vienna. And there is a stamp duty of nearly a cent upon each copy of a newspaper's issue. Every American paper that reaches me has a stamp upon it, which has been pasted there in the post-office or down-stairs in the hotel office; but no matter who put it there, I have to pay for it, and that is the main thing. Sometimes friends send me so many papers that it takes all I can earn that week to keep this government going.

I must take passing notice of another point in the government's measures for maintaining tranquillity. Everybody says it does not like to see any individual attain to commanding influence in the country, since such a man can become a disturber and an inconvenience. "We have as much talent as the other nations," says the citizen, resignedly, and without bitterness, "but for the sake of the general good of the country we are discouraged from making it overconspicuous; and not only discouraged, but tactfully and skillfully prevented from doing it, if we show too much persistence. Consequently we have no renowned men; in centuries we have seldom produced one—that is, seldom allowed one to produce himself. We can say to-day what no other nation of first importance in the family of Christian civilizations can say: that there exists no Austrian who has made an enduring name for himself which is familiar all around the globe."

Another helper toward tranquillity is the army. It is as pervasive as the atmosphere. It is everywhere. All the mentioned creators, promoters, and preservers of the public tranquillity do their several shares in the quieting work. They make a restful and comfortable serenity and reposefulness. This is disturbed sometimes for a little while: a mob assembles to protest against something; it gets noisy—noisier—still noisier—finally *too* noisy; then the persuasive soldiery come charging down upon it, and in a few minutes all is quiet again, and there is no mob.

There is a Constitution and there is a Parliament. The House draws its membership of 425 deputies from the nineteen or twenty states heretofore mentioned. These men represent peoples who speak eleven languages. That means eleven distinct varieties of jealousies, hostilities, and warring interests. This could be expected to furnish forth a parliament of a pretty inharmonious sort, and make legislation difficult at times—and it does that. The parliament is split up into many parties —the Clericals, the Progressists, the German Nationalists, the Young

Czechs, the Social Democrats, the Christian Socialists, and some others —and it is difficult to get up working combinations among them. They prefer to fight apart sometimes.

The recent troubles have grown out of Count Badeni's necessities. He could not carry on his government without a majority vote in the House at his back, and in order to secure it he had to make a trade of some sort. He made it with the Czechs—the Bohemians. The terms were not easy for him: he must pass a bill making the Czech tongue the official language in Bohemia in place of the German. This created a storm. All the Germans in Austria were incensed. In numbers they form but a fourth part of the empire's population, but they urge that the country's public business should be conducted in one common tongue, and that tongue a world language—which German is.

However, Badeni secured his majority. The German element in parliament was apparently become helpless. The Czech deputies were exultant.

Then the music began. Badeni's voyage, instead of being smooth, was disappointingly rough from the start. The government must get the *Ausgleich* through. It must not fail. Badeni's majority was ready to carry it through; but the minority was determined to obstruct it and delay it until the obnoxious Czech-language measure should be shelved.

The *Ausgleich* is an Adjustment, Arrangement, Settlement, which holds Austria and Hungary together. It dates from 1867, and has to be renewed every ten years. It establishes the share which Hungary must pay toward the expenses of the imperial government. Hungary is a kingdom (the Emperor of Austria is its King), and has its own parliament and governmental machinery. But it has no foreign office, and it has no army—at least its army is a part of the imperial army, is paid out of the imperial treasury, and is under the control of the imperial war office.

The ten-year rearrangement was due a year ago, but failed to connect. At least completely. A year's compromise was arranged. A new arrangement must be effected before the last day of this year. Otherwise the two countries become separate entities. The Emperor would still be King of Hungary—that is, King of an independent foreign country. There would be Hungarian custom-houses on the Austrian frontier, and there would be a Hungarian army and a Hungarian foreign office. Both countries would be weakened by this, both would suffer damage.

The Opposition in the House, although in the minority, had a good weapon to fight with in the pending *Ausgleich*. If it could delay the

Ausgleich a few weeks, the government would doubtless have to withdraw the hated language bill or lose Hungary.

The Opposition began its fight. Its arms were the Rules of the House. It was soon manifest that by applying these Rules ingeniously it could make the majority helpless, and keep it so as long as it pleased. It could shut off business every now and then with a motion to adjourn. It could require the ayes and noes on the motion, and use up thirty minutes on that detail. It could call for the reading and verification of the minutes of the preceding meeting, and use up half a day in that way. It could require that several of its members be entered upon the list of permitted speakers previously to the opening of a sitting; and as there is no time limit, further delays could thus be accomplished.

These were all lawful weapons, and the men of the Opposition (technically called the Left) were within their rights in using them. They used them to such dire purpose that all parliamentary business was paralyzed. The Right (the government side) could accomplish nothing. Then it had a saving idea. This idea was a curious one. It was to have the President and the Vice-Presidents of the parliament trample the Rules under foot upon occasion!

This, for a profoundly embittered minority constructed out of fire and gun-cotton! It was time for idle strangers to go and ask leave to look down out of a gallery and see what would be the result of it.

II. A MEMORABLE SITTING

And now took place that memorable sitting of the House which broke two records. It lasted the best part of two days and a night, surpassing by half an hour the longest sitting known to the world's previous parliamentary history, and breaking the long-speech record with Dr. Lecher's twelve-hour effort, the longest flow of unbroken talk that ever came out of one mouth since the world began.

At 8.45, on the evening of the 28th of October, when the House had been sitting a few minutes short of ten hours, Dr. Lecher was granted the floor. It was a good place for theatrical effects. I think that no other Senate House is so shapely as this one, or so richly and showily decorated. Its plan is that of an opera-house. Up toward the straight side of it—the stage side—rise a couple of terraces of desks for the ministry, and the official clerks or secretaries—terraces thirty feet long, and each supporting about half a dozen desks with spaces between them. Above these is the President's terrace, against the wall. Along it are distributed the proper accommodations for the presiding officer and his assistants. The wall is of richly colored marble highly polished, its paneled sweep relieved by fluted columns and pilasters of distinguished grace and dignity, which glow softly and frostily in the electric light. Around the spacious half-circle of the floor bends the great two-storied curve of the boxes, its frontage elaborately ornamented and sumptuously gilded. On the floor of the House the four hundred and twenty-five desks radiate fanwise from the President's tribune.

The galleries are crowded on this particular evening, for word has gone about that the *Ausgleich* is before the House; that the President, Ritter von Abrahamowicz, has been throttling the Rules; that the Opposition are in an inflammable state in consequence, and that the night session is likely to be of an exciting sort.

The gallery guests are fashionably dressed, and the finery of the women makes a bright and pretty show under the strong electric light. But down on the floor there is no costumery.

The deputies are dressed in day clothes; some of the clothes neat and trim, others not; there may be three members in evening dress, but not more. There are several Catholic priests in their long black gowns, and with crucifixes hanging from their necks. No member wears his hat. One may see by these details that the aspects are not those of an evening sitting of an English House of Commons, but rather those of a sitting of our House of Representatives.

In his high place sits the President, Abrahamowicz, object of the Opposition's limitless hatred. He is sunk back in the depths of his arm-chair, and has his chin down. He brings the ends of his spread fingers together in front of his breast, and reflectively taps them together, with the air of one who would like to begin business, but must wait, and be as patient as he can. It makes you think of Richelieu. Now and then he swings his head up to the left or to the right and answers something which some one has bent down to say to him. Then he taps his fingers again. He looks tired, and maybe a trifle harassed. He is a gray-haired, long, slender man, with a colorless long face, which, in repose, suggests a death-mask; but when not in repose is tossed and rippled by a turbulent smile which washes this way and that, and is not easy to keep up with—a pious smile, a holy smile, a saintly smile, a deprecating smile, a beseeching and supplicating smile; and when it is at work the large mouth opens and the flexible lips crumple, and unfold, and crumple again, and move around in a genial and persuasive and angelic way, and expose large glimpses of the teeth; and that interrupts the sacredness of the smile and gives it momentarily a mixed worldly and political and satanic cast. It is a most

interesting face to watch. And then the long hands and the body—
they furnish great and frequent help to the face in the business of
adding to the force of the statesman's words.

To change the tense. At the time of which I have just been speaking
the crowds in the galleries were gazing at the stage and the pit with
rapt interest and expectancy. One half of the great fan of desks was
in effect empty, vacant; in the other half several hundred members
were bunched and jammed together as solidly as the bristles in a brush;
and they also were waiting and expecting. Presently the Chair delivered this utterance:

"Dr. Lecher has the floor."

Then burst out such another wild and frantic and deafening clamor
as has not been heard on this planet since the last time the Comanches
surprised a white settlement at midnight. Yells from the Left, counter-
yells from the Right, explosions of yells from all sides at once, and all
the air sawed and pawed and clawed and cloven by a writhing confusion of gesturing arms and hands. Out of the midst of this thunder
and turmoil and tempest rose Dr. Lecher, serene and collected, and
the providential length of him enabled his head to show out above it.
He began his twelve-hour speech. At any rate, his lips could be seen
to move, and that was evidence. On high sat the President imploring
order, with his long hands put together as in prayer, and his lips visibly but not hearably speaking. At intervals he grasped his bell and
swung it up and down with vigor, adding its keen clamor to the storm
weltering there below.

Dr. Lecher went on with his pantomime speech, contented, un-
troubled. Here and there and now and then powerful voices burst
above the din, and delivered an ejaculation that was heard. Then the
din ceased for a moment or two, and gave opportunity to hear what
the Chair might answer; then the noise broke out again. Apparently
the President was being charged with all sorts of illegal exercises of
power in the interest of the Right (the government side): among these,
with arbitrarily closing an Order of Business before it was finished;
with an unfair distribution of the right to the floor; with refusal of the
floor, upon quibble and protest, to members entitled to it; with stopping a speaker's speech upon quibble and protest; and with other
transgressions of the Rules of the House. One of the interrupters who
made himself heard was a young fellow of slight build and neat dress,
who stood a little apart from the solid crowd and leaned negligently,
with folded arms and feet crossed, against a desk. Trim and handsome, strong face and thin features; black hair roughed up; parsimoni-

ous mustache; resonant great voice, of good tone and pitch. It is Wolf, capable and hospitable with sword and pistol; fighter of the recent duel with Count Badeni, the head of the government. He shot Badeni through the arm, and then walked over in the politest way and inspected his game, shook hands, expressed regret, and all that. Out of him came early this thundering peal, audible above the storm:

"I demand the floor. I wish to offer a motion."

In the sudden lull which followed, the President answered, "Dr. Lecher has the floor."

Wolf. "I move the close of the sitting!"

P. "Representative Lecher has the floor." [Stormy outburst from the Left—that is, the Opposition.]

Wolf. "I demand the floor for the introduction of a formal motion. [Pause.] Mr. President, are you going to grant it, or not? [Crash of approval from the Left.] I will keep on demanding the floor till I get it."

P. "I call Representative Wolf to order. Dr. Lecher has the floor."

Wolf. "Mr. President, are you going to observe the Rules of this House?" [Tempest of applause and confused ejaculations from the Left—a boom and roar which long endured, and stopped all business for the time being.]

"*Dr. von Pessler.* "By the Rules motions are in order, and the Chair *must* put them to vote."

For answer the President (who is a Pole—I make this remark in passing) began to jangle his bell with energy at the moment that that wild pandemonium of voices burst out again.

Wolf (hearable above the storm). "Mr. President, I demand the floor. We intend to find out, here and now, which is the hardest, *a Pole's skull or a German's!*"

This brought out a perfect cyclone of satisfaction from the Left. In the midst of it some one again moved an adjournment. The President blandly answered that Dr. Lecher had the floor. Which was true; and he was speaking, too, calmly, earnestly, and argumentatively; and the official stenographers had left their places and were at his elbows taking down his words, he leaning and orating into their ears—a most curious and interesting scene.

Dr. von Pessler (to the Chair). "Do not drive us to extremities!"

The tempest burst out again; yells of approval from the Left, catcalls, and ironical laughter from the Right. At this point a new and most effective noise-maker was pressed into service. Each desk has an extension, consisting of a removable board eighteen inches long, six wide, and a

half-inch thick. A member pulled one of these out and began to bela-
bor the top of his desk with it. Instantly other members followed suit,
and perhaps you can imagine the result. Of all conceivable rackets it
is the most ear-splitting, intolerable, and altogether fiendish.

The persecuted President leaned back in his chair, closed his eyes,
clasped his hands in his lap, and a look of pathetic resignation crept
over his long face. It is the way a country schoolmaster used to look
in days long past when he had refused his school a holiday and it
had risen against him in ill-mannered riot and violence and insurrection. Twice a motion to adjourn had been offered—a motion always in
order in other Houses, and doubtless so in this one also. The President
had refused to put these motions. By consequence, he was not in a
pleasant place now, and was having a right hard time. Votes upon
motions, whether carried or defeated, could make endless delay, and
postpone the *Ausgleich* to next century.

In the midst of these sorrowful circumstances and this hurricane of
yells and screams and satanic clatter of desk-boards, Representative
Dr. Kronawetter unfeelingly reminds the Chair that a motion has been
offered, and adds: "Say yes, or no! What do you sit there for, and give
no answer?"

P. "After I have given a speaker the floor, I cannot give it to another.
After Dr. Lecher is through, I will put your motion." [Storm of indignation from the Left.]

Wolf (to the Chair). "Thunder and lightning! look at the Rule governing the case!"

Kronawetter. "I move the close of the sitting! And I demand the
ayes and noes!"

Dr. Lecher. "Mr. President, have I the floor?"

P. "You have the floor."

Wolf (to the Chair, in a stentorian voice which cleaves its way
through the storm). "It is by such brutalities as these that you drive
us to extremities! Are you waiting till some one shall throw into your
face the word that shall describe what you are bringing about?[1] [Tem-
pest of insulted fury from the Right.] *Is that what you are waiting for,
old Grayhead?*" [Long-continued clatter of desk-boards from the Left,
with shouts of "The vote! the vote!" An ironical shout from the Right,
"Wolf is boss!"]

Wolf keeps on demanding the floor for his motion. At length:

P. "I call Representative Wolf to order! Your conduct is unheard-of,

[1] That is, *revolution.*—M.T.

sir! You forget that you are in a parliament; you must remember where
you are, sir." [Applause from the Right. Dr. Lecher is still peacefully
speaking, the stenographers listening at his lips.]

Wolf (banging on his desk with his desk-board). "I demand the floor
for my motion! I won't stand this trampling of the Rules under foot—
no, not if I die for it! I will never yield! You have got to stop me by
force. Have I the floor?"

P. "Representative Wolf, what kind of behavior is this? I call you
to order again. You should have some regard for your dignity."

Dr. Lecher speaks on. Wolf turns upon him with an offensive innuendo.

Dr. Lecher. "Mr. Wolf, I beg you to refrain from that sort of suggestions." [Storm of hand-clapping from the Right.]

This was applause from the enemy, for Lecher himself, like Wolf,
was an Obstructionist.

Wolf growls to Lecher: "You can scribble that applause in your al-
bum!"

P. "Once more I call Representative Wolf to order! Do not forget
that you are a Representative, sir!"

Wolf (slam-banging with his desk-board). "I will force this matter!
Are you going to grant me the floor, or not?"

And still the sergeant-at-arms did not appear. It was because there
wasn't any. It is a curious thing, but the Chair has no effectual means of
compelling order.

After some more interruptions:

Wolf (banging with his board). "I demand the floor. I will not yield!"

P. "I have no recourse against Representative Wolf. In the presence
of behavior like this it is to be regretted that such is the case." [A shout
from the Right, "Throw him out!"]

It is true, he had no effective recourse. He had an official called an
"Ordner," whose help he could invoke in desperate cases, but apparently the Ordner is only a persuader, not a compeller. Apparently he
is a sergeant-at-arms who is not loaded; a good enough gun to look at,
but not valuable for business.

For another twenty or thirty minutes Wolf went on banging with
his board and demanding his rights; then at last the weary President
threatened to summon the dread order-maker. But both his manner
and his words were reluctant. Evidently it grieved him to have to resort to this dire extremity. He said to Wolf, "If this goes on, I shall feel
obliged to summon the Ordner, and beg him to restore order in the
House."

Wolf. "I'd like to see you do it! Suppose you fetch in a few police-men, too! [Great tumult.] Are you going to put my motion to adjourn, or not?"

Dr. Lecher continues his speech. Wolf accompanies him with his board-clatter.

The President despatches the Ordner, Dr. Lang (himself a deputy), on his order-restoring mission. Wolf, with his board uplifted for de-fense, confronts the Ordner with a remark which Boss Tweed might have translated into "Now let's see what you are going to do about it!" [Noise and tumult all over the House.]

Wolf stands upon his rights, and says he will maintain them till he is killed in his tracks. Then he resumes his banging, the President jan-gles his bell and begs for order, and the rest of the House augments the racket the best it can.

Wolf. "I require an adjournment, because I find myself personally threatened. [Laughter from the Right.] Not that I fear for myself; I am only anxious about what will happen to the man who touches me."

The Ordner. "I am not going to fight with you."

Nothing came of the efforts of the angel of peace, and he presently melted out of the scene and disappeared. Wolf went on with his noise and with his demands that he be granted the floor, resting his board at intervals to discharge criticisms and epithets at the Chair. Once he re-minded the Chairman of his violated promise to grant him (Wolf) the floor, and said, "Whence I came, we call promise-breakers rascals!" And he advised the Chairman to take his conscience to bed with him and use it as a pillow. Another time he said that the Chair was making itself ridiculous before all Europe. In fact, some of Wolf's language was almost unparliamentary. By and by he struck the idea of beating out a *tune* with his board. Later he decided to stop asking for the floor, and to confer it upon himself. And so he and Dr. Lecher now spoke at the same time, and mingled their speeches with the other noises, and nobody heard either of them. Wolf rested himself now and then from speech-making by reading, in his clarion voice, from a pamphlet.

I will explain that Dr. Lecher was not making a twelve-hour speech for pastime, but for an important purpose. It was the government's intention to push the *Ausgleich* through its preliminary stages in this one sitting (for which it was the Order of the Day), and then by vote refer it to a select committee. It was the Majority's scheme—as charged by the Opposition—to drown debate upon the bill by pure noise—drown it out and stop it. The debate being thus ended, the vote upon the reference would follow—with victory for the government. But into the government's calculations had not entered the possibility of a single-barreled speech which should occupy the entire time-limit of the sitting, and also get itself delivered in spite of all the noise. Goliath was not expecting David. But David was there; and during twelve hours he tranquilly pulled statistical, historical, and argumentative pebbles out of his scrip and slung them at the giant; and when he was done he was victor, and the day was saved.

In the English House an obstructionist has held the floor with Bible-readings and other outside matters; but Dr. Lecher could not have that restful and recuperative privilege—he must confine himself strictly to the subject before the House. More than once, when the President could not hear him because of the general tumult, he sent persons to listen and report as to whether the orator was speaking to the subject or not.

The subject was a peculiarly difficult one, and it would have troubled any other deputy to stick to it three hours without exhausting his ammunition, because it required a vast and intimate knowledge—detailed and particularized knowledge—of the commercial, railroading, financial, and international banking relations existing between two great sovereignties, Hungary and the Empire. But Dr. Lecher is President of the Board of Trade of his city of Brünn, and was master of the situation. His speech was not formally prepared. He had a few notes jotted down for his guidance; he had his facts in his head; his heart was in his work; and for twelve hours he stood there, undisturbed by the clamor around him, and with grace and ease and confidence poured out the riches of his mind, in closely reasoned arguments, clothed in eloquent and faultless phrasing.

He is a young man of thirty-seven. He is tall and well proportioned, and has cultivated and fortified his muscle by mountain-climbing. If he were a little handsomer he would sufficiently reproduce for me the Chauncey Depew of the great New England dinner nights of some years ago; he has Depew's charm of manner and graces of language and delivery.

There was but one way for Dr. Lecher to hold the floor—he must stay on his legs. If he should sit down to rest a moment, the floor would be taken from him by the enemy in the Chair. When he had been talking three or four hours he himself proposed an adjournment, in order that he might get some rest from his wearing labors; but he limited his motion with the condition that if it was lost he should be allowed to continue his speech, and if it carried he should have the floor at the next sitting. Wolf was now appeased, and withdrew his own thousand-times offered motion, and Dr. Lecher's was voted upon—and lost. So he went on speaking.

By one o'clock in the morning, excitement and noise-making had tired out nearly everybody but the orator. Gradually the seats of the Right underwent depopulation; the occupants had slipped out to the refreshment-rooms to eat and drink, or to the corridors to chat. Some one remarked that there was no longer a quorum present, and moved a call of the House. The Chair (Vice-President Dr. Kramarz) refused to put it to a vote. There was a small dispute over the legality of this ruling, but the Chair held its ground.

The Left remained on the battle-field to support their champion. He went steadily on with his speech; and always it was strong, virile, felicitous, and to the point. He was earning applause, and this enabled his party to turn that fact to account. Now and then they applauded him a couple of minutes on a stretch, and during that time he could stop speaking and rest his voice without having the floor taken from him.

At a quarter to two a member of the Left demanded that Dr. Lecher be allowed a recess for rest, and said that the Chairman was "heartless." Dr. Lecher himself asked for ten minutes. The Chair allowed him five. Before the time had run out Dr. Lecher was on his feet again.

Wolf burst out again with a motion to adjourn. Refused by the Chair. Wolf said the whole parliament wasn't worth a pinch of powder. The Chair retorted that that was true in a case where a single member was able to make all parliamentary business impossible. Dr. Lecher continued his speech.

The members of the Majority went out by detachments from time to time and took naps upon sofas in the reception-rooms; and also refreshed themselves with food and drink—in quantities nearly unbelievable—but the Minority stayed loyally by their champion. Some distinguished deputies of the Majority stayed by him, too, compelled thereto by admiration of his great performance. When a man has been speaking eight hours, is it conceivable that he can still be interesting, still fascinating? When Dr. Lecher had been speaking eight hours he was still compactly surrounded by friends who would not leave him and by foes (of all parties) who *could* not; and all hung enchanted and wondering upon his words, and all testified their admiration with constant and cordial outbursts of applause. Surely this was a triumph without precedent in history.

During the twelve-hour effort friends brought to the orator three glasses of wine, four cups of coffee, and one glass of beer—a most stingy reinforcement of his wasting tissues, but the hostile Chair would permit no addition to it. But no matter, the Chair could not beat that man. He was a garrison holding a fort, and was not to be starved out.

When he had been speaking eight hours his pulse was seventy-two; when he had spoken twelve, it was one hundred.

He finished his long speech in these terms, as nearly as a permissibly free translation can convey them:

"I will now hasten to close my examination of the subject. I conceive that we of the Left have made it clear to the honorable gentlemen of the other side of the House that we are stirred by no intemperate enthusiasm for this measure in its present shape. . . .

"What we require, and shall fight for with all lawful weapons, is a formal, comprehensive, and definitive solution and settlement of these vexed matters. We desire the restoration of the earlier condition of things; the cancellation of all this incapable government's pernicious trades with Hungary; and then—release from the sorry burden of the Badeni ministry!

"I voice the hope—I know not if it will be fulfilled—I voice the deep and sincere and patriotic hope that the committee into whose hands this bill will eventually be committed will take its stand upon high ground, and will return the *Ausgleich-Provisorium* to this House in a form which shall make it the protector and promoter alike of the great interests involved and of the honor of our fatherland." After a pause, turning toward the government benches: "But in any case, gentlemen of the Majority, make sure of this: henceforth, as before, you will find us at our post. The Germans of Austria will neither surrender nor die!"

Then burst a storm of applause which rose and fell, rose and fell, burst out again and again and again, explosion after explosion, hurricane after hurricane, with no apparent promise of ever coming to an end; and meantime the whole Left was surging and weltering about the champion, all bent upon wringing his hand and congratulating him and glorifying him.

Finally he got away, and went home and ate five loaves and twelve baskets of fishes, read the morning papers, slept three hours, took a short drive, then returned to the House and sat out the rest of the thirty-three-hour session.

To merely *stand up* in one spot twelve hours on a stretch is a feat which very few men could achieve; to add to the task the utterance of a hundred thousand words would be beyond the possibilities of the most of those few; to superimpose the requirement that the words should be put into the form of a compact, coherent, and symmetrical oration would probably rule out the rest of the few, bar Dr. Lecher.

III. CURIOUS PARLIAMENTARY ETIQUETTE

In consequence of Dr. Lecher's twelve-hour speech and the other obstructions furnished by the Minority, the famous thirty-three-hour sitting of the House accomplished nothing. The government side had made a supreme effort, assisting itself with all the helps at hand, both lawful and unlawful, yet had failed to get the *Ausgleich* into the hands of a committee. This was a severe defeat. The Right was mortified, the Left jubilant.

Parliament was adjourned for a week—to let the members cool off, perhaps—a sacrifice of precious time, for but two months remained in which to carry the all-important *Ausgleich* to a consummation.

If I have reported the behavior of the House intelligibly, the reader has been surprised at it, and has wondered whence these lawmakers come and what they are made of; and he has probably supposed that the conduct exhibited at the Long Sitting was far out of the common, and due to special excitement and irritation. As to the make-up of the House, it is this: the deputies come from all the walks of life and from all the grades of society. There are princes, counts, barons, priests, peasants, mechanics, laborers, lawyers, judges, physicians, professors, merchants, bankers, shopkeepers. They are religious men, they are earnest, sincere, devoted, and they hate the Jews. The title of Doctor is so common in the House that one may almost say that the deputy who does not bear it is by that reason conspicuous. I am assured that it is not a self-granted title, and not an honorary one, but an *earned* one; that in Austria it is very seldom conferred as a mere compliment; that in Austria the degrees of Doctor of Music, Doctor of Philosophy, and so on, are not conferred by the seats of learning; and so, when an Austrian is called Doctor it means that he is either a lawyer or a physician, and that he is not a self-educated man, but is college-bred, and has been diplomaed for merit.

That answers the question of the constitution of the House. Now as to the House's curious manners. The manners exhibited by this convention of Doctors were not at that time being tried as a wholly new experiment. I will go back to a previous sitting in order to show that the deputies had already had some practice.

There had been an incident. The dignity of the House had been wounded by improprieties indulged in in its presence by a couple of the members. This matter was placed in the hands of a committee to determine where the guilt lay, and the degree of it, and also to suggest the punishment. The chairman of the committee brought in his report. By this it appeared that, in the course of a speech, Deputy Schrammel said that religion had no proper place in the public schools —it was a private matter. Whereupon Deputy Gregorig shouted, "How about free love!"

To this, Deputy Iro flung out this retort: "Soda-water at the Wimberger!"

This appeared to deeply offend Deputy Gregorig, who shouted back at Iro, "You cowardly blatherskite, say that again!"

The committee had sat three hours. Gregorig had apologized; Iro had explained. Iro explained that he didn't say anything about soda-water at the Wimberger. He explained in writing, and was very explicit: "I declare *upon my word of honor* that I did not say the words attributed to me."

Unhappily for his word of honor, it was proved by the official stenographers and by the testimony of several deputies that he *did* say them.

The committee did not officially know why the apparently inconsequential reference to soda-water at the Wimberger should move Deputy Gregorig to call the utterer of it a cowardly blatherskite; still, after proper deliberation, it was of the opinion that the House ought to formally censure the whole business. This verdict seems to have been regarded as sharply severe. I think so because Deputy Dr. Lueger, Bürgermeister of Vienna, felt it a duty to soften the blow to his friend Gregorig by showing that the soda-water remark was not so innocuous as it might look; that indeed Gregorig's tough retort was justifiable— and he proceeded to explain why. He read a number of scandalous post-cards which he intimated had proceeded from Iro, as indicated by the handwriting, though they were anonymous. Some of them were posted to Gregorig at his place of business, and could have been read by all his subordinates; the others were posted *to Gregorig's wife.* Lueger did not say—but everybody knew—that the cards referred to a matter of town gossip which made Mr. Gregorig a chief actor in a tavern scene where siphon-squirting played a prominent and humorous part, and wherein women had a share.

There were several of the cards; more than several, in fact; no fewer than five were sent in one day. Dr. Lueger read some of them, and described others. Some of them had pictures on them; one a picture of a hog with a monstrous snout, and beside it a squirting soda-siphon; below it some sarcastic doggerel.

Gregorig deals in shirts, cravats, etc. One of the cards bore these words: "Much respected Deputy and collar-sewer—or *stealer*."

Another: "Hurrah for the Christian-Social work among the women assemblages! Hurrah for the soda-squirter!" Comment by Dr. Lueger: "I cannot venture to read the rest of that one, nor the signature, either."

Another: "Would you mind telling me if . . ."

Comment by Dr. Lueger: "The rest of it is not properly readable."

To Deputy Gregorig's wife: "Much respected Madam Gregorig,— The undersigned desires an invitation to the next soda-squirt." Comment by Dr. Lueger: "Neither the rest of the card nor the signature can I venture to read to the House, so vulgar are they."

The purpose of this card—to expose Gregorig to his family—was repeated in others of these anonymous missives.

The House, by vote, censured the two improper deputies.

This may have had a modifying effect upon the phraseology of the membership for a while, and upon its general exuberance also, but it was not for long. As has been seen, it had become lively once more on the night of the Long Sitting. At the next sitting after the long one there was certainly no lack of liveliness. The President was persistently ignoring the Rules of the House in the interest of the government side, and the Minority were in an unappeasable fury about it. The ceaseless din and uproar, the shouting and stamping and desk-banging, were deafening, but through it all burst voices now and then that made themselves heard. Some of the remarks were of a very candid sort, and I believe that if they had been uttered in our House of Representatives they would have attracted attention. I will insert some samples here. Not in their order, but selected on their merits:

Dr. Mayreder (to the President). "You have lied! You conceded the floor to me; make it good, or you have lied!"

Mr. Glöckner (to the President). "Leave! Get out!"

Wolf (indicating the President). "There sits a man to whom a certain title belongs!"

Unto Wolf, who is continuously reading, in a powerful voice, from a newspaper, arrive these personal remarks from the Majority: "Oh, shut your mouth!" "Put him out!" "Out with him!" Wolf stops reading a moment to shout at Dr. Lueger, who has the floor, but cannot get a hearing, "Please, Betrayer of the People, begin!"

Dr. Lueger. "Meine Herren—" ["Oho!" and groans.]

Wolf. "*That's* the holy light of the Christian Socialists!"

Mr. Kletzenbauer (Christian Socialist). "Dam—nation! are you ever going to quiet down?"

Wolf discharges a galling remark at Mr. Wohlmeyer.

Wohlmeyer (responding). "You Jew, you!"

There is a moment's lull, and Dr. Lueger begins his speech. Graceful, handsome man, with winning manners and attractive bearing, a bright and easy speaker, and is said to know how to trim his political sails to catch any favoring wind that blows. He manages to say a few words, then the tempest overwhelms him again.

Wolf stops reading his paper a moment to say a drastic thing about Lueger and his Christian-Social pieties, which sets the C. S.'s in a sort of frenzy.

Mr. Vielohlawek. "You leave the Christian Socialists alone, you word-of-honor-breaker! Obstruct all you want to, but you leave *them* alone! You've no business in this House; you belong in a gin-mill!"

Mr. Prochazka. "In a lunatic asylum, you mean!"

Vielohlawek. "It's a pity that such a man should be leader of the Germans; he disgraces the German name!"

Dr. Scheicher. "It's a shame that the like of him should insult us."

Strohbach (to Wolf). "Contemptible cub—we will bounce thee out of this!" [It is inferable that the "thee" is not intended to indicate affection this time, but to reinforce and emphasize Mr. Strohbach's scorn.]

Dr. Scheicher. "His insults are of no consequence. He wants his ears boxed."

Dr. Lueger (to Wolf). "You'd better worry a trifle over your Iro's word of honor. You are behaving like a street arab."

Dr. Scheicher. "It's infamous!"

Dr. Lueger. "And *these* shameless creatures are the leaders of the German People's Party!"

Meantime Wolf goes whooping along with his newspaper-readings in great contentment.

Dr. Pattai. "Shut up! Shut up! Shut *up!* You haven't the floor!"

Strohbach. "The miserable cub!"

Dr. Lueger (to Wolf, raising his voice strenuously above the storm). "You are a wholly honorless street brat!" [A voice, "Fire the rapscallion out!" But Wolf's soul goes marching noisily on, just the same.]

Schönerer (vast and muscular, and endowed with the most powerful voice in the Reichsrath; comes plowing down through the standing crowds, red, and choking with anger; halts before Deputy Wohlmeyer, grabs a rule and smashes it with a blow upon a desk, threatens Wohlmeyer's face with his fist, and bellows out some personalities, and a promise). "Only you wait—we'll teach you!" [A whirlwind of offensive retorts assails him from the band of meek and humble Christian Socialists compacted around their leader, that distinguished religious expert, Dr. Lueger, Bürgermeister of Vienna. Our breath comes in excited gasps now, and we are full of hope. We imagine that we are back fifty years ago in the Arkansas Legislature, and we think we know what is going to happen, and are glad we came, and glad we are up in the gallery, out of the way, where we can see the whole thing and yet not have to supply any of the material for the inquest. However, as it turns out, our confidence is abused, our hopes are misplaced.]

Dr. Pattai (wildly excited). "You quiet down, or we shall turn ourselves loose! There will be a cuffing of ears!"

Prochazka (in a fury). "Not—*not* ear-boxing, but genuine *blows!*"

Vielohlawek. "I would rather take my hat off to a Jew than to Wolf!"

Strohbach (to Wolf). "Jew-flunky! Here we have been fighting the Jews for ten years, and now you are helping them to power again. How much do you get for it?"

Holansky. "What he wants is a strait-jacket!"

Wolf continues his readings. It is a market report now.

Remark flung across the House to Schönerer: *"Die Grossmutter auf dem Misthaufen erzeugt worden!"*[2]

It will be judicious not to translate that. Its flavor is pretty high, in any case, but it becomes particularly gamey when you remember that the first gallery was well stocked with ladies.

Apparently it was a great hit. It fetched thunders of joyous enthusiasm out of the Christian Socialists, and in their rapture they flung biting epithets with wasteful liberality at specially detested members of the Opposition; among others, this one at Schönerer: *"Bordell in der Krugerstrasse!"* Then they added these words, which they whooped, howled, and also even sang, in a deep-voiced chorus: *"Schmul lieb' Kohn! Schmul lieb' Kohn! Schmul lieb' Kohn!"* and made it splendidly audible above the banging of desk-boards and the rest of the roaring cyclone of fiendish noises. [A gallery witticism comes flitting by from mouth to mouth around the great curve: "The swan-song of Austrian representative government!" You can note its progress by the applausive smiles and nods it gets as it skims along.]

[2] "Your grandmother was conceived on a dungpile!"—C.N.

Kletzenbauer. "Holofernes, where is Judith?" [Storm of laughter.]

Gregorig (the shirt-merchant). "This Wolf-Theater is costing six thousand florins!"

Wolf (with sweetness). "Notice him, gentlemen; it is Mr. Gregorig." [Laughter.]

Vielohlawek (to Wolf). "You Judas!"

Schneider. "Brothel-Knight!"

Chorus of Voices. "East-German offal-tub!"

And so the war of epithets crashes along, with never-diminishing energy, for a couple of hours.

The ladies in the gallery were learning. That was well; for by and by ladies will form a part of the membership of all the legislatures in the world; as soon as they can prove competency they will be admitted. At present, men only are competent to legislate; therefore they look down upon women, and would feel degraded if they had to have them for colleagues in their high calling.

Wolf is yelling another market report now.

Gessman. "Shut up, infamous louse-brat!"

During a momentary lull Dr. Lueger gets a hearing for three sentences of his speech. They demand and require that the President shall suppress the four noisiest members of the Opposition.

Wolf (with a that-settles-it toss of the head). "The shifty trickster of Vienna has spoken!"

Iro belonged to Schönerer's party. The word-of-honor incident has given it a new name. Gregorig is a Christian Socialist, and hero of the post-cards and the Wimberger soda-squirting incident. He stands vast and conspicuous, and conceited and self-satisfied, and roosterish and inconsequential, at Lueger's elbow, and is proud and cocky to be in such great company. He looks very well indeed; really majestic, and aware of it. He crows out his little empty remark, now and then, and looks as pleased as if he had been delivered of the *Ausgleich.* Indeed, he does look notably fine. He wears almost the only dress vest on the floor: it exposes a continental spread of white shirt-front; his hands are posed at ease in the lips of his trousers pockets; his head is tilted back complacently; he is attitudinizing; he is playing to the gallery. However, they are all doing that. It is curious to see. Men who only vote, and can't make speeches, and don't know how to invent witty ejaculations, wander about the vacated parts of the floor, and stop in a good place and strike attitudes—attitudes suggestive of weighty thought, mostly—and glance furtively up at the galleries to see how it works; or a couple will come together and shake hands in an artificial way, and laugh a gay manufactured laugh, and do some constrained and self-conscious attitudinizing; and *they* steal glances at the galleries to see if they are getting notice. It is like a scene on the stage—by-play by minor actors at the back while the stars do the great work at the front. Even Count Badeni attitudinizes for a moment; strikes a reflective Napoleonic attitude of fine picturesqueness—but soon thinks better of it and desists. There are two who do not attitudinize—poor harried and insulted President Abrahamowicz, who seems wholly miserable, and can find no way to put in the dreary time but by swinging his bell and by discharging occasional remarks which nobody can hear; and a resigned and patient priest, who sits lonely in a great vacancy on Majority territory and munches an apple.

Schönerer uplifts his fog-horn of a voice and shakes the roof with an insult discharged at the Majority.

Dr. Lueger. "The Honorless Party would better keep still here!"

Gregorig (the echo, swelling out his shirt-front). "Yes, keep quiet, pimp!"

Schönerer (to Lueger). "Political mountebank!"

Prochazka (to Schönerer). "Drunken clown!"

During the final hour of the sitting many happy phrases were distributed through the proceedings. Among them were these—and they are strikingly good ones:

Blatherskite!

Blackguard!

Scoundrel!

Brothel-daddy!

This last was the contribution of Dr. Gessman, and gave great satisfaction. And deservedly. It seems to me that it was one of the most sparkling things that was said during the whole evening.

At half-past two in the morning the House adjourned. The victory was with the Opposition. No; not quite that. The effective part of it was snatched away from them by an unlawful exercise of Presidential force—another contribution toward driving the mistreated Minority out of their minds.

At other sittings of the parliament, gentlemen of the Opposition, shaking their fists toward the President, addressed him as "Polish Dog." At one sitting an angry deputy turned upon a colleague and shouted:

"———!"

You must try to imagine what it was. If I should offer it even in the original it would probably not get by the Magazine editor's blue pencil; to offer a translation would be to waste my ink, of course. This remark was frankly printed in its entirety by one of the Vienna dailies, but the others disguised the toughest half of it with stars.

If the reader will go back over this chapter and gather its array of extraordinary epithets into a bunch and examine them, he will marvel at two things: how this convention of gentlemen could consent to use such gross terms; and why the users were allowed to get out of the place alive. There is no way to understand this strange situation. If every man in the House were a professional blackguard, and had his home in a sailor boarding-house, one could still not understand it; for although that sort do use such terms, they never *take* them. These men are not professional blackguards; they are mainly gentlemen, and educated; yet they use the terms, and take them, too. They really seem to attach no consequence to them. One cannot say that they act like school-boys; for that is only almost true, not entirely. School-boys blackguard each other fiercely, and by the hour, and one would think that nothing would ever come of it but noise; but that would be a mistake. Up to a certain limit the result would be noise only, but that limit overstepped, trouble would follow right away. There are certain phrases—phrases of a peculiar character—phrases of the nature of that reference to Schönerer's grandmother, for instance, which not even the most spiritless school-boy in the English-speaking world would allow to pass unavenged. One difference between school-boys and the lawmakers of the Reichsrath seems to be that the lawmakers have no limit, no danger-line. Apparently they may call each other what they please, and go home unmutilated.

Now, in fact, they did have a scuffle on two occasions, but it was not on account of names called. There has been no scuffle where *that* was the cause.

It is not to be inferred that the House lacks a sense of honor because it lacks delicacy. That would be an error. Iro was caught in a lie, and it profoundly disgraced him. The House cut him, turned its back upon him. He resigned his seat; otherwise he would have been expelled. But it was lenient with Gregorig, who had called Iro a cowardly blatherskite in debate. It merely went through the form of mildly censuring him. That did not trouble Gregorig.

The Viennese say of themselves that they are an easy-going, pleasure-loving community, making the best of life, and not taking it very seriously. Nevertheless, they are grieved about the ways of their parliament, and say quite frankly that they are ashamed. They claim that the low condition of the parliament's manners is new, not old. A gentleman who was at the head of the government twenty years ago confirms this, and says that in his time the parliament was orderly and well behaved. An English gentleman of long residence here indorses this, and says that a low order of politicians originated the present forms of questionable speech on the stump some years ago, and imported them into the parliament.[3] However, some day there will be a Minister of Etiquette and a sergeant-at-arms, and then things will go better. I mean if parliament and the Constitution survive the present storm.

IV. THE HISTORIC CLIMAX

During the whole of November things went from bad to worse. The all-important *Ausgleich* remained hard aground, and could not be sparred off. Badeni's government could not withdraw the Language Ordinance and keep its majority, and the Opposition could not be placated on easier terms. One night, while the customary pandemonium was crashing and thundering along at its best, a fight broke out. It was a surging, struggling, shoulder-to-shoulder scramble. A great many blows were struck. Twice Schönerer lifted one of the heavy ministerial fauteuils—some say with one hand—and threatened members of the Majority with it, but it was wrenched away from him; a member hammered Wolf over the head with the President's bell, and another member choked him; a professor was flung down and belabored with fists and choked; he held up an open penknife as a defense against the blows; it was snatched from him and flung to a distance; it hit a peaceful Christian Socialist who wasn't doing anything, and brought blood from his hand. This was the only blood drawn. The men who got hammered and choked looked sound and well next day. The fists and the bell were not properly handled, or better results would have been apparent. I am quite sure that the fighters were not in earnest.

On Thanksgiving day the sitting was a history-making one. On that day the harried, bedeviled, and despairing government went insane. In order to free itself from the thraldom of the Opposition it committed this curiously juvenile crime: it moved an important change of the Rules of the House, forbade debate upon the motion, put it to a stand-up vote instead of ayes and noes, and then gravely claimed that it

[3] "In that gracious bygone time when a mild and good-tempered spirit was the atmosphere of our House, when the manner of our speakers was studiously formal and academic, and the storms and explosions of to-day were wholly unknown," etc.—*Translation of the opening remark of an editorial in this morning's* Neue Freie Presse, *December 1, 1897.*—M.T.

had been adopted; whereas, to even the dullest witness—if I without immodesty may pretend to that place—it was plain that nothing legitimately to be called a vote had been taken at all.

I think that Saltpeter never uttered a truer thing than when he said, "Whom the gods would destroy they first make mad."

Evidently the government's mind was tottering when this bald insult to the House was the best way it could contrive for getting out of the frying-pan.

The episode would have been funny if the matter at stake had been a trifle; but in the circumstances it was pathetic. The usual storm was raging in the House. As usual, many of the Majority and the most of the Minority were standing up—to have a better chance to exchange epithets and make other noises. Into this storm Count Falkenhayn entered, with his paper in his hand; and at once there was a rush to get near him and hear him read his motion. In a moment he was walled in by listeners. The several clauses of his motion were loudly applauded by these allies, and as loudly disapplauded—if I may invent a word—by such of the Opposition as could hear his voice. When he took his seat the President promptly put the motion—persons desiring to vote in the affirmative, *stand up!* The House was already standing up; had been standing for an hour; and before a third of it had found out what the President had been saying, he had proclaimed the adoption of the motion! And only a few heard *that.* In fact, when that House is legislating you can't tell it from artillery practice.

You will realize what a happy idea it was to sidetrack the lawful ayes and noes and substitute a stand-up vote by this fact: that a little later, when a deputation of deputies waited upon the President and asked him if he was actually willing to claim that that measure had been passed, he answered, "Yes—and *unanimously.*" It shows that in effect the whole house was on its feet when that trick was sprung.

The "Lex Falkenhayn," thus strangely born, gave the President power to suspend for three days any deputy who should continue to be disorderly after being called to order twice, and it also placed at his disposal such force as might be necessary to make the suspension effective. So the House had a sergeant-at-arms at last, and a more formidable one, as to power, than any other legislature in Christendom had ever possessed. The Lex Falkenhayn also gave the House itself authority to suspend members for *thirty* days.

On these terms the *Ausgleich* could be put through in an hour—apparently. The Opposition would have to sit meek and quiet, and stop obstructing, or be turned into the street, deputy after deputy, leaving the Majority an unvexed field for its work.

Certainly the thing looked well. The government was out of the fry-ing-pan at last. It congratulated itself, and was almost girlishly happy. Its stock rose suddenly from less than nothing to a premium. It con-fessed to itself, with pride, that its Lex Falkenhayn was a master-stroke —a work of genius.

However, there were doubters; men who were troubled, and be-lieved that a grave mistake had been made. It might be that the Op-position was crushed, and profitably for the country, too; but the *man-ner* of it—the *manner* of it! That was the serious part. It could have far-reaching results; results whose gravity might transcend all guessing. It might be the initial step toward a return to government by force, a restoration of the irresponsible methods of obsolete times.

There were no vacant seats in the galleries next day. In fact, stand-ing-room outside the building was at a premium. There were crowds there, and a glittering array of helmeted and brass-buttoned police, on foot and on horseback, to keep them from getting too much excited. No one could guess what was going to happen, but every one felt that *something* was going to happen, and hoped he might have a chance to see it, or at least get the news of it while it was fresh.

At noon the House was empty—for I do not count myself. Half an hour later the two galleries were solidly packed, the floor still empty. Another half-hour later Wolf entered and passed to his place; then other deputies began to stream in, among them many forms and faces grown familiar of late. By one o'clock the membership was present in full force. A band of Socialists stood grouped against the ministerial desks, in the shadow of the Presidential tribune. It was observable that these official strongholds were now protected against rushes by bolted gates, and that these were in ward of servants wearing the House's livery. Also the removable desk-boards had been taken away, and noth-ing left for disorderly members to slat with.

There was a pervading, anxious hush—at least what stood very well for a hush in that house. It was believed by many that the Opposition was cowed, and that there would be no more obstruction, no more noise. That was an error.

Presently the President entered by the distant door to the right, fol-lowed by Vice-President Fuchs, and the two took their way down past the Polish benches toward the tribune. Instantly the customary storm of noises burst out, and rose higher and higher, and wilder and wilder, and really seemed to surpass anything that had gone before it in that place. The President took his seat, and begged for order, but no one could hear him. His lips moved—one could see that; he bowed his body forward appealingly, and spread his great hand eloquently over his breast—one could see that; but as concerned his uttered words, he probably could not hear them himself. Below him was that crowd of two dozen Socialists glaring up at him, shaking their fists at him, roaring imprecations and insulting epithets at him. This went on for some time. Suddenly the Socialists burst through the gates and stormed up through the ministerial benches, and a man in a red cravat reached up and snatched and documents that lay on the President's desk and flung them abroad. The next moment he and his allies were struggling and fighting with the half-dozen uniformed servants who were there to protect the new gates. Meantime a detail of Socialists had swarmed up the side-steps and overflowed the President and the Vice, and were crowding and shouldering and shoving them out of the place. They crowded them out, and down the steps and across the House, past the Polish benches; and all about them swarmed hostile Poles and Czechs, who resisted them. One could see fists go up and come down, with other signs and shows of a heady fight; then the President and the Vice disappeared through the door of entrance, and the victorious Socialists turned and marched back, mounted the tribune, flung the President's bell and his remaining papers abroad, and then stood there in a compact little crowd, eleven strong, and held the place as if it were a fortress. Their friends on the floor were in a frenzy of triumph, and manifested it in their deafening way. The whole House was on its feet, amazed and wondering.

It was an astonishing situation, and imposingly dramatic. Nobody had looked for this. The unexpected had happened. What next? But there *can* be no next; the play is over; the grand climax is reached; the possibilities are exhausted: ring down the curtain.

Not yet. That distant door opens again. And now we see what history will be talking of five centuries hence: a uniformed and helmeted battalion of bronzed and stalwart men marching in double file down the floor of the House—a free parliament profaned by an invasion of brute force.

It was an odious spectacle—odious and awful. For one moment it was an unbelievable thing—a thing beyond all credibility; it must be a delusion, a dream, a nightmare. But no, it was real—pitifully real, shamefully real, hideously real. These sixty policemen had been soldiers, and they went at their work with the cold unsentimentality of their trade. They ascended the steps of the tribune, laid their hands upon the inviolable persons of the representatives of a nation, and dragged and tugged and hauled them down the steps and out at the door; then ranged themselves in stately military array in front of the ministerial *estrade,* and so stood.

It was a tremendous episode. The memory of it will outlast all the thrones that exist to-day. In the whole history of free parliaments the like of it had been seen but three times before. It takes its imposing place among the world's unforgetable things. I think that in my life-time I have not twice seen abiding history made before any eyes, but I know that I have seen it once.

Some of the results of this wild freak followed instantly. The Badeni government came down with a crash; there was a popular outbreak or two in Vienna; there were three or four days of furious rioting in Prague, followed by the establishing there of martial law; the Jews and Germans were harried and plundered, and their houses destroyed; in other Bohemian towns there was rioting—in some cases the Germans being the rioters, in others the Czechs—and in all cases the Jew had to roast, no matter which side he was on. We are well along in De-cember now,[4] the new Minister-President has not been able to patch up a peace among the warring factions of the parliament, therefore there is no use in calling it together again for the present; public opin-ion believes that parliamentary government and the Constitution are actually threatened with extinction, and that the permanency of the monarchy itself is a not absolutely certain thing!

Yes, the Lex Falkenhayn was a great invention, and did what was claimed for it—it got the government out of the frying-pan.

1898

Concerning the Jews

Some months ago I published a magazine article descriptive of a remarkable scene in the Imperial Parliament in Vienna. Since then I have received from Jews in America several letters of inquiry. They were difficult letters to answer, for they were not very definite. But at last I received a definite one. It is from a lawyer, and he really asks

[4] It is the 9th.—M.T.

the questions which the other writers probably believed they were asking. By help of this text I will do the best I can to publicly answer
this correspondent, and also the others—at the same time apologizing
for having failed to reply privately. The lawyer's letter reads as follows:

I have read "Stirring Times in Austria." One point in particular is of
vital import to not a few thousand people, including myself, being a point
about which I have often wanted to address a question to some disinterested person. The show of military force in the Austrian Parliament,
which precipitated the riots, was not introduced by any Jew. No Jew was
a member of that body. No Jewish question was involved in the *Ausgleich*
or in the language proposition. No Jew was insulting anybody. In short,
no Jew was doing any mischief toward anybody whatsoever. In fact, the
Jews were the only ones of the nineteen different races in Austria which
did not have a party—they are absolutely non-participants. Yet in your
article you say that in the rioting which followed, all classes of people
were unanimous only on one thing—*viz.,* in being against the Jews. Now
will you kindly tell me why, in your judgment, the Jews have thus ever
been, and are even now, in these days of supposed intelligence, the butt
of baseless, vicious animosities? I dare say that for centuries there has been
no more quiet, undisturbing, and well-behaving citizens, as a class, than
that same Jew. It seems to me that ignorance and fanaticism cannot alone
account for these horrible and unjust persecutions.
Tell me, therefore, from your vantage-point of cold view, what in your
mind is the cause. Can American Jews do anything to correct it either in
America or abroad? Will it ever come to an end? Will a Jew be permitted
to live honestly, decently, and peaceably like the rest of mankind? What
has become of the golden rule?

I will begin by saying that if I thought myself prejudiced against the
Jew, I should hold it fairest to leave this subject to a person not crippled in that way. But I think I have no such prejudice. A few years
ago a Jew observed to me that there was no uncourteous reference to
his people in my books, and asked how it happened. It happened because the disposition was lacking. I am quite sure that (bar one) I
have no race prejudices, and I think I have no color prejudices nor
caste prejudices nor creed prejudices. Indeed, I know it. I can stand
any society. All that I care to know is that a man is a human being—
that is enough for me; he can't be any worse. I have no special regard
for Satan; but I can at least claim that I have no prejudice against
him. It may even be that I lean a little his way, on account of his not
having a fair show. All religions issue bibles against him, and say the

most injurious things about him, but we never hear *his* side. We have
none but the evidence for the prosecution, and yet we have rendered
the verdict. To my mind, this is irregular. It is un-English; it is un-
American; it is French. Without this precedent Dreyfus could not have
been condemned. Of course Satan has some kind of a case, it goes
without saying. It may be a poor one, but that is nothing; that can be
said about any of us. As soon as I can get at the facts I will undertake his rehabilitation myself, if I can find an unpolitic publisher. It
is a thing which we ought to be willing to do for any one who is under
a cloud. We may not pay him reverence, for that would be indiscreet,
but we can at least respect his talents. A person who has for untold
centuries maintained the imposing position of spiritual head of four-
fifths of the human race, and political head of the whole of it, must be
granted the possession of executive abilities of the loftiest order. In
his large presence the other popes and politicians shrink to midges for
the microscope. I would like to see him. I would rather see him and
shake him by the tail than any other member of the European Concert.
In the present paper I shall allow myself to use the word Jew as if
it stood for both religion and race. It is handy; and, besides, that is
what the term means to the general world.

In the above letter one notes these points:

1. The Jew is a well-behaved citizen.

2. Can ignorance and fanaticism *alone* account for his unjust treatment?

3. Can Jews do anything to improve the situation?

4. The Jews have no party; they are non-participants.

5. Will the persecution ever come to an end?

6. What has become of the golden rule?

Point No. 1.—We must grant proposition No. 1, for several sufficient
reasons. The Jew is not a disturber of the peace of any country. Even
his enemies will concede that. He is not a loafer, he is not a sot, he is
not noisy, he is not a brawler nor a rioter, he is not quarrelsome. In the
statistics of crime his presence is conspicuously rare—in all countries.
With murder and other crimes of violence he has but little to do: he is
a stranger to the hangman. In the police court's daily long roll of "assaults" and "drunk and disorderlies" his name seldom appears. That
the Jewish home is a home in the truest sense is a fact which no one
will dispute. The family is knitted together by the strongest affections;
its members show each other every due respect; and reverence for the
elders is an inviolate law of the house. The Jew is not a burden on the

charities of the state nor of the city; these could cease from their functions without affecting him. When he is well enough, he works; when
he is incapacitated, his own people take care of him. And not in a poor
and stingy way, but with a fine and large benevolence. His race is
entitled to be called the most benevolent of all the races of men. A
Jewish beggar is not impossible, perhaps; such a thing may exist, but
there are few men that can say they have seen that spectacle. The Jew
has been staged in many uncomplimentary forms, but, so far as I know,
no dramatist has done him the injustice to stage him as a beggar. Whenever a Jew has real need to beg, his people save him from the necessity
of doing it. The charitable institutions of the Jews are supported by
Jewish money, and amply. The Jews make no noise about it; it is done
quietly; they do not nag and pester and harass us for contributions;
they give us peace, and set us an example—an example which we have
not found ourselves able to follow; for by nature we are not free givers,
and have to be patiently and persistently hunted down in the interest
of the unfortunate.

These facts are all on the credit side of the proposition that the Jew
is a good and orderly citizen. Summed up, they certify that he is quiet,
peaceable, industrious, unaddicted to high crimes and brutal dispositions; that his family life is commendable; that he is not a burden upon
public charities; that he is not a beggar; that in benevolence he is above
the reach of competition. These are the very quintessentials of good
citizenship. If you can add that he is as honest as the average of his
neighbors— But I think that question is affirmatively answered by the
fact that he is a successful business man. The basis of successful business is honesty; a business cannot thrive where the parties to it cannot
trust each other. In the matter of numbers the Jew counts for little in
the overwhelming population of New York; but that his honesty counts
for much is guaranteed by the fact that the immense wholesale business
of Broadway, from the Battery to Union Square, is substantially in his
hands.

I suppose that the most picturesque example in history of a trader's
trust in his fellow-trader was one where it was not Christian trusting
Christian, but Christian trusting Jew. That Hessian Duke who used to
sell his subjects to George III. to fight George Washington with got
rich at it; and by and by, when the wars engendered by the French
Revolution made his throne too warm for him, he was obliged to fly
the country. He was in a hurry, and had to leave his earnings behind—
nine million dollars. He had to risk the money with some one without
security. He did not select a Christian, but a Jew—a Jew of only mod-

est means, but of high character; a character so high that it left him lonesome—Rothschild of Frankfort. Thirty years later, when Europe had become quiet and safe again, the Duke came back from overseas, and the Jew returned the loan, with interest added.[1]

The Jew has his other side. He has some discreditable ways, though he has not a monopoly of them, because he cannot get entirely rid of vexatious Christian competition. We have seen that he seldom transgresses the laws against crimes of violence. Indeed, his dealings with courts are almost restricted to matters connected with commerce. He has a reputation for various small forms of cheating, and for practising oppressive usury, and for burning himself out to get the insurance, and arranging for cunning contracts which leave him an exit but lock the other man in, and for smart evasions which find him safe and comfortable just within the strict letter of the law, when court and jury know

[1] Here is another piece of picturesque history; and it reminds us that shabbiness and dishonesty are not the monopoly of any race or creed, but are merely human:

"Congress passed a bill to pay $379.56 to Moses Pendergrass, of Libertyville, Missouri. The story of the reason of this liberality is pathetically interesting, and shows the sort of pickle that an honest man may get into who undertakes to do an honest job of work for Uncle Sam. In 1886 Moses Pendergrass put in a bid for the contract to carry the mail on the route from Knob Lick to Libertyville and Coffman, thirty miles a day, from July 1, 1887, for one year. He got the postmaster at Knob Lick to write the letter for him, and while Moses intended that his bid should be $400, his scribe carelessly made it $4. Moses got the contract, and did not find out about the mistake until the end of the first quarter, when he got his first pay. When he found at what rate he was working he was sorely cast down, and opened communication with the Post Office Department. The department informed him that he must either carry out his contract or throw it up, and that if he threw it up his bondsmen would have to pay the government $1,459.85 damages. So Moses carried out his contract, walked thirty miles every weekday for a year, and carried the mail, and received for his labor $4—or, to be accurate, $6.84; for, the route being extended after his bid was accepted, the pay was proportionately increased. Now, after ten years, a bill was finally passed to pay to Moses the difference between what he earned in that unlucky year and what he received."

The *Sun*, which tells the above story, says that bills were introduced in three or four Congresses for Moses' relief, and that committees repeatedly investigated his claim.

It took six Congresses, containing in their persons the compressed virtues of 70,000,000 of people, and cautiously and carefully giving expression to those virtues in the fear of God and the next election, eleven years to find out some way to cheat a fellow-Christian out of about $13 on his honestly executed contract, and out of nearly $300 due him on its enlarged terms. And they succeeded. During the same time they paid out $1,000,000,000 in pensions—a third of it unearned and undeserved. This indicates a splendid all-around competency in theft, for it starts with farthings, and works its industries all the way up to ship-loads. It may be possible that the Jews can beat this, but the man that bets on it is taking chances.

very well that he has violated the spirit of it. He is a frequent and faithful and capable officer in the civil service, but he is charged with a unpatriotic disinclination to stand by the flag as a soldier—like the Christian Quaker.

Now if you offset these discreditable features by the creditable ones summarized in a preceding paragraph beginning with the words, "These facts are all on the credit side," and strike a balance, what must the verdict be? This, I think: that, the merits and demerits being fairly weighed and measured on both sides, the Christian can claim no superiority over the Jew in the matter of good citizenship.

Yet, in all countries, from the dawn of history, the Jew has been persistently and implacably hated, and with frequency persecuted.

Point No. 2.—"Can fanaticism *alone* account for this?"

Years ago I used to think that it was responsible for nearly all of it, but latterly I have come to think that this was an error. Indeed, it is now my conviction that it is responsible for hardly any of it. In this connection I call to mind Genesis, chapter xlvii.

We have all thoughtfully—or unthoughtfully—read the pathetic story of the years of plenty and the years of famine in Egypt, and how Joseph, with that opportunity, made a corner in broken hearts, and the crusts of the poor, and human liberty—a corner whereby he took a nation's money all away, to the last penny; took a nation's land away, to the last acre; then took the nation itself, buying it for bread, man by man, woman by woman, child by child, till all were slaves; a corner which took everything, left nothing; a corner so stupendous that, by comparison with it, the most gigantic corners in subsequent history are but baby things, for it dealt in hundreds of millions of bushels, and its profits were reckonable by hundreds of millions of dollars, and it was a disaster so crushing that its effects have not wholly disappeared from Egypt to-day, more than three thousand years after the event.

Is it presumable that the eye of Egypt was upon Joseph, the foreign Jew, all this time? I think it likely. Was it friendly? We must doubt it. Was Joseph establishing a character for his race which would survive long in Egypt? And in time would his name come to be familiarly used to express that character—like Shylock's? It is hardly to be doubted. Let us remember that this was *centuries before the crucifixion.*

I wish to come down eighteen hundred years later and refer to a remark made by one of the Latin historians. I read it in a translation many years ago, and it comes back to me now with force. It was alluding to a time when people were still living who could have seen the

Saviour in the flesh. Christianity was so new that the people of Rome
had hardly heard of it, and had but confused notions of what it was.
The substance of the remark was this: Some Christians were persecuted in Rome through error, they being *"mistaken for Jews."*

The meaning seems plain. These pagans had nothing against Christians, but they were quite ready to persecute Jews. For some reason
or other they hated a Jew before they even knew what a Christian
was. May I not assume, then, that the persecution of Jews is a thing
which *antedates* Christianity and was not born of Christianity? I think
so. What was the origin of the feeling?

When I was a boy, in the back settlements of the Mississippi Valley,
where a gracious and beautiful Sunday-school simplicity and unpracti-
cality prevailed, the "Yankee" (citizen of the New England states) was
hated with a splendid energy. But religion had nothing to do with it.
In a trade, the Yankee was held to be about five times the match of the
Westerner. His shrewdness, his insight, his judgment, his knowledge,
his enterprise, and his formidable cleverness in applying these forces
were frankly confessed, and most competently cursed.

In the cotton states, after the war, the simple and ignorant negroes
made the crops for the white planter on shares. The Jews came down in
force, set up shop on the plantation, supplied all the negro's wants on
credit, and at the end of the season was proprietor of the negro's share
of the present crop and of part of his share of the next one. Before
long, the whites detested the Jew, and it is doubtful if the negro loved
him.

The Jew is being legislated out of Russia. The reason is not concealed. The movement was instituted because the Christian peasant
and villager stood no chance against his commercial abilities. He was
always ready to lend money on a crop, and sell vodka and other neces-
saries of life on credit while the crop was growing. When settlement
day came he owned the crop; and next year or year after he owned the
farm, like Joseph.

In the dull and ignorant England of John's time everybody got into
debt to the Jew. He gathered all lucrative enterprises into his hands; he
was the king of commerce; he was ready to be helpful in all profitable
ways; he even financed crusades for the rescue of the Sepulcher. To
wipe out his account with the nation and restore business to its natural
and incompetent channels he had to be banished the realm.

For the like reasons Spain had to banish him four hundred years ago,
and Austria about a couple of centuries later.

In all the ages Christian Europe has been obliged to curtail his activities. If he entered upon a mechanical trade, the Christian had to retire from it. If he set up as a doctor, he was the best one, and he took the business. If he exploited agriculture, the other farmers had to get at something else. Since there was no way to successfully compete with him in any vocation, the law had to step in and save the Christian from the poorhouse. Trade after trade was taken away from the Jew by statute till practically none was left. He was forbidden to engage in agriculture; he was forbidden to practise law; he was forbidden to practise medicine, except among Jews; he was forbidden the handi-crafts. Even the seats of learning and the schools of science had to be closed against this tremendous antagonist. Still, almost bereft of em-ployments, he found ways to make money, even ways to get rich. Also ways to invest his takings well, for usury was not denied him. In the hard conditions suggested, the Jew without brains could not survive, and the Jew with brains had to keep them in good training and well sharpened up, or starve. Ages of restriction to the one tool which the law was not able to take from him—his brain—have made that tool singularly competent; ages of compulsory disuse of his hands have atro-phied them, and he never uses them now. This history has a very, very commercial look, a most sordid and practical commercial look, the busi-ness aspect of a Chinese cheap-labor crusade. Religious prejudices may account for one part of it, but not for the other nine.

Protestants have persecuted Catholics, but they did not take their livelihoods away from them. The Catholics have persecuted the Prot-estants with bloody and awful bitterness, but they never closed agri-culture and the handicrafts against them. Why was that? That has the candid look of genuine religious persecution, not a trade-union boycott in a religious disguise.

The Jews are harried and obstructed in Austria and Germany, and lately in France; but England and America give them an open field and yet survive. Scotland offers them an unembarrassed field too, but there are not many takers. There are a few Jews in Glasgow, and one in Aberdeen; but that is because they can't earn enough to get away. The Scotch pay themselves that compliment, but it is authentic.

I feel convinced that the Crucifixion has not much to do with the world's attitude toward the Jew; that the reasons for it are older than that event, as suggested by Egypt's experience and by Rome's regret for having persecuted an unknown quantity called a Christian, under the mistaken impression that she was merely persecuting a Jew. *Merely* a Jew—a skinned eel who was used to it, presumably. I am persuaded that in Russia, Austria, and Germany nine-tenths of the hostility to the

Jews comes from the average Christian's inability to compete successfully with the average Jew in business—in either straight business or
the questionable sort.

In Berlin, a few years ago, I read a speech which frankly urged the
expulsion of the Jews from Germany; and the agitator's *reason* was as
frank as his proposition. It was this: *that eighty-five per cent.* of the
successful lawyers of Berlin were Jews, and that about the same percentage of the great and lucrative businesses of all sorts in Germany
were in the hands of the Jewish race! Isn't it an amazing confession?
It was but another way of saying that in a population of 48,000,000, of
whom only 500,000 were registered as Jews, eighty-five per cent. of
the brains and honesty of the whole was lodged in the Jews. I must
insist upon the honesty—it is an essential of successful business, taken
by and large. Of course it does not rule out rascals entirely, even among
Christians, but it is a good working rule, nevertheless. The speaker's
figures may have been inexact, but *the motive of persecution* stands
out as clear as day.

The man claimed that in Berlin the banks, the newspapers, the theaters, the great mercantile, shipping, mining, and manufacturing interests, the big army and city contracts, the tramways, and pretty much
all other properties of high value, and *also* the small businesses—were
in the hands of the Jews. He said the Jew was pushing the Christian
to the wall all along the line; that it was all a Christian could do to
scrape together a living; and that the Jew *must* be banished, and soon—
there was no other way of saving the Christian. Here in Vienna, last
autumn, an agitator said that all these disastrous details were true of
Austria-Hungary also; and in fierce language he demanded the expulsion of the Jews. When politicians come out without a blush and read
the baby act in this frank way, *unrebuked,* it is a very good indication
that they have a market back of them, and know where to fish for votes.

You note the crucial point of the mentioned agitation; the argument
is that the Christian cannot *compete* with the Jew, and that hence his
very bread is in peril. To human beings this is a much more hate-inspir-
ing thing than is any detail connected with religion. With most people,
of a necessity, bread and meat take first rank, religion second. I am
convinced that the persecution of the Jew is not due in any large
degree to religious prejudice.

No, the Jew is a money-getter; and in getting his money he is a very
serious obstruction to less capable neighbors who are on the same
quest. I think that that is the trouble. In estimating worldly values the
Jew is not shallow, but deep. With precocious wisdom he found out in

the morning of time that some men worship rank, some worship heros, some worship power, some worship God, and that over these ideals they dispute and cannot unite—but that they all worship money; so he made it the end and aim of his life to get it. He was at it in Egypt thirty-six centuries ago; he was at it in Rome when that Christian got persecuted by mistake for him; he has been at it ever since. The cost to him has been heavy; his success has made the whole human race his enemy—but it has paid, for it has brought him envy, and that is the only thing which men will sell both soul and body to get. He long ago observed that a millionaire commands respect, a two-millionaire homage, a multi-millionaire the deepest deeps of adoration. We all know that feeling; we have seen it express itself. We have noticed that when the average man mentions the name of a multi-millionaire he does it with that mixture in his voice of awe and reverence and lust which burns in a Frenchman's eye when it falls on another man's centime.

Point No. 4.—"The Jews have no party; they are non-participants."

Perhaps you have let the secret out and given yourself away. It seems hardly a credit to the race that it is able to say that; or to you, sir, that you can say it without remorse; more, that you should offer it as a plea against maltreatment, injustice, and oppression. Who gives the Jew the right, who gives any race the right, to sit still, in a free country, and let somebody else look after its safety? The oppressed Jew was entitled to all pity in the former times under brutal autocracies, for he was weak and friendless, and had no way to help his case. But he has ways now, and he has had them for a century, but I do not see that he has tried to make serious use of them. When the Revolution set him free in France it was an act of grace—the grace of other people; he does not appear in it as a helper. I do not know that he helped when England set him free. Among the Twelve Sane Men of France who have stepped forward with great Zola at their head to fight (and win, I hope and believe[2]) the battle for the most infamously misused Jew of modern times, do you find a great or rich or illustrious Jew helping? In the United States he was created free in the beginning—he did not need to help, of course. In Austria, and Germany, and France he has a vote, but of what considerable use is it to him? He doesn't seem to know how to apply it to the best effect. With all his splendid capacities and all his fat wealth he is to-day not politically important in any country. In America, as early as 1854, the ignorant Irish hod-carrier, who had a spirit of his own and a way of exposing it to the

[2] The article was written in the summer of 1898.—Editor, *Harper's Magazine.*

weather, made it apparent to all that he must be politically reckoned with; yet fifteen years before that we hardly knew what an Irishman looked like. As an intelligent force, and numerically, he has always been away down, but he has governed the country just the same. It was because he was *organized*. It made his vote valuable—in fact, essential.

You will say the Jew is everywhere numerically feeble. That is nothing to the point—with the Irishman's history for an object-lesson. But I am coming to your numerical feebleness presently. In all parliamentary countries you could no doubt elect Jews to the legislatures—and even *one* member in such a body is sometimes a force which counts. How deeply have you concerned yourselves about this in Austria, France, and Germany? Or even in America for that matter? You remark that the Jews were not to blame for the riots in this Reichsrath here, and you add with satisfaction that there wasn't one in that body. That is not strictly correct; if it were, would it not be in order for you to explain it and apologize for it, not try to make a merit of it? But I think that the Jew was by no means in as large force there as he ought to have been, with his chances. Austria opens the suffrage to him on fairly liberal terms, and it must surely be his own fault that he is so much in the background politically.

As to your numerical weakness. I mentioned some figures awhile ago —500,000—as the Jewish population of Germany. I will add some more —6,000,000 in Russia, 5,000,000 in Austria, 250,000 in the United States. I take them from memory; I read them in the *Encyclopædia Britannica* about ten years ago. Still, I am entirely sure of them. If those statistics are correct, my argument is not as strong as it ought to be as concerns America, but it still has strength. It is plenty strong enough as concerns Austria, for ten years ago 5,000,000 was nine per cent. of the empire's population. The Irish would govern the Kingdom of Heaven if they had a strength there like that.

I have some suspicions; I got them at second hand, but they have remained with me these ten or twelve years. When I read in the *E.B.* that the Jewish population of the United States was 250,000, I wrote the editor, and explained to him that I was personally acquainted with more Jews than that in my country, and that his figures were without doubt a misprint for 25,000,000. I also added that I was personally acquainted with *that* many there; but that was only to raise his confidence in me, for it was not true. His answer miscarried, and I never got it; but I went around talking about the matter, and people told me they had reason to suspect that for business reasons many Jews whose dealings were mainly with the Christians did not report themselves as Jews in the census. It looked plausible; it looks plausible yet. Look at the city of New York; and look at Boston, and Philadelphia, and New Orleans, and Chicago, and Cincinnati, and San Francisco—how your race swarms in those places!—and everywhere else in America, down to the least little village. Read the signs on the marts of commerce, and on the shops: Goldstein (gold stone), Edelstein (precious stone), Blumenthal (flower-vale), Rosenthal (rose-vale), Verlchenduft (violet odor), Singvogel (song-bird), Rosenzweig (rose branch), and all the amazing list of beautiful and enviable names which Prussia and Austria glorified you with so long ago. It is another instance of Europe's coarse and cruel persecution of your race; not that it was coarse and cruel to outfit it with pretty and poetical names like those, but that it was coarse and cruel to make it *pay* for them or else take such hideous and often indecent names that to-day their owners never use them; or, if they do, only on official papers. And it was the many, not the few, who got the odious names, they being too poor to bribe the officials to grant better ones.

Now why was the race renamed? I have been told that in Prussia it was given to using fictitious names, and often changing them, so as to beat the tax-gatherer, escape military service, and so on; and that finally the idea was hit upon of furnishing all the inmates of a house with *one and the same surname*, and then holding the house responsible right along for those inmates, and accountable for any disappearances that might occur; it made the Jews keep track of *each other*, for self-interest's sake, and saved the government the trouble.[3]

If that explanation of how the Jews of Prussia came to be renamed is correct, if it is true that they fictitiously registered themselves to gain certain advantages, it may possibly be true that in America they refrain from registering themselves as Jews to fend off the damaging prejudices of the Christian customer. I have no way of knowing whether this notion is well founded or not. There may be other and better ways of explaining why only that poor little 250,000 of our Jews got into the

[3] In Austria the renaming was merely done because the Jews in some newly acquired regions had no surnames, but were mostly named Abraham and Moses, and therefore the tax-gatherer could not tell t'other from which, and was likely to lose his reason over the matter. The renaming was put into the hands of the War Department, and a charming mess the graceless young lieutenants made of it. To them a Jew was of no sort of consequence, and they labeled the race in a way to make the angels weep. As an example take these two! *Abraham Bellyache* and *Schmul Godbedamned.—Culled from "Namens Studien," by Karl Emil Franzos.*

Encyclopædia. I may, of course, be mistaken, but I am strongly of the opinion that we have an immense Jewish population in America.

Point No. 3.—"Can Jews do anything to improve the situation?"

I think so. If I may make a suggestion without seeming to be trying to teach my grandmother how to suck eggs, I will offer it. In our days we have learned the value of combination. We apply it everywhere—in railway systems, in trusts, in trade-unions, in Salvation Armies, in minor politics, in major politics, in European Concerts. Whatever our strength may be, big or little, we *organize* it. We have found out that that is the only way to get the most out of it that is in it. We know the weakness of individual sticks, and the strength of the concentrated fagot. Suppose you try a scheme like this, for instance. In England and America put every Jew on the census-book *as* a Jew (in case you have not been doing that). Get up volunteer regiments composed of Jews solely, and, when the drum beats, fall in and go to the front, so as to remove the reproach that you have few Massénas among you, and that you feed on a country but don't like to fight for it. Next, in politics, organize your strength, band together, and deliver the casting vote where you can, and, where you can't, compel as good terms as possible. You huddle to yourselves already in all countries, but you huddle to no sufficient purpose, politically speaking. You do not seem to be organized, except for your charities. There you are omnipotent; there you compel your due of recognition—you do not have to beg for it. It shows what you can do when you band together for a definite purpose.

And then from America and England you can encourage your race in Austria, France, and Germany, and materially help it. It was a pathetic tale that was told by a poor Jew in Galicia a fortnight ago during the riots, after he had been raided by the Christian peasantry and despoiled of everything he had. He said his vote was of no value to him, and he wished he could be excused from casting it, for indeed casting it was a sure *damage* to him, since no matter which party he voted for, the other party would come straight and take its revenge out of him. Nine per cent. of the population of the empire, these Jews, and apparently they cannot put a plank into any candidate's platform! If you will send our Irish lads over here I think they will organize your race and change the aspect of the Reichsrath.

You seem to think that the Jews take no hand in politics here, that they are "absolutely non-participants." I am assured by men competent to speak that this is a very large error, that the Jews are exceedingly active in politics all over the empire, but that they scatter

their work and their votes among the numerous parties, and thus lose
the advantages to be had by concentration. I think that in America
they scatter too, but you know more about that than I do.

Speaking of concentration, Dr. Herzl has a clear insight into the
value of that. Have you heard of his plan? He wishes to gather the
Jews of the world together in Palestine, with a government of their
own—under the suzerainty of the Sultan, I suppose. At the convention
of Berne, last year, there were delegates from everywhere, and the
proposal was received with decided favor. I am not the Sultan, and I
am not objecting; but if that concentration of the cunningest brains in
the world was going to be made in a free country (bar Scotland), I
think it would be politic to stop it. It will not be well to let that race
find out its strength. If the horses knew theirs, we should not ride any
more.

Point No. 5.—"Will the persecution of the Jews ever come to an
end?"

On the score of religion, I think it has already come to an end. On the
score of race prejudice and trade, I have the idea that it will continue.
That is, here and there in spots about the world, where a barbarous
ignorance and a sort of mere animal civilization prevail; but I do not
think that elsewhere the Jew need now stand in any fear of being
robbed and raided. Among the high civilizations he seems to be very
comfortably situated indeed, and to have more than his proportionate
share of the prosperities going. It has that look in Vienna. I suppose
the race prejudice cannot be removed; but he can stand that; it is no
particular matter. By his make and ways he is substantially a foreigner
wherever he may be, and even the angels dislike a foreigner. I am using
this word foreigner in the German sense—*stranger.* Nearly all of us have
an antipathy to a stranger, even of our own nationality. We pile grip-
sacks in a vacant seat to keep him from getting it; and a dog goes further, and does as a savage would—challenges him on the spot. The German dictionary seems to make no distinction between a stranger and a
foreigner; in its view a stranger *is* a foreigner—a sound position, I think.
You will always be by ways and habits and predilections substantially
strangers—foreigners—wherever you are, and that will probably keep
the race prejudice against you alive.

But you were the favorites of Heaven originally, and your manifold
and unfair prosperities convince me that you have crowded back into
that snug place again. Here is an incident that is significant. Last week
in Vienna a hail-storm struck the prodigious Central Cemetery and
made wasteful destruction there. In the Christian part of it, according

to the official figures, 621 window-panes were broken; more than 900 singing-birds were killed; five great trees and many small ones were torn to shreds and the shreds scattered far and wide by the wind; the ornamental plants and other decorations of the graves were ruined, and more than a hundred tomb-lanterns shattered; and it took the cemetery's whole force of 300 laborers more than three days to clear away the storm's wreckage. In the report occurs this remark—and in its italics you can hear it grit its Christian teeth: ". . . lediglich die *israelitische* Abtheilung des Friedhofes vom Hagelwetter *ganzlich verschont* worden war." Not a hailstone hit the Jewish reservation! Such nepotism makes me tired.

Point No. 6.—"What has become of the golden rule?"

It exists, it continues to sparkle, and is well taken care of. It is Exhibit A in the Church's assets, and we pull it out every Sunday and give it an airing. But you are not permitted to try to smuggle it into this discussion, where it is irrelevant and would not feel at home. It is strictly religious furniture, like an acolyte, or a contribution-plate, or any of those things. It has never been intruded into business; and Jewish persecution is not a religious passion, it is a business passion.

To conclude.—If the statistics are right, the Jews constitute but *one per cent.* of the human race. It suggests a nebulous dim puff of star dust lost in the blaze of the Milky Way. Properly the Jew ought hardly to be heard of; but he is heard of, has always been heard of. He is as prominent on the planet as any other people, and his commercial importance is extravagantly out of proportion to the smallness of his bulk. His contributions to the world's list of great names in literature, science, art, music, finance, medicine, and abstruse learning are also away out of proportion to the weakness of his numbers. He has made a marvelous fight in this world, in all the ages; and has done it with his hands tied behind him. He could be vain of himself, and be excused for it. The Egyptian, the Babylonian, and the Persian rose, filled the planet with sound and splendor, then faded to dream-stuff and passed away; the Greek and the Roman followed, and made a vast noise, and they are gone; other peoples have sprung up and held their torch high for a time, but it burned out, and they sit in twilight now, or have vanished. The Jew saw them all, beat them all, and is now what he always was, exhibiting no decadence, no infirmities of age, no weakening of his parts, no slowing of his energies, no dulling of his alert and aggressive mind. All things are mortal but the Jew; all other forces pass, but he remains. What is the secret of his immortality?

Postscript—THE JEW AS SOLDIER

When I published the above article in HARPER'S MONTHLY,[4] I was ignorant—like the rest of the Christian world—of the fact that the Jew had a record as a soldier. I have since seen the official statistics, and I find that he furnished soldiers and high officers to the Revolution, the War of 1812, and the Mexican War. In the Civil War he was represented in the armies and navies of both the North and the South by 10 per cent. of his numerical strength—the same percentage that was furnished by the Christian populations of the two sections. This large fact means more than it seems to mean; for it means that the Jew's patriotism was not merely level with the Christian's, but overpassed it. When the Christian volunteer arrived in camp he got a welcome and applause, but as a rule the Jew got a snub. His company was not desired, and he was made to feel it. That he nevertheless conquered his wounded pride and sacrificed both that and his blood for his flag raises the average and quality of his patriotism above the Christian's. His record for capacity, for fidelity, and for gallant soldiership in the field is as good as any one's. This is true of the Jewish private soldiers and the Jewish generals alike. Major-General O. O. Howard speaks of one of his Jewish staff-officers as being "of the bravest and best"; of another—killed at Chancellorsville—as being "a true friend and a brave officer"; he highly praises two of his Jewish brigadier-generals; finally, he uses these strong words: "Intrinsically there are no more patriotic men to be found in the country than those who claim to be of Hebrew descent, and who served with me in parallel commands or more directly under my instructions."

Fourteen Jewish Confederate and Union families contributed, between them, fifty-one soldiers to the war. Among these, a father and three sons; and another, a father and four sons.

In the above article I was not able to endorse the common reproach that the Jew is willing to feed upon a country but not to fight for it, because I did not know whether it was true or false. I supposed it to be true, but it is not allowable to endorse wandering maxims upon supposition—except when one is trying to make out a case. That slur upon the Jew cannot hold up its head in presence of the figures of the War Department. It has done its work, and done it long and faithfully, and with high approval: it ought to be pensioned off now, and retired from active service.

1899

* September 1899.—C.N.

Diplomatic Pay and Clothes

Vienna, *January* 5.—I find in this morning's papers the statement that the government of the United States has paid to the two members of the Peace Commission entitled to receive money for their services one hundred thousand dollars each for their six weeks' work in Paris.

I hope that this is true. I will allow myself the satisfaction of considering that it *is* true, and of treating it as a thing finished and settled.

It is a precedent; and ought to be a welcome one to our country. A precedent always has a chance to be valuable (as well as the other way); and its best chance to be valuable (or the other way) is when it takes such a striking form as to fix a whole nation's attention upon it. If it come justified out of the discussion which will follow, it will find a career ready and waiting for it.

We realize that the edifice of public justice is built of precedents, from the ground upward; but we do not always realize that all the other details of our civilization are likewise built of precedents. The changes also which they undergo are due to the intrusion of new precedents, which hold their ground against opposition, and keep their place. A precedent may die at birth, or it may live—it is mainly a matter of luck. If it be imitated once, it has a chance; if twice, a better chance; if three times it is reaching a point where account must be taken of it; if four, five, or six times, it has probably come to stay—for a whole century, possibly. If a town start a new bow, or a new dance, or a new temperance project, or a new kind of hat, and can get the precedent adopted in the next town, the career of that precedent is begun; and it will be unsafe to bet as to where the end of its journey is going to be. It may not get this start at all, and may have no career; but if a crown prince introduce the precedent, it will attract vast attention, and its chances for a career are so great as to amount almost to a certainty.

For a long time we have been reaping damage from a couple of disastrous precedents. One is the precedent of shabby pay to public servants standing for the power and dignity of the Republic in foreign lands; the other is a precedent condemning them to exhibit themselves officially in clothes which are not only without grace or dignity, but are a pretty loud and pious rebuke to the vain and frivolous costumes worn by the other officials. To our day an American ambassador's official costume remains under the reproach of these defects. At a public function in a European court all foreign representatives except ours wear clothes which in some way distinguish them from the unofficial throng, and mark them as standing for their *countries*. But our representative appears in a plain black swallow-tail, which stands for neither country nor people. It has no nationality. It is found in all countries; it is as international as a night-shirt. It has no particular meaning: but our government tries to give it one; it tries to make it stand for Republican Simplicity, modesty and unpretentiousness. Tries, and without doubt fails, for it is not conceivable that this loud ostentation of simplicity deceives any one. The statue that advertises its modesty with a fig-leaf really brings its modesty under suspicion. Worn officially, our non-conforming swallow-tail is a declaration of ungracious independence in the matter of manners, and is uncourteous. It says to all around: "In Rome we do not choose to do as Rome does; we refuse to respect your tastes and your traditions; we make no sacrifices to any one's customs and prejudices; we yield no jot to the courtesies of life; we prefer our manners, and intrude them here."

That is not the true American spirit, and those clothes misrepresent us. When a foreigner comes among us and trespasses against our customs and our code of manners, we are offended, and justly so: but our government commands our ambassadors to wear abroad an official dress which is an offense against foreign manners and customs; and the discredit of it falls upon the nation.

We did not dress our public functionaries in undistinguished raiment before Franklin's time; and the change would not have come if he had been an obscurity. But he was such a colossal figure in the world that whatever he did of an unusual nature attracted the world's attention, and became a precedent. In the case of clothes, the next representative after him, and the next, had to imitate it. After that, the thing was custom: and custom is a petrifaction; nothing but dynamite can dislodge it for a century. We imagine that our queer official costumery was deliberately devised to symbolize our Republican Simplicity—a quality which we have never possessed, and are too old to acquire now, if we had any use for it or any leaning toward it. But it is not so; there was nothing deliberate about it: it grew naturally and heedlessly out of the precedent set by Franklin.

If it had been an intentional thing, and based upon a principle, it would not have stopped where it did; we should have applied it further. Instead of clothing our admirals and generals, for courts-martial and other public functions, in superb dress uniforms blazing with color and gold, the government would put them in swallow-tails and white cravats, and make them look like ambassadors and lackeys. If I am wrong in making Franklin the father of our curious official clothes, it is no matter—he will be able to stand it.

It is my opinion—and I make no charge for the suggestion—that, whenever we appoint an ambassador or a minister, we ought to confer upon him the temporary rank of admiral or general, and allow him to wear the corresponding uniform at public functions in foreign countries. I would recommend this for the reason that it is not consonant with the dignity of the United States of America that her representative should appear upon occasions of state in a dress which makes him glaringly conspicuous; and that is what his present undertaker-outfit does when it appears, with its dismal smudge, in the midst of the butterfly splendors of a Continental court. It is a most trying position for a shy man, a modest man, a man accustomed to being like other people. He is the most striking figure present; there is no hiding from the multitudinous eyes. It would be funny, if it were not such a cruel spectacle, to see the hunted creature in his solemn sables scuffling around in that sea of vivid color, like a mislaid Presbyterian in perdition. We are all aware that our representative's dress should not compel too much attention; for anybody but an Indian chief knows that that is a vulgarity. I am saying these things in the interest of our national pride and dignity. Our representative is the flag. He is the Republic. He is the United States of America. And when these embodiments pass by, we do not want them scoffed at; we desire that people shall be obliged to concede that they are worthily clothed, and politely.

Our government is oddly inconsistent in this matter of official dress. When its representative is a civilian who has not been a soldier, it restricts him to the black swallow-tail and white tie; but if he is a civilian who has been a soldier, it allows him to wear the uniform of his former rank as an official dress. When General Sickles was minister to Spain, he always wore, when on official duty, the dress uniform of a major-general. When General Grant visited foreign courts, he went handsomely and properly ablaze in the uniform of a full general, and was introduced by diplomatic survivals of his own Presidential Administration. The latter, by official necessity, went in the meek and lowly swallow-tail—a deliciously sarcastic contrast: the one dress representing the honest and honorable dignity of the nation; the other, the cheap hypocrisy of the Republican Simplicity tradition. In Paris our present representative can perform his official functions reputably clothed; for he was an officer in the Civil War. In London our late ambassador was similarly situated; for he also was an officer in the Civil War. But Mr. Choate must represent the Great Republic—even at official breakfast at seven in the morning—in that same old funny swallow-tail.

Our government's notions about proprieties of costume are indeed very, very odd—as suggested by that last fact. The swallow-tail is recognized the world over as not wearable in the daytime; it is a night-dress, and a night-dress only—a night-shirt is not more so. Yet, when our representative makes an official visit in the morning, he is obliged by his government to go in that night-dress. It makes the very cab-horses laugh.

The truth is, that for a while during the present century, and up to something short of forty years ago, we had a lucid interval, and dropped the Republican Simplicity sham, and dressed our foreign representatives in a handsome and becoming official costume. This was discarded by and by, and the swallow-tail substituted. I believe it is not now known which statesman brought about this change; but we all know that, stupid as he was to diplomatic proprieties in dress, he would not have sent his daughter to a state ball in a corn-shucking costume, nor to a corn-shucking in a state ball costume, to be harshly criticized as an ill-mannered offender against the proprieties of custom in both places. And we know another thing,—*viz.* that he himself would not have wounded the tastes and feelings of a family of mourners by attending a funeral in their house in a costume which was an offense against the dignities and decorum prescribed by tradition and sanctified by custom. Yet that man was so heedless as not to reflect that *all* the social customs of civilized peoples are entitled to respectful observance, and that no man with a right spirit of courtesy in him ever has any disposition to transgress these customs.

There is still another argument for a rational diplomatic dress—a business argument. We are a trading nation; and our representative is our business agent. If he is respected, esteemed, and liked where he is stationed, he can exercise an influence which can extend our trade and forward our prosperity. A considerable number of his business activities have their field in his social relations; and clothes which do not offend against local manners and customs and prejudices are a valuable part of his equipment in this matter—would be, if Franklin had died earlier.

I have not done with gratis suggestions yet. We made a great and valuable advance when we instituted the office of ambassador. That lofty rank endows its possessor with several times as much influence, consideration, and effectiveness as the rank of minister bestows. For the sake of the country's dignity and for the sake of her advantage commercially, we should have ambassadors, not ministers, at the great courts of the world.

But not at present salaries! No; if we are to maintain present salaries, let us make no more ambassadors; and let us unmake those we have already made. The great position, without the means of respectably maintaining it—there could be no wisdom in that. A foreign representative, to be valuable to his country, must be on good terms with the officials of the capital and with the rest of the influential folk. He must mingle with this society; he cannot sit at home—it is not business, it butters no commercial parsnips. He must attend the dinners, banquets, suppers, balls, receptions, and must *return* these hospitalities. He should return as good as he gets, too, for the sake of the dignity of his country, and for the sake of Business. Have we ever had a minister or an ambassador who could do this on his salary? No—not once, from Franklin's time to ours. Other countries understand the commercial value of properly lining the pockets of their representatives; but apparently our government has not learned it. England is the most successful trader of the several trading nations; and she takes good care of the watchmen who keep guard in her commercial towers. It has been a long time, now, since we needed to blush for our representatives abroad. It has become custom to send our fittest. We send men of distinction, cultivation, character—our ablest, our choicest, our best. Then we cripple their efficiency through the meagerness of their pay. Here is a list of salaries for English and American ministers and ambassadors:

CITY	SALARIES	
	American	English
Paris	$17,500	$45,000
Berlin	17,500	40,000
Vienna	12,000	40,000
Constantinople	10,000	40,000
St. Petersburg	17,500	39,000
Rome	12,000	35,000
Washington	————	32,500

Sir Julian Pauncefote, the English ambassador at Washington, has a very fine house besides—at no damage to his salary.

English ambassadors pay no house-rent; they live in palaces owned by England. Our representatives pay house-rent out of their salaries. You can judge by the above figures what kind of houses the United States of America has been used to living in abroad, and what sort of return-entertaining she has done. There is not a salary in our list which would properly house the representative receiving it, and, in addition, pay three thousand dollars toward his family's bacon and doughnuts—the strange but economical and customary fare of the American ambassador's household, except on Sundays, when petrified Boston crackers are added.

The ambassadors and ministers of foreign nations not only have generous salaries, but their governments provide them with money wherewith to pay a considerable part of their hospitality bills. I believe our government pays no hospitality bills except those incurred by the navy. Through this concession to the navy, that arm is able to do us credit in foreign parts; and certainly that is well and politic. But why the government does not think it well and politic that our diplomats should be able to do us like credit abroad is one of those mysterious inconsistencies which have been puzzling me ever since I stopped trying to understand baseball and took up statesmanship as a pastime.

To return to the matter of house-rent. Good houses, properly furnished, in European capitals, are not to be had at small figures. Consequently, our foreign representatives have been accustomed to live in garrets—sometimes on the roof. Being poor men, it has been the best they could do on the salary which the government has paid them. How could they adequately return the hospitalities shown them? It was impossible. It would have exhausted the salary in three months. Still, it was their official duty to entertain the influentials after some sort of fashion; and they did the best they could with their limited purse. In return for champagne they furnished lemonade; in return for game they furnished ham; in return for whale they furnished sardines; in return for liquors they furnished condensed milk; in return for the battalion of liveried and powdered flunkeys they furnished the hired girl; in return for the fairy wilderness of sumptuous decorations they draped the stove with the American flag; in return for the orchestra they furnished zither and ballads by the family, in return for the ball—but they didn't return the ball, except in cases where the United States lived on the roof and had room.

Is this an exaggeration? It can hardly be called that. I saw nearly the equivalent of it once, a good many years ago. A minister was trying to create influential friends for a project which might be worth ten millions a year to the agriculturists of the Republic; and our government had furnished him ham and lemonade to persuade the opposition with. The minister did not succeed. He might not have succeeded if his salary had been what it ought to have been—fifty or sixty thousand dollars a year—but his chances would have been very greatly improved. And in any case, he and his dinners and his country would not have been joked about by the hard-hearted and pitied by the compassionate.

Any experienced "drummer" will testify that, when you want to do business, there is no economy in ham and lemonade. The drummer takes his country customer to the theater, the opera, the circus; dines him, wines him, entertains him all the day and all the night in luxurious style; and plays upon his human nature in all seductive ways. For he knows, by old experience, that this is the best way to get a profitable order out of him. He has his reward. All governments except our own play the same policy, with the same end in view; and they also have their reward. But ours refuses to do business by business ways, and sticks to ham and lemonade. This is the most expensive diet known to the diplomatic service of the world.

Ours is the only country of first importance that pays its foreign representatives trifling salaries. If we were poor, we could not find great fault with these economies, perhaps—at least one could find a sort of plausible excuse for them. But we are not poor; and the excuse fails. As shown above, some of our important diplomatic representatives receive $12,000, others $17,500. These salaries are all ham and lemonade, and unworthy of the flag. When we have a rich ambassador in London or Paris, he lives as the ambassador of a country like ours ought to live, and it costs him $100,000 a year to do it. But why should we allow him to pay that out of his private pocket? There is nothing fair about it, and the Republic is no proper subject for any one's charity. In several cases our salaries of $12,000 should be $50,000; and all of the salaries of $17,500 ought to be $75,000 or $100,000, since we pay no representative's house-rent. Our State Department realizes the mistake which we are making, and would like to rectify it, but it has not the power.

When a young girl reaches eighteen she is recognized as being a woman. She adds six inches to her skirt, she unplaits her dangling braids and balls her hair on top of her head, she stops sleeping with her little sister and has a room to herself, and becomes in many ways a thundering expense. But she is in society now; and papa has to stand it. There is no avoiding it. Very well. The Great Republic lengthened her skirts last year, balled up her hair, and entered the world's society. This means that, if she would prosper and stand fair with society, she must put aside some of her dearest and darlingest young ways and superstitions, and do as society does. Of course, she can decline if she wants to; but this would be unwise. She ought to realize, now that she has "come out," that this is a right and proper time to change a part of her style. She is in Rome; and it has long been granted that when one is in Rome it is good policy to do as Rome does. To advantage Rome? No—to advantage herself.

If our government has really paid representatives of ours on the Paris Commission one hundred thousand dollars apiece for six weeks' work, I feel sure that it is the best cash investment the nation has made in many years. For it seems quite impossible that, with that precedent on the books, the government will be able to find excuses for continuing its diplomatic salaries at the present mean figure.

P.S.—VIENNA, *January 10.*—I see, by this morning's telegraphic news, that I am not to be the new ambassador here, after all. This—well, I hardly know what to say. I—well, of course, I do not care anything about it; but it is at least a surprise. I have for many months been using my influence at Washington to get this diplomatic see expanded into an ambassadorship, with the idea, of course, th— But never mind. Let it go. It is of no consequence. I say it calmly; for I am calm. But at the same time— However, the subject has no interest for me, and never had. I never really intended to take the place, anyway—I made up my mind to it months and months ago, nearly a year. But now, while I am calm, I would like to say this—that so long as I shall continue to possess an American's proper pride in the honor and dignity of his country, I will not take any ambassadorship in the gift of the flag at a salary short of seventy-five thousand dollars a year. If I shall be charged with wanting to live beyond my country's means, I cannot help it. A country which cannot afford ambassadors' wages should be ashamed to have ambassadors.

Think of a seventeen-thousand-five-hundred-dollar ambassador! Particularly for *America*. Why, it is the most ludicrous spectacle, the most inconsistent and incongruous spectacle contrivable by even the most diseased imagination. It is a billionaire in a paper-collar, a king in a breechclout, an archangel in a tin halo. And, for pure sham and hypocrisy, the salary is just the match of the ambassador's official clothes— that boastful advertisement of a Republican Simplicity which manifests itself at home in Fifty-thousand-dollar salaries to insurance presidents and railway lawyers, and in domestic palaces whose fittings and furnishings often transcend in costly display and splendor and richness the fittings and furnishings of the palaces of the sceptered masters of Europe; and which has invented and exported to the Old World the palace-car, the sleeping-car, the tram-car, the electric trolley, the best bicycles, the best motor-cars, the steam-heater, the best and smartest systems of electric calls and telephonic aids to laziness and comfort, the elevator, the private bath-room (hot and cold water on tap), the palace hotel, with its multifarious conveniences, comforts, shows, and luxuries, the—oh, the list is interminable! In a word, Republican Simplicity found Europe with one shirt on her back, so to speak, as far as *real* luxuries, conveniences, and the comforts of life go, and has clothed her to the chin with the latter. We are the lavishest and showiest and most luxury-loving people on the earth; and at our masthead we fly one true and honest symbol, the gaudiest flag the world has ever seen. Oh, Republican Simplicity, there are many, many humbugs in the world, but none to which you need take off *your* hat!

1899

My Début as a Literary Person

In those early days I had already published one little thing ("The Jumping Frog") in an Eastern paper, but I did not consider that that counted. In my view, a person who published things in a mere newspaper could not properly claim recognition as a Literary Person: he must rise away above that; he must appear in a magazine. He would then be a Literary Person; also, he would be famous—right away. These two ambitions were strong upon me. This was in 1866. I prepared my contribution, and then looked around for the best magazine to go up to glory in. I selected the most important one in New York. The contribution was accepted. I signed it "MARK TWAIN"; for that name had some currency on the Pacific coast, and it was my idea to spread it all over the world, now, at this one jump. The article appeared in the December number, and I sat up a month waiting for the January number; for that one would contain the year's list of contributors, my name would be in it, and I should be famous and could give the banquet I was meditating.

I did not give the banquet. I had not written the "MARK TWAIN" distinctly; it was a fresh name to Eastern printers, and they put it "Mike Swain" or "MacSwain," I do not remember which. At any rate, I was not celebrated, and I did not give the banquet. I was a Literary Person, but that was all—a buried one; buried alive.

My article was about the burning of the clipper-ship *Hornet* on the line, May 3, 1866. There were thirty-one men on board at the time, and I was in Honolulu when the fifteen lean and ghostly survivors arrived there after a voyage of forty-three days in an open boat, through the blazing tropics, on *ten days' rations* of food. A very remarkable trip; but it was conducted by a captain who was a remarkable man, otherwise there would have been no survivors. He was a New-Englander of the best sea-going stock of the old capable times—Captain Josiah Mitchell.

I was in the islands to write letters for the weekly edition of the Sacramento *Union*, a rich and influential daily journal which hadn't any use for them, but could afford to spend twenty dollars a week for nothing. The proprietors were lovable and well-beloved men: long ago dead, no doubt, but in me there is at least one person who still holds them in grateful remembrance; for I dearly wanted to see the islands, and they listened to me and gave me the opportunity when there was but slender likelihood that it could profit them in any way.

I had been in the islands several months when the survivors arrived. I was laid up in my room at the time, and unable to walk.[1] Here was a great occasion to serve my journal, and I not able to take advantage of it. Necessarily I was in deep trouble. But by good luck his Excellency Anson Burlingame was there at the time, on his way to take up his post in China, where he did such good work for the United States. He came and put me on a stretcher and had me carried to the hospital where the shipwrecked men were, and I never needed to ask a question. He attended to all of that himself, and I had nothing to do but make the notes. It was like him to take that trouble. He was a great man and a great American, and it was in his fine nature to come down from his high office and do a friendly turn whenever he could.

We got through with this work at six in the evening. I took no dinner, for there was no time to spare if I would beat the other correspondents. I spent four hours arranging the notes in their proper order,

---

[1] It was a case of saddle sores.—C.N.

then wrote all night and beyond it; with this result: that I had a very long and detailed account of the *Hornet* episode ready at nine in the morning, while the correspondents of the San Francisco journals had nothing but a brief outline report—for they didn't sit up. The now-and-then schooner was to sail for San Francisco about nine; when I reached the dock she was free forward and was just casting off her stern-line. My fat envelope was thrown by a strong hand, and fell on board all right, and my victory was a safe thing. All in due time the ship reached San Francisco, but it was my complete report which made the stir and was telegraphed to the New York papers, by Mr. Cash; he was in charge of the Pacific bureau of the New York *Herald* at the time.

When I returned to California by and by, I went up to Sacramento and presented a bill for general correspondence at twenty dollars a week. It was paid. Then I presented a bill for "special" service on the *Hornet* matter of three columns of solid nonpareil at *a hundred dollars a column*. The cashier didn't faint, but he came rather near it. He sent for the proprietors, and they came and never uttered a protest. They only laughed in their jolly fashion, and said it was robbery, but no matter; it was a grand "scoop" (the bill or my *Hornet* report, I didn't know which); "pay it. It's all right." The best men that ever owned a newspaper.

The *Hornet* survivors reached the Sandwich Islands the 15th of June. They were mere skinny skeletons; their clothes hung limp about them and fitted them no better than a flag fits the flagstaff in a calm. But they were well nursed in the hospital; the people of Honolulu kept them supplied with all the dainties they could need; they gathered strength fast, and were presently nearly as good as new. Within a fortnight the most of them took ship for San Francisco; that is, if my dates have not gone astray in my memory. I went in the same ship, a sailing-vessel. Captain Mitchell of the *Hornet* was along; also the only passengers the *Hornet* had carried. These were two young gentlemen from Stamford, Connecticut—brothers: Samuel Ferguson, aged twenty-eight, a graduate of Trinity College, Hartford, and Henry Ferguson, aged eighteen, a student of the same college. The elder brother had had some trouble with his lungs, which induced his physician to prescribe a long sea-voyage. This terrible disaster, however, developed the disease which later ended fatally. The younger brother is still living, and is fifty years old this year (1898). The *Hornet* was a clipper of the first class and a fast sailer; the young men's quarters were roomy and comfortable, and were well stocked with books, and also with canned meats and fruits to help out the ship-fare with; and when the ship cleared from New York harbor in the first week of January, there was promise that she would make quick and pleasant work of the fourteen or fifteen thousand miles in front of her. As soon as the cold latitudes were left behind and the vessel entered summer weather, the voyage became a holiday picnic. The ship flew southward under a cloud of sail which needed no attention, no modifying or change of any kind, for days together. The young men read, strolled the ample deck, rested and drowsed in the shade of the canvas, took their meals with the captain, and when the day was done they played dummy whist with him till bedtime. After the snow and ice and tempests of the Horn, the ship bowled northward into summer weather again, and the trip was a picnic once more.

Until the early morning of the 3d of May. Computed position of the ship 112°10′ west longitude; latitude 2° above the equator; no wind, no sea—dead calm; temperature of the atmosphere, tropical, blistering, unimaginable by one who has not been roasted in it. There was a cry of fire. An unfaithful sailor had disobeyed the rules and gone into the booby-hatch with an open light to draw some varnish from a cask. The proper result followed, and the vessel's hours were numbered.

There was not much time to spare, but the captain made the most of it. The three boats were launched—long-boat and two quarter-boats. That the time was very short and the hurry and excitement considerable is indicated by the fact that in launching the boats a hole was stove in the side of one of them by some sort of collision, and an oar driven through the side of another. The captain's first care was to have four sick sailors brought up and placed on deck out of harms' way— among them a "portyghee." This man had not done a day's work on the voyage, but had lain in his hammock four months nursing an abscess. When we were taking notes in the Honolulu hospital and a sailor told this to Mr. Burlingame, the third mate, who was lying near, raised his head with an effort, and in weak voice made this correction—with solemnity and feeling:

"*Raising* abscesses! He had a family of them. He done it to keep from standing his watch."

Any provisions that lay handy were gathered up by the men and the two passengers and brought and dumped on the deck where the "Portyghee" lay; then they ran for more. The sailor who was telling this to Mr. Burlingame added:

"We pulled together thirty-two days' rations for the thirty-one men that way."

The third mate lifted his head again and made another correction —with bitterness:

"The Portyghee et twenty-two of them while he was soldiering there and nobody noticing. A damned hound."

The fire spread with great rapidity. The smoke and flame drove the men back, and they had to stop their incomplete work of fetching provisions, and take to the boats with only ten days' rations secured.

Each boat had a compass, a quadrant, a copy of Bowditch's *Navigator*, and a nautical almanac, and the captain's and chief mate's boats had chronometers. There were thirty-one men all told. The captain took an account of stock, with the following result: four hams, nearly thirty pounds of salt pork, half-box of raisins, one hundred pounds of bread, twelve two-pound cans of oysters, clams, and assorted meats, a keg containing four pounds of butter, twelve gallons of water in a forty-gallon "scuttle-butt," four one-gallon demijohns full of water, three bottles of brandy (the property of passengers), some pipes, matches, and a hundred pounds of tobacco. No medicines. Of course the whole party had to go on short rations at once.

The captain and the two passengers kept diaries. On our voyage to San Francisco we ran into a calm in the middle of the Pacific, and did not move a rod during fourteen days; this gave me a chance to copy the diaries. Samuel Ferguson's is the fullest; I will draw upon it now. When the following paragraph was written the ship was about one hundred and twenty days out from port, and all hands were putting in the lazy time about as usual, as no one was forecasting disaster.

May 2. Latitude 1°28′ N., longitude 111°38′ W. Another hot and sluggish day; at one time, however, the clouds promised wind, and there came a slight breeze—just enough to keep us going. The only thing to chronicle to-day is the quantities of fish about; nine bonitos were caught this forenoon, and some large albacores seen. After dinner the first mate hooked a fellow which he could not hold, so he let the line go to the captain, who was on the bow. He, holding on, brought the fish to with a jerk, and snap went the line, hook and all. We also saw astern, swimming lazily after us, an enormous shark, which must have been nine or ten feet long. We tried him with all sorts of lines and a piece of pork, but he declined to take hold. I suppose he had appeased his appetite on the heads and other remains of the bonitos we had thrown overboard.

Next day's entry records the disaster. The three boats got away, retired to a short distance, and stopped. The two injured ones were leaking badly; some of the men were kept busy bailing, others

patched the holes as well as they could. The captain, the two passengers, and eleven men were in the long-boat, with a share of the provisions and water, and with no room to spare, for the boat was only
twenty-one feet long, six wide, and three deep. The chief mate and
eight men were in one of the small boats, the second mate and seven
men in the other. The passengers had saved no clothing but what
they had on, excepting their overcoats. The ship, clothed in flame and
sending up a vast column of black smoke into the sky, made a grand
picture in the solitudes of the sea, and hour after hour the outcasts sat
and watched it. Meantime the captain ciphered on the immensity of
the distance that stretched between him and the nearest available land,
and then scaled the rations down to meet the emergency: half a biscuit for breakfast; one biscuit and some canned meat for dinner; half
a biscuit for tea; a few swallows of water for each meal. And so hunger
began to gnaw while the ship was still burning.

May 4. The ship burned all night very brightly, and hopes are that
some ship has seen the light and is bearing down upon us. None seen,
however, this forenoon, so we have determined to go together north
and a little west to some islands in 18° or 19° north latitude and 114°
to 115° west longitude, hoping in the mean time to be picked up by some
ship. The ship sank suddenly at about 5 A.M. We find the sun very hot and
scorching, but all try to keep out of it as much as we can.

They did a quite natural thing now: waited several hours for that
possible ship that might have seen the light to work her slow way to
them through the nearly dead calm. Then they gave it up and set about
their plans. If you will look at the map you will say that their course
could be easily decided. Albemarle Island (Galapagos group) lies
straight eastward nearly a thousand miles; the islands referred to in the
diary indefinitely as "some islands" (Revillagigedo Islands) lie, as they
think, in some widely uncertain region northward about one thousand
miles and westward one hundred or one hundred and fifty miles.
Acapulco, on the Mexican coast, lies about northeast something short
of one thousand miles. You will say random rocks in the ocean are not
what is wanted; let them strike for Acapulco and the solid continent.
That does look like the rational course, but one presently guesses from
the diaries that the thing would have been wholly irrational—indeed,
suicidal. If the boats struck for Albemarle they would be in the doldrums all the way; and that means a watery perdition, with winds
which are wholly crazy, and blow from all points of the compass at

once and also perpendicularly. If the boats tried for Acapulco they would get out of the doldrums when half-way there—in case they ever got half-way—and then they would be in a lamentable case, for there they would meet the northeast trades coming down in their teeth, and these boats were so rigged that they could not sail within eight points of the wind. So they wisely started northward, with a slight slant to the west. They had but ten days' short allowance of food; the long-boat was towing the others; they could not depend on making any sort of definite progress in the doldrums, and they had four or five hundred miles of doldrums in front of them yet. *They* are the real equator, a tossing, roaring, rainy belt, ten or twelve hundred miles broad, which girdles the globe.

It rained hard the first night, and all got drenched, but they filled up their water-butt. The brothers were in the stern with the captain, who steered. The quarters were cramped; no one got much sleep. "Kept on our course till squalls headed us off."

Stormy and squally the next morning, with drenching rains. A heavy and dangerous "cobbling" sea. One marvels how such boats could live in it. It is called a feat of desperate daring when one man and a dog cross the Atlantic in a boat the size of a long-boat, and indeed it is; but this long-boat was overloaded with men and other plunder, and was only three feet deep. "We naturally thought often of all at home, and were glad to remember that it was Sacrament Sunday, and that prayers would go up from our friends for us, although they know not our peril."

The captain got not even a cat-nap during the first three days and nights, but he got a few winks of sleep the fourth night. "The worst sea yet." About ten at night the captain changed his course and headed east-northeast, hoping to make Clipperton Rock. If he failed, no matter; he would be in a better position to make those other islands. I will mention here that he did not find that rock.

On the 8th of May no wind all day; sun blistering hot; they take to the oars. Plenty of dolphins, but they couldn't catch any. "I think we are all beginning to realize more and more the awful situation we are in." "It often takes a ship a week to get through the doldrums; how much longer, then, such a craft as ours." "We are so crowded that we cannot stretch ourselves out for a good sleep, but have to take it any way we can get it."

Of course this feature will grow more and more trying, but it will be human nature to cease to set it down; there will be five weeks of it yet—

we must try to remember that for the diarist; it will make our beds the softer.

The 9th of May the sun gives him a warning: "Looking with both eyes, the horizon crossed thus+." "Henry keeps well, but broods over our troubles more than I wish he did." They caught two dolphins; they tasted well. "The captain believed the compass out of the way, but the long-invisible north star came out—a welcome sight—and indorsed the compass."

May 10, "latitude 7°0'3" N., longitude 111°32' W." So they have made about three hundred miles of northing in the six days since they left the region of the lost ship. "Drifting in calms all day." And baking hot, of course; I have been down there, and I remember that detail. "Even as the captain says, all romance has long since vanished, and I think the most of us are beginning to look the fact of our awful situation full in the face."

"We are making but little headway on our course." Bad news from the rearmost boat: the men are improvident; "they have eaten up all of the canned meats brought from the ship, and are now growing discontented." Not so with the chief mate's people—they are evidently under the eye of a *man*.

Under date of May 11: "Standing still! or worse; we lost more last night than we made yesterday." In fact, they have lost three miles of the three hundred of northing they had so laboriously made." "The cock that was rescued and pitched into the boat while the ship was on fire still lives, and crows with the breaking of dawn, cheering us a good deal." What has he been living on for a week? Did the starving men feed him from their dire poverty? "The second mate's boat out of water again, showing that they overdrink their allowance. The captain spoke pretty sharply to them." It is true: I have the remark in my old notebook; I got it of the third mate in the hospital at Honolulu. But there is not room for it here, and it is too combustible, anyway. Besides, the third mate admired it, and what he admired he was likely to enhance.

They were still watching hopefully for ships. The captain was a thoughtful man, and probably did not disclose to them that that was substantially a waste of time. "In this latitude the horizon is filled with little upright clouds that look very much like ships." Mr. Ferguson saved three bottles of brandy from his private stores when he left the ship, and the liquor came good in these days. "The captain serves out two tablespoonfuls of brandy and water—half and half—to our crew." He means the watch that is on duty; they stood regular watches—four hours on and four off. The chief mate was an excellent officer—a self-possessed, resolute, fine, all-round man. The diarist makes the following note—there is character in it: "I offered one bottle of brandy to the chief mate, but he declined, saying he could keep the after-boat quiet, and we had not enough for all."

HENRY FERGUSON'S DIARY TO DATE, GIVEN IN FULL

May 4, 5, 6, doldrums. May 7, 8, 9, doldrums. May 10, 11, 12, doldrums. Tells it all. Never saw, never felt, never heard, never experienced such heat, such darkness, such lightning and thunder, and wind and rain, in my life before.

That boy's diary is of the economical sort that a person might properly be expected to keep in such circumstances—and be forgiven for the economy, too. His brother, perishing of consumption, hunger, thirst, blazing heat, drowning rains, loss of sleep, lack of exercise, was persistently faithful and circumstantial with his diary from the first day to the last—an instance of noteworthy fidelity and resolution. In spite of the tossing and plunging boat he wrote it close and fine, in a hand as easy to read as print. They can't seem to get north of 7° N.; they are still there the next day:

May 12. A good rain last night and we caught a good deal, though not enough to fill up our tank, pails, etc. Our object is to get out of these doldrums, but it seems as if we cannot do it. To-day we have had it very variable, and hope we are on the northern edge, though we are not much above 7 °. This morning we all thought we had made out a sail; but it was one of those deceiving clouds. Rained a good deal to-day, making all hands wet and uncomfortable; we filled up pretty nearly all our waterpots, however. I hope we may have a fine night, for the captain certainly wants rest, and while there is any danger of squalls, or danger of any kind, he is always on hand. I never would have believed that open boats such as ours, with their loads, could live in some of the seas we have had.

During the night, 12th—13th, "the cry of *A ship!* brought us to our feet." It seemed to be the glimmer of a vessel's signal-lantern rising out of the curve of the sea. There was a season of breathless hope while they stood watching, with their hands shading their eyes, and their hearts in their throats; then the promise failed: the light was a rising star. It is a long time ago—thirty-two years—and it doesn't matter now, yet one is sorry for their disappointment. "Thought often of those at home to-day, and of the disappointment they will feel next Sunday at not hearing from us by telegraph from San Francisco." It will be many weeks yet before the telegram is received, and it will come as a

268   THE COMPLETE ESSAYS OF MARK TWAIN

thunder-clap of joy then, and with the seeming of a miracle, for it
will raise from the grave men mourned as dead. "To-day our rations
were reduced to a quarter of a biscuit a meal, with about half a pint
of water." This is on the 13th of May, with more than a month of voyaging in front of them yet! However, as they do not know that, "we are
all feeling pretty cheerful."

In the afternoon of the 14th there was a thunderstorm, "which
toward night seemed to close in around us on every side, making it
very dark and squally." "Our situation is becoming more and more desperate," for they were making very little northing, "and every day di-
minishes our small stock of provisions." They realize that the boats must
soon separate, and each fight for its own life. Towing the quarter-boats
is a hindering business.

That night and next day, light and baffling winds and but little progress. Hard to bear, that persistent standing still, and the food wasting
away. "Everything in a perfect sop; and all so cramped, and no change
of clothes." Soon the sun comes out and roasts them. "Joe caught
another dolphin to-day; in his maw we found a flying-fish and two skip-
jacks." There is an event, now, which rouses an enthusiasm of hope:
a land-bird arrives! It rests on the yard for a while, and they can look
at it all they like, and envy it, and thank it for its message. As a subject of talk it is beyond price—a fresh, new topic for tongues tired to
death of talking upon a single theme: Shall we ever see the land again;
and when? Is the bird from Clipperton Rock? They hope so; and they
take heart of grace to believe so. As it turned out, the bird had no message; it merely came to mock.

May 16, "the cock still lives, and daily carols forth His praise." It
will be a rainy night, "but I do not care if we can fill up our water-
butts."

On the 17th one of those majestic specters of the deep, a water-
spout, stalked by them, and they trembled for their lives. Young Henry
set it down in his scanty journal with the judicious comment that "it
might have been a fine sight from a ship."

From Captain Mitchell's log for this day: *Only half a bushel of
bread-crumbs left.*" (And a month to wander the seas yet.)

It rained all night and all day; everybody uncomfortable. Now came
a swordfish chasing a bonito; and the poor thing, seeking help and
friends, took refuge under the rudder. The big swordfish kept hovering
around, scaring everybody badly. The men's mouths watered for him,
for he would have made a whole banquet; but no one dared to touch

him, of course, for he would sink a boat promptly if molested. Providence protected the poor bonito from the cruel swordfish. This was just and right. Providence next befriended the shipwrecked sailors: they got the bonito. This was also just and right. But in the distribution of mercies the swordfish himself got overlooked. He now went away; to muse over these subtleties, probably. "The men in all the boats seem pretty well; the feeblest of the sick ones (not able for a long time to stand his watch on board the ship) is wonderfully recovered." This is the third mate's detested "Portyghee" that raised the family of abscesses.

Passed a most awful night. Rained hard nearly all the time, and blew in squalls, accompanied by terrific thunder and lightning, from all points of the compass.—*Henry's Log.*

Most awful night I ever witnessed.—*Captain's Log.*

Latitude, May 18, 11°11'. So they have averaged but forty miles of northing a day during the fortnight. Further talk of separating. "Too bad, but it must be done for the safety of the whole." "At first I never dreamed, but now hardly shut my eyes for a cat-nap without conjuring up something or other—to be accounted for by weakness, I suppose." But for their disaster they think they would be arriving in San Francisco about this time. "I should have liked to send B—— the telegram for her birthday." This was a young sister.

On the 19th the captain called up the quarter-boats and said one would have to go off on its own hook. The long-boat could no longer tow both of them. The second mate refused to go, but the chief mate was ready; in fact, he was always ready when there was a man's work to the fore. He took the second mate's boat; six of its crew elected to remain, and two of his own crew came with him (nine in the boat, now, including himself). He sailed away, and toward sunset passed out of sight. The diarist was sorry to see him go. It was natural; one could have better spared the "Portyghee." After thirty-two years I find my prejudice against this "Portyghee" reviving. His very looks have long passed out of my memory; but no matter, I am coming to hate him as religiously as ever. "Water will now be a scarce article, for as we get out of the doldrums we shall get showers only now and then in the trades. This life is telling severely on my strength. Henry holds out first rate." Henry did not start well, but under hardships he improved straight along.

Latitude, Sunday, May 20, 12°0'9". They ought to be well out of the doldrums now, but they are not. No breeze—the longed-for trades still missing. They are still anxiously watching for a sail, but they have only "visions of ships that come to naught—the shadow without the substance." The second mate catches a booby this afternoon, a bird which consists mainly of feathers; "but as they have no other meat, it will go well."

May 21, they strike the trades at last! The second mate catches three more boobies, and gives the long-boat one. Dinner "Half a can of mincemeat divided up and served around, which strengthened us some-what." They have to keep a man bailing all the time; the hole knocked in the boat when she was launched from the burning ship was never efficiently mended. "Heading about northwest now." They hope they have easting enough to make some of those indefinite isles. Failing that, they think they will be in a better position to be picked up. It was an infinitely slender chance, but the captain probably refrained from mentioning that.

The next day is to be an eventful one.

May 22. Last night wind headed us off, so that part of the time we had to steer east-southeast and then west-northwest, and so on. This morning we were all startled by a cry of "Sail ho!" Sure enough we could see it! And for a time we cut adrift from the second mate's boat and steered so as to attract its attention. This was about half-past five A.M. After sailing in a state of high excitement for almost twenty minutes we made it out to be the chief mate's boat. Of course we were glad to see them and have them report all well; but still it was a bitter disappointment to us all. Now that we are in the trades it seems impossible to make northing enough to strike the isles. We have determined to do the best we can and get in the route of vessels. Such being the determination, it became necessary to cast off the other boat, which, after a good deal of unpleasantness, was done, we again dividing water and stores, and taking Cox into our boat. This makes our number fifteen. The second mate's crew wanted to all get in with us and cast the other boat adrift. It was a very painful separation.

So those isles that they have struggled for so long and so hopefully have to be given up. What with lying birds that come to mock, and isles that are but a dream, and "visions of ships that come to naught," it is a pathetic time they are having, with much heartbreak in it. It was odd that the vanished boat, three days lost to sight in that vast solitude, should appear again. But it brought Cox—we can't be certain why. But if it hadn't, the diarist would never have seen the land again.

Our chances as we go west increase in regard to being picked up, but each day our scanty fare is so much reduced. Without the fish, turtle, and birds sent us, I do not know how we should have got along. The other day I offered to read prayers morning and evening for the captain, and last night commenced. The men, although of various nationalities and religions, are very attentive, and always uncovered. May God grant my weak endeavor its issue.

Latitude, May 24, 14°18′ N. Five oysters apiece for dinner and three spoonfuls of juice, a gill of water, and a piece of biscuit the size of a silver dollar. "We are plainly getting weaker—God have mercy upon us all!" That night heavy seas break over the weather side and make everybody wet and uncomfortable, besides requiring constant bailing. Next day, "nothing particular happened." Perhaps some of us would have regarded it differently. "Passed a spar, but not near enough to see what it was." They saw some whales blow; there were flying-fish skimming the seas, but none came aboard. Misty weather, with fine rain, very penetrating.

Latitude, May 26, 15°50′. They caught a flying fish and a booby, but had to eat them raw. "The men grow weaker, and I think, despondent; they say very little, though." And so, to all the other imaginable and unimaginable horrors, silence is added—the muteness and brooding of coming despair. "It seems our best chance to get in the track of ships, with the hope that some one will run near enough to our speck to see it." He hopes the other boats stood west and have been picked up. (They will never be heard of again in this world.)

Sunday, May 27. Latitude 16°0′5″; longitude, by chronometer, 117° 22′. Our fourth Sunday! When we left the ship we reckoned on having about ten days' supplies, and now we hope to be able, by rigid economy, to make them last another week if possible.[2] Last night the sea was comparatively quiet, but the wind headed us off to about west-northwest, which has been about our course all day to-day. Another flying-fish came aboard last night, and one more to-day—both small ones. No birds. A booby is a great catch, and a good large one makes a small dinner for the fifteen of us—that is, of course, as dinners go in the *Hornet's* long-boat. Tried this morning to read the full service to myself, with the communion, but found it too much; am too weak, and get sleepy, and cannot give strict attention; so I put off half till this afternoon. I trust God will hear the prayers gone up for us at home to-day, and graciously answer them by sending us succor and help in this our season of deep distress.

[2] There are nineteen days of voyaging ahead yet.—M.T.

The next day was "a good day for seeing a ship." But none was seen. The diarist "still feels pretty well," though very weak; his brother Henry "bears up and keeps his strength the best of any on board." "I do not feel despondent at all, for I fully trust that the Almighty will hear our and the home prayers, and He who suffers not a sparrow to fall sees and cares for us, His creatures."

Considering the situation and circumstances, the record for next day, May 29, is one which has a surprise in it for those dull people who think that nothing but medicines and doctors can cure the sick. A little starvation can really do more for the average sick man than can the best medicines and the best doctors. I do not mean a restricted diet; I mean *total abstention from food for one or two days*. I speak from experience; starvation has been my cold and fever doctor for fifteen years, and has accomplished a cure in all instances. The third mate told me in Honolulu that the "Portyghee" had lain in his hammock for months, raising his family of abscesses and feeding like a cannibal. We have seen that in spite of dreadful weather, deprivation of sleep, scorching, drenching, and all manner of miseries, thirteen days of starvation "wonderfully recovered" him. There were four sailors down sick when the ship was burned. Twenty-five days of pitiless starvation have followed, and now we have this curious record: *"All the men are hearty and strong; even the ones that were down sick are well, except poor Peter."* When I wrote an article some months ago urging temporary abstention from food as a remedy for an inactive appetite and for disease, I was accused of jesting, but I was in earnest. *"We are all wonderfully well and strong, comparatively speaking."* On this day the starvation regimen drew its belt a couple of buckle-holes tighter: the bread ration was reduced from the usual piece of cracker the size of a silver dollar *to the half of that, and one meal was abolished from the daily three*. This will weaken the men physically, but if there are any diseases of an ordinary sort left in them they will disappear.

Two quarts bread-crumbs left, one-third of a ham, three small cans of oysters, and twenty gallons of water.—*Captain's Log*.

The hopeful tone of the diaries is persistent. It is remarkable. Look at the map and see where the boat is: latitude 16°44′, longitude 119° 20′. It is more than two hundred miles west of the Revillagigedo Islands, so they are quite out of the question against the trades, rigged as this boat is. The nearest land available for such a boat is the American group, *six hundred and fifty miles away*, westward; still, there is no note of surrender, none even of discouragement! Yet,

May 30, "we have now left: *one can of oysters; three pounds of raisins; one can of soup; one-third of a ham; three pints of biscuit-crumbs.*" And fifteen starved men to live on it while they creep and crawl six hundred and fifty miles. "Somehow I feel much encouraged by this change of course (west by north) which we have made to-day." Six hundred and fifty miles on a hatful of provisions! Let us be thankful, even after thirty-two years, that they are mercifully ignorant of the fact that it isn't six hundred and fifty that they must creep on the hatful, but *twenty-two hundred!* Isn't the situation romantic enough just as it stands? No. Providence added a startling detail: pulling an oar in that boat, for common seaman's wages, was a *banished duke*—Danish. We hear no more of him; just that mention, that is all, with the simple remark that "he is one of our best men"—a high enough compliment for a duke or any other man in those manhood-testing circumstances. With that little glimpse of him at his oar, and that fine word of praise, he vanishes out of our knowledge for all time. For all time, unless he should chance upon this note and reveal himself.

The last day of May is come. And now there is a disaster to report: think of it, reflect upon it, and try to understand how much it means, when you sit down with your family and pass your eye over your breakfast-table. Yesterday there were three pints of bread-crumbs; this morning the little bag is found open and *some of the crumbs missing.* "We dislike to suspect any one of such a rascally act, but there is no question that this grave crime has been committed. Two days will certainly finish the remaining morsels. God grant us strength to reach the American group!" The third mate told me in Honolulu that in these days the men remembered with bitterness that the "Portyghee" had devoured twenty-two days' rations while he lay waiting to be transferred from the burning ship, and that now they cursed him and swore an oath that if it came to cannibalism he should be the first to suffer for the rest.

The captain has lost his glasses, and therefore he cannot read our pocket prayer-books as much as I think he would like, though he is not familiar with them.

Further of the captain: "He is a good man, and has been most kind to us—almost fatherly. He says that if he had been offered the command of the ship sooner he should have brought his two daughters with him." It makes one shudder yet to think how narrow an escape it was.

The two meals (rations) a day are as follows: fourteen raisins and a piece of cracker the size of a cent, for tea; a gill of water, and a piece of ham and a piece of bread, each the size of a cent, for breakfast.—*Captain's Log.*

He means a cent in *thickness* as well as in circumference. Samuel Ferguson's diary says the ham was shaved "about as thin as it could be cut."

June 1. Last night and to-day sea very high and cobbling, breaking over and making us all wet and cold. Weather squally, and there is no doubt that only careful management—with God's protecting care—preserved us through both the night and the day; and really it is most marvelous how every morsel that passes our lips is blessed to us. It makes me think daily of the miracle of the loaves and fishes. Henry keeps up wonderfully, which is a great consolation to me. I somehow have great confidence, and hope that our afflictions will soon be ended, though we are running rapidly across the track of both outward and inward bound vessels, and away from them; our chief hope is a whaler, man-of-war, or some Australian ship. The isles we are steering for are put down in Bowditch, but on my map are said to be doubtful. God grant they may be there!
Hardest day yet.—*Captain's Log.*

Doubtful! It was worse than that. A week later *they sailed straight over them.*

June 2. Latitude 18°9′. Squally, cloudy, a heavy sea. . . . I cannot help thinking of the cheerful and comfortable time we had aboard the *Hornet.*
Two day's scanty supplies left—ten rations of water apiece and a little morsel of bread. *But the sun shines, and God is merciful.—Captain's Log.*
Sunday, June 3. Latitude 17°54′. Heavy sea all night, and from 4 A.M. very wet, the sea breaking over us in frequent sluices, and soaking everything aft, particularly. All day the sea has been very high, and it is a wonder that we are not swamped. Heaven grant that it may go down this evening! Our suspense and condition are getting terrible. I managed this morning to crawl, more than step, to the forward end of the boat, and was surprised to find that I was so weak, especially in the legs and knees. The sun has been out again, and I have dried some things, and hope for a better night.
June 4. Latitude 17°6′, longitude 131°30′. Shipped hardly any sea last night, and to-day the sea has gone down somewhat, although it is still too high for comfort, as we have an occasional reminder that water is wet. The sun has been out all day, and so we have had a good drying. I have been trying for the last ten or twelve days to get a pair of drawers dry enough to put on, and at last succeeded. I mention this to show the state in which

we have lived. If our chronometer is anywhere near right, we ought to see the American Isles to-morrow or next day. If they are not there, we have only the chance for a few days, of a stray ship, for we cannot eke out the provisions more than five or six days longer, and our strength is failing very fast. I was much surprised to-day to note how my legs have wasted away above my knees: they are hardly thicker than my upper arm used to be. Still, I trust in God's infinite mercy, and feel sure he will do what is best for us. To survive, as we have done, thirty-two days in an open boat, with only about ten days' fair provisions for thirty-one men in the first place, and these divided twice subsequently, is more than mere unassisted *human* art and strength could have accomplished and endured.

Bread and raisins all gone.—*Captain's Log.*

Men growing dreadfully discontented, and awful grumbling and un-pleasant talk is arising. God save us from all strife of men; and if we must die now, take us himself, and not embitter our bitter death still more.—*Henry's Log.*

June 5. Quiet night and pretty comfortable day, though our sail and block show signs of failing, and need taking down—which latter is some-thing of a job, as it requires the climbing of the mast. We also had news from forward, there being discontent and some threatening complaints of unfair allowances, etc., all as unreasonable as foolish; still, these things bid us be on our guard. I am getting miserably weak, but try to keep up the best I can. If we cannot find those isles we can only try to make north-west and get in the track of Sandwich Island bound vessels, living as best we can in the mean time. To-day we changed to one meal, and that at about noon, with a small ration of water at 8 or 9 A.M., another at 12 M., and a third at 5 or 6 P.M.

Nothing left but a little piece of ham and a gill of water, all around.—*Captain's Log.*

They are down to *one* meal a day now—such as it is—and *fifteen hundred miles to crawl yet!* And now the horrors deepen, and though they escape actual mutiny, the attitude of the men became alarming. Now we seem to see why that curious accident happened, so long ago: I mean Cox's return, after he had been far away and out of sight sev-eral days in the chief mate's boat. If he had not come back the captain and the two young passengers would have been slain by these sailors, who were becoming crazed through their sufferings.

NOTE SECRETLY PASSED BY HENRY TO HIS BROTHER

Cox told me last night that there is getting to be a good deal of ugly talk among the men against the captain and us aft. They say that the cap-tain is the cause of all; that he did not try to save the ship at all, nor to get provisions, and even would not let the men put in some they had; and that partiality is shown us in apportioning our rations aft. —— asked Cox the other day if he would starve first or eat human flesh. Cox answered he would starve. —— then told him he would be only killing himself. If we do not find these islands we would do well to prepare for anything. —— is the loudest of all.

REPLY

We can depend on ——, I think, and ——, and Cox, can we not?

SECOND NOTE

I guess so, and very likely on ——; but there is no telling. —— and Cox are certain. There is nothing definite said or hinted as yet, as I understand Cox; but starving men are the same as maniacs. It would be well to keep a watch on your pistol, so as to have it and the cartridges safe from theft.

Henry's Log, June 5. Dreadful forebodings. God spare us from all such horrors! Some of the men getting to talk a good deal. Nothing to write down. Heart very sad.

Henry's Log, June 6. Passed some seaweed, and something that looked like the trunk of an old tree, but no birds; beginning to be afraid islands not there. To-day it was said to the captain, in the hearing of all, that some of the men would not shrink, when a man was dead, from using the flesh, though they would not kill. Horrible! God give us all full use of our reason, and spare us from such things! "From plague, pestilence, and famine, from battle and murder, and from sudden death, good Lord, deliver us!"

June 6. Latitude 16°30′, longitude (chron.) 134°. Dry night and wind steady enough to require no change in sail; but this A.M. an attempt to lower it proved abortive. First the third mate tried and got up to the block, and fastened a temporary arrangement to reeve the halyards through, but had to come down, weak and almost fainting, before finishing; then Joe tried, and after twice ascending, fixed it and brought down the block; but it was very exhausting work, and afterward he was good for nothing all day. The clue-iron which we are trying to make serve for the broken block works, however, very indifferently, and will, I am afraid, soon cut the rope. It is very necessary to get everything connected with the sail in good, easy running order before we get too weak to do anything with it.

Only three meals left.—*Captain's Log*.

June 7. Latitude 16°35′ N., longitude 136°30′ W. Night wet and uncomfortable. To-day shows us pretty conclusively that the American Isles are not there, though we have had some signs that looked like them. At noon we decided to abandon looking any farther for them, and to-night haul a little more northerly, so as to get in the way of Sandwich Island vessels, which fortunately come down pretty well this way—say to latitude

19° to 20°—to get the benefit of the trade-winds. Of course all the westing we have made is gain, and I hope the chronometer is wrong in our favor, for I do not see how any such delicate instrument can keep good time with the constant jarring and thumping we get from the sea. With the strong trade we have, I hope that a week from Sunday will put us in sight of the Sandwich Islands, if we are not safe by that time by being picked up.

It is twelve hundred miles to the Sandwich Islands; the provisions are virtually exhausted, but not the perishing diarist's pluck.

June 8. My cough troubled me a good deal last night, and therefore I got hardly any sleep at all. Still, I make out pretty well, and should not complain. Yesterday the third mate mended the block, and this P.M. the sail, after some difficulty, was got down, and Harry got to the top of the mast and rove the halyards through after some hardship, so that it now works easy and well. This getting up the mast is no easy matter at any time with the sea we have, and is very exhausting in our present state. We could only reward Harry by an extra ration of water. We have made good time and course to-day. Heading her up, however, makes the boat ship seas and keeps us all wet; however, it cannot be helped. Writing is a rather precarious thing these times. Our meal to-day for the fifteen consists of half a can of "soup and boullie"; the other half is reserved for to-morrow. Henry still keeps up grandly, and is a great favorite. God grant he may be spared!

A better feeling prevails among the men.—*Captain's Log*

June 9. Latitude 17°53'. Finished to-day, I may say, our whole stock of provisions.[3] We have only left a lower end of a ham-bone, with some of the outer rind and skin on. In regard to the water, however, I think we have got ten days' supply at our present rate of allowance. This, with what nourishment we can get from boot-legs and such chewable matter, we hope will enable us to weather it out till we get to the Sandwich Islands, or, sailing in the mean time in the track of vessels thither bound, be picked up. My hope is in the latter, for in all human probability I cannot stand the other. Still we have been marvelously protected, and God, I hope, will preserve us all in his own good time and way. The men are getting weaker, but are still quiet and orderly.

Sunday, June 10. Latitude 18°40', longitude 142°34'. A pretty good night last night, with some wettings, and again another beautiful Sunday. I cannot but think how we should all enjoy it at home, and what a contrast is here! How terrible their suspense must begin to be! God grant that it may be relieved before very long, and he certainly seems to be with us in everything we do, and has preserved this boat miraculously; for since

[3] Six days to sail yet, nevertheless.—M.T.

we left the ship we have sailed considerably over three thousand miles, which, taking into consideration our meager stock of provisions, is almost unprecedented. As yet I do not feel the stint of food so much as I do that of water. Even Henry, who is naturally a good water-drinker, can save half of his allowance from time to time, when I cannot. My diseased throat may have something to do with that, however.

Nothing is now left which by any flattery can be called food. But they must manage somehow for five days more, for at noon they have still eight hundred miles to go. It is a race for life now.

This is no time for comments or other interruptions from me—every moment is valuable. I will take up the boy brother's diary at this point, and clear the seas before it and let it fly.

HENRY FERGUSON'S LOG

Sunday, June 10. Our ham-bone has given us a taste of food to-day, and we have got left a little meat and the remainder of the bone for to-morrow. Certainly never was there such a sweet knuckle-bone, or one that was so thoroughly appreciated. . . . I do not know that I feel any worse than I did last Sunday, notwithstanding the reduction of diet; and I trust that we may all have strength given us to sustain the sufferings and hardships of the coming week. We estimate that we are within seven hundred miles of the Sandwich Islands, and that our average daily, is somewhat over a hundred miles, so that our hopes have some foundation in reason. Heaven send we may all live to see land!

June 11. Ate the meat and rind of our ham-bone, and have the bone and the greasy cloth from around the ham left to eat to-morrow. God send us birds or fish, and let us not perish of hunger, or be brought to the dreadful alternative of feeding on human flesh! As I feel now, I do not think anything could persuade me; but you cannot tell what you will do when you are reduced by hunger and your mind wandering. I hope and pray we can make out to reach the islands before we get to this strait; but we have one or two desperate men aboard, though they are quiet enough now. *It is my firm trust and belief that we are going to be saved.* All food gone.—*Captain's Log.*[4]

June 12. Stiff breeze, and we are fairly flying—dead ahead of it—and toward the islands. Good hope, but the prospects of hunger are awful. Ate hambone to-day. It is the captain's birthday; he is fifty-four years old.

June 13. The ham-rags are not quite all gone yet, and the boot-legs, we

[4] It was at this time discovered that the crazed sailors had gotten the delusion that the captain had *a million dollars* in gold concealed aft, and they were conspiring to kill him and the two passengers and seize it.—M.T.

find, are very palatable after we get the salt out of them. A little smoke, I think, does some little good; but I don't know.

June 14. Hunger does not pain us much, but we are dreadfully weak. Our water is getting frightfully low. God grant we may see land soon! *Nothing to eat,* but feel better than I did yesterday. Toward evening saw a magnificent rainbow—*the first we had seen.* Captain said, "Cheer up, boys; it's a prophecy—*it's the bow of promise!*"

June 15. God be forever praised for his infinite mercy! LAND IN SIGHT! Rapidly neared it and soon were *sure* of it. . . . Two noble Kanakas swam out and took the boat ashore. We were joyfully received by two white men —Mr. Jones and his steward Charley—and a crowd of native men, women, and children. They treated us splendidly—aided us, and carried us up the bank, and brought us water, poi, bananas, and green cocoanuts; but the white men took care of us and prevented those who would have eaten too much from doing so. Everybody overjoyed to see us, and all sympathy expressed in faces, deeds, and words. We were then helped up to the house; and help we needed. Mr. Jones and Charley are the only white men here. Treated us splendidly. Gave us first about a teaspoonful of spirits in water, and then to each a cup of warm tea, with a little bread. Takes *every* care of us. Gave us later another cup of tea, and bread the same, and then let us go to rest. *It is the happiest day of my life.* . . . God in his mercy has heard our prayer. . . . Everybody is so kind. Words cannot tell.

June 16. Mr. Jones gave us a delightful bed, and we surely had a good night's rest; but not sleep—we were too happy to sleep; would keep the reality and not let it turn to a delusion—dreaded that we might wake up and find ourselves in the boat again.

It is an amazing adventure. There is nothing of its sort in history that surpasses it in impossibilities made possible. In one extraordinary detail—the survival of *every person* in the boat—it probably stands alone in the history of adventures of its kind. Usually merely a part of a boat's company survive—officers, mainly, and other educated and tenderly reared men, unused to hardship and heavy labor; the untrained, roughly reared hard workers succumb. But in this case even the rudest and roughest stood the privations and miseries of the voyage almost as well as did the college-bred young brothers and the captain. I mean, physically. The minds of most of the sailors broke down in the fourth week and went to temporary ruin, but physically the endurance exhibited was astonishing. Those men did not survive by any merit of their own, of course, but by merit of the character and intelligence of the captain; they lived by the mastery of his spirit. Without him they would have been children without a nurse; they would have exhausted their provisions in a week, and their pluck would not have lasted even as long as the provisions.

The boat came near to being wrecked at the last. As it approached the shore the sail was let go, and came down with a run; then the captain saw that he was drifting swiftly toward an ugly reef, and an effort was made to hoist the sail again: but it could not be done; the men's strength was wholly exhausted; they could not even pull an oar. They were helpless, and death imminent. It was then that they were discovered by the two Kanakas who achieved the rescue. They swam out and manned the boat and piloted her through a narrow and hardly noticeable break in the reef—the only break in it in a stretch of thirty-five miles! The spot where the landing was made was the only one in that stretch where footing could have been found on the shore; everywhere else precipices came sheer down into forty fathoms of water. Also, in all that stretch this was the only spot where anybody lived.

Within ten days after the landing all the men but one were up and creeping about. Properly, they ought to have killed themselves with the "food" of the last few days—some of them, at any rate—men who had freighted their stomachs with strips of leather from old boots and with chips from the butter-cask; a freightage which they did not get rid of by digestion, but by other means. The captain and the two passengers did not eat strips and chips, as the sailors did, but *scraped* the boot-leather and the wood, and made a pulp of the scrapings by moistening them with water. The third mate told me that the boots were old and full of holes; then added thoughtfully, "but the holes digested the best." Speaking of digestion, here is a remarkable thing, and worth noting: during this strange voyage, and for a while afterward on shore, the bowels of some of the men virtually ceased from their functions; in some cases there was no action for twenty and thirty days, and in one case for forty-four! Sleeping also came to be rare. Yet the men did very well without it. During many days the captain did not sleep at all—twenty-one, I think, on one stretch.

When the landing was made, all the men were successfully protected from overeating except the "Portyghee"; he escaped the watch and ate an incredible number of bananas: a hundred and fifty-two, the third mate said, but this was undoubtedly an exaggeration; I think it was a hundred and fifty-one. He was already nearly full of leather; it was hanging out of his ears. (I do not state this on the third mate's authority, for we have seen what sort of person he was; I state it on my own.) The "Portyghee" ought to have died, of course, and even now it seems a pity that he didn't; but he got well, and as early as any

of them; and all full of leather, too, the way he was, and butter-timber
and handkerchiefs and bananas. Some of the men did eat handkerchiefs
in those last days, also socks; and he was one of them.

It is to the credit of the men that they did not kill the rooster that
crowed so gallantly mornings. He lived eighteen days, and then stood
up and stretched his neck and made a brave, weak effort to do his
duty once more, and died in the act. It is a picturesque detail; and so
is that rainbow, too—the only one seen in the forty-three days—raising
its triumphal arch in the skies for the sturdy fighters to sail under to
victory and rescue.

With ten days' provisions Captain Josiah Mitchell performed this
memorable voyage of forty-three days and eight hours in an open boat,
sailing four thousand miles in reality and thirty-three hundred and
sixty by direct courses, and brought every man safe to land. A bright,
simple-hearted, unassuming, plucky, and most companionable man. I
walked the deck with him twenty-eight days—when I was not copying
diaries—and I remember him with reverent honor. If he is alive he is
eighty-six years old now.

If I remember rightly, Samuel Ferguson died soon after we reached
San Francisco. I do not think he lived to see his home again; his
disease had been seriously aggravated by his hardships.

For a time it was hoped that the two quarter-boats would presently
be heard of, but this hope suffered disappointment. They went down
with all on board, no doubt, not even sparing that knightly chief mate.

The authors of the diaries allowed me to copy them exactly as they
were written, and the extracts that I have given are without any
smoothing over or revision. These diaries are finely modest and unaffected, and with unconscious and unintentional art they rise toward
the climax with graduated and gathering force and swing and dramatic
intensity; they sweep you along with a cumulative rush, and when the
cry rings out at last, "Land in sight!" your heart is in your mouth, and
for a moment you think it is you that have been saved. The last two
paragraphs are not improvable by anybody's art; they are literary gold;
and their very pauses and uncompleted sentences have in them an
eloquence not reachable by any words.

The interest of this story is unquenchable; it is of the sort that time
cannot decay. I have not looked at the diaries for thirty-two years, but
I find that they have lost nothing in that time. Lost? They have gained;
for by some subtle law all tragic human experiences gain in pathos by
the perspective of time. We realize this when in Naples we stand musing over the poor Pompeian mother, lost in the historic storm of vol-

canic ashes eighteen centuries ago, who lies with her child gripped close to her breast, trying to save it, and whose despair and grief have been preserved for us by the fiery envelope which took her life but eternalized her form and features. She moves us, she haunts us, she stays in our thoughts for many days, we do not know why, for she is nothing to us, she has been nothing to any one for eighteen centuries; whereas of the like case to-day we should say, "Poor thing! it is pitiful," and forget it in an hour.

1899

To the Person Sitting in Darkness[1]

Christmas will dawn in the United States over a people full of hope and aspiration and good cheer. Such a condition means contentment and happiness. The carping grumbler who may here and there go forth will find few to listen to him. The majority will wonder what is the matter with him and pass on.—*New York Tribune,* on Christmas Eve.

From the *Sun,* of New York:

The purpose of this article is not to describe the terrible offenses against humanity committed in the name of Politics in some of the most notorious East Side districts. *They could not be described, even verbally.* But it is the intention to let the great mass of more or less careless citizens of this beautiful metropolis of the New World get some conception of the havoc and ruin wrought to man, woman, and child in the most densely populated and least-known section of the city. Name, date, and place can be supplied to those of little faith—or to any man who feels himself aggrieved. It is a plain statement of record and observation, written without license and without garnish.

Imagine, if you can, a section of the city territory completely dominated by one man, without whose permission neither legitimate nor illegitimate business can be conducted; *where illegitimate business is encouraged and legitimate business discouraged;* where the respectable residents have to fasten their doors and windows summer nights and sit in their rooms with asphyxiating air and 100-degree temperature, rather than try to catch the faint whiff of breeze in their natural breathing places, the stoops of their homes; *where naked women dance by night in the streets, and un-*

[1] This essay and the essay following it appeared first in the *North American Review.*—C.N.

sexed men prowl like vultures through the darkness on "business" not only permitted but encouraged by the police; *where the education of infants begins with the knowledge of prostitution* and the training of little girls is training in the arts of Phryne; where *American* girls brought up with the refinements of *American* homes are imported from small towns up-state, Massachusetts, Connecticut, and New Jersey, and kept as virtually prisoners as if they were locked up behind jail bars until they have lost all semblance of womanhood; *where small boys are taught to solicit for the women of disorderly houses;* where there is an organized society of young men *whose sole business in life is to corrupt young girls and turn them over to bawdy houses;* where men walking with their wives along the street are openly insulted; *where children that have adult diseases are the chief patrons of the hospitals and dispensaries;* where it is the rule, rather than the exception, that *murder, rape, robbery, and theft go unpunished*—in short where the Premium of the most awful forms of Vice is the Profit of the politicians.

The following news from China appeared in the *Sun,* of New York, on Christmas Eve. The italics are mine:

The Rev. Mr. Ament, of the American Board of Foreign Missions, has returned from a trip which he made for the purpose of collecting indemnities for damages done by Boxers. *Everywhere he went he compelled the Chinese to pay.* He says that all his native Christians are now provided for. He had 700 of them under his charge, and 300 were killed. He has *collected 300 taels for each of these murders,* and has *compelled full payment for all the property belonging to Christians* that was destroyed. He also assessed *fines* amounting to THIRTEEN TIMES the amount of the indemnity. *This money will be used for the propagation of the Gospel.*

Mr. Ament declares that the compensation he has collected is *moderate* when compared with the amount secured by the Catholics, who demand, in addition to money, *head for head.* They collect 500 taels for each murder of a Catholic. In the Wenchiu country, 680 Catholics were killed, and for this the European Catholics here demand 750,000 strings of cash and 680 *heads.*

In the course of a conversation, Mr. Ament referred to the attitude of the missionaries toward the Chinese. He said:

"I deny emphatically that the missionaries are *vindictive,* that they *generally* looted, or that they have done anything *since* the siege that *the circumstances did not demand.* I criticize the Americans. *The soft hand of the Americans is not as good as the mailed fist of the Germans.* If you deal with the Chinese with a soft hand they will take advantage of it.

"The statement that the French government will return the loot taken by the French soldiers is the source of the greatest amusement here. The

French soldiers were more systematic looters than the Germans, and it is a fact that to-day *Catholic Christians,* carrying French flags and armed with modern guns, *are looting villages* in the Province of Chili."

By happy luck, we get all these glad tidings on Christmas Eve— just in time to enable us to celebrate the day with proper gayety and enthusiasm. Our spirits soar, and we find we can even make jokes: Taels, I win, Heads you lose.

Our Reverend Ament is the right man in the right place. What we want of our missionaries out there is, not that they shall merely represent in their acts and persons the grace and gentleness and charity and loving-kindness of our religion, but that they shall also represent the American spirit. The oldest Americans are the Pawnees. Macallum's History says:

When a white Boxer kills a Pawnee and destroys his property, the other Pawnees do not trouble to seek *him* out, they kill any white person that comes along; also, they make some white village pay deceased's heirs the full cash value of deceased, together with full cash value of the property destroyed; they also make the village pay, in addition, *thirteen times* the value of that property into a fund for the dissemination of the Pawnee religion, which they regard as the best of all religions for the softening and humanizing of the heart of man. It is their idea that it is only fair and right that the innocent should be made to suffer for the guilty, and that it is better that ninety and nine innocent should suffer than that one guilty person should escape.

Our Reverend Ament is justifiably jealous of those enterprising Catholics, who not only get big money for each lost convert, but get "head for head" besides. But he should soothe himself with the reflections that the entirety of their exactions are for their own pockets, whereas he, less selfishly, devotes only 300 taels per head to that service, and gives the whole vast thirteen repetitions of the property-indemnity to the service of propagating the Gospel. His magnanimity has won him the approval of his nation, and will get him a monument. Let him be content with these rewards. We all hold him dear for manfully defending his fellow missionaries from exaggerated charges which were beginning to distress us, but which his testimony has so considerably modified that we can now contemplate them without noticeable pain. For now we know that, even before the siege, the missionaries were not "generally" out looting, and that, "since the siege," they have acted quite handsomely, except when "circumstances" crowded them. I am arranging for the monument. Subscriptions for it can be sent to the

American Board; designs for it can be sent to me. Designs must allegor-
ically set forth the Thirteen Reduplications of the Indemnity, and the
Object for which they were exacted; as Ornaments, the designs must
exhibit 680 Heads, so disposed as to give a pleasing and pretty effect;
for the Catholics have done nicely, and are entitled to notice in the
monument. Mottos may be suggested, if any shall be discovered that
will satisfactorily cover the ground.

Mr. Ament's financial feat of squeezing a thirteenfold indemnity out
of the pauper peasants to square other people's offences, thus condemning them and their women and innocent little children to inevitable
starvation and lingering death, in order that the blood money so acquired might be *"used for the propagation of the Gospel,"* does not
flutter my serenity; although the act and the words, taken together,
concrete a blasphemy so hideous and so colossal that, without doubt,
its mate is not findable in the history of this or of any other age. Yet, if
a layman had done that thing and justified it with those words, I
should have shuddered, I know. Or, if I had done the thing and said
the words myself— However, the thought is unthinkable, irreverent as
some imperfectly informed people think me. Sometimes an ordained
minister sets out to be blasphemous. When this happens, the layman is
out of the running; he stands no chance.

We have Mr. Ament's impassioned assurance that the missionaries
are not "vindictive." Let us hope and pray that they will never become
so, but will remain in the almost morbidly fair and just and gentle
temper which is affording so much satisfaction to their brother and
champion to-day.

The following is from the New York *Tribune* of Christmas Eve.
It comes from that journal's Tokyo correspondent. It has a strange and
impudent sound, but the Japanese are but partially civilized as yet.
When they become wholly civilized they will not talk so:

The missionary question, of course, occupies a foremost place in the discussion. It is now felt as essential that the Western Powers take cogni-
zance of the sentiment here, that religious invasions of Oriental countries
by powerful Western organizations are tantamount to filibustering ex-
peditions, and should not only be discountenanced, but that stern measures should be adopted for their suppression. The feeling here is that
the missionary organizations constitute a constant menace to peaceful
international relations.

Shall we? That is, shall we go on conferring our Civilization upon
the peoples that sit in darkness, or shall we give those poor things a
rest? Shall we bang right ahead in our old-time, loud, pious way, and

commit the new century to the game; or shall we sober up and sit down and think it over first? Would it not be prudent to get our Civilization tools together, and see how much stock is left on hand in the way of Glass Beads and Theology, and Maxim Guns and Hymn Books, and Trade Gin and Torches of Progress and Enlightenment (patent adjustable ones, good to fire villages with, upon occasion), and balance the books, and arrive at the profit and loss, so that we may intelligently decide whether to continue the business or sell out the property and start a new Civilization Scheme on the proceeds?

Extending the Blessings of Civilization to our Brother who Sits in Darkness has been a good trade and has paid well, on the whole; and there is money in it yet, if carefully worked—but not enough, in my judgment, to make any considerable risk advisable. The people that Sit in Darkness are getting to be too scarce—too scarce and too shy. And such darkness as is now left is really of but an indifferent quality, and not dark enough for the game. The most of those People that Sit in Darkness have been furnished with more light than was good for them or profitable for us. We have been injudicious.

The Blessings-of-Civilization Trust, wisely and cautiously administered, is a Daisy. There is more money in it, more territory, more sovereignty, and other kinds of emolument, than there is in any other game that is played. But Christendom has been playing it badly of late years, and must certainly suffer by it, in my opinion. She has been so eager to get every stake that appeared on the green cloth, that the People who Sit in Darkness have noticed it—they have noticed it, and have begun to show alarm. They have become suspicious of the Blessings of Civilization. More—they have begun to examine them. This is not well. The Blessings of Civilization are all right, and a good commercial property; there could not be a better, in a dim light. In the right kind of a light, and at a proper distance, with the goods a little out of focus, they furnish this desirable exhibit to the Gentlemen who Sit in Darkness:

LOVE,	LAW AND ORDER,
JUSTICE,	LIBERTY,
GENTLENESS,	EQAULITY,
CHRISTIANITY,	HONORABLE DEAL-
PROTECTION TO THE	ING,
WEAK,	MERCY,
TEMPERANCE,	EDUCATION,

—and so on.

There. Is it good? Sir, it is pie. It will bring into camp any idiot that sits in darkness anywhere. But not if we adulterate it. It is proper to be emphatic upon that point. This brand is strictly for Export—apparently. *Apparently*. Privately and confidentially, it is nothing of the kind. Privately and confidentially, it is merely an outside cover, gay and pretty and attractive, displaying the special patterns of our Civilization which we reserve for Home Consumption, while *inside* the bale is the Actual Thing that the Customer Sitting in Darkness buys with his blood and tears and land and liberty. That Actual Thing is, indeed, Civilization, but it is only for Export. Is there a difference between the two brands? In some of the details, yes.

We all know that the Business is being ruined. The reason is not far to seek. It is because our Mr. McKinley, and Mr. Chamberlain, and the Kaiser, and the Tsar and the French have been exporting the Actual Thing *with the outside cover left off*. This is bad for the Game. It shows that these new players of it are not sufficiently acquainted with it.

It is a distress to look on and note the mismoves, they are so strange and so awkward. Mr. Chamberlain manufactures a war of materials so inadequate and so fanciful that they make the boxes grieve and the gallery laugh, and he tries hard to persuade himself that it isn't purely a private raid for cash, but has a sort of dim, vague respectability about it somewhere, if he could only find the spot; and that, by and by, he can scour the flag clean again after he has finished dragging it through the mud, and make it shine and flash in the vault of heaven once more as it had shone and flashed there a thousand years in the world's respect until he laid his unfaithful hand upon it. It is bad play—bad. For it exposes the Actual Thing to Them that Sit in Darkness, and they say: "What! Christian against Christian? And only for money? Is *this* a case of magnanimity, forbearance, love, gentleness, mercy, protection of the weak—this strange and overshowy onslaught of an elephant upon a nest of field mice, on the pretext that the mice had squeaked an insolence at him—conduct which "no self-respecting government could allow to pass unavenged"? as Mr. Chamberlain said. Was that a good pretext in a small case, when it had not been a good pretext in a large one?—for only recently Russia had affronted the elephant three times and survived alive and unsmitten. Is this Civilization and Progress? Is it something better than we already possess? These harryings and burnings and desert-makings in the Transvaal—is this an improvement on our darkness? Is it, perhaps, possible that there are two kinds of Civilization—one for home consumption and one for the heathen market?"

Then They that Sit in Darkness are troubled, and shake their heads; and they read this extract from a letter of a British private, recounting his exploits in one of Methuen's victories, some days before the affair of Magersfontein, and they are troubled again:

We tore up the hill and into the intrenchments, and the Boers saw we had them; so they dropped their guns and went down on their knees and put up their hands clasped, and begged for mercy. And we gave it them— *with the long spoon.*

The long spoon is the bayonet. See *Lloyd's Weekly,* London, of those days. The same number—and the same column—contained some quite unconscious satire in the form of shocked and bitter upbraidings of the Boers for their brutalities and inhumanities!

Next, to our heavy damage, the Kaiser went to playing the game without first mastering it. He lost a couple of missionaries in a riot in Shantung, and in his account he made an overcharge for them. China had to pay a hundred thousand dollars apiece for them, in money; twelve miles of territory, containing several millions of inhabitants and worth twenty million dollars; and to build a monument, and also a Christian church; whereas the people of China could have been depended upon to remember the missionaries without the help of these expensive memorials. This was all bad play. Bad, because it would not, and could not and will not now or ever, deceive the Person Sitting in Darkness. He knows that it was an overcharge. He knows that a missionary is like any other man: he is worth merely what you can supply his place for, and no more. He is useful, but so is a doctor, so is a sheriff, so is an editor; but a just Emperor does not charge war prices for such. A diligent, intelligent, but obscure missionary, and a diligent, intelligent country editor are worth much, and we know it; but they are not worth the earth. We esteem such an editor, and we are sorry to see him go; but, when he goes, we should consider twelve miles of territory, and a church, and a fortune, overcompensation for his loss. I mean, if he was a Chinese editor, and we had to settle for him. It is no proper figure for an editor or a missionary; one can get shop-worn kings for less. It was bad play on the Kaiser's part. It got this property, true; but it *produced the Chinese revolt,* the indignant uprising of China's traduced patriots, the Boxers. The results have been expensive to Germany, and to the other Disseminators of Progress and the Blessings of Civilization. The Kasier's claim was paid, yet it was bad play, for it could not fail to have an evil effect upon Persons Sitting in Darkness in China. They would muse upon the event, and be likely to say: "Civilization is gracious and beautiful, for such is its reputation; but can we afford it? There are rich Chinamen, perhaps they can afford it; but this tax is not laid upon them, it is laid upon the peasants of Shantung; it is they that must pay this mighty sum, and their wages are but four cents a day. Is this a better civilization than ours, and holier and higher and nobler? Is not this rapacity? Is not this extortion? Would Germany charge America two hundred thousand dollars for two missionaries, and shake the mailed fist in her face, and send warships, and send soldiers, and say: 'Seize twelve miles of territory, worth twenty millions of dollars, as additional pay for the missionaries; and make those peasants build a monument to the missionaries, and a costly Christian church to remember them by?' And later would Germany say to her soldiers: 'March through America and slay, *giving no quarter;* make the German face there, as has been our Hun-face here, a terror for a thousand years; march through the Great Republic and slay, slay, slay, carving a road for our offended religion through its heart and bowels?' Would Germany do like this to America, to England, to France, to Russia? Or only to China, the helpless—imitating the elephant's assault upon the field mice? Had we better invest in this Civilization—this Civilization which called Napoleon a buccaneer for carrying off Venice's bronze horses, but which steals our ancient astronomical instruments from our walls, and goes looting like common bandits—that is, all the alien soldiers except America's; and (Americans again excepted) storms frightened villages and cables the result to glad journals at home every day: 'Chinese losses, 450 killed; ours, *one officer and two men wounded.* Shall proceed against neighboring village to-morrow, where a *massacre* is reported.' Can we afford Civilization?"

And next Russia must go and play the game injudiciously. She affronts England once or twice—with the Person Sitting in Darkness observing and noting; by moral assistance of France and Germany, she robs Japan of her hard-earned spoil, all swimming in Chinese blood—Port Arthur—with the Person again observing and noting; then she seizes Manchuria, raids its villages, and chokes its great river with the swollen corpses of countless massacred peasants—that astonished Person still observing and noting. And perhaps he is saying to himself: "It is yet *another* Civilized Power, with its banner of the Prince of Peace in one hand and its loot basket and its butcher knife in the other. Is there no salvation for us but to adopt Civilization and lift ourselves down to its level?"

And by and by comes America, and our Master of the Game plays it badly—plays it as Mr. Chamberlain was playing it in South Africa. It was a mistake to do that; also, it was one which was quite unlooked for in a Master who was playing it so well in Cuba. In Cuba, he was playing the usual and regular *American* game, and it was winning, for there is no way to beat it. The Master, contemplating Cuba, said: "Here is an oppressed and friendless little nation which is willing to fight to be free; we go partners, and put up the strength of seventy million sympathizers and the resources of the United States: play!" Nothing but Europe combined could call that hand: and Europe cannot combine on anything. There, in Cuba, he was following our great traditions in a way which made us very proud of him, and proud of the deep dissatisfaction which his play was provoking in continental Europe. Moved by a high inspiration, he threw out those stirring words which proclaimed that forcible annexation would be "criminal aggression"; and in that utterance fired another "shot heard round the world." The memory of that fine saying will be outlived by the remembrance of no act of his but one—that he forgot it within the twelvemonth, and its honorable gospel along with it.

For, presently, came the Philippine temptation. It was strong; it was too strong, and he made that bad mistake: he played the European game, the Chamberlain game. It was a pity; it was a great pity, that error; that one grievous error, that irrevocable error. For it was the very place and time to play the American game again. And at no cost. Rich winnings to be gathered in, too; rich and permanent; indestructible; a fortune transmissible forever to the children of the flag. Not land, not money, not dominion—no, something worth many times more than that dross: our share, the spectacle of a nation of long harrassed and persecuted slaves set free through our influence; our posterity's share, the golden memory of that fair deed. The game was in our hands. If it had been played according to the American rules, Dewey would have sailed away from Manila as soon as he had destroyed the Spanish fleet—after putting up a sign on shore guaranteeing foreign property and life against damage by the Filipinos, and warning the Powers that interference with the emancipated patriots would be regarded as an act unfriendly to the United States. The Powers cannot combine, in even a bad cause, and the sign would not have been molested.

Dewey could have gone about his affairs elsewhere, and left the competent Filipino army to starve out the little Spanish garrison and

send it home, and the Filipino citizens to set up the form of government they might prefer, and deal with the friars and their doubtful
acquisitions according to Filipino ideas of fairness and justice—ideas
which have since been tested and found to be of as high an order as
any that prevail in Europe or America.

But we played the Chamberlain game, and lost the chance to add
another Cuba and another honorable deed to our good record.

The more we examine the mistake, the more clearly we perceive
that it is going to be bad for the Business. The Person Sitting in Darkness is almost sure to say: "There is something curious about this—
curious and unaccountable. There must be two Americans; one that
sets the captive free, and one that takes a once-captive's new freedom
away from him, and picks a quarrel with him with nothing to found
it on; then kills him to get his land."

The truth is, the Person Sitting in Darkness *is* saying things like that;
and for the sake of the Business we must persuade him to look at the
Philippine matter in another and healthier way. We must arrange his
opinions for him. I believe it can be done; for Mr. Chamberlain has
arranged England's opinion of the South African matter, and done it
most cleverly and successfully. He presented the facts—some of the
facts—and showed those confiding people what the facts meant. He
did it statistically, which is a good way. He used the formula: "Twice
2 are 14, and 2 from 9 leaves 35." Figures are effective; figures will
convince the elect.

Now, my plan is a still bolder one than Mr. Chamberlain's, though
apparently a copy of it. Let us be franker than Mr. Chamberlain; let
us audaciously present the whole of the facts, shirking none, then explain them according to Mr. Chamberlain's formula. This daring
truthfulness will astonish and dazzle the Person Sitting in Darkness,
and he will take the Explanation down before his mental vision has
had time to get back into focus. Let us say to him:

"Our case is simple. On the 1st of May, Dewey destroyed the Spanish
fleet. This left the Archipelago in the hands of its proper and rightful
owners, the Filipino nation. Their army numbered 30,000 men, and
they were competent to whip out or starve out the little Spanish garrison; then the people could set up a government of their own devising.
Our traditions required that Dewey should now set up his warning
sign, and go away. But the Master of the Game happened to think of
another plan—the European plan. He acted upon it. This was, to send
out an army—ostensibly to help the native patriots put the finishing

touch upon their long and plucky struggle for independence, but really
to take their land away from them and keep it. That is, in the interest of
Progress and Civilization. The plan developed, stage by stage, and
quite satisfactorily. We entered into a military alliance with the trusting
Filipinos, and they hemmed in Manila on the land side, and by their
valuable help the place, with its garrison of 8,000 or 10,000 Spaniards,
was captured—a thing which we could not have accomplished unaided
at that time. We got their help by—by ingenuity. We knew they were
fighting for their independence, and that they had been at it for two
years. We knew they supposed that we also were fighting in their
worthy cause—just as we had helped the Cubans fight for Cuban independence—and we allowed them to go on thinking so. *Until Manila
was ours and we could get along without them.* Then we showed our
hand. Of course, they were surprised—that was natural; surprised and
disappointed; disappointed and grieved. To them it looked un-Amer-
ican; uncharacteristic; foreign to our established traditions. And this
was natural, too; for we were only playing the American Game in
public—in private it was the European. It was neatly done, very neatly,
and it bewildered them. They could not understand it; for we had
been so friendly—so affectionate, even—with those simple-minded
patriots! We, our own selves, had brought back out of exile their
leader, their hero, their hope, their Washington—Aguinaldo; brought
him in a warship, in high honor, under the sacred shelter and hospitality of the flag; brought him back and restored him to his people,
and got their moving and eloquent gratitude for it. Yes, we had been
so friendly to them, and had heartened them up in so many ways!
We had lent them guns and ammunition; advised with them; ex-
changed pleasant courtesies with them; placed our sick and wounded
in their kindly care; intrusted our Spanish prisoners to their humane
and honest hands; fought shoulder to shoulder with them against "the
common enemy" (our own phrase); praised their courage, praised
their gallantry, praised their mercifulness, praised their fine and honorable conduct; borrowed their trenches, borrowed strong positions
which they had previously captured from the Spaniards; petted them,
lied to them—officially proclaiming that our land and naval forces
came to give them their freedom and displace the bad Spanish
Government—fooled them, used them until we needed them no
longer; then derided the sucked orange and threw it away. We kept
the positions which we had beguiled them of; by and by, we moved
a force forward and overlapped patriot ground—a clever thought, for

we needed trouble, and this would produce it. A Filipino soldier, crossing the ground, where no one had a right to forbid him, was shot by our sentry. The badgered patriots resented this with arms, without waiting to know whether Aguinaldo, who was absent, would approve or not. Aguinaldo did not approve; but that availed nothing. What we wanted, in the interest of Progress and Civilization, was the Archipelago, unencumbered by patriots struggling for independence; and War was what we needed. We clinched our opportunity. It is Mr. Chamberlain's case over again—at least in its motive and intention; and we played the game as adroitly as he played it himself."

At this point in our frank statement of fact to the Person Sitting in Darkness, we should throw in a little trade taffy about the Blessings of Civilization—for a change, and for the refreshment of his spirit—then go on with our tale:

"We and the patriots having captured Manila, Spain's ownership of the Archipelago and her sovereignty over it were at an end—obliterated—annihilated—not a rag or shred of either remaining behind. It was then that we conceived the divinely humorous idea of *buying* both of these specters from Spain! [It is quite safe to confess this to the Person Sitting in Darkness, since neither he nor any other sane person will believe it.] In buying those ghosts for twenty millions, we also contracted to take care of the friars and their accumulations. [I think we also agreed to propagate leprosy and smallpox, but as to this there is doubt. But it is not important; persons afflicted with the friars do not mind other diseases.]

"With our Treaty ratified, Manila subdued, and our Ghosts secured, we had no further use for Aguinaldo and the owners of the Archipelago. We forced a war, and we have been hunting America's guest and ally through the woods and swamps ever since."

At this point in the tale, it will be well to boast a little of our war work and our heriosms in the field, so as to make our performance look as fine as England's in South Africa; but I believe it will not be best to emphasize this too much. We must be cautious. Of course, we must read the war telegrams to the Person, in order to keep up our frankness; but we can throw an air of humorousness over them, and that will modify their grim eloquence a little, and their rather indiscret exhibitions of gory exultation. Before reading to him the following display heads of the dispatches of November 18, 1900, it will be well to practice on them in private first, so as to get the right tang of lightness and gayety into them:

"ADMINISTRATION WEARY OF
PROTRACTED HOSTILITIES!"

"REAL WAR AHEAD FOR FILIPINO
REBELS"[2]

"WILL SHOW NO MERCY!"
"KITCHENER'S PLAN ADOPTED!"

Kitchener knows how to handle disagreeable people who are fighting for their homes and their liberties, and we must let on that we are
merely imitating Kitchener, and have no national interest in the matter, further than to get ourselves admired by the Great Family of Nations, in which august company our Master of the Game has bought a
place for us in the back row.

Of course, we must not venture to ignore our General MacArthur's
reports—oh, why do they keep on printing those embarrassing things?
—we must drop them trippingly from the tongue and take the chances:

During the last ten months our losses have been 268 killed and 750
wounded; Filipino loss, *three thousand two hundred and twenty-seven
killed*, and 694 wounded.

We must stand ready to grab the Person Sitting in Darkness, for he
will swoon away at this confession, saying: "Good God! those 'niggers'
spare their wounded, and the Americans massacre theirs!"

We must bring him to, and coax him and coddle him, and assure
him that the ways of Providence are best, and that it would not become us to find fault with them; and then, to show him that we are
only imitators, not originators, we must read the following passage
from the letter of an American soldier lad in the Philippines to his
mother, published in *Public Opinion*, of Decorah, Iowa, describing the
finish of a victorious battle:

"We never left one alive. If one was wounded, we would run
our bayonets through him.

Having now laid all the historical facts before the Person Sitting
in Darkness, we should bring him to again, and explain them to him.
We should say to him:

"They look doubtful, but in reality they are not. There have been
lies; yes, but they were told in a good cause. We have been treacherous;

but that was only in order that real good might come out of apparent evil. True, we have crushed a deceived and confiding people; we have turned against the weak and the friendless who trusted us; we have stamped out a just and intelligent and well-ordered republic; we have stabbed an ally in the back and slapped the face of a guest; we have bought a Shadow from an enemy that hadn't it to sell; we have robbed a trusting friend of his land and his liberty; we have invited our clean young men to shoulder a discredited musket and do bandits' work under a flag which bandits have been accustomed to fear, not to follow; we have debauched America's honor and blackened her face before the world; but each detail was for the best. We know this. The Head of every State and Sovereignty in Christendom and 90 per cent. of every legislative body in Christendom, including our Congress and our fifty state legislatures, are members not only of the church, but also of the Blessings-of-Civilization Trust. This world-girdling accumulation of trained morals, high principles, and justice cannot do an unright thing, an unfair thing, an ungenerous thing, an unclean thing. It knows what it is about. Give yourself no uneasiness; it is all right."

Now then, that will convince the Person. You will see. It will restore the Business. Also, it will elect the Master of the Game to the vacant place in the Trinity of our national gods; and there on their high thrones the Three will sit, age after age, in the people's sight, each bearing the Emblem of his service: Washington, the Sword of the Liberator; Lincoln, the Slave's Broken Chains; the Master, the Chains Repaired.

It will give the Business a splendid new start. You will see.

Everything is prosperous, now; everything is just as we should wish it. We have got the Archipelago, and we shall never give it up. Also, we have every reason to hope that we shall have an opportunity before very long to slip out of our congressional contract with Cuba and give her something better in the place of it. It is a rich country, and many of us are already beginning to see that the contract was a sentimental mistake. But now—right now—is the best time to do some profitable rehabilitating work—work that will set us up and make us comfortable, and discourage gossip. We cannot conceal from ourselves that, privately, we are a little troubled about our uniform. It is one of our prides; it is acquainted with honor; it is familiar with great deeds and noble; we love it, we revere it; and so this errand it is on makes us uneasy. And our flag—another pride of ours, our chiefest! We have worshipped it so; and when we have seen it in far lands—glimpsing

it unexpectedly in that strange sky, waving its welcome and bene-
diction to us—we have caught our breaths, and uncovered our heads,
and couldn't speak, for a moment, for the thought of what it was to us
and the great ideals it stood for. Indeed, we *must* do something about
these things; it is easily managed. We can have a special one—our
states do it: we can have just our usual flag, with the white stripes
painted black and the stars replaced by the skull and crossbones.

And we do not need that Civil Commission out there. Having no
powers, it has to invent them, and that kind of work cannot be effectively done by just anybody; an expert is required. Mr. Croker can be
spared. We do not want the United States represented there, but only
the Game.

By help of these suggested amendments, Progress and Civilization
in that country can have a boom, and it will take in the Persons who
are Sitting in Darkness, and we can resume Business at the old stand.

1901

To My Missionary Critics

I have received many newspaper cuttings; also letters from several
clergymen; also a note from the Rev. Dr. Judson Smith, Corresponding
Secretary of the American Board of Foreign Missions—all of a like
tenor; all saying, substantially, what is said in the cutting here copied:

AN APOLOGY DUE FROM MR. CLEMENS

The evidence of the past day or two should induce Mark Twain to make
for the amen corner and formulate a prompt apology for his scathing attack
on the Rev. Dr. Ament, the veteran Chinese missionary. The assault was
based on a Peking dispatch to the New York *Sun*, which said that Dr.
Ament had collected from the Chinese in various places damages thirteen times in excess of actual losses. So Mark Twain charged Mr. Ament
with bullyragging, extortion, and things. A Peking dispatch to the *Sun*
yesterday, however, explains that the amount collected was not thirteen
times the damage sustained, but *one-third in excess of the indemnities*,
and that the blunder was due to a cable error in transmission. The 1-3d got
converted into 13. Yesterday the Rev. Judson Smith, Secretary of the
American Board, received a dispatch from Dr. Ament, calling attention

to the cable blunder, and declaring that all the collections which he made
were *approved by the Chinese officials.* The fractional amount that was
collected in *excess* of actual losses, he explains, is being *used for the support of widows and orphans.*

So collapses completely—and convulsively—Mark Twain's sensational
and ugly bombardment of a missionary whose character and services
should have exempted him from such an assault.

From the charge the underpinning has been knocked out. To Dr.
Ament Mr. Clemens has done an injustice which is gross but unintentional. If Mark Twain is the man we take him to be he won't be long in
filing a retraction, plus an apology.

I have no prejudice against apologies. I trust I shall never withhold
one when it is due; I trust I shall never even have a disposition to do
so. These letters and newspaper paragraphs are entitled to my best
attention; respect for their writers and for the humane feeling which
has prompted their utterances requires this of me. It may be barely
possible that, if these requests for an apology had reached me before
the 20th of February, I might have had a sort of qualified chance to
apologize; but on that day appeared the two little cablegrams referred
to in the newspaper cutting copied above—one from the Rev. Dr. Smith
to the Rev. Dr. Ament, the other from Dr. Ament to Dr. Smith—and
my small chance died then. In my opinion, these cablegrams ought to
have been suppressed, for it seems clear that they give Dr. Ament's
case entirely away. Still, that is only an opinion, and may be a mistake. It will be best to examine the case from the beginning, by the
light of the documents connected with it.

EXHIBIT A

This is a dispatch from Mr. Chamberlain,[1] chief of the *Sun's* correspondence staff in Peking. It appeared in the *Sun* last Christmas
Eve, and in referring to it hereafter I will call it the "C.E. dispatch"
for short:

The Rev. Mr. Ament, of the American Board of Foreign Missions, has
returned from a trip which he made for the purpose of collecting indemnities for damages done by Boxers. Everywhere he went he compelled the
Chinese to pay. He says that all his native Christians are now provided for.
He had seven hundred of them under his charge, and three hundred were
killed. He has collected 300 taels for each of these murders, and has compelled full payment for all the property belonging to Christians that was

[1] Testimony of the manager of the *Sun.*—M.T.

destroyed. He also assessed fines amounting to thirteen times[2] the amount of the indemnity. This money will be used for the propagation of the Gospel.

Mr. Ament declares that the compensation he has collected is moderate when compared with the amount secured by the Catholics, who demand, in addition to money, head for head. They collect 500 taels for each murder of a Catholic. In the Wen-Chiu country 680 Catholics were killed, and for this the European Catholics here demand 750,000 strings of cash and 680 heads.

In the course of a conversation Mr. Ament referred to the attiude of the missionaries toward the Chinese. He said:

"I deny emphatically that the missionaries are vindictive, that they generally looted, or that they have done anything since the siege that the circumstances did not demand. I criticize the Americans. The soft hand of the Americans is not as good as the mailed fist of the Germans. If you deal with the Chinese with a soft hand they will take advantage of it."

In an article addressed "To the Person Sitting in Darkness," published in the *North American Review* for February, I made some comments upon this C.E. dispatch.

In an Open Letter to me, from the Rev. Dr. Smith, published in the *Tribune* of February 15th, doubt is cast upon the authenticity of the dispatch.

Up to the 20th of February, this doubt was an important factor in the case: Dr. Ament's brief cablegram, published on that date, took the importance all out of it.

In the Open Letter, Dr. Smith quotes this passage from a letter from Dr. Ament, dated November 13th. The italics are mine:

This time I proposed to settle affairs *without the aid of soldiers or* legations.

This cannot mean two things, but only one: that, previously, he *had* collected by armed force.

Also, in the Open Letter, Dr. Smith quotes some praises of Dr. Ament and the Rev. Mr. Tewksbury, furnished by the Rev. Dr. Sheffield, and says:

Dr. Sheffield is not accustomed to speak thus of *thieves*, or *extortioners*, or *braggarts*.

[2] Cable error. For "thirteen times" read "one third." This correction was made by Dr. Ament in his brief cablegram published February 20th, previously referred to.—M.T.

What can he mean by those vigorous expressions? Can he mean that the first two would be applicable to a missionary who should collect from B, with the "aid of soldiers," indemnities possibly due by A, and upon occasion go out looting?

EXHIBIT B

Testimony of George Lynch (indorsed as entirely trustworthy by the *Tribune* and the *Herald*), war correspondent in the Cuban and South African wars, and in the march upon Peking for the rescue of the legations. The italics are mine:

When the *soldiers* were prohibited from looting, no such prohibitions seemed to operate with the *missionaries*. For instance, the *Rev. Mr. Tewksbury held a great sale of looted goods, which lasted several days.*

A day or two after the relief, when looking for a place to sleep in, I met the Rev. Mr. Ament, of the American Board of Foreign Missions. *He told me* he was going to take possession of the house of a wealthy Chinaman who was an old enemy of his, as he had interfered much in the past with his missionary labors in Peking. A couple of days afterwards *he did so,* and held a *great sale of his enemy's effects.* I bought a sable cloak at it for $125, and a couple of statues of Buddha. As the stock became depleted *it was replenished by the efforts of his converts, who were ransacking the houses in the neighborhood.*—New York *Herald*, February 18th.

It is Dr. Smith, not I, who has suggested that persons who act in this way are "thieves and extortioners."

EXHIBIT C

Sir Robert Hart, in the *Fortnightly Review* for January, 1901. This witness has been for many years the most prominent and important Englishman in China, and bears an irreproachable reputation for moderation, fairness, and truth-speaking. In closing a description of the revolting scenes which followed the occupation of Peking, when the Christain armies (with the proud exception of the American soldiery, let us be thankful for that) gave themselves up to a ruthless orgy of robbery and spoliation, he says (the italics are mine):

And even some *missionaries* took such a *leading* part in "spoiling the Egyptians" for the greater glory of God that a bystander was heard to say: *"For a century to come Chinese converts will consider looting and vengeance Christian virtues."*

It is Dr. Smith, not I, who has suggested that persons who act in this way are "thieves and extortioners." According to Mr. Lynch and Mr. Martin (another war correspondent), Dr. Ament helped to spoil several of those Egyptians. Mr. Martin took a photograph of the scene. It was reproduced in the *Herald.* I have it.

EXHIBIT D

In a brief reply to Dr. Smith's Open Letter to me, I said this in the *Tribune.* I am italicizing several words—for a purpose:

Whenever he (Dr. Smith) can produce from the Rev. Mr. Ament an assertion that the *Sun's* character-blasting dispatch was not authorized *by him,* and whenever Dr. Smith can buttress Mr. Ament's disclaimer with a confession from *Mr. Chamberlain,* the head of the Laffan News Service in China, that that dispatch was a false invention *and unauthorized,* the case against Mr. Ament will fall at once to the ground.

EXHIBIT E

Brief cablegrams, referred to above, which passed between Dr. Smith and Dr. Ament, and were published on February 20th:

Ament, Peking, Reported December 24 your collecting thirteen times actual losses; using for propagating the Gospel. Are these statements true? Cable specific answer. SMITH.

Statement untrue. Collected 1-3 for church expenses, additional actual damages; now supporting widows and orphans. Publication thirteen times blunder cable. All collections received approval Chinese officials, who are urging further settlements same line. AMENT.

Only two questions are asked; "specific" answers required; no perilous wanderings among the other details of the unhappy dispatch desired.

EXHIBIT F

Letter from Dr. Smith to me, dated March 8th. The italics are mine; they tag inaccuracies of statement:

Permit me to call your attention to the marked paragraphs in the inclosed papers, and to ask you to note their relation to the two conditions named in your letter to the New York *Tribune* of February 15th.

The first is *Dr. Ament's denial of the truth of the dispatch in the New York "Sun,"* of December 24th, on which your criticisms of him in the *North American Review* of February were founded. The second is a correction by the "*Sun's*" *special correspondent* in Peking of the dispatch printed in the *Sun* of December 24th.

Since, as you state in your letter to the *Tribune,* "the case against Mr. Ament would fall to the ground" *if Mr. Ament denied the truth* of the *Sun's* first dispatch, and *if the 'Sun's' news agency* in Peking also *declared that dispatch false,* and these two conditions *have thus been fulfilled,* I am sure that upon having these *facts* brought to your attention you will gladly withdraw the criticisms that were *founded on a "cable blunder."*

I think Dr. Smith ought to read me more carefully; then he would not make so many mistakes. Within the narrow space of two paragraphs, totaling eleven lines, he has scored nine departures from fact out of a possible 9½. Now, is that parliamentary? I do not treat him like that. Whenever I quote him, I am particular not to do him the least wrong, or make him say anything he did not say.

(1) Mr. Ament doesn't "deny the truth of the C.E. dispatch"; he merely changes one of its phrases, without materially changing the meaning, and (immaterially) corrects a cable blunder (which correction I accept). He was asked no question about the other four fifths of the C.E. dispatch. (2) I said nothing about "special" correspondents; I named the right and responsible man—Mr. Chamberlain. The "correction" referred to is a repetition of the one I have just accepted, which (immaterially) changes "thirteen times" to "one third" extra tax. (3) I did not say anything about "the *Sun's* news agency"; I said "Chamberlain." I have every confidence in Mr. Chamberlain, but I am not personally acquainted with the others. (4) Once more—Mr. Ament didn't "deny the truth" of the C.E. dispatch, but merely made unimportant emendations of a couple of its many details. (5) I did not say "if Mr. Ament denied the truth" of the C.E. dispatch: I said, if he would assert that the dispatch was not "authorized" *by him.* For example, I did not suppose that the charge that the Catholic missionaries wanted 680 Chinamen beheaded was true; but I did want to know if Dr. Ament personally authorized that statement and the others, as coming from his lips. Another detail: one of my conditions was that Mr. Chamberlain must not stop with confessing that the C.E. was a "false invention," he must also confess that it was "*unauthorized.*" Dr. Smith has left out that large detail. (6) The *Sun's* news agency did not "declare the C.E. dispatch false," but confined itself to correcting one unimportant detail of its long list—the change of "13 times" to "one third" extra. (7) The "two conditions" have not "been fulfilled"—far from it. (8) Those details labeled "facts" are only fancies. (9) Finally,

my criticisms were by no means confined to that detail of the C.E. dispatch which we now accept as having been a "cable blunder."

Setting to one side these nine departures from fact, I find that what is left of the eleven lines is straight and true. I am not blaming Dr. Smith for these discrepancies—it would not be right, it would not be fair. I make the proper allowances. He has not been a journalist, as I have been—a trade wherein a person is brought to book by the rest of the press so often for divergencies that, by and by, he gets to be almost morbidly afraid to indulge in them. It is so with me. I always have the disposition to tell what is not so; I was born with it; we all have it. But I try not to do it now, because I have found out that it is unsafe. But with the Doctor of course it is different.

EXHIBIT G

I wanted to get at the whole of the facts as regards the C.E. dispatch, and so I wrote to China for them, when I found that the Board was not going to do it. But I am not allowed to wait. It seemed quite within the possibilities that a full detail of the facts might furnish me a chance to make an apology to Mr. Ament—a chance which, I give you my word, I would have honestly used, and not abused. But it is no matter. If the Board is not troubled about the bulk of that lurid dispatch, why should I be? I answered the apology-urging letters of several clergymen with the information that I had written to China for the details, and said I thought it was the only sure way of getting into a position to do fair and full justice to all concerned; but a couple of them replied that it was not a matter that could wait. That is to say, groping your way out of a jungle in the dark with guesses and conjectures is better than a straight march out in the sunlight of fact. It seems a curious idea.

However, those two clergymen were in a large measure right—from their point of view and the Board's; which is, putting it in the form of a couple of questions:

1. *Did Dr. Ament collect the assessed damages and thirteen times over?* The answer is: He did *not*. He collected only *a third* over.

2. *Did he apply the third to the "propagation of the Gospel?"* The answer is this correction: He applied it to "church expenses." Part or all of the outlay, it appears, goes to "supporting widows and orphans." It may be that church expenses and supporting widows and orphans are not part of the machinery for propagating the Gospel. I supposed they were, but it isn't any matter; I prefer this phrasing; it is not so blunt as the other.

In the opinion of the two clergymen and of the Board, these two points are *the only important ones* in the whole C.E. dispatch.

I accept that. Therefore let us throw out the rest of the dispatch as being no longer a part of Dr. Ament's case.

EXHIBIT H

The two clergymen and the Board are quite content with Dr. Ament's answers upon the two points.

Upon the first point of the two, my own viewpoint may be indicated by a question:

Did Dr. Ament collect from B (whether by compulsion or simple demand) even so much as a penny in payment for murders or depredations, without knowing, beyond question, that B, and not another, committed the murders or the depredations?

Or, in other words:

Did Dr. Ament ever, by chance or through ignorance, make the innocent pay the debts of the guilty?

In the article entitled "To the Person Sitting in Darkness," I put forward that point in a paragraph taken from Macallum's (imaginary) "History":

EXHIBIT I

When a white Boxer kills a Pawnee and destroys his property the other Pawnees do not trouble to seek *him* out; they kill any white person that comes along; also, they make some white village pay deceased's heirs the full cash value of deceased, together with full cash value of the property destroyed; they also make the village pay, in addition, *thirteen times* [3] the value of that property into a fund for the dissemination of the Pawnee religion, which they regard as the best of all religions for the softening and humanizing of the heart of man. It is their idea that it is only fair and right *that the innocent should be made to suffer for the guilty,* and that it is better that 90 and 9 innocent should suffer than one guilty person should escape.

We all know that Dr. Ament did not bring suspected persons into a duly organized court and try them by just and fair Christian and civilized methods, but proclaimed his "conditions," and collected damages from the innocent and the guilty alike, without any court pro-

---

[3] For "thirteen times" read "one third."—M.T.

ceedings at all.[4] That he himself, and not the villagers, made the
"conditions," we learn from his letter of November 13th, already
quoted from—the one in which he remarked that, upon *that* occasion
he brought no soldiers with him. The italics are mine:

After our *conditions* were known many villagers came of their own
accord and brought their money with them.

Not all, but "many." The Board really believes that those hunted
and harried paupers out there were not only willing to strip themselves
to pay Boxer damages, whether they owed them or not, but were
sentimentally eager to do it. Mr. Ament says, in his letter: "The villagers were extremely grateful because I brought no foreign soldiers,
and were glad to settle on the terms proposed." Some of those people
know more about theology than they do about human nature. I do not
remember encountering even a Christian who was "glad" to pay
money he did not owe; and as for a Chinaman doing it, why, dear me,
the thing is unthinkable. We have all seen Chinamen, many Chinamen, but not that kind. It is a new kind: an invention of the Board—
and "soldiers."

CONCERNING THE COLLECTIONS

What was the "one third extra"? Money due? No. Was it a theft,
then? Putting aside the "one third extra," what was the *remainder*
of the exacted indemnity, if collected from persons not *known* to owe
it, and without Christian and civilized forms of procedure? Was *it* theft,
was it robbery? In America it would be that; in Christian Europe it
would be that. I have great confidence in Dr. Smith's judgment concerning this detail, and he calls it "theft and extortion"—even in China;
for he was talking about the "thirteen times" at the time that he gave
it that strong name.[5] It is his idea that, when you make guilty and

[4] In civilized countries, if a mob destroy property in a town, the damage is
paid out of the town treasury, and no taxpayer suffers a disproportionate share
of the burden; the mayor is not privileged to distribute the burden according to
his private notions, sparing himself and his friends, and fleecing persons he holds
a spite against—as in the Orient—and the citizen who is too poor to be a taxpayer pays no part of the fine at all.—M.T.

[5] In his Open Letter, Dr. Smith cites Dr. Ament's letter of November 13th,
which contains an account of Dr. Ament's collecting tour; then Dr. Smith makes
this comment: "Nothing is said of securing 'thirteen times' the amount of the
losses." Farther down, Dr. Smith quotes praises of Dr. Ament and his work

innocent villagers pay the appraised damages, and then make them pay thirteen times that, besides, the *thirteen* stand for "theft and extortion."

Then what does *one third* extra stand for? Will he give that one third a name? Is it Modified Theft and Extortion? Is that it? The girl who was rebuked for having borne an illegitimate child excused herself by saying, "But it is such a *little* one."

When the "thirteen-times-extra" was alleged, it stood for theft and extortion, in Dr. Smith's eyes, and he was shocked. But when Dr. Ament showed that he had taken only a *third* extra, instead of thirteenfold, Dr. Smith was relieved, content, happy. I declare I cannot imagine why. That editor—quoted at the head of this article—was happy about it, too. I cannot think why. He thought I ought to "make for the amen corner and formulate a prompt apology." To whom, and for what? It is too deep for me.

To Dr. Smith, the "thirteenfold extra" clearly stood for "theft and extortion," and he was right, distinctly right, indisputably right. He manifestly thinks that when it got scaled away down to a mere "one third," a little thing like that was something other than "theft and extortion." Why? Only the Board knows! I will try to explain this difficult problem, so that the Board can get an idea of it. If a pauper owes me a dollar, and I catch him unprotected and make him pay me fourteen dollars, thirteen of it is "theft and extortion"; if I make him pay only a dollar and thirty-three and a third cents the thirty-three and a third cents are "theft and extortion" just the same. I will put it in another way, still simpler. If a man owes me one dog—any kind of a dog, the breed is of no consequence—and I— But let it go; the Board would never understand it. It *can't* understand these involved and difficult things.

But *if* the Board could understand, then I could furnish some more instruction—which is this. The one third, obtained by "theft and extortion," is *tainted money*, and cannot be purified even by defraying "church expenses" and "supporting widows and orphans" with it. It has to be restored to the people it was taken from.

Also, there is another view of these things. By our Christian code of morals and law, the *whole* $1.33⅓, if taken from a man not formally *proven* to have committed the damage the dollar represents, is, "theft and extortion." It cannot be honestly used for any purpose at all. It must be handed back to the man it was taken from.

Is there no way, then, to justify these thefts and extortions and make them clean and fair and honorable? Yes, there is. It can be done; it has been done; it continues to be done—by revising the Ten Commandments and bringing them down to date: for use in pagan lands. For example:

Thou shalt not steal—except when it is the custom of the country.

This way out is recognized and *approved* by all the best authorities, including the Board. I will cite witnesses.

The newspaper cutting, above: "Dr. Ament declares that all the collections which he made were approved by the *Chinese* officials." The editor is satisfied.

Dr. Ament's cable to Dr. Smith: "All collections received approval *Chinese* officials." Dr. Ament is satisfied.

Letters from eight clergymen—all to the same effect: Dr. Ament merely did as the *Chinese* do. So they are satisfied.

Mr. Ward, of the "Independent."

The Rev. Dr. Washington Gladden.

I have mislaid the letters of these gentlemen and cannot quote their words, but they are of the satisfied.

The Rev. Dr. Smith, in his Open Letter, published in the *Tribune:* "The whole procedure [Dr. Ament's] is in accordance with a custom among the *Chinese,* of holding a village responsible for wrongs suffered in that village, and especially making the head man of the village accountable for wrongs committed there." Dr. Smith is satisfied. Which means that the Board is satisfied.

The "head man"! Why, then, this poor rascal, innocent or guilty, must pay the whole bill, if he cannot squeeze it out of his poor-devil neighbors. But, indeed, he can be depended upon to try, even to the skinning them of their last brass farthing, their last rag of clothing, their last ounce of food. He can be depended upon to get the indemnity out of them, though it cost stripes and blows, blood-tears, and flesh.

THE TALE OF THE KING AND HIS TREASURER

How strange and remote and romantic and Oriental and Arabian-Nighty it all seems—and is. It brings back the old forgotten tales, and we hear the King say to his Treasurer:

"Bring me 30,000 gold tomauns."

"Allah preserve us, Sire! the treasury is empty."

"Do you hear? Bring the money—in ten days. Else, send me your head in a basket."

"I hear and obey."

The Treasurer summons the head men of a hundred villages, and says to one:

"Bring me a hundred gold tomauns." To another, "Bring me five hundred." To another, "Bring a thousand. In ten days. Your head is the forfeit."

"Your slaves kiss your feet! Ah, high and mighty lord, be merciful to our hard-pressed villagers; they are poor, they are naked, they starve; oh, these impossible sums! even the half——"

"Go! Grind it out of them, crush it out of them, turn the blood of the fathers, the tears of the mothers, the milk of the babes to money— or take the consequences. Have you heard?"

"His will be done, Who is the Fount of love and mercy and compassion, Who layeth this heavy burden upon us by the hand of His anointed servants—blessed be His holy Name! The father shall bleed, the mother shall faint for hunger, the babe shall perish at the dry breast. The chosen of God have commanded: it shall be as they say."

I am not meaning to object to the substitution of pagan customs for Christian, here and there and now and then, when the Christian ones are inconvenient. No; I like it and admire it. I do it myself. And I admire the alertness of the Board in watching out for chances to trade Board morals for Chinese morals, and get the best of the swap; for I cannot endure those people, they are yellow, and I have never considered yellow becoming. I have always been like the Board—perfectly well-meaning, but destitute of the Moral Sense. Now, one of the main reasons why it is so hard to make the Board understand that there is no moral difference between a big filch and a little filch, but only a legal one, is that vacancy in its make-up. Morally, there are no degrees in stealing. The Commandment merely says, "Thou shalt not *steal,*" and stops there. It doesn't recognize any difference between stealing a third and stealing thirteenfold. If I could think of a way to put it before the Board in such a plain and—

THE WATERMELONS

I have it, now. Many years ago, when I was studying for the gallows, I had a dear comrade, a youth who was not in my line, but still a thoroughly good fellow, though devious. He was preparing to qualify for a place on the Board, for there was going to be a vacancy by superannua-

tion in about five years. This was down South, in the slavery days. It
was the nature of the negro then, as now, to steal watermelons. They
stole three of the melons of an adoptive brother of mine, the only good
ones he had. I suspected three of a neighbor's negroes, but there was
no proof: and, besides, the watermelons in those negroes' private
patches were all green and small, and not up to indemnity standard.
But in the private patches of three other negroes there were a number
of competent melons. I consulted with my comrade, the understudy of
the Board. He said that if I would approve his arrangements, he
would arrange. I said, "Consider me the Board; I approve: arrange."
So he took a gun, and went and collected three large melons for my
brother-on-the-half-shell, and one over. I was greatly pleased, and
asked:

"Who gets the extra one?"

"Widows and orphans."

"A good idea, too. Why didn't you take thirteen?"

"It would have been wrong; a crime, in fact—Theft and Extortion."

"What is the one third extra—the odd melon—the same?"

It caused him to reflect. But there was no result.

The justice of the peace was a stern man. On the trial, he found
fault with the scheme, and required us to explain upon what we based
our strange conduct—as he called it. The understudy said:

"On the custom of the niggers. They all do it."

The justice forgot his dignity, and descended to sarcasm:

"Custom of the niggers! Are our morals so inadequate that we have
to borrow of niggers?" Then he said to the jury: "Three melons were
owing; they were collected from persons not proven to owe them; this
is theft. They were collected by compulsion; this is extortion. A melon
was added—for the widows and orphans. It was owed by no one. It is
another theft, another extortion. Return it whence it came, with the
others. It is not permissable, here, to apply to any object goods dishonestly obtained—not even to the feeding of widows and orphans,
for that would be to put a shame upon charity and dishonor it."

He said it in open court, before everybody, and to me it did not seem
very kind.

A clergyman, in a letter to me, reminds me, with a touch of reproach,
that "many of the missionaries are good men, kind-hearted, earnest,
devoted to their work." Certainly they are. No one is disputing it.
Instead of "many," he could have said "almost all," and still said
the truth, no doubt. I know many missionaries; I have met them all
about the globe, and have known only one or two who could not fill

that bill and answer to that description. "Almost all" comes near to being a proportion and a description applicable also to lawyers, authors, editors, merchants, manufacturers—in fact, to most guilds and vocations. Without a doubt, Dr. Ament did what he believed to be right, and I concede that when a man is doing what he believes to be right, there is argument on his side. I differ with Dr. Ament, but that is only because he got his training from the Board and I got mine outside. Neither of us is responsible, altogether.

RECAPITULATION

But there is no need to sum up. Mr. Ament has acknowledged the "one third extra"—no other witness is necessary. The Rev. Dr. Smith has carefully considered the act and labeled it with a stern name, and his verdict seems to have no flaw in it. The morals of the act are Chinese, but are approved by the Board, and by some of the clergy and some of the newspapers, as being a valuable improvement upon Christian ones—which leaves me with a closed mouth, though with a pain in my heart.

IS THE AMERICAN BOARD ON TRIAL?

Do I think that Dr. Ament and certain of his fellow missionaries are as bad as their conduct? No, I do not. They are the product of their training; and now that I understand the whole case, and where they got their ideals, and that they are merely subordinates and subject to authority, I comprehend that they are rather accessories than principals and that their acts only show faulty heads curiously trained, not bad hearts. Mainly, as it seems to me, it is the American Board that is on trial. And again, it is a case of the head, not of the heart. That it has a heart which has never harbored an evil intention, no one will deny, no one will question; the Board's history can silence any challenge on that score. The Board's heart is not in court: it is its head that is on trial.

It is a sufficiently strange head. Its ways baffle comprehension; its ideas are like no one else's, its methods are novelties to the practical world; its judgments are surprises. When one thinks it is going to speak and must speak, it is silent; when one thinks it ought to be silent and must be silent, it speaks. Put your finger where you think it ought to be, it is not there; put it where you think it ought not to be, there you find it.

When its servant in China seemed to be charging himself with amazing things, in a reputable journal—in a dispatch which was copied into many other papers—the Board was as silent about it as any dead man could have been who was informed that his house was burning over his head. An exchange of cablegrams could have enabled it, within two days, to prove to the world—possibly—that the damaging dispatch had not proceeded from the mouth of its servant; yet it sat silent and asked no questions about the matter.

It was silent during thirty-eight days. Then the dispatch came into prominence again. It chanced that I was the occasion of it. A break in the stillness followed. In what form? An exchange of cablegrams, resulting in proof that the damaging dispatch had not been authorized? No, in the form of an Open Letter by the Corresponding Secretary of the American Board, the Rev. Dr. Smith, in which it was *argued* that Dr. Ament could not have said and done the things set forth in the dispatch.

Surely, this was bad politics. A repudiating telegram would have been worth more than a library of argument.

An extension of the silence would have been better than the Open Letter, I think. I thought so at the time. It seemed to me that mistakes enough had been made and harm enough done. I thought it questionable policy to publish the Letter, for I "did not think it likely that Dr. Ament would disown the dispatch," and I telegraphed that to the Rev. Dr. Smith. Personally, I had nothing against Dr. Ament, and that is my attitude yet.

Once more it was a good time for an extension of the silence. But no; the Board has its own ways, and one of them is to do the unwise thing, when occasion offers. After having waited fifty-six days, it cabled to Dr. Ament. No one can divine why it did so then, instead of fifty-six days earlier.[6] It got a fatal reply—and was not aware of it. That was that curious confession about the "one third extra"; its application, not to the "propagation of the Gospel," but only to "church expenses," support of widows and orphans; and, on top of this confession, that other strange one revealing the dizzying fact that our missionaries, who went to China to teach Christian morals and justice, had adopted pagan morals and justice in their place. *That cablegram was dynamite.*

It seems odd that the Board did not see that that revelation made the case far worse than it was before; for there was a saving doubt, before—a doubt which was a Gibraltar for strength, and should have been carefully left undisturbed. Why did the Board allow that revela-

[6] The cablegram went on the day (February 18th) that Mr. George Lynch's account of the looting was published. See "Exhibit B." It seems a pity it did not inquire about the looting and get it denied.—M.T.

tion to get into print? Why did the Board not suppress it and keep still? But no; in the Board's opinion, this was once more the time for speech. Hence Dr. Smith's latest letter to me, suggesting that I speak also—a letter which is a good enough letter, barring its nine defects, but is another evidence that the Board's head is not as good as its heart.

A missionary is a man who is pretty nearly all heart, else he would not be in a calling which requires of him such large sacrifices of one kind and another. He is made up of faith, zeal, courage, sentiment, emotion, enthusiasm; and so he is a mixture of poet, devotee, and knight errant. He exiles himself from home and friends and the scenes and associations that are dearest to him; patiently endures discomforts, privations, discouragements; goes with good pluck into dangers which he knows may cost him his life; and when he must suffer death, willingly makes that supreme sacrifice for his cause.

Sometimes the headpiece of that kind of a man can be of an inferior sort, and error of judgment can result—as we have seen. Then, for his protection, as it seems to me, he ought to have at his back a Board able to know a blunder when it sees one, and prompt to bring him back upon his right course when he strays from it. That is to say, I think the captain of a ship ought to understand navigation. Whether he does or not, he will have to take a captain's share of the blame, if the crew bring the vessel to grief.

1901

Thomas Brackett Reed

He wore no shell. His ways were frank and open, and the road to his large sympathies was straight and unobstructed. His was a nature which invited affection—compelled it, in fact—and met it halfway. Hence he was "Tom" to the most of his friends, and to half of the nation. The abbreviating of such a man's name is a patent of nobility, and is conferred from the heart. Mr. Reed had a very strong and decided character, and he may have had enemies; I do not know; if he had them—outside of politics—they did not know the man. He was transparently honest and honorable, there were no furtivenesses about him, and whoever came to know him trusted him and was not disappointed. He was wise, he was shrewd and alert, he was a clear and capable thinker, a logical reasoner, and a strong and convincing speaker. His manner was easy and engaging, his speeches sparkled with felicities of phrasing thrown off without apparent effort, and when he needed the happy help of humor he had a mine of it as deep and rich as Kimberly to draw from. His services to his country were great, and they were gratefully acknowledged.

I cannot remember back to a time when he was not "Tom" Reed to me, nor to a time when he would have been offended at being so addressed by me. I cannot remember back to a time when I could let him alone in an after-dinner speech if he was present, nor to a time when he did not take my extravagances concerning him and misstatements about him in good part, nor yet to a time when he did not pay them back with usury when his turn came. The last speech he made was at my birthday dinner at the end of November, when naturally I was his text; my last word to him was in a letter the next day; a day later I was illustrating a fantastic article on Art with his portrait among others—a portrait now to be laid reverently away among the jests that begin in humor and end in pathos. These things happened only eight days ago, and now he is gone from us, and the nation is speaking of him as one who *was*. It seems incredible, impossible. Such a man, such a friend, seems to us a permanent possession; his vanishing from our midst is unthinkable; as unthinkable as was the vanishing of the Campanile, that had stood for a thousand years, and was turned to dust in a moment.

I have no wish, at this time, to enter upon light and humorous reminiscences connected with yachting voyages with Mr. Reed in northern and southern seas, nor with other recreations in his company in other places—they do not belong in this paper, they do not invite me, they would jar upon me. I have only wished to say how fine and beautiful was his life and character, and to take him by the hand and say goodby, as to a fortunate friend who has done well his work and goes a pleasant journey.

1902

Saint Joan of Arc

CHAPTER I

The evidence furnished at the Trials and Rehabilitation sets forth Joan of Arc's strange and beautiful history in clear and minute detail. Among all the multitude of biographies that freight the shelves of the world's libraries, *this is the only one whose validity is confirmed to us by oath.* It gives us a vivid picture of a career and a personality of so extraordinary a character that we are helped to accept them as actualities by the very fact that both are beyond the inventive reach of fiction. The public part of the career occupied only a mere breath of time—it covered but two years; but what a career it was! The personality which made it possible is one to be reverently studied, loved, and marveled at, but not to be wholly understood and accounted for by even the most searching analysis.

In Joan of Arc at the age of sixteen there was no promise of a romance. She lived in a dull little village on the frontiers of civilization; she had been nowhere and had seen nothing; she knew none but simple shepherd folk; she had never seen a person of note; she hardly knew what a soldier looked like; she had never ridden a horse, nor had a warlike weapon in her hand; she could neither read nor write: she could spin and sew; she knew her catechism and her prayers and the fabulous histories of the saints, and this was all her learning. That

Note.—The Official Record of the Trials and Rehabilitation of Joan of Arc is the most remarkable history that exists in any language; yet there are few people in the world who can say they have read it: in England and America it has hardly been heard of.

Three hundred years ago Shakespeare did not know the true story of Joan of Arc; in his day it was unknown even in France. For four hundred years it existed rather as a vaguely defined romance than as definite and authentic history. The true story remained buried in the official archives of France from the Rehabilitation of 1456 until Quicherat dug it out and gave it to the world two generations ago, in lucid and understandable modern French. It is a deeply fascinating story. But only in the Official Trials and Rehabilitation can it be found in its entirety.—M.T.

was Joan at sixteen. What did she know of law? of evidence? of courts? of the attorney's trade? of legal procedure? Nothing. Less than nothing. Thus exhaustively equipped with ignorance, she went before the court at Toul to contest a false charge of breach of promise of marriage; she conducted her cause herself, without any one's help or advice or any one's friendly sympathy, and won it. She called no witnesses of her own, but vanquished the prosecution by using with deadly effectiveness its own testimony. The astonished judge threw the case out of court, and spoke of her as "this marvelous child."

She went to the veteran Commandant of Vaucouleurs and demanded an escort of soldiers, saying she must march to the help of the King of France, since she was commissioned of God to win back his lost kingdom for him and set the crown upon his head. The Commandant said, "What, you? You are only a child." And he advised that she be taken back to her village and have her ears boxed. But she said she must obey God, and would come again, and again, and yet again, and finally she would get the soldiers. She said truly. In time he yielded, after months of delay and refusal, and gave her the soldiers; and took off his sword and gave her that, and said, "Go—and let come what may." She made her long and perilous journey through the enemy's country, and spoke with the King, and convinced him. Then she was summoned before the University of Poitiers to prove that she *was* commissioned of God and not of Satan, and daily during three weeks she sat before that learned congress unafraid, and capably answered their deep questions out of her ignorant but able head and her simple and honest heart; and again she won her case, and with it the wondering admiration of all that august company.

And now, aged seventeen, she was made Commander-in-Chief, with a prince of the royal house and the veteran generals of France for subordinates; and at the head of the first army she had ever seen, she marched to Orleans, carried the commanding fortresses of the enemy by storm in three desperate assaults, and in ten days raised a siege which had defied the might of France for seven months.

After a tedious and insane delay caused by the King's instability of character and the treacherous counsels of his ministers, she got permission to take the field again. She took Jargeau by storm; then Meung; she forced Beaugency to surrender; then—in the open field—she won the memorable victory of Patay against Talbot, "the English lion," and broke the back of the Hundred Years' War. It was a campaign which cost but seven weeks of time; yet the political results would have been cheap if the time expended had been fifty years.

Patay, that unsung and now long-forgotten battle, was the Moscow of the English power in France; from the blow struck that day it was destined never to recover. It was the beginning of the end of an alien dominion which had ridden France intermittently for three hundred years.

Then followed the great campaign of the Loire, the capture of Troyes by assault, and the triumphal march past surrendering towns and fortresses to Rheims, where Joan put the crown upon her King's head in the Cathedral, amid wild public rejoicings, and with her old peasant father there to see these things and believe his eyes if he could. She had restored the crown and the lost sovereignty; the King was grateful for once in his shabby poor life, and asked her to name her reward and have it. She asked for nothing for herself, but begged that the taxes of her native village might be remitted forever. The prayer was granted, and the promise kept for three hundred and sixty years. Then it was broken, and remains broken to-day. France was very poor then, she is very rich now; but she has been collecting those taxes for more than a hundred years.

Joan asked one other favor: that now that her mission was fulfilled she might be allowed to go back to her village and take up her humble life again with her mother and the friends of her childhood; for she had no pleasure in the cruelties of war, and the sight of blood and suffering wrung her heart. Sometimes in battle she did not draw her sword, lest in the splendid madness of the onset she might forget herself and take an enemy's life with it. In the Rouen Trials, one of her quaintest speeches—coming from the gentle and girlish source it did—was her naïve remark that she had "never killed any one." Her prayer for leave to go back to the rest and peace of her village home was not granted.

Then she wanted to march at once upon Paris, take it, and drive the English out of France. She was hampered in all the ways that treachery and the King's vacillation could devise, but she forced her way to Paris at last, and fell badly wounded in a successful assault upon one of the gates. Of course her men lost heart at once—she was the only heart they had. They fell back. She begged to be allowed to remain at the front, saying victory was sure. "I will take Paris now or die!" she said. But she was removed from the field by force; the King ordered a retreat, and actually disbanded his army. In accordance with a beautiful old military custom Joan devoted her silver armor and hung it up in the Cathedral of St. Denis. Its great days were over.

Then, by command, she followed the King and his frivolous court and endured a gilded captivity for a time, as well as her free spirit could; and whenever inaction became unbearable she gathered some men together and rode away and assaulted a stronghold and captured it.

At last in a sortie against the enemy, from Compiègne, on the 24th of May (when she was turned eighteen), she was herself captured, after a gallant fight. It was her last battle. She was to follow the drums no more.

Thus ended the briefest epoch-making military career known to history. It lasted only a year and a month, but it found France an English province, and furnishes the reason that France is France to-day and not an English province still. Thirteen months! It was, indeed, a short career; but in the centuries that have since elapsed five hundred millions of Frenchmen have lived and died blest by the benefactions it conferred; and so long as France shall endure, the mighty debt must grow. And France is grateful; we often hear her say it. Also thrifty: she collects the Domremy taxes.

CHAPTER II

Joan was fated to spend the rest of her life behind bolts and bars. She was a prisoner of war, not a criminal, therefore hers was recognized as an honorable captivity. By the rules of war she must be held to ransom, and a fair price could not be refused if offered. John of Luxembourg paid her the just compliment of requiring a prince's ransom for her. In that day that phrase represented a definite sum—61,125 francs. It was, of course, supposable that either the King or grateful France, or both, would fly with the money and set their fair young benefactor free. But this did not happen. In five and a half months neither King nor country stirred a hand nor offered a penny. Twice Joan tried to escape. Once by a trick she succeeded for a moment, and locked her jailer in behind her, but she was discovered and caught; in the other case she let herself down from a tower sixty feet high, but her rope was too short, and she got a fall that disabled her and she could not get away.

Finally, Cauchon, Bishop of Beauvais, paid the money and bought Joan—ostensibly for the Church, to be tried for wearing male attire and for other impieties, but really for the English, the enemy into whose hands the poor girl was so piteously anxious not to fall. She was now shut up in the dungeons of the Castle of Rouen and kept in an iron cage, with her hands and feet and neck chained to a pillar; and from that time forth during all the months of her imprisonment, till the end, several rough English soldiers stood guard over her night and day—and not outside her room, but in it. It was a dreary and hideous captivity, but it did not conquer her: nothing could break that invincible spirit. From first to last she was a prisoner a year; and she spent the last three months of it on trial for her life before a formidable array of ecclesiastical judges, and disputing the ground with them foot by foot and inch by inch with brilliant generalship and dauntless pluck. The spectacle of that solitary girl, forlorn and friendless, without advocate or adviser, and without the help and guidance of any copy of the charges brought against her or rescript of the complex and voluminous daily proceedings of the court to modify the crushing strain upon her astonishing memory, fighting that long battle serene and undismayed against these colossal odds, stands alone in its pathos and its sublimity; it has nowhere its mate, either in the annals of fact or in the inventions of fiction.

And how fine and great were the things she daily said, how fresh and crisp—and she so worn in body, so starved, and tired, and harried! They run through the whole gamut of feeling and expression—from scorn and defiance, uttered with soldierly fire and frankness, all down the scale to wounded dignity clothed in words of noble pathos; as when her patience was exhausted by the pestering delvings and gropings and searchings of her persecutors to find out what kind of devil's witchcraft she had employed to rouse the war spirit in her timid soldiers, she burst out with, "What I said was, 'Ride these English down'—and I did it myself!" and as, when insultingly asked why it was that *her* standard had place at the crowning of the King in the Cathedral of Rheims rather than the standards of the other captains, she uttered that touching speech, "It had borne the burden, it had earned the honor"—a phrase which fell from her lips without premeditation, yet whose moving beauty and simple grace it would bankrupt the arts of language to surpass.

Although she was on trial for her life, she was the only witness called on either side; the only witness summoned to testify before a packed jury commissioned with a definite task: to find her guilty, whether she was guilty or not. She must be convicted out of her own mouth, there being no other way to accomplish it. Every advantage that learning has over ignorance, age over youth, experience over inexperience, chicane over artlessness, every trick and trap and gin devisable by malice and the cunning of sharp intellects practised in setting snares for the unwary—all these were employed against her without shame; and when these arts were one by one defeated by the marvelous intuitions of her alert and penetrating mind, Bishop Cauchon stooped to a final baseness which it degrades human speech to describe: a priest who pretended to come from the region of her own home and to be a pitying friend and anxious to help her in her sore need was smuggled into her cell, and he misused his sacred office to steal her confidence; she confided to him the things sealed from revealment by her Voices, and which her prosecutors had tried so long in vain to trick her into betraying. A concealed confederate set it all down and delivered it to Cauchon, who used Joan's secrets, thus obtained, for her ruin.

Throughout the Trials, whatever the foredoomed witness said was twisted from its true meaning when possible, and made to tell against her; and whenever an answer of hers was beyond the reach of twisting it was not allowed to go upon the record. It was upon one of these latter occasions that she uttered that pathetic reproach—to Cauchon: "Ah, you set down everything that is against me, but you will not set down what is for me."

That this untrained young creature's genius for war was wonderful, and her generalship worthy to rank with the ripe products of a tried and trained military experience, we have the sworn testimony of two of her veteran subordinates—one, the Duc d'Alençon, the other the greatest of the French generals of the time, Dunois, Bastard of Orleans; that her genius was as great—possibly even greater—in the subtle warfare of the forum we have for witness the records of the Rouen Trials, that protracted exhibition of intellectual fence maintained with credit against the master-minds of France; that her moral greatness was peer to her intellect we call the Rouen Trials again to witness, with their testimony to a fortitude which patiently and steadfastly endured during twelve weeks the wasting forces of captivity, chains, loneliness, sickness, darkness, hunger, thirst, cold, shame, insult, abuse, broken sleep, treachery, ingratitude, exhausting sieges of cross-examination, the threat of torture, with the rack before her and the executioner standing ready: yet never surrendering, never asking quarter, the frail wreck of her as unconquerable the last day as was her invincible spirit the first.

Great as she was in so many ways, she was perhaps even greatest of all in the lofty things just named—her patient endurance, her steadfastness, her granite fortitude. We may not hope to easily find her mate and twin in these majestic qualities; where we lift our eyes highest we find only a strange and curious contrast—there in the captive eagle beating his broken wings on the Rock of St. Helena.

CHAPTER III

The Trials ended with her condemnation. But as she had conceded nothing, confessed nothing, this was victory for her, defeat for Cauchon. But his evil resources were not yet exhausted. She was persuaded to agree to sign a paper of slight import, then by treachery a paper was substituted which contained a recantation and a detailed confession of everything which had been charged against her during the Trials and denied and repudiated by her persistently during the three months; and this false paper she ignorantly signed. This was a victory for Cauchon. He followed it eagerly and pitilessly up by at once setting a trap for her which she could not escape. When she realized this she gave up the long struggle, denounced the treason which had been practised against her, repudiated the false confession, reasserted the truth of the testimony which she had given in the Trials, and went to her martyrdom with the peace of God in her tired heart, and on her lips endearing words and loving prayers for the cur she had crowned and the nation of ingrates she had saved.

When the fires rose about her and she begged for a cross for her dying lips to kiss, it was not a friend but an enemy, not a Frenchman but an alien, not a comrade in arms but an English soldier, that answered that pathetic prayer. He broke a stick across his knee, bound the pieces together in the form of the symbol she so loved, and gave it her; and his gentle deed is not forgotten, nor will be.

CHAPTER IV

Twenty-five years afterward the Process of Rehabilitation was instituted, there being a growing doubt as to the validity of a sovereignty that had been rescued and set upon its feet by a person who had been proven by the Church to be a witch and a familiar of evil spirits. Joan's old generals, her secretary, several aged relations and other villagers of Domremy, surviving judges and secretaries of the Rouen and Poitiers Processes—a cloud of witnesses, some of whom had been her enemies and persecutors—came and made oath and testified; and what they said was written down. In that sworn testimony the moving and beautiful history of Joan of Arc is laid bare, from her childhood to her martyrdom. From the verdict she rises stainlessly pure, in mind and heart, in speech and deed and spirit, and will so endure to the end of time.

She is the Wonder of the Ages. And when we consider her origin,

her early circumstances, her sex, and that she did all the things upon
which her renown rests while she was still a young girl, we recognize
that while our race continues she will be also the *Riddle* of the Ages.
When we set about accounting for a Napoleon or a Shakespeare or a
Raphael or a Wagner or an Edison or other extraordinary person, we
understand that the measure of his talent will not explain the whole
result, nor even the largest part of it; no, it is the atmosphere in which
the talent was cradled that explains; it is the training which it received
while it grew, the nurture it got from reading, study, example, the encouragement it gathered from self-recognition and recognition from the
outside at each stage of its development: when we know all these details, then we know why the man was ready when his opportunity
came. We should expect Edison's surroundings and atmosphere to have
the largest share in discovering him to himself and to the world; and
we should expect him to live and die undiscovered in a land where an
inventor could find no comradeship, no sympathy, no ambition-rousing
atmosphere of recognition and applause—Dahomey, for instance. Dahomey could not find an Edison out; in Dahomey an Edison could not
find himself out. Broadly speaking, genius is not born with sight, but
blind; and it is not itself that opens its eyes, but the subtle influences
of a myriad of stimulating exterior circumstances.

We all know this to be not a guess, but a mere commonplace fact, a
truism. Lorraine was Joan of Arc's Dahomey. And there the Riddle
confronts us. We can understand how she could be born with military
genius, with leonine courage, with incomparable fortitude, with a mind
which was in several particulars a prodigy—a mind which included
among its specialties the lawyer's gift of detecting traps laid by the adversary in cunning and treacherous arrangements of seemingly innocent words, the orator's gift of eloquence, the advocate's gift of pre-
senting a case in clear and compact form, the judge's gift of sorting
and weighing evidence, and finally, something recognizable as more
than a mere trace of the statesman's gift of understanding a political
situation and how to make profitable use of such opportunities
as it offers; we can comprehend how she could be born with these
great qualities, but we cannot comprehend how they became immediately usable and effective without the developing forces of a sympathetic atmosphere and the training which comes of teaching, study,
practice—years of practice—and the crowning and perfecting help of a
thousand mistakes. We can understand how the possibilities of the
future perfect peach are all lying hid in the humble bitter-almond,
but we cannot conceive of the peach springing directly from the al-

mond without the intervening long seasons of patient cultivation and development. Out of a cattle-pasturing peasant village lost in the remotenesses of an unvisited wilderness and atrophied with ages of stupefaction and ignorance we cannot see a Joan of Arc issue equipped to the last detail for her amazing career and hope to be able to explain the riddle of it, labor at it as we may.

It is beyond us. All the rules fail in this girl's case. In the world's history she stands alone—quite alone. Others have been great in their first public exhibitions of generalship, valor, legal talent, diplomacy, fortitude; but always their previous years and associations had been in a larger or smaller degree a preparation for these things. There have been no exceptions to the rule. But Joan was competent in a law case at sixteen without ever having seen a law-book or a court-house before; she had no training in soldiership and no associations with it, yet she was a competent general in her first campaign; she was brave in her first battle, yet her courage had had no education—not even the education which a boy's courage gets from never-ceasing reminders that it is not permissible in a boy to be a coward, but only in a girl; friendless, alone, ignorant, in the blossom of her youth, she sat week after week, a prisoner in chains, before her assemblage of judges, enemies hunting her to her death, the ablest minds in France, and answered them out of an untaught wisdom which overmatched their learning, baffled their tricks and treacheries with a native sagacity which compelled their wonder, and scored every day a victory against these incredible odds and camped unchallenged on the field. In the history of the human intellect, untrained, inexperienced, and using only its birthright equipment of untried capacities, there is nothing which approaches this. Joan of Arc stands alone, and must continue to stand alone, by reason of the unfellowed fact that in the things wherein she was great she was so without shade or suggestion of help from preparatory teaching, practice, environment, or experience. There is no one to compare her with, none to measure her by; for all others among the illustrious *grew* toward their high place in an atmosphere and surroundings which discovered their gift to them and nourished it and promoted it, intentionally or unconsciously. There have been other young generals, but they were not girls; young generals, but they had been soldiers before they were generals: she *began* as a general; she commanded the first army she ever saw; she led it from victory to victory, and never lost a battle with it; there have been young commanders-in-chief, but none so young as she: she is the only soldier in history who has held the supreme command of a nation's armies at the age of seventeen.

Her history has still another feature which sets her apart and leaves her without fellow or competitor: there have been many uninspired prophets, but she was the only one who ever ventured the daring detail of naming, along with a foretold event, the event's precise nature, the special time-limit within which it would occur, and the place—*and scored fulfilment*. At Vaucouleurs she said she must go to the King and be made his general, and break the English power, and crown her sovereign—"at Rheims." It all happened. It was all to happen "next year"—and it did. She foretold her first wound and its character and date a month in advance, and the prophecy was recorded in a public record-book three weeks in advance. She repeated it the morning of the date named, and it was fulfilled before night. At Tours she foretold the limit of her military career—saying it would end in one year from the time of its utterance—and she was right. She foretold her martyrdom—using *that word*, and naming a time three months away— and again she was right. At a time when France seemed hopelessly and permanently in the hands of the English she twice asserted in her prison before her judges that within seven years the English would meet with a mightier disaster than had been the fall of Orleans: it happened within five—the fall of Paris. Other prophecies of hers came true, both as to the event named and the time-limit prescribed.

She was deeply religious, and believed that she had daily speech with angels; that she saw them face to face, and that they counseled her, comforted and heartened her, and brought commands to her direct from God. She had a childlike faith in the heavenly origin of her apparitions and her Voices, and not any threat of any form of death was able to frighten it out of her loyal heart. She was a beautiful and simple and lovable character. In the records of the Trials this comes out in clear and shining detail. She was gentle and winning and affectionate; she loved her home and friends and her village life; she was miserable in the presence of pain and suffering; she was full of compassion: on the field of her most splendid victory she forgot her triumphs to hold in her lap the head of a dying enemy and comfort his passing spirit with pitying words; in an age when it was common to slaughter prisoners she stood dauntless between hers and harm, and saved them alive; she was forgiving, generous, unselfish, magnanimous; she was pure from all spot or stain of baseness. And always she was a *girl*; and dear and worshipful, as is meet for that estate: when she fell wounded, the first time, she was frightened, and cried when she saw her blood gushing from her breast; but she was Joan of Arc! and when presently she found that her generals were sounding the retreat, she staggered to her feet and led the assault again and took that place by storm.

There is no blemish in that rounded and beautiful character.

How strange it is!—that almost invariably the artist remembers only one detail—one minor and meaningless detail of the personality of Joan of Arc: to wit, that she was a peasant girl—and forgets all the rest; and so he paints her as a strapping middle-aged fishwoman, with costume to match, and in her face the spirituality of a ham. He is slave to his one idea, and forgets to observe that the supremely great souls are never lodged in gross bodies. No brawn, no muscle, could endure the work that their bodies must do; they do their miracles by the spirit, which has fifty times the strength and staying-power of brawn and muscle. The Napoleons are little, not big; and they work twenty hours in the twenty-four, and come up fresh, while the big soldiers with the little hearts faint around them with fatigue. We know what Joan of Arc was like, without asking—merely by what she did. The artist should paint her *spirit*—then he could not fail to paint her body aright. She would rise before us, then, a vision to win us, not repel: a lithe young slender figure, instinct with "the unbought grace of youth," dear and bonny and lovable, the face beautiful, and transfigured with the light of that lustrous intellect and the fires of that unquenchable spirit.

Taking into account, as I have suggested before, all the circumstances—her origin, youth, sex, illiteracy, early environment, and the obstructing conditions under which she exploited her high gifts and made her conquests in the field and before the courts that tried her for her life—she is easily and by far the most extraordinary person the human race has ever produced.

1904

The First Writing-Machines

FROM MY UNPUBLISHED AUTOBIOGRAPHY[1]

Some days ago a correspondent sent in an old typewritten sheet, faded by age, containing the following letter over the signature of Mark Twain.

"HARTFORD, *March 19, 1875.*
"Please do not use my name in any way. Please do not even divulge the fact that I own a machine. I have entirely stopped using the typewriter, for the reason that I never could write a letter with it to anybody without receiving a request by return mail that I would not only describe the machine, but state what progress I had made in the use of it, etc., etc. I don't like to write letters, and so I don't want people to know I own this curiosity-breeding little joker."

A note was sent to Mr. Clemens asking him if the letter was genuine and whether he really had a typewriter as long ago as that. Mr. Clemens replied that his best answer is in the following chapter from his unpublished autobiography:

1904. *Villa Quarto, Florence, January.*
Dictating autobiography to a typewriter is a new experience for me, but it goes very well, and is going to save time and "language"—the kind of language that soothes vexation.

I have dictated to a typewriter before—but not autobiography. Between that experience and the present one there lies a mighty gap—more than thirty years! It is a sort of lifetime. In that wide interval much has happened—to the type-machine as well as to the rest of us. At the beginning of that interval a type-machine was a curiosity. The person who owned one was a curiosity, too. But now it is the other way about: the person who *doesn't* own one is a curiosity. I saw a type-

---

[1] Over a period of many years Clemens amassed an extensive autobiographical manuscript, which was a sort of attic in which, he believed, almost anything could be shoved that came to mind. He took a curious delight at times in labelling certain of his works (as in the present instance) as having been lifted from his autobiography.—C.N.

machine for the first time in—what year? I suppose it was 1873—because Nasby was with me at the time, and it was in Boston. We must have been lecturing, or we could not have been in Boston, I take it. I quitted the platform that season.

But never mind about that, it is no matter. Nasby and I saw the machine through a window, and went in to look at it. The salesman explained it to us, showed us samples of its work, and said it could do fifty-seven words a minute—a statement which we frankly confessed that we did not believe. So he put his type-girl to work, and we timed her by the watch. She actually did the fifty-seven in sixty seconds. We were partly convinced, but said it probably couldn't happen again. But it did. We timed the girl over and over again—with the same result always: she won out. She did her work on narrow slips of paper, and we pocketed them as fast as she turned them out, to show as curiosities. The price of the machine was one hundred and twenty-five dollars. I bought one, and we went away very much excited.

At the hotel we got out our slips and were a little disappointed to find that they all contained the same words. The girl had economized time and labor by using a formula which she knew by heart. However, we argued—safely enough—that the *first* type-girl must naturally take rank with the first billiard-player: neither of them could be expected to get out of the game any more than a third or a half of what was in it. If the machine survived—*if* it survived—experts would come to the front, by and by, who would double this girl's output without a doubt. They would do one hundred words a minute—my talking speed on the platform. That score has long ago been beaten.

At home I played with the toy, repeating and repeating and repeating "The Boy stood on the Burning Deck," until I could turn that boy's adventure out at the rate of twelve words a minute; then I resumed the pen, for business, and only worked the machine to astonish inquiring visitors. They carried off many reams of the boy and his burning deck.

By and by I hired a young woman, and did my first dictating (letters, merely), and my last until now. The machine did not do both capitals and lower case (as now), but only capitals. Gothic capitals they were, and sufficiently ugly. I remember the first letter I dictated. It was to Edward Bok, who was a boy then. I was not acquainted with him at that time. His present enterprising spirit is not new—he had it in that early day. He was accumulating autographs, and was not content with mere signatures, he wanted a whole autograph *letter*. I fur-

nished it—in type-machine capitals, *signature and all.* It was long; it
was a sermon; it contained advice; also reproaches. I said writing was
my *trade,* my bread-and-butter; I said it was not fair to ask a man to
give away samples of his trade; would he ask the blacksmith for a
horseshoe? would he ask the doctor for a corpse?

Now I come to an important matter—as I regard it. In the year '74
the young woman copied a considerable part of a book of mine *on the
machine.* In a previous chapter of this Autobiography I have claimed
that I was the first person in the world that ever had a telephone in
his house for practical purposes; I will now claim—until dispossessed
—that I was the first person in the world to *apply the type-machine to
literature.* That book must have been *The Adventures of Tom Sawyer.*
I wrote the first half of it in '72, the rest of it in '74. My machinist
type-copied a book for me in '74, so I concluded it was that one.

That early machine was full of caprices, full of defects—devilish ones.
It had as many immoralities as the machine of to-day has virtues. After
a year or two I found that it was degrading my character, so I thought
I would give it to Howells. He was reluctant, for he was suspicious of
novelties and unfriendly toward them, and he remains so to this day.
But I persuaded him. He had great confidence in me, and I got him to
believe things about the machine that I did not believe myself. He took
it home to Boston, and my morals began to improve, but his have never
recovered.

He kept it six months, and then returned it to me. I gave it away
twice after that, but it wouldn't stay; it came back. Then I gave it to
our coachman, Patrick McAleer, who was very grateful, because he
did not know the animal, and thought I was trying to make him wiser
and better. As soon as he got wiser and better he traded it to a heretic
for a side-saddle which he could not use, and there my knowledge of
its history ends.

1905

A Helpless Situation

Once or twice a year I get a letter of a certain pattern, a pattern that never materially changes, in form and substance, yet I cannot get used to that letter—it always astonishes me. It affects me as the locomotive always affects me: I say to myself, "I have seen you a thousand times, you always look the same way, yet you are always a wonder, and you are always impossible; to contrive you is clearly beyond human genius—you can't exist, you don't exist, yet here you are!"

I have a letter of that kind by me, a very old one. I yearn to print it, and where is the harm? The writer of it is dead years ago, no doubt, and if I conceal her name and address—her this-world address—I am sure her shade will not mind. And with it I wish to print the answer which I wrote at the time but probably did not send. If it went—which is not likely—it went in the form of a copy, for I find the original still here, pigeonholed with the said letter. To that kind of letters we all write answers which we do not send, fearing to hurt where we have no desire to hurt; I have done it many a time, and this is doubtless a case of the sort.

THE LETTER

X——., CALIFORNIA, *June 3, 1879.*

Mr. S. L. Clemens, *Hartford, Conn.*

DEAR SIR,—You will doubtless be surprised to know who has presumed to write and ask a favor of you. Let your memory go back to your days in the Humboldt mines—'62–'63. You will remember, you and Clagett and Oliver and the old blacksmith Tillou lived in a lean-to which was half-way up the gulch, and there were six log cabins in the camp—strung pretty well separated up the gulch from its mouth at the desert to where the last claim was, at the divide. The lean-to you lived in was the one with a canvas roof that the cow fell down through one night, as told about by you in *Roughing It*—my uncle Simmons remembers it very well. He lived in the principal cabin, half-way up the divide, along with Dixon and Parker and Smith. It had two rooms, one for kitchen and the other for bunks, and was the only one that had. You and your party were there on the great night, the time they had dried-apple-pie, Uncle Simmons often speaks of it. It seems curious that dried-apple-pie should have seemed such a great thing, but it was, and it shows how far Humboldt was out of the world and difficult to get to, and how slim the regular bill of fare was. Sixteen years ago—it is a long time. I was a little girl then, only fourteen. I never saw you, I lived in Washoe. But Uncle Simmons ran across you every now and then, all during those weeks that you and party were there working your claim which was like the rest. The camp played out long and long ago, there wasn't silver enough in it to make a button. You never saw my husband, but he was there after you left, *and lived in that very lean-to,* a bachelor then but married to me now. He often wishes there had been a photographer there in those days, he would have taken the lean-to. He got hurt in the old Hal Clayton claim that was abandoned like the others putting in a blast and not climbing out quick enough, though he scrambled the best he could. It landed him clear down on the trail and hit a Piute. For weeks they thought he would not get over it but he did, and is all right, now. Has been ever since. This is a long introduction but it is the only way I can make myself known. The favor I ask I feel assured your generous heart will grant: Give me some advice about a book I have written. I do not claim anything for it only it is mostly true and as interesting as most of the books of the times. I am unknown in the literary world and you know what that means unless one has some one of influence (like yourself) to help you by speaking a good word for you. I would like to place the book on royalty basis plan with any one you would suggest.

This is a secret from my husband and family. I intend it as a surprise in case I get it published.

Feeling you will take an interest in this and if possible write me a letter to some publisher, or, better still, if you could see them for me and then let me hear.

I appeal to you to grant me this favor. With deepest gratitude I thank you for your attention.

One knows, without inquiring, that the twin of that embarrassing letter is forever and ever flying in this and that and the other direction across the continent in the mails, daily, nightly, hourly, unceasingly, unrestingly. It goes to every well-known merchant, and railway official, and manufacturer, and capitalist, and Mayor, and Congressman, and

Governor, and editor, and publisher, and author, and broker, and banker—in a word, to every person who is supposed to have "influence." It always follows the one pattern: "You do not know me, *but you once knew a relative of mine,*" etc., etc. We should all like to help the applicants, we should all be glad to do it, we should all like to return the sort of answer that is desired, but— Well, there is not a thing we can do that would be a help, for not in any instance does that letter ever come from anyone who *can* be helped. The struggler whom you *could* help does his own helping; it would not occur to him to apply to you, a stranger. He has talent and knows it, and he goes into his fight eagerly and with energy and determination—all alone, preferring to be alone. That pathetic letter which comes to you from the incapable, the unhelpable—how do you who are familiar with it answer it? What do you find to say? You do not want to inflict a wound; you hunt ways to avoid that. What do you find? How do you get out of your hard place with a contented conscience? Do you try to explain? The old reply of mine to such a letter shows that I tried that once. Was I satisfied with the result? Possibly; and possibly not; probably not; almost certainly not. I have long ago forgotten all about it. But, anyway, I append my effort:

THE REPLY

I know Mr. H., and I will go to him, dear madam, if upon reflection you find you still desire it. There will be a conversation. I know the form it will take. It will be like this:

Mr. H. How do her books strike you?
Mr. Clemens. I am not acquainted with them.
H. Who has been her publisher?
C. I don't know.
H. She *has* one, I suppose?
C. I—I think not.
H. Ah. You think this is her first book?
C. Yes—I suppose so. I think so.
H. What is it about? What is the character of it?
C. I believe I do not know.
H. Have you seen it?
C. Well—no, I haven't.
H. Ah-h. How long have you known her?
C. I don't know her.
H. Don't know her?

C. No.

H. Ah-h. How did you come to be interested in her book, then?

C. Well, she—she wrote and asked me to find a publisher for her, and mentioned you.

H. Why should she apply to you instead of to me?

C. She wished me to use my influence.

H. Dear me, what has *influence* to do with such a matter?

C. Well, I think she thought you would be more likely to examine her book if you were influenced.

H. Why, what we are here *for* is to examine books—anybody's book that comes along. It's our *business*. Why should we turn away a book unexamined because it's a stranger's? It would be foolish. No publisher does it. On what ground did she request your influence, since you do not know her? She must have thought you knew her literature and could speak for it. Is that it?

C. No; she knew I didn't.

H. Well, what then? She had a reason of *some* sort for believing you competent to recommend her literature, and also under obligations to do it?

C. Yes, I—I knew her uncle.

H. Knew her *uncle?*

C. Yes.

H. Upon my word! So, you knew her uncle; her uncle knows her literature; he indorses it to you; the chain is complete, nothing further needed; you are satisfied, and therefore—

C. No, that isn't all, there are other ties. I know the cabin her uncle lived in, in the mines; I knew his partners, too; also I came near knowing her husband before she married him, and I *did* know the abandoned shaft where a premature blast went off and he went flying through the air and clear down to the trail and hit an Indian in the back with almost fatal consequences.

H. To *him*, or to the Indian?

C. She didn't say which it was.

H. (*With a sigh*). It certainly beats the band! You don't know *her*, you don't know her literature, you don't know who got hurt when the blast went off, you don't know a single thing for us to build an estimate of her book upon, so far as I—

C. I knew her uncle. You are forgetting her uncle.

H. Oh, what use is *he?* Did you know him long? How long was it?

C. Well, I don't know that I really knew him, but I must have met him, anyway. I think it was that way; you can't tell about these things, you know, except when they are recent.

H. Recent? When was all this?

C. Sixteen years ago.

H. What a basis to judge a book upon! At first you said you knew him, and now you don't know whether you did or not.

C. Oh yes, I knew him; anyway, I think I thought I did; I'm perfectly certain of it.

H. What makes you think you thought you knew him?

C. Why, she says I did, herself.

H. She says so!

C. Yes, she does, and I *did* know him, too, though I don't remember it now.

H. Come—how can you know it when you don't remember it.

C. I don't know. That is, I don't know the process, but I *do* know lots of things that I don't remember, and remember lots of things that I don't know. It's so with every educated person.

H. (After a pause.) Is your time valuable?

C. No—well, not very.

H. Mine is.

So I came away then, because he was looking tired. Overwork, I reckon; I never do that; I have seen the evil effects of it. My mother was always afraid I would overwork myself, but I never did.

Dear madam, you see how it would happen if I went there. He would ask me those questions, and I would try to answer them to suit him, and he would hunt me here and there and yonder and get me embarrassed more and more all the time, and at last he would look tired on account of overwork, and there it would end and nothing done. I wish I could be useful to you, but, you see, they do not care for uncles or any of those things; it doesn't move them, it doesn't have the least effect, they don't care for anything but the literature itself, and they as good as despise influence. But they do care for books, and are eager to get them and examine them, no matter whence they come, nor from whose pen. If you will send yours to a publisher—any publisher—he will certainly examine it, I can assure you of that.

1905

A Humane Word from Satan

[The following letter, signed by Satan and purporting to come from him, we have reason to believe was not written by him, but by Mark Twain.—EDITOR.]

To the Editor of Harper's Weekly.

DEAR SIR AND KINSMAN,—Let us have done with this frivolous talk. The American Board accepts contributions from me every year: then why shouldn't it from Mr. Rockefeller? In all the ages, three-fourths of the support of the great charities has been conscience-money, as my books will show: then what becomes of the sting when that term is applied to Mr. Rockefeller's gift? The American Board's trade is financed mainly from the graveyards. Bequests, you understand. Conscience-money. Confession of an old crime and deliberate perpetration of a new one; for deceased's contribution is a robbery of his heirs. Shall the Board decline bequests because they stand for one of these offenses every time and generally for both?

Allow me to continue. The charge most persistently and resentfully and remorselessly dwelt upon is that Mr. Rockefeller's contribution is incurably tainted by perjury—perjury proved against him in the courts. *It makes us smile*—down in my place! Because there isn't a rich man in your vast city who doesn't perjure himself every year before the tax board. They are all caked with perjury, many layers thick. Iron-clad, so to speak. If there is one that isn't, I desire to acquire him for my museum, and will pay Dinosaur rates. Will you say it isn't infraction of law, but only annual evasion of it? Comfort yourselves with that nice distinction if you like—*for the present.* But by and by, when you arrive, I will show you something interesting: a whole hell-full of evaders! Sometimes a frank lawbreaker turns up elsewhere, but I get those others every time.

To return to my muttons. I wish you to remember that my rich perjurers are contributing to the American Board with frequency: it is money filched from the sworn-off personal tax; therefore it is the wages of sin; therefore it is my money; therefore it is *I* that contribute it; and, finally, it is therefore as I have said: since the Board daily accepts contributions from me, why should it decline them from Mr. Rockefeller, who is as good as I am, let the courts say what they may?

SATAN.

1905

A Monument to Adam

Some one has revealed to the *Tribune* that I once suggested to Rev. Thomas K. Beecher, of Elmira, New York, that we get up a monument to Adam, and that Mr. Beecher favored the project. There is more to it than that. The matter started as a joke, but it came somewhat near to materializing.

It is long ago—thirty years. Mr. Darwin's *Descent of Man* had been in print five or six years, and the storm of indignation raised by it was still raging in pulpits and periodicals. In tracing the genesis of the human race back to its sources, Mr. Darwin had left Adam out altogether. We had monkeys, and "missing links," and plenty of other kinds of ancestors, but no Adam. Jesting with Mr. Beecher and other friends in Elmira, I said there seemed to be a likelihood that the world would discard Adam and accept the monkey, and that in the course of time Adam's very name would be forgotten in the earth; therefore this calamity ought to be averted; a monument would accomplish this, and Elmira ought not to waste this honorable opportunity to do Adam a favor and herself a credit.

Then the unexpected happened. Two bankers came forward and took hold of the matter—not for fun, not for sentiment, but because they saw in the monument certain commercial advantages for the town. The project had seemed gently humorous before—it was more than that now, with this stern business gravity injected into it. The bankers discussed the monument with me. We met several times. They proposed an indestructible memorial, to cost twenty-five thousand dollars. The insane oddity of a monument set up in a village to preserve a name that would outlast the hills and the rocks without any such help, would advertise Elmira to the ends of the earth—and draw custom. It would be the only monument on the planet to Adam, and in the matter of interest and impressiveness could never have a rival until somebody should set up a monument to the Milky Way.

People would come from every corner of the globe and stop off to look at it, no tour of the world would be complete that left out Adam's monument. Elmira would be a Mecca; there would be pilgrim ships at pilgrim rates, pilgrim specials on the continent's railways, libraries would be written about the monument, every tourist would kodak it, models of it would be for sale everywhere in the earth, its form would become as familiar as the figure of Napoleon.

One of the bankers subscribed five thousand dollars, and I think the other one subscribed half as much, but I do not remember with certainty now whether that was the figure or not. We got designs made—some of them came from Paris.

In the beginning—as a detail of the project when it was as yet a joke—I had framed a humble and beseeching and perfervid petition to Congress begging the government to build the monument, as a testimony of the Great Republic's gratitude to the Father of the Human Race and as a token of her loyalty to him in this dark day of his humiliation when his older children were doubting him and deserting him. It seemed to me that this petition ought to be presented, now—it would be widely and feelingly abused and ridiculed and cursed, and would advertise our scheme and make our ground-floor stock go off briskly. So I sent it to General Joseph R. Hawley, who was then in the House, and he said he would present it. But he did not do it. I think he explained that when he came to read it he was afraid of it: it was too serious, too gushy, too sentimental—the House might take it for earnest.

We ought to have carried out our monument scheme; we could have managed it without any great difficulty, and Elmira would now be the most celebrated town in the universe.

Very recently I began to build a book in which one of the minor characters touches incidentally upon a project for a monument to Adam, and now the *Tribune* has come upon a trace of the forgotten jest of thirty years ago. Apparently mental telegraphy is still in business. It is odd; but the freaks of mental telegraphy are usually odd.

1906

What Is Man?

I

a. MAN THE MACHINE b. PERSONAL MERIT

[The OLD MAN and the YOUNG MAN had been conversing. The OLD MAN had asserted that the human being is merely a machine, and nothing more. The YOUNG MAN objected, and asked him to go into particulars and furnish his reasons for his position.]

Old Man. What are the materials of which a steam-engine is made?

Young Man. Iron, steel, brass, white-metal, and so on.

O. M. Where are these found?

Y. M. In the rocks.

O. M. In a pure state?

Y. M. No—in ores.

O. M. Are the metals suddenly deposited in the ores?

Y. M. No—it is the patient work of countless ages.

O. M. You could make the engine out of the rocks themselves?

Y. M. Yes, a brittle one and not valuable.

O. M. You would not require much, of such an engine as that?

Y. M. No—substantially nothing.

O. M. To make a fine and capable engine, how would you proceed?

Y. M. Drive tunnels and shafts into the hills; blast out the iron ore; crush it, smelt it, reduce it to pig-iron; put some of it through the Bessemer process and make steel of it. Mine and treat and combine the several metals of which brass is made.

O. M. Then?

Y. M. Out of the perfected result, build the fine engine.

O. M. You would require much of this one?

Y. M. Oh, indeed yes.

O. M. It could drive lathes, drills, planers, punches, polishers, in a word all the cunning machines of a great factory?

Y. M. It could.

O. M.   What could the stone engine do?

Y. M.   Drive a sewing-machine, possibly—nothing more, perhaps.

O. M.   Men would admire the other engine and rapturously praise it?

Y. M.   Yes.

O. M.   But not the stone one?

Y. M.   No.

O. M.   The merits of the metal machine would be far above those of the stone one?

Y. M.   Of course.

O. M.   Personal merits?

Y. M.   *Personal* merits? How do you mean?

O. M.   It would be personally entitled to the credit of its own performance?

Y. M.   The engine? Certainly not.

O. M.   Why not?

Y. M.   Because its performance is not personal. It is a result of the law of its construction. It is not a *merit* that it does the things which it is set to do—it can't *help* doing them.

O. M.   And it is not a personal demerit in the stone machine that it does so little?

Y. M.   Certainly not. It does no more and no less than the law of its make permits and compels it to do. There is nothing *personal* about it; it cannot choose. In this process of "working up to the matter" is it your idea to work up to the proposition that man and a machine are about the same thing, and that there is no personal merit in the performance of either?

O. M.   Yes—but do not be offended; I am meaning no offense. What makes the grand difference between the stone engine and the steel one? Shall we call it training, education? Shall we call the stone engine a savage and the steel one a civilized man? The original rock contained the stuff of which the steel one was built—but along with it a lot of sulphur and stone and other obstructing inborn heredities, brought down from the old geologic ages—prejudices, let us call them. Prejudices which nothing within the rock itself had either *power* to remove or any *desire* to remove. Will you take note of that phrase?

Y. M.   Yes. I have written it down; "Prejudices which nothing within the rock itself had either power to remove or any desire to remove." Go on.

O. M.   Prejudices which must be removed by *outside influences* or not at all. Put that down.

Y. M. Very well; "Must be removed by outside influences or not at all." Go on.

O. M. The iron's prejudice against ridding itself of the cumbering rock. To make it more exact, the iron's absolute *indifference* as to whether the rock be removed or not. Then comes the *outside influence* and grinds the rock to powder and sets the ore free. The *iron* in the ore is still captive. An *outside influence* smelts it free of the clogging ore. The iron is emancipated iron, now, but indifferent to further progress. An *outside influence* beguiles it into the Bessemer furnace and refines it into steel of the first quality. It is educated, now —its training is complete. And it has reached its limit. By no possible process can it be educated into *gold*. Will you set that down?

Y. M. Yes. "Everything has its limit—iron ore cannot be educated into gold."

O. M. There are gold men, and tin men, and copper men, and leaden men, and steel men, and so on—and each has the limitations of his nature, his heredities, his training, and his environment. You can build engines out of each of these metals, and they will all perform, but you must not require the weak ones to do equal work with the strong ones. In each case, to get the best results, you must free the metal from its obstructing prejudicial ores by education— smelting, refining, and so forth.

Y. M. You have arrived at man, now?

O. M. Yes. Man the machine—man the impersonal engine. Whatsoever a man is, is due to his *make*, and to the *influences* brought to bear upon it by his heredities, his habitat, his associations. He is moved, directed, COMMANDED, by *exterior* influences—*solely*. He *originates* nothing, not even a thought.

Y. M. Oh, come! Where did I get my opinion that this which you are talking is all foolishness?

O. M. It is a quite natural opinion—indeed an inevitable opinion —but *you* did not create the materials out of which it is formed. They are odds and ends of thoughts, impressions, feelings, gathered unconsciously from a thousand books, a thousand conversations, and from streams of thought and feeling which have flowed down into your heart and brain out of the hearts and brains of centuries of ancestors. *Personally* you did not create even the smallest microscopic fragment of the materials out of which your opinion is made; and personally you cannot claim even the slender merit of *putting the borrowed materials together*. That was done *automatically*—by your mental machinery, in strict accordance with the law of that machinery's construction. And you not only did not make that machinery yourself, but you have *not even any command over it.*

Y. M. This is too much. You think I could have formed no opinion but that one?

O. M. Spontaneously? No. And *you did not form that one;* your machinery did it for you—automatically and instantly, without reflection or the need of it.

Y. M. Suppose I had reflected? How then?

O. M. Suppose you try?

Y. M. (*After a quarter of an hour.*) I have reflected.

O. M. You mean you have tried to change your opinion—as an experiment?

Y. M. Yes.

O. M. With success?

Y. M. No. It remains the same; it is impossible to change it.

O. M. I am sorry, but you see, yourself, that your mind is merely a machine, nothing more. You have no command over it, it has no command over itself—it is worked *solely from the outside.* That is the law of its make; it is the law of all machines.

Y. M. Can't I *ever* change one of these automatic opinions?

O. M. No. You can't yourself, but *exterior influences* can do it.

Y. M. And exterior ones *only?*

O. M. Yes—exterior ones only.

Y. M. That position is untenable—I may say ludicrously untenable.

O. M. What makes you think so?

Y. M. I don't merely think it, I know it. Suppose I resolve to enter upon a course of thought, and study, and reading, with the deliberate purpose of changing that opinion; and suppose I succeed. *That* is not the work of an exterior impulse, the whole of it is mine and personal: for I originated the project.

O. M. Not a shred of it. *It grew out of this talk with me.* But for that it would never have occurred to you. No man ever orginates anything. All his thoughts, all his impulses, come *from the outside.*

Y. M. It's an exasperating subject. The *first* man who had orginal thoughts, anyway; there was nobody to draw from.

O. M. It is a mistake. Adams's thoughts came to him from the outside. *You* have a fear of death. You did not invent that—you got it from outside, from talking and teaching. Adam had no fear of death—none in the world.

Y. M. Yes, he had.

O. M. When he was created?

Y. M. No.

O. M. When, then?

Y. M. When he was threatened with it.

O. M. Then it came from the *outside*. Adam is quite big enough; let us not try to make a god of him. *None but gods have ever had a thought which did not come from the outside.* Adam probably had a good head, but it was of no sort of use to him until it was filled up *from the outside.* He was not able to invent the triflingest little thing with it. He had not a shadow of a notion of the difference between good and evil—he had to get the idea *from the outside.* Neither he nor Eve was able to originate the idea that it was immodest to go naked: the knowledge came in with the apple *from the outside.* A man's brain is so constructed that *it can originate nothing whatever.* It can only use material obtained *outside.* It is merely a machine; and it works automatically, not by will-power. *It has no command over itself, its owner has no command over it.*

Y. M. Well, never mind Adam: but certainly Shakespeare's creations—

O. M. No, you mean Shakespeare's *imitations.* Shakespeare created nothing. He correctly observed, and he marvelously painted. He exactly portrayed people whom *God* had created; but he created none himself. Let us spare him the slander of charging him with trying. Shakespeare could not create. *He was a machine, and machines do not create.*

Y. M. Where *was* his excellence, then?

O. M. In this. He was not a sewing-machine, like you and me; he was a Gobelin loom. The threads and the colors came into him *from the outside;* outside influences, suggestions, *experiences* (reading, seeing plays, playing plays, borrowing ideas, and so on), framed the patterns in his mind and started up its complex and admirable machinery, and *it automatically* turned out that pictured and gorgeous fabric which still compels the astonishment of the world. If Shakespeare had been born and bred on a barren and unvisited rock in the ocean his mighty intellect would have had no *outside material* to work with, and could have invented none; and *no outside influences,* teaching, moldings, persuasions, inspirations, of a valuable sort, and could have invented none; and so Shakespeare would have produced nothing. In Turkey he would have produced something—something up to the highest limit of Turkish influences, associations, and training. In France he would have produced something better—something up to the highest limit of the French influences and training. In England he rose to the highest limit attainable through the *outside helps afforded by that land's ideals, influences, and training.* You and I are but sewing-machines. We must turn out what we can; we must do our endeavor and care nothing at all when the unthinking reproach us for not turning out Gobelins.

Y. M.   And so we are mere machines! And machines may not boast, nor feel proud of their performance, nor claim personal merit for it, nor applause and praise. It is an infamous doctrine.

O. M.   It isn't a doctrine, it is merely a fact.

Y. M.   I suppose, then, there is no more merit in being brave than in being a coward?

O. M.   *Personal* merit? No. A brave man does not *create* his bravery. He is entitled to no personal credit for possessing it. It is born to him. A baby born with a billion dollars—where is the personal merit in that? A baby born with nothing—where is the personal de-merit in that? The one is fawned upon, admired, worshipped, by sycophants, the other is neglected and despised—where is the sense in it?

Y. M.   Sometimes a timid man sets himself the task of conquering his cowardice and becoming brave—and succeeds. What do you say to that?

O. M.   That it shows the value of *training in right directions over training in wrong ones.* Inestimably valuable is training, influence, education, in right directions—*training one's self-approbation to elevate its ideals.*

Y. M.   But as to merit—the personal merit of the victorious coward's project and achievement?

O. M.   There isn't any. In the world's view he is a worthier man than he was before, but *he* didn't achieve the change—the merit of it is not his.

Y. M.   Whose, then?

O. M.   His *make,* and the influences which wrought upon it from the outside.

Y. M.   His make?

O. M.   To start with, he was *not* utterly and completely a coward, or the influences would have had nothing to work upon. He was not afraid of a cow, though perhaps of a bull: not afraid of a woman, but afraid of a man. There was something to build upon. There was a *seed.* No seed, no plant. Did he make that seed himself, or was it born in him? It was no merit of *his* that the seed was there.

Y. M. Well, anyway, the idea of *cultivating* it, the resolution to cultivate it, was meritorious, and he originated that.

O. M. He did nothing of the kind. It came whence *all* impulses, good or bad, come—from *outside*. If that timid man had lived all his life in a community of human rabbits, had never read of brave deeds, had never heard speak of them, had never heard any one praise them nor express envy of the heroes that had done them, he would have had no more idea of bravery than Adam had of modesty, and it could never by any possibility have occurrred to him to *resolve* to become brave. He *could not originate the idea*—it had to come to him from the *outside*. And so, when he heard bravery extolled and cowardice derided, it woke him up. He was ashamed. Perhaps his sweetheart turned up her nose and said, "I am told that you are a coward!" It was not *he* that turned over the new leaf—she did it for him. *He* must not strut around in the merit of it—it is not his.

Y. M. But, anyway, he reared the plant after she watered the seed.

O. M. No. Outside influences reared it. At the command—and trembling—he marched out into the field—with other soldiers and in the daytime, not alone and in the dark. He had the *influence of example,* he drew courage from his comrades' courage; he was afraid, and wanted to run, but he did not dare; he was *afraid* to run, with all those soldiers looking on. He was progressing, you see—the moral fear of shame had risen superior to the physical fear of harm. By the end of the campaign experience will have taught him that not *all* who go into battle get hurt—an outside influence which will be helpful to him; and he will also have learned how sweet it is to be praised for courage and be huzza'd at with tear-choked voices as the war-worn regiment marches past the worshiping multitude with flags flying and the drums beating. After that he will be as securely brave as any veteran in the army—and there will not be a shade nor suggestion of *personal merit* in it anywhere; it will all have come from the *outside*. The Victoria Cross breeds more heroes than—

Y. M. Hang it, where is the sense in his becoming brave if he is to get no credit for it?

O. M. Your question will answer itself presently. It involves an important detail of man's make which we have not yet touched upon.

Y. M. What detail is that?

O. M. The impulse which moves a person to do things—the only impulse that ever moves a person to do a thing.

Y. M. The *only* one! Is there but one?

O. M. That is all. There is only one.

Y. M. Well, certainly that is a strange enough doctrine. What is the sole impulse that ever moves a person to do a thing?

O. M. The impulse to *content his own spirit*—the *necessity* of contenting his own spirit and *winning its approval.*

Y. M. Oh, come, that won't do!

O. M. Why won't it?

Y. M. Because it puts him in the attitude of always looking out for his own comfort and advantage; whereas an unselfish man often does a thing solely for another person's good when it is a positive disadvantage to himself.

O. M. It is a mistake. The act must do *him* good, FIRST; otherwise he will not do it. He may *think* he is doing it solely for the other person's sake, but it is not so; he is contenting his own spirit first—the other person's benefit has to always take *second* place.

Y. M. What a fantastic idea! What becomes of self-sacrifice? Please answer me that.

O. M. What is self-sacrifice?

Y. M. The doing good to another person where no shadow nor suggestion of benefit to one's self can result from it.

II

MAN'S SOLE IMPULSE—THE SECURING OF HIS OWN
APPROVAL

Old Man. There have been instances of it—you think?

Young Man. *Instances?* Millions of them!

O. M. You have not jumped to conclusions? You have examined them—critically?

Y. M. They don't need it: the acts themselves reveal the golden impulse back of them.

O. M. For instance?

Y. M. Well, then, for instance. Take the case in the book here. The man lives three miles up-town. It is bitter cold, snowing hard, midnight. He is about to enter the horse-car when a gray and ragged old woman, a touching picture of misery, puts out her lean hand and begs for rescue from hunger and death. The man finds that he has but a quarter in his pocket, but he does not hesitate: he gives it her and trudges home through the storm. There—it is noble, it is beautiful; its grace is marred by no fleck or blemish or suggestion of self-interest.

O. M. What makes you think that?

Y. M. Pray what else could I think? Do you imagine that there is some other way of looking at it?

O. M. Can you put yourself in the man's place and tell me what he felt and what he thought?

Y. M. Easily. The sight of that suffering old face pierced his generous heart with a sharp pain. He could not bear it. He could endure the three-mile walk in the storm, but he could not endure the tortures his conscience would suffer if he turned his back and left that poor old creature to perish. He would not have been able to sleep, for thinking of it.

O. M. What was his state of mind on his way home?

Y. M. It was a state of joy which only the self-sacrificer knows. His heart sang, he was unconscious of the storm.

O. M. He felt well?

Y. M. One cannot doubt it.

O. M. Very well. Now let us add up the details and see how much he got for his twenty-five cents. Let us try to find out the *real* why of his making the investment. In the first place *he* couldn't bear the pain which the old suffering face gave him. So he was thinking of *his* pain—this good man. He must buy a salve for it. If he did not succor the old woman *his* conscience would torture him all the way home. Thinking of *his* pain again. He must buy relief from that. If he didn't relieve the old woman *he* would not get any sleep. He must buy some sleep—still thinking of *himself,* you see. Thus, to sum up, he bought himself free of a sharp pain in his heart, he bought himself free of the tortures of a waiting conscience, he bought a whole night's sleep—all for twenty-five cents! It should make Wall Street ashamed of itself. On his way home his heart was joyful, and it sang— profit on top of profit! The impulse which moved the man to succor the old woman was—*first*—to *content his own spirit;* secondly to relieve *her* sufferings. Is it your opinion that men's acts proceed from one central and unchanging and inalterable impulse, or from a variety of impulses?

Y. M. From a variety, of course—some high and fine and noble, others not. What is your opinion?

O. M. Then there is but *one* law, one source.

Y. M. That both the noblest impulses and the basest proceed from that one source?

O. M. Yes.

Y. M. Will you put that law into words?

O. M. Yes. This is the law, keep it in your mind. *From his cradle*

to his grave a man never does a single thing which has any FIRST AND
FOREMOST *object but one—to secure peace of mind, spiritual comfort,
for* HIMSELF.

Y. M.   Come! He never does anything for any one else's comfort,
spiritual or physical?

O. M.   No. *Except on those distinct terms*—that it shall *first* secure
his own spiritual comfort. Otherwise he will not do it.

Y. M.   It will be easy to expose the falsity of that proposition.

O. M.   For instance?

Y. M.   Take that noble passion, love of country, patriotism. A man
who loves peace and dreads pain, leaves his pleasant home and his
weeping family and marches out to manfully expose himself to hunger,
cold, wounds, and death. Is that seeking spiritual comfort?

O. M.   He loves peace and dreads pain?

Y. M.   Yes.

O. M.   Then perhaps there is something that he loves *more* than he
loves peace—*the approval of his neighbors and the public.* And perhaps there is something which he dreads more than he dreads pain
—the *disapproval* of his neighbors and the public. If he is sensitive
to shame he will go to the field—not because his spirit will be *entirely*
comfortable there, but because it will be more comfortable there
than it would be if he remained at home. He will always do the
thing which will bring him the *most* mental comfort—for that is *the
sole law of his life.* He leaves the weeping family behind; he is
sorry to make them uncomfortable, but not sorry enough to sacrifice
his *own* comfort to secure theirs.

Y. M.   Do you really believe that mere public opinion could force
a timid and peaceful man to—

O. M.   Go to war? Yes—public opinion can force some men to do
anything.

Y. M.   *Anything?*

O. M.   Yes—anything.

Y. M.   I don't believe that. Can it force a right-principled man to
do a wrong thing?

O. M.   Yes.

Y. M.   Can it force a kind man to do a cruel thing?

O. M.   Yes.

Y. M.   Give an instance.

O. M.   Alexander Hamilton was a conspicuously high-principled
man. He regarded dueling as wrong, and as opposed to the teachings
of religion—but in deference to *public opinion* he fought a duel.

He deeply loved his family, but to buy public approval he treacherously deserted them and threw his life away, ungenerously leaving them to lifelong sorrow in order that he might stand well with a foolish world. In the then condition of the public standards of honor he could not have been comfortable with the stigma upon him of having refused to fight. The teachings of religion, his devotion to his family, his kindness of heart, his high principles, all went for nothing when they stood in the way of his spiritual comfort. A man will do *anything*, no matter what it is, *to secure his spiritual comfort;* and he can neither be forced nor persuaded to any act which has not that goal for its object. Hamilton's act was compelled by the inborn necessity of contenting his own spirit; in this it was like all the other acts of his life, and like all the acts of all men's lives. Do you see where the kernel of the matter lies? A man cannot be comfortable without *his own* approval. He will secure the largest share possible of that, at all costs, all sacrifices.

Y. M. A minute ago you said Hamilton fought that duel to get *public* approval.

O. M. I did. By refusing to fight the duel he would have secured his family's approval and a large share of his own; but the public approval was more valuable in his eyes than all other approvals put together—in the earth or above it; to secure that would furnish him the *most* comfort of mind, the most *self*-approval; so he sacrificed all other values to get it.

Y. M. Some noble souls have refused to fight duels, and have manfully braved the public contempt.

O. M. They acted *according to their make*. They valued their principles and the approval of their familes *above* the public approval. They took the thing they valued *most* and let the rest go. They took what would give them the *largest* share of *personal contentment and approval*—a man *always* does. Public opinion cannot force that kind of men to go to the wars. When they go it is for other reasons. Other spirit-contenting reasons.

Y. M. Always spirit-contenting reasons?

O. M. There are no others.

Y. M. When a man sacrifices his life to save a little child from a burning building, what do you call that?

O. M. When he does it, it is the law of *his* make. *He* can't bear to see the child in that peril (a man of different make *could*), and so he tries to save the child, and loses his life. But he has got what he was after—*his own approval.*

Y. M.   What do you call Love, Hate, Charity, Revenge, Humanity, Magnanimity, Forgiveness?

O. M.   Different results of the one Master Impulse: the necessity of securing one's self-approval. They wear diverse clothes and are subject to diverse moods, but in whatsoever ways they masquerade they are the *same person* all the time. To change the figure, the *compulsion* that moves a man—and there is but the one—is the necessity of securing the contentment of his own spirit. When it stops, the man is dead.

Y. M.   This is foolishness. Love—

O. M.   Why, love is that impulse, that law, in its most uncompromising form. It will squander life and everything else on its object. Not *primarily* for the object's sake, but for *its own*. When its object is happy *it* is happy—and that is what it is unconsciously after.

Y. M.   You do not even except the lofty and gracious passion of mother-love?

O. M.   No, *it* is the absolute slave of that law. The mother will go naked to clothe her child; she will starve that it may have food; suffer torture to save it from pain; die that it may live. She takes a living *pleasure* in making these sacrifices. *She does it for that reward* —that self-approval, that contentment, that peace, that comfort. *She would do it for your child* IF SHE COULD GET THE SAME PAY.

Y. M.   This is an infernal philosophy of yours.

O. M.   It isn't a philosophy, it is a fact.

Y. M.   Of course you must admit that there are some acts which—

O. M.   No. There is *no* act, large or small, fine or mean, which springs from any motive but the one—the necessity of appeasing and contenting one's own spirit.

Y. M.   The world's philanthropists—

O. M.   I honor them, I uncover my head to them—from habit and training; but *they* could not know comfort or happiness or self-approval if they did not work and spend for the unfortunate. It makes *them* happy to see others happy; and so with money and labor they buy what they are after—*happiness, self-approval*. Why don't misers do the same thing? Because they can get a thousandfold more happiness by *not* doing it. There is no other reason. They follow the law of their make.

Y. M.   What do you say of duty for duty's sake?

O. M.   That *it does not exist*. Duties are not performed for duty's *sake*, but because their *neglect* would make the man *uncomfortable*. A man performs but *one* duty—the duty of contenting his spirit, the duty of making himself agreeable to himself. If he can most satisfyingly perform this sole and only duty by *helping* his neighbor, he will do it; if he can most satisfyingly perform it by *swindling* his neighbor, he will do that. But he always looks out for Number One—*first;* the effects upon others are a *secondary* matter. Men pretend to self-sacrifices, but this is a thing which, in the ordinary value of the phrase, *does not exist and has not existed.* A man often honestly *thinks* he is sacrificing himself merely and solely for some one else, but he is deceived; his bottom impulse is to content a requirement of his nature and training, and thus acquire peace for his soul.

Y. M. Apparently, then all men, both good and bad ones, devote their lives to contenting their consciences?

O. M. Yes. That is a good enough name for it: Conscience—that independent Sovereign, that insolent absolute Monarch inside of a man who is the man's Master. There are all kinds of consciences, because there are all kinds of men. You satisfy an assassin's conscience in one way, a philanthropist's in another, a miser's in another, a burglar's in still another. As a *guide* or *incentive* to any authoritatively prescribed line of morals or conduct (leaving *training* out of the account), a man's conscience is totally valueless. I know a kind-hearted Kentuckian whose self-approval was lacking—whose conscience was troubling him, to phrase it with exactness—*because he had neglected to kill a certain man*—a man whom he had never seen. The stranger had killed this man's friend in a fight, this man's Kentucky training made it a duty to kill the stranger for it. He neglected his duty—kept dodging it, shirking it, putting it off, and his unrelenting conscience kept persecuting him for this conduct. At last, to get ease of mind, comfort, self-approval, he hunted up the stranger and took his life. It was an immense act of *self-sacrifice* (as per the usual definition), for he did not want to do it, and he never would have done it if he could have bought a contented spirit and an unworried mind at smaller cost. But we are so made that we will pay *anything* for that contentment—even another man's life.

Y. M. You spoke a moment ago of *trained* consciences. You mean that we are not *born* with consciences competent to guide us aright?

O. M. If we were, children and savages would know right from wrong, and not have to be taught it.

Y. M. But consciences can be *trained?*

O. M. Yes.

Y. M. Of course by parents, teachers, the pulpit, and books.

O. M. Yes—they do their share; they do what they can.

Y. M. And the rest is done by—

O. M. Oh, a million unnoticed influences—for good or bad: influences which work without rest during every waking moment of a man's life, from cradle to grave.

Y. M. You have tabulated these?

O. M. Many of them—yes.

Y. M. Will you read me the result?

O. M. Another time, yes. It would take an hour.

Y. M. A conscience can be trained to shun evil and prefer good?

O. M. Yes.

Y. M. But will prefer it for spirit-contenting reasons only?

O. M. It *can't* be trained to do a thing for any *other* reason. The thing is impossible.

Y. M. There *must* be a genuinely and utterly self-sacrificing act recorded in human history somewhere.

O. M. You are young. You have many years before you. Search one out.

Y. M. It does seem to me that when a man sees a fellow-being struggling in the water and jumps in at the risk of his life to save him—

O. M. Wait. Describe the *man*. Describe the *fellow-being*. State if there is an *audience* present; or if they are *alone*.

Y. M. What have these things to do with the splendid act?

O. M. Very much. Shall we suppose, as a beginning, that the two are alone, in a solitary place, at midnight?

Y. M. If you choose.

O. M. And that the fellow-being is the man's daughter?

Y. M. Well, n-no—make it some one else.

O. M. A filthy drunken ruffian, then?

Y. M. I see. Circumstances alter cases. I suppose that if there was no audience to observe the act, the man wouldn't perform it.

O. M. But there is here and there a man who *would*. People, for instance, like the man who lost his life trying to save the child from the fire; and the man who gave the needy old woman his twenty-five cents and walked home in the storm—there are here and there men like that who would do it. And why? Because they couldn't *bear* to see a fellow-being struggling in the water and not jump in and help. It would give *them* pain. They would save the fellow-being on that account. *They wouldn't do it otherwise.* They strictly obey the law which I have been insisting upon. You must remember and always distinguish the people who *can't bear* things from the people who *can.* It will throw light upon a number of apparently "self-sacrificing" cases.

Y. M.   Oh, dear, it's all so disgusting.

O. M.   Yes. And so true.

Y. M.   Come—take the good boy who does things he doesn't want to do, in order to gratify his mother.

O. M.   He does seven-tenths of the act because it gratifies *him* to gratify his mother. Throw the bulk of advantage the other way and the good boy would not do the act. He *must* obey the iron law. None can escape it.

Y. M.   Well, take the case of a bad boy who—

O. M.   You needn't mention it, it is a waste of time. It is no matter about the bad boy's act. Whatever it was, he had a spirit-contenting reason for it. Otherwise you have been misinformed, and he didn't do it.

Y. M.   It is very exasperating. A while ago you said that a man's conscience is not a born judge of morals and conduct, but has to be taught and trained. Now I think conscience can get drowsy and lazy, but I don't think it can go wrong; and if you wake it up—

A Little Story

O. M.   I will tell you a little story:

Once upon a time an Infidel was guest in the house of a Christian widow whose little boy was ill and near to death. The Infidel often watched by the bedside and entertained the boy with talk, and he used these opportunities to satisfy a strong longing of his nature—that desire which is in us all to better other people's condition by having them think as we think. He was successful. But the dying boy, in his last moments, reproached him and said:

"I believed, and was happy in it; you have taken my belief away, and my comfort. Now I have nothing left, and I die miserable; for the things which you have told me do not take the place of that which I have lost."

And the mother, also, reproached the Infidel, and said:

"My child is forever lost, and my heart is broken. How could you do this cruel thing? We have done you no harm, but only kindness; we made our house your home, you were welcome to all we had, and this is our reward."

The heart of the Infidel was filled with remorse for what he had done, and he said:

"It was wrong—I see it now; but I was only trying to do him good. In my view he was in error; it seemed my duty to teach him the truth."

Then the mother said:

"I had taught him, all his little life, what I believed to be the truth, and in his believing faith both of us were happy. Now he is dead—and lost; and I am miserable. Our faith came down to us through centuries of being ancestors; what right had you, or any one, to disturb it? Where was your honor, where was your shame?"

Y. M.   He was a miscreant, and deserved death!

O. M.   He thought so himself, and said so.

Y. M.   Ah—you see, *his conscience was awakened!*

O. M.   Yes, his Self-Disapproval was. It *pained* him to see the mother suffer. He was sorry he had done a thing which brought *him* pain. It did not occur to him to think of the mother when he was misteaching the boy, for he was absorbed in providing *pleasure* for himself, then. Providing it by satisfying what he believed to be a call of duty.

Y. M.   Call it what you please, it is to me a case of *awakened conscience*. That awakened conscience could never get itself into that species of trouble again. A cure like that is a *permanent* cure.

O. M.   Pardon—I had not finished the story. We are creatures of *outside influences*—we originate *nothing* within. Whenever we take a new line of thought and drift into a new line of belief and action, the impulse is *always* suggested from the *outside*. Remorse so preyed upon the Infidel that it dissolved his harshness toward the boy's religion and made him come to regard it with tolerance, next with kindness, for the boy's sake and the mother's. Finally he found himself examining it. From that moment his progress in his new trend was steady and rapid. He became a believing Christian. And now his remorse for having robbed the dying boy of his faith and his salvation was bitterer than ever. It gave him no rest, no peace. He *must* have rest and peace—it is the law of our nature. There seemed but one way to get it; he must devote himself to saving imperiled souls. He became a missionary. He landed in a pagan country ill and helpless. A native widow took him into her humble home and nursed him back to convalescence. Then her young boy was taken hopelessly ill, and the grateful missionary helped her tend him. Here was his first opportunity to repair a part of the wrong done to the other boy by doing a precious service for this one by undermining his foolish faith in his false gods. He was successful. But the dying boy in his last moments reproached him and said:

"I believed, and was happy in it; you have taken my belief away, and my comfort. Now I have nothing left, and I die miserable; for the things which you have told me do not take the place of that which I have lost."

And the mother, also, reproached the missionary, and said:

"My child is forever lost, and my heart is broken. How could you do this cruel thing? We had done you no harm, but only kindness; we made our house your home, you were welcome to all we had, and this is our reward."

The heart of the missionary was filled with remorse for what he had done, and he said:

"It was wrong—I see it now; but I was only trying to do him good. In my view he was in error; it seemed my duty to teach him the truth."

Then the mother said:

"I had taught him, all his little life, what I believed to be the truth, and in his believing faith both of us were happy. Now he is dead—and lost; and I am miserable. Our faith came down to us through centuries of believing ancestors; what right had you, or any one, to disturb it? Where was your honor, where was your shame?"

The missionary's anguish of remorse and sense of treachery were as bitter and persecuting and unappeasable, now, as they had been in the former case. The story is finished. What is your comment?

Y. M. The man's conscience was a fool! It was morbid. It didn't know right from wrong.

O. M. I am not sorry to hear you say that. If you grant that *one* man's conscience doesn't know right from wrong, it is an admission that there are others like it. This single admission pulls down the whole doctrine of infallibility of judgment in consciences. Meantime there is one thing which I ask you to notice.

Y. M. What is that?

O. M. That in both cases the man's *act* gave him no spiritual discomfort, and that he was quite satisfied with it and got pleasure out of it. But afterward when it resulted in *pain to him,* he was sorry. Sorry it had inflicted pain upon the others, *but for no reason under the sun except that their pain gave* HIM *pain.* Our consciences take *no* notice of pain inflicted upon others until it reaches a point where it gives pain to *us.* In *all* cases without exception we are absolutely indifferent to another person's pain until his sufferings make us uncomfortable. Many an infidel would not have been troubled by that Christian mother's distress. Don't you believe that?

Y. M.   Yes. You might almost say it of the *average* infidel, I think.

O. M.   And many a missionary, sternly fortified by his sense of duty, would not have been troubled by the pagan mother's distress—Jesuit missionaries in Canada in the early French times, for instance; see episodes quoted by Parkman.

Y. M.   Well, let us adjourn. Where have we arrived?

O. M.   At this. That we (mankind) have ticketed ourselves with a number of qualities to which we have given misleading names. Love, Hate, Charity, Compassion, Avarice, Benevolence, and so on. I mean we attach misleading *meanings* to the names. They are all forms of self-contentment, self-gratification, but the names so disguise them that they distract our attention from the fact. Also we have smuggled a word into the dictionary which ought not to be there at all—Self-Sacrifice. It describes a thing which does not exist. But worst of all, we ignore and never mention the Sole Impulse which dictates and compels a man's every act: the imperious necessity of securing his own approval, in every emergency and at all costs. To it we owe all that we are. It is our breath, our heart, our blood. It is our only spur, our whip, our goad, our only impelling power; we have no other. Without it we should be mere inert images, corpses; no one would do anything, there would be no progress, the world would stand still. We ought to stand reverently uncovered when the name of that stupendous power is uttered.

Y. M.   I am not convinced.

O. M.   You will be when you think.

III

INSTANCES IN POINT

Old Man.   Have you given thought to the Gospel of Self-Approval since we talked?

Young Man.   I have.

O. M.   It was I that moved you to it. That is to say an *outside influence* moved you to it—not one that originated in your own head. Will you try to keep that in mind and not forget it?

Y. M.   Yes. Why?

O. M.   Because by and by in one of our talks, I wish to further impress upon you that neither you, nor I, nor any man ever originates a thought in his own head. *The utterer of a thought always utters a second-hand one.*

Y. M.   Oh, now—

O. M. Wait. Reserve your remark till we get to that part of our discussion—to-morrow or next day, say. Now, then, have you been considering the proposition that no act is ever born of any but a self-contenting impulse—(primarily). You have sought. What have you found?

Y. M. I have not been very fortunate. I have examined many fine and apparently self-sacrificing deeds in romances and biographies, but—

O. M. Under searching analysis the ostensible self-sacrifice disappeared? It naturally would.

Y. M. But here in this novel is one which seems to promise. In the Adirondack woods is a wage-earner and lay preacher in the lumber-camps who is of noble character and deeply religious. An earnest and practical laborer in the New York slums comes up there on vacation—he is leader of a section of the University Settlement. Holme, the lumberman, is fired with a desire to throw away his excellent worldly prospects and go down and save souls on the East Side. He counts it happiness to make this sacrifice for the glory of God and for the cause of Christ. He resigns his place, makes the sacrifice cheerfully, and goes to the East Side and preaches Christ and Him crucified every day and every night to little groups of half-civilized foreign paupers who scoff at him. But he rejoices in the scoffings, since he is suffering them in the great cause of Christ. You have so filled my mind with suspicions that I was constantly expecting to find a hidden questionable impulse back of all this, but I am thankful to say I have failed. This man saw his duty, and for *duty's sake* he sacrificed self and assumed the burden it imposed.

O. M. Is that as far as you have read?

Y. M. Yes.

O. M. Let us read further, presently. Meantime, in sacrificing himself—*not* for the glory of God, *primarily,* as *he* imagined, but *first* to content that exacting and inflexible master within him—*did he sacrifice anybody else?*

Y. M. How do you mean?

O. M. He relinquished a lucrative post and got mere food and lodging in place of it. Had he dependants?

Y. M. Well—yes.

O. M. In what way and to what extent did his self-sacrifice affect *them?*

Y. M. He was the support of a superannuated father. He had a young sister with a remarkable voice—he was giving her a musical education, so that her longing to be self-supporting might be gratified. He was furnishing the money to put a young brother through a polytechnic school and satisfy his desire to become a civil engineer.

O. M. The old father's comforts were now curtailed?

Y. M. Quite seriously. Yes.

O. M. The sister's music-lessons had to stop?

Y. M. Yes.

O. M. The young brother's education—well, an extinguishing blight fell upon that happy dream, and he had to go to sawing wood to support the old father, or something like that?

Y. M. It is about what happened. Yes.

O. M. What a handsome job of self-sacrificing he did do! It seems to me that he sacrificed everybody *except* himself. Haven't I told you that no man *ever* sacrifices himself; that there is no instance of it upon record anywhere; and that when a man's Interior Monarch requires a thing of its slave for either its *momentary* or its *permanent* contentment, that thing must and will be furnished and that command obeyed, no matter who may stand in the way and suffer disaster by it? That man *ruined his family* to please and content his Interior Monarch—

Y. M. And help Christ's cause.

O. M. Yes—*secondly*. Not firstly. *He* thought it was firstly.

Y. M. Very well, have it so, if you will. But it could be that he argued that if he saved a hundred souls in New York—

O. M. The sacrifice of the *family* would be justified by that great profit upon the—the—what shall we call it?

Y. M. Investment?

O. M. Hardly. How would *speculation* do? How would *gamble* do? Not a solitary soul-capture was sure. He played for a possible thirty-three-hundred-per-cent. profit. It was *gambling*—with his family for "chips." However, let us see how the game came out. Maybe we can get on the track of the secret original impulse, the *real* impulse, that moved him to so nobly self-sacrifice his family in the Saviour's cause under the superstition that he was sacrificing himself. I will read a chapter or so. . . . Here we have it! It was bound to expose itself sooner or later. He preached to the East-Side rabble a season, then went back to his old dull, obscure life in the lumber-camps *"hurt to the heart, his pride humbled."* Why? Were not his efforts acceptable to the Saviour, for Whom alone they were made? Dear me, that detail is *lost sight of,* is not even referred to, the fact that it started out as a motive is entirely forgotten! Then what is the trouble? The authoress quite innocently and unconsciously gives the whole business away. The trouble was this: this man merely *preached* to the poor; that is not the University Settlement's way; it deals in larger and better things than that, and it did not enthuse over that crude Salvation-Army eloquence. It was courteous to Holme— but cool. It did not pet him, did not take him to its bosom. *"Perished were all his dreams of distinction, the praise and grateful approval of—"* Of whom? The Saviour? No; the Saviour is not mentioned. Of whom, then? Of "his *fellow-workers.*" Why did he want that? Because the Master inside of him wanted it, and would not be content without it. That emphasized sentence quoted above, reveals the secret we have been seeking, the original impulse, the *real* impulse, which moved the obscured and unappreciated Adirondack lumberman to sacrifice his family and go on that crusade to the East Side —which said original impulse was this, to wit: without knowing it *he went there to show a neglected world the large talent that was in him, and rise to distinction.* As I have warned you before, *no* act springs from any but the one law, the one motive. But I pray you, do not accept this law upon my say-so; but diligently examine for yourself. Whenever you read of a self-sacrificing act or hear of one, or of a duty done for *duty's sake,* take it to pieces and look for the *real* motive. It is always there.

Y. M. I do it every day. I cannot help it, now that I have gotten started upon the degrading and exasperating quest. For it is hatefully interesting!—in fact, fascinating is the word. As soon as I come across a golden deed in a book I have to stop and take it apart and examine it, I cannot help myself.

O. M. Have you ever found one that defeated the rule?

Y. M. No—at least, not yet. But take the case of servant-tipping in Europe. You pay the *hotel* for service; you owe the servants *nothing,* yet you pay them besides. Doesn't that defeat it?

O. M. In what way?

Y. M. You are not *obliged* to do it, therefore its source is compassion for their ill-paid condition, and—

O. M. Has that custom ever vexed you, annoyed you, irritated you?

Y. M. Well—yes.

O. M. Still you succumbed to it?

Y. M. Of course.

O. M. Why of course?

Y. M. Well, custom is law, in a way, and laws must be submitted to—everybody recognizes it as a *duty.*

O. M. Then you pay the irritating tax for *duty's* sake?

Y. M. I suppose it amounts to that.

O. M. Then the impulse which moves you to submit to the tax is not *all* compassion, charity, benevolence?

Y. M. Well—perhaps not.

O. M. Is *any* of it?

Y. M. I—perhaps I was too hasty in locating its source.

O. M. Perhaps so. In case you ignored the custom would you get prompt and effective service from the servants?

Y. M. Oh, hear yourself talk! Those European servants? Why, you wouldn't get any at all, to speak of.

O. M. Couldn't *that* work as an impulse to move you to pay the tax?

Y. M. I am not denying it.

O. M. Apparently, then, it is a case of for-duty's-sake with a little self-interest added?

Y. M. Yes, it has the look of it. But here is a point: we pay that tax knowing it to be unjust and an extortion; yet we go away with a pain at the heart if we think we have been stingy with the poor fellows; and we heartily wish we were back again, so that we could do the right thing, and *more* than the right thing, the *generous* thing. I think it will be difficult for you to find any thought of self in that impulse.

O. M. I wonder why you should think so. When you find service charged in the *hotel* bill does it annoy you?

Y. M. No.

O. M. Do you ever complain of the amount of it?

Y. M. No, it would not occur to me.

O. M. The *expense*, then, is not the annoying detail. It is a fixed charge, and you pay it cheerfully, you pay it without a murmur. When you came to pay the servants, how would you like it if each of the men and maids had a fixed charge?

Y. M. Like it? I should rejoice!

O. M. Even if the fixed tax were a shade *more* than you had been in the habit of paying in the form of tips?

Y. M. Indeed, yes!

O. M. Very well, then. As I understand it, it isn't really compassion nor yet duty that moves you to pay the tax, and it isn't the *amount* of the tax that annoys you. Yet *something* annoys you. What is it?

Y. M. Well, the trouble is, you never know *what* to pay, the tax varies so, all over Europe.

O. M. So you have to guess?

Y. M. There is no other way. So you go on thinking and thinking, and calculating and guessing, and consulting with other people and getting their views; and it spoils your sleep nights, and makes you distraught in the daytime, and while you are pretending to look at the sights you are only guessing and guessing and guessing all the time, and being worried and miserable.

O. M. And all about a debt which you don't owe and don't have to pay unless you want to! Strange. What is the purpose of the guessing?

Y. M. To guess out what is right to give them, and not be unfair to any of them.

O. M. It has quite a noble look—taking so much pains and using up so much valuable time in order to be just and fair to a poor servant to whom you owe nothing but who needs money and is ill paid.

Y. M. I think, myself, that if there is any ungracious motive back of it it will be hard to find.

O. M. How do you know when you have not paid a servant fairly?

Y. M. Why, he is silent; does not thank you. Sometimes he gives you a look that makes you ashamed. You are too proud to rectify your mistake there, with people looking, but afterward you keep on wishing and wishing you *had* done it. My, the shame and the pain of it! Sometimes you see, by the signs, that you have hit it *just right,* and you go away mightily satisfied. Sometimes the man is so effusively thankful that you know you have given him a good deal *more* than was necessary.

O. M. *Necessary?* Necessary for what?

Y. M. To content him.

O. M. How do you feel *then?*

Y. M. Repentant.

O. M. It is my belief that you have *not* been concerning yourself in guessing out his just dues, but only in ciphering out what would *content* him. And I think you had a self-deluding reason for that.

Y. M. What was it?

O. M. If you fell short of what he was expecting and wanting, you would get a look which would *shame you before folk.* That would give you *pain. You*—for you are only working for yourself, not *him.* If you gave him too much you would be *ashamed of yourself* for it, and that would give *you* pain—another case of thinking of *yourself,* protecting yourself, *saving yourself from discomfort.* You never think of the servant once—except to guess out how to get *his approval.* If you get that, you get your *own* approval, and that is the sole and only thing you are after. The Master inside of you is then satisfied, contented, comfortable; there was *no other* thing at stake, as a matter of *first* interest, anywhere in the transaction.

Further Instances

Y. M. Well, to think of it: Self-Sacrifice for others, the grandest thing in man, ruled out! non-existent!

O. M. Are you accusing me of saying that?

Y. M. Why, certainly.

O. M. I haven't said it.

Y. M. What did you say, then?

O. M. That no man has ever sacrificed himself in the common meaning of that phrase—which is, self-sacrifice for another *alone*. Men make daily sacrifices for others, but it is for their own sake *first*. The act must content their own spirit *first*. The other beneficiaries come second.

Y. M. And the same with duty for duty's sake?

O. M. Yes. No man performs a duty for mere duty's sake; the act must content his spirit *first*. He must feel better for *doing* the duty than he would for shirking it. Otherwise he will not do it.

Y. M. Take the case of the *Berkeley Castle.*

O. M. It was a noble duty, greatly performed. Take it to pieces and examine it, if you like.

Y. M. A British troop-ship crowded with soldiers and their wives and children. She struck a rock and began to sink. There was room in the boats for the women and children only. The colonel lined up his regiment on the deck and said "it is our duty to die, that they may be saved." There was no murmur, no protest. The boats carried away the women and children. When the death-moment was come, the colonel and his officers took their several posts, the men stood at shoulder-arms, and so, as on dress-parade, with their flag flying and the drums beating, they went down, a sacrifice to duty for duty's sake. Can you view it as other than that?

O. M. It was something as fine as that, as exalted as that. Could you have remained in those ranks and gone down to your death in that unflinching way?

Y. M. Could I? No, I could not.

O. M. Think. Imagine yourself there, with that watery doom creeping higher and higher around you.

Y. M. I can imagine it. I feel all the horror of it. I could not have endured it, I could not have remained in my place. I know it.

O. M. Why?

Y. M. There is no why about it: I know myself, and I know I couldn't *do* it.

O. M. But it would be your *duty* to do it.

Y. M. Yes, I know—but I couldn't.

O. M. It was more than a thousand men, yet not one of them flinched. Some of them must have been born with your temperament; if they could do that great duty for duty's *sake*, why not you? Don't you know that you could go out and gather together a thousand clerks and mechanics and put them on that deck and ask them to die for duty's sake, and not two dozen of them would stay in the ranks to the end?

Y. M. Yes, I know that.

O. M. But you *train* them, and put them through a campaign or two; then they would be soldiers; soldiers, with a soldier's pride, a soldier's self-respect, a soldier's ideals. They would have to content a *soldier's* spirit then, not a clerk's, not a mechanic's. They could not content that spirit by shirking a soldier's duty, could they?

Y. M. I suppose not.

O. M. Then they would do the duty not for the *duty's* sake, but for their *own* sake—primarily. The *duty* was *just the same*, and just as imperative, when they were clerks, mechanics, raw recruits, but they wouldn't perform it for that. As clerks and mechanics they had other ideals, another spirit to satisfy, and they satisfied it. They *had* to; it is the law. *Training* is potent. Training toward higher and higher, and even higher ideals is worth any man's thought and labor and diligence.

Y. M. Consider the man who stands by his duty and goes to the stake rather than be recreant to it.

O. M. It is his make and his training. He has to content the spirit that is in him, though it cost him his life. Another man, just as sincerely religious, but of different temperament, will fail of that duty, though recognizing it as a duty, and grieving to be unequal to it: but he must content the spirit that is in him—he cannot help it. He could not perform that duty for duty's *sake*, for that would not content his spirit, and the contenting of his spirit must be looked to *first*. It takes precedence of all other duties.

Y. M. Take the case of a clergyman of stainless private morals who votes for a thief for public office, on his own party's ticket, and against an honest man on the other ticket.

O. M. He has to content his spirit. He has no public morals; he has no private ones, where his party's prosperity is at stake. He will always be true to his make and training.

IV

TRAINING

Young Man. You keep using that word—training. By it do you particularly mean—

Old Man. Study, instruction, lectures, sermons? That is a part of it —but not a large part. I mean *all* the outside influences. There are a million of them. From the cradle to the grave, during all his waking hours, the human being is under training. In the very first rank of his trainers stands *association*. It is his human environment which influences his mind and his feelings, furnishes him his ideals, and sets him on his road and keeps him in it. If he leave that road he will find himself shunned by the people whom he most loves and esteems, and whose approval he most values. He is a chameleon; by the law of his nature he takes the color of his place of resort. The influences about him create his preferences, his aversions, his politics, his tastes, his morals, his religion. He creates none of these things for himself. He *thinks* he does, but that is because he has not examined into the matter. You have seen Presbyterians?

Y. M. Many.

O. M. How did they happen to be Presbyterians and not Congregationalists? And why were the Congregationalists not Baptists, and the Baptists Roman Catholics, and the Roman Catholics Buddhists, and the Buddhists Quakers, and the Quakers Episcopalians, and the Episcopalians Millerites and the Millerites Hindoos, and the Hindoos Atheists, and the Atheists Spiritualists, and the Spiritualists Agnostics, and the Agnostics Methodists, and the Methodists Confucians, and the Confucians Unitarians, and the Unitarians Mohammedans, and the Mohammedans Salvation Warriors, and the Salvation Warriors Zoroastrians, and the Zoroastrians Christian Scientists, and the Christian Scientists Mormons—and so on?

Y. M. You may answer your question yourself.

O. M. That list of sects is not a record of *studies*, searchings, seekings after light; it mainly (and sarcastically) indicates what *association* can do. If you know a man's nationality you can come within a split hair of guessing the complexion of his religion: English—Protestant;

American—ditto; Spaniard, Frenchman, Irishman, Italian, South American, Austrian—Roman Catholic; Russian—Greek Catholic; Turk—Mohammedan; and so on. And when you know the man's religious complexion, you know what sort of religious books he reads when he wants some more light, and what sort of books he avoids, lest by accident he get more light than he wants. In America if you know which party-collar a voter wears, you know what his associations are, and how he came by his politics, and which breed of newspaper he reads to get light, and which breed he diligently avoids, and which breed of mass-meetings he attends in order to broaden his political knowledge, and which breed of mass-meetings he doesn't attend, except to refute its doctrines with brickbats. We are always hearing of people who are around *seeking after Truth.* I have never seen a (permanent) specimen. I think he has never lived. But I have seen several entirely sincere people who *thought* they were (permanent) Seekers after Truth. They sought diligently, persistently, carefully, cautiously, profoundly, with perfect honesty and nicely adjusted judgment—until they believed that without doubt or question they had found the Truth. *That was the end of the search.* The man spent the rest of his life hunting up shingles wherewith to protect his Truth from the weather. If he was seeking after political Truth he found it in one or another of the hundred political gospels which govern men in the earth; if he was seeking after the Only True Religion he found it in one or another of the three thousand that are on the market. In any case, when he found the Truth *he sought no further;* but from that day forth, with his soldering-iron in one hand and his bludgeon in the other he tinkered its leaks and reasoned with objectors. There have been innumerable Temporary Seekers after Truth—have you ever heard of a permanent one? In the very nature of man such a person is impossible. However, to drop back to the text—training: all training is one form or another of *outside influence,* and *association* is the largest part of it. A man is never anything but what his outside influences have made him. They train him downward or they train him upward—but they *train* him; they are at work upon him all the time.

Y. M.   Then if he happen by the accidents of life to be evilly placed there is no help for him, according to your notions—he must train downward.

O. M.   No help for him? No help for this chameleon? It is a mistake. It is in his chameleonship that his greatest good fortune lies. He has only to change his habitat—his *associations.* But the impulse to do it must come from the *outside*—he cannot originate it himself, with that purpose in view. Sometimes a very small and accidental thing can furnish him the initiatory impulse and start him on a new road, with a new deal. The chance remark of a sweetheart, "I hear that you are a coward," may water a seed that shall sprout and bloom and flourish, and end in producing a surprising fruitage—in the fields of war. The history of man is full of such accidents. The accident of a broken leg brought a profane and ribald soldier under religious influences and furnished him a new ideal. From that accident sprang the Order of the Jesuits, and it has been shaking thrones, changing policies, and doing other tremendous work for two hundred years—and will go on. The chance reading of a book or of a paragraph in a newspaper can start a man on a new track and make him renounce his old associations and seek new ones that are *in sympathy with his new ideal:* and the result, for that man, can be an entire change of his way of life.

Y. M. Are you hinting at a scheme of procedure?

O. M. Not a new one—an old one. Old as mankind.

Y. M. What is it?

O. M. Merely the laying of traps for people. Traps baited with *Initiatory Impulses toward high ideals.* It is what the tract-distributer does. It is what the missionary does. It is what governments ought to do.

Y. M. Don't they?

O. M. In one way they do, in another way they don't. They separate the smallpox patients from the healthy people, but in dealing with crime they put the healthy into the pest-house along with the sick. That is to say, they put the beginners in with the confirmed criminals. This would be well if man were naturally inclined to good, but he isn't, and so *association* makes the beginners worse than they were when they went into captivity. It is putting a very severe punishment upon the comparatively innocent at times. They hang a man—which is a trifling punishment; this breaks the hearts of his family—which is a heavy one. They comfortably jail and feed a wife-beater, and leave his innocent wife and children to starve.

Y. M. Do you believe in the doctrine that man is equipped with an intuitive perception of good and evil?

O. M. Adam hadn't it.

Y. M. But has man acquired it since?

O. M. No. I think he has no intuitions of any kind. He gets *all* his ideas, all his impressions, from the outside. I keep repeating this, in the hope that I may so impress it upon you that you will be interested to observe and examine for yourself and see whether it is true or false.

Y. M. Where did you get your own aggravating notions?

O. M. From the *outside*. I did not invent them. They are gathered from a thousand unknown sources. Mainly *unconsciously* gathered.

Y. M. Don't you believe that God could make an inherently honest man?

O. M. Yes. I know He could. I also know that He never did make one.

Y. M. A wiser observer than you has recorded the fact that "an honest man's the noblest work of God."

O. M. He didn't record a fact, he recorded a falsity. It is windy, and sounds well, but it is not true. God makes a man with honest and dishonest *possibilities* in him and stops there. The man's *associations* develop the possibilities—the one set or the other. The result is accordingly an honest man or a dishonest one.

Y. M. And the honest one is not entitled to—

O. M. Praise? No. How often must I tell you that? *He* is not the architect of his honesty.

Y. M. Now then, I will ask you where there is any sense in training people to lead virtuous lives. What is gained by it?

O. M. The man himself gets large advantages out of it, and that is the main thing—to *him*. He is not a peril to his neighbors, he is not a damage to them—and so *they* get an advantage out of his virtues. That is the main thing to *them*. It can make this life comparatively comfortable to the parties concerned; the *neglect* of this training can make this life a constant peril and distress to the parties concerned.

Y. M. You have said that training is everything; that training is the man *himself*, for it makes him what he is.

O. M. I said training and *another* thing. Let that other thing pass, for the moment. What were you going to say?

Y. M. We have an old servant. She had been with us twenty-two years. Her service used to be faultless, but now she has become very forgetful. We are all fond of her; we all recognize that she cannot help the infirmity which age has brought her; the rest of the family do not scold her for her remissnesses, but at times I do—I can't seem to control myself. Don't I try? I do try. Now, then, when I was ready to dress, this morning, no clean clothes had been put out. I lost my temper; I lose it easiest and quickest in the early morning. I rang; and immediately began to warn myself not to show temper, and to be careful and speak gently. I safeguarded myself most carefully. I even chose the very words I would use: "You've forgotten the clean clothes, Jane." When she appeared in the door I opened my mouth to say that phrase—and out of it, moved by an instant surge of passion which I was not expecting and hadn't time to put under control, came the hot rebuke, "You've forgotten them again!" You say a man always does the thing which will best please his Interior Master. Whence came the impulse to make careful preparation to save the girl the humiliation of a rebuke? Did that come from the Master, who is always primarily concerned about *himself?*

O. M.   Unquestionably. There is no other source for any impulse. *Secondarily* you made preparation to save the girl, but *primarily* its object was to save yourself, by contenting the Master.

Y. M.   How do you mean?

O. M.   Has any member of the family ever implored you to watch your temper and not fly out at the girl?

Y. M.   Yes. My mother.

O. M.   You love her?

Y. M.   Oh, more than that!

O. M.   You would always do anything in your power to please her?

Y. M.   It is a delight to me to do anything to please her!

O. M.   Why? *You would do it for pay, solely*—for *profit.* What profit would you expect and certainly receive from the investment?

Y. M.   Personally? None. To please *her* is enough.

O. M.   It appears, then, that your object, primarily, *wasn't* to save the girl a humiliation, but to *please your mother.* It also appears that to please your mother gives *you* a strong pleasure. Is not that the profit which you get out of the investment? Isn't that the *real* profit and *first* profit?

Y. M.   Oh, well? Go on.

O. M.   In *all* transactions, the Interior Master looks to it that *you get the first profit.* Otherwise there is no transaction.

Y. M.   Well, then, if I was so anxious to get that profit and so intent upon it, why did I throw it away by losing my temper?

O. M.   In order to get *another* profit which suddenly superseded it in value.

Y. M.   Where was it?

O. M.   Ambushed behind your born temperament, and waiting for a chance. Your native warm temper suddenly jumped to the front, and *for the moment* its influence was more powerful than your mother's, and abolished it. In that instance you were eager to flash out a hot rebuke and enjoy it. You did enjoy it, didn't you?

Y. M.   For—for a quarter of a second. Yes—I did.

O. M.   Very well, it is as I have said: the thing which will give you the *most* pleasure, the most satisfaction, in any moment or *fraction* of a moment, is the thing you will always do. You must content the Master's *latest* whim, whatever it may be.

Y. M. But when the tears came into the old servant's eyes I could have cut my hand off for what I had done.

O. M. Right. You had humiliated *yourself*, you see, you had given yourself *pain*. Nothing is of *first* importance to a man except results which damage *him* or profit him—all the rest is *secondary*. Your Master was displeased with you, although you had obeyed him. He required a prompt *repentance;* you obeyed again; you *had* to—there is never any escape from his commands. He is a hard master and fickle; he changes his mind in the fraction of a second, but you must be ready to obey, and you will obey, *always*. If he requires repentance, to content him, you will always furnish it. He must be nursed, petted, coddled, and kept contented, let the terms be what they may.

Y. M. Training! Oh, what is the use of it? Didn't I, and didn't my mother try to train me up to where I would no longer fly out at that girl?

O. M. Have you never managed to keep back a scolding?

Y. M. Oh, certainly—many times.

O. M. More times this year than last?

Y. M. Yes, a good many more.

O. M. More times last year than the year before?

Y. M. Yes.

O. M. There is a large improvement, then, in the two years?

Y. M. Yes, undoubtedly.

O. M. Then your question is answered. You see there *is* use in training. Keep on. Keep faithfully on. You are doing well.

Y. M. Will my reform reach perfection?

O. M. It will. Up to *your* limit.

Y. M. My limit? What do you mean by that?

O. M. You remember that you said that I said training was *everything*. I corrected you, and said "training and *another* thing." That other thing is *temperament*—that is, the disposition you were born with. *You can't eradicate your disposition nor any rag of it*—you can only put a pressure on it and keep it down and quiet. You have a warm temper?

Y. M. Yes.

O. M. You will never get rid of it; but by watching it you can keep it down nearly all the time. *Its presence is your limit*. Your reform will never quite reach perfection, for your temper will beat you now and then, but you will come near enough. You have made valuable progress and can make more. There *is* use in training. Immense use. Presently you will reach a new stage of development, then your progress will be easier; will proceed on a simpler basis, anyway.

Y. M. Explain.

O. M. You keep back your scoldings now, to please *yourself* by pleasing your *mother;* presently the mere triumphing over your temper will delight your vanity and confer a more delicious pleasure and satisfaction upon you than even the approbation of your *mother* confers upon you now. You will then labor for yourself directly and at *first hand,* not by the roundabout way through your mother. It simplifies the matter, and it also strengthens the impulse.

Y. M. Ah, dear! But I sha'n't ever reach the point where I will spare the girl for *her* sake *primarily,* not mine?

O. M. Why—yes. In heaven.

Y. M. (*After a reflective pause.*) Temperament. Well, I see one must allow for temperament. It is a large factor, sure enough. My mother is thoughtful, and not hot-tempered. When I was dressed I went to her room; she was not there; I called, she answered from the bathroom. I heard the water running. I inquired. She answered, without temper, that Jane had forgotten her bath, and she was preparing it herself. I offered to ring, but she said, "No, don't do that; it would only distress her to be confronted with her lapse, and would be a rebuke; she doesn't deserve that—she is not to blame for the tricks her memory serves her." I say—has my mother an Interior Master?—and where was he?

O. M. He was there. There, and looking out for his own peace and pleasure and contentment. The girl's distress would have pained *your mother.* Otherwise the girl would have been rung up, distress and all. I know women who would have gotten a No. 1 *pleasure* out of ringing Jane up—and so they would infallibly have pushed the button and obeyed the law of their make and training, which are the servants of their Interior Masters. It is quite likely that a part of your mother's forbearance came from training. The *good* kind of training—whose best and highest function is to see to it that every time it confers a satisfaction upon its pupil a benefit shall fall at second hand upon others.

Y. M. If you were going to condense into an admonition your plan for the general betterment of the race's condition, how would you word it?

Admonition

O. M. Diligently train your ideals *upward* and *still upward* toward a summit where you will find your chiefest pleasure in conduct which, while contenting you, will be sure to confer benefits upon your neighbor and the community.

Y. M. Is that a new gospel?

O. M. No.

Y. M. It has been taught before?

O. M. For ten thousand years.

Y. M. By whom?

O. M. All the great religions—all the great gospels.

Y. M. Then there is nothing new about it?

O. M. Oh yes, there is. It is candidly stated, this time. That has not been done before.

Y. M. How do you mean?

O. M. Haven't I put *you* FIRST, and your neighbor and the community *afterward?*

Y. M. Well, yes, that is a difference, it is true.

O. M. The difference between straight speaking and crooked; the difference between frankness and shuffling.

Y. M. Explain.

O. M. The others offer you a hundred bribes to be good, thus conceding that the Master inside of you must be conciliated and contented first, and that you will do nothing at *first hand* but for his sake; then they turn square around and require you to do good for *others'* sake *chiefly;* and to do your duty for duty's *sake,* chiefly; and to do acts of *self-sacrifice.* Thus at the outset we all stand upon the same ground—recognition of the supreme and absolute Monarch that resides in man, and we all grovel before him and appeal to him; then those others dodge and shuffle, and face around and unfrankly and inconsistently and illogically change the form of their appeal and direct its persuasions to man's *second-place* powers and to powers which have *no existence* in him, thus advancing them to *first* place; whereas in my Admonition I stick logically and consistently to the original position: I place the Interior Master's requirements *first,* and keep them there.

Y. M. If we grant, for the sake of argument, that your scheme and the other schemes aim at and produce the same result—*right living*—has yours an advantage over the others?

O. M. One, yes—large one. It has no concealments, no deceptions.

When a man leads a right and valuable life under it he is not deceived as to the *real* chief motive which impels him to it—in those other cases he is.

Y. M.   Is that an advantage? Is it an advantage to live a lofty life for a mean reason? In the other cases he lives the lofty life under the *impression* that he is living it for a lofty reason. Is not that an advantage?

O. M.   Perhaps so. The same advantage he might get out of thinking himself a duke, and living a duke's life and parading in ducal fuss and feathers, when he wasn't a duke at all, and could find it out if he would only examine the herald's records.

Y. M.   But anyway, he is obliged to do a duke's part; he puts his hand in his pocket and does his benevolences on as big a scale as he can stand, and that benefits the community.

O. M.   He could do that without being a duke.

Y. M.   But would he?

O. M.   Don't you see where you are arriving?

Y. M.   Where?

O. M.   At the standpoint of the other schemes: That it is good morals to let an ignorant duke do showy benevolences for his pride's sake, a pretty low motive, and go on doing them unwarned, lest if he were made acquainted with the actual motive which prompted them he might shut up his purse and cease to be good?

Y. M.   But isn't it best to leave him in ignorance, as long as he *thinks* he is doing good for others' sake?

O. M.   Perhaps so. It is the position of the other schemes. They think humbug is good enough morals when the dividend on it is good deeds and handsome conduct.

Y. M.   It is my opinion that under your scheme of a man's doing a good deed for his *own* sake first-off, instead of first for the *good deed's* sake, no man would ever do one.

O. M.   Have you committed a benevolence lately?

Y. M.   Yes. This morning.

O. M.   Give the particulars.

Y. M.   The cabin of the old negro woman who used to nurse me when I was a child and who saved my life once at the risk of her own, was burned last night, and she came mourning this morning, and pleading for money to build another one.

O. M.   You furnished it?

Y. M.   Certainly.

O. M.   You were glad you had the money?

Y. M. Money? I hadn't. I sold my horse.

O. M. You were glad you had the horse?

Y. M. Of course I was; for if I hadn't had the horse I should have been incapable, and my *mother* would have captured the chance to set old Sally up.

O. M. You were cordially glad you were not caught out and incapable?

Y. M. Oh, I just was.

O. M. Now, then—

Y. M. Stop where you are! I know your whole catalogue of questions, and I could answer every one of them without your wasting the time to ask them; but I will summarize the whole thing in a single remark: I did the charity knowing it was because the act would give *me* a splendid pleasure, and because old Sally's moving gratitude and delight would give *me* another one; and because the reflection that she would be happy now and out of her trouble would fill *me* full of happiness. I did the whole thing with my eyes open and recognizing and realizing that I was looking out for *my* share of the profits *first*. Now then, I have confessed. Go on.

O. M. I haven't anything to offer; you have covered the whole ground. Could you have been any *more* strongly moved to help Sally out of her trouble—could you have done the deed any more eagerly— if you had been under the delusion that you were doing it for *her* sake and profit only?

Y. M. No! Nothing in the world could have made the impulse which moved me more powerful, more masterful, more thoroughly irresistible. I played the limit!

O. M. Very well. You begin to suspect—and I claim to *know*—that when a man is a shade *more strongly moved* to do *one* of two things or of two dozen things than he is to do any one of the *others*, he will infallibly do that *one* thing, be it good or be it evil; and if it be good, not all the beguilements of all the casuistries can increase the strength of the impulse by a single shade or add a shade to the comfort and contentment he will get out of the act.

Y. M. Then you believe that such tendency toward doing good as is in men's hearts would not be diminished by the removal of the delusion that good deeds are done primarily for the sake of No. 2 instead of for the sake of No. 1?

O. M. That is what I fully believe.

Y. M. Doesn't it somehow seem to take from the dignity of the deed?

O. M.   If there is dignity in falsity, it does. It removes that.

Y. M.   What is left for the moralist to do?

O. M.   Teach unreservedly what he already teaches with one side of his mouth and takes back with the other: Do right *for your own sake,* and be happy in knowing that your *neighbor* will certainly share in the benefits resulting.

Y. M.   Repeat your Admonition.

O. M.   *Diligently train your ideals upward and still upward toward a summit where you will find your chiefest pleasure in conduct which, while contenting you, will be sure to confer benefits upon your neighbor and the community.*

Y. M.   One's *every* act proceeds from *exterior influences,* you think?

O. M.   Yes.

Y. M.   If I conclude to rob a person, I am not the *originator* of the idea, but it comes in from the *outside?* I see him handling money—for instance—and *that* moves me to the crime?

O. M.   That, by itself? Oh, certainly not. It is merely the *latest* outside influence of a procession of preparatory influences stretching back over a period of years. No *single* outside influence can make a man do a thing which is at war with his training. The most it can do is to start his mind on a new tract and open it to the reception of *new* influences—as in the case of Ignatius Loyola. In time these influences can train him to a point where it will be consonant with his new character to yield to the *final* influence and do that thing. I will put the case in a form which will make my theory clear to you, I think. Here are two ingots of virgin gold. They shall represent a couple of characters which have been refined and perfected in the virtues by years of diligent right training. Suppose you wanted to break down these strong and well-compacted characters—what influence would you bring to bear upon the ingots?

Y. M.   Work it out yourself. Proceed.

O. M.   Suppose I turn upon one of them a steam-jet during a long succession of hours. Will there be a result?

Y. M.   None that I know of.

O. M.   Why?

Y. M.   A steam-jet cannot break down such a substance.

O. M.   Very well. The steam is an *outside influence,* but it is ineffective because the gold *takes no interest in it.* The ingot remains as it was. Suppose we add to the steam some quicksilver in a vaporized condition, and turn the jet upon the ingot, will there be an instantaneous result?

Y. M. No.

O. M. The *quicksilver* is an outside influence which gold (by its peculiar nature—say *temperament, disposition*) *cannot be indifferent to.* It stirs the interest of the gold, although we do not perceive it; but a *single* application of the influence works no damage. Let us continue the application in a steady stream, and call each minute a year. By the end of ten or twenty minutes—ten or twenty years—the little ingot is sodden with quicksilver, its virtues are gone, its character is degraded. At last it is ready to yield to a temptation which it would have taken no notice of, ten or twenty years ago. We will apply that temptation in the form of a pressure of my finger. You note the result?

Y. M. Yes; the ingot has crumbled to sand. I understand, now. It is not the *single* outside influence that does the work, but only the *last* one of a long and disintegrating accumulation of them. I see, now, how my *single* impulse to rob the man is not the one that makes me do it, but only the *last* one of a preparatory series. You might illustrate it with a parable.

A Parable

O. M. I will. There was once a pair of New England boys—twins. They were alike in good dispositions, fleckless morals, and personal appearance. They were the models of the Sunday-school. At fifteen George had an opportunity to go as cabin-boy in a whale-ship, and sailed away for the Pacific. Henry remained at home in the village. At eighteen George was a sailor before the mast, and Henry was teacher of the advanced Bible class. At twenty-two George, through fighting-habits and drinking-habits acquired at sea and in the sailor boarding-houses of the European and Oriental ports, was a common rough in Hong-Kong, and out of a job; and Henry was superintendent of the Sunday-school. At twenty-six George was a wanderer, a tramp, and Henry was pastor of the village church. Then George came home, and was Henry's guest. One evening a man passed by and turned down the lane, and Henry said, with a pathetic smile, "Without intending me a discomfort, that man is always keeping me reminded of my pinching poverty, for he carries heaps of money about him, and goes by here every evening of his life." That *outside influence*—that remark—was enough for George, but *it* was not the one that made him ambush the man and rob him, it merely represented the eleven years' accumulation of such influences, and gave birth to the act for which their long gestation had made preparation. It had never entered the head of Henry to rob the man—his ingot had been subjected to clean steam only; but George's had been subjected to vaporized quicksilver.

MORE ABOUT THE MACHINE

NOTE.—When Mrs. W. asks how can a millionaire give a single dollar to colleges and museums while one human being is destitute of bread, she has answered her question herself. Her feeling for the poor shows that she has a standard of benevolence; therefore she has conceded the millionaire's privilege of having a standard; since she evidently requires him to adopt her standard, she is by that act requiring herself to adopt his. The human being, always looks down when he is examining another person's standard; he never finds one that he has to examine by looking up.

The Man-Machine Again

Young Man. You really think man is a mere machine?

Old Man. I do.

Y. M.   And that his mind works automatically and is independent of his control—carries on thought on its own hook?

O. M.   Yes. It is diligently at work, unceasingly at work, during every waking moment. Have you never tossed about all night, imploring, beseeching, commanding your mind to stop work and let you go to sleep?—you who perhaps imagine that your mind is your servant and must obey your orders, think what you tell it to think, and stop when you tell it to stop. When it chooses to work, there is no way to keep it still for an instant. The brightest man would not be able to supply it with subjects if he had to hunt them up. If it needed the man's help it would wait for him to give it work when he wakes in the morning.

Y. M.   Maybe it does.

O. M.   No, it begins right away, before the man gets wide enough awake to give it a suggestion. He may go to sleep saying, "The moment I wake I will think upon such and such a subject," but he will fail. His mind will be too quick for him; by the time he has become nearly enough awake to be half conscious, he will find that it is already at work upon another subject. Make the experiment and see.

Y. M.   At any rate, he can make it stick to a subject if he wants to.

O. M.   Not if it finds another that suits it better. As a rule it will listen to neither a dull speaker nor a bright one. It refuses all persuasion. The dull speaker wearies it and sends it far away in idle dreams; the bright speaker throws out stimulating ideas which it goes chasing after and is at once unconscious of him and his talk. You cannot keep your mind from wandering, if it wants to; it is master, not you.

After an Interval of Days

O. M. Now, dreams—but we will examine that later. Meantime, did you try commanding your mind to wait for orders from you, and not do any thinking on its own hook?

Y. M. Yes, I commanded it to stand ready to take orders when I should wake in the morning.

O. M. Did it obey?

Y. M. No. It went to thinking of something of its own initiation, without waiting for me. Also—as you suggested—at night I appointed a theme for it to begin on in the morning, and commanded it to begin on that one and no other.

O. M. Did it obey?

Y. M. No.

O. M. How many times did you try the experiment?

Y. M. Ten.

O. M. How many successes did you score?

Y. M. Not one.

O. M. It is as I have said: the mind is independent of the man. He has no control over it; it does as it pleases. It will take up a subject in spite of him; it will stick to it in spite of him; it will throw it aside in spite of him. It is entirely independent of him.

Y. M. Go on. Illustrate.

O. M. Do you know chess?

Y. M. I learned it a week ago.

O. M. Did your mind go on playing the game all night that first night?

Y. M. Don't mention it!

O. M. It was eagerly, unsatisfiably interested; it rioted in the combinations; you implored it to drop the game and let you get some sleep?

Y. M. Yes. It wouldn't listen; it played right along. It wore me out and I got up haggard and wretched in the morning.

O. M.   At some time or other you have been captivated by a ridiculous rhyme-jingle?

Y. M.   Indeed, yes!

> "I saw Esau kissing Kate,
> And she saw I saw Esau;
> I saw Esau, he saw Kate,
> And she saw—"

And so on. My mind went mad with joy over it. It repeated it all day and all night for a week in spite of all I could do to stop it, and it seemed to me that I must surely go crazy.

O. M.   And the new popular song?

Y. M.   Oh yes! "In the Swee-eet By and By"; etc. Yes, the new popular song with the taking melody sings through one's head day and night, asleep and awake, till one is a wreck. There is no getting the mind to let it alone.

O. M.   Yes, asleep as well as awake. The mind is quite independent. It is master. You have nothing to do with it. It is so apart from you that it can conduct its affairs, sing its songs, play its chess, weave its complex and ingeniously constructed dreams, while you sleep. It has no use for your help, no use for your guidance, and never uses either, whether you be asleep or awake. You have imagined that you could originate a thought in your mind, and you have sincerely believed you could do it.

Y. M.   Yes, I have had that idea.

O. M.   Yet you can't originate a dream-thought for it to work out, and get it accepted?

Y. M.   No.

O. M.   And you can't dictate its procedure after it has originated a dream-thought for itself?

Y. M.   No. No one can do it. Do you think the waking mind and the dream mind are the same machine?

O. M.   There is argument for it. We have wild and fantastic day-thoughts? Things that are dream-like?

Y. M.   Yes—like Mr. Wells's man who invented a drug that made him invisible; and like the Arabian tales of the Thousand Nights.

O. M.   And there are dreams that are rational, simple, consistent, and unfantastic?

Y. M.   Yes. I have dreams that are like that. Dreams that are just like real life; dreams in which there are several persons with distinctly differentiated characters—inventions of my mind and yet strangers to me: a vulgar person; a refined one; a wise person; a fool; a cruel person; a kind and compassionate one; a quarrelsome person; a peacemaker; old persons and young; beautiful girls and homely ones. They talk in character, each preserves his own characteristics. There are vivid fights, vivid and biting insults, vivid love-passages; there are tragedies and comedies, there are griefs that go to one's heart, there are sayings and doings that make you laugh: indeed, the whole thing is exactly like real life.

O. M. Your dreaming mind originates the scheme, consistently and artistically develops it, and carries the little drama creditably through —all without help or suggestion from you?

Y. M. Yes.

O. M. It is argument that it could do the like awake without help or suggestion from you—and I think it does. It is argument that it is the same old mind in both cases, and never needs your help. I think the mind is purely a machine, a thoroughly independent machine, an automatic machine. Have you tried the other experiment which I suggested to you?

Y. M. Which one?

O. M. The one which was to determine how much influence you have over your mind—if any.

Y. M. Yes, and got more or less entertainment out of it. I did as you ordered: I placed two texts before my eyes—one a dull one and barren of interest, the other one full of interest, inflamed with it, white-hot with it. I commanded my mind to busy itself solely with the dull one.

O. M. Did it obey?

Y. M. Well, no, it didn't. It busied itself with the other one.

O. M. Did you try hard to make it obey?

Y. M. Yes, I did my honest best.

O. M. What was the text which it refused to be interested in or think about?

Y. M. It was this question: If A owes B a dollar and a half, and B owes C two and three-quarters, and C owes A thirty-five cents, and D and A together owe E and B three-sixteenths of—of—I don't remember the rest, now, but anyway it was wholly uninteresting, and I could not force my mind to stick to it even half a minute at a time; it kept flying off to the other text.

O. M. What was the other text?

Y. M. It is no matter about that.

O. M. But what was it?

Y. M.   A photograph.

O. M.   Your own?

Y. M.   No. It was hers.

O. M.   You really made an honest good test. Did you make a second trial?

Y. M.   Yes. I commanded my mind to interest itself in the morning paper's report of the pork-market, and at the same time I reminded it of an experience of mine of sixteen years ago. It refused to consider the pork and gave its whole blazing interest to that ancient incident.

O. M.   What was the incident?

Y. M.   An armed desperado slapped my face in the presence of twenty spectators. It makes me wild and murderous every time I think of it.

O. M.   Good tests, both; very good tests. Did you try my other suggestion?

Y. M.   The one which was to prove to me that if I would leave my mind to its own devices it would find things to think about without any of my help, and thus convince me that it was a machine, an automatic machine, set in motion by exterior influences, and as independent of me as it could be if it were in some one else's skull? Is that the one?

O. M.   Yes.

Y. M.   I tried it. I was shaving. I had slept well, and my mind was very lively, even gay and frisky. It was reveling in a fantastic and joyful episode of my remote boyhood which had suddenly flashed up in my memory—moved to this by the spectacle of a yellow cat picking its way carefully along the top of the garden wall. The color of this cat brought the bygone cat before me, and I saw her walking along the side-step of the pulpit; saw her walk on to a large sheet of sticky fly-paper and get all her feet involved; saw her struggle and fall down, helpless and dissatisfied, more and more urgent, more and more unreconciled, more and more mutely profane; saw the silent congregation quivering like jelly, and the tears running down their faces. I saw it all. The sight of the tears whisked my mind to a far distant and a sadder scene—in Terra del Fuego—and with Darwin's eyes I saw a naked great savage hurl his little boy against the rocks for a trifling fault; saw the poor mother gather up her dying child and hug it to her breast and weep, uttering no word. Did my mind stop to mourn with that nude black sister of mine? No—it was far away from that scene in an instant, and was busying itself with an ever-recurring and disagreeable dream of mine. In this dream I always find myself, stripped to my shirt, cringing and dodging about in the midst of a great drawing-room throng of finely dressed ladies and gentlemen, and wondering how I got there. And so on and so on, picture after picture, incident after incident, a drifting panorama of ever-changing, ever-dissolving views manufactured by my mind without any help from me—why, it would take me two hours to merely name the multitude of things my mind tallied off and photographed in fifteen minutes, let alone describe them to you.

O. M.   A man's mind left free, has no use for his help. But there is one way whereby he can get its help when he desires it.

Y. M.   What is that way?

O. M.   When your mind is racing along from subject to subject and strikes an inspiring one, open your mouth and begin talking upon that matter—or take your pen and use that. It will interest your mind and concentrate it, and it will pursue the subject with satisfaction. It will take full charge, and furnish the words itself.

Y. M.   But don't I tell it what to say?

O. M.   There are certainly occasions when you haven't time. The words leap out before you know what is coming.

Y. M.   For instance?

O. M.   Well, take a "flash of wit"—repartee. Flash is the right word. It is out instantly. There is no time to arrange the words. There is no thinking, no reflecting. Where there is a wit-mechanism it is automatic in its action and needs no help. Where the wit-mechanism is lacking, no amount of study and reflection can manufacture the product.

Y. M.   You really think a man originates nothing, creates nothing.

The Thinking-Process

O. M.   I do. Men perceive, and their brain-machines automatically combine the things perceived. That is all.

Y. M.   The steam-engine?

O. M.   It takes fifty men a hundred years to invent it. One meaning of invent is discover. I use the word in that sense. Little by little they discover and apply the multitude of details that go to make the perfect engine. Watt noticed that confined steam was strong enough to lift the lid of the teapot. He didn't create the idea, he merely discovered the fact; the cat had noticed it a hundred times. From the teapot he evolved the cylinder—from the displaced lid he evolved the piston-rod. To attach something to the piston-rod to be moved by it, was a simple matter—crank and wheel. And so there was a working engine.[1]

One by one, improvements were discovered by men who used their eyes, not their creating powers—for they hadn't any—and now, after a hundred years the patient contributions of fifty or a hundred observers stand compacted in the wonderful machine which drives the ocean liner.

Y. M.   A Shakespearian play?

O. M.   The process is the same. The first actor was a savage. He reproduced in his theatrical war-dances, scalp-dances, and so on, incidents which he had seen in real life. A more advanced civilization produced more incidents, more episodes; the actor and the story-teller borrowed them. And so the drama grew, little by little, stage by stage. It is made up of the facts of life, not creations. It took centuries to develop the Greek drama. It borrowed from preceding ages; it lent to the ages that came after. Men observe and combine, that is all. So does a rat.

Y. M.   How?

O. M.   He observes a smell, he infers a cheese, he seeks and finds. The astronomer observes this and that; adds his this and that to the this-and-thats of a hundred predecessors, infers an invisible planet, seeks it and finds it. The rat gets into a trap; gets out with trouble; infers that cheese in traps lacks value, and meddles with that trap no more. The astronomer is very proud of his achievement, the rat is proud of his. Yet both are machines; they have done machine work, they have originated nothing, they have no right to be vain; the whole credit belongs to their Maker. They are entitled to no honors, no praises, no monuments when they die, no remembrance. One is a complex and elaborate machine, the other a simple and limited machine, but they are alike in principle, function, and process, and neither of them works otherwise than automatically, and neither of them may righteously claim a *personal* superiority or a personal dignity above the other.

Y. M.   In earned personal dignity, then, and in personal merit for what he does, it follows of necessity that he is on the same level as a rat?

O. M.   His brother the rat; yes, that is how it seems to me. Neither of them being entitled to any personal merit for what he does, it fol-

[1] The Marquess of Worcester had done all of this more than a century earlier.

lows of necessity that neither of them has a right to arrogate to himself (personally created) superiorities over his brother.

Y. M. Are you determined to go on believing in these insanities? Would you go on believing in them in the face of able arguments backed by collated facts and instances?

O. M. I have been a humble, earnest, and sincere Truth-Seeker.

Y. M. Very well?

O. M. The humble, earnest, and sincere Truth-Seeker is always convertible by such means.

Y. M. I am thankful to God to hear you say this, for now I know that your conversion—

O. M. Wait. You misunderstand. I said I have *been* a Truth-Seeker.

Y. M. Well?

O. M. I am not that now. Have you forgotten? I told you that there are none but temporary Truth-Seekers; that a permanent one is a human impossibility; that as soon as the Seeker finds what he is thoroughly convinced is the Truth, he seeks no further, but gives the rest of his days to hunting junk to patch it and caulk it and prop it with, and make it weather-proof and keep it from caving in on him. Hence the Presbyterian remains a Presbyterian, the Mohammedan a Mohammedan, the Spiritualist a Spiritualist, the Democrat a Democrat, the Republican a Republican, the Monarchist a Monarchist; and if a humble, earnest, and sincere Seeker after Truth should find it in the proposition that the moon is made of green cheese nothing could ever budge him from that position; for he is nothing but an automatic machine, and must obey the laws of his construction.

Y. M. And so—

O. M. Having found the Truth; perceiving that beyond question man has but one moving impulse—the contenting of his own spirit —and is merely a machine and entitled to no personal merit for anything he does, it is not humanly possible for me to seek further. The rest of my days will be spent in patching and painting and puttying and caulking my priceless possession and in looking the other way when an imploring argument or a damaging fact approaches.

VI

INSTINCT AND THOUGHT

Young Man. It is odious. Those drunken theories of yours, advanced a while ago—concerning the rat and all that—strip Man bare of all his dignities, grandeurs, sublimities.

Old Man He hasn't any to strip—they are shams, stolen clothes. He claims credits which belong solely to his Maker.

Y. M. But you have no right to put him on a level with a rat.

O. M. I don't—morally. That would not be fair to the rat. The rat is well above him, there.

Y. M. Are you joking?

O. M. No, I am not.

Y. M. Then what do you mean?

O. M. That comes under the head of the Moral Sense. It is a large question. Let us finish with what we are about now, before we take it up.

Y. M. Very well. You have seemed to concede that you place Man and the rat on *a* level. What is it? The intellectual?

O. M. In form—not in degree.

Y. M. Explain.

O. M. I think that the rat's mind and the man's mind are the same machine, but of unequal capacities—like yours and Edison's; like the African pygmy's and Homer's; like the Bushman's and Bismarck's.

Y. M. How are you going to make that out, when the lower animals have no mental quality but instinct, while man possesses reason?

O. M. What is instinct?

Y. M. It is merely unthinking and mechanical exercise of inherited habit.

O. M. What originated the habit?

Y. M. The first animal started it, its descendants have inherited it.

O. M. How did the first one come to start it?

Y. M. I don't know; but it didn't *think* it out.

O. M. How do you know it didn't?

Y. M. Well—I have a right to suppose it didn't, anyway.

O. M. I don't believe you have. What is thought?

Y. M. I know what you call it: the mechanical and automatic putting together of impressions received from outside, and drawing an inference from them.

O. M. Very good. Now my idea of the meaningless term "instinct" is, that it is merely *petrified thought;* solidified and made inanimate by habit; thought which was once alive and awake, but is become unconscious—walks in its sleep, so to speak.

Y. M. Illustrate it.

O. M. Take a herd of cows, feeding in a pasture. Their heads are all turned in one direction. They do that instinctively; they gain nothing by it, they have no reason for it, they don't know why they do it. It is an inherited habit which was originally thought—that is to say, observation of an exterior fact, and a valuable inference drawn from that observation and confirmed by experience. The original wild ox noticed that with the wind in his favor he could smell his enemy in time to escape; then he inferred that it was worth while to keep his nose to the wind. That is the process which man calls reasoning. Man's thought-machine works just like the other animals', but it is a better one and more Edisonian. Man, in the ox's place, would go further, reason wider: he would face part of the herd the other way and protect both front and rear.

Y. M.   Did you say the term instinct is meaningless?

O. M.   I think it is a bastard word. I think it confuses us; for as a rule it applies itself to habits and impulses which had a far-off origin in thought, and now and then breaks the rule and applies itself to habits which can hardly claim a thought-origin.

Y. M.   Give an instance.

O. M.   Well, in putting on trousers a man always inserts the same old leg first—never the other one. There is no advantage in that, and no sense in it. All men do it, yet no man thought it out and adopted it of set purpose, I imagine. But it is a habit which is transmitted, no doubt, and will continue to be transmitted.

Y. M.   Can you prove that the habit exists?

O. M.   You can prove it, if you doubt. If you will take a man to a clothing-store and watch him try on a dozen pairs of trousers, you will see.

Y. M.   The cow illustration is not—

O. M.   Sufficient to show that a dumb animal's mental machine is just the same as a man's and its reasoning processes the same? I will illustrate further. If you should hand Mr. Edison a box which you caused to fly open by some concealed device he would infer a spring, and would hunt for it and find it. Now an uncle of mine had an old horse who used to get into the closed lot where the corncrib was and dishonestly take the corn. I got the punishment myself, as it was supposed that I had heedlessly failed to insert the wooden pin which kept the gate closed. These persistent punishments fatigued me; they also caused me to infer the existence of a culprit, somewhere; so I hid myself and watched the gate. Presently the horse came and pulled the pin out with his teeth and went in. Nobody taught him that; he had observed—then thought it out for himself. His process did not differ from Edison's; he put this and that together and drew an inference—and the peg, too; but I made him sweat for it.

Y. M.   It has something of the seeming of thought about it. Still it is not very elaborate. Enlarge.

O. M.   Suppose that Edison has been enjoying some one's hospitalities. He comes again by and by, and the house is vacant. He infers that his host has moved. A while afterward, in another town, he sees the man enter a house; he infers that that is the new home, and follows to inquire. Here, now, is the experience of a gull, as related by a naturalist. The scene is a Scotch fishing village where the gulls were kindly treated. This particular gull visited a cottage; was fed; came next day and was fed again; came into the house, next time, and ate with the family; kept on doing this almost daily, thereafter. But, once the gull was away on a journey for a few days, and when it returned the house was vacant. Its friends had removed to a village three miles distant. Several months later it saw the head of the family on the street there, followed him home, entered the house without excuse or apology, and became a daily guest again. Gulls do not rank high mentally, but this one had memory and the reasoning faculty, you see, and applied them Edisonially.

Y. M.   Yet it was not an Edison and couldn't be developed into one.

O. M.   Perhaps not. Could you?

Y. M.   That is neither here nor there. Go on.

O. M.   If Edison were in trouble and a stranger helped him out of it and next day he got into the same difficulty again, he would infer the wise thing to do in case he knew the stranger's address. Here is a case of a bird and a stranger as related by a naturalist. An Englishman saw a bird flying around about his dog's head, down in the grounds, and uttering cries of distress. He went there to see about it. The dog had a young bird in his mouth—unhurt. The gentleman rescued it and put it on a bush and brought the dog away. Early the next morning the mother bird came for the gentleman, who was sitting on his veranda, and by its manœuvers persuaded him to follow it to a distant part of the grounds—flying a little way in front of him and waiting for him to catch up, and so on; and keeping to the winding path, too, instead of flying the near way across lots. The distance covered was four hundred yards. The same dog was the culprit; he had the young bird again, and once more he had to give it up. Now the mother bird had reasoned it all out: since the stranger had helped her once, she inferred that he would do it again; she knew where to find him, and she went upon her errand with confidence. Her mental processes were what Edison's would have been. She put this and that together—and that is all that thought *is*—and out of them built her logical arrangement of inferences. Edison couldn't have done it any better himself.

Y. M. Do you believe that many of the dumb animals can think?

O. M. Yes—the elephant, the monkey, the horse, the dog, the parrot, the macaw, the mocking-bird, and many others. The elephant whose mate fell into a pit, and who dumped dirt and rubbish into the pit till the bottom was raised high enough to enable the captive to step out, was equipped with the reasoning quality. I conceive that all animals that can learn things through teaching and drilling have to know how to observe, and put this and that together and draw an inference—the process of thinking. Could you teach an idiot the manual of arms, and to advance, retreat, and go through complex field manœuvers at the word of command?

Y. M. Not if he were a thorough idiot.

O. M. Well, canary-birds can learn all that; dogs and elephants learn all sorts of wonderful things. They must surely be able to notice, and to put things together, and say to themselves, "I get the idea, now: when I do so and so, as per order, I am praised and fed; when I do differently I am punished." Fleas can be taught nearly anything that a Congressman can.

Y. M. Granting, then, that dumb animals are able to think upon a low plane, is there any that can think upon a high one? Is there one that is well up toward man?

O. M. Yes. As a thinker and planner the ant is the equal of any savage race of men; as a self-educated specialist in several arts she is the superior of any savage race of men; and in one or two high mental qualities she is above the reach of any man, savage or civilized!

Y. M. Oh, come! you are abolishing the intellectual frontier which separates man and beast.

O. M. I beg your pardon. One cannot abolish what does not exist.

Y. M. You are not in earnest, I hope. You cannot mean to seriously say there is no such frontier.

O. M. I do say it seriously. The instances of the horse, the gull, the mother bird, and the elephant show that those creatures put their this's and thats together just as Edison would have done it and drew the same inferences that he would have drawn. Their mental machinery was just like his, also its manner of working. Their equipment was as inferior to his in elaboration as a Waterbury is inferior to the Strasburg clock, but that is the only difference—there is no frontier.

Y. M. It looks exasperatingly true; and is distinctly offensive. It elevates the dumb beasts to—to—

O. M.   Let us drop that lying phrase, and call them the Unrevealed Creatures; so far as we can know, there is no such thing as a dumb beast.

Y. M.   On what grounds do you make that assertion?

O. M.   On quite simple ones. "Dumb" beast suggests an animal that has no thought-machinery, no understanding, no speech, no way of communicating what is in its mind. We know that a hen *has* speech. We cannot understand everything she says, but we easily learn two or three of her phrases. We know when she is saying, "I have laid an egg"; we know when she is saying to the chicks, "Run here, dears, I've found a worm"; we know what she is saying when she voices a warning: "Quick! hurry! gather yourselves under mamma, there's a hawk coming!" We understand the cat when she stretches herself out, purring with affection and contentment and lifts up a soft voice and says, "Come, kitties, supper's ready"; we understand her when she goes mourning about and says, "Where can they be? They are lost. Won't you help me hunt for them?" and we understand the disreputable Tom when he challenges at midnight from his shed, "You come over here, you product of immoral commerce, and I'll make your fur fly!" We understand a few of a dog's phrases and we learn to understand a few of the remarks and gestures of any bird or other animal that we domesticate and observe. The clearness and exactness of the few of the hen's speeches which we understand is argument that she can communicate to her kind a hundred things which we cannot comprehend—in a word, that she can converse. And this argument is also applicable in the case of others of the great army of the Unrevealed. It is just like man's vanity and impertinence to call an animal dumb because it is dumb to his dull perceptions. Now as to the ant—

Y. M.   Yes, go back to the ant, the creature that—as you seem to think—sweeps away the last vestige of an intellectual frontier between man and the Unrevealed.

O. M.   That is what she surely does. In all his history the aboriginal Australian never thought out a house for himself and built it. The ant is an amazing architect. She is a wee little creature, but she builds a strong and enduring house eight feet high—a house which is as large in proportion to her size as is the largest capitol or cathedral in the world compared to man's size. No savage race has produced architects who could approach the ant in genius or culture. No civilized race has produced architects who could plan a house better for the uses proposed than can hers. Her house contains a throne-room; nurseries for her young; granaries; apartments for her soldiers, her workers, etc.; and they and the multifarious halls and corridors which communicate with them are arranged and distributed with an educated and experienced eye for convenience and adaptability.

Y. M. That could be mere instinct.

O. M. It would elevate the savage if he had it. But let us look further before we decide. The ant has soldiers—battalions, regiments, armies; and they have their appointed captains and generals, who lead them to battle.

Y. M. That could be instinct, too.

O. M. We will look still further. The ant has a system of government; it is well planned, elaborate, and is well carried on.

Y. M. Instinct again.

O. M. She has crowds of slaves, and is a hard and unjust employer of forced labor.

Y. M. Instinct.

O. M. She has cows, and milks them.

Y. M. Instinct, of course.

O. M. In Texas she lays out a farm twelve feet square, plants it, weeds it, cultivates it, gathers the crop and stores it away.

Y. M. Instinct, all the same.

O. M. The ant discriminates between friend and stranger. Sir John Lubbock took ants from two different nests, made them drunk with whisky and laid them, unconscious, by one of the nests, near some water. Ants from the nest came and examined and discussed these disgraced creatures, then carried their friends home and threw the strangers overboard. Sir John repeated the experiment a number of times. For a time the sober ants did as they had done at first—carried their friends home and threw the strangers overboard. But finally they lost patience, seeing that their reformatory efforts went for nothing, and threw both friends and strangers overboard. Come—is this instinct, or is it thoughtful and intelligent discussion of a thing new—absolutely new—to their experience; with a verdict arrived at, sentence passed, and judgment executed? Is it instinct?—thought petrified by ages of habit—or isn't it brand-new thought, inspired by the new occasion, the new circumstances?

Y. M. I have to concede it. It was not a result of habit; it has all the look of reflection, thought, putting this and that together, as you phrase it. I believe it was thought.

O. M. I will give you another instance of thought. Franklin had a cup of sugar on a table in his room. The ants got at it. He tried several preventives; the ants rose superior to them. Finally he contrived one which shut off access—probably set the table's legs in pans of water, or drew a circle of tar around the cup, I don't remember. At any rate, he watched to see what they would do. They tried various schemes—failures, every one. The ants were badly puzzled. Finally they held a consultation, discussed the problem, arrived at a decision—and this time they beat that great philosopher. They formed in procession, crossed the floor, climbed the wall, marched across the ceiling to a point just over the cup, then one by one they let go and fell down into it! Was that instinct—thought petrified by ages of inherited habit?

Y. M. No, I don't believe it was. I believe it was a newly reasoned scheme to meet a new emergency.

O. M. Very well. You have conceded the reasoning power in two instances. I come now to a mental detail wherein the ant is a long way the superior of any human being. Sir John Lubbock proved by many experiments that an ant knows a stranger ant of her own species in a moment, even when the stranger is disguised—with paint. Also he proved that an ant knows every individual in her hive of five hundred thousand souls. Also, after a year's absence of one of the five hundred thousand she will straightway recognize the returned absentee and grace the recognition with an affectionate welcome. How are these recognitions made? Not by color, for painted ants were recognized. Not by smell, for ants that had been dipped in chloroform were recognized. Not by speech and not by antennæ signs nor contacts, for the drunken and motionless ants were recognized and the friend discriminated from the stranger. The ants were all of the same species, therefore the friends had to be recognized by form and feature—friends who formed part of a hive of five hundred thousand! Has any man a memory for form and feature approaching that?

Y. M. Certainly not.

O. M. Franklin's ants and Lubbocks's ants show fine capacities of putting this and that together in new and untried emergencies and deducting smart conclusions from the combinations—a man's mental process exactly. With memory to help, man preserves his observations and reasonings, reflects upon them, adds to them, recombines, and so proceeds, stage by stage, to far results—from the teakettle to the ocean greyhound's complex engine; from personal labor to slave labor; from wigwam to palace; from the capricious chase to agriculture and stored food; from nomadic life to stable government and concentrated authority; from incoherent hordes to massed armies. The ant has observation, the reasoning faculty, and the preserving adjunct of a prodigious memory; she has duplicated man's development and the essential features of his civilization, and you call it all instinct!

Y. M. Perhaps I lacked the reasoning faculty myself.

O. M. Well, don't tell anybody, and don't do it again.

Y. M. We have come a good way. As a result—as I understand it—I am required to concede that there is absolutely no intellectual frontier separating Man and the Unrevealed Creatures?

O. M. That is what you are required to concede. There is no such frontier—there is no way to get around that. Man has a finer and more capable machine in him than those others, but it is the same machine and works in the same way. And neither he nor those others can command the machine—it is strictly automatic, independent of control, works when it pleases, and when it doesn't please, it can't be forced.

Y. M. Then man and the other animals are all alike, as to mental machinery, and there isn't any difference of any stupendous magnitude between them, except in quality, not in kind.

O. M. That is about the state of it—intellectuality. There are pronounced limitations on both sides. We can't learn to understand much of their language, but the dog, the elephant, etc., learn to understand a very great deal of ours. To that extent they are our superiors. On the other hand, they can't learn reading, writing, etc., nor any of our fine and high things, and there we have a large advantage over them.

Y. M. Very well, let them have what they've got, and welcome; there is still a wall, and a lofty one. They haven't got the Moral Sense; we have it, and it lifts us immeasurably above them.

O. M. What makes you think that?

Y. M. Now look here—let us call a halt. I have stood the other infamies and insanities and that is enough; I am not going to have man and the other animals put on the same level morally.

O. M. I wasn't going to hoist man up to that.

Y. M. This is too much! I think it is not right to jest about such things.

O. M. I am not jesting, I am merely reflecting a plain and simple truth—and without uncharitableness. The fact that man knows right from wrong proves his *intellectual* superiority to the other creatures; but the fact that he can *do* wrong proves his *moral* inferiority to any creature that *cannot*. It is my belief that this position is not assailable.

Free Will

Y. M.   What is your opinion regarding Free Will?

O. M.   That there is no such thing. Did the man possess it who gave the old woman his last shilling and trudged home in the storm?

Y. M.   He had the choice between succoring the old woman and leaving her to suffer. Isn't it so?

O. M.   Yes, there was a choice to be made, between bodily comfort on the one hand and the comfort of the spirit on the other. The body made a strong appeal, of course—the body would be quite sure to do that; the spirit made a counter appeal. A choice had to be made between the two appeals, and was made. Who or what determined that choice?

Y. M.   Any one but you would say that the man determined it, and that in doing it he exercised Free Will.

O. M.   We are constantly assured that every man is endowed with Free Will, and that he can and must exercise it where he is offered a choice between good conduct and less-good conduct. Yet we clearly saw that in that man's case he really had no Free Will: his temperament, his training, and the daily influences which had molded him and made him what he was, *compelled* him to rescue the old woman and thus save *himself*—save himself from spiritual pain, from unendurable wretchedness. He did not make the choice, it was made *for* him by forces which he could not control. Free Will has always existed in *words*, but it stops there, I think—stops short of *fact*. I would not use those words—Free Will—but others.

Y. M.   What others?

O. M.   Free Choice.

Y. M.   What is the difference?

O. M.   The one implies untrammeled power to *act* as you please, the other implies nothing beyond a mere *mental process:* the critical ability to determine which of two things is nearest right and just.

Y. M.   Make the difference clear, please.

O. M.   The mind can freely *select, choose, point out* the right and just one—its function stops there. It can go no further in the matter. It has no authority to say that the right one shall be acted upon and the wrong one discarded. That authority is in other hands.

Y. M.   The man's?

O. M.   In the machine which stands for him. In this born disposition and the character which has been built around it by training and environment.

Y. M. It will act upon the right one of the two?

O. M. It will do as it pleases in the matter. George Washington's machine would act upon the right one; Pizarro's mind would know which was the right one and which the wrong, but the Master inside of Pizarro would act upon the wrong one.

Y. M. Then as I understand it a bad man's mental machinery calmly and judicially points out which of two things is right and just—

O. M. Yes, and his *moral* machinery will freely act upon the one or the other, according to its make, and be quite indifferent to the *mind's* feelings concerning the matter—that is, *would* be, if the mind had any feelings; which it hasn't. It is merely a thermometer: it registers the heat and the cold, and cares not a farthing about either.

Y. M. Then we must not claim that if a man *knows* which of two things is right he is absolutely *bound* to do that thing?

O. M. His temperament and training will decide what he shall do, and he will do it; he cannot help himself, he has no authority over the matter. Wasn't it right for David to go out and slay Goliath?

Y. M. Yes.

O. M. Then it would have been equally *right* for any one else to do it?

Y. M. Certainly.

O. M. Then it would have been *right* for a born coward to attempt it?

Y. M. It would—yes.

O. M. You know that no born coward ever would have attempted it, don't you?

Y. M. Yes.

O. M. You know that a born coward's make and temperament would be an absolute and insurmountable bar to his ever essaying such a thing, don't you?

Y. M. Yes, I know it.

O. M. He clearly perceives that it would be *right* to try it?

Y. M. Yes.

O. M. His mind has Free Choice in determining that it would be *right* to try it?

Y. M. Yes.

O. M. Then if by reason of his inborn cowardice he simply can *not* essay it, what becomes of his Free Will? Where is his Free Will? Why claim that he has Free Will when the plain facts show that he hasn't? Why contend that because he and David *see* the right alike, both must *act* alike? Why impose the same laws upon goat and lion?

Y. M. There is really no such thing as Free Will?

O. M. It is what I think. There is *Will*. But it has nothing to do with *intellectual perceptions of right and wrong*, and is not under their command. David's temperament and training had Will, and it was a compulsory force; David had to obey its decrees, he had no choice. The coward's temperament and training possess Will, and *it* is compulsory; it commands him to avoid danger, and he obeys, he has no choice. But neither the Davids nor the cowards possess Free Will— will that may do the right or do the wrong, as their *mental* verdict shall decide.

Not Two Values, but Only One

Y. M. There is one thing which bothers me: I can't tell where you draw the line between *material* covetousness and *spiritual* covetousness.

O. M. I don't draw any.

Y. M. How do you mean?

O. M. There is no such thing as *material* covetousness. All covetousness is spiritual.

Y. M. *All* longings, desires, ambitions *spiritual*, never material?

O. M. Yes. The Master in you requires that in *all* cases you shall content his *spirit*—that alone. He never requires anything else, he never interests himself in any other matter.

Y. M. Ah, come! When he covets somebody's money—isn't that rather distinctly material and gross?

O. M. No. The money is merely a symbol—it represents in visible and concrete form a *spiritual desire*. Any so-called material thing that you want is merely a symbol: you want it not for *itself*, but because it will content your spirit for the moment.

Y. M. Please particularize.

O. M. Very well. Maybe the thing longed for is a new hat. You get it and your vanity is pleased, your spirit contented. Suppose your friends deride the hat, make fun of it: at once it loses its value; you are ashamed of it, you put it out of your sight, you never want to see it again.

Y. M. I think I see. Go on.

O. M. It is the same hat, isn't it? It is in no way altered. But it wasn't the *hat* you wanted, but only what it stood for—a something to please and content your *spirit*. When it failed of that, the whole of its value was gone. There are no *material* values; there are only spiritual ones. You will hunt in vain for a material value that is *actual, real*— there is no such thing. The only value it possesses, for even a moment, is the spiritual value back of it: remove that and it is at once worthless— like the hat.

Y. M. Can you extend that to money?

O. M. Yes. It is merely a symbol, it has no *material* value; you think you desire it for its own sake, but it is not so. You desire it for the spiritual content it will bring; if it fail of that, you discover that its value is gone. There is that pathetic tale of the man who labored like a slave, unresting, unsatisfied, until he had accumulated a fortune, and was happy over it, jubilant about it; then in a single week a pestilence swept away all whom he held dear and left him desolate. His money's value was gone. He realized that his joy in it came not from the money itself, but from the spiritual contentment he got out of his family's enjoyment of the pleasures and delights it lavished upon them. Money has no *material* value; if you remove its spiritual value nothing is left but dross. It is so with all things, little or big, majestic or trivial—there are no exceptions. Crowns, scepters, pennies, paste jewels, village notoriety, world-wide fame—they are all the same, they have no *material* value: while they content the *spirit* they are precious, when this fails they are worthless.

A Difficult Question

Y. M. You keep me confused and perplexed all the time by your elusive terminology. Sometimes you divide a man up into two or three separate personalities, each with authorities, jurisdictions, and responsibilities of its own, and when he is in that condition I can't grasp him. Now when *I* speak of a man, he is *the whole thing in one*, and easy to hold and contemplate.

O. M. That is pleasant and convenient, if true. When you speak of "my body" who is the "my"?

Y. M. It is the "me."

O. M. The body is a property, then, and the Me owns it. Who is the Me?

Y. M. The Me is *the whole thing*; it is a common property; an undivided ownership, vested in the whole entity.

O. M. If the Me admires a rainbow, is it the whole Me that admires it, including the hair, hands, heels, and all?

Y. M. Certainly not. It is my *mind* that admires it.

O. M.   So *you* divide the Me yourself. Everybody does; everybody must. What, then, definitely, is the Me?

Y. M.   I think it must consist of just those two parts—the body and the mind.

O. M.   You think so? If you say "I believe the world is round," who is the "I" that is speaking?

Y. M.   The mind.

O. M.   If you say "I grieve for the loss of my father," who is the "I"?

Y. M.   The mind.

O. M.   Is the mind exercising an intellectual function when it examines and accepts the evidence that the world is round?

Y. M.   Yes.

O. M.   Is it exercising an intellectual function when it grieves for the loss of your father?

Y. M.   No. That is not cerebration, brain-work, it is a matter of *feeling*.

O. M.   Then its source is not in your mind, but in your *moral* territory?

Y. M.   I have to grant it.

O. M.   Is your mind a part of your *physical* equipment?

Y. M.   No. It is independent of it; it is spiritual.

O. M.   Being spiritual, it cannot be affected by physical influences?

Y. M.   No.

O. M.   Does the mind remain sober when the body is drunk?

Y. M.   Well—no.

O. M.   There *is* a physical effect present, then?

Y. M.   It looks like it.

O. M.   A cracked skull has resulted in a crazy mind. Why should that happen if the mind is spiritual, and *independent* of physical influences?

Y. M.   Well—I don't know.

O. M.   When you have a pain in your foot, how do you know it?

Y. M.   I feel it.

O. M.   But you do not feel it until a nerve reports the hurt to the brain. Yet the brain is the seat of the mind, is it not?

Y. M.   I think so.

O. M.   But isn't spiritual enough to learn what is happening in the outskirts without the help of the *physical* messenger? You perceive that the question of who or what the Me is, is not a simple one at all. You say "I admire the rainbow," and "I believe the world is round," and in these cases we find that the Me is not all speaking, but only the *mental* part. You say "I grieve," and again the Me is not all speaking, but only the *moral* part. You say the mind is wholly spiritual; then you say "I have a pain" and find that this time the Me is mental *and* spiritual combined. We all use the "I" in this indeterminate fashion, there is no help for it. We imagine a Master and King over what you call The Whole Thing, and we speak of him as "I," but when we try to define him we find we cannot do it. The intellect and the feelings can act quite *independently* of each other; we recognize that, and we look around for a Ruler who is master over both, and can serve as a *definite and indisputable "I,"* and enable us to know what we mean and who or what we are talking about when we use that pronoun, but we have to give it up and confess that we cannot find him. To me, Man is a machine, made up of many mechanisms, the moral and mental ones acting automatically in accordance with the impulses of an interior Master who is built out of born-temperament and an accumulation of multitudinous outside influences and trainings; a machine whose *one* function is to secure the spiritual contentment of the Master, be his desires good or be they evil; a machine whose Will is absolute and must be obeyed, and always *is* obeyed.

Y. M.   Maybe the Me is the Soul?

O. M.   Maybe it is. What is the Soul?

Y. M.   I don't know.

O. M.   Neither does any one else.

The Master Passion

Y. M.   What is the Master?—or, in common speech, the Conscience? Explain it.

O. M.   It is that mysterious autocrat, lodged in a man, which compels the man to content its desires. It may be called the Master Passion—the hunger for Self-Approval.

Y. M.   Where is its seat?

O. M.   In man's moral constitution.

Y. M.   Are its commands for the man's good?

O. M.   It is indifferent to the man's good; it never concerns itself about anything but the satisfying of its own desires. It can be *trained* to prefer things which will be for the man's good, but it will prefer them only because they will content *it* better than other things would.

Y. M.   Then even when it is trained to high ideals it is still looking out for its own contentment, and not for the man's good?

O. M.   True. Trained or untrained, it cares nothing for the man's good, and never concerns itself about it.

Y. M.   It seems to be an *immoral* force seated in the man's moral constitution?

O. M.   It is a *colorless* force seated in the man's moral constitution. Let us call it an instinct—a blind, unreasoning instinct, which cannot and does not distinguish between good morals and bad ones, and cares nothing for results to the man provided its own contentment be secured; and it will *always* secure that.

Y. M.   It seeks money, and it probably considers that that is an advantage for the man?

O. M.   It is not always seeking money, it is not always seeking power, nor office, nor any other *material* advantage. In *all* cases it seeks a *spiritual* contentment, let the *means* be what they may. Its desires are determined by the man's temperament—and it is lord over that. Temperament, Conscience, Susceptibility, Spiritual Appetite, are, in fact, the same thing. Have you ever heard of a person who cared nothing for money?

Y. M.   Yes. A scholar who would not leave his garret and his books to take a place in a business house at large salary.

O. M.   He had to satisfy his master—that is to say, his temperament, his Spiritual Appetite—and it preferred the books to money. Are there other cases?

Y. M.   Yes, the hermit.

O. M.   It is a good instance. The hermit endures solitude, hunger, cold, and manifold perils, to content his autocrat, who prefers these things, and prayer and contemplation, to money or to any show or luxury that money can buy. Are there others?

Y. M.   Yes. The artist, the poet, the scientist.

O. M.   Their autocrat prefers the deep pleasures of these occupations, either well paid or ill paid, to any others in the market, at any price. You *realize* that the Master Passion—the contentment of the spirit—concerns itself with many things besides so-called material advantage, material prosperity, cash, and all that?

Y. M.   I think I must concede it.

O. M.   I believe you must. There are perhaps as many Temperaments that would refuse the burdens and vexations and distinctions of public office as there are that hunger after them. The one set of Temperaments seek the contentment of the spirit, and that alone; and this is exactly the case with the other set. Neither set seeks anything *but* the contentment of the spirit. If the one is sordid, both are sordid; and equally so, since the end in view is precisely the same in both cases. And in both cases Temperament decides the preference—and Temperament is *born*, not made.

Conclusion

O. M.   You have been taking a holiday?

Y. M.   Yes; a mountain tramp covering a week. Are you ready to talk?

O. M.   Quite ready. What shall we begin with?

Y. M.   Well, lying abed resting up, two days and nights, I have thought over all these talks, and passed them carefully in review. With this result: that . . . that . . . are you intending to publish your notions about Man some day?

O. M.   Now and then, in these past twenty years, the Master inside of me has half-intended to order me to set them to paper and publish them. Do I have to tell you why the order has remained unissued, or can you explain so simple a thing without my help?

Y. M.   By your doctrine, it is simplicity itself: outside influences moved your interior Master to give the order; stronger outside influences deterred him. Without the outside influences, neither of these impulses could ever have been born, since a person's brain is incapable of originating an idea within itself.

O. M.   Correct. Go on.

Y. M.   The matter of publishing or withholding is still in your Master's hands. If some day an outside influence shall determine him to publish, he will give the order, and it will be obeyed.

O. M.   That is correct. Well?

Y. M.   Upon reflection I have arrived at the conviction that the publication of your doctrines would be harmful. Do you pardon me?

O. M.   Pardon *you?* You have done nothing. You are an instrument —a speaking-trumpet. Speaking-trumpets are not responsible for what is said through them. Outside influences—in the form of lifelong teachings, trainings, notions, prejudices, and other second-hand importations—have persuaded the Master within you that the publication of these doctrines would be harmful. Very well, this is quite natural, and was to be expected; in fact, was inevitable. Go on; for the sake of ease and convenience, stick to habit: speak in the first person, and tell me what your Master thinks about it.

Y. M.   Well, to begin: it is a desolating doctrine; it is not inspiring, enthusing, uplifting. It takes the glory out of man, it takes the pride out of him, it takes the heroism out of him, it denies him all personal credit, all applause; it not only degrades him to a machine, but allows him no control over the machine; makes a mere coffee-mill of him, and neither permits him to supply the coffee nor turn the crank, his sole and piteously humble function being to grind coarse or fine, according to his make, outside impulses doing all the rest.

O. M.   It is correctly stated. Tell me—what do men admire most in each other?

Y. M.   Intellect, courage, majesty of build, beauty of countenance, charity, benevolence, magnanimity, kindliness, heroism, and—and—

O. M.   I would not go any further. These are *elementals*. Virtue, fortitude, holiness, truthfulness, loyalty, high ideals—these, and all the related qualities that are named in the dictionary, are *made of the elementals*, by blendings, combinations, and shadings of the elementals, just as one makes green by blending blue and yellow, and makes several shades and tints of red by modifying the elemental red. There are several elemental colors; they are all in the rainbow; out of them we manufacture and name fifty shades of them. You have named the elementals of the human rainbow, and also one *blend*—heroism, which is made out of courage and magnanimity. Very well, then; which of these elements does the possessor of it manufacture for himself? Is it intellect?

Y. M.   No.

O. M.   Why?

Y. M.   He is born with it.

O. M.   Is it courage?

Y. M.   No. He is born with it.

O. M.   Is it majesty of build, beauty of countenance?

Y. M.   No. They are birthrights.

O. M.   Take those others—the elemental moral qualities—charity, benevolence, magnanimity, kindliness; fruitful seeds, out of which spring, through cultivation by outside influences, all the manifold blends and combinations of virtues named in the dictionaries: does man manufacture any one of those seeds, or are they all born in him?

Y. M.   Born in him.

O. M.   Who manufactures them, then?

Y. M.   God.

O. M.   Where does the credit of it belong?

Y. M.   To God.

O. M.   And the glory of which you spoke, and the applause?

Y. M.   To God.

O. M. Then it is *you* who degrade man. You make him claim glory, praise, flattery, for every valuable thing he possesses—*borrowed* finery, the whole of it; no rag of it earned by himself, not a detail of it produced by his own labor. *You* make man a humbug; have I done worse by him?

Y. M. You have made a machine of him.

O. M. Who devised that cunning and beautiful mechanism, a man's hand?

Y. M. God.

O. M. Who devised the law by which it automatically hammers out of a piano an elaborate piece of music, without error, while the man is thinking about something else, or talking to a friend?

Y. M. God.

O. M. Who devised the blood? Who devised the wonderful machinery which automatically drives its renewing and refreshing streams through the body, day and night, without assistance or advice from the man? Who devised the man's mind, whose machinery works automatically, interests itself in what it pleases, regardless of his will or desire, labors all night when it likes, deaf to his appeals for mercy? God devised all these things. *I* have not made man a machine, God made him a machine. I am merely calling attention to the fact, nothing more. Is it wrong to call attention to the fact? Is it a crime?

Y. M. I think it is wrong to *expose* a fact when harm can come of it.

O. M. Go on.

Y. M. Look at the matter as it stands now. Man has been taught that he is the supreme marvel of the Creation; he believes it; in all the ages he has never doubted it, whether he was a naked savage, or clothed in purple and fine linen, and civilized. This has made his heart buoyant, his life cheery. His pride in himself, his sincere admiration of himself, his joy in what he supposed were his own and unassisted achievements, and his exultation over the praise and applause which they evoked—these have exalted him, enthused him, ambitioned him to higher and higher flights; in a word, made his life worth the living. But by your scheme, all this is abolished; he is degraded to a machine, he is a nobody, his noble prides wither to mere vanities; let him strive as he may, he can never be any better than his humblest and stupidest neighbor; he would never be cheerful again, his life would not be worth the living.

O. M. You really think that?

Y. M. I certainly do.

O. M. Have you ever seen me uncheerful, unhappy?

Y. M.   No.

O. M.   Well, *I* believe these things. Why have they not made me unhappy?

Y. M.   Oh, well—temperament, of course! You never let *that* escape from your scheme.

O. M.   That is correct. If a man is born with an unhappy temperament, nothing can make him happy; if he is born with a happy temperament, nothing can make him unhappy.

Y. M.   What—not even a degrading and heart-chilling system of beliefs?

O. M.   Beliefs? Mere beliefs? Mere convictions? They are powerless. They strive in vain against inborn temperament.

Y. M.   I can't believe that, and I don't.

O. M.   Now you are speaking hastily. It shows that you have not studiously examined the facts. Of all your intimates, which one is the happiest? Isn't it Burgess?

Y. M.   Easily.

O. M.   And which one is the unhappiest? Henry Adams?

Y. M.   Without a question!

O. M.   I know them well. They are extremes, abnormals; their temperaments are as opposite as the poles. Their life-histories are about alike—but look at the results! Their ages are about the same—around about fifty. Burgess has always been buoyant, hopeful, happy; Adams has always been cheerless, hopeless, despondent. As young fellows both tried country journalism—and failed. Burgess didn't seem to mind it; Adams couldn't smile, he could only mourn and groan over what had happened and torture himself with vain regrets for not having done so and so instead of so and so—*then* he would have succeeded. They tried the law—and failed. Burgess remained happy—because he couldn't help it. Adams was wretched—because he couldn't help it. From that day to this, those two men have gone on trying things and failing: Burgess has come out happy and cheerful every time; Adams the reverse. And we do absolutely know that these men's inborn temperaments have remained unchanged through all the vicissitudes of their material affairs. Let us see how it is with their immaterials. Both have been zealous Democrats; both have been zealous Republicans; both have been zealous Mugwumps. Burgess has always found happiness and Adams unhappiness in these several political beliefs and in their migrations out of them. Both of these men have been Presbyterians, Universalists, Methodists, Catholics—then Presbyterians again, then Methodists again. Burgess has always found rest in these excursions, and Adams unrest. They are trying Christian Science, now, with the customary result, the inevitable result. No political or religious belief can make Burgess unhappy or the other man happy. I assure you it is purely a matter of temperament. Beliefs are *acquirements*, temperaments are *born*, beliefs are subject to change, nothing whatever can change temperament.

    Y. M. You have instanced extreme temperaments.

    O. M. Yes. The half-dozen others are modifications of the extremes. But the law is the same. Where the temperament is two-thirds happy, or two-thirds unhappy, no political or religious beliefs can change the proportions. The vast majority of temperaments are pretty equally balanced; the intensities are absent, and this enables a nation to learn to accommodate itself to its political and religious circumstances and like them, be satisfied with them, at last prefer them. Nations do not *think*, they only *feel*. They get their feelings at second hand through their temperaments, not their brains. A nation can be brought—by force of circumstances, not argument—to reconcile itself to *any kind of government or religion that can be devised;* in time it will fit itself to the required conditions; later, it will prefer them and will fiercely fight for them. As instances, you have all history: the Greeks, the Romans, the Persians, the Egyptians, the Russians, the Germans, the French, the English, the Spaniards, the Americans, the South Americans, the Japanese, the Chinese, the Hindoos, the Turks —a thousand wild and tame religions, every kind of government that can be thought of, from tiger to house-cat, each nation *knowing* it has the only true religion and the only sane system of government, each despising all the others, each an ass and not suspecting it, each proud of its fancied supremacy, each perfectly sure it is the pet of God, each with undoubting confidence summoning Him to take command in time of war, each surprised when He goes over to the enemy, but by habit able to excuse it and resume compliments—in a word, the whole human race content, always content, persistently content, indestructibly content, happy, thankful, proud, *no matter what its religion is, nor whether its master be tiger or house-cat.* Am I stating facts? You know I am. Is the human race cheerful? You know it is. Considering what it can stand, and be happy, you do me too much honor when you think that *I* can place before it a system of plain cold facts that can take the cheerfulness out of it. Nothing can do that. Everything has been tried. Without success. I beg you not to be troubled.

1906

William Dean Howells

Is it true that the sun of a man's mentality touches noon at forty and then begins to wane toward setting? Doctor Osler is charged with saying so. Maybe he said it, maybe he didn't; I don't know which it is. But if he said it, I can point him to a case which proves his rule. Proves it by being an exception to it. To this place I nominate Mr. Howells.

I read his *Venetian Days* about forty years ago. I compare it with his paper on Machiavelli in a late number of *Harper*, and I cannot find that his English has suffered any impairment. For forty years his English has been to me a continual delight and astonishment. In the sustained exhibition of certain great qualities—clearness, compression, verbal exactness, and unforced and seemingly unconscious felicity of phrasing—he is, in my belief, without his peer in the English-writing world. *Sustained.* I intrench myself behind that protecting word. There are others who exhibit those great qualities as greatly as does he, but only by intervaled distributions of rich moonlight, with stretches of veiled and dimmer landscape between; whereas Howells's moon sails cloudless skies all night and all the nights.

In the matter of verbal exactness Mr. Howells has no superior, I suppose. He seems to be almost always able to find that elusive and shifty grain of gold, the *right word*. Others have to put up with approximations, more or less frequently; he has better luck. To me, the others are miners working with the gold-pan—of necessity some of the gold washes over and escapes; whereas, in my fancy, he is quicksilver raiding down a riffle—no grain of the metal stands much chance of eluding him. A powerful agent is the right word: it lights the reader's way and makes it plain; a close approximation to it will answer, and much traveling is done in a well-enough fashion by its help, but we do not welcome it and applaud it and rejoice in it as we do when *the* right one blazes out on us. Whenever we come upon one of those intensely right words in a book or a newspaper the resulting effect is physical as well as spiritual, and electrically prompt: it tingles exquisitely around through the walls of the mouth and tastes as tart and crisp and good as the autumn-butter that creams the sumac-berry. One has no time to examine the word and vote upon its rank and standing, the automatic recognition of its supremacy is so immediate. There is a plenty of acceptable literature which deals largely in approximations, but it may be likened to a fine landscape seen through the rain; the right word would dismiss the rain, then you would see it better. It doesn't rain when Howells is at work.

And where does he get the easy and effortless flow of his speech? and its cadenced and undulating rhythm? and its architectural felicities of construction, its graces of expression, its pemmican quality of compression, and all that? Born to him, no doubt. All in shining good order in the beginning, all extraordinary; and all just as shining, just as extraordinary to-day, after forty years of diligent wear and tear and use. He passed his fortieth year long and long ago; but I think his English of to-day—his perfect English, I wish to say—can throw down the glove before his English of that antique time and not be afraid.

I will go back to the paper on Machiavelli now, and ask the reader to examine this passage from it which I append. I do not mean examine it in a bird's-eye way; I mean search it, study it. And, of course, read it aloud. I may be wrong, still it is my conviction that one cannot get out of finely wrought literature all that is in it by reading it mutely:

Mr. Dyer is rather of the opinion, first luminously suggested by Macaulay, that Machiavelli was in earnest, but must not be judged as a political moralist of our time and race would be judged. He thinks that Machiavelli was in earnest, as none but an idealist can be, and he is the first to imagine him an idealist immersed in realities, who involuntarily transmutes the events under his eye into something like the visionary issues of reverie. The Machiavelli whom he depicts does not cease to be politically a republican and socially a just man because he holds up an atrocious despot like Caesar Borgia as a mirror for rulers. What Machiavelli beheld round him in Italy was a civic disorder in which there was oppression without statecraft, and revolt without patriotism. When a miscreant like Borgia appeared upon the scene and reduced both tyrants and rebels to an apparent quiescence, he might very well seem to such a dreamer the savior of society whom a certain sort of dreamers are always looking for. Machiavelli was no less honest when he honored the diabolical force of Caesar Borgia than Carlyle was when at different times he extolled the strong man who destroys liberty in creating order. But Carlyle has only just ceased to be mistaken for a reformer, while it is still Machiavelli's hard fate to be so trammeled in his material that his name stands for whatever is most malevolent and perfidious in human nature.

You see how easy and flowing it is; how unvexed by ruggednesses, clumsinesses, broken meters; how simple and—so far as you or I can make out—unstudied; how clear, how limpid, how understandable, how confused by cross-currents, eddies, undertows; how seemingly unadorned, yet is all adornment, like the lily-of-the-valley; and how compressed, how compact, without a complacency-signal hung out anywhere to call attention to it.

There are twenty-three lines in the quoted passage. After reading it several times aloud, one perceives that a good deal of matter is crowded into that small space. I think it is a model of compactness. When I take its materials apart and work them over and put them together in my way, I find I cannot crowd the result back into the same hole, there not being room enough. I find it a case of a woman packing a man's trunk: he can get the things out, but he can't ever get them back again.

The proffered paragraph is a just and fair sample; the rest of the article is as compact as it is; there are no waste words. The sample is just in other ways: limpid, fluent, graceful, and rhythmical as it is, it holds no superiority in these respects over the rest of the essay. Also, the choice phrasing noticeable in the sample is not lonely; there is a plenty of its kin distributed through the other paragraphs. This is claiming much when that kin must face the challenge of a phrase like the one in the middle sentence: "an idealist immersed in realities who involuntarily transmutes the events under his eye into something like the visionary issues of reverie." With a hundred words to do it with, the literary artisan could catch that airy thought and tie it down and reduce it to a concrete condition, visible, substantial, understandable and all right, like a cabbage; but the artist does it with twenty, and the result is a flower.

The quoted phrase, like a thousand others that have come from the same source, has the quality of certain scraps of verse which take hold of us and stay in our memories, we do not understand why, at first: all the words being the right words, none of them is conspicuous, and so they all seem inconspicuous, therefore we wonder what it is about them that makes their message take hold.

> The mossy marbles rest
> On the lips that he has prest
> 　　In their bloom,
> And the names he loved to hear
> Have been carved for many a year
> 　　On the tomb.

It is like a dreamy strain of moving music, with no sharp notes in it. The words are all "right" words, and all the same size. We do not notice it at first. We get the effect, it goes straight home to us, but we do not know why. It is when the right words are conspicuous that they thunder:

The glory that was Greece and the grandeur that was Rome!

When I go back from Howells old to Howells young I find him arranging and clustering English words well, but not any better than now. He is not more felicitous in concreting abstractions now than he was in translating, then, the visions of the eyes of flesh into words that reproduced their forms and colors:

In Venetian streets they give the fallen snow no rest. It is at once shoveled into the canals by hundreds of half-naked *facchini;* and now in St. Mark's Place the music of innumerable shovels smote upon my ear; and I saw the shivering legion of poverty as it engaged the elements in a struggle for the possession of the Piazza. But the snow continued to fall, and through the twilight of the descending flakes all this toil and encounter looked like that weary kind of effort in dreams, when the most determined industry seems only to renew the task. The lofty crest of the bell-tower was hidden in the folds of falling snow, and I could no longer see the golden angel upon its summit. But looked at across the Piazza, the beautiful outline of St. Mark's Church was perfectly penciled in the air, and the shifting threads of the snowfall were woven into a spell of novel enchantment around the structure that always seemed to me too exquisite in its fantastic loveliness to be anything but the creation of magic. The tender snow had compassionated the beautiful edifice for all the wrongs of time, and so hid the stains and ugliness of decay that it looked as if just from the hand of the builder—or, better said, just from the brain of the architect. There was marvelous freshness in the colors of the mosaics in the great arches of the façade, and all that gracious harmony into which the temple rises, of marble scrolls and leafy exuberance airily supporting the statues of the saints, was a hundred times etherealized by the purity and whiteness of the drifting flakes. The snow lay lightly on the golden globes that tremble like peacock-crests above the vast domes, and plumed them with softest white; it robed the saints in ermine; and it danced over all its work, as if exulting in its beauty—beauty which filled me with subtle, selfish yearning to keep such evanescent loveliness for the little-while-longer of my whole life, and with despair to think that even the poor lifeless shadow of it could never be fairly reflected in picture or poem.

Through the wavering snowfall, the Saint Theodore upon one of the

granite pillars of the Piazzetta did not show so grim as his wont is, and
the winged lion on the other might have been a winged lamb, so gentle
and mild he looked by the tender light of the storm. The towers of the
island churches loomed faint and far away in the dimness; the sailors in
the rigging of the ships that lay in the Basin wrought like phantoms
among the shrouds; the gondolas stole in and out of the opaque distance
more noiselessly and dreamily than ever; and a silence, almost palpable,
lay upon the mutest city in the world.

The spirit of Venice is there: of a city where Age and Decay, fagged
with distributing damage and repulsiveness among the other cities of
the planet in accordance with the policy and business of their profession, come for rest and play between seasons, and treat themselves
to the luxury and relaxation of sinking the shop and inventing and
squandering charms all about, instead of abolishing such as they find,
as is their habit when not on vacation.

In the working season they do business in Boston sometimes, and a
character in *The Undiscovered Country* takes accurate note of pathetic
effects wrought by them upon the aspects of a street of once dignified
and elegant homes whose occupants have moved away and left them
a prey to neglect and gradual ruin and progressive degradation; a
descent which reaches bottom at last, when the street becomes a roost
for humble professionals of the faith-cure and fortune-telling sort.

What a queer, melancholy house, what a queer, melancholy street! I
don't think I was ever in a street before where quite so many professional
ladies, with English surnames, preferred Madam to Mrs. on their door-
plates. And the poor old place has such a desperately conscious air of going
to the deuce. Every house seems to wince as you go by, and button itself
up to the chin for fear you should find out it had no shirt on—so to speak.
I don't know what's the reason, but these material tokens of a social decay
afflict me terribly: a tipsy woman isn't dreadfuler than a haggard old house,
that's once been a home, in a street like this.

Mr. Howells's pictures are not mere stiff, hard, accurate photographs; they are photographs with feeling in them, and sentiment,
photographs taken in a dream, one might say.

As concerns his humor, I will not try to say anything, yet I would
try, if I had the words that might approximately reach up to its high
place. I do not think any one else can play with humorous fancies so
gracefully and delicately and deliciously as he does, nor has so many
to play with, nor can come so near making them look as if they were
doing the playing themselves and he was not aware that they were
at it. For they are unobtrusive, and quiet in their ways, and well

conducted. His is a humor which flows softly all around about and over and through the mesh of the page, pervasive, refreshing, health-giving, and makes no more show and no more noise than does the circulation of the blood.

There is another thing which is contentingly noticeable in Mr. Howells's books. That is his "stage directions"—those artifices which authors employ to throw a kind of human naturalness around a scene and a conversation, and help the reader to see the one and get at meanings in the other which might not be perceived if intrusted unexplained to the bare words of the talk. Some authors overdo the stage directions, they elaborate them quite beyond necessity; they spend so much time and take up so much room in telling us how a person said a thing and how he looked and acted when he said it that we get tired and vexed and wish he hadn't said it at all. Other authors' directions are brief enough, but it is seldom that the brevity contains either wit or information. Writers of this school go in rags, in the matter of stage directions; the majority of them have nothing in stock but a cigar, a laugh, a blush, and a bursting into tears. In their poverty they work these sorry things to the bone. They say:

". . . replied Alfred, flipping the ash from his cigar." (This explains nothing; it only wastes space.)

". . . responded Richard, with a laugh." (There was nothing to laugh about; there never is. The writer puts it in from habit—automatically; he is paying no attention to his work, or he would see that there is nothing to laugh at; often, when a remark is unusually and poignantly flat and silly, he tries to deceive the reader by enlarging the stage direction and making Richard break into "frenzies of uncontrollable laughter." This makes the reader sad.)

". . . murmured Gladys, blushing." (This poor old shop-worn blush is a tiresome thing. We get so we would rather Gladys would fall out of the book and break her neck than do it again. She is always doing it, and usually irrelevantly. Whenever it is her turn to murmur she hangs out her blush; it is the only thing she's got. In a little while we hate her, just as we do Richard.)

". . . repeated Evelyn, bursting into tears." (This kind keep a book damp all the time. They can't say a thing without crying. They cry so much about nothing that by and by when they have something to cry *about* they have gone dry; they sob, and fetch nothing; we are not moved. We are only glad.)

They gravel me, these stale and overworked stage directions, these carbon films that got burnt out long ago and cannot now carry any faintest thread of light. It would be well if they could be relieved from duty and flung out in the literary back yard to rot and disappear along with the discarded and forgotten "steeds" and "halidomes" and similar stage-properties once so dear to our grandfathers. But I am friendly to Mr. Howells's stage directions; more friendly to them than to any one else's, I think. They are done with a competent and discriminating art, and are faithful to the requirements of a stage direction's proper and lawful office, which is to inform. Sometimes they convey a scene and its conditions so well that I believe I could see the scene and get the spirit and meaning of the accompanying dialogue if some one would read merely the stage directions to me and leave out the talk. For instance, a scene like this, from *The Undiscovered Country:*

". . . and she laid her arms with a beseeching gesture on her father's shoulder."

". . . she answered, following his gesture with a glance."

". . . she said, laughing nervously."

". . . she asked, turning swiftly upon him that strange, searching glance."

". . . she answered, vaguely."

". . . she reluctantly admitted."

". . . but her voice died wearily away, and she stood looking into his face with puzzled entreaty."

Mr. Howells does not repeat his forms, and does not need to; he can invent fresh ones without limit. It is mainly the repetition over and over again, by the third-rates, of worn and commonplace and juiceless forms that makes their novels such a weariness and vexation to us, I think. We do not mind one or two deliveries of their wares, but as we turn the pages over and keep on meeting them we presently get tired of them and wish they would do other things for a change:

". . . replied Alfred, flipping the ash from his cigar."

". . . responded Richard, with a laugh."

". . . murmured Gladys, blushing."

". . . repeated Evelyn, bursting into tears."

". . . replied the Earl, flipping the ash from his cigar."

". . . responded the undertaker, with a laugh."

". . . murmured the chambermaid, blushing."

". . . repeated Evelyn, bursting into tears."

". . . replied the conductor, flipping the ash from his cigar."

". . . responded Arkwright, with a laugh."

". . . murmured the chief of police, blushing."

". . . repeated the house-cat, bursting into tears." And so on and so on; till at last it ceases to excite. I always notice stage directions, because they fret me and keep me trying to get out of their way, just as the automobiles do. At first; then by and by they become monotonous and I get run over.

Mr. Howells has done much work, and the spirit of it is as beautiful as the make of it. I have held him in admiration and affection so many years that I know by the number of those years that he is old now; but his heart isn't, nor his pen: and years do not count. Let him have plenty of them: there is profit in them for us.

1906

Is Shakespeare Dead?

(FROM MY AUTOBIOGRAPHY)[1]

I

Scattered here and there through the stacks of unpublished manuscript which constitute this formidable Autobiography and Diary of mine, certain chapters will in some distant future be found which deal with "Claimants"—claimants historically notorious: Satan, Claimant; the Golden Calf, Claimant; the Veiled Prophet of Khorassan, Claimant; Louis XVII., Claimant; William Shakespeare, Claimant; Arthur Orton, Claimant; Mary Baker G. Eddy, Claimant—and the rest of them. Eminent Claimants, successful Claimants, defeated Claimants, royal Claimants, pleb Claimants, showy Claimants, shabby Claimants, revered Claimants, despised Claimants, twinkle star-like here and there and yonder through the mists of history and legend and tradition—and, oh, all the darling tribe are clothed in mystery and romance, and we read about them with deep interest and discuss them with loving sympathy or with rancorous resentment, according

[1] Here again, as in "The First Writing-Machines," Clemens announces the birthplace of one of his essays. "Is Shakespeare Dead?" obviously does not belong in his autobiography, unless the word "autobiography" is stretched entirely out of recognizable shape. Although much of his autobiography had to wait for posthumous publication, he saw the present essay through the press the year before his death.—C.N.

to which side we hitch ourselves to. It has always been so with the human race. There was never a Claimant that couldn't get a hearing, nor one that couldn't accumulate a rapturous following, no matter how flimsy and apparently unauthentic his claim might be. Arthur Orton's claim that he was the lost Tichborne baronet come to life again was as flimsy as Mrs. Eddy's that she wrote *Science and Health* from the direct dictation of the Deity; yet in England near forty years ago Orton had a huge army of devotees and incorrigible adherents, many of whom remained stubbornly unconvinced after their fat god had been proven an impostor and jailed as a perjurer, and to-day Mrs. Eddy's following is not only immense, but is daily augmenting in numbers and enthusiasm. Orton had many fine and educated minds among his adherents, Mrs. Eddy has had the like among hers from the beginning. Her Church is as well equipped in those particulars as is any other Church. Claimants can always count upon a following, it doesn't matter who they are, nor what they claim, nor whether they come with documents or without. It was always so. Down out of the long-vanished past, across the abyss of the ages, if you listen, you can still hear the believing multitudes shouting for Perkin Warbeck and Lambert Simnel.

A friend has sent me a new book, from England—*The Shakespeare Problem Restated*—well restated and closely reasoned; and my fifty years' interest in that matter—asleep for the last three years—is excited once more. It is an interest which was born of Delia Bacon's book—away back in that ancient day—1857, or maybe 1856. About a year later my pilot-master, Bixby, transferred me from his own steamboat to the *Pennsylvania,* and placed me under the orders and instructions of George Ealer—dead now, these many, many years. I steered for him a good many months—as was the humble duty of the pilot-apprentice: stood a daylight watch and spun the wheel under the severe superintendence and correction of the master. He was a prime chess-player and an idolater of Shakespeare. He would play chess with anybody; even with me, and it cost his official dignity something to do that. Also—quite uninvited—he would read Shakespeare to me; not just casually, but by the hour, when it was his watch and I was steering. He read well, but not profitably for me, because he constantly injected commands into the text. That broke it all up, mixed it all up, tangled it all up—to that degree, in fact, that if we were in a risky and difficult piece of river an ignorant person couldn't have told, sometimes, which observations were Shakespeare's and which were Ealer's. For instance:

What man dare, I dare!

Approach thou *what* are you laying in the leads for? what a hell of an idea! like the rugged ease her off a little, ease her off! rugged Russian bear, the armed rhinoceros or the *there* she goes! meet her, meet her! didn't you *know* she'd smell the reef if you crowded it like that? Hyrcan tiger; take any shape but that and my firm nerves she'll be in the *woods* the first you know! stop the starboard! come ahead strong on the larboard! back the starboard! . . . *Now* then, you're all right; come ahead on the starboard; straighten up and go 'long, never tremble: or be alive again, and dare me to the desert *damnation* can't you keep away from that greasy water? pull her down! snatch her! snatch her baldheaded! with thy sword; if trembling I inhabit then, lay in the leads!—no, only the starboard one, leave the other alone, protest me the baby of a girl. Hence horrible shadow! eight bells—that watchman's asleep again, I reckon, go down and call Brown yourself, unreal mockery, hence!

He certainly was a good reader, and splendidly thrilling and stormy and tragic, but it was a damage to me, because I have never since been able to read Shakespeare in a calm and sane way. I cannot rid it of his explosive interlardings, they break in everywhere with their irrelevant, "What in hell are you up to *now!* pull her down! more! *more!*—there now, steady as you go," and the other disorganizing interruptions that were always leaping from his mouth. When I read Shakespeare now I can hear them as plainly as I did in that long-departed time—fifty-one years ago. I never regarded Ealer's readings as educational. Indeed, they were a detriment to me.

His contributions to the text seldom improved it, but barring that detail he was a good reader; I can say that much for him. He did not use the book, and did not need to; he knew his Shakespeare as well as Euclid ever knew his multiplication table.

Did he have something to say—this Shakespeare-adoring Mississippi pilot—anent Delia Bacon's book?

Yes. And he said it; said it all the time, for months—in the morning watch, the middle watch, and dog watch; and probably kept it going in his sleep. He bought the literature of the dispute as fast as it appeared, and we discussed it all through thirteen hundred miles of river four times traversed in every thirty-five days—the time required by that swift boat to achieve two round trips. We discussed, and discussed, and discussed, and disputed and disputed and disputed; at any rate, *he* did, and I got in a word now and then when he slipped a cog and there was a vacancy. He did his arguing with heat, with energy, with violence; and I did mine with the reserve and moderation of a subordinate who does not like to be flung out of a pilot-house that is perched forty feet above the water. He was fiercely loyal to Shakespeare and cordially scornful of Bacon and of all the pretensions of the Baconians. So was I—at first. And at first he was glad that that was my attitude. There were even indications that he admired it; indications dimmed, it is true, by the distance that lay between the lofty boss-pilotical altitude and my lowly one, yet perceptible to me; perceptible, and translatable into a compliment—compliment coming down from above the snow-line and not well thawed in the transit, and not likely to set anything afire, not even a cub-pilot's self-conceit; still a detectable compliment, and precious.

Naturally it flattered me into being more loyal to Shakespeare—if possible—than I was before, and more prejudiced against Bacon—if possible—than I was before. And so we discussed and discussed, both on the same side, and were happy. For a while. Only for a while. Only for a very little while, a very, very, very little while. Then the atmosphere began to change; began to cool off.

A brighter person would have seen what the trouble was, earlier than I did, perhaps, but I saw it early enough for all practical purposes. You see, he was of an argumentative disposition. Therefore it took him but a little time to get tired of arguing with a person who agreed with everything he said and consequently never furnished him a provocative to flare up and show what he could do when it came to clear, cold, hard, rose-cut, hundred-faceted, diamond-flashing *reasoning*. That was his name for it. It has been applied since, with complacency, as many as several times, in the Bacon-Shakespeare scuffle. On the Shakespeare side.

Then the thing happened which has happened to more persons than to me when principle and personal interest found themselves in opposition to each other and a choice had to be made: I let principle go, and went over to the other side. Not the entire way, but far enough to answer the requirements of the case. That is to say, I took this attitude—to wit, I only *believed* Bacon wrote Shakespeare, whereas I *knew* Shakespeare didn't. Ealer was satisfied with that, and the war broke loose. Study, practice, experience in handling my end of the matter presently enabled me to take any new position almost seriously; a little bit later, utterly seriously; a little later still, lovingly, gratefully, devotedly; finally: fiercely, rabidly, uncompromisingly. After that I was welded to my faith, I was theoretically ready to die for it, and I looked down with compassion not unmixed with scorn upon everybody else's faith that didn't tally with mine. That faith, imposed upon me by self-interest in that ancient day, remains my faith to-day, and in it I find comfort, solace, peace, and never-failing joy. You see how curiously theological it is. The "rice Christian" of the Orient goes through the very same steps, when he is after rice and the missionary is after *him;* he goes for rice, and remains to worship.

Ealer did a lot of our "reasoning"—not to say substantially all of it. The slaves of his cult have a passion for calling it by that large name. We others do not call our inductions and deductions and re-ductions by any name at all. They show for themselves what they are, and we can with tranquil confidence leave the world to ennoble them with a title of its own choosing.

Now and then when Ealer had to stop to cough, I pulled my induction-talents together and hove the controversial lead myself: always getting eight feet, eight and a half, often nine, sometimes even quarter-less-twain—as *I* believed; but always "no bottom," as *he* said.

I got the best of him only once. I prepared myself. I wrote out a passage from Shakespeare—it may have been the very one I quoted awhile ago, I don't remember—and riddled it with his wild steamboat-ful interlardings. When an unrisky opportunity offered, one lovely sum-mer day, when we had sounded and buoyed a tangled patch of crossings known as Hell's Half Acre, and were aboard again and he had sneaked the *Pennsylvania* triumphantly through it without once scraping sand, and the *A. T. Lacey* had followed in our wake and got stuck, and he was feeling good, I showed it to him. It amused him. I asked him to fire it off—*read* it; read it, I diplomatically added, as only *he* could read dramatic poetry. The compliment touched him where he lived. He did read it; read it with surpassing fire and spirit; read it as it will never be read again; for *he* knew how to put the right music into those thunderous interlardings and make them seem a part of the text, make them sound as if they were bursting from Shakespeare's own soul, each one of them a golden inspiration and not to be left out without damage to the massed and magnificent whole.

I waited a week, to let the incident fade; waited longer; waited until he brought up for reasonings and vituperation my pet position, my pet argument, the one which I was fondest of, the one which I prized far above all others in my ammunition-wagon—to wit, that Shakespeare couldn't have written Shakespeare's works, for the reason that the man who wrote them was limitlessly familiar with the laws, and the law-courts, and law-proceedings, and lawyer-talk, and lawyer-ways—and if Shakespeare was possessed of the infinitely divided star-dust that constituted this vast wealth, *how* did he get it, and *where*, and *when?*

"From books."

From books! That was always the idea. I answered as my read-ings of the champions of my side of the great controversy had taught me to answer: that a man can't handle glibly and easily and com-fortably and successfully the argot of a trade at which he has not personally served. He will make mistakes; he will not, and cannot, get the trade-phrasings precisely and exactly right; and the mo-ment he departs, by even a shade, from a common trade-form, the reader who has served that trade will know the writer *hasn't*. Ealer would not be convinced; he said a man could learn how to correctly handle the subtleties and mysteries and free-masonries of *any* trade by careful reading and studying. But when I got him to read again the passage from Shakespeare with the interlardings, he perceived, himself, that books couldn't teach a student a bewildering multitude of pilot-phrases so thoroughly and perfectly that he could talk them off in book and play or conversation and make no mistake that a pilot would not immediately discover. It was a triumph for me. He was silent awhile, and I knew what was happening—he was losing his temper. And I knew he would presently close the session with the same old argument that was always his stay and his support in time of need; the same old argument, the one I couldn't answer, because I dasn't—the argument that I was an ass, and better shut up. He delivered it, and I obeyed.

Oh dear, how long ago it was—how pathetically long ago! And here am I, old, forsaken, forlorn, and alone, arranging to get that argument out of somebody again.

When a man has a passion for Shakespeare, it goes without saying that he keeps company with other standard authors. Ealer always had several high-class books in the pilot-house, and he read the same ones over and over again, and did not care to change to newer and fresher ones. He played well on the flute, and greatly enjoyed hearing himself play. So did I. He had a notion that a flute would keep its health better if you took it apart when it was not standing a watch; and so, when it was not on duty it took its rest, disjointed, on the compass-shelf under the breastboard. When the *Pennsylvania* blew up and became a drifting rack-heap freighted with wounded and dying poor souls (my young brother Henry among them), pilot Brown had the watch below, and was probably asleep and never knew what killed him; but Ealer escaped unhurt. He and his pilot-house were shot up into the air; then they fell, and Ealer sank through the ragged cavern where the hurricane-deck and the boiler-deck had been, and landed in a nest of ruins on the main deck, on top of one of the unexploded boilers, where he lay prone in a fog of scald and deadly steam. But not for long. He did not lose his head—long familiarity with danger had taught him to keep it, in any and all emergencies. He held his coat-lapels to his nose with one hand, to keep out the steam, and scrabbled around with the other till he found the joints of his flute, then he took measures to save himself alive, and was successful. I was not on board. I had been put ashore in New Orleans by Captain Klinefelter. The reason—however, I have told all about it in the book called *Old Times on the Mississippi,* and it isn't important, anyway, it is so long ago.

II

When I was a Sunday-school scholar, something more than sixty years ago, I became interested in Satan, and wanted to find out all I could about him. I began to ask questions, but my class-teacher, Mr. Barclay, the stone-mason, was reluctant about answering them, it seemed to me. I was anxious to be praised for turning my thoughts to serious subjects when there wasn't another boy in the village who could be hired to do such a thing. I was greatly interested in the incident of Eve and the serpent, and thought Eve's calmness was perfectly noble. I asked Mr. Barclay if he had ever heard of another woman who, being approached by a serpent, would not excuse herself and break for the nearest timber. He did not answer my question, but rebuked me for inquiring into matters above my age and comprehension. I will say for Mr. Barclay that he was willing to tell me the facts of Satan's history, but he stopped there: he wouldn't allow any discussion of them.

In the course of time we exhausted the facts. There were only five or six of them; you could set them all down on a visiting-card. I was disappointed. I had been meditating a biography, and was grieved to find that there were no materials. I said as much, with the tears running down. Mr. Barclay's sympathy and compassion were aroused, for he was a most kind and gentle-spirited man, and he patted me on the head and cheered me up by saying there was a whole vast ocean of materials! I can still feel the happy thrill which these blessed words shot through me.

Then he began to bail out that ocean's riches for my encouragement and joy. Like this: it was "conjectured"—though not established—that Satan was originally an angel in heaven; that he fell; that he rebelled, and brought on a war; that he was defeated, and banished to perdition. Also, "we have reason to believe" that later he did so and so; that "we are warranted in supposing" that at a subsequent time he traveled extensively, seeking whom he might devour; that a couple of centuries afterward, "as tradition instructs us," he took up the cruel trade of tempting people to their ruin, with vast and fearful results; that by and by, "as the probabilities seem to indicate," he may have done certain things, he might have done certain other things, he must have done still other things.

And so on and so on. We set down the five known facts by themselves, on a piece of paper, and numbered it "page 1"; then on fifteen hundred other pieces of paper we set down the "conjectures," and "suppositions," and "maybes," and "perhapses," and "doubtlesses," and "rumors," and "guesses," and "probabilities," and "likelihoods," and "we are permitted to thinks," and "we are warranted in believings," and "might have beens," and "could have beens," and "must have beens," and "unquestionablys," and "without a shadow of doubts"—and behold!

Materials? Why, we had enough to build a biography of Shakespeare!

Yet he made me put away my pen; he would not let me write the history of Satan. Why? Because, as he said, he had suspicions—suspicions that my attitude in this matter was not reverent, and that a person must be reverent when writing about the sacred characters. He said any one who spoke flippantly of Satan would be frowned upon by the religious world and also be brought to account.

I assured him, in earnest and sincere words, that he had wholly misconceived my attitude; that I had the highest respect for Satan, and that my reverence for him equaled, and possibily even exceeded, that of any member of any church. I said it wounded me deeply to perceive by his words that he thought I would make fun of Satan, and deride him, laugh at him, scoff at him; whereas in truth I had never thought of such a thing, but had only a warm desire to make fun of those others and laugh at *them*. "What others?" "Why, the Supposers, the Perhapsers, the Might-Have-Beeners, the Could-Have-Beeners, the Must-Have-Beeners, the Without-a-Shadow-of-Doubters, the We-Are-Warranted-in-Believingers, and all that funny crop of solemn architects who have taken a good solid foundation of five indisputable and unimportant facts and built upon it a Conjectural Satan thirty miles high."

What did Mr. Barclay do then? Was he disarmed? Was he silenced? No. He was shocked. He was so shocked that he visibly shuddered. He said the Satanic Traditioners and Perhapsers and Conjecturers were *themselves* sacred! As sacred as their work. So sacred that whoso ventured to mock them or make fun of their work, could not afterward enter any respectable house, even by the back door.

How true were his words, and how wise! How fortunate it would have been for me if I had heeded them. But I was young, I was but seven years of age, and vain, foolish, and anxious to attract attention. I wrote the biography, and have never been in a respectable house since.

III

How curious and interesting is the parallel—as far as poverty of biographical details is concerned—between Satan and Shakespeare. It is wonderful, it is unique, it stands quite alone, there is nothing resembling it in history, nothing resembling it in romance, nothing approaching it even in tradition. How sublime is their position, and how over-topping, how sky-reaching, how supreme—the two Great Unknowns, the two Illustrious Conjecturabilities! They are the best-known unknown persons that have ever drawn breath upon the planet.

For the instruction of the ignorant I will make a list, now, of those details of Shakespeare's history which are *facts*—verified facts, established facts, undisputed facts.

FACTS

He was born on the 23d of April, 1564.

Of good farmer-class parents who could not read, could not write, could not sign their names.

At Stratford, a small back settlement which in that day was shabby and unclean, and densely illiterate. Of the nineteen important men charged with the government of the town, thirteen had to "make their mark" in attesting important documents, because they could not write their names.

Of the first eighteen years of his life *nothing* is known. They are a blank.

On the 27th of November (1582) William Shakespeare took out a license to marry Anne Whateley.

Next day William Shakespeare took out a license to marry Anne Hathaway. She was eight years his senior.

William Shakespeare married Anne Hathaway. In a hurry. By grace of a reluctantly granted dispensation there was but one publication of the banns.

Within six months the first child was born.

About two (blank) years followed, during which period *nothing at all happened to Shakespeare,* so far as anybody knows.

Then came twins—1585. February.

Two blank years follow.

Then—1587—he makes a ten-year visit to London, leaving the family behind.

Five blank years follow. During this period *nothing happened to him,* as far as anybody actually knows.

Then—1592—there is mention of him as an actor.

Next year—1593—his name appears in the official list of players.

Next year—1594—he played before the queen. A detail of no consequence: other obscurities did it every year of the forty-five of her reign. And remained obscure.

Three pretty full years follow. Full of play-acting. Then

In 1597 he bought New Place, Stratford.

Thirteen or fourteen busy years follow; years in which he accumulated money, and also reputation as actor and manager.

Meantime his name, liberally and variously spelt, had become associated with a number of great plays and poems, as (ostensibly) author of the same.

Some of these, in these years and later, were pirated, but he made no protest.

Then—1610-11—he returned to Stratford and settled down for good and all, and busied himself in lending money, trading in tithes, trading in land and houses; shirking a debt of forty-one shillings, borrowed by his wife during his long desertion of his family; suing debtors for shillings and coppers; being sued himself for shillings and coppers; and acting as confederate to a neighbor who tried to rob the town of its rights in a certain common, and did not succeed.

He lived five or six years—till 1616—in the joy of these elevated pursuits. Then he made a will, and signed each of its three pages with his name.

A thoroughgoing business man's will. It named in minute detail every item of property he owned in the world—houses, lands, sword, silver-gilt bowl, and so on—all the way down to his "second-best bed" and its furniture.

It carefully and calculatingly distributed his riches among the members of his family, overlooking no individual of it. Not even his wife: the wife he had been enabled to marry in a hurry by urgent grace of a special dispensation before he was nineteen; the wife whom he had left husbandless so many years; the wife who had had to borrow forty-one shillings in her need, and which the lender was never able to collect of the prosperous husband, but died at last with the money still lacking. No, even this wife was remembered in Shakespeare's will.

He left her that "second-best bed."

And *not another thing;* not even a penny to bless her lucky widowhood with.

It was eminently and conspicuously a business man's will, not a poet's.

It mentioned *not a single book.*

Books were much more precious than swords and silver-gilt bowls and second-best beds in those days, and when a departing person owned one he gave it a high place in his will.

The will mentioned *not a play, not a poem, not an unfinished literary work, not a scrap of manuscript of any kind.*

Many poets have died poor, but this is the only one in history that has died *this* poor; the others all left literary remains behind. Also a book. Maybe two.

If Shakespeare had owned a dog—but we need not go into that: we know he would have mentioned it in his will. If a good dog, Susanna would have got it; if an inferior one his wife would have got a dower interest in it. I wish he had had a dog, just so we could see how painstakingly he would have divided that dog among the family, in his careful business way.

He signed the will in three places.

In earlier years he signed two other official documents.

These five signatures still exist.

There are *no other specimens of his penmanship in existence.* Not a line.

Was he prejudiced against the art? His granddaughter, whom he loved, was eight years old when he died, yet she had had no teaching, he left no provision for her education, although he was rich, and in her mature womanhood she couldn't write and couldn't tell her husband's manuscript from anybody else's—she thought it was Shakespeare's.

When Shakespeare died in Stratford *it was not an event.* It made no more stir in England than the death of any other forgotten theater-actor would have made. Nobody came down from London; there were no lamenting poems, no eulogies, no national tears—there was merely silence, and nothing more. A striking contrast with what happened when Ben Jonson, and Francis Bacon, and Spenser, and Raleigh, and the other distinguished literary folk of Shakespeare's time passed from life! No praiseful voice was lifted for the lost Bard of Avon; even Ben Jonson waited seven years before he lifted his.

So far as anybody actually knows and can prove, Shakespeare of Stratford-on-Avon never wrote a play in his life.

So far as anybody knows and can prove, he never wrote a letter to anybody in his life.

So far as any one knows, he received only one letter during his life.

So far as any one *knows and can prove,* Shakespeare of Stratford wrote only one poem during his life. This one is authentic. He did write that one—a fact which stands undisputed; he wrote the whole of it; he wrote the whole of it out of his own head. He commanded that this work of art be engraved upon his tomb, and he was obeyed. There it abides to this day. This is it:

> Good friend for Iesus sake forbeare
> To digg the dust encloased heare:
> Blest be ye man yt spares thes stones
> And curst be he yt moves my bones.

In the list as above set down will be found *every positively known* fact of Shakespeare's life, lean and meager as the invoice is. Beyond these details we know *not a thing* about him. All the rest of his vast history, as furnished by the biographers, is built up, course upon course, of guesses, inferences, theories, conjectures—an Eiffel Tower of artificialities rising sky-high from a very flat and very thin foundation of inconsequential facts.

IV

CONJECTURES

The historians "suppose" that Shakespeare attended the Free School in Stratford from the time he was seven years old till he was thirteen. There is no *evidence* in existence that he ever went to school at all.

The historians "infer" that he got his Latin in that school—the school which they "suppose" he attended.

They "suppose" his father's declining fortunes made it necessary for him to leave the school they supposed he attended, and get to work and help support his parents and their ten children. But there is no evidence that he ever entered or returned from the school they suppose he attended.

They "suppose" he assisted his father in the butchering business; and that, being only a boy, he didn't have to do full-grown butchering, but only slaughtered calves. Also, that whenever he killed a calf he made a high-flown speech over it. This supposition rests upon the testimony of a man who wasn't there at the time; a man who got it from a man who could have been there, but did not say whether he was or not; and neither of them thought to mention it for decades, and decades, and decades, and two more decades after Shakespeare's death (until old age and mental decay had refreshed and vivified their memories). They hadn't two facts in stock about the long-dead distinguished citizen, but only just the one: he slaughtered calves and broke into oratory while he was at it. Curious. They had only one fact, yet the distinguished citizen had spent twenty-six years in that little town—just half his lifetime. However, rightly viewed, it was the most important fact, indeed almost the only important fact, of Shakespeare's life in Stratford. Rightly viewed. For experience is an author's most valuable asset; experience is the thing that puts the muscle and the breath and the warm blood into the book he writes. Rightly viewed, calf-butchering accounts for "Titus Andronicus," the only play—ain't it? —that the Stratford Shakespeare ever wrote; and yet it is the only one everybody tries to chouse him out of, the Baconians included.

The historians find themselves "justified in believing" that the young Shakespeare poached upon Sir Thomas Lucy's deer preserves and got haled before that magistrate for it. But there is no shred of respectworthy evidence that anything of the kind happened.

The historians, having argued the thing that *might* have happened

into the thing that *did* happen, found no trouble in turning Sir Thomas
Lucy into Mr. Justice Shallow. They have long ago convinced the
world—on surmise and without trustworthy evidence—that Shallow *is*
Sir Thomas.

The next addition to the young Shakespeare's Stratford history
comes easy. The historian builds it out of the surmised deer-stealing,
and the surmised trial before the magistrate, and the surmised venge-
ance-prompted satire upon the magistrate in the play: result, the young
Shakespeare was a wild, wild, wild, oh, *such* a wild young scamp,
and that gratuitous slander is established for all time! It is the very
way Professor Osborn and I built the colossal skeleton brontosaur that
stands fifty-seven feet long and sixteen feet high in the Natural History
Museum, the awe and admiration of all the world, the stateliest skeleton that exists on the planet. We had nine bones, and we built the
rest of him out of plaster of Paris. We ran short of plaster of Paris, or
we'd have built a brontosaur that could sit down beside the Stratford
Shakespeare and none but an expert could tell which was biggest or
contained the most plaster.

Shakespeare pronounced "Venus and Adonis" "the first heir of his invention," apparently implying that it was his first effort at literary composition. He should not have said it. It has been an embarrassment
to his historians these many, many years. They have to make him write
that graceful and polished and flawless and beautiful poem before he
escaped from Stratford and his family—1586 or '87—age, twenty-two,
or along there; because within the next five years he wrote five great
plays, and could not have found time to write another line.

It is sorely embarrassing. If he began to slaughter calves, and poach
deer, and rollick around, and learn English, at the earliest likely moment—say at thirteen, when he was supposably wrenched from that
school where he was supposably storing up Latin for future literary
use—he had his youthful hands full, and much more than full. He
must have had to put aside his Warwickshire dialect, which wouldn't
be understood in London, and study English very hard. Very hard
indeed; incredibly hard, almost, if the result of that labor was to be
the smooth and rounded and flexible and letter-perfect English of
the "Venus and Adonis" in the space of ten years; and at the same
time learn great and fine and unsurpassable literary *form.*

However, it is "conjectured" that he accomplished all this and more,
much more: learned law and its intricacies; and the complex procedure
of the law-courts; and all about soldiering, and sailoring, and the man-

ners and customs and ways of royal courts and aristocratic society; and likewise accumulated in his one head every kind of knowledge the learned then possessed, and every kind of humble knowledge possessed by the lowly and the ignorant; and added thereto a wider and more intimate knowledge of the world's great literatures, ancient and modern, than was possessed by any other man of his time—for he was going to make brilliant and easy and admiration-compelling use of these splendid treasures the moment he got to London. And according to the surmisers, that is what he did. Yes, although there was no one in Stratford able to teach him these things, and no library in the little village to dig them out of. His father could not read, and even the surmisers surmise that he did not keep a library.

It is surmised by the biographers that the young Shakespeare got his vast knowledge of the law and his familiar and accurate acquaintance with the manners and customs and shop-talk of lawyers through being for a time the *clerk of a Stratford court;* just as a bright lad like me, reared in a village on the banks of the Mississippi, might become perfect in knowledge of the Bering Strait whale-fishery and the shop-talk of the veteran exercises of that adventure-bristling trade through catching catfish with a "trot-line" Sundays. But the surmise is damaged by the fact that there is no evidence—and not even tradition—that the young Shakespeare was ever clerk of a lawcourt.

It is further surmised that the young Shakespeare accumulated his law-treasures in the first years of his sojourn in London, through "amusing himself" by learning book-law in his garret and by picking up lawyer-talk and the rest of it through loitering about the lawcourts and listening. But it is only surmise; there is no *evidence* that he ever did either of those things. They are merely a couple of chunks of plaster of Paris.

There is a legend that he got his bread and butter by holding horses in front of the London theaters, mornings and afternoons. Maybe he did. If he did, it seriously shortened his law-study hours and his recreation-time in the courts. In those very days he was writing great plays, and needed all the time he could get. The horse-holding legend ought to be strangled; it too formidably increases the historian's difficulty in accounting for the young Shakespeare's erudition—an erudition which he was acquiring, hunk by hunk and chunk by chunk, every day in those strenuous times, and emptying each day's catch into next day's imperishable drama.

He had to acquire a knowledge of war at the same time; and a knowledge of soldier-people and sailor-people and their ways and talk; also a knowledge of some foreign lands and their languages: for he was daily emptying fluent streams of these various knowledges, too, into his dramas. How did he acquire these rich assets?

In the usual way: by surmise. It is *surmised* that he traveled in Italy and Germany and around, and qualified himself to put their scenic and social aspects upon paper; that he perfected himself in French, Italian, and Spanish on the road; that he went in Leicester's expedition to the Low Countries, as soldier or sutler or something, for several months or years—or whatever length of time a surmiser needs in his business—and thus became familiar with soldiership and soldier-ways and soldier-talk and generalship and general-ways and general-talk, and seamanship and sailor-ways and sailor-talk.

Maybe he did all these things, but I would like to know who held the horses in the mean time; and who studied the books in the garret; and who frollicked in the law-courts for recreation. Also, who did the call-boying and the play-acting.

For he became a call-boy; and as early as '93 he became a "vagabond"—the law's ungentle term for an unlisted actor; and in '94 a "regular" and properly and officially listed member of that (in those days) lightly valued and not much respected profession.

Right soon thereafter he became a stockholder in two theaters, and manager of them. Thenceforward he was a busy and flourishing business man, and was raking in money with both hands for twenty years. Then in a noble frenzy of poetic inspiration he wrote his one poem— his only poem, his darling—and laid him down and died:

> Good friend for Iesus sake forbeare
> To digg the dust encloased heare:
> Blest be ye man yt spares thes stones
> And curst be he yt moves my bones.

He was probably dead when he wrote it. Still, this is only conjecture. We have only circumstantial evidence. Internal evidence.

Shall I set down the rest of the Conjectures which constitute the giant Biography of William Shakespeare? It would strain the Unabridged Dictionary to hold them. He is a brontosaur: nine bones and six hundred barrels of plaster of Paris.

V

"WE MAY ASSUME"

In the Assuming trade three separate and independent cults are transacting business. Two of these cults are known as the Shakespearites and the Baconians, and I am the other one—the Brontosaurian.

The Shakespearite knows that Shakespeare wrote Shakespeare's Works; the Baconian knows that Francis Bacon wrote them; the Brontosaurian doesn't really know which of them did it, but is quite composedly and contentedly sure that Shakespeare *didn't*, and strongly suspects that Bacon *did*. We all have to do a good deal of assuming, but I am fairly certain that in every case I can call to mind the Baconian assumers have come out ahead of the Shakespearites. Both parties handle the same materials, but the Baconians seem to me to get much more reasonable and rational and persuasive results out of them than is the case with the Shakespearites. The Shakespearite conducts his assuming upon a definite principle, an unchanging and immutable law: which is: 2 and 8 and 7 and 14, added together, make 165. I believe this to be an error. No matter, you cannot get a habit-sodden Shakespearite to cipher-up his materials upon any other basis. With the Baconian it is different. If you place before him the above figures and set him to adding them up, he will never in any case get more than 45 out of them, and in nine cases out of ten he will get just the proper 31.

Let me try to illustrate the two systems in a simple and homely way calculated to bring the idea within the grasp of the ignorant and unintelligent. We will suppose a case: take a lap-bred, house-fed, uneducated, inexperienced kitten; take a rugged old Tom that's scarred from stem to rudder-post with the memorials of strenuous experience, and is so cultured, so educated, so limitlessly erudite that one may say of him "all cat-knowledge is his province"; also, take a mouse. Lock the three up in a holeless, crackless, exitless prison-cell. Wait half an hour, then open the cell, introduce a Shakespearite and a Baconian, and let them cipher and assume. The mouse is missing: the question to be decided is, where it is? You can guess both verdicts beforehand. One verdict will say the kitten contains the mouse; the other will as certainly say the mouse is in the tom-cat.

The Shakespearite will Reason like this—(that is not my word, it is his). He will say the kitten *may have been* attending school when

nobody was noticing; therefore *we are warranted in assuming* that
it did so; also, it *could have been* training in a court-clerk's office when
no one was noticing; since that could have happened, *we are justified
in assuming* that it did happen; it *could have studied catology in a
garret* when no one was noticing—therefore it *did;* it *could have* attended cat-assizes on the shed-roof nights, for recreation, when no one
was noticing, and have harvested a knowledge of cat court-forms and
cat lawyer-talk in that way: it *could* have done it, therefore without
a doubt it *did;* it *could have* gone soldiering with a war-tribe when
no one was noticing, and learned soldier-wiles and soldier-ways, and
what to do with a mouse when opportunity offers; the plain inference,
therefore, is that that is what it *did.* Since all these manifold things
could have occurred, we have *every right to believe* they did occur.
These patiently and painstakingly accumulated vast acquirements and
competences needed but one thing more—opportunity—to convert
themselves into triumphant action. The opportunity came, we have the
result; *beyond shadow of question* the mouse is in the kitten.

It is proper to remark that when we of the three cults plant a *"We
think we may assume,"* we expect it, under careful watering and
fertilizing and tending, to grow up into a strong and hardy and
weather-defying *"there isn't a shadow of a doubt"* at last—and it usually happens.

We know what the Baconian's verdict would be: *"There is not a rag
of evidence that the kitten has had any training, any education, any
experience qualifying it for the present occasion, or is indeed equipped
for any achievement above lifting such unclaimed milk as comes its
way; but there is abundant evidence—unassailable proof, in fact—that
the other animal is equipped, to the last detail, with every qualification
necessary for the event. Without shadow of doubt the tom-cat contains
the mouse."*

VI

When Shakespeare died, in 1616, great literary productions attributed to him as author had been before the London world and in high
favor for twenty-four years. Yet his death was not an event. It made
no stir, it attracted no attention. Apparently his eminent literary contemporaries did not realize that a celebrated poet had passed from
their midst. Perhaps they knew a play-actor of minor rank had dis-

appeared, but did not regard him as the author of his Works. "We are justified in assuming" this.

His death was not even an event in the little town of Stratford. Does this mean that in Stratford he was not regarded as a celebrity of *any* kind?

"We are privileged to assume"—no, we are indeed *obliged* to assume —that such was the case. He had spent the first twenty-two or twenty-three years of his life there, and of course knew everybody and was known by everybody of that day in the town, including the dogs and the cats and the horses. He had spent the last five or six years of his life there, diligently trading in every big and little thing that had money in it; so we are compelled to assume that many of the folk there in those said latter days knew him personally, and the rest by sight and hearsay. But not as a *celebrity?* Apparently not. For everybody soon forgot to remember any contact with him or any incident connected with him. The dozens of townspeople, still alive, who had known of him or known about him in the first twenty-three years of his life were in the same unremembering condition: if they knew of any incident connected with that period of his life they didn't tell about it. Would they if they had been asked? It is most likely. Were they asked? It is pretty apparent that they were not. Why weren't they? It is a very plausible guess that nobody there or elsewhere was interested to know.

For seven years after Shakespeare's death nobody seems to have been interested in him. Then the quarto was published, and Ben Jonson awoke out of his long indifference and sang a song of praise and put it in the front of the book. Then silence fell *again.*

For sixty years. Then inquiries into Shakespeare's Stratford life began to be made, of Stratfordians. Of Stratfordians who had known Shakespeare or had seen him? No. Then of Stratfordians who had seen people who had known or seen people who had seen Shakespeare? No. Apparently the inquiries were only made of Stratfordians who were not Stratfordians of Shakespeare's day, but later comers; and what they had learned had come to them from persons who had not seen Shakespeare; and what they had learned was not claimed as *fact,* but only as legend—dim and fading and indefinite legend; legend of the calf-slaughtering rank, and not worth remembering either as history or fiction.

Has it ever happened before—or since—that a celebrated person who had spent exactly half of a fairly long life in the village where he was

born and reared, was able to slip out of this world and leave that
village voiceless and gossipless behind him—utterly voiceless, utterly
gossipless? And permanently so? I don't believe it has happened in
any case except Shakespeare's. And couldn't and wouldn't have happened in his case if he had been regarded as a celebrity at the time
of his death.

When I examine my own case—but let us do that, and see if it will
not be recognizable as exhibiting a condition of things quite likely to
result, most likely to result, indeed substantially *sure* to result in the
case of a celebrated person, a benefactor of the human race. Like me.

My parents brought me to the village of Hannibal, Missouri, on the
banks of the Mississippi, when I was two and a half years old. I entered school at five years of age, and drifted from one school to another in the village during nine and a half years. Then my father
died, leaving his family in exceedingly straitened circumstances;
wherefore my book-education came to a standstill forever, and I became a printer's apprentice, on board and clothes, and when the
clothes failed I got a hymn-book in place of them. This for summer
wear, probably. I lived in Hannibal fifteen and a half years, altogether, then ran away, according to the custom of persons who are intending to become celebrated. I never lived there afterward. Four
years later I became a "cub" on a Mississippi steamboat in the St.
Louis and New Orleans trade, and after a year and a half of hard
study and hard work the U.S. inspectors rigorously examined me
through a couple of long sittings and decided that I knew every inch
of the Mississippi—thirteen hundred miles—in the dark and in the day
—as well as a baby knows the way to its mother's paps day or night.
So they licensed me as a pilot—knighted me, so to speak—and I rose
up clothed with authority, a responsible servant of the United States
Government.

Now then. Shakespeare died young—he was only fifty-two. He had
lived in his native village twenty-six years, or about that. He died celebrated (if you believe everything you read in the books). Yet when he
died nobody there or elsewhere took any notice of it; and for sixty
years afterward no townsman remembered to say anything about him
or about his life in Stratford. When the inquirer came at last he got
but one fact—no, *legend*—and got that one at second hand, from a
person who had only heard it as a rumor and didn't claim copyright
in it as a production of his own. He couldn't, very well, for its date
antedated his own birth-date. But necessarily a number of persons

were still alive in Stratford who, in the days of their youth, had seen Shakespeare nearly every day in the last five years of his life, and they would have been able to tell that inquirer some first-hand things about him if he had in those last days been a celebrity and therefore a person of interest to the villagers. Why did not the inquirer hunt them up and interview them? Wasn't it worth while? Wasn't the matter of sufficient consequence? Had the inquirer an engagement to see a dog-fight and couldn't spare the time?

It all seems to mean that he never had any literary celebrity, there or elsewhere, and no considerable repute as actor and manager.

Now then, I am away along in life—my seventy-third year being already well behind me—yet *sixteen* of my Hannibal schoolmates are still alive to-day, and can tell—and do tell—inquirers dozens and dozens of incidents of their young lives and mine together; things that happened to us in the morning of life, in the blossom of our youth, in the good days, the dear days, "the days when we went gipsying, a long time ago." Most of them creditable to me, too. One child to whom I paid court when she was five years old and I eight still lives in Hannibal, and she visited me last summer, traversing the necessary ten or twelve hundred miles of railroad without damage to her patience or to her old-young vigor. Another little lassie to whom I paid attention in Hannibal when she was nine years old and I the same, is still alive—in London—and hale and hearty, just as I am. And on the few surviving steamboats—those lingering ghosts and remembrancers of great fleets that plied the big river in the beginning of my water-career—which is exactly as long ago as the whole invoice of the life-years of Shakespeare numbers—there are still findable two or three river-pilots who saw me do creditable things in those ancient days; and several white-headed engineers; and several roustabouts and mates; and several deck-hands who used to heave the lead for me and send up on the still night air the "Six—feet—*scant!*" that made me shudder, and the "M-a-r-k—*twain!*" that took the shudder away, and presently the darling "By the d-e-e-p—*four!*" that lifted me to heaven for joy.[2] They know about me, and can tell. And so do printers, from St. Louis to New York; and so do newspaper reporters, from Nevada to San Francisco. And so do the police. If Shakespeare had really been celebrated, like me, Stratford could have told things about him; and if my experience goes for anything, they'd have done it.

[2] Four fathoms—twenty-four feet.—M.T.

VII

If I had under my superintendence a controversy appointed to decide whether Shakespeare wrote Shakespeare or not, I believe I would
place before the debaters only the one question, *Was Shakespeare
ever a practising lawyer?* and leave everything else out.

It is maintained that the man who wrote the plays was not merely
myriad-minded, but also myriad-accomplished: that he not only knew
some thousands of things about human life in all its shades and grades,
and about the hundred arts and trades and crafts and professions
which men busy themselves in, but that he could *talk* about the men
and their grades and trades accurately, making no mistakes. Maybe
it is so, but have the experts spoken, or is it only Tom, Dick, and
Harry? Does the exhibit stand upon wide, and loose, and eloquent
generalizing—which is not evidence, and not proof—or upon details,
particulars, statistics, illustrations, demonstrations?

Experts of unchallengeable authority have testified definitely as to
only one of Shakespeare's multifarious craft-equipments, so far as my
recollections of Shakespeare-Bacon talk abide with me—his law-equip-
ment. I do not remember that Wellington or Napoleon ever examined
Shakespeare's battles and sieges and strategies, and then decided and
established for good and all that they were militarily flawless; I do not
remember that any Nelson, or Drake, or Cook ever examined his seamanship and said it showed profound and accurate familiarity with
that art; I don't remember that any king or prince or duke has ever
testified that Shakespeare was letter-perfect in his handling of royal
court-manners and the talk and manners of aristocracies; I don't remember that any illustrious Latinist or Grecian or Frenchman or
Spaniard or Italian has proclaimed him a past-master in those languages; I don't remember—well, I don't remember that there is *testimony*—great testimony—imposing testimony—unanswerable and unat-
tackable testimony as to any of Shakespeare's hundred specialties,
except one—the law.

Other things change, with time, and the student cannot trace back
with certainty the changes that various trades and their processes and
technicalities have undergone in the long stretch of a century or two
and find out what their processes and technicalities were in those
early days, but with the law it is different: it is mile-stoned and
documented all the way back, and the master of that wonderful trade,
that complex and intricate trade, that awe-compelling trade, has com-

petent ways of knowing whether Shakespeare-law is good law or not; and whether his law-court procedure is correct or not, and whether his legal shop-talk is the shop-talk of a veteran practitioner or only a machine-made counterfeit of it gathered from books and from occasional loiterings in Westminster.

Richard H. Dana served two years before the mast, and had every experience that falls to the lot of the sailor before the mast of our day. His sailor-talk flows from his pen with the sure touch and the ease and confidence of a person who has *lived* what he is talking about, not gathered it from books and random listenings. Hear him:

Having hove short, cast off the gaskets, and made the bunt of each sail fast by the jigger, with a man on each yard, at the word the whole canvas of the ship was loosed, and with the greatest rapidity possible everything was sheeted home and hoisted up, the anchor tripped and cat-headed, and the ship under headway.

Again:

The royal yards were all crossed at once, and royals and skysails set, and, as we had the wind free, the booms were run out, and all were aloft, active as cats, laying out on the yards and booms, reeving the studding-sail gear; and sail after sail the captain piled upon her, until she was covered with canvas, her sails looking like a great white cloud resting upon a black speck.

Once more. A race in the Pacific:

Our antagonist was in her best trim. Being clear of the point, the breeze became stiff, and the royal-masts bent under our sails, but we would not take them in until we saw three boys spring into the rigging of the *California;* then they were all furled at once, but with orders to our boys to stay aloft at the top-gallant mast-heads and loose them again at the word. It was my duty to furl the fore-royal; and while standing by to loose it again, I had a fine view of the scene. From where I stood, the two vessels seemed nothing but spars and sails, while their narrow decks, far below, slanting over by the force of the wind aloft, appeared hardly capable of supporting the great fabrics raised upon them. The *California* was to windward of us, and had every advantage; yet, while the breeze was stiff we held our own. As soon as it began to slacken she ranged a little ahead, and the order was given to loose the royals. In an instant the gaskets were off and the bunt dropped. "Sheet home the fore-royal!"—"Weather sheet's home!"—"Lee sheet's home!"—"Hoist away, sir!" is bawled from aloft. "Overhaul your clewlines!" shouts the mate. "Aye-aye, sir, all clear!"—"Taut leech! belay! Well the lee brace; haul taut to windward!" and the royals are set.

What would the captain of any sailing-vessel of our time say to that? He would say, "The man that wrote that didn't learn his trade out of a book, he has *been* there!" But would this same captain be competent to sit in judgment upon Shakespeare's seamanship—considering the changes in ships and ship-talk that have necessarily taken place, unrecorded, unremembered, and lost to history in the last three hundred years? It is my conviction that Shakespeare's sailor-talk would be Choctaw to him. For instance—from "The Tempest":

Master. Boatswain!
Boatswain. Here, master; what cheer?
Master. Good, speak to the mariners: fall to 't, yarely, or we run ourselves to ground; bestir, bestir!
(*Enter mariners.*)
Boatswain. Heigh, my hearts! cheerly, cheerly, my hearts! yare, yare! Take in the topsail. Tend to the master's whistle. . . . Down with the topmast! yare! lower, lower! Bring her to try wi' the main course. . . . Lay her a-hold, a-hold! Set her two courses. Off to sea again; lay her off.

That will do, for the present; let us yare a little, now, for a change.

If a man should write a book and in it make one of his characters say, "Here, devil, empty the quoins into the standing galley and the imposing-stone into the hell-box; assemble the comps around the frisket and let them jeff for takes and be quick about it," I should recognize a mistake or two in the phrasing, and would know that the writer was only a printer theoretically, not practically.

I have been a quartz miner in the silver regions—a pretty hard life; I know all the palaver of that business: I know all about discovery claims and the subordinate claims; I know all about lodes, ledges, outcroppings, dips, spurs, angles, shafts, drifts, inclines, levels, tunnels, air-shafts, "horses," clay casings, granite casings; quartz mills and their batteries; arastras, and how to charge them with quicksilver and sulphate of copper; and how to clean them up, and how to reduce the resulting amalgam in the retorts, and how to cast the bullion into pigs; and finally I know how to screen tailings, and also how to hunt for something less robust to do, and find it. I know the argot of the quartz-mining and milling industry familiarly; and so whenever Bret Harte introduces that industry into a story, the first time one of his miners opens his mouth I recognize from his phrasing that Harte got the phrasing by listening—like Shakespeare—I mean the Stratford one—

not by experience. No one can talk the quartz dialect correctly without learning it with pick and shovel and drill and fuse.

I have been a surface miner—gold—and I know all its mysteries, and the dialect that belongs with them; and whenever Harte introduces that industry into a story I know by the phrasing of his characters that neither he nor they have ever served that trade.

I have been a "pocket" miner—a sort of gold mining not findable in any but one little spot in the world, so far as I know. I know how, with horn and water, to find the trail of a pocket and trace it step by step and stage by stage up the mountain to its source, and find the compact little nest of yellow metal reposing in its secret home under the ground. I know the language of that trade, that capricious trade, that fascinating buried-treasure trade, and can catch any writer who tries to use it without having learned it by the sweat of his brow and the labor of his hands.

I know several other trades and the argot that goes with them; and whenever a person tries to talk the talk peculiar to any of them without having learned it at its source I can trap him always before he gets far on his road.

And so, as I have already remarked, if I were required to superintend a Bacon-Shakespeare controversy, I would narrow the matter down to a single question—the only one, so far as the previous controversies have informed me, concerning which illustrious experts of unimpeachable competency have testified: *Was the author of Shakespeare's Works a lawyer?*—a lawyer deeply read and of limitless experience? I would put aside the guesses and surmises, and perhapses, and might-have-beens, and could-have-beens, and must-have-beens, and we-are-justified-in-presumings, and the rest of those vague specters and shadows and indefinitenesses, and stand or fall, win or lose, by the verdict rendered by the jury upon that single question. If the verdict was Yes, I should feel quite convinced that the Stratford Shakespeare, the actor, manager, and trader who died so obscure, so forgotten, so destitute of even village consequence, that sixty years afterward no fellow-citizen and friend of his later days remembered to tell anything about him, did not write the Works.

Chapter XIII of *The Shakespeare Problem Restated* bears the heading "Shakespeare as a Lawyer," and comprises some fifty pages of expert testimony, with comments thereon, and I will copy the first nine, as being sufficient all by themselves, as it seems to me, to settle the question which I have conceived to be the master-key to the Shakespeare-Bacon puzzle.

VIII

SHAKESPEARE AS A LAWYER[3]

The Plays and Poems of Shakespeare supply ample evidence that their author not only had a very extensive and accurate knowledge of law, but that he was well acquainted with the manners and customs of members of the Inns of Court and with legal life generally.

"While novelists and dramatists are constantly making mistakes as to the laws of marriage, of wills, and inheritance, to Shakespeare's law, lavishly as he expounds it, there can neither be demurrer, nor bill of exceptions, nor writ of error." Such was the testimony borne by one of the most distinguished lawyers of the nineteenth century who was raised to the high office of Lord Chief Justice in 1850, and subsequently became Lord Chancellor. Its weight will, doubtless, be more appreciated by lawyers than by laymen, for only lawyers know how impossible it is for those who have not served an apprenticeship to the law to avoid displaying their ignorance if they venture to employ legal terms and to discuss legal doctrines. "There is nothing so dangerous," wrote Lord Campbell, "as for one not of the craft to tamper with our freemasonry." A layman is certain to betray himself by using some expression which a lawyer would never employ. Mr. Sidney Lee himself supplies us with an example of this. He writes (p. 164): "On February 15, 1609, Shakespeare . . . obtained judgment from a jury against Addenbroke for the payment of No. 6, and No. 1, 5s. od. costs." Now a lawyer would never have spoken of obtaining "judgment from a jury," for it is the function of a jury not to deliver judgment (which is the prerogative of the court), but to find a verdict on the facts. The error is, indeed, a venial one, but it is just one of those little things which at once enable a lawyer to know if the writer is a layman or "one of the craft."

But when a layman ventures to plunge deeply into legal subjects, he is naturally apt to make an exhibition of his incompetence. "Let a non-professional man, however acute," writes Lord Campbell again, "presume to talk law, or to draw illustrations from legal science in discussing other subjects, and he will speedily fall into laughable absurdity."

And what does the same high authority say about Shakespeare? He had "a deep technical knowledge of the law," and an easy familiarity with "some of the most abstruse proceedings in English jurisprudence." And again: "Whenever he indulges this propensity he uniformly lays down good law." Of "Henry IV.," Part 2, he says: "If Lord Eldon could be supposed to have written the play, I do not see how he could be chargeable with having forgotten any of his law while writing it." Charles and Mary

[3]From Chapter XIII of *The Shakespeare Problem Restated*. By George G. Greenwood, M.P. John Lane Company, publishers.

Cowden Clarke speak of "the marvelous intimacy which he displays with legal terms, his frequent adoption of them in illustration, and his curiously technical knowledge of their form and force." Malone, himself a lawyer, wrote: "His knowledge of legal terms is not merely such as might be acquired by the casual observation of even his all-comprehending mind; it has the appearance of technical skill." Another lawyer and well-known Shakespearian, Richard Grant White, says: "No dramatist of the time, not even Beaumont, who was the younger son of a judge of the Common Pleas, and who after studying in the Inns of Court abandoned law for the drama, used legal phrases with Shakespeare's readiness and exactness. And the significance of this fact is heightened by another, that it is only to the language of the law that he exhibits this inclination. The phrases peculiar to other occupations serve him on rare occasions by way of description, comparison, or illustration, generally when something in the scene suggests them, but legal phrases flow from his pen as part of his vocabulary and parcel of his thought. Take the word 'purchase' for instance, which, in ordinary use, means to acquire by giving value, but applies in law to all legal modes of obtaining property except by inheritance or descent, and in this peculiar sense the word occurs five times in Shakespeare's thirty-four plays, and only in one single instance in the fifty-four plays of Beaumont and Fletcher. It has been suggested that it was in attendance upon the courts in London that he picked up his legal vocabulary. But this supposition not only fails to account for Shakespeare's peculiar freedom and exactness in the use of that phraseology, it does not even place him in the way of learning those terms his use of which is most remarkable, which are not such as he would have heard at ordinary proceedings at *nisi prius*, but such as refer to the tenure or transfer of real property, 'fine and recovery,' 'statutes merchant,' 'purchase,' 'indenture,' 'tenure,' 'double voucher,' 'fee simple,' 'fee farm,' 'remainder,' 'reversion,' 'forfeiture,' etc. This conveyancer's jargon could not have been picked up by hanging round the courts of law in London two hundred and fifty years ago, when suits as to the title of real property were comparatively rare. And besides, Shakespeare uses his law just as freely in his first plays, written in his first London years, as in those produced at a later period. Just as exactly, too; for the correctness and propriety with which these terms are introduced have compelled the admiration of a Chief Justice and a Lord Chancellor."

Senator Davis wrote: "We seem to have something more than a sciolist's temerity of indulgence in the terms of an unfamiliar art. No legal solecisms will be found. The abstrusest elements of the common law are impressed into a disciplined service. Over and over again, where such knowledge is unexampled in writers unlearned in the law, Shakespeare appears in perfect possession of it. In the law of real property, its rules of tenure and descents, its entails, its fines and recoveries, their vouchers and double vouchers, in the procedure of the Courts, the method of bringing writs and arrests, the nature of actions, the rules of pleading, the law of escapes and of contempt of court, in the principles of evidence, both technical and philosophical, in the distinction between the temporal and spiritual tribunals, in the law of attainder and forfeiture, in the requisites of a valid marriage, in the presumption of legitimacy, in the learning of the law of prerogative, in the inalienable character of the Crown, this mastership appears with surprising authority."

To all this testimony (and there is much more which I have not cited) may now be added that of a great lawyer of our own times, *viz.*: Sir James Plaisted Wilde, Q.C. 1855, created a Baron of the Exchequer in 1860, promoted to the post of Judge-Ordinary and Judge of the Courts of Probate and Divorce in 1863, and better known to the world as Lord Penzance, to which dignity he was raised in 1869. Lord Penzance, as all lawyers know, and as the late Mr. Inderwick, K.C., has testified, was one of the first legal authorities of his day, famous for his "remarkable grasp of legal principles," and "endowed by nature with a remarkable facility for marshaling facts, and for a clear expression of his views."

Lord Penzance speaks of Shakespeare's "perfect familiarity with not only the principles, axioms, and maxims, but the technicalities of English law, a knowledge so perfect and intimate that he was never incorrect and never at fault. . . . The mode in which this knowledge was pressed into service on all occasions to express his meaning and illustrate his thoughts was quite unexampled. He seems to have had a special pleasure in his complete and ready mastership of it in all its branches. As manifested in the plays, this legal knowledge and learning had therefore a special character which places it on a wholly different footing from the rest of the multifarious knowledge which is exhibited in page after page of the plays. At every turn and point at which the author required a metaphor, simile, or illustration, his mind ever turned *first* to the law. He seems almost to have *thought* in legal phrases, the commonest of legal expressions were ever at the end of his pen in description or illustration. That he should have descanted in lawyer language when he had a forensic subject in hand, such as Shylock's bond, was to be expected, but the knowledge of law in 'Shakespeare' was exhibited in a far different manner: it protruded itself on all occasions, appropriate or inappropriate, and mingled itself with strains of thought widely divergent from forensic subjects." Again: "To acquire a perfect familiarity with legal principles, and an accurate and ready use of the technical terms and phrases not only of the conveyancer's office, but of the pleader's chambers and the Courts at Westminster, nothing short of employment in some career involving constant contact with legal questions and general legal work would be requisite. But a continuous employment involves the element of time, and time was just what the manager of two theaters had not at his disposal. In what portion of Shakespeare's (*i.e.*, Shakspere's) career would it be possible to point out that time could be found for the interposition of a legal employment in the chambers or offices of practising lawyers?"

Stratfordians, as is well known, casting about for some possible explanation of Shakespeare's extraordinary knowledge of law, have made the suggestion that Shakespeare might, conceivably, have been a clerk in an attorney's office before he came to London. Mr. Collier wrote to Lord Campbell to ask his opinion as to the probability of this being true. His answer was as follows: "You require us to believe implicitly a fact, of which, if true, positive and irrefragable evidence in his own handwriting might have been forthcoming to establish it. Not having been actually enrolled as an attorney, neither the records of the local court at Stratford nor of the superior Courts at Westminster would present his name as being concerned in any suit as an attorney, but it might reasonably have been expected that there would be deeds or wills witnessed by him still extant, and after a very diligent search none such can be discovered."

Upon this Lord Penzance comments: "It cannot be doubted that Lord Campbell was right in this. No young man could have been at work in an attorney's office without being called upon continually to act as a witness, and in many other ways leaving traces of his work and name." There is not a single fact or incident in all that is known of Shakespeare, even by rumor or tradition, which supports this notion of a clerkship. And after much argument and surmise which has been indulged in on this subject, we may, I think, safely put the notion on one side, for no less an authority than Mr. Grant White says finally that the idea of having been clerk to an attorney has been "blown to pieces."

It is altogether characteristic of Mr. Churton Collins that he, nevertheless, adopts this exploded myth. "That Shakespeare was in early life employed as a clerk in an attorney's office may be correct. At Stratford there was by royal charter a Court of Record sitting every fortnight, with six attorneys, besides the town clerk, belonging to it, and it is certainly not straining probability to suppose that the young Shakespeare may have had employment in one of them. There is, it is true, no tradition to this effect, but such traditions as we have about Shakespeare's occupation between the time of leaving school and going to London are so loose and baseless that no confidence can be placed in them. It is, to say the least, more probable that he was in an attorney's office than that he was a butcher killing calves 'in a high style,' and making speeches over them."

This is a charming specimen of Stratfordian argument. There is, as we have seen, a very old tradition that Shakespeare was a butcher's apprentice. John Dowdall, who made a tour in Warwickshire in 1693, testifies to it as coming from the old clerk who showed him over the church, and it is unhesitatingly accepted as true by Mr. Halliwell-Phillipps. (Vol. I, p. 11, and Vol. II, pp. 71, 72.) Mr. Sidney Lee sees nothing improbable in it, and it is supported by Aubrey, who must have written his account some time before 1680, when his manuscript was completed. Of the attorney's clerk hypothesis, on the other hand, there is not the faintest vestige of a tradition. It has been evolved out of the fertile imaginations of embarrassed Stratfordians, seeking for some explanation of the Stratford rustic's marvelous acquaintance with law and legal terms and legal life. But Mr. Churton Collins has not the least hesitation in throwing over the tradition which has the warrant of antiquity and setting up in its stead this ridiculous invention, for which not only is there no shred of positive evidence, but which, as Lord Campbell and Lord Penzance point out, is really put out of court by the negative evidence, since "no young man could have been at work in an attorney's office without being called upon continually to act as a witness, and in many other ways leaving traces of his work and name." And as Mr. Edwards further points out, since the day when Lord Campbell's book was published (between forty and fifty years ago), "every old deed or will, to say nothing of other legal papers, dated during the period of William Shakespeare's youth, has been scrutinized over half a dozen shires, and not one signature of the young man has been found."

Moreover, if Shakespeare had served as clerk in an attorney's office it is clear that he must have so served for a considerable period in order to have gained (if, indeed, it is credible that he could have so gained) his remarkable knowledge of law. Can we then for a moment believe that, if this had been so, tradition would have been absolutely silent on the matter? That Dowdall's old clerk, over eighty years of age, should have never heard of it (though he was sure enough about the butcher's apprentice), and that all the other ancient witnesses should be in similar ignorance!

But such are the methods of Stratfordian controversy. Tradition is to be scouted when it is found inconvenient, but cited as irrefragable truth when it suits the case. Shakespeare of Stratford was the author of the Plays and Poems, but the author of the Plays and Poems could not have been a butcher's apprentice. Away, therefore, with tradition. But the author of the Plays and Poems *must* have had a very large and a very accurate knowledge of the law. Therefore, Shakespeare of Stratford must have been an attorney's clerk! The method is simplicity itself. By similar reasoning Shakespeare has been made a country schoolmaster, a soldier, a physician, a printer, and a good many other things besides, according to the inclination and the exigencies of the commentator. It would not be in the least surprising to find that he was studying Latin as a schoolmaster and law in an attorney's office at the same time.

However, we must do Mr. Collins the justice of saying that he has fully recognized, what is indeed tolerably obvious, that Shakespeare must have had a sound legal training. "It may, of course, be urged," he writes, "that Shakespeare's knowledge of medicine, and particularly that branch of it which related to morbid psychology, is equally remarkable, and that no one has ever contended that he was a physician. (Here Mr. Collins is wrong; that contention also has been put forward.) It may be urged that his acquaintance with the technicalities of other crafts and callings, notably of marine and military affairs, was also extraordinary, and yet no one has suspected him of being a sailor or a soldier. (Wrong again. Why, even Messrs. Garnett and Gosse "suspect" that he was a soldier!) This may be conceded, but the concession hardly furnishes an analogy. To these and all other subjects he recurs occasionally, and in season, but with reminiscences of the law his memory, as is abundantly clear, was simply saturated. In season and out of season now in manifest, now in recondite application, he presses it into the service of expression and illustration. At least a third of his myriad metaphors are derived from it. It would indeed be difficult to find a single act in any of his dramas, nay, in some of them, a single scene, the diction and imagery of which are not colored by it. Much of his law may have been acquired from three books easily accessible to him—namely, Tottell's *Precedents* (1572), Pulton's *Statutes* (1578), and Fraunce's *Lawier's Logike* (1588), works with which he certainly seems to have been familiar; but much of it could only have come from one who had an intimate acquaintance with legal proceedings. We quite agree with Mr. Castle that Shakespeare's legal knowledge is not what could have been picked up in an attorney's office, but could only have been learned by an actual attendance at the Courts, at a Pleader's Chambers, and on circuit, or by associating intimately with members of the Bench and Bar."

This is excellent. But what is Mr. Collins's explanation? "Perhaps the simplest solution of the problem is to accept the hypothesis that in early life he was in an attorney's office (!), that he there contracted a love for the law which never left him, that as a young man in London he continued to study or dabble in it for his amusement, to stroll in leisure hours into the Courts, and to frequent the society of lawyers. On no other supposition is it possible to explain the attraction which the law evidently had for him, and his minute and undeviating accuracy in a subject where no layman who has indulged in such copious and ostentatious display of legal technicalities has ever yet succeeded in keeping himself from tripping."

A lame conclusion. "No other supposition" indeed! Yes, there is another, and a very obvious supposition—namely, that Shakespeare was himself a lawyer, well versed in his trade, versed in all the ways of the courts, and living in close intimacy with judges and members of the Inns of Court.

One is, of course, thankful that Mr. Collins has appreciated the fact that Shakespeare must have had a sound legal training, but I may be forgiven if I do not attach quite so much importance to his pronouncements on this branch of the subject as to those of Malone, Lord Campbell, Judge Holmes, Mr. Castle, K.C., Lord Penzance, Mr. Grant White, and other lawyers, who have expressed their opinion on the matter of Shakespeare's legal acquirements. . . .

Here it may, perhaps, be worth while to quote again from Lord Penzance's book as to the suggestion that Shakespeare had somehow or other managed "to acquire a perfect familiarity with legal principles, and an accurate and ready use of the technical terms and phrases, not only of the conveyancer's office, but of the pleader's chambers and the Courts at Westminster." This, as Lord Penzance points out, "would require nothing short of employment in some career involving *constant contact* with legal questions and general legal work." But "in what portion of Shakespeare's career would it be possible to point out that time could be found for the interposition of a legal employment in the chambers or offices of practising lawyers? . . . It is beyond doubt that at an early period he was called upon to abandon his attendance at school and assist his father, and was soon after, at the age of sixteen, bound apprentice to a trade. While under the obligation of this bond he could not have pursued any other employment. Then he leaves Stratford and comes to London. He has to provide himself with the means of a livelihood, and this he did in some capacity at the theater. No one doubts that. The holding of horses is scouted by many, and perhaps with justice, as being unlikely and certainly unproved; but whatever the nature of his employment was at the theater, there is hardly room for the belief that it could have been other than continuous, for his progress there was so rapid. Ere long he had been taken into the company as an actor, and was soon spoken of as a 'Johannes Factotum.' His rapid accumulation of wealth speaks volumes for the constancy and activity of his services. One fails to see when there could be a break in the current of his life at this period of it, giving room or opportunity for legal or indeed any other employment. 'In 1589,' says Knight, 'we have undeniable evidence that he had not only a casual engagement, was not only a salaried servant, as many players were, but was a shareholder in the company of the Queen's players with other shareholders below him on the list.' This (1589) would be within two years after his arrival in London, which is placed by White and Halliwell-Phillipps about the year 1587. The difficulty in supposing that, starting with a state of ignorance in 1587, when he is supposed to have come to London, he was induced to enter upon a course of most extended study and mental culture, is almost insuperable. Still it was physically possible, provided always that he could have had access to the needful books. But this legal training seems to me to stand on a different footing. It is not only unaccountable and incredible, but it is actually negatived by the known facts of his career." Lord Penzance then refers to the fact that "by 1592 (according to the best authority, Mr. Grant White) several of the plays had been written. 'The Comedy of Errors' in 1589, 'Love's Labour's Lost' in 1589, 'Two Gentlemen of Verona' in 1589 or 1590," and so forth, and then asks, "with this catalogue of dramatic work on hand . . . was it possible that he could have taken a leading part in the management and conduct of two theaters, and if Mr. Phillipps is to be relied upon, taken his share in the performances of the provincial tours of his company—and at the same time devoted himself to the study of the law in all its branches so efficiently as to make himself complete master of its principles and practice, and saturate his mind with all its most technical terms?"

I have cited this passage from Lord Penzance's book, because it lay before me, and I had already quoted from it on the matter of Shakespeare's legal knowledge; but other writers have still better set forth the insuperable difficulties, as they seem to me, which beset the idea that Shakespeare might have found time in some unknown period of early life, amid multifarious other occupations, for the study of classics, literature, and law, to say nothing of languages and a few other matters. Lord Penzance further asks his readers: "Did you ever meet with or hear of an instance in which a young man in this country gave himself up to legal studies and engaged in legal employments, which is the only way of becoming familiar with the technicalities of practice, unless with the view of practising in that profession? I do not believe that it would be easy, or indeed possible, to produce an instance in which the law has been seriously studied in all its branches, except as a qualification for practice in the legal profession."

This testimony is so strong, so direct, so authoritative; and so uncheapened, unwatered by guesses, and surmises, and maybe-so's, and might-have-beens, and could-have-beens, and must-have-beens, and the rest of that ton of plaster of Paris out of which the biographers have built the colossal brontosaur which goes by the Stratford actor's name, that it quite convinces me that the man who wrote Shakespeare's Works knew all about law and lawyers. Also, that that man could not have been the Stratford Shakespeare—and *wasn't*.

Who did write these Works, then?

I wish I knew.

IX

Did Francis Bacon write Shakespeare's Works?

Nobody knows.

We cannot say we *know* a thing when that thing has not been proved. *Know* is too strong a word to use when the evidence is not final and absolutely conclusive. We can infer, if we want to, like those slaves. . . . No, I will not write that word, it is not kind, it is not courteous. The upholders of the Stratford-Shakespeare superstition call *us* the hardest names they can think of, and they keep doing it all the time; very well, if they like to descend to that level, let them do it, but I will not so undignify myself as to follow them. I cannot call them harsh names; the most I can do is to indicate them by terms reflecting my disapproval; and this without malice, without venom.

To resume. What I was about to say was, those thugs have built their entire superstition upon *inferences*, not upon known and established facts. It is a weak method, and poor, and I am glad to be able to say our side never resorts to it while there is anything else to resort to.

But when we must, we must; and we have now arrived at a place of that sort. . . . Since the Stratford Shakespeare couldn't have written the Works, we infer that somebody did. Who was it, then? This requires some more inferring.

Ordinarily when an unsigned poem sweeps across the continent like a tidal wave whose roar and boom and thunder are made up of admiration, delight, and applause, a dozen obscure people rise up and claim the authorship. Why a dozen, instead of only one or two? One reason is, because there are a dozen that are recognizably competent to do that poem. Do you remember "Beautiful Snow"? Do you remember "Rock Me to Sleep, Mother, Rock Me to Sleep"? Do you remember "Backward, turn backward, O Time, in thy flight! Make me a child again just for to-night"? I remember them very well. Their authorship was claimed by most of the grown-up people who were alive at the time, and every claimant had one plausible argument in his favor, at least—to wit, he could have done the authoring; he was competent.

Have the Works been claimed by a dozen? They haven't. There was good reason. The world knows there was but one man on the planet at the time who was competent—not a dozen, and not two. A long time ago the dwellers in a far country used now and then to find a procession of prodigious footprints stretching across the plain—footprints that were three miles apart, each footprint a third of a mile long and a furlong deep, and with forests and villages mashed to mush in it. Was there any doubt as to who made that mighty trail? Were there a dozen claimants? Were there two? No—the people knew who it was that had been along there: there was only one Hercules.

There has been only one Shakespeare. There couldn't be two; certainly there couldn't be two at the same time. It takes ages to bring forth a Shakespeare, and some more ages to match him. This one was not matched before his time; nor during his time; and hasn't been matched since. The prospect of matching him in our time is not bright.

The Baconians claim that the Stratford Shakespeare was not qualified to write the Works, and that Francis Bacon was. They claim that Bacon possessed the stupendous equipment—both natural and acquired—for the miracle; and that no other Englishman of his day possessed the like; or, indeed, anything closely approaching it.

Macaulay, in his Essay, has much to say about the splendor and horizonless magnitude of that equipment. Also, he has synopsized Bacon's history—a thing which cannot be done for the Stratford Shakespeare, for he hasn't any history to synopsize. Bacon's history is open to the world, from his boyhood to his death in old age—a history consisting of known facts, displayed in minute and multitudinous detail; *facts*, not guesses and conjectures and might-have-beens.

Whereby it appears that he was born of a race of statesmen, and had a Lord Chancellor for his father, and a mother who was "distinguished both as a linguist and a theologian: she corresponded in Greek with Bishop Jewell, and translated his *Apologia* from the Latin so correctly that neither he nor Archbishop Parker could suggest a single alteration." It is the atmosphere we are reared in that determines how our inclinations and aspirations shall tend. The atmosphere furnished by the parents to the son in this present case was an atmosphere saturated with learning; with thinkings and ponderings upon deep subjects; and with polite culture. It had its natural effect. Shakespeare of Stratford was reared in a house which had no use for books, since its owners, his parents, were without education. This may have had an effect upon the son, but we do not know, because we have no history of him of an informing sort. There were but few books anywhere, in that day, and only the well-to-do and highly educated possessed them, they being almost confined to the dead languages. "All the valuable books then extant in all the vernacular dialects of Europe would hardly have filled a single shelf"—imagine it! The few existing books were in the Latin tongue mainly. "A person who was ignorant of it was shut out from all acquaintance—not merely with Cicero and Virgil, but with the most interesting memoirs, state papers, and pamphlets of his own time"—a literature necessary to the Stratford lad, for his fictitious reputation's sake, since the writer of his Works would begin to use it wholesale and in a most masterly way before the lad was hardly more than out of his teens and into his twenties.

At fifteen Bacon was sent to the university, and he spent three years there. Thence he went to Paris in the train of the English Ambassador, and there he mingled daily with the wise, the cultured, the great, and the aristocracy of fashion, during another three years. A total of six years spent at the sources of knowledge; knowledge both of books and of men. The three spent at the university were coeval with the second and last three spent by the little Stratford lad at Stratford school supposedly, and perhapsedly, and maybe, and by inference—with nothing to infer from. The second three of the Baconian six were "presumably" spent by the Stratford lad as apprentice to a butcher. That is, the thugs presume it—on no evidence of any kind. Which is their way, when they want a historical fact. Fact and presumption are, for business purposes, all the same to them. They know the difference, but they also know how to blink it. They know, too, that while in history-building a fact is better than a presumption, it doesn't take a presumption long to bloom into a fact when *they* have the handling of it. They know by old experience that when they get hold of a presumption-tadpole he is not going to *stay* tadpole in their history-tank; no, they know how to develop him into the giant four-legged bullfrog of *fact*, and make him sit up on his hams, and puff out his chin, and look important and insolent and come-to-stay; and assert his genuine simon-pure authenticity with a thundering bellow that will convince everybody because it is so loud. The thug is aware that loudness convinces sixty persons where reasoning convinces but one. I wouldn't be a thug, not even if—but never mind about that, it has nothing to do with the argument, and it is not noble in spirit besides. If I am better than a thug, is the merit mine? No, it is His. Then to Him be the praise. That is the right spirit.

They "presume" the lad severed his "presumed" connection with the Stratford school to become apprentice to a butcher. They also "presume" that the butcher was his father. They don't know. There is no written record of it, nor any other actual evidence. If it would have helped their case any, they would have apprenticed him to thirty butchers, to fifty butchers, to a wilderness of butchers—all by their patented method "presumption." If it will help their case they will do it yet; and if it will further help it, they will "presume" that all those butchers were his father. And the week after, they will *say* it. Why, it is just like being the past tense of the compound reflexive adverbial incandescent hypodermic irregular accusative Noun of Multitude; which is father to the expression which the grammarians call Verb. It is like a whole ancestry, with only one posterity.

To resume. Next, the young Bacon took up the study of law, and mastered that abstruse science. From that day to the end of his life he was daily in close contact with lawyers and judges; not as a casual onlooker in intervals between holding horses in front of a theater, but as a practising lawyer—a great and successful one, a renowned one, a Launcelot of the bar, the most formidable lance in the high brother-hood of the legal Table Round; he lived in the law's atmosphere thenceforth, all his years, and by sheer ability forced his way up its difficult steeps to its supremest summit, the Lord-Chancellorship, leaving behind him no fellow-craftsman qualified to challenge his divine right to that majestic place.

When we read the praises bestowed by Lord Penzance and the other illustrious experts upon the legal condition and legal aptnesses, brilliances, profundities, and felicities so prodigally displayed in the Plays, and try to fit them to the historyless Stratford stage-manager, they sound wild, strange, incredible, ludicrous; but when we put them in the mouth of Bacon they do not sound strange, they seem in their natural and rightful place, they seem at home there. Please turn back and read them again. Attributed to Shakespeare of Stratford they are meaningless, they are inebriate extravagancies—intemperate admirations of the dark side of the moon, so to speak; attributed to Bacon, they are admirations of the golden glories of the moon's front side, the moon at the full—and not intemperate, not overwrought, but sane and right, and justified. "At every turn and point at which the author required a metaphor, simile, or illustration, his mind ever turned *first* to the law; he seems almost to have *thought* in legal phrases; the commonest legal phrases, the commonest of legal expressions, were ever at the end of his pen." That could happen to no one but a person whose *trade* was the law; it could not happen to a dabbler in it. Veteran mariners fill their conversation with sailor-phrases and draw all their similes from the ship and the sea and the storm, but no mere *passenger* ever does it, be he of Stratford or elsewhere; or could do it with anything resembling accuracy, if he were hardy enough to try. Please read again what Lord Campbell and the other great authorities have said about Bacon when they thought they were saying it about Shakespeare of Stratford.

X

THE REST OF THE EQUIPMENT

The author of the Plays was equipped, beyond every other man of his time, with wisdom, erudition, imagination, capaciousness of mind, grace, and majesty of expression. Every one has said it, no one doubts it. Also, he had humor, humor in rich abundance, and always wanting to break out. We have no evidence of any kind that Shakespeare of

Stratford possessed any of these gifts or any of these acquirements.
The only lines he ever wrote, so far as we know, are substantially
barren of them—barren of all of them.

> Good friend for Iesus sake forbeare
> To digg the dust encloased heare:
> Blest be ye man yt spares thes stones
> And curst be he yt moves my bones.

Ben Jonson says of Bacon, as orator:

His language, *where he could spare and pass by a jest,* was nobly
censorious. No man ever spoke more neatly, more pressly, more weightily,
or suffered less emptiness, less idleness, in what he uttered. No member
of his speech but consisted of his (its) own graces. . . . The fear of every
man that heard him was lest he should make an end.

From Macaulay:

He continued to distinguish himself in Parliament, particularly by his
exertions in favor of one excellent measure on which the King's heart was
set—the union of England and Scotland. It was not difficult for such an
intellect to discover many irresistible arguments in favor of such a scheme.
He conducted the great case of the *Post Nati* in the Exchequer Chamber;
and the decision of the judges—a decision the legality of which may be
questioned, but the beneficial effect of which must be acknowledged—was
in a great measure attributed to his dexterous management.

Again:

While actively engaged in the House of Commons and in the courts of
law, he still found leisure for letters and philosophy. The noble treatise on
the *Advancement of Learning,* which at a later period was expanded into
the *De Augmentis,* appeared in 1605.

The *Wisdom of the Ancients,* a work which, if it had proceeded from
any other writer, would have been considered as a masterpiece of wit and
learning, was printed in 1609.

In the mean time the *Novum Organum* was slowly proceeding. Several
distinguished men of learning had been permitted to see portions of that
extraordinary book, and they spoke with the greatest admiration of his
genius.

Even Sir Thomas Bodley, after perusing the *Cogitata et Visa,* one of
the most precious of those scattered leaves out of which the great oracular
volume was afterward made up, acknowledged that "in all proposals
and plots in that book, Bacon showed himself a master workman"; and that
"it could not be gainsaid but all the treatise over did abound with choice

conceits of the present state of learning, and with worthy contemplations of the means to procure it."

In 1612 a new edition of the *Essays* appeared, with additions surpassing the original collection both in bulk and quality.

Nor did these pursuits distract Bacon's attention from a work the most arduous, the most glorious, and the most useful that even his mighty powers could have achieved, "the reducing and recompiling," to use his own phrase, "of the laws of England."

To serve the exacting and laborious offices of Attorney-General and Solicitor-General would have satisfied the appetite of any other man for hard work, but Bacon had to add the vast literary industries just described, to satisfy his. He was a born worker.

The service which he rendered to letters during the last five years of his life, amid ten thousand distractions and vexations, increase the regret with which we think on the many years which he had wasted, to use the words of Sir Thomas Bodley, "on such study as was not worthy such a student."

He commenced a digest of the laws of England, a History of England under the Princes of the House of Tudor, a body of National History, a Philosophical Romance. He made extensive and valuable additions to his Essays. He published the inestimable *Treatise De Augmentis Scientiarum*.

Did these labors of Hercules fill up his time to his contentment, and quiet his appetite for work? Not entirely:

The trifles with which he amused himself in hours of pain and languor bore the mark of his mind. *The best jest-book in the world* is that which he dictated from memory, without referring to any book, on a day on which illness had rendered him incapable of serious study.

Here are some scattered remarks (from Macaulay) which throw light upon Bacon, and seem to indicate—and maybe demonstrate— that he was competent to write the Plays and Poems:

With great minuteness of observation he had an amplitude of comprehension such as has never yet been vouchsafed to any other human being.

The *Essays* contain abundant proofs that no nice feature of character, no peculiarity in the ordering of a house, a garden, or a court-masque, could escape the notice of one whose mind was capable of taking in the whole world of knowledge.

His understanding resembled the tent which the fairy Paribanou gave to Prince Ahmed: fold it, and it seemed a toy for the hand of a lady;

spread it, and the armies of powerful Sultans might repose beneath its shade.

The knowledge in which Bacon excelled all men was a knowledge of the mutual relations of all departments of knowledge.

In a letter written when he was only thirty-one, to his uncle, Lord Burleigh, he said, "I have taken all knowledge to be my province."

Though Bacon did not arm his philosophy with the weapons of logic, he adorned her profusely with all the richest decorations of rhetoric.

The practical faculty was powerful in Bacon; but not, like his wit, so powerful as occasionally to usurp the place of his reason and to tyrannize over the whole man.

There are too many places in the Plays where this happens. Poor old dying John of Gaunt volleying second-rate puns at his own name, is a pathetic instance of it. "We may assume" that it is Bacon's fault, but the Stratford Shakespeare has to bear the blame.

No imagination was ever at once so strong and so thoroughly subjugated. It stopped at the first check from good sense.

In truth, much of Bacon's life was passed in a visionary world—amid things as strange as any that are described in the *Arabian Tales* . . . amid buildings more sumptuous than the palace of Aladdin, fountains more wonderful than the golden water of Parizade, conveyances more rapid than the hippogryph of Ruggiero, arms more formidable than the lance of Astolfo, remedies more eficacious than the balsam of Fierabras. Yet in his magnificent day-dreams there was nothing wild—nothing but what sober reason sanctioned.

Bacon's greatest performance is the first book of the *Novum Organum*. . . . Every part of it blazes with wit, but with wit which is employed only to illustrate and decorate truth. No book ever made so great a revolution in the mode of thinking, overthrew so many prejudices, introduced so many new opinions.

But what we most admire is the vast capacity of that intellect which, without effort, takes in at once all the domains of science—all the past, the present and the future, all the errors of two thousand years, all the encouraging signs of the passing times, all the bright hopes of the coming age.

He had a wonderful talent for packing thought close and rendering it portable.

His eloquence would alone have entitled him to a high rank in literature.

It is evident that he had each and every one of the mental gifts and each and every one of the acquirements that are so prodigally displayed in the Plays and Poems, and in much higher and richer degree than any other man of his time or of any previous time. He was a genius without a mate, a prodigy not matable. There was only one of him; the planet could not produce two of him at one birth, nor in one age. He could have written anything that is in the Plays and Poems. He could have written this:

> The cloud-cap'd towers, the gorgeous palaces,
> The solemn temples, the great globe itself,
> Yea, all which it inherit, shall dissolve,
> And, like an insubstantial pageant faded,
> Leave not a rack behind. We are such stuff
> As dreams are made on, and our little life
> Is rounded with a sleep.

Also, he could have written this, but he refrained:

> Good friend for Iesus sake forbeare
> To digg the dust encloased heare:
> Blest be ye man yt spares thes stones
> And curst be he yt moves my bones.

When a person reads the noble verses about the cloud-cap'd towers, he ought not to follow it immediately with Good friend for Iesus sake forbeare, because he will find the transition from great poetry to poor prose too violent for comfort. It will give him a shock. You never notice how commonplace and unpoetic gravel is until you bite into a layer of it in a pie.

XI

Am I trying to convince anybody that Shakespeare did not write Shakespeare's Works? Ah, now, what do you take me for? Would I be so soft as that, after having known the human race familiarly for nearly seventy-four years? It would grieve me to know that any one could think so injuriously of me, so uncomplimentarily, so unadmiringly of me. No, no, I am aware that when even the brightest mind in our world has been trained up from childhood in a superstition of any kind, it will never be possible for that mind, in its maturity, to examine sincerely, dispassionately, and conscientiously any evidence or any circumstance which shall seem to cast a doubt upon the validity of that superstition. I doubt if I could do it myself. We always get at second hand our notions about systems of government; and high tariff

and low tariff; and prohibition and anti-prohibition; and the holiness
of peace and the glories of war; and codes of honor and codes of
morals; and approval of the duel and disapproval of it; and our beliefs
concerning the nature of cats; and our ideas as to whether the murder
of helpless wild animals is base or is heroic; and our preferences in the
matter of religious and political parties; and our acceptance or rejec-
tion of the Shakespeares and the Arthur Ortons and the Mrs. Eddys.
We get them all at second hand, we reason none of them out for ourselves. It is the way we are made. It is the way we are all made, and
we can't help it, we can't change it. And whenever we have been
furnished a fetish, and have been taught to believe in it, and love it
and worship it, and refrain from examining it, there is no evidence,
howsoever clear and strong, that can persuade us to withdraw from
it our loyalty and our devotion. In morals, conduct, and beliefs we take
the color of our environment and associations, and it is a color that
can safely be warranted to wash. Whenever we have been furnished
with a tar baby ostensibly stuffed with jewels, and warned that it will
be dishonorable and irreverent to disembowel it and test the jewels,
we keep our sacrilegious hands off it. We submit, not reluctantly, but
rather gladly, for we are privately afraid we should find, upon examination, that the jewels are of the sort that are manufactured at North
Adams, Mass.

I haven't any idea that Shakespeare will have to vacate his pedestal
this side of the year 2209. Disbelief in him cannot come swiftly, disbelief in a healthy and deeply-loved tar baby has never been known
to disintegrate swiftly; it is a very slow process. It took several thousand years to convince our fine race—including every splendid intellect in it—that there is no such thing as a witch; it has taken several
thousand years to convince that same fine race—including every splendid intellect in it—that there is no such person as Satan; it has taken
several centuries to remove perdition from the Protestant Church's
program of post-mortem entertainments; it has taken a weary long
time to persuade American Presbyterians to give up infant damnation
and try to bear it the best they can; and it looks as if their Scotch
brethren will still be burning babies in the everlasting fires when
Shakespeare comes down from his perch.

We are The Reasoning Race. We can't prove it by the above examples, and we can't prove it by the miraculous "histories" built by
those Stratfordolaters out of a hatful of rags and a barrel of sawdust,
but there is a plenty of other things we can prove it by, if I could
think of them. We are The Reasoning Race, and when we find a vague

file of chipmunk-tracks stringing through the dust of Stratford village, we know by our reasoning powers that Hercules has been along there. I feel that our fetish is safe for three centuries yet. The bust, too—there in the Stratford Church. The precious bust, the priceless bust, the calm bust, the serene bust, the emotionless bust, with the dandy mustache, and the putty face, unseamed of care—that face which has looked passionlessly down upon the awed pilgrim for a hundred and fifty years and will still look down upon the awed pilgrim three hundred more, with the deep, deep, deep, subtle, subtle, subtle, expression of a bladder.

XII

IRREVERENCE

One of the most trying defects which I find in these—these—what shall I call them? for I will not apply injurious epithets to them, the way they do to us, such violations of courtesy being repugnant to my nature and my dignity. The farthest I can go in that direction is to call them by names of limited reverence—names merely descriptive, never unkind, never offensive, never tainted by harsh feeling. If *they* would do like this, they would feel better in their hearts. Very well, then—to proceed. One of the most trying defects which I find in these Stratfordolaters, these Shakesperiods, these thugs, these bangalores, these troglodytes, these herumfrodites, these blatherskites, these buccaneers, these bandoleers, is their spirit of irreverence. It is detectable in every utterance of theirs when they are talking about us. I am thankful that in me there is nothing of that spirit. When a thing is sacred to me it is impossible for me to be irreverent toward it. I cannot call to mind a single instance where I have ever been irreverent, except toward the things which were sacred to other people. Am I in the right? I think so. But I ask no one to take my unsupported word; no, look at the dictionary; let the dictionary decide. Here is the definition:

Irreverence. The quality or condition of irreverence toward God and sacred things.

What does the Hindu say? He says it is correct. He says irreverence is lack of respect for Vishnu, and Brahma, and Chrishna, and his other gods, and for his sacred cattle, and for his temples and the things within them. He indorses the definition, you see; and there are 300,000,000 Hindus or their equivalents back of him.

The dictionary had the acute idea that by using the capital G it could restrict irreverence to lack of reverence for *our* Deity and our sacred things, but that ingenious and rather sly idea miscarried: for by the simple process of spelling *his* deities with capitals the Hindu confiscates the definition and restricts it to his own sects, thus making it clearly compulsory upon us to revere *his* gods and *his* sacred things, and nobody's else. We can't say a word, for he has our own dictionary at his back, and its decision is final.

This law, reduced to its simplest terms, is this: 1. Whatever is sacred to the Christian must be held in reverence by everybody else; 2. whatever is sacred to the Hindu must be held in reverence by everybody else; 3. therefore, by consequence, logically, and indisputably, whatever is sacred to *me* must be held in reverence by everybody else.

Now then, what aggravates me is that these troglodytes and muscovites and bandoleers and buccaneers are *also* trying to crowd in and share the benefit of the law, and compel everybody to revere their Shakespeare and hold him sacred. We can't have that: there's enough of us already. If you go on widening and spreading and inflating the privilege, it will presently come to be conceded that each man's sacred things are the *only* ones, and the rest of the human race will have to be humbly reverent toward them or suffer for it. That can surely happen, and when it happens, the word Irreverence will be regarded as the most meaningless, and foolish, and self-conceited, and insolent, and impudent, and dictatorial word in the language. And people will say, "Whose business is it what gods I worship and what things hold sacred? Who has the right to dictate to my conscience, and where did he get that right?"

We cannot afford to let that calamity come upon us. We must save the word from this destruction. There is but one way to do it, and that is to stop the spread of the privilege and strictly confine it to its present limits—that is, to all the Christian sects, to all the Hindu sects, and me. We do not need any more, the stock is watered enough, just as it is.

It would be better if the privilege were limited to me alone. I think so because I am the only sect that knows how to employ it gently, kindly, charitably, dispassionately. The other sects lack the quality of self-restraint. The Catholic Church says the most irreverent things about matters which are sacred to the Protestants, and the Protestant Church retorts in kind about the confessional and other matters which Catholics hold sacred; then both of these irreverencers turn upon

Thomas Paine and charge *him* with irreverence. This is all unfortunate, because it makes it difficult for students equipped with only a low grade of mentality to find out what Irreverence really *is*.

It will surely be much better all around if the privilege of regulating the irreverent and keeping them in order shall eventually be withdrawn from all the sects but me. Then there will be no more quarreling, no more bandying of disrespectful epithets, no more heartburnings.

There will then be nothing sacred involved in this Bacon-Shakespeare controversy except what is sacred to me. That will simplify the whole matter, and trouble will cease. There will be irreverence no longer, because I will not allow it. The first time those criminals charge me with irreverence for calling their Stratford myth an Arthur - Orton - Mary - Baker - Thompson - Eddy - Louis - the - Seventeenth - Veiled - Prophet - of - Khorassan will be the last. Taught by the methods found effective in extinguishing earlier offenders by the Inquisition, of holy memory, I shall know how to quiet them.

XIII

Isn't it odd, when you think of it, that you may list all the celebrated Englishmen, Irishmen, and Scotchmen of modern times, clear back to the first Tudors—a list containing five hundred names, shall we say?—and you can go to the histories, biographies, and cyclopedias and learn the particulars of the lives of every one of them. Every one of them except one—the most famous, the most renowned—by far the most illustrious of them all—Shakespeare! You can get the details of the lives of all the celebrated ecclesiastics in the list; all the celebrated tragedians, comedians, singers, dancers, orators, judges, lawyers, poets, dramatists, historians, biographers, editors, inventors, reformers, statesmen, generals, admirals, discoverers, prize-fighters, murderers, pirates, conspirators, horse-jockeys, bunco-steerers, misers, swindlers, explorers, adventurers by land and sea, bankers, financiers, astronomers, naturalists, claimants, impostors, chemists, biologists, geologists, philologists, college presidents and professors, architects, engineers, painters, sculptors, politicians, agitators, rebels, revolutionists, patriots, demagogues, clowns, cooks, freaks, philosophers, burglars, highwaymen, journalists, physicians, surgeons—you can get the life-histories of all of them but *one*. Just *one*—the most extraordinary and the most celebrated of them all—Shakespeare!

You may add to the list the thousand celebrated persons furnished by the rest of Christendom in the past four centuries, and you can find out the life-histories of all those people, too. You will then have listed fifteen hundred celebrities, and you can trace the authentic life-histories of the whole of them. Save one—far and away the most colossal prodigy of the entire accumulation—Shakespeare! About him you can find out *nothing*. Nothing of even the slightest importance. Nothing worth the trouble of stowing away in your memory. Nothing that even remotely indicates that he was ever anything more than a distinctly commonplace person—a manager, an actor of inferior grade, a small trader in a small village that did not regard him as a person of any consequence, and had forgotten all about him before he was fairly cold in his grave. We can go to the records and find out the life-history of every renowned *race-horse* of modern times—but not Shakespeare's! There are many reasons why, and they have been furnished in cart-loads (of guess and conjecture) by those troglodytes; but there is one that is worth all the rest of the reasons put together, and is abundantly sufficient all by itself—*he hadn't any history to record*. There is no way of getting around that deadly fact. And no sane way has yet been discovered of getting around its formidable significance.

Its quite plain significance—to any but those thugs (I do not use the term unkindly) is, that Shakespeare had no prominence while he lived, and none until he had been dead two or three generations. The Plays enjoyed high fame from the beginning; and if he wrote them it seems a pity the world did not find it out. He ought to have explained that he was the author, and not merely a *nom de plume* for another man to hide behind. If he had been less intemperately solicitous about his bones, and more solicitous about his Works, it would have been better for his good name, and a kindness to us. The bones were not important. They will moulder away, they will turn to dust, but the Works will endure until the last sun goes down.

P.S. March 25.[4] About two months ago I was illuminating this Autobiography with some notions of mine concerning the Bacon-Shakespeare controversy, and I then took occasion to air the opinion that the Stratford Shakespeare was a person of no public consequence or celebrity during his lifetime, but was utterly obscure and unimportant. And not only in great London, but also in the little village where he was born, where he lived a quarter of a century, and where

[4] Year not given, but from the internal evidence which follows I gather it is 1909. The essay was copyrighted April 1909.—C.N.

he died and was buried. I argued that if he had been a person of any note at all, aged villagers would have had much to tell about him many and many a year after his death, instead of being unable to furnish inquirers a single fact connected with him. I believed, and I still believe, that if he had been famous, his notoriety would have lasted as long as mine has lasted in my native village out in Missouri. It is a good argument, a prodigiously strong one, and a most formidable one for even the most gifted and ingenious and plausible Stratfordolater to get around or explain away. To-day a Hannibal *Courier-Post* of recent date has reached me, with an article in it which reinforces my contention that a really celebrated person cannot be forgotten in his village in the short space of sixty years. I will make an extract from it:

Hannibal, as a city, may have many sins to answer for, but ingratitude is not one of them, or reverence for the great men she has produced, and as the years go by her greatest son, Mark Twain, or S. L. Clemens as a few of the unlettered call him, grows in the estimation and regard of the residents of the town he made famous. His name is associated with every old building that is torn down to make way for the modern structures demanded by a rapidly growing city, and with every hill or cave over or through which he might by any possibility have roamed, while the many points of interest which he wove into his stories, such as Holiday Hill, Jackson's Island, or Mark Twain Cave, are now monuments to his genius. Hannibal is glad of any opportunity to do him honor as he has honored her.

So it has happened that the "old timers" who went to school with Mark or were with him on some of his usual escapades have been honored with large audiences whenever they were in a reminiscent mood and condescended to tell of their intimacy with the ordinary boy who came to be a very extraordinary humorist and whose every boyish act is now seen to have been indicative of what was to come. Like Aunt Becky and Mrs. Clemens, they can now see that Mark was hardly appreciated when he lived here and that the things he did as a boy and was whipped for doing were not all bad, after all. So they have been in no hesitancy about drawing out the bad things he did as well as the good in their efforts to get a "Mark Twain" story, all incidents being viewed in the light of his present fame, until the volume of "Twainiana" is already considerable and growing in proportion as the "old timers" drop away and the stories are retold second and third hand by their descendants. With some seventy-three years young and living in a villa instead of a house, he is a fair target, and let him incorporate, copyright, or patent himself as he will, there are some of his "works" that will go swooping up Hannibal chimneys as long as graybeards gather about the fires and begin with; "I've heard father tell," or possibly, "Once when I."

The Mrs. Clemens referred to is my mother—*was* my mother.

And here is another extract from a Hannibal paper, of date twenty days ago:

Miss Becca Blankenship died at the home of William Dickason, 408 Rock Street, at 2.30 o'clock yesterday afternoon aged 72 years. The deceased was a sister of "Huckleberry Finn," one of the famous characters in Mark Twain's *Tom Sawyer.* She had been a member of the Dickason family—the housekeeper—for nearly forty-five years, and was a highly respected lady. For the past eight years she had been an invalid, but was as well cared for by Mr. Dickason and his family as if she had been a near relative. She was a member of the Park Methodist Church and a Christian woman.

I remember her well. I have a picture of her in my mind which was graven there, clear and sharp and vivid, sixty-three years ago. She was at that time nine years old, and I was about eleven. I remember where she stood, and how she looked; and I can still see her bare feet, her bare head, her brown face, and her short tow-linen frock. She was crying. What it was about I have long ago forgotten. But it was the tears that preserved the picture for me, no doubt. She was a good child, I can say that for her. She knew me nearly seventy years ago. Did she forget me, in the course of time? I think not. If she had lived in Stratford in Shakespeare's time, would she have forgotten him? Yes. For he was never famous during his lifetime, he was utterly obscure in Stratford, and there wouldn't be any occasion to remember him after he had been dead a week.

"Injun Joe," "Jimmy Finn," and "General Gaines" were prominent and very intemperate ne'er-do-weels in Hannibal two generations ago. Plenty of grayheads there remember them to this day, and can tell you about them. Isn't it curious that two "town drunkards" and one half-breed loafer should leave behind them, in a remote Missourian village, a fame a hundred times greater and several hundred times more particularized in the matter of definite facts than Shakespeare left behind him in the village where he had lived the half of his lifetime?

1909

Marjorie Fleming, the Wonder Child

Marjorie has been in her tiny grave a hundred years; and still the tears fall for her, and will fall. What an intensely human little creature she was! How vividly she lived her small life; how impulsive she was; how sudden, how tempestuous, how tender, how loving, how sweet, how loyal, how rebellious, how repentant, how wise, how unwise, how bursting with fun, how frank, how free, how honest, how innocently bad, how natively good, how charged with quaint philosophies, how winning, how precious, how adorable—and how perennially and indestructibly interesting! And all this exhibited, proved, and recorded before she reached the end of her ninth year and "fell on sleep."

Geographically considered, the lassie was a Scot; but in fact she had no frontiers, she was the world's child, she was the human race in little. It is one of the prides of my life that the first time I ever heard her name it came from the lips of Dr. John Brown—his very own self —Dr. John Brown of Edinburgh—Dr. John Brown of *Rab and His Friends*—Dr. John Brown of the beautiful face and the sweet spirit, whose friends loved him with a love that was worship—Dr. John Brown, who was Marjorie's biographer, and who had clasped an aged hand that had caressed Marjorie's fifty years before, thus linking me with that precious child by an unbroken chain of handshakes, for I had shaken hands with Dr. John. This was in Edinburgh thirty-six years ago. He gave my wife his little biography of Marjorie, and I have it yet.

Is Marjorie known in America? No—at least to only a few. When Mr. L. MacBean's new and enlarged and charming biography[1] of her was published five years ago it sent over here in sheets, the market not being large enough to justify recomposing and reprinting it on our side of the water. I find that there are even cultivated Scotchmen among us who have not heard of Marjorie Fleming.

She was born in Kirkcaldy in 1803, and she died when she was eight

---

[1] *Marjorie Fleming*. By L. MacBean. G. P. Putnam's Sons, publishers, London and New York.
Permission to use the extracts quoted from Marjorie's Journal in this article has been granted me by the publishers.—M.T.

years and eleven months old. By the time she was five years old she was become a devourer of various kinds of literature—both heavy and light—and was also become a quaint and free-spoken and charming little thinker and philosopher whose views were a delightful jumble of first-hand cloth of gold and second-hand rags.

When she was six she opened up that rich mine, her journals, and continued to work it by spells during the remainder of her brief life. She was a pet of Walter Scott, from the cradle, and when he could have her society for a few hours he was content, and required no other. Her little head was full of noble passages from Shakespeare and other favorites of hers, and the fact that she could deliver them with moving effect is proof that her elocution was a born gift with her, and not a mechanical reproduction of somebody else's art, for a child's parrot-work does not move. When she was a little creature of seven years, Sir Walter Scott "would read ballads to her in his own glorious way, the two getting wild with excitement over them; and he would take her on his knee and make her repeat Constance's speeches in *King John* till he swayed to and fro, sobbing his fill." [Dr. John Brown.]

"*Sobbing his fill*"—that great man—over that little thing's inspired interpretations. It is a striking picture; there is no mate to it. Sir Walter said of her:

"She's the most extraordinary creature I ever met with, and her repeating of Shakespeare overpowers me as nothing else does."

She spent the whole of her little life in a Presbyterian heaven; yet she was not affected by it; she could not have been happier if she had been in the other heaven.

She was made out of thunderstorms and sunshine, and not even her little perfunctory pieties and shop-made holiness could squelch her spirits or put out her fires for long. Under pressure of a pestering sense of duty she heaves a shovelful of trade godliness into her journals every little while, but it does not offend, for none of it is her own; it is all borrowed, it is a convention, a custom of her environment, it is the most innocent of hypocrisies, and this tainted butter of hers soon gets to be as delicious to the reader as are the stunning and worldly sincerities she splatters around it every time her pen takes a fresh breath. The adorable child! she hasn't a discoverable blemish in her make-up anywhere.

Marjorie's first letter was written before she was six years old; it was to her cousin, Isa Keith, a young lady of whom she was passionately fond. It was done in a sprawling hand, ten words to the page—and in those foolscap days a page was a spacious thing:

"MY DEAR ISA—

"I now sit down on my botom to answer all the kind & beloved letters which you was so so good as to write to me. This is the first time I ever wrote a letter in my life.

"Miss Potune, a lady of my acquaintance, praises me dreadfully. I repeated something out of Deen Swift & she said I was fit for the stage, & you may think I was primmed up with majestick Pride, but upon my word I felt myself turn a little birsay—birsay is a word which is a word that William composed which is as you may suppose a little enraged. This horid fat Simpliton says that my Aunt is beautifull which is intirely impossible for that is not her nature."

Frank? Yes, Marjorie was that. And during the brief moment that she enchanted this dull earth with her presence she was the bewitchingest speller and punctuator in all Christendom.

The average child of six "prints" its correspondence in rickety and reeling Roman capitals, or dictates to mamma, who puts the little chap's message on paper. The sentences are labored, repetitious, and slow; there are but three or four of them; they deal in information solely, they contain no ideas, they venture no judgments, no opinions; they inform papa that the cat has had kittens again; that Mary has a new doll that can wink; that Tommy has lost his top; and will papa come soon and bring the writer something nice? But with Marjorie it is different.

She needs no amanuensis, she puts her message on paper herself; and not in weak and tottering Roman capitals, but in a thundering hand that can be heard a mile and be read across the square without glasses. And she doesn't have to study, and puzzle, and search her head for something to say; no, she had only to connect the pen with the paper and turn on the current; the words spring forth at once, and go chasing after each other like leaves dancing down a stream. For she has a faculty, has Marjorie! Indeed yes; when she sits down on her bottom to do a letter, there isn't going to be any lack of materials, nor of fluency, and neither is her letter going to be wanting in pepper, or vinegar, or vitriol, or any of the other condiments employed by genius to save a literary work of art from flatness and vapidity. And as for judgments and opinions, they are as commodiously in her line as they are in the Lord Chief Justice's. They have weight, too, and are convincing: for instance, for thirty-six years they have damaged that "horid Simpliton" in my eyes; and, more than that, they

have even imposed upon me—and most unfairly and unwarrantably
—an aversion to the horid fat Simpliton's name; a perfectly innocent name, and yet, because of the prejudice against it with which
this child has poisoned my mind for a generation I cannot see "Potune"
on paper and keep my gorge from rising.

In her journals Marjorie changes her subject whenever she wants to
—and that is pretty often. When the deep moralities pay her a passing
visit she registers them. Meantime if a cherished love passage drifts
across her memory she shoves it into the midst of the moralities—it
is nothing to her that it may not feel at home there:

"We should not be happy at the death of our fellow creatures, for
they love life like us love your neighbor & he will love you Bountiful-
ness and Mercifulness are always rewarded. In my travels I met with
a handsome lad named Charles Balfour Esge [Esqr.] and from him
I got offers of marage—ofers of marage did I say? nay plainly [he]
loved me. Goodness does not belong to the wicked but badness dishonor befals wickedness but not virtue, no disgrace befals virtue perciverence overcomes almost al difficulties no I am rong in saying almost I should say always as it is so perciverence is a virtue my Csosin
says pacience is a cristain virtue, which is true."

She is not copying these profundities out of a book, she is getting
them out of her memory; her spelling shows that the book is not before her. The easy and effortless flow of her talk is a marvelous thing
in a baby of her age. Her interests are as wide and varied as a grown
person's: she discusses all sorts of books, and fearlessly delivers judgment upon them; she examines whomsoever crosses the field of her
vision, and again delivers a verdict; she dips into religion and history,
and even into politics; she takes a shy at the news of the day, and
comments upon it; and now and then she drops into poetry—into
rhyme, at any rate.

Marjorie would not intentionally mislead anyone, but she has just
been making a remark which moves me to hoist a danger-signal for
the protection of the modern reader. It is this one: *"In my travels."*
Naturally we are apt to clothe a word with its present-day meaning
—the meaning we are used to, the meaning we are familiar with; and
so—well, you get the idea: some words that are giants to-day were
very small dwarfs a century ago, and if we are not careful to take
that vast enlargement into account when we run across them in the
literatures of the past, they are apt to convey to us a distinctly wrong
impression. To-day, when a person says *"in my travels"* he means that
he has been around the globe nineteen or twenty times, and we so un-

derstand him; and so, when Marjorie says it, it startles us for a moment, for it gives us the impression that *she* has been around it fourteen or fifteen times; whereas, such is not at all the case. She has traveled prodigiously for *her* day, but not for ours. She had "traveled," altogether, three miles by land and eight by water—per ferryboat. She is fairly and justly proud of it, for it is the exact equivalent, in grandeur and impressiveness, in the case of a child of our day, to two trips across the Atlantic and a thousand miles by rail.

"In the love novels all the heroins are very desperate Isabella will not allow me to speak about lovers and heroins, and tiss too refined for my taste a loadstone is a curous thing indeed it is true Heroic love doth never win disgrace this is my maxum and I will follow it forever Miss Eguards [Edgeworth] tails are very good particularly some that are very much adopted for youth as Lazy Lawrence Tarelton False Key &c &c Persons of the parlement house are as I think caled Advocakes Mr Cay & Mr Crakey has that honour. This has been a very mild winter. Mr Banestors Budget is to-night I hope it will be a good one. A great many authors have expressed themselfs too sentimentaly. . . . The Mercandile Afares are in a perilous situation sickness & a delicante frame I have not & I do not know what it is, but Ah me perhaps I shall have it.[2] Grandure reigns in Edinburgh. . . . Tomson is a beautifull author and Pope but nothing is like Shakespear of which I have a little knolegde of. An unfortunate death James the 5 had for he died of greif Macbeth is a pretty composition but awful one Macbeth is so bad & wicked, but Lady Macbeth is so hardened in guilt she does not mind her sins & faults No.

". . . A sailor called here to say farewell, it must be dreadful to leave his native country where he might get a wife or perhaps me, for I love him very much & with all my heart, but O I forgot Isabella forbid me to speak about love. . . . I wish everybody would follow her example & be as good as pious & virtious as she is & they would get husbands soon enough, love is a parithatick [pathetic] thing as well as troublesome & tiresome but O Isabella forbid me to speak about it."

But the little rascal can't *keep* from speaking about it, because it is her supreme interest in life; her heart is not capacious enough to hold all the product that is engendered by the ever-recurring inflaming spectacle of man-creatures going by, and the surplus is obliged to spill over; Isa's prohibitions are no sufficient dam for such a discharge.

---

[2] It is a whole century since the dimly conscious little prophet said it, but the pathos of it is still there.—M.T.

"Love I think is the fasion for everybody is marring [marrying].
. . . Yesterday a marrade man named Mr John Balfour Esg [Esq.]
offered to kiss me, & offered to marry me though the man was espused
[espoused], & his wife was present & said he must ask her permission
but he did not, I think he was ashamed or confounded before 3 gentleman Mr Jobson and two Mr Kings."

I must make room here for another of Marjorie's second-hand high-
morality outbreaks. They give me a sinful delight which I ought to
grieve at, I suppose, but I can't seem to manage it:

"James Macary is to be transported for murder in the flower of his
youth O passion is a terrible thing for it leads people from sin to sin
at last it gets so far as to come to greater crimes than we thought we
could comit and it must be dreadful to leave his native country and
his friends and to be so disgraced and affronted."

That is Marjorie talking shop, dear little diplomat—to please and
comfort mamma and Isa, no doubt.

This wee little child has a marvelous range of interests. She reads
philosophies, novels, baby books, histories, the mighty poets—reads
them with burning interest, and frankly and freely criticizes them all;
she revels in storms, sunsets, cloud effects, scenery of mountain,
plain, ocean, and forest, and all the other wonders of nature, and sets
down her joy in them all; she loves people, she detests people,
according to mood and circumstances, and delivers her opinion of
them, sometimes seasoned with attar of roses, sometimes with vitriol;
in games, and all kinds of childish play she is an enthusiast; she adores
animals, adores them all; none is too forlorn to fail of favor in her
friendly eyes, no creature so humble that she cannot find something in
it on which to lavish her caressing worship.

"I am going to-morrow to a delightfull place, Braehead by name,
belonging to Mrs. Crraford [Crauford], where there is ducks cocks
hens bobblyjocks 2 dogs 2 cats and swine which is delightful. I think
it is shocking to think that the dog and cat should bear them and they
are drowned after all."

She is a dear child, a bewitching little scamp; and never dearer,
I think, than when the devil has had her in possession and she is
breaking her stormy little heart over the remembrance of it:

"I confess I have been very more like a little young divil than a
creature for when Isabella went up stairs to teach me religion and my
multiplication and to be good and all my other lessons I stamped with
my foot and threw my new hat which she had made on the ground

and was sulky and was dreadfully passionate, but she never whiped me but said Marjory go into another room and think what a great crime you are committing letting your temper git the better of you. But I went so sulkily that the devil got the better of me but she never never never whips me so that I think I would be the better of it & the next time that I behave ill I think she should do it for she never does it. . . . Isabella has given me praise for checking my temper for I was sulky even when she was kneeling an whole hour teaching me to write."

The wise Isabella, the sweet and patient Isabella! It is just a hundred years now (May, 1909) since the grateful child made that golden picture of you and laid your good heart bare for distant generations to see and bless; a hundred years—but if the picture endures a thousand it will still bring you the blessing, and with it the reverent homage that is your due. You had the seeing eye and the wise head. A fool would have punished Marjorie and wrecked her, but you held your hand, as knowing that when her volcanic fires went down she would repent, and grieve, and punish herself, and be saved.

Sometimes when Marjorie was miraculously good, she got a penny for it, and once when she got an entire sixpence, she recognized that it was wealth. This wealth brought joy to her heart. Why? Because she could spent it on somebody else! We who know Marjorie would know that without being told it. I am sorry—often sorry, often grieved—that I was not there and looking over her shoulder when she was writing down her valued penny rewards: I would have said, "Save that scrap of manuscript, dear; make a will, and leave it to your posterity, to save them from want when penury shall threaten them; a day will come when it will be worth a thousand guineas, and a later day will come when it will be worth five thousand; here you are, rejoicing in copper farthings, and don't know that your magic pen is showering gold coin all over the paper." But I was not there to say it; those who were there did not think to say it; and so there is not a line of that quaint precious cacography in existence to-day.

I have adored Marjorie for six-and-thirty years; I have adored her in detail, I have adored the whole of her; but above all other details —just a little above all other details—I have adored her because she detested that odious and confusing and unvanquishable and unlearnable and shameless invention, the multiplication table:

"I am now going to tell you the horible and wretched plaege [plague] that my multiplication gives me you can't conceive it the most Devilish thing is 8 times 8 & 7 times 7 it is what nature itself cant endure."

I stand reverently uncovered in the presence of that holy verdict.

Here is that person again whom I so dislike—and for no reason at all except that my Marjorie doesn't like her:

"Miss Potune is very fat she pretends to be very learned she says she saw a stone that dropt from the skies, but she is a good christian."

Of course, stones have fallen from the skies, but I don't believe this "horid fat Simpliton" had ever seen one that had done it; but even if she had, it was none of her business, and she could have been better employed than in going around exaggerating it and carrying on about it and trying to make trouble with a little child that had never done *her* any harm.

". . . The Birds do chirp the Lambs do leap and Nature is clothed with the garments of green yellow, and white, purple, and red."

". . . There is a book that is called the Newgate Calender that contains all the Murders: all the Murders did I say, nay all Thefts & Forgeries that ever were committed & fills me with horror & consternation."

Marjorie is a diligent little student, and her education is always storming along and making great time and lots of noise:

"Isabella this morning taught me some French words one of which is bon suar the interpretation is good morning."

It slanders Isabella, but the slander is not intentional. The main thing to notice is that big word, "interpretation." Not many children of Marjorie's age can handle a five syllable team in that easy and confident way. It is observable that she frequently employs words of an imposingly formidable size, and is manifestly quite familiar with them and not at all afraid of them.

"Isa is teaching me to make Simecolings nots of interrigations periods & commas &c. As this is Sunday I will meditate uppon senciable & Religious subjects first I should be very thankful I am not a beggar as many are."

That was the "first." She didn't get to her second subject, but got side-tracked by a saner interest, and used her time to better purpose.

"It is melancholy to think, that I have so many talents, & many there are that have not had the attention paid to them that I have, & yet they contrive to be better then me.

". . . Isabella is far too indulgent to me & even the Miss Crafords say that they wonder at her patience with me & it is indeed true for my temper is a bad one."

The daring child wrote a (synopsized) history of Mary Queen of Scots and of five of the royal Jameses in rhyme—but never mind, we have no room to discuss it here. Nothing was entirely beyond her literary jurisdiction; if it had occurred to her that the laws of Rome needed codifying she would have taken a chance at it.

Here is a sad note:

"My religion is greatly falling off because I dont pray with so much attention when I am saying my prayers and my character is lost a-mong the Breahead people I hope I will be religious again but as for regaining my character I despare of it."

When religion and character go, they leave a large vacuum. But there are ways to fill it:

"I've forgot to say, but I've four lovers, the other one is Harry Watson, a very delightful boy. . . . James Keith hardly ever Spoke to me, he said Girl! make less noise. . . . Craky hall . . . I walked to that delightfull place with a delightful young man beloved by all his friends and espacialy by me his loveress but I must not talk any longer about him for Isa said it is not proper for to speak of gentalman but I will never forget him. . . .

"The Scythians tribe live very coarsely for a Gluton Introduced to Arsaces the Captain of the Army, 1 man who Dressed hair & another man who was a good cook but Arsaces said that he would keep 1 for brushing his horses tail and the other to fead his pigs. . . .

"On Saturday I expected no less than three well-made bucks, the names of whom is here advertised. Mr. Geo. Crakey [Cragie], and Wm. Keith and Jn Keith—the first is the funniest of every one of them. Mr. Crakey and I walked to Craky-hall [Craigiehall] hand and hand in Innocence and matitation sweet thinking on the kind love which flows in our tender hearted mind which is overflowing with majestic pleasure no one was ever so polite to me in the hole state of my existence. Mr. Craky you must know is a great Buck and pretty good-looking."

For a purpose, I wish the reader to take careful note of these statistics:

"I am going to tell you of a melancholy story. A young turkie of 2 or 3 months old, would you believe it, the father broke its leg, & he killed another! I think he ought to be transported or hanged."

Marjorie wrote some verses about this tragedy—I think. I cannot be quite certain it is this one, for in the verses there are three deaths, whereas these statistics do not furnish so many. Also in the statistics the father of the deceased is indifferent about the loss he has sustained, whereas in the verses he is not. Also in the third verse, the *mother*, too, exhibits feeling, whereas in the two closing verses of the poem she—at least it seems to be she—is indifferent. At least it looks like indifference to me, and I believe it *is* indifference:

> "Three turkeys fair their last have breathed,
> And now this world forever leaved;
> Their father, and their mother too,
> They sighed and weep as well as you;
> Indeed, the rats their bones have cranched.
> Into eternity theire launched.
> A direful death indeed they had,
> As wad put any parent mad;
> But she was more than usual calm,
> She did not give a single dam."

The naughty little scamp! I mean, for not leaving out the *l* in the word "Calm," so as to perfect the rhyme. It seems a pity to damage with a lame rhyme a couplet that is otherwise without a blemish.

Marjorie wrote four journals. She began the first one in January, 1809, when she was just six years old, and finished it five months later, in June.

She began the second in the following month, and finished it six months afterward (January, 1810), when she was just seven.

She began the third one in April, 1810, and finished it in the autumn.

She wrote the fourth in the winter of 1810–11, and the last entry in it bears date July 19, 1811, and she died exactly five months later, December 19th, aged eight years and eleven months. It contains her rhymed Scottish histories.

Let me quote from Dr. John Brown:

"The day before her death, Sunday, she sat up in bed, worn and thin, her eye gleaming as with the light of a coming world, and with a tremulous, old voice repeated a long poem by Burns—heavy with the shadow of death, and lit with the fantasy of the judgment seat—the publican's prayer in paraphrase, beginning:

> " 'Why am I loth to leave this earthly scene?
> Have I so found it full of pleasing charms?
> Some drops of joy, with draughts of ill between,
> Some gleams of sunshine 'mid renewing storms.'

"It is more affecting than we care to say to read her mother's and Isabella Keith's letters written immediately after her death. Old and withered, tattered and pale, they are now; but when you read them, how quick, how throbbing with life and love! how rich in that language of affection which only women, and Shakespeare, and Luther can use—that power of detaining the soul over the beloved object and its loss."

Fifty years after Marjorie's death her sister, writing to Dr. Brown, said:

"My mother was struck by the patient quietness manifested by Marjorie during this illness, unlike her ardent, impulsive nature; but love and poetic feeling were unquenched. When Dr. Johnstone rewarded her submissiveness with a sixpence, the request speedily followed that she might get out ere New Year's Day came. When asked why she was so desirous of getting out, she immediately rejoined: 'Oh, I am so anxious to buy something with my sixpence for my dear Isa Keith.' Again, when lying very still, her mother asked her if there was anything she wished: 'Oh yes, if you would just leave the room door open a wee bit, and play the *Land o' the Leal*, and I will lie and *think* and enjoy myself' (this is just as stated to me by her mother and mine). Well, the happy day came, alike to parents and child, when Marjorie was allowed to come forth from the nursery to the parlor. It was Sabbath evening, and after tea. My father, who idolized this child, and never afterward in my hearing mentioned her name, took her in his arms; and while walking her up and down the room she said: 'Father, I will repeat something to you; what would you like?' He said, 'Just choose for yourself, Maidie.' She hesitated for a moment between the paraphrase, 'Few are thy days and full of woe,' and the lines of Burns already quoted but decided on the latter; a remarkable choice for a child. The repeating of these lines seemed to stir up the depths of feeling in her soul. She asked to be allowed to write a poem. There was a doubt whether it would be right to allow her, in case of hurting her eyes. She pleaded earnestly, 'Just this once'; the point was yielded, her slate was given her, and with great rapidity she wrote an address of fourteen lines 'To my loved cousin on the author's recovery.'"

The cousin was Isa Keith.

"She went to bed apparently well, awoke in the middle of the night with the old cry of woe to a mother's heart, 'My head, my head!' Three days of the dire malady, 'water in the head,' followed, and the end came."

1909

The New Planet

(The astronomers at Harvard have observed "perturbations in the orbital movement of Neptune," such as might be caused by the presence of a new planet in the vicinity.)

I believe in the new planet. I was eleven years old in 1846, when Leverrier and Adams and Mary Somerville discovered Neptune through the disturbance and discomfort it was causing Uranus. "Perturbations," they call that kind of disturbance. I had been having those perturbations myself, for more than two months; in fact, all through watermelon time, for they used to keep dogs in some of the patches in those days. You notice that these recent perturbations are considered remarkable because they perturbate through three seconds of arc, but really that is nothing: often I used to perturbate through as much as half an hour if it was a dog that was attending to the perturbating. There isn't any Neptune that can outperturbate a dog; and I know, because I am not speaking from hearsay. Why, if there was a planet two hundred and fifty thousand "light-years" the other side of Neptune's orbit, Professor Pickering would discover it in a minute if it could perturbate equal to a dog. Give me a dog every time, when it comes to perturbating. You let a dog jump out at you all of a sudden in the dark of the moon, and you will see what a small thing three seconds of arc is: the shudder that goes through you then would open the seams of Noah's Ark itself, from figurehead to rudder post, and you would drop that melon the same as if you had never had any but just a casual interest in it. I know about these things, because this is not tradition I am writing, but history.

Now then, notice this. About the end of August, 1846, a change came over me and I resolved to lead a better life, so I reformed; but it was just as well, anyway, because they had got to having guns and dogs both. Although I was reformed, the perturbations did not stop! Does that strike you? They did not stop, they went right on and on and on, for three weeks, clear up to the 23d of September; then Neptune was discovered and the whole mystery stood explained. It shows that I am so sensitively constructed that I perturbate when any other planet is disturbed. This has been going on all my life. It only happens in the watermelon season, but that has nothing to do with it and has no significance: geologists and anthropologists and horticulturists all tell me it is only ancestral and hereditary, and that is what I think myself. Now then, I got to perturbating again, this summer—all summer through; all through watermelon time: and *where,* do you think? Up here on my farm in Connecticut. Is that significant? Unquestionably it is, for you couldn't raise a watermelon on this farm with a derrick.

That perturbating was caused by the new planet. That Washington Observatory may throw as much doubt as it wants to, it cannot affect me, because I know there *is* a new planet. I know it because I don't perturbate for nothing. There has got to be a dog or a planet, one or the other; and there isn't any dog around here, so there's *got* to be a planet. I hope it is going to be named after me; I should just love it if I can't have a constellation.

1909

The Old-fashioned Printer

ADDRESS AT THE TYPOTHETAE DINNER GIVEN AT DELMONICO'S, JANUARY 18, 1886, COMMEMORATING THE BIRTH-DAY OF BENJAMIN FRANKLIN

The chairman's historical reminiscences of Gutenberg have caused me to fall into reminiscences, for I myself am something of an antiquity. All things change in the procession of years, and it may be that I am among strangers. It may be that the printer of to-day is not the printer of thirty-five years ago. I was no stranger to him. I knew him well. I built his fire for him in the winter mornings; I brought his water from the village pump; I swept out his office; I picked up his type from under his stand; and, if he were there to see, I put the good type in his case and the broken ones among the "hell matter"; and if he wasn't there to see, I dumped it all with the "pi" on the imposing stone—for that was the furtive fashion of the cub, and I was a cub. I wetted down the paper Saturdays, I turned it Sundays—for this was a country weekly; I rolled, I washed the rollers, I washed the forms, I folded the papers, I carried them around at dawn Thursday mornings. The carrier was then an object of interest to all the dogs in town. If I had saved up all the bites I ever received, I could keep M. Pasteur busy for a year. I enveloped the papers that were for the mail—we had a hundred town subscribers and three hundred and fifty country ones; the town subscribers paid in groceries and the country ones in cabbages and cordwood—when they paid at all which was merely sometimes, and then we always stated the fact in the paper, and gave them a puff; and if we forgot it they stopped the paper. Every man on the town list helped edit the thing—that is, he gave orders as to how it was to be edited; dictated its opinions, marked out its course for it, and every time the boss failed to connect he stopped his paper. We were just infested with critics, and we tried to satisfy them all over. We had one subscriber who paid cash, and he was more trouble than all the rest. He bought us once a year, body and soul, for two dollars. He used to modify our politics every which way, and he made us change our religion four times in five years. If we ever tried to reason with him, he would threaten to stop his paper, and, of course, that meant bankruptcy and destruction. That man used to write articles a column and a half long, leaded long primer, and sign them "Junius," or "Veritas," or "Vox Populi," or some other high-sounding rot; and then, after it was set up, he would come in and say he had changed his mind—which was a gilded figure of speech, because he hadn't any—and order it to be left out. We couldn't afford "bogus" in that office, so we always took the leads out, altered the signature, credited the article to the rival paper, in the next village, and put it in. Well, we did have one or two kinds of "bogus." Whenever there was a barbecue, or a circus, or a baptizing, we knocked off for half a day, and then to make up for short matter we would "turn over ads"—turn over the whole pages and duplicate it. The other "bogus" was deep philosophical stuff, which we judged nobody ever read; so we kept a galley of it standing, and kept on slapping the same old batches of it in, every now and then, till it got dangerous. Also, in the early days of the telegraph we used to economize on the news. We picked out the items that were pointless and barren of information and stood them on a galley, and changed the dates and localities, and used them over and over again till the public interest in them was worn to the bone. We marked the ads, but we seldom paid any attention to the marks afterward; so the life of a "td" ad and a "tf" ad was equally eternal. I have seen a "td" notice of a sheriff's sale still booming serenely along two years after the sale was over, the sheriff dead, and the whole circumstance become ancient history. Most of the yearly ads were patent-medicine stereotypes, and we used to fence with them.

I can see that printing office of prehistoric times yet with its horse bills on the walls, its "d" boxes clogged with tallow, because we always stood the candle in the "k" box nights, its towel, which was not considered soiled until it could stand alone, and other signs and symbols that marked the establishment of that kind in the Mississippi Valley; and I can see, also, the tramping "jour," who flitted by in the summer and tarried a day, with his wallet stuffed with one shirt and a hatful of handbills, for if he couldn't get any type to set he would do a temperance lecture. His way of life was simple, his needs not complex; all he wanted was plate and bed and money enough to get drunk on, and he was satisfied. But it may be, as I have said, that I am among strangers, and sing the glories of a forgotten age to unfamiliar ears, so I will "make even" and stop.

1910

Seventieth Birthday

Address at a dinner given in New York, December 5, 1950, to celebrate Mark Twain's seventieth birthday. Mark Twain was introduced by William Dean Howells.

"Now, ladies and gentlemen, and Colonel Harvey, I will try to be greedy on your behalf in wishing the health of our honored and, in view of his great age, our revered guest. I will not say, 'O King, live forever!' but 'O King, live as long as you like!'" [Amid great applause and waving of napkins all rose and drank to Mark Twain.]

Well, if I had made that joke, it would be the best one I ever made, and in the prettiest language, too. I never can get quite to that height. But I appreciate that joke, and I shall remember it—and I shall use it when occasion requires.

I have had a great many birthdays in my time. I remember the first one very well, and I always think of it with indignation; everything was so crude, unaesthetic, primeval. Nothing like this at all. No proper appreciative preparation made; nothing really ready. Now, for a person born with high and delicate instincts—why, even the cradle wasn't whitewashed—nothing ready at all. I hadn't any hair, I hadn't my teeth, I hadn't any clothes, I had to go to my first banquet just like that. Well, everybody came swarming in. It was the merest little bit of a village—hardly that, just a little hamlet, in the backwoods of Missouri, where nothing ever happened, and the people were all interested, and they all came; they looked me over to see if there was anything fresh in my line. Why, nothing ever happened in that village —I—why, I was the only thing that had really happened there for months and months and months; and although I say it myself that shouldn't, I came the nearest to being a real event that had happened in that village in more than two years. Well, those people came, they came with that curiosity which is so provincial, with that frankness which also is so provincial, and they examined me all around and gave their opinion. Nobody asked them, and I shouldn't have minded if anybody had paid me a compliment, but nobody did. Their opinions were all just green with prejudice, and I feel those opinions to this day. Well, I stood that as long as—you know I was courteous, and I stood it to the limit. I stood it an hour, and then the worm turned. I was the worm; it was my turn to turn, and I turned. I knew very well the strength of my position; I knew that I was the only spotlessly pure and innocent person in that whole town, and I came out and said so. And they could not say a word. It was so true. They blushed; they were embarrassed. Well, that was the first after-dinner speech I ever made. I think it was after dinner.

It's a long stretch between that first birthday speech and this one. That was my cradle song, and this is my swan song, I suppose. I am used to swan songs; I have sung them several times.

This is my seventieth birthday, and I wonder if you all rise to the size of that proposition, realizing all the significance of that phrase, seventieth birthday.

The seventieth birthday! It is the time of life when you arrive at a new and awful dignity; when you may throw aside the decent reserves which have oppressed you for a generation and stand unafraid and unabashed upon your seven-terraced summit and look down and teach—unrebuked. You can tell the world how you got there. It is what they all do. You shall never get tired of telling by what delicate arts and deep moralities you climb up to that great place. You will explain the process and dwell on the particulars with senile rapture. I have been anxious to explain my own system this long time, and now at last I have the right.

I have achieved my seventy years in the usual way: by sticking strictly to a scheme of life which would kill anybody else. It sounds like an exaggeration, but that is really the common rule for attaining old age. When we examine the programme of any of these garrulous old people we always find that the habits which have preserved them would have decayed us; that the way of life which enabled them to live upon the property of their heirs so long, as Mr. Choate says, would have put us out of commission ahead of time. I will offer here, as a sound maxim, this: That we can't reach old age by another man's road.

I will now teach, offering my way of life to whomsoever desires to commit suicide by the scheme which has enabled me to beat the doctor and the hangman for seventy years. Some of the details may sound untrue, but they are not. I am not here to deceive; I am here to teach.

We have no permanent habits until we are forty. Then they begin to harden, presently they petrify, then business begins. Since forty I have been regular about going to bed and getting up—and that is one of the main things. I have made it a rule to go to bed when there wasn't anybody left to sit up with; and I have made it a rule to get up when I had to. This has resulted in an unswerving regularity of irregularity. It has saved me sound, but it would injure another person.

In the matter of diet—which is another main thing—I have been persistently strict in sticking to the things which didn't agree with me until one or the other of us got the best of it. Until lately I got the best of it myself. But last spring I stopped frolicking with mince pie after midnight; up to then I had always believed it wasn't loaded. For thirty years I have taken coffee and bread at eight in the morning, and no bite nor sup until seven-thirty in the evening. Eleven hours. That is all right for me, and is wholesome, because I have never had a headache in my life, but headachy people would not reach seventy comfortably by that road, and they would be foolish to try it. And I wish to urge upon you this—which I think is wisdom—that if you find you can't make seventy by any but an uncomfortable road, don't you go. When they take off the Pullman and retire you to the rancid smoker, put on your things, count your checks, and get out at the first way station where there's a cemetery.

I have made it a rule never to smoke more than one cigar at a time. I have no other restriction as regards smoking. I do not know just when I began to smoke, I only know that it was in my father's lifetime, and that I was discreet. He passed from this life early in

1847, when I was a shade past eleven; ever since than I have smoked publicly. As an example to others, and not that I care for moderation myself, it has always been my rule never to smoke when asleep, and never to refrain when awake. It is a good rule. I mean, for me; but some of you know quite well that it wouldn't answer for everybody that's trying to get to be seventy.

I smoke in bed until I have to go to sleep; I wake up in the night, sometimes once, sometimes twice, sometimes three times, and I never waste any of these opportunities to smoke. This habit is so old and dear and precious to me that I would feel as you, sir, would feel if you should lose the only moral you've got—meaning the chairman—if you've got one: I am making no charges. I will grant, here, that I have stopped smoking now and then, for a few months at a time, but it was not on principle, it was only to show off; it was to pulverize those critics who said I was a slave to my habits and couldn't break my bonds.

To-day it is all of sixty years since I began to smoke the limit. I have never bought cigars with life belts around them. I early found that those were too expensive for me. I have always bought cheap cigars—reasonably cheap, at any rate. Sixty years ago they cost me four dollars a barrel, but my taste has improved, latterly, and I pay seven now. Six or seven. Seven, I think. Yes, it's seven. But that includes the barrel. I often have smoking parties at my house; but the people that come have always just taken the pledge. I wonder why that is?

As for drinking, I have no rule about that. When the others drink I like to help; otherwise I remain dry, by habit and preference. This dryness does not hurt me, but it could easily hurt you, because you are different. You let it alone.

Since I was seven years old I have seldom taken a dose of medicine, and have still seldomer needed one. But up to seven I lived exclusively on allopathic medicines. Not that I needed them, for I don't think I did; it was for economy; my father took a drug store for a debt, and it made cod-liver oil cheaper than the other breakfast foods. We had nine barrels of it, and it lasted me seven years. Then I was weaned. The rest of the family had to get along with rhubarb and ipecac and such things, because I was the pet. I was the first Standard Oil Trust. I had it all. By the time the drug store was exhausted my health was established and there has never been much the matter with me since. But you know very well it would be foolish for the average child to start for seventy on that basis. It happened to be just the thing for me, but that was merely an accident; it couldn't happen again in a century.

I have never taken any exercise, except sleeping and resting, and I never intend to take any. Exercise is loathsome. And it cannot be any benefit when you are tired; and I was always tired. But let another person try my way, and see whence he will come out.

I desire now to repeat and emphasize that maxim: We can't reach old age by another man's road. My habits protect my life, but they would assassinate you.

I have lived a severely moral life. But it would be a mistake for other people to try that, or for me to recommend it. Very few would succeed: you have to have a perfectly colossal stock of morals; and you can't get them on a margin; you have to have the whole thing, and put them in your box. Morals are an acquirement—like music, like a foreign language, like piety, poker, paralysis—no man is born with them. I wasn't myself, I started poor. I hadn't a single moral. There is hardly a man in this house that is poorer than I was then. Yes, I started like that—the world before me, not a moral in the slot. Not even an insurance moral. I can remember the first one I ever got. I can remember the landscape, the weather, the—I can remember how everything looked. It was an old moral, an old second-hand moral, all out of repair, and didn't fit, anyway. But if you are careful with a thing like that, and keep it in a dry place, and save it for processions, and Chautauquas, and World's Fairs, and so on, and disinfect it now and then, and give it a fresh coat of whitewash once in a while, you will be surprised to see how well she will last and how long she will keep sweet, or at least inoffensive. When I got that mouldy old moral, she had stopped growing, because she hadn't any exercise; but I worked her hard, I worked her Sundays and all. Under this culti- vation she waxed in might and stature beyond belief, and served me well and was my pride and joy for sixty-three years; then she got to associating with insurance presidents, and lost flesh and character, and was a sorrow to look at and no longer competent for business. She was a great loss to me. Yet not all loss. I sold her—ah, pathetic skeleton, as she was—I sold her to Leopold, the pirate King of Bel- gium; he sold her to our Metropolitan Museum, and it was very glad to get her, for without a rag on, she stands 57 feet long and 16 feet high, and they think she's a brontosaur. Well, she looks it. They be- lieve it will take nineteen geological periods to breed her match.

Morals are of inestimable value, for every man is born crammed with sin microbes, and the only thing that can extirpate these sin microbes is morals. Now you take a sterilized Christian—I mean, you take *the* sterilized Christian, for there's only one. Dear sir, I wish you wouldn't look at me like that.

Threescore years and ten!

It is the Scriptural statute of limitations. After that, you owe no active duties; for you the strenuous life is over. You are a time-expired man, to use Kipling's military phrase: You have served your term, well or less well, and you are mustered out. You are become an honorary member of the republic, you are emancipated, compulsions are not for you, nor any bugle call but "lights out." You pay the time-worn duty bills if you choose, or decline if you prefer—and without prejudice—for they are not legally collectable.

The previous-engagement plea, which in forty years has cost you so many twinges, you can lay aside forever; on this side of the grave you will never need it again. If you shrink at thought of night, and winter, and the late home-coming from the banquet and the lights and the laughter through the deserted streets—a desolation which would not remind you now, as for a generation it did, that your friends are sleeping, and you must creep in a-tiptoe and not disturb them, but would only remind you that you need not tiptoe, you can never disturb them more—if you shrink at thought of these things, you need only reply, "Your invitation honors me, and pleases me because you still keep me in your remembrance, but I am seventy; seventy, and would nestle in the chimney corner, and smoke my pipe, and read my book, and take my rest, wishing you well in all affection, and that when you in your turn shall arrive at pier No. 70 you may step aboard your waiting ship with a reconciled spirit, and lay your course toward the sinking sun with a contented heart."

1910

Taxes and Morals

Address at Carnegie Hall, New York, January 22, 1906

I came here in the responsible capacity of policeman to watch Mr. Choate. This is an occasion of grave and serious importance, and it seems necessary for me to be present, so that if he tried to work off any statement that required correction, reduction, refutation, or exposure, there would be a tried friend of the public to protect the house. He has not made one statement whose veracity fails to tally exactly with my own standard. I have never seen a person improve so. This makes me thankful and proud of a country that can produce such men—two such men. And all in the same country. We can't be with you always; we are passing away, and then—well, everything will have to stop, I reckon. It is a sad thought. But in spirit I shall still be with you. Choate, too—if he can.

Every born American among the eighty millions, let his creed or destitution of creed be what it may, is indisputably a Christian to this degree—that his moral constitution is Christian.

There are two kinds of Christian morals, one private and the other public. These two are so distinct, so unrelated, that they are no more akin to each other than are archangels and politicians. During three hundred and sixty-three days in the year the American citizen is true to his Christian private morals, and keeps undefiled the nation's character at its best and highest; then in the other two days of the year he leaves his Christian private morals at home and carries his Christian public morals to the tax office and the polls, and does the best he can to damage and undo his whole year's faithful and righteous work. Without a blush he will vote for an unclean boss if that boss is his party's Moses, without compunction he will vote against the best man in the whole land if he is on the other ticket. Every year in a number of cities and States he helps put corrupt men in office, whereas if he would but throw away his Christian public morals, and carry his Christian private morals to the polls, he could promptly purify the public service and make the possession of office a high and honorable distinction.

Once a year he lays aside his Christian private morals and hires a ferry-boat and piles up his bonds in a warehouse in New Jersey for three days, and gets out his Christian public morals and goes to the tax office and holds up his hands and swears he wishes he may never-never if he's got a cent in the world, so help him. The next day the list appears in the papers—a column and a quarter of names, in fine print, and every man in the list a billionaire and member of a couple of churches. I know all those people. I have friendly, social, and criminal relations with the whole lot of them. They never miss a sermon when they are so's to be around, and they never miss swearing-off day, whether they are so's to be around or not.

I used to be an honest man. I am crumbling. No—I have crumbled.

When they assessed me at $75,000 a fortnight ago I went out and tried to borrow the money, and couldn't; then when I found they were letting a whole crop of millionaires live in New York at a third of the price they were charging me I was hurt, I was indignant, and said: "This is the last feather. I am not going to run this town all by myself." In that moment—in that memorable moment—I began to crumble. In fifteen minutes the disintegration was complete. In fifteen minutes I had become just a mere moral sand pile; and I lifted up my hand along with those seasoned and experienced deacons and swore off every rag of personal property I've got in the world, clear down to cork leg, glass eye, and what is left of my wig.

Those tax officers were moved; they were profoundly moved. They had long been accustomed to seeing hardened old grafters act like that, and they could endure the spectacle; but they were expecting better things of me, a chartered, professional moralist, and they were saddened.

I fell visibly in their respect and esteem, and I should have fallen in my own, except that I had already struck bottom, and there wasn't any place to fall to.

At Tuskegee they will jump to misleading conclusions from insufficient evidence, along with Doctor Parkhurst, and they will deceive the student with the superstition that no gentleman ever swears.

Look at those good millionaires; aren't they gentlemen? Well, they swear. Only once in a year, maybe, but there's enough bulk to it to make up for the lost time. And do they lose anything by it? No, they don't; they save enough in three minutes to support the family seven years. When they swear, do we shudder? No—unless they say "damn!" Then we do. It shrivels us all up. Yet we ought not to feel so about it because we all swear—everybody. Including the ladies. Including Doctor Parkhurst, that strong and brave and excellent citizen, but superficially educated.

For it is not the word that is the sin, it is the spirit back of the word. When an irritated lady says "oh!" the spirit back of it is "damn!" and that is the way it is going to be recorded against her. It always makes me so sorry when I hear a lady swear like that. But if she says "damn," and says it in an amiable, nice way, it isn't going to be recorded at all.

The idea that no gentleman ever swears is all wrong; he can swear and still be a gentleman if he does it in a nice and benevolent and affectionate way. The historian, John Fiske, whom I knew well and loved, was a spotless and most noble and upright Christian gentleman, and yet he swore once. Not exactly that, maybe; still, he—but I will tell you about it.

One day, when he was deeply immersed in his work, his wife came in, much moved and profoundly distressed, and said: "I am sorry to disturb you, John, but I must, for this is a serious matter, and needs to be attended to at once."

Then, lamenting, she brought a grave accusation against their little son. She said: "He has been saying his Aunt Mary is a fool and his Aunt Martha is a damned fool." Mr. Fiske reflected upon the matter a minute, then said: "Oh, well, it's about the distinction I should make between them myself."

Mr. Washington, I beg you to convey these teachings to your great and prosperous and most beneficent education institution, and add them to the prodigal mental and moral riches wherewith you equip your fortunate protégés for the struggle of life.

1910

The Turning-point of My Life

I

If I understand the idea, the *Bazaar*[1] invites several of us to write upon the above text. It means the change in my life's course which introduced what must be regarded by me as the most *important* condition of my career. But it also implies—without intention, perhaps—that that turning-point *itself* was the creator of the new condition. This gives it too much distinction, too much prominence, too much credit. It is only the *last* link in a very long chain of turning-points commissioned to produce the cardinal result; it is not any more important than the humblest of its ten thousand predecessors. Each of the ten thousand did its appointed share, on its appointed date, in forwarding the scheme, and they were all necessary; to have left out any one of them would have defeated the scheme and brought about *some other* result. I know we have a fashion of saying "such and such an event was the turning-point in my life," but we shouldn't say it. We should merely grant that its place as *last* link in the chain

---

[1] *Harper's Bazaar.* Henry James also wrote on the suggested text.—C.N.

makes it the most *conspicuous* link; in real importance it has no advantage over any one of its predecessors.

Perhaps the most celebrated turning-point recorded in history was the crossing of the Rubicon. Suetonius says:

> Coming up with his troops on the banks of the Rubicon, he halted for a while, and, revolving in his mind the importance of the step he was on the point of taking, he turned to those about him and said, "We may still retreat; but if we pass this little bridge, nothing is left for us but to fight it out in arms."

This was a stupendously important moment. And all the incidents, big and little, of Caesar's previous life had been leading up to it, stage by stage, link by link. This was the *last* link—merely the last one, and no bigger than the others; but as we gaze back at it through the inflating mists of our imagination, it looks as big as the orbit of Neptune.

You, the reader, have a *personal* interest in that link, and so have I; so has the rest of the human race. It was one of the links in your life-chain, and it was one of the links in mine. We may wait, now, with bated breath, while Caesar reflects. Your fate and mine are involved in his decision.

While he was thus hesitating, the following incident occurred. A person remarked for his noble mien and graceful aspect appeared close at hand, sitting and playing upon a pipe. When not only the shepherds, but a number of soldiers also, flocked to listen to him, and some trumpeters among them, he snatched a trumpet from one of them, ran to the river with it, and, sounding the advance with a piercing blast, crossed to the other side. Upon this, Caesar exclaimed: "Let us go whither the omens of the gods and the iniquity of our enemies call us. *The die is cast.*"

So he crossed—and changed the future of the whole human race, for all time. But that stranger was a link in Caesar's life-chain, too; and a necessary one. We don't know his name, we never hear of him again; he was very casual; he acts like an accident; but he was no accident, he was there by compulsion of *his* life-chain, to blow the electrifying blast that was to make up Caesar's mind for him, and thence go piping down the aisles of history forever.

If the stranger hadn't been there! But he *was*. And Caesar crossed. With such results! Such vast events—each a link in the *human* race's life-chain; each event producing the next one, and that one the next one, and so on: the destruction of the republic; the founding of the empire; the breaking up of the empire; the rise of Christianity upon its ruins; the spread of the religion to other lands—and so on: link by link took its appointed place at its appointed time, the discovery of America being one of them; our Revolution another; the inflow of English and other immigrants another; their drift westward (my ancestors among them) another; the settlement of certain of them in Missouri, which resulted in *me*. For I was one of the unavoidable results of the crossing of the Rubicon. If the stranger, with his trumpet blast, had stayed away (which he *couldn't*, for he was an appointed link) Caesar would not have crossed. What would have happened, in that case, we can never guess. We only know that the things that did happen would not have happened. They might have been replaced by equally prodigious things, of course, but their nature and results are beyond our guessing. But the matter that interests me personally is that I would not be *here* now, but somewhere else; and probably black—there is no telling. Very well, I am glad he crossed. And very really and thankfully glad, too, though I never cared anything about it before.

II

To me, the most important feature of my life is its literary feature. I have been professionally literary something more than forty years. There have been many turning-points in my life, but the one that was the last link in the chain appointed to conduct me to the literary guild is the most *conspicuous* link in that chain. *Because* it was the last one. It was not any more important than its predecessors. All the other links have an inconspicuous look, except the crossing of the Rubicon; but as factors in making me literary they are all of the one size, the crossing of the Rubicon included.

I know how I came to be literary, and I will tell the steps that led up to it and brought it about.

The crossing of the Rubicon was not the first one, it was hardly even a recent one; I should have to go back ages before Caesar's day to find the first one. To save space I will go back only a couple of generations and start with an incident of my boyhood. When I was twelve and a half years old, my father died. It was in the spring. The summer came, and brought with it an epidemic of measles. For a time, a child died almost every day. The village was paralyzed with fright, distress, despair. Children that were not smitten with the disease

were imprisoned in their homes to save them from the infection. In
the homes there were no cheerful faces, there was no music, there
was no singing but of solemn hymns, no voice but of prayer, no
romping was allowed, no noise, no laughter, the family moved
spectrally about on tiptoe, in a ghostly hush. I was a prisoner. My soul
was steeped in this awful dreariness—and in fear. At some time or
other every day and every night a sudden shiver shook me to the
marrow, and I said to myself, "There, I've got it! and I shall die." Life
on these miserable terms was not worth living, and at last I made up
my mind to get the disease and have it over, one way or the other.
I escaped from the house and went to the house of a neighbor where
a playmate of mine was very ill with the malady. When the chance
offered I crept into his room and got into bed with him. I was discovered by his mother and sent back into captivity. But I had the
disease; they could not take that from me. I came near to dying. The
whole village was interested, and anxious, and sent for news of me
every day; and not only once a day, but several times. Everybody believed I would die; but on the fourteenth day a change came for the
worse and they were disappointed.

This was a turning-point of my life. (Link number one.) For when
I got well my mother closed my school career and apprenticed me to
a printer. She was tired of trying to keep me out of mischief, and
the adventure of the measles decided her to put me into more masterful hands than hers.

I became a printer, and began to add one link after another to
the chain which was to lead me into the literary profession. A long
road, but I could not know that; and as I did not know what its goal
was, or even that it had one, I was indifferent. Also contented.

A young printer wanders around a good deal, seeking and finding
work; and seeking again, when necessity commands. N. B. Necessity
is a *Circumstance;* Circumstance is man's master—and when Circumstance commands, he must obey; he may argue the matter—that is his
privilege, just as it is the honorable privilege of a falling body to
argue with the attraction of gravitation—but it won't do any good, he
must *obey.* I wandered for ten years, under the guidance and dictator-
ship of Circumstance, and finally arrived in a city of Iowa, where I
worked several months. Among the books that interested me in those
days was one about the Amazon. The traveler told an alluring tale
of his long voyage up the great river from Para to the sources of the
Madeira, through the heart of an enchanted land, a land wastefully
rich in tropical wonders, a romantic land where all the birds and

flowers and animals were of the museum varieties, and where the alligator and the crocodile and the monkey seemed as much at home
as if they were in the Zoo. Also, he told an astonishing tale about *coca*,
a vegetable product of miraculous powers, asserting that it was so
nourishing and so strength-giving that the native of the mountains
of the Madeira region would tramp up hill and down all day on a
pinch of powdered coca and require no other sustenance.

I was fired with a longing to ascend the Amazon. Also with a longing to open up a trade in coca with all the world. During months I
dreamed that dream, and tried to contrive ways to get to Para and
spring that splendid enterprise upon an unsuspecting planet. But all
in vain. A person may *plan* as much as he wants to, but nothing of
consequence is likely to come of it until the magician *Circumstance*
steps in and takes the matter off his hands. At last Circumstance came
to my help. It was in this way. Circumstance, to help or hurt another
man, made him lose a fifty-dollar bill in the street; and to help or
hurt me, made me find it. I advertised the find, and left for the
Amazon the same day. This was another turning-point, another link.

Could Circumstance have ordered another dweller in that town to
go to the Amazon and open up a world-trade in coca on a fifty-dollar
basis and been obeyed? No, I was the only one. There were other
fools there—shoals and shoals of them—but they were not of my kind.
I was the only one of my kind.

Circumstance is powerful, but it cannot work alone; it has to have
a partner. Its partner is man's *temperament*—his natural disposition.
His temperament is not his invention, it is *born* in him, and he has
no authority over it, neither is he responsible for its acts. He cannot
change it, nothing can change it, nothing can modify it—except temporarily. But it won't stay modified. It is permanent, like the color
of the man's eyes and the shape of his ears. Blue eyes are gray in
certain unusual lights; but they resume their natural color when that
stress is removed.

A Circumstance that will coerce one man will have no effect upon
a man of a different temperament. If Circumstance had thrown the
bank-note in Caesar's way, his temperament would not have made
him start for the Amazon. His temperament would have compelled
him to do something with the money, but not that. It might have made
him advertise the note—and *wait*. We can't tell. Also, it might have
made him go to New York and buy into the Government, with results
that would leave Tweed nothing to learn when it came his turn.

Very well, Circumstance furnished the capital, and my temperament told me what to do with it. Sometimes a temperament is an ass. When that is the case the owner of it is an ass, too, and is going to remain one. Training, experience, association, can temporarily so polish him, improve him, exalt him that people will think he is a mule, but they will be mistaken. Artificially he *is* a mule, for the time being, but at bottom he is an ass yet, and will remain one.

By temperament I was the kind of person that *does* things. Does them, and reflects afterward. So I started for the Amazon without reflecting and without asking any questions. That was more than fifty years ago. In all that time my temperament has not changed, by even a shade. I have been punished many and many a time, and bitterly, for doing things and reflecting afterward, but these tortures have been of no value to me: I still do the thing commanded by Circumstance and Temperament, and reflect afterward. Always violently. When I am reflecting, on those occasions, even deaf persons can hear me think.

I went by the way of Cincinnati, and down the Ohio and Mississippi. My idea was to take ship, at New Orleans, for Para. In New Orleans I inquired, and found there was no ship leaving for Para. Also, that there never had *been* one leaving for Para. I reflected. A policeman came and asked me what I was doing, and I told him. He made me move on, and said if he caught me reflecting in the public street again he would run me in.

After a few days I was out of money. Then Circumstance arrived, with another turning-point of my life—a new link. On my way down, I had made the acquaintance of a pilot. I begged him to teach me the river, and he consented. I became a pilot.

By and by Circumstance came again—introducing the Civil War, this time, in order to push me ahead another stage or two toward the literary profession. The boats stopped running, my livelihood was gone.

Circumstance came to the rescue with a new turning-point and a fresh link. My brother was appointed secretary to the new Territory of Nevada, and he invited me to go with him and help him in his office. I accepted.

In Nevada, Circumstance furnished me the silver fever and I went into the mines to make a fortune, as I supposed; but that was not the idea. The idea was to advance me another step toward literature. For amusement I scribbled things for the Virginia City *Enterprise*. One isn't a printer ten years without setting up acres of good and bad literature, and learning—unconsciously at first, consciously later—to discriminate between the two, within his mental limitations; and meantime he is unconsciously acquiring what is called a "style." One of my efforts attracted attention, and the *Enterprise* sent for me and put me on its staff.

And so I became a journalist—another link. By and by Circumstance and the Sacramento *Union* sent me to the Sandwich Islands for five or six months, to write up sugar. I did it; and threw in a good deal of extraneous matter that hadn't anything to do with sugar. But it was this extraneous matter that helped me to another link.

It made me notorious, and San Francisco invited me to lecture. Which I did. And profitably. I had long had a desire to travel and see the world, and now Circumstance had most kindly and unexpectedly hurled me upon the platform and furnished me the means. So I joined the "Quaker City Excursion."

When I returned to America, Circumstance was waiting on the pier—with the *last* link—the conspicuous, the consummating, the victorious link: I was asked to *write a book*, and I did it, and called it *The Innocents Abroad*. Thus I became at last a member of the literary guild. That was forty-two years ago, and I have been a member ever since. Leaving the Rubicon incident away back where it belongs, I can say with truth that the reason I am in the literary profession is because I had the measles when I was twelve years old.

III

Now what interests me, as regards these details, is not the details themselves, but the fact that none of them was foreseen by me, none of them was planned by me, I was the author of none of them. Circumstance, working in harness with my temperament, created them all and compelled them all. I often offered help, and with the best intentions, but it was rejected—as a rule, uncourteously. I could never plan a thing and get it to come out the way I planned it. It came out some other way—some way I had not counted upon.

And so I do not admire the human being—as an intellectual marvel—as much as I did when I was young, and got him out of books, and did not know him personally. When I used to read that such and such a general did a certain brilliant thing, I believed it. Whereas it was not so. Circumstance did it by help of his temperament. The circumstance would have failed of effect with a general of another temperament: he might see the chance, but lose the advantage by being by nature too slow or too quick or too doubtful. Once General

Grant was asked a question about a matter which had been much debated by the public and the newspapers; he answered the question without any hesitancy. "General, who planned the march through Georgia?" "The enemy!" He added that the enemy usually makes your plans for you. He meant that the enemy by neglect or through force of circumstances leaves an opening for you, and you see your chance and take advantage of it.

Circumstances do the planning for us all, no doubt, by help of our temperaments. I see no great difference between a man and a watch, except that the man is conscious and the watch isn't, and the man *tries* to plan things and the watch doesn't. The watch doesn't wind itself and doesn't regulate itself—these things are done exteriorly. Outside influences, outside circumstances, wind the *man* and regulate him. Left to himself, he wouldn't get regulated at all, and the sort of time he would keep would not be valuable. Some rare men are wonderful watches, with gold case, compensation balance, and all those things, and some men are only simple and sweet and humble Waterburys. I am a Waterbury. A Waterbury of that kind, some say.

A nation is only an individual multiplied. It makes plans and Circumstance comes and upsets them—or enlarges them. Some patriots throw the tea overboard; some other patriots destroy a Bastille. The *plans* stop there; then Circumstance comes in, quite unexpectedly, and turns these modest riots into a revolution.

And there was poor Columbus. He elaborated a deep plan to find a new route to an old country. Circumstance revised his plan for him, and he found a new *world*. And *he* gets the credit of it to this day. He hadn't anything to do with it.

Necessarily the scene of the real turning-point of my life (and of yours) was the Garden of Eden. It was there that the first link was forged of the chain that was ultimately to lead to the emptying of me into the literary guild. Adam's *temperament* was the first command the Deity ever issued to a human being on this planet. And it was the only command Adam would *never* be able to disobey. It said, "Be weak, be water, be characterless, be cheaply persuadable." The later command, to let the fruit alone, was certain to disobeyed. Not by Adam himself, but by his *temperament*—which he did not create and had no authority over. For the *temperament* is the man; the thing tricked out with clothes and named Man is merely its Shadow, nothing more. The law of the tiger's temperament is, Thou shalt kill; the law of the sheep's temperament is, Thou shalt not kill. To issue later commands requiring the tiger to let the fat stranger alone, and requiring the sheep to imbue its hands in the blood of the lion is not worth while, for those commands *can't* be obeyed. They would invite to violations of the law of *temperament,* which is supreme, and takes precedence of all other authorities. I cannot help feeling disappointed in Adam and Eve. That is, in their temperaments. Not in *them,* poor helpless young creatures—afflicted with temperaments made out of butter; which butter was commanded to get into contact with fire and *be melted.* What I cannot help wishing is, that Adam and Eve had been postponed, and Martin Luther and Joan of Arc put in their place—that splendid pair equipped with temperaments not made of butter, but of asbestos. By neither sugary persuasions nor by hell fire could Satan have beguiled *them* to eat the apple.

There would have been results! Indeed, yes. The apple would be intact to-day; there would be no human race; there would be no *you;* there would be no *me.* And the old, old creation-dawn scheme of ultimately launching me into the literary guild would have been defeated.

1910

The Death of Jean

The death of Jean Clemens occurred early in the morning of December 24, 1909. Mr. Clemens was in great stress of mind when I first saw him, but a few hours later I found him writing steadily.

"I am setting it down," he said, "everything. It is a relief to me to write it. It furnishes me an excuse for thinking." At intervals during that day and the next I looked in, and usually found him writing. Then on the evening of the 26th, when he knew that Jean had been laid to rest in Elmira, he came to my room with the manuscript in his hand.

"I have finished it," he said; "read it. I can form no opinion of it myself. If you think it worthy, some day—at the proper time—it can end my autobiography. It is the final chapter."[1]

Four months later—almost to the day—(April 21st) he was with Jean.

ALBERT BIGELOW PAINE.

[1] The chapter appeared posthumously in *Harper's Magazine,* January 1911, and was reprinted by Paine in *What Is Man?* in 1917. Paine did not use it in his edition of the autobiography (1924). I used it as the concluding chapter of my edition (1959).—C.N.

Jean is dead!

Has any one ever tried to put upon paper all the little happenings connected with a dear one—happenings of the twenty-four hours preceding the sudden and unexpected death of that dear one? Would a book contain them? Would two books contain them? I think not. They pour into the mind in a flood. They are little things that have been always happening every day, and were always so unimportant and easily forgetable before—but now! Now, how different! how precious they are, how dear, how unforgetable, how pathetic, how sacred, how clothed with dignity!

Last night Jean, all flushed with splendid health, and I the same, from the wholesome effects of my Bermuda holiday, strolled hand in hand from the dinner-table and sat down in the library and chatted, and planned, and discussed, cheerily and happily (and how unsuspectingly!—until nine—which is late for us—then went up-stairs, Jean's friendly German dog following. At my door Jean said, "I can't kiss you good night, father: I have a cold, and you could catch it." I bent and kissed her hand. She was moved—I saw it in her eyes—and she impulsively kissed my hand in return. Then with the usual gay "Sleep well, dear!" from both, we parted.

At half past seven this morning I woke, and heard voices outside my door. I said to myself, "Jean is starting on her usual horseback flight to the station for the mail." Then Katy[2] entered, stood quaking and gasping at my bedside a moment, then found her tongue:

"Miss Jean is dead!"

Possibly I know now what the soldier feels when a bullet crashes through his heart.

In her bathroom there she lay, the fair young creature, stretched upon the floor and covered with a sheet. And looking so placid, so natural, and as if asleep. We knew what had happened. She was an epileptic: she had been seized with a convulsion and heart failure in her bath. The doctor had to come several miles. His efforts, like our previous ones, failed to bring her back to life.

It is noon, now. How lovable she looks, how sweet and how tranquil! It is a noble face, and full of dignity; and that was a good heart that lies there so still.

In England, thirteen years ago, my wife and I were stabbed to the

---

[2] Katy Leary, who had been in the service of the Clemens family for twenty-nine years.—A.B.P.

heart with a cablegram which said, "Susy was mercifully released to-day." I had to send a like shock to Clara, in Berlin, this morning. With the peremptory addition, "You must not come home." Clara and her husband sailed from here on the 11th of this month. How will Clara bear it? Jean, from her babyhood, was a worshiper of Clara.

Four days ago I came back from a month's holiday in Bermuda in perfected health; but by some accident the reporters failed to perceive this. Day before yesterday, letters and telegrams began to arrive from friends and strangers which indicated that I was supposed to be dangerously ill. Yesterday Jean begged me to explain my case through the Associated Press. I said it was not important enough; but she was distressed and said I must think of Clara. Clara would see the report in the German papers, and as she had been nursing her husband day and night for four months[3] and was worn out and feeble, the shock might be disastrous. There was reason in that; so I sent a humorous paragraph by telephone to the Associated Press denying the "charge" that I was "dying," and saying "I would not do such a thing at my time of life."

Jean was a little troubled, and did not like to see me treat the matter so lightly; but I said it was best to treat it so, for there was nothing serious about it. This morning I sent the sorrowful facts of this day's irremediable disaster to the Associated Press. Will both appear in this evening's papers?—the one so blithe, the other so tragic.

I lost Susy thirteen years ago; I lost her mother—her incomparable mother!—five and a half years ago; Clara has gone away to live in Europe; and now I have lost Jean. How poor I am, who was once so rich! Seven months ago Mr. Rogers died—one of the best friends I ever had, and the nearest perfect, as man and gentleman, I have yet met among my race; within the last six weeks Gilder has passed away, and Laffan—old, old friends of mine. Jean lies yonder, I sit here; we are strangers under our own roof; we kissed hands good-by at this door last night—and it was forever, we never suspecting it. She lies there, and I sit here—writing, busying myself, to keep my heart from breaking. How dazzlingly the sunshine is flooding the hills around! It is like a mockery.

Seventy-four years old twenty-four days ago. Seventy-four years old yesterday. Who can estimate my age to-day?

I have looked upon her again. I wonder I can bear it. She looks just

---

[3] Mr. Gabrilowitsch had been operated on for appendicitis.—A.B.P.

as her mother looked when she lay dead in that Florentine villa so long ago. The sweet placidity of death! it is more beautiful than sleep.

I saw her mother buried. I said I would never endure that horror again; that I would never again look into the grave of any one dear to me. I have kept to that. They will take Jean from this house tomorrow, and bear her to Elmira, New York, where lie those of us that have been released, but I shall not follow.

Jean was on the dock when the ship came in, only four days ago. She was at the door, beaming a welcome, when I reached this house the next evening. We played cards, and she tried to teach me a new game called "Mark Twain." We sat chatting cheerily in the library last night, and she wouldn't let me look into the loggia, where she was making Christmas preparations. She said she would finish them in the morning, and then her little French friend would arrive from New York—the surprise would follow; the surprise she had been working over for days. While she was out for a moment I disloyally stole a look. The loggia floor was clothed with rugs and furnished with chairs and sofas; and the uncompleted surprise was there; in the form of a Christmas tree that was drenched with silver film in a most wonderful way; and on a table was a prodigal profusion of bright things which she was going to hang upon it to-day. What desecrating hand will ever banish that eloquent unfinished surprise from that place? Not mine, surely. All these little matters have happened in the last four days. "Little." Yes—*then*. But not now. Nothing she said or thought or did is little now. And all the lavish humor!—what is become of it? It is pathos, now. Pathos, and the thought of it brings tears.

All these little things happened such a few hours ago—and now she lies yonder. Lies yonder, and cares for nothing any more. Strange—marvelous—incredible! I have had this experience before; but it would still be incredible if I had had it a thousand times.

"Miss Jean is dead!"

That is what Katy said. When I heard the door open behind the bed's head without a preliminary knock, I supposed it was Jean coming to kiss me good morning, she being the only person who was used to entering without formalities.

And so—

I have been to Jean's parlor. Such a turmoil of Christmas presents for servants and friends! They are everywhere; tables, chairs, sofas, the floor—everything is occupied, and over-occupied. It is many and many a year since I have seen the like. In that ancient day Mrs. Clemens and I used to slip softly into the nursery at midnight on Christmas Eve and look the array of presents over. The children were little then. And now here is Jean's parlor looking just as that nursery used to look. The presents are not labeled—the hands are forever idle that would have labeled them to-day. Jean's mother always worked herself down with her Christmas preparations. Jean did the same yesterday and the preceding days, and the fatigue has cost her her life. The fatigue caused the convulsion that attacked her this morning. She had had no attack for months.

Jean was so full of life and energy that she was constantly in danger of overtaxing her strength. Every morning she was in the saddle by half past seven, and off to the station for her mail. She examined the letters and I distributed them: some to her, some to Mr. Paine, the others to the stenographer and myself. She despatched her share and then mounted her horse again and went around superintending her farm and her poultry the rest of the day. Sometimes she played billiards with me after dinner, but she was usually too tired to play, and went early to bed.

Yesterday afternoon I told her about some plans I had been devising while absent in Bermuda, to lighten her burdens. We would get a housekeeper; also we would put her share of the secretary-work into Mr. Paine's hands.

No—she wasn't willing. She had been making plans herself. The matter ended in a compromise, I submitted. I always did. She wouldn't audit the bills and let Paine fill out the checks—she would continue to attend to that herself. Also, she would continue to be housekeeper, and let Katy assist. Also, she would continue to answer the letters of personal friends for me. Such was the compromise. Both of us called it by that name, though I was not able to see where any formidable change had been made.

However, Jean was pleased, and that was sufficient for me. She was proud of being my secretary, and I was never able to persuade her to give up any part of her share in that unlovely work.

In the talk last night I said I found everything going so smoothly that if she were willing I would go back to Bermuda in February and get blessedly out of the clash and turmoil again for another month. She was urgent that I should do it, and said that if I would put off the trip until March she would take Katy and go with me. We struck hands upon that, and said it was settled. I had a mind to write to Ber-

muda by to-morrow's ship and secure a furnished house and servants.
I meant to write the letter this morning. But it will never be written,
now.

For she lies yonder, and before her is another journey than that.

Night is closing down; the rim of the sun barely shows above the
sky-line of the hills.

I have been looking at that face again that was growing dearer and
dearer to me every day. I was getting acquainted with Jean in these
last nine months. She had been long an exile from home when she
came to us three-quarters of a year ago. She had been shut up in
sanitariums, many miles from us. How eloquently glad and grateful
she was to cross her father's threshold again!

Would I bring her back to life if I could do it? I would not. If a
word would do it, I would beg for strength to withhold the word. And
I would have the strength; I am sure of it. In her loss I am almost
bankrupt, and my life is a bitterness, but I am content: for she has
been enriched with the most precious of all gifts—that gift which
makes all other gifts mean and poor—death. I have never wanted any
released friend of mine restored to life since I reached manhood. I
felt in this way when Susy passed away; and later my wife, and later
Mr. Rogers. When Clara met me at the station in New York and told
me Mr. Rogers had died suddenly that morning, my thought was, Oh,
favorite of fortune—fortunate all his long and lovely life—fortunate to
his latest moment! The reporters said there were tears of sorrow in
my eyes. True—but they were for *me*, not for him. He had suffered no
loss. All the fortunes he had ever made before were poverty compared with this one.

Why did I build this house, two years ago? To shelter this vast
emptiness? How foolish I was! But I shall stay in it. The spirits of the
dead hallow a house, for me. It was not so with other members of my
family. Susy died in the house we built in Hartford. Mrs. Clemens
would never enter it again. But it made the house dearer to me. I
have entered it once since, when it was tenantless and silent and forlorn, but to me it was a holy place and beautiful. It seemed to me that
the spirits of the dead were all about me, and would speak to me
and welcome me if they could: Livy, and Susy, and George, and
Henry Robinson, and Charles Dudley Warner. How good and kind
they were, and how lovable their lives! In fancy I could see them all
again, I could call the children back and hear them romp again with
George—that peerless black ex-slave and children's idol who came one

day—a flitting stranger—to wash windows, and stayed eighteen years. Until he died. Clara and Jean would never enter again the New York hotel which their mother had frequented in earlier days. They could not bear it. But I shall stay in this house. It is dearer to me to-night than ever it was before. Jean's spirit will make it beautiful for me always. Her lonely and tragic death—but I will not think of that now.

Jean's mother always devoted two or three weeks to Christmas shopping, and was always physically exhausted when Christmas Eve came. Jean was her very own child—she wore herself out present-hunting in New York these latter days. Paine has just found on her desk a long list of names—fifty, he thinks—people to whom she sent presents last night. Apparently she forgot no one. And Katy found there a roll of bank-notes, for the servants.

Her dog has been wandering about the grounds to-day, comradeless and forlorn. I have seen him from the windows. She got him from Germany. He has tall ears and looks exactly like a wolf. He was educated in Germany, and knows no language but the German. Jean gave him no orders save in that tongue. And so, when the burglar-alarm made a fierce clamor at midnight a fortnight ago, the butler, who is French and knows no German, tried in vain to interest the dog in the supposed burglar. Jean wrote me, to Bermuda, about the incident. It was the last letter I was ever to receive from her bright head and her competent hand. The dog will not be neglected.

There was never a kinder heart than Jean's. From her childhood up she always spent the most of her allowance on charities of one kind and another. After she became secretary and had her income doubled she spent her money upon these things with a free hand. Mine too, I am glad and grateful to say.

She was a loyal friend to all animals, and she loved them all, birds, beasts, and everything—even snakes—an inheritance from me. She knew all the birds: she was high up in that lore. She became a member of various humane societies when she was still a little girl—both here and abroad—and she remained an active member to the last. She founded two or three societies for the protection of animals, here and in Europe.

She was an embarrassing secretary, for she fished my correspondence out of the waste-basket and answered the letters. She thought all letters deserved the courtesy of an answer. Her mother brought her up in that kindly error.

She could write a good letter, and was swift with her pen. She had but an indifferent ear for music, but her tongue took to languages with an easy facility. She never allowed her Italian, French, and German to get rusty through neglect.

The telegrams of sympathy are flowing in, from far and wide, now, just as they did in Italy five years and a half ago, when this child's mother laid down her blameless life. They cannot heal the hurt, but they take away some of the pain. When Jean and I kissed hands and parted at my door last, how little did we imagine that in twenty-two hours the telegraph would be bringing words like these:

"From the bottom of our hearts we send our sympathy, dearest of friends."

For many and many a day to come, wherever I go in this house, remembrancers of Jean will mutely speak to me of her. Who can count the number of them?

She was in exile two years with the hope of healing her malady—epilepsy. There are no words to express how grateful I am that she did not meet her fate in the hands of strangers, but in the loving shelter of her own home.

"Miss Jean is dead!"

It is true. Jean is dead.

A month ago I was writing bubbling and hilarious articles for magazines yet to appear, and now I am writing—this.

Christmas Day. Noon.—Last night I went to Jean's room at intervals, and turned back the sheet and looked at the peaceful face, and kissed the cold brow, and remembered that heartbreaking night in Florence so long ago, in that cavernous and silent vast villa, when I crept down-stairs so many times, and turned back a sheet and looked at a face just like this one—Jean's mother's face—and kissed a brow that was just like this one. And last night I saw again what I had seen then—that strange and lovely miracle—the sweet, soft contours of early maidenhood restored by the gracious hand of death! When Jean's mother lay dead, all trace of care, and trouble, and suffering, and the corroding years had vanished out of the face, and I was looking again upon it as I had known and worshiped it in its young bloom and beauty a whole generation before.

About three in the morning, while wandering about the house in the deep silences, as one does in times like these, when there is a dumb sense that something has been lost that will never be found again, yet must be sought, if only for the employment the useless seeking gives, I came upon Jean's dog in the hall down-stairs, and noted that he did not spring to greet me, according to his hospitable habit, but came slow and sorrowfully; also I remembered that he had not visited Jean's apartment since the tragedy. Poor fellow, did he know? I think so. Always when Jean was abroad in the open he was with her; always when she was in the house he was with her, in the night as well as in the day. Her parlor was his bedroom. Whenever I happened upon him on the ground floor he always followed me about, and when I went up-stairs he went too—in a tumultuous gallop. But now it was different: after patting him a little I went to the library— he remained behind; when I went up-stairs he did not follow me, save with his wistful eyes. He has wonderful eyes—big, and kind, and eloquent. He can talk with them. He is a beautiful creature, and is of the breed of the New York police-dogs. I do not like dogs, because they bark when there is no occasion for it; but I have liked this one from the beginning, because he belonged to Jean, and because he never barks except when there is occasion—which is not oftener than twice a week.

In my wanderings I visited Jean's parlor. On a shelf I found a pile of my books, and I knew what it meant. She was waiting for me to come home from Bermuda and autograph them, then she would send them away. If I only knew whom she intended them for! But I shall never know. I will keep them. Her hand has touched them—it is an accolade—they are noble, now.

And in a closet she had hidden a surprise for me—a thing I have often wished I owned: a noble big globe. I couldn't see it for the tears. She will never know the pride I take in it, and the pleasure. Today the mails are full of loving remembrances for her: full of those old, old kind words she loved so well, "Merry Christmas to Jean!" If she could only have lived one day longer!

At last she ran out of money, and would not use mine. So she sent to one of those New York homes for poor girls all the clothes she could spare—and more, most likely.

Christmas Night.—This afternoon they took her away from her room. As soon as I might, I went down to the library, and there she lay, in her coffin, dressed in exactly the same clothes she wore when she stood at the other end of the same room on the 6th of October last, as Clara's chief bridesmaid. Her face was radiant with happy excitement then; it was the same face now, with the dignity of death and the peace of God upon it.

They told me the first mourner to come was the dog. He came uninvited, and stood up on his hind legs and rested his fore paws upon the trestle, and took a last long look at the face that was so dear to him, then went his way as silently as he had come. *He knows.*

At mid-afternoon it began to snow. The pity of it—that Jean could not see it! She so loved the snow.

The snow continued to fall. At six o'clock the hearse drew up to the door to bear away its pathetic burden. As they lifted the casket, Paine began playing on the orchestrelle Schubert's "Impromptu," which was Jean's favorite. Then he played the Intermezzo; that was for Susy; then he played the Largo; that was for their mother. He did this at my request. Elsewhere in my Autobiography I have told how the Intermezzo and the Largo came to be associated in my heart with Susy and Livy in their last hours in this life.

From my windows I saw the hearse and the carriages wind along the road and gradually grow vague and spectral in the falling snow, and presently disappear. Jean was gone out of my life, and would not come back any more. Jervis, the cousin she had played with when they were babies together—he and her beloved old Katy—were conducting her to her distant childhood home, where she will lie by her mother's side once more, in the company of Susy and Langdon.

December 26th. The dog came to see me at eight o'clock this morning. He was very affectionate, poor orphan! My room will be his quarters hereafter.

The storm raged all night. It has raged all the morning. The snow drives across the landscape in vast clouds, superb, sublime—and Jean not here to see.

2.30 P.M.—It is the time appointed. The funeral has begun. Four hundred miles away, but I can see it all, just as if I were there. The scene is the library in the Langdon homestead. Jean's coffin stands where her mother and I stood, forty years ago, and were married; and where Susy's coffin stood thirteen years ago, where her mother's stood five years and a half ago; and where mine will stand after a little time.

Five o'clock.—It is all over.

When Clara went away two weeks ago to live in Europe, it was hard, but I could bear it, for I had Jean left. I said *we* would be a family. We said we would be close comrades and happy—just we two. That fair dream was in my mind when Jean met me at the steamer last Monday; it was in my mind when she received me at the door last Tuesday evening. We were together; *we were a family!* the dream had come true—oh, precisely true, contentedly true, satisfyingly true! and remained true two whole days.

And now? Now Jean is in her grave!

In the grave—if I can believe it. God rest her sweet spirit!

1911

How to Make History Dates Stick

These chapters are for children, and I shall try to make the words large enough to command respect. In the hope that you are listening, and that you have confidence in me, I will proceed. Dates are difficult things to acquire; and after they are acquired it is difficult to keep them in the head. But they are very valuable. They are like the cattle-pens of a ranch—they shut in the several brands of historical cattle, each within its own fence, and keep them from getting mixed together. Dates are hard to remember because they consist of figures; figures are monotonously unstriking in appearance, and they don't take hold, they form no pictures, and so they give the eye no chance to help. Pictures are the thing. Pictures can make dates stick. They can make nearly anything stick—particularly *if you make the pictures yourself.* Indeed, that is the great point—make the pictures *yourself.* I know about this from experience. Thirty years ago I was delivering a memorized lecture every night, and every night I had to help myself with a page of notes to keep from getting myself mixed. The notes consisted of beginnings of sentences, and were eleven in number, and they ran something like this:

"*In that region the weather—*"

"*At that time it was a custom—*"

"*But in California one never heard—*"

Eleven of them. They initialed the brief divisions of the lecture and protected me against skipping. But they all looked about alike on the page; they formed no picture; I had them by heart, but I could never with certainty remember the order of their succession; therefore I always had to keep those notes by me and look at them every little while. Once I mislaid them; you will not be able to imagine the terrors of that evening. I now saw that I must invent some other protection. So I got ten of the initial letters by heart in their proper order—I, A, B, and so on—and I went on the platform the next night with these marked in ink on my finger-nails. But it didn't answer. I kept track of the fingers for a while; then I lost it, and after that I was never quite sure which finger I had used last. I couldn't lick off a letter after using it, for while that would have made success certain it would also have provoked too much curiosity. There was curiosity enough without that. To the audience I seemed more interested in my fingernails than I was in my subject; one or two persons asked me afterward what was the matter with my hands.

It was now that the idea of pictures occurred to me; then my troubles passed away. In two minutes I made six pictures with a pen, and they did the work of the eleven catch-sentences, and did it perfectly. I threw the pictures away as soon as they were made, for I was sure I could shut my eyes and see them any time. That was a quarter of a century ago; the lecture vanished out of my head more than twenty years ago, but I could rewrite it from the pictures—for they remain. Here are three of them: (Fig. 1).

FIG. 1

The first one is a haystack—below it a rattlesnake—and it told me where to begin to talk ranch-life in Carson Valley. The second one told me where to begin to talk about a strange and violent wind that used to burst upon Carson City from the Sierra Nevadas every afternoon at two o'clock and try to blow the town away. The third picture, as you easily perceive, is lightning; its duty was to remind me when it was time to begin to talk about San Francisco weather, where there *is* no lightning—nor thunder, either—and it never failed me.

I will give you a valuable hint. When a man is making a speech and you are to follow him don't jot down notes to speak from, jot down *pictures*. It is awkward and embarrassing to have to keep referring to notes; and besides it breaks up your speech and makes it ragged and non-coherent; but you can tear up your pictures as soon as you have made them—they will stay fresh and strong in your memory in the order and sequence in which you scratched them down. And many will admire to see what a good memory you are furnished with, when perhaps your memory is not any better than mine.

Sixteen years ago when my children were little creatures the governess was trying to hammer some primer histories into their heads. Part of this fun—if you like to call it that—consisted in the memorizing of the accession dates of the thirty-seven personages who had ruled over England from the Conqueror down. These little people found it a bitter, hard contract. It was all dates, they all looked alike, and they wouldn't stick. Day after day of the summer vacation dribbled by, and still the kings held the fort; the children couldn't conquer any six of them.

With my lecture experience in mind I was aware that I could invent some way out of the trouble with pictures, but I hoped a way could be found which would let them romp in the open air while they learned the kings. I found it, and then they mastered all the monarchs in a day or two.

The idea was to make them *see* the reigns with their eyes; that would be a large help. We were at the farm then. From the house-porch the grounds sloped gradually down to the lower fence and rose on the right to the high ground where my small work den stood. A carriage-road wound through the grounds and up the hill. I staked it out with the English monarchs, beginning with the Conqueror, and you could stand on the porch and clearly see every reign and its length, from the Conquest down to Victoria, then in the forty-sixth year of her reign—*eight hundred and seventeen years* of English history under your eye at once!

English history was an unusually live topic in America just then. The world had suddenly realized that while it was not noticing the Queen had passed Henry VIII., passed Henry VI. and Elizabeth, and gaining in length every day. Her reign had entered the list of the long ones; everybody was interested now—it was watching a race. Would she pass the long Edward? There was a possibility of it. Would she pass the long Henry? Doubtful, most people said. The long George? Impossible! Everybody said it. But we have lived to see her leave him two years behind.

I measured off 817 feet of the roadway, a foot representing a year, and at the beginning and end of each reign I drove a three-foot white-pine stake in the turf by the roadside and wrote the name and dates on it. Abreast the middle of the porch-front stood a great granite flower-vase overflowing with a cataract of bright-yellow flowers—I can't think of their name. The vase was William the Conqueror. We put his name on it and his accession date, 1066. We started from that and measured off twenty-one feet of the road, and drove William Rufus's stake; then thirteen feet and drove the first Henry's stake; then thirty-five feet and drove Stephen's; then nineteen feet, which brought us just past the summerhouse on the left; then we staked out thirty-five, ten, and seventeen for the second Henry and Richard and John; turned the curve and entered upon just what was needed for Henry III.—a level, straight stretch of fifty-six feet of road without a crinkle in it. And it lay exactly in front of the house, in the middle of the grounds. There couldn't have been a better place for that long reign; you could stand on the porch and see those two wide-apart stakes almost with your eyes shut. (Fig. 2.)

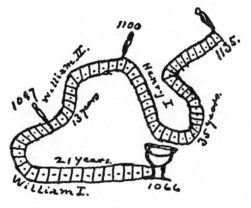

FIG. 2

That isn't the shape of the road—I have bunched it up like that to save room. The road had some great curves in it, but their gradual sweep was such that they were no mar to history. No, in our road one could tell at a glance who was who by the size of the vacancy between stakes—with *locality* to help, of course.

Although I am away off here in a Swedish village[1] and those stakes

---

[1] Summer of 1899.—M.T. (The essay was published posthumously in 1914.— C.N.)

did not stand till the snow came, I can see them to-day as plainly as ever; and whenever I think of an English monarch his stakes rise before me of their own accord and I notice the large or small space which he takes up on our road. Are your kings spaced off in your mind? When you think of Richard III. and of James II. do the durations of their reigns seem about alike to you? It isn't so to me; I always notice that there's a foot's difference. When you think of Henry III. do you see a great long stretch of straight road? I do; and just at the end where it joins on to Edward I. I always see a small pear-bush with its green fruit hanging down. When I think of the Commonwealth I see a shady little group of these small saplings which we called the oak parlor; when I think of George III. I see him stretching up the hill, part of him occupied by a flight of stone steps; and I can locate Stephen to an inch when he comes into my mind, for he just filled the stretch which went by the summer-house. Victoria's reign reached almost to my study door on the first little summit; there's sixteen feet to be added now; I believe that that would carry it to a big pine-tree that was shattered by some lightning one summer when it was trying to hit me.

We got a good deal of fun out of the history road; and exercise, too. We trotted the course from the Conqueror to the study, the children calling out the names, dates, and length of reigns as we passed the stakes, going a good gait along the long reigns, but slowing down when we came upon people like Mary and Edward VI., and the short Stuart and Plantagenet, to give time to get in the statistics. I offered prizes, too—apples. I threw one as far as I could send it, and the child that first shouted the reign it fell in got the apple.

The children were encouraged to stop locating things as being "over by the arbor," or "in the oak parlor," or "up at the stone steps," and say instead that the things were in Stephen, or in the Commonwealth, or in George III. They got the habit without trouble. To have the long road mapped out with such exactness was a great boon for me, for I had the habit of leaving books and other articles lying around everywhere, and had not previously been able to definitely name the place, and so had often been obliged to go to fetch them myself, to save time and failure; but now I could name the reign I left them in, and send the children.

Next I thought I would measure off the French reigns, and peg them alongside the English ones, so that we could always have contemporaneous French history under our eyes as we went our English rounds. We pegged them down to the Hundred Years' War, then threw the idea aside, I do not now remember why. After that we made the English pegs fence in European and American history as well as English, and that answered very well. English and alien poets, statesmen, artists, heroes, battles, plagues, cataclysms, revolutions—we shoveled them all into the English fences according to their dates. Do you understand? We gave Washington's birth to George II.'s pegs and his death to George III.'s; George II. got the Lisbon earthquake and George III. the Declaration of Independence. Goethe, Shakespeare, Napoleon, Savonarola, Joan of Arc, the French Revolution, the Edict of Nantes, Clive, Wellington, Waterloo, Plassey, Patay, Cowpens, Saratoga, the Battle of the Boyne, the invention of the logarithms, the microscope, the steam-engine, the telegraph—anything and everything all over the world—we dumped it all in among the English pegs according to its date and regardless of its nationality.

If the road-pegging scheme had not succeeded I should have lodged the kings in the children's heads by means of pictures—that is, I should have tried. It might have failed, for the pictures could only be effective *when made by the pupil,* not the master, for it is the work put upon the drawing that makes the drawing stay in the memory, and my children were too little to make drawings at that time. And, besides, they had no talent for art, which is strange, for in other ways they are like me.

But I will develop the picture plan now, hoping that you will be able to use it. It will come good for indoors when the weather is bad and one cannot go outside and peg a road. Let us imagine that the kings are a procession, and that they have come out of the Ark and down Ararat for exercise and are now starting back again up the zigzag road. This will bring several of them into view at once, and each zigzag will represent the length of a king's reign.

And so on. You will have plenty of space, for by my project you will use the parlor wall. You do not mark on the wall; that would cause trouble. You only attach bits of paper to it with pins or thumbtacks. These will leave no mark.

Take your pen now, and twenty-one pieces of white paper, each two inches square, and we will do the twenty-one years of the Conqueror's reign. On each square draw a picture of a whale and write the dates and term of service. We choose the whale for several reasons: its name and William's begin with the same letter; it is the biggest fish that swims, and William is the most conspicuous figure in

English history in the way of a landmark; finally, a whale is about the easiest thing to draw. By the time you have drawn twenty-one whales and written "William I.—1066–1087—twenty-one years" twenty-one times, those details will be your property; you cannot dislodge them from your memory with anything but dynamite. I will make a sample for you to copy: (Fig. 3).

William I

1066 — 1087

21 years

FIG. 3

I have got his chin up too high, but that is no matter; he is looking for Harold. It may be that a whale hasn't that fin up there on his back, but I do not remember; and so, since there is a doubt, it is best to err on the safe side. He looks better, anyway, than he would without it.

Be very careful and *attentive* while you are drawing your first whale from my sample and writing the word and figures under it, so that you will not need to copy the sample any more. Compare your copy with the sample; examine closely; if you find you have got everything right and can shut your eyes and see the picture and call the words and figures, then turn the sample and the copy upside down and make the next copy from memory; and also the next and next, and so on, always drawing and writing from memory until you have finished the whole twenty-one. This will take you twenty minutes, or thirty, and by that time you will find that you can make a whale in less time than an un-practised person can make a sardine; also, up to the time you die you will always be able to furnish William's dates to any ignorant person that inquires after them.

You will now take thirteen pieces of *blue* paper, each two inches square, and do William II. (Fig. 4.)

FIG. 4

Make him spout his water forward instead of backward; also make him small, and stick a harpoon in him and give him that sick look in the eye. Otherwise you might seem to be continuing the other William, and that would be confusing and a damage. It is quite right to make him small; he was only about a No. II whale, or along there somewhere; there wasn't room in him for his father's great spirit. The barb of that harpoon ought not to show like that, because it is down inside the whale and ought to be out of sight, but it cannot be helped; if the barb were removed people would think some one had stuck a whip-stock into the whale. It is best to leave the barb the way it is, then every one will know it is a harpoon and attending to business. Remember—draw from the copy only once; make your other twelve and the inscription from memory.

Now the truth is that whenever you have copied a picture and its inscription once from my sample and two or three times from memory the details will stay with you and be hard to forget. After that, if you like, you may make merely the whale's *head and water-spout* for the Conqueror till you end his reign, each time *saying* the inscription in place of writing it; and in the case of William II. make the *harpoon* alone, and say over the inscription each time you do it. You see, it will take nearly twice as long to do the first set as it will to do the second, and that will give you a marked sense of the difference in length of the two reigns.

Next do Henry I. on thirty-five squares of *red* paper. (Fig. 5.)

FIG. 5

That is a hen, and suggests Henry by furnishing the first syllable. When you have repeated the hen and the inscription until you are perfectly sure of them, draw merely the hen's head the rest of the thirty-five times, saying over the inscription each time. Thus: (Fig. 6.).

FIG. 6

You begin to understand now how this procession is going to look when it is on the wall. First, there will be the Conqueror's twenty-one whales and water spouts, the twenty-one white squares joined to one another and making a white stripe three and one-half feet long; the thirteen blue squares of William II. will be joined to that—a blue stripe two feet, two inches long, followed by Henry's red stripe five feet, ten inches long, and so on. The colored divisions will smartly show to the eye the difference in the length of the reigns and impress the proportions on the memory and the understanding. (Fig. 7.)

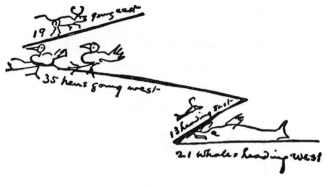

FIG. 7

Stephen of Blois comes next. He requires nineteen two-inch squares of *yellow* paper. (Fig. 8.)

FIG. 8

That is a steer. The sound suggests the beginning of Stephen's name. I choose it for that reason. I can make a better steer than that when I am not excited. But this one will do. It is a good-enough steer for history. The tail is defective, but it only wants straightening out.

Next comes Henry II. Give him thirty-five squares of *red* paper. These hens must face west, like the former ones. (Fig. 9.)

FIG. 9

This hen differs from the other one. He is on his way to inquire what has been happening at Canterbury.

Now we arrive at Richard I., called Richard of the Lion-heart because he was a brave fighter and was never so contented as when he was leading crusades in Palestine and neglecting his affairs at home. Give him ten squares of *white* paper. (Fig. 10.)

FIG. 10

That is a lion. His office is to remind you of the lion-hearted Richard. There is something the matter with his legs, but I do not quite know what it is, they do not seem right. I think the hind ones are the most unsatisfactory; the front ones are well enough, though it would be better if they were rights and lefts.

Next comes King John, and he was a poor circumstance. He was called Lackland. He gave his realm to the Pope. Let him have seventeen squares of *yellow* paper. (Fig. 11.)

FIG. 11

That creature is a jamboree. It looks like a trademark, but that is only an accident and not intentional. It is prehistoric and extinct. It used to roam the earth in the Old Silurian times, and lay eggs and catch fish and climb trees and live on fossils; for it was of a mixed breed, which was the fashion then. It was very fierce, and the Old Silurians were afraid of it, but this is a tame one. Physically it has no representative now, but its mind has been transmitted. First I drew it sitting down, but have turned it the other way now because I think it looks more attractive and spirited when one end of it is galloping. I love to think that in this attitude it gives us a pleasant idea of John coming all in a happy excitement to see what the barons have been arranging for him at Runnymede, while the other one gives us an idea of him sitting down to wring his hands and grieve over it.

We now come to Henry III.; *red* squares again, of course—fifty-six of them. We must make all the Henrys of the same color; it will make their long reigns show up handsomely on the wall. Among all the eight Henrys there were but two short ones. A lucky name, as far as longevity goes. The reigns of six of the Henrys cover 227 years. It might have been well to name all the royal princes Henry, but this was overlooked until it was too late. (Fig. 12.)

FIG. 12

That is the best one yet. He is on his way (1265) to have a look at the first House of Commons in English history. It was a monumental event, the situation of the House, and was the second great liberty landmark which the century had set up. I have made Henry looking glad, but this was not intentional.

Edward I. comes next; *light-brown* paper, thirty-five squares. (Fig. 13.)

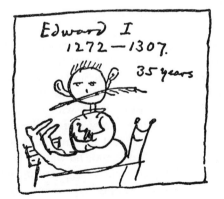

FIG. 13

That is an editor. He is trying to think of a word. He props his feet on the chair, which is the editor's way; then he can think better. I do not care much for this one; his ears are not alike; still, editor suggests the sound of Edward, and he will do. I could make him better if I had a model, but I made this one from memory. But it is no particular matter; they all look alike, anyway. They are conceited and troublesome, and don't pay enough. Edward was the first really English king that had yet occupied the throne. The editor in the picture probably looks just as Edward looked when it was first borne in upon him that this was so. His whole attitude expressed gratification and pride mixed with stupefaction and astonishment.

Edward II. now; twenty *blue* squares. (Fig. 14.)

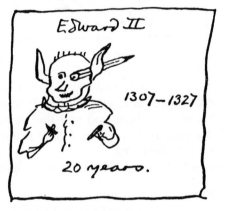

FIG. 14

Another editor. That thing behind his ear is his pencil. Whenever he finds a bright thing in your manuscript he strikes it out with that. That does him good, and makes him smile and show his teeth, the way he is doing in the picture. This one has just been striking out a smart thing, and now he is sitting there with his thumbs in his vest-holes, gloating. They are full of envy and malice, editors are. This picture will serve to remind you that Edward II. was the first English king who was *deposed*. Upon demand, he signed his deposition himself. He had found kingship a most aggravating and disagreeable occupation, and you can see by the look of him that he is glad he resigned. He has put his blue pencil up for good now. He had struck out many a good thing with it in his time.

Edward III. next; fifty *red* squares. (Fig. 15.)

FIG. 15

This editor is a critic. He has pulled out his carving-knife and his tomahawk and is starting after a book which he is going to have for breakfast. This one's arms are put on wrong. I did not notice it at first, but I see it now. Somehow he has got his right arm on his left shoulder, and his left arm on the right shoulder, and this shows us the back of his hands in both instances. It makes him left-handed all around, which is a thing which has never happened before, except perhaps in a museum. That is the way with art, when it is not acquired but born to you: you start in to make some simple little thing, not suspecting that your genius is beginning to work and swell and strain in secret, and all of a sudden there is a convulsion and you fetch out something astonishing. This is called inspiration. It is an accident; you never know when it is coming. I might have tried as much as a year to think of such a strange thing as an all-around left-handed man and I could not have done it, for the more you try to think of an un-thinkable thing the more it eludes you; but it can't elude inspiration; you have only to bait with inspiration and you will get it every time. Look at Botticelli's "Spring." Those snaky women were unthinkable, but inspiration secured them for us, thanks to goodness. It is too late to reorganize this editor-critic now; we will leave him as he is. He will serve to remind us.

Richard II. next; twenty-two *white* squares. (Fig. 16.)

FIG. 16

We use the lion again because this is another Richard. Like Edward II., he was *deposed*. He is taking a last sad look at his crown before they take it away. There was not room enough and I have made it too small; but it never fitted him, anyway.

Now we turn the corner of the century with a new line of monarchs —the Lancastrian kings.

Henry IV.; fourteen squares of *yellow* paper. (Fig. 17.)

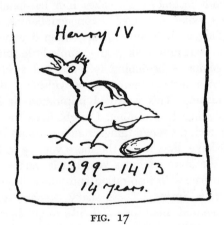

FIG. 17

This hen has laid the egg of a new dynasty and realizes the imposing magnitude of the event. She is giving notice in the usual way. You notice that I am improving in the construction of hens. At first I made them too much like other animals, but this one is orthodox. I mention this to encourage you. You will find that the more you practise the more accurate you will become. I could always draw animals, but before I was educated I could not tell what kind they were when I got them done, but now I can. Keep up your courage; it will be the same with you, although you may not think it. This Henry died the year after Joan of Arc was born.

Henry V.; nine *blue* squares. (Fig. 18.)

FIG. 18

There you see him lost in meditation over the monument which records the amazing figures of the battle of Agincourt. French history says 20,000 Englishmen routed 80,000 Frenchmen there; and English historians say that the French loss, in killed and wounded, was 60,000.

Henry V.; nine *blue* squares. (Fig. 18.)

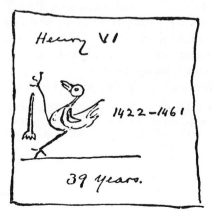

FIG. 19

This is poor Henry VI., who reigned long and scored many mis-fortunes and humiliations. Also two great disasters: he lost France to Joan of Arc and he lost the throne and ended the dynasty which Henry IV. had started in business with such good prospects. In the picture we see him sad and weary and downcast, with the scepter falling from his nerveless grasp. It is a pathetic quenching of a sun which had risen in such splendor.

Edward IV.; twenty-two *light-brown* squares. (Fig. 20.)

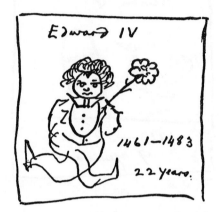

FIG. 20

That is a society editor, sitting there elegantly dressed, with his legs crossed in that indolent way, observing the clothes the ladies wear, so that he can describe them for his paper and make them out finer than they are and get bribes for it and become wealthy. That flower which he is wearing in his buttonhole is a rose—a white rose, a York rose—and will serve to remind us of the Wars of the Roses, and that the white one was the winning color when Edward got the throne and dis-possessed the Lancastrian dynasty.

Edward V.; one-third of a *black* square.[2] (Fig. 21.)

[2] *Well* now, what happened to old Clemens's arithmetic—or am I batty? Don't three months make a quarter rather than a third of a square? Apparently not, if you're a genius. Actually, Edward V did not reign a full three months. He reigned from April 9 to June 26.—C.N.

FIG. 21

His uncle Richard had him murdered in the tower. When you get the reigns displayed upon the wall this one will be conspicuous and easily remembered. It is the shortest one in English history except Lady Jane Grey's, which was only nine days. She is never officially recognized as a monarch of England, but if you or I should ever occupy a throne we should like to have proper notice taken of it; and it would be only fair and right, too, particularly if we gained nothing by it and lost our lives besides.

Richard III.; two *white* squares. (Fig. 22.)

FIG. 22

That is not a very good lion, but Richard was not a very good king. You would think that this lion has two heads, but that is not so; one is only a shadow. There would be shadows for the rest of him, but there was not light enough to go round, it being a dull day, with only fleeting sun-glimpses now and then. Richard had a humped back and a hard heart, and fell at the battle of Bosworth. I do not know the name of that flower in the pot, but we will use it as Richard's trade-mark, for it is said that it grows in only one place in the world—Bosworth Field—and tradition says it never grew there until Richard's royal blood warmed its hidden seed to life and made it grow.

Henry VII.; twenty-four *blue* squares. (Fig. 23.)

FIG. 23

Henry VII. had no liking for wars and turbulence; he preferred peace and quiet and the general prosperity which such conditions create. He liked to sit on that kind of eggs on his own private account as well as the nation's, and hatch them out and count up the result. When he died he left his heir £2,000,000, which was a most unusual fortune for a king to possess in those days. Columbus's great achievement gave him the discovery-fever, and he sent Sebastian Cabot to the New World to search out some foreign territory for England. That is Cabot's ship up there in the corner. This was the first time that England went far abroad to enlarge her estate—but not the last.

Henry VIII.; thirty-eight *red* squares. (Fig. 24.)

FIG. 24

That is Henry VIII. suppressing a monastery in his arrogant fashion.
Edward VI.; six squares of *yellow* paper. (Fig. 25.)

FIG. 25

He is the last Edward to date. It is indicated by that thing over his
head, which is a *last*—shoemaker's last.

Mary; five squares of *black* paper. (Fig. 26.)

FIG. 26

The picture represents a burning martyr. He is in back of the smoke. The first three letters of Mary's name and the first three of the word martyr are the same. Martyrdom was going out in her day and martyrs were becoming scarcer, but she made several. For this reason she is sometimes called Bloody Mary.

This brings us to the reign of Elizabeth, after passing through a period of nearly five hundred years of England's history—492 to be exact. I think you may now be trusted to go the rest of the way without further lessons in art or inspirations in the matter of ideas. You have the scheme now, and something in the ruler's name or career will suggest the pictorial symbol. The effort of inventing such things will not only help your memory, but will develop originality in art. See what it has done for me. If you do not find the parlor wall big enough for all of England's history, continue it into the dining-room and into other rooms. This will make the walls interesting and instructive and really worth something instead of being just flat things to hold the house together.

1914

A Scrap of Curious History

Marion City, on the Mississippi River, in the State of Missouri—a village; time, 1845. La Bourboule-les-Bains, France—a village; time, the end of June, 1894. I was in the one village in that early time; I am in the other now. These times and places are sufficiently wide apart, yet today I have the strange sense of being thrust back into that Missourian village and of reliving certain stirring days that I lived there so long ago.

Last Saturday night the life of the President of the French Republic was taken by an Italian assassin. Last night a mob surrounded our hotel, shouting, howling, singing the "Marseillaise," and pelting our windows with sticks and stones; for we have Italian waiters, and the mob demanded that they be turned out of the house instantly—to be drubbed, and then driven out of the village. Everybody in the hotel remained up until far into the night, and experienced the several kinds of terror which one reads about in books which tell of night attacks by Indians and by French mobs: the growing roar of the oncoming crowd; the arrival, with rain of stones and crash of glass; the withdrawal to rearrange plans—followed by a silence ominous, threatening, and harder to bear than even the active siege and the noise. The landlord and the two village policemen stood their ground, and at last the mob was persuaded to go away and leave our Italians in peace. To-day four of the ringleaders have been sentenced to heavy punishment of a public sort—and are become local heroes, by consequence.

That is the very mistake which was at first made in the Missourian village half a century ago. The mistake was repeated and repeated—just as France is doing in these latter months.

In our village we had our Ravochals, our Henrys, our Vaillants; and in a humble way our Cesario—I hope I have spelled this name wrong. Fifty years ago we passed through, in all essentials, what France has been passing through during the past two or three years, in the matter of periodical frights, horrors, and shudderings.

In several details the parallels are quaintly exact. In that day, for a man to speak out openly and proclaim himself an enemy of negro slavery was simply to proclaim himself a madman. For he was blaspheming against the holiest thing known to a Missourian, and could *not* be in his right mind. For a man to proclaim himself an anarchist in France, three years ago, was to proclaim himself a madman—he could not be in his right mind.

Now the original old first blasphemer against any institution profoundly venerated by a community is quite sure to be in earnest; his followers and imitators may be humbugs and self-seekers, but he himself is sincere—his heart is in his protest.

Robert Hardy was our first *abolitionist*—awful name! He was a journeyman cooper, and worked in the big cooper-shop belonging to the great pork-packing establishment which was Marion City's chief pride and sole source of prosperity. He was a New-Englander, a stranger. And, being a stranger, he was of course regarded as an inferior person—for that has been human nature from Adam down—and of course, also, he was made to feel unwelcome, for this is the ancient law with man and the other animals. Hardy was thirty years old, and a bachelor; pale, given to reverie and reading. He was reserved, and seemed to prefer the isolation which had fallen to his lot. He was treated to many side remarks by his fellows, but as he did not resent them it was decided that he was a coward.

All of a sudden he proclaimed himself an abolitionist—straight out and publicly! He said that negro slavery was a crime, an infamy. For a moment the town was paralyzed with astonishment; then it broke into a fury of rage and swarmed toward the cooper-shop to lynch Hardy. But the Methodist minister made a powerful speech to them and stayed their hands. He proved to them that Hardy was insane and not responsible for his words; that no man *could* be sane and utter such words.

So Hardy was saved. Being insane, he was allowed to go on talking. He was found to be good entertainment. Several nights running he made abolition speeches in the open air, and all the town flocked to hear and laugh. He implored them to believe him sane and sincere, and have pity on the poor slaves, and take measures for the restoration of their stolen rights, or in no long time blood would flow—blood, blood, rivers of blood!

It was great fun. But all of a sudden the aspect of things changed. A slave came flying from Palmyra, the county-seat, a few miles back, and was about to escape in a canoe to Illinois and freedom in the dull twilight of the approaching dawn, when the town constable seized him.

Hardy happened along and tried to rescue the negro; there was a struggle, and the constable did not come out of it alive. Hardy crossed the river with the negro, and then came back to give himself up. All this took time, for the Mississippi is not a French brook, like the Seine, the Loire, and those other rivulets, but is a real river nearly a mile wide. The town was on hand in force by now, but the Methodist preacher and the sheriff had already made arrangements in the interest of order; so Hardy was surrounded by a strong guard and safely conveyed to the village calaboose in spite of all the effort of the mob to get hold of him. The reader will have begun to perceive that this Methodist minister was a prompt man; a prompt man, with active hands and a good headpiece. Williams was his name—Damon Williams; Damon Williams in public, Damnation Williams in private, because he was so powerful on that theme and so frequent.

The excitement was prodigious. The constable was the first man who had ever been killed in the town. The event was by long odds the most imposing in the town's history. It lifted the humble village into sudden importance; its name was in everybody's mouth for twenty miles around. And so was the name of Robert Hardy—Robert Hardy, the stranger, the despised. In a day he was become the person of most consequence in the region, the only person talked about. As to those other coopers, they found their position curiously changed—they were important people, or unimportant, now, in proportion as to how large or how small had been their intercourse with the new celebrity. The two or three who had really been on a sort of familiar footing with him found themselves objects of admiring interest with the public and of envy with their shopmates.

The village weekly journal had lately gone into new hands. The new man was an enterprising fellow, and he made the most of the tragedy. He issued an extra. Then he put up posters promising to devote his whole paper to matters connected with the great event—there would be a full and intensely interesting biography of the murderer, and even a portrait of him. He was as good as his word. He carved the portrait himself, on the back of a wooden type—and a terror it was to look at. It made a great commotion, for this was the first time the village paper had ever contained a picture. The village was very proud. The output of the paper was ten times as great as it had ever been before, yet every copy was sold.

When the trial came on, people came from all the farms around, and from Hannibal, and Quincy, and even from Keokuk; and the court-house could hold only a fraction of the crowd that applied for admission. The trial was published in the village paper, with fresh and still more trying pictures of the accused.

Hardy was convicted, and hanged—a mistake. People came from miles around to see the hanging; they brought cakes and cider, also the women and children, and made a picnic of the matter. It was the largest crowd the village had ever seen. The rope that hanged Hardy was eagerly bought up, in inch samples, for everybody wanted a memento of the memorable event.

Martyrdom gilded with notoriety has its fascinations. Within one week afterward four young light-weights in the village proclaimed themselves abolitionists! In life Hardy had not been able to make a convert; everybody laughed at him; but nobody could laugh at his legacy. The four swaggered around with their slouch-hats pulled down over their faces, and hinted darkly at awful possibilities. The people were troubled and afraid, and showed it. And they were stunned, too; they could not understand it. "Abolitionist" had always been a term of shame and horror; yet here were four young men who were not only not ashamed to bear that name, but were grimly proud of it. Respectable young men they were, too—of good families, and brought up in the church. Ed Smith, the printer's apprentice, nineteen, had been the head Sunday-school boy, and had once recited three thousand Bible verses without making a break. Dick Savage, twenty, the baker's apprentice; Will Joyce, twenty-two, journeyman blacksmith; and Henry Taylor, twenty-four, tobacco-stemmer—were the other three. They were all of a sentimental cast; they were all romance-readers; they all wrote poetry, such as it was; they were all vain and foolish; but they had never before been suspected of having anything bad in them.

They withdrew from society, and grew more and more mysterious and dreadful. They presently achieved the distinction of being denounced by names from the pulpit—which made an immense stir! This was grandeur, this was fame. They were envied by all the other young fellows now. This was natural. Their company grew—grew alarmingly. They took a name. It was a secret name, and was divulged to no outsider; publicly they were simply the abolitionists. They had pass-words, grips, and signs; they had secret meetings; their initiations were conducted with gloomy pomps and ceremonies, at midnight.

They always spoke of Hardy as "the Martyr," and every little while they moved through the principal street in procession—at midnight, black-robed, masked, to the measured tap of the solemn drum—on pilgrimage to the Martyr's grave, where they went through with some majestic fooleries and swore vengeance upon his murderers. They gave previous notice of the pilgrimage by small posters, and warned everybody to keep indoors and darken all houses along the route, and leave the road empty. These warnings were obeyed, for there was a skull and crossbones at the top of the poster.

When this kind of thing had been going on about eight weeks, a quite natural thing happened. A few men of character and grit woke up out of the nightmare of fear which had been stupefying their faculties, and began to discharge scorn and scoffings at themselves and the community for enduring this child's-play; and at the same time they proposed to end it straightway. Everybody felt an uplift; life was breathed into their dead spirits; their courage rose and they began to feel like men again. This was on a Saturday. All day the new feeling grew and strengthened; it grew with a rush; it brought inspiration and cheer with it. Midnight saw a united community, full of zeal and pluck, and with a clearly defined and welcome piece of work in front of it. The best organizer and strongest and bitterest talker on that great Saturday was the Presbyterian clergyman who had denounced the original four from his pulpit—Rev. Hiram Fletcher—and he promised to use his pulpit in the public interest again now. On the morrow he had revelations to make, he said—secrets of the dreadful society.

But the revelations were never made. At half past two in the morning the dead silence of the village was broken by a crashing explosion, and the town patrol saw the preacher's house spring in a wreck of whirling fragments into the sky. The preacher was killed, together with a negro woman, his only slave and servant.

The town was paralyzed again, and with reason. To struggle against a visible enemy is a thing worth while, and there is a plenty of men who stand always ready to undertake it; but to struggle against an invisible one—an invisible one who sneaks in and does his awful work in the dark and leaves no trace—that is another matter. That is a thing to make the bravest tremble and hold back.

The cowed populace were afraid to go to the funeral. The man who was to have had a packed church to hear him expose and denounce the common enemy had but a handful to see him buried. The coroner's jury had brought in a verdict of "death by the visitation of God," for no witness came forward; if any existed they prudently kept out of the way. Nobody seemed sorry. Nobody wanted to see the terrible secret

society provoked into the commission of further outrages. Everybody
wanted the tragedy hushed up, ignored, forgotten, if possible.

And so there was a bitter surprise and an unwelcome one when Will
Joyce, the blacksmith's journey-man, came out and proclaimed himself the assassin! Plainly he was not minded to be robbed of his glory.
He made his proclamation, and stuck to it. Stuck to it, and insisted
upon a trial. Here was an ominous thing; here was a new and peculiarly
formidable terror, for a motive was revealed here which society could
not hope to deal with successfully—*vanity,* thirst for notoriety. If men
were going to kill for notoriety's sake, and to win the glory of newspaper renown, a big trial, and a showy execution, what possible invention of man could discourage or deter them? The town was in a
sort of panic; it did not know what to do.

However, the grand jury had to take hold of the matter—it had no
choice. It brought in a true bill, and presently the case went to the
county court. The trial was a fine sensation. The prisoner was the
principal witness for the prosecution. He gave a full account of the
assassination; he furnished even the minutest particulars: how he
deposited his keg of powder and laid his train—from the house to
such-and-such a spot; how George Ronalds and Henry Hart came
along just then, smoking, and he borrowed Hart's cigar and fired the
train with it, shouting, "Down with all slave-tyrants!" and how Hart
and Ronalds made no effort to capture him, but ran away, and had
never come forward to testify yet.

But they had to testify now, and they did—and pitiful it was to see
how reluctant they were, and how scared. The crowded house listened to Joyce's fearful tale with a profound and breathless interest,
and in a deep hush which was not broken till he broke it himself, in
concluding, with a roaring repetition of his "Death to all slave-tyrants!"
—which came so unexpectedly and so startlingly that it made every
one present catch his breath and gasp.

The trial was put in the paper, with biography and large portrait,
with other slanderous and insane pictures, and the edition sold beyond imagination.

The execution of Joyce was a fine and picturesque thing. It drew a
vast crowd. Good places in trees and seats on rail fences sold for
half a dollar apiece; lemonade and gingerbread-stands had great
prosperity. Joyce recited a furious and fantastic and denunciatory
speech on the scaffold which had imposing passages of school-boy
eloquence in it, and gave him a reputation on the spot as an orator, and
the name, later, in the society's records, of the "Martyr Orator." He

went to his death breathing slaughter and charging his society to "avenge his murder." If he knew anything of human nature he knew that to plenty of young fellows present in that great crowd he was a grand hero—and enviably situated.

He was hanged. It was a mistake. Within a month from his death the society which he had honored had twenty new members, some of them earnest, determined men. They did not court distinction in the same way, but they celebrated his martyrdom. The crime which had been obscure and despised had become lofty and glorified.

Such things were happening all over the country. Wild-brained martyrdom was succeeded by uprising and organization. Then, in natural order, followed riot, insurrection, and the wrack and restitutions of war. It was bound to come, and it would naturally come in that way. It has been the manner of reform since the beginning of the world.

1914

As Concerns Interpreting the Deity

I

This line of hieroglyphs was for fourteen years the despair of all the scholars who labored over the mysteries of the Rosetta stone:

After five years of study Champollion translated it thus:

Therefore let the worship of Epiphanes be maintained in all the temples; this upon pain of death.

That was the twenty-fourth translation that had been furnished by scholars. For a time it stood. But only for a time. Then doubts began to assail it and undermine it, and the scholars resumed their labors. Three years of patient work produced eleven new translations; among them, this, by Grünfeldt, was received with considerable favor:

The horse of Epiphanes shall be maintained at the public expense; this upon pain of death.

But the following rendering, by Gospodin, was received by the learned world with yet greater favor:

The priest shall explain the wisdom of Epiphanes to all these people, and these shall listen with reverence, upon pain of death.

Seven years followed, in which twenty-one fresh and widely varying renderings were scored—none of them quite convincing. But now, at last, came Rawlinson, the youngest of all the scholars, with a translation which was immediately and universally recognized as being the correct version, and his name became famous in a day. So famous, indeed, that even the children were familiar with it; and such a noise did the achievement itself make that not even the noise of the monumental political event of that same year—the flight from Elba—was able to smother it to silence. Rawlinson's version reads as follows:

Therefore, walk not away from the wisdom of Epiphanes, but turn and follow it; so shall it conduct thee to the temple's peace, and soften for thee the sorrows of life and the pains of death.

Here is another difficult text:

It is demotic—a style of Egyptian writing and a phase of the language which had perished from the knowledge of all men twenty-five hundred years before the Christian era.

Our red Indians have left many records, in the form of pictures, upon our crags and boulders. It has taken our most gifted and painstaking students two centuries to get at the meanings hidden in these pictures; yet there are still two little lines of hieroglyphs among the figures grouped upon the Dighton Rocks which they have not succeeded in interpreting to their satisfaction. These:

The suggested solutions of this riddle are practically innumerable; they would fill a book.

Thus we have infinite trouble in solving man-made mysteries; it is only when we set out to discover the secret of God that our difficulties disappear. It was always so. In antique Roman times it was the custom of the Deity to try to conceal His intentions in the entrails of birds, and this was patiently and hopefully continued century after century, although the attempted concealment never succeeded, in a single recorded instance. The augurs could read entrails as easily as a modern child can read coarse print. Roman history is full of the marvels of interpretation which these extraordinary men performed. These strange and wonderful achievements move our awe and compel our admiration. Those men could piece to the marrow of a mystery instantly. If the Rosetta-stone idea had been introduced it would have defeated them, but entrails had no embarrassments for them. Entrails have gone out, now—entrails and dreams. It was at last found out that as hiding-places for the divine intentions they were inadequate.

A part of the wall of Valletri having in former times been struck with thunder, the response of the soothsayers was, that a native of that town would some time or other arrive at supreme power.—*Bohn's Suetonius*, p. 138.

"Some time or other." It looks indefinite, but no matter, it happened, all the same; one needed only to wait, and be patient, and keep watch, then he would find out that the thunder-stroke had Caesar Augustus in mind, and had come to give notice.

There were other advance-advertisements. One of them appeared just before Caesar Augustus was born, and was most poetic and touching and romantic in its feelings and aspects. It was a dream. It was dreamed by Caesar Augustus's mother, and interpreted at the usual rates:

Atia, before her delivery, dreamed that her bowels stretched to the stars and expanded through the whole circuit of heaven and earth.—*Suetonius*, p. 139.

That was in the augur's line, and furnished him no difficulties, but it would have taken Rawlinson and Champollion fourteen years to make sure of what it meant, because they would have been surprised and dizzy. It would have been too late to be valuable, then, and the bill for service would have been barred by the statute of limitation.

In those old Roman days a gentleman's education was not complete until he had taken a theological course at the seminary and learned how to translate entrails. Caesar Augustus's education received this final polish. All through his life, whenever he had poultry on the menu he saved the interiors and kept himself informed of the Deity's plans by exercising upon those interiors the arts of augury.

In his first consulship, while he was observing the auguries, twelve vultures presented themselves, as they had done to Romulus. And when he offered sacrifice, the livers of all the victims were folded inward in the lower part; a circumstance which was regarded by those present who had skill in things of that nature, as an indubitable prognostic of great and wonderful fortune.—*Suetonius*, p. 141.

"Indubitable" is a strong word, but no doubt it was justified, if the livers were really turned that way. In those days chicken livers were strangely and delicately sensitive to coming events, no matter how far off they might be; and they could never keep still, but would curl and squirm like that, particularly when vultures came and showed interest in that approaching great event and in breakfast.

II

We may now skip eleven hundred and thirty or forty years, which brings us down to enlightened Christian times and the troubled days of King Stephen of England. The augur has had his day and has been long ago forgotten; the priest had fallen heir to his trade.

King Henry is dead; Stephen, that bold and outrageous person, comes flying over from Normandy to steal the throne from Henry's daughter. He accomplished his crime, and Henry of Huntington, a priest of high degree, mourns over it in his Chronicle. The Archbishop of Canterbury consecrated Stephen: "wherefore the Lord visited the Archbishop with the same judgment which he had inflicted upon him who struck Jeremiah the great priest: he died within a year."

Stephen's was the greater offense, but Stephen could wait; not so the Archbishop, apparently.

The kingdom was a prey to intestine wars; slaughter, fire, and rapine spread ruin throughout the land; cries of distress, horror, and woe rose in every quarter.

That was the result of Stephen's crime. These unspeakable conditions continued during nineteen years. Then Stephen died as comfortably as any man ever did, and was honorably buried. It makes one pity the poor Archbishop, and wish that he, too, could have been let off as leniently. How did Henry of Huntington know that the Archbishop was sent to his grave by judgment of God for consecrating Stephen? He does not explain. Neither does he explain why Stephen was awarded a pleasanter death than he was entitled to, while the aged King Henry, his predecessor, who had ruled England thirty-five years to the people's strongly worded satisfaction, was condemned to close his life in circumstances most distinctly unpleasant, inconvenient, and disagreeable. His was probably the most uninspiring funeral that is set down in history. There is not a detail about it that is attractive. It seems to have been just the funeral for Stephen, and even at this far-distant day it is matter of just regret that by an indiscretion the wrong man got it.

Whenever God punishes a man, Henry of Huntington knows why it was done, and tells us; and his pen is eloquent with admiration; but when a man has earned punishment, and escapes, he does not explain. He is evidently puzzled, but he does not say anything. I think it is often apparent that he is pained by these discrepancies, but loyally tries his best not to show it. When he cannot praise, he delivers himself of a silence so marked that a suspicious person could mistake it for suppressed criticism. However, he had plenty of opportunities to feel contented with the way things go—his book is full of them.

King David of Scotland . . . under color of religion caused his followers to deal most barbarously with the English. They ripped open women, tossed children on the points of spears, butchered priests at the altars, and, cutting off the heads from the images on crucifixes, placed them on the bodies of the slain, while in exchange they fixed on the crucifixes the heads of their victims. Wherever the Scots came, there was the same scene of horror and cruelty: women shrieking, old men lamenting, amid the groans of the dying and the despair of the living.

But the English got the victory.

Then the chief of the men of Lothian fell, pierced by an arrow, and all his followers were put to flight. For the Almighty was offended at them and their strength was rent like a cobweb.

Offended at them for what? For committing those fearful butcheries? No, for that was the common custom on both sides, and not open to criticism. Then was it for doing the butcheries "under cover of religion"? No, that was not it; religious feeling was often expressed in that fervent way all through those old centuries. The truth is, He was not offended at "them" at all; He was only offended at their king, who had been false to an oath. Then why did not He put the punishment upon the king instead of upon "them"? It is a difficult question. One can see by the Chronicle that the "judgments" fell rather customarily upon the wrong person, but Henry of Huntington does not explain why. Here is one that went true; the chronicler's satisfaction in it is not hidden:

> In the month of August, Providence displayed its justice in a remarkable manner; for two of the nobles who had converted monasteries into fortifications, expelling the monks, their sin being the same, met with a similar punishment. Robert Marmion was one, Godfrey de Mandeville the other. Robert Marmion, issuing forth against the enemy, was slain under the walls of the monastery, being the only one who fell, though he was surrounded by his troops. Dying excommunicated, he became subject to death everlasting. In like manner Earl Godfrey was singled out among his followers, and shot with an arrow by a common foot-soldier. He made light of the wound, but he died of it in a few days, under excommunication. See here the like judgment of God, memorable through all ages!

This exaltation jars upon me; not because of the death of the men, for they deserved that, but because it is death eternal, in white-hot fire and flame. It makes my flesh crawl. I have not known more than three men, or perhaps four, in my whole lifetime, whom I would rejoice to see writhing in those fires for even a year, let alone forever. I believe I would relent before the year was up, and get them out if I could. I think that in the long run, if a man's wife and babies, who had not harmed me, should come crying and pleading, I couldn't stand it; I know I should forgive him and let him go, even if he had violated a monastery. Henry of Huntington has been watching Godfrey and Marmion for nearly seven hundred and fifty years, now, but I couldn't do it, I know I couldn't. I am soft and gentle in my nature, and I should have forgiven them seventy-and-seven times, long ago. And I think God has; but this is only an opinion, and not authoritative, like Henry of Huntington's interpretations. I could learn to interpret, but I have never tried; I get so little time.

All through his book Henry exhibits his familiarity with the intentions of God, and with the reasons for his intentions. Sometimes—very often, in fact—the act follows the intention after such a wide interval of time that one wonders how Henry could fit one act out of a hundred to one intention out of a hundred and get the thing right every time when there was such abundant choice among acts and intentions. Sometimes a man offends the Deity with a crime, and is punished for it thirty years later; meantime he has committed a million other crimes: no matter, Henry can pick out the one that brought the worms. Worms were generally used in those days for the slaying of particularly wicked people. This has gone out, now, but in old times it was a favorite. It always indicated a case of "wrath." For instance:

. . . the just God avenging Robert Fitzhildebrand's perfidy, a worm grew in his vitals, which gradually gnawing its way through his intestines fattened on the abandoned man till, tortured with excruciating sufferings and venting himself in bitter moans, he was by a fitting punishment brought to his end.—(P. 400.)

It was probably an alligator, but we cannot tell; we only know it was a particular breed, and only used to convey wrath. Some authorities think it was an ichthyosaurus, but there is much doubt.

However, one thing we do know; and that is that that worm had been due years and years. Robert F. had violated a monastery once; he had committed unprintable crimes since, and they had been permitted—under disapproval—but the ravishment of the monastery had not been forgotten nor forgiven, and the worm came at last.

Why were these reforms put off in this strange way? What was to be gained by it? Did Henry of Huntington really know his facts, or was he only guessing? Sometimes I am half persuaded that his is only a guesser, and not a good one. The divine wisdom must surely be of the better quality than he makes it out to be.

Five hundred years before Henry's time some forecasts of the Lord's purposes were furnished by a pope, who perceived, by certain perfectly trustworthy signs furnished by the Deity for the information of His familiars, that the end of the world was

. . . about to come. But as this end of the world draws near many things are at hand which have not before happened, as changes in the air, terrible signs in the heavens, tempests out of the common order of the seasons, wars, famines, pestilences, earthquakes in various places; all which will not happen in our days, but after our days all will come to pass.

Still, the end was so near that these signs were "sent before that we may be careful for our souls and be found prepared to meet the impending judgment."

That was thirteen hundred years ago. This is really no improvement on the work of the Roman augurs.

1917

The Bee

It was Maeterlinck who introduced me to the bee. I mean, in the psychical and in the poetical way. I had had a business introduction earlier. It was when I was a boy. It is strange that I should remember a formality like that so long; it must be nearly sixty years.

Bee scientists always speaks of the bee as she. It is because all the important bees are of that sex. In the hive there is one married bee, called the queen; she has fifty thousand children; of these, about one hundred are sons; the rest are daughters. Some of the daughters are young maids, some are old maids, and are virgins and remain so.

Every spring the queen comes out of the hive and flies away with one of her sons and marries him. The honeymoon lasts only an hour or two; then the queen divorces her husband and returns home competent to lay two million eggs. This will be enough to last the year, but not more than enough, because hundreds of bees get drowned every day, and other hundreds are eaten by birds, and it is the queen's business to keep the population up to standard—say, fifty thousand. She must always have that many children on hand and efficient during the busy season, which is summer, or winter would catch the community short of food. She lays from two thousand to three thousand eggs a day, according to the demand; and she must exercise judgment, and not lay more than are needed in a slim flower-harvest, nor fewer than are required in a prodigal one, or the board of directors will dethrone her and elect a queen that has more sense.

There are always a few royal heirs in stock and ready to take her place—ready and more than anxious to do it, although she is their own mother. These girls are kept by themselves, and are regally fed and tended from birth. No other bees get such fine food as they get, or live such a high and luxurious life. By consequence they are larger and longer and sleeker than their working sisters. And they have a curved sting, shaped like a simitar, while the others have a straight one.

A common bee will sting any one or anybody, but a royalty stings royalties only. A common bee will sting and kill another common bee, for cause, but when it is necessary to kill the queen other ways are employed. When a queen has grown old and slack and does not lay eggs enough one of her royal daughters is allowed to come to attack her, the rest of the bees looking on at the duel and seeing fair play. It is a duel with the curved stings. If one of the fighters gets hard pressed and gives it up and runs, she is brought back and must try again—once, maybe twice; then, if she runs yet once more for her life, judicial death is her portion; her children pack themselves into a ball around her person and hold her in that compact grip two or three days, until she starves to death or is suffocated. Meantime the victor bee is receiving royal honors and performing the one royal function— laying eggs.

As regards the ethics of the judicial assassination of the queen, that is a matter of politics, and will be discussed later, in its proper place.

During substantially the whole of her short life of five or six years the queen lives in the Egyptian darkness and stately seclusion of the royal apartments, with none about her but plebeian servants, who give her empty lip-affection in place of the love which her heart hungers for; who spy upon her in the interest of her waiting heirs, and report and exaggerate her defects and deficiencies to them; who fawn upon her and flatter her to her face and slander her behind her back; who grovel before her in the day of her power and forsake her in her age and weakness. There she sits, friendless, upon her throne through the long night of her life, cut off from the consoling sympathies and sweet companionship and loving endearments which she craves, by the gilded barriers of her awful rank; a forlorn exile in her own house and home, weary object of formal ceremonies and machine-made worship, winged child of the sun, native to the free air and the blue skies and the flowery fields, doomed by the splendid accident of her birth to trade this priceless heritage for a black captivity, a tinsel grandeur, and a loveless life, with shame and insult at the end and a cruel death—and condemned by the human instinct in her to hold the bargain valuable!

Huber, Lubbock, Maeterlinck—in fact, all the great authorities— are agreed in denying that the bee is a member of the human family. I do not know why they have done this, but I think it is from dishonest motives. Why, the innumerable facts brought to light by their own painstaking and exhaustive experiments prove that if there is a master fool in the world, it is the bee. That seems to settle it.

But that is the way of the scientist. He will spend thirty years in building up a mountain range of facts with the intent to prove a certain theory; then he is so happy in his achievement that as a rule he overlooks the main chief fact of all—that his accumulation proves an entirely different thing. When you point out this miscarriage to him he does not answer your letters; when you call to convince him, the servant prevaricates and you do not get in. Scientists have odious manners, except when you prop up their theory; then you can borrow money of them.

To be strictly fair, I will concede that now and then one of them will answer your letter, but when they do they avoid the issue—you cannot pin them down. When I discovered that the bee was human I wrote about it to all those scientists whom I have just mentioned. For evasions, I have seen nothing to equal the answers I got.

After the queen, the personage next in importance in the hive is the virgin. The virgins are fifty thousand or one hundred thousand in number, and they are the workers, the laborers. No work is done, in the hive or out of it, save by them. The males do not work, the queen does no work, unless laying eggs is work, but it does not seem so to me. There are only two million of them, anyway, and all of five months to finish the contract in. The distribution of work in a hive is as cleverly and elaborately specialized as it is in a vast American machine-shop or factory. A bee that has been trained to one of the many and various industries of the concern doesn't know how to exercise any other, and would be offended if asked to take a hand in anything outside of her profession. She is as human as a cook; and if you should ask the cook to wait on the table, you know what would happen. Cooks will play the piano if you like, but they draw the line there. In my time I have asked a cook to chop wood, and I know about these things. Even the hired girl has her frontiers; true, they are vague, they are ill-defined, even flexible, but they are there. This is not conjecture; it is founded on the absolute. And then the butler. You ask the butler to wash the dog. It is just as I say; there is much to be learned in these ways, without going to books. Books are very well, but books do not cover the whole domain of esthetic human culture. Pride of profession is one of the boniest bones of existence, if not the boniest. Without doubt it is so in the hive.

1917

Concerning Tobacco[1]

As concerns tobacco, there are many superstitions. And the chiefest is this—that there is a *standard* governing the matter, whereas there is nothing of the kind. Each man's own preference is the only standard for him, the only one which he can accept, the only one which can command him. A congress of all the tobacco-lovers in the world could not elect a standard which would be binding upon you or me, or would even much influence us.

The next superstition is that a man has a standard of his own. He hasn't. He thinks he has, but he hasn't. He thinks he can tell what he regards as a good cigar from what he regards as a bad one—but he can't. He goes by the brand, yet imagines he goes by the flavor. One may palm off the worst counterfeit upon him; if it bears his brand he will smoke it contentedly and never suspect.

Children of twenty-five, who have seven years of experience, try to tell me what is a good cigar and what isn't. Me, who never learned to smoke, but always smoked; me, who came into the world asking for a light.

No one can tell me what is a good cigar—for me. I am the only judge. People who claim to know say that I smoke the worst cigars in the world. They bring their own cigars when they come to my house. They betray an unmanly terror when I offer them a cigar; they tell lies and hurry away to meet engagements which they have not made when they are threatened with the hospitalities of my box. Now then, observe what superstition, assisted by a man's reputation, can do. I was to have twelve personal friends to supper one night. One of them was as notorious for costly and elegant cigars as I was for cheap and devilish ones. I called at his house and when no one was looking borrowed a double handful of his very choicest; cigars which cost him forty cents apiece and bore red-and-gold labels in sign of their nobility. I removed the labels and put the cigars into a box with my favorite brand on it—a brand which those people all knew, and which cowed

[1] Paine says this was written "about 1893." It was first published in 1917. See the interesting "Smoking as Inspiration" in *Mark Twain: Life As I Find It*, pp. 202–3.—C.N.

them as men are cowed by an epidemic. They took these cigars when
offered at the end of the supper, and lit them and sternly struggled
with them—in dreary silence, for hilarity died when the fell brand came
into view and started around—but their fortitude held for a short time
only; then they made excuses and filed out, treading on one another's
heels with indecent eagerness; and in the morning when I went out
to observe results the cigars lay all between the front door and the
gate. All except one—that one lay in the plate of the man from whom
I had cabbaged the lot. One or two whiffs was all he could stand. He
told me afterward that some day I would get shot for giving people
that kind of cigars to smoke.

Am I certain of my own standard? Perfectly; yes, absolutely—unless
somebody fools me by putting my brand on some other kind of
cigar; for no doubt I am like the rest, and know my cigar by the brand
instead of by the flavor. However, my standard is a pretty wide one
and covers a good deal of territory. To me, almost any cigar is good
that nobody else will smoke, and to me almost all cigars are bad that
other people consider good.[2] Nearly any cigar will do me, except a
Havana. People think they hurt my feelings when they come to my
house with their life preservers on—I mean, with their own cigars in
their pockets. It is an error; I take care of myself in a similar way.
When I go into danger—that is, into rich people's houses, where, in
the nature of things, they will have high-tariff cigars, red-and-gilt
girdled and nested in a rosewood box along with a damp sponge,
cigars which develop a dismal black ash and burn down the side and
smell, and will grow hot to the fingers, and will go on growing hotter
and hotter, and go on smelling more and more infamously and un-
endurably the deeper the fire tunnels down inside below the thimble-
ful of honest tobacco that is in the front end, the furnisher of it praising it all the time and telling you how much the deadly thing cost—
yes, when I go into that sort of peril I carry my own defense along;
I carry my own brand—twenty-seven cents a barrel—and I live to see
my family again. I may seem to light his red-gartered cigar, but that
is only for courtesy's sake; I smuggle it into my pocket for the poor, of
whom I know many, and light one of my own; and while he praises it
I join in, but when he says it cost forty-five cents I say nothing, for I
know better.

However, to say true, my tastes are so catholic that I have never
seen any cigar that I really could not smoke, except those that cost a

---

[2] Clemens held similar views regarding literary materials, which made good
sense and good fortune.—C.N.

dollar apiece. I have examined those and know that they are made of dog-hair, and not good dog-hair at that.

I have a thoroughly satisfactory time in Europe, for all over the Continent one finds cigars which not even the most hardened newsboys in New York would smoke. I brought cigars with me, the last time; I will not do that any more. In Italy, as in France, the Government is the only cigar-peddler. Italy has three or four domestic brands: the Minghetti, the Trabuco, the Virginia, and a very coarse one which is a modification of the Virginia. The Minghettis are large and comely, and cost three dollars and sixty cents a hundred; I can smoke a hundred in seven days and enjoy every one of them. The Trabucos suit me, too; I don't remember the price. But one has to learn to like the Virginia, nobody is born friendly to it. It looks like a rattail file, but smokes better, some think. It has a straw through it; you pull this out, and it leaves a flue, otherwise there would be no draught, not even as much as there is to a nail. Some prefer a nail at first. However, I like all the French, Swiss, German, and Italian domestic cigars, and have never cared to inquire what they are made of; and nobody would know, anyhow, perhaps. There is even a brand of European smoking-tobacco that I like. It is a brand used by the Italian peasants. It is loose and dry and black, and looks like tea-grounds. When the fire is applied it expands, and climbs up and towers above the pipe, and presently tumbles off inside of one's vest. The tobacco itself is cheap, but it raises the insurance. It is as I remarked in the beginning—the taste for tobacco is a matter of superstition. There are no standards—no real standards. Each man's preference is the only standard for him, the only one which he can accept, the only one which can command him.

1917

The Memorable Assassination

NOTE.—The assassination of the Empress of Austria at Geneva, September 10, 1898, occurred during Mark Twain's Austrian residence. The news came to him at Kaltenleutgeben, a summer resort a little way out of Vienna. To his friend, the Rev. Jos. H. Twichell, he wrote:

"That good and unoffending lady, the Empress, is killed by a madman, and I am living in the midst of world-history again. The Queen's Jubilee last year, the invasion of the Reichsrath by the police, and now this murder, which will still be talked of and described and painted a thousand years from now. To have a personal friend of the wearer of two crowns burst in at the gate in the deep dusk of the evening and say, in a voice broken with tears, 'My God! the Empress is murdered,' and fly toward her home before we can utter a question—why, it brings the giant event home to you, makes you a part of it and personally interested; it is as if your neighbor, Antony, should come flying and say, 'Caesar is butchered—the head of the world is fallen!'

"Of course there is no talk but of this. The mourning is universal and genuine, the consternation is stupefying. The Austrian Empire is being draped with black. Vienna will be a spectacle to see by next Saturday, when the funeral cortège marches."

He was strongly moved by the tragedy, impelled to write concerning it. He prepared the article which here follows, but did not offer it for publication, perhaps feeling that his own close association with the court circles at the moment prohibited this personal utterance.

ALBERT BIGELOW PAINE

The more one thinks of the assassination, the more imposing and tremendous the event becomes. The destruction of a city is a large event, but it is one which repeats itself several times in a thousand years; the destruction of a third part of a nation by plague and famine is a large event, but it has happened several times in history; the murder of a king is a large event, but it has been frequent.

The murder of an empress is the largest of all large events. One must go back about two thousand years to find an instance to put with this one. The oldest family of unchallenged descent in Christendom lives in Rome and traces its line back seventeen hundred years, but no member of it has been present in the earth when an empress was murdered, until now. Many a time during these seventeen centuries members of that family have been startled with the news of extraordinary events—the destruction of cities, the fall of thrones, the murder of kings, the wreck of dynasties, the extinction of religions, the birth of new systems of government; and their descendants have been by to hear of it and talk about it when all these things were repeated once, twice, or a dozen times—but to even that family has come news at last which is not staled by use, has no duplicates in the long reach of its memory.

It is an event which confers a curious distinction upon every individual now living in the world: he has stood alive and breathing in the presence of an event such as has not fallen within the experience of any traceable or untraceable ancestor of his for twenty centuries, and it is not likely to fall within the experience of any descendant of his for twenty more.

Time has made some great changes since the Roman days. The murder of an empress then—even the assassination of Caesar himself —could not electrify the world as this murder has electrified it. For one reason, there was then not much of a world to electrify; it was a small world, as to known bulk, and it had rather a thin population, besides; and for another reason, the news traveled so slowly that its tremendous initial thrill wasted away, week by week and month by month, on the journey, and by the time it reached the remoter regions there was but little of it left. It was no longer a fresh event it was a thing of the far past; it was not properly news, it was history. But the world is enormous now, and prodigiously populated—that is one change; and another is the lightning swiftness of the flight of tidings, good and bad. "The Empress is murdered!" When those amazing words struck upon my ear in this Austrian village last Saturday, three hours after the disaster, I knew that it was already old news in London, Paris, Berlin, New York, San Francisco, Japan, China, Melbourne, Cape Town, Bombay, Madras, Calcutta, and that the entire globe, with a single voice, was cursing the perpetrator of it. Since the telegraph first began to stretch itself wider and wider about the earth, larger and increasingly larger areas of the world have, as time went on, received simultaneously the shock of a great calamity; but this is the first time in history that the entire surface of the globe has been swept in a single instant with the thrill of so gigantic an event.

And who is the miracle-worker who has furnished to the world this spectacle? All the ironies are compacted in the answer. He is at the bottom of the human ladder, as the accepted estimates of degree and value go: a soiled and patched young loafer, without gifts, without talents, without education, without morals, without character, without any born charm or any acquired one that wins or beguiles or attracts; without a single grace of mind or heart or hand that any tramp or prostitute could envy him; an unfaithful private in the ranks, an incompetent stone-cutter, an inefficient lackey; in a word, a mangy, offensive, empty, unwashed, vulgar, gross, mephitic, timid, sneaking, human polecat. And it was within the privileges and powers of this sarcasm upon the human race to reach up—up—up—and strike from its far summit in the social skies the world's accepted ideal of Glory and Might and Splendor and Sacredness! It realizes to us what sorry shows and shadows we are. Without our clothes and our pedestals we are poor things and much of a size; our dignities are not real, our pomps are shams. At our best and stateliest we are not suns, as we pretended, and teach, and believe, but only candles; and any bummer can blow us out.

And now we get realized to us once more another thing which we often forget—or try to: that no man has a wholly undiseased mind; that in one way or another all men are mad. Many are mad for money. When this madness is in a mild form it is harmless and the man passes for sane; but when it develops powerfully and takes possession of the man, it can make him cheat, rob, and kill; and when he has got his fortune and lost it again it can land him in the asylum or the suicide's coffin. Love is a madness; if thwarted it develops fast; it can grow to a frenzy of despair and make an otherwise sane and highly gifted prince, like Rudolph, throw away the crown of an empire and snuff out his own life. All the whole list of desires, predilections, aversions, ambitions, passions, cares, griefs, regrets, remorses, are incipient madness, and ready to grow, spread, and consume, when the occasion comes. There are no healthy minds, and nothing saves any man but accident—the accident of not having his malady put to the supreme test.

One of the commonest forms of madness is the desire to be noticed, the pleasure derived from being noticed. Perhaps it is not merely common, but universal. In its mildest form it doubtless is universal. Every child is pleased at being noticed; many intolerable children put in their whole time in distressing and idiotic effort to attract the attention of visitors; boys are always "showing off"; apparently all men and women are glad and grateful when they find that they have done a thing which has lifted them for a moment out of obscurity and caused wondering talk. This common madness can develop, by nurture, into a hunger for notoriety in one, for fame in another. It is this madness for being noticed and talked about which has invented kingship and the thousand other dignities, and tricked them out with pretty and showy fineries; it has made kings pick one another's pockets, scramble for one another's crowns and estates, slaughter one another's subjects; it has raised up prize-fighters, and poets, and village mayors, and little and big politicians, and big and little charity-founders, and bicycle champions, and banditti chiefs, and frontier desperadoes, and Napoleons. Anything to get notoriety; anything to set the village, or the township, or the city, or the State, or the nation, or the planet shouting, "Look—there he goes—that is the man!" And in five minutes' time, at no cost of brain, or labor, or genius this mangy Italian tramp has beaten them all, transcended them all, outstripped them all, for in time their names will perish; but by the friendly help of the insane newspapers and courts and kings and historians, his is safe to live and thunder in the world all down the ages as long as human speech shall endure! Oh, if it were not so tragic how ludicrous it would be!

She was so blameless, the Empress; and so beautiful, in mind and heart, in person and spirit; and whether with a crown upon her head or without it and nameless, a grace to the human race, and almost a justi- fication of its creation; *would* be, indeed, but that the animal that struck her down re-establishes the doubt.

In her character was every quality that in woman invites and en- gages respect, esteem, affection, and homage. Her tastes, her instincts, and her aspirations were all high and fine and all her life her heart and brain were busy with activities of a noble sort. She had had bitter griefs, but they did not sour her spirit, and she had had the highest honors in the world's gift, but she went her simple way unspoiled. She knew all ranks, and won them all, and made them her friends. An English fisherman's wife said, "When a body was in trouble she didn't send her help, she brought it herself." Crowns have adorned others, but she adorned her crowns.

It was a swift celebrity the assassin achieved. And it is marked by some curious contrasts. At noon last Saturday there was no one in the world who would have considered acquaintanceship with him a thing worth claiming or mentioning; no one would have been vain of such an acquaintanceship; the humblest honest boot-black would not have valued the fact that he had met him or seen him at some time or other; he was sunk in abysmal obscurity, he was away beneath the notice of the bottom grades of officialdom. Three hours later he was the one subject of conversation in the world, the gilded generals and admirals and governors were discussing him, all the kings and queens and em- perors had put aside their other interests to talk about him. And wherever there was a man, at the summit of the world or the bottom of it, who by chance had at some time or other come across that creature, he remembered it with a secret satisfaction, and *mentioned* it—for it was a distinction, now! It brings human dignity pretty low, and for a moment the thing is not quite realizable—but it is perfectly true. If there is a king who can remember, now, that he once saw that creature in a time past, he has let that fact out, in a more or less studiedly casual and indifferent way, some dozens of times during the past week. For a king is merely human; the inside of him is exactly like the inside of any other person; and it is human to find satisfaction in being in a kind of personal way connected with amazing events. We are all privately vain of such a thing; we are all alike; a king is a king by accident; the reason the rest of us are not kings is merely due to another accident; we are all made out of the same clay, and it is a sufficiently poor quality.

Below the kings, these remarks are in the air these days; I know it as well as if I were hearing them:

The Commander: "He was in my army."

The General: "He was in my corps."

The Colonel: "He was in my regiment. A brute. I remember him well."

The Captain: "He was in my company. A troublesome scoundrel. I remember him well."

The Sergeant: "Did I know him? As well as I know you. Why, every morning I used to—" etc., etc.; a glad, long story, told to devouring ears.

The Landlady: "Many's the time he boarded with me. I can show you his very room, and the very bed he slept in. And the charcoal mark there on the wall—he made that. My little Johnny saw him do it with his own eyes. Didn't you, Johnny?"

It is easy to see, by the papers, that the magistrate and the constables and the jailer treasure up the assassin's daily remarks and doings as precious things, and as wallowing this week in seas of blissful distinction. The interviewer, too; he tries to let on that he is not vain of his privilege of contact with this man whom few others are allowed to gaze upon, but he is human, like the rest, and can no more keep his vanity corked in than could you or I.

Some think that this murder is a frenzied revolt against the criminal militarism which is impoverishing Europe and driving the starving poor mad. That has many crimes to answer for, but not this one, I think. One may not attribute to this man a generous indignation against the wrongs done the poor; one may not dignify him with a generous impulse of any kind. When he saw his photograph and said, "I shall be celebrated," he laid bare the impulse that prompted him. It was a mere hunger for notoriety. There is another confessed case of the kind which is as old as history—the burning of the temple of Ephesus.

Among the inadequate attempts to account for the assassination we must concede high rank to the many which have described it as a "peculiarly brutal crime" and then added that it was "ordained from above." I think this verdict will not be popular "above." If the deed was ordained from above, there is no rational way of making this prisoner even partially responsible for it, and the Genevan court cannot condemn him without manifestly committing a crime. Logic is logic, and by disregarding its laws even the most pious and showy theologian may be beguiled into preferring charges which should not be ventured upon except in the shelter of plenty of lightning-rods.

I witnessed the funeral procession, in company with friends, from the windows of the Krantz, Vienna's sumptuous new hotel. We came into town in the middle of the forenoon, and I went on foot from the station. Black flags hung down from all the houses; the aspects were Sunday-like; the crowds on the sidewalks were quiet and moved slowly; very few people were smoking; many ladies wore deep mourning, gentlemen were in black as a rule; carriages were speeding in all directions, with footmen and coachmen in black clothes and wearing black cocked hats; the shops were closed; in many windows were pictures of the Empress: as a a beautiful young bride of seventeen; as a serene and majestic lady with added years; and finally in deep black and without ornaments—the costume she always wore after the tragic death of her son nine years ago, for her heart broke then, and life lost almost all its value for her. The people stood grouped before these pictures, and now and then one saw women and girls turn away wiping the tears from their eyes.

In front of the Krantz is an open square; over the way was the church where the funeral services would be held. It is small and old and severely plain, plastered outside and whitewashed or painted, and with no ornament but a statue of a monk in a niche over the door, and above that a small black flag. But in its crypt lie several of the great dead of the House of Habsburg, among them Maria Theresa and Napoleon's son, the Duke of Reichstadt. Hereabouts was a Roman camp, once, and in it the Emperor Marcus Aurelius died a thousand years before the first Habsburg ruled in Vienna, which was six hundred years ago and more.

The little church is packed in among great modern stores and houses, and the windows of them were full of people. Behind the vast plate-glass windows of the upper floors of a house on the corner one glimpsed terraced masses of fine-clothed men and women, dim and shimmery, like people under water. Under us the square was noiseless, but it was full of citizens; officials in fine uniforms were flitting about on errands, and in a doorstep sat a figure in the uttermost raggedness of poverty, the feet bare, the head bent humbly down; a youth of eighteen or twenty, he was, and through the field-glass one could see that he was tearing apart and munching riffraff that he had gathered somewhere. Blazing uniforms flashed by him, making a sparkling contrast with his drooping ruin of moldy rags, but he took no notice; he was not there to grieve for a nation's disaster; he had his own cares, and deeper. From two directions two long files of infantry came plowing through the pack and press in silence; there was a low, crisp order and the crowd vanished, the square save the sidewalks was empty, the private mourner was gone. Another order, the soldiers fell apart and inclosed the square in a double-ranked human fence. It was all so swift, noiseless, exact—like a beautifully ordered machine.

It was noon, now. Two hours of stillness and waiting followed. Then carriages began to flow past and deliver the two or three hundred court personages and high nobilities privileged to enter the church. Then the square filled up; not with civilians, but with army and navy officers in showy and beautiful uniforms. They filled it compactly, leaving only a narrow carriage path in front of the church, but there was no civilian among them. And it was better so; dull clothes would have marred the radiant spectacle. In the jam in front of the church, on its steps, and on the sidewalk was a bunch of uniforms which made a blazing splotch of color—intense red, gold, and white—which dimmed the brilliancies around them; and opposite them on the other side of the path was a bunch of cascaded bright-green plumes above pale-blue shoulders which made another splotch of splendor emphatic and conspicuous in its glowing surroundings. It was a sea of flashing color all about, but these two groups were the high notes. The green plumes were worn by forty or fifty Austrian generals, the group opposite them were chiefly Knights of Malta and knights of a German order. The mass of heads in the square were covered by gilt helmets and by military caps roofed with a mirror-like glaze, and the movements of the wearers caused these things to catch the sunrays, and the effect was fine to see—the square was like a garden of richly colored flowers with a multitude of blinding and flashing little suns distributed over it.

Think of it—it was by command of that Italian loafer yonder on his imperial throne in the Geneva prison that this splendid multitude was assembled there; and the kings and emperors that were entering the church from a side street were there by his will. It is so strange, so unrealizable.

At three o'clock the carriages were still streaming by in single file. At three-five a cardinal arrives with his attendants; later some bishops; then a number of archdeacons—all in striking colors that add to the show. At three-ten a procession of priests passes along, with crucifix. Another one, presently; after an interval, two more; at three-fifty another one—very long, with many crosses, gold-embroidered robes, and much white lace; also great pictured banners, at intervals, receding into the distance.

A hum of tolling bells makes itself heard, but not sharply. At three-fifty-eight a waiting interval. Presently a long procession of gentlemen in evening dress comes in sight and approaches until it is near to the square, then falls back against the wall of soldiers at the sidewalk, and the white shirt-fronts show like snowflakes and are very conspicuous where so much warm color is all about.

A waiting pause. At four-twelve the head of the funeral procession comes into view at last. First, a body of cavalry, four abreast, to widen the path. Next, a great body of lancers, in blue, with gilt helmets. Next, three six-horse mourning-coaches; outriders and coachmen in black, with cocked hats and white wigs. Next, troops in splendid uniforms, red, gold, and white, exceedingly showy.

Now the multitude uncover. The soldiers present arms; there is a low rumble of drums; the sumptuous great hearse approaches, drawn at a walk by eight black horses plumed with black bunches of nodding ostrich feathers; the coffin is borne into the church, the doors are closed.

The multitude cover their heads, and the rest of the procession moves by; first the Hungarian Guard in their indescribably brilliant and picturesque and beautiful uniform, inherited from the ages of barbaric splendor, and after them other mounted forces, a long and showy array.

Then the shining crowd in the square crumbled apart, a wrecked rainbow, and melted away in radiant streams, and in the turn of a wrist the three dirtiest and raggedest and cheerfulest little slum-girls in Austria were capering about in the spacious vacancy. It was a day of contrasts.

Twice the Empress entered Vienna in state. The first time was in 1854, when she was a bride of seventeen, and then she rode in measureless pomp and with blare of music through a fluttering world of gay flags and decorations, down streets walled on both hands with a press of shouting and welcoming subjects; and the second time was last Wednesday, when she entered the city in her coffin and moved down the same streets in the dead of the night under swaying black flags, between packed human walls again; but everywhere was a deep stillness, now—a stillness emphasized, rather than broken, by the muffled hoofbeats of the long cavalcade over pavements cushioned with sand, and the low sobbing of gray-headed women who had witnessed the first entry forty-four years before, when she and they were young—and unaware!

A character in Baron von Berger's recent fairy drama "Habsburg" tells about that first coming of the girlish Empress-Queen, and in his history draws a fine picture: I cannot make a close translation of it, but will try to convey the spirit of the verses:

> I saw the stately pagaent pass:
> In her high place I saw the Empress-Queen:
> I could not take my eyes away
> From that fair vision, spirit-like and pure,
> That rose serene, sublime, and figured to my sense
> A noble Alp far lighted in the blue,
> That in the flood of morning rends its veil of cloud
> And stands a dream of glory to the gaze
> Of them that in the Valley toil and plod.

1917

A Simplified Alphabet

I have had a kindly feeling, a friendly feeling, a cousinly feeling toward Simplified Spelling, from the beginning of the movement three years ago, but nothing more inflamed than that. It seemed to me to merely propose to substitute one inadequacy for another; a sort of patching and plugging poor old dental relics with cement and gold and porcelain paste; what was really wanted was a new set of teeth. That is to say, a new *alphabet*.

The heart of our trouble is with our foolish alphabet. It doesn't know how to spell, and can't be taught. In this it is like all other alphabets except one—the phonographic. That is the only competent alphabet in the world. It can spell and correctly pronounce any word in our language.

That admirable alphabet, that brilliant alphabet, that inspired alphabet, can be learned in an hour or two. In a week the student can

learn to write it with some little facility, and to read it with considerable ease. I know, for I saw it tried in a public school in Nevada
forty-five years ago, and was so impressed by the incident that it has
remained in my memory ever since.

I wish we could adopt it in place of our present written (and
printed) character. I mean *simply* the alphabet; simply the consonants
and the vowels—I don't mean any *reductions* or abbreviations of
them, such as the shorthand writer uses in order to get compression
and speed. No, I would *spell every word out.*

I will insert the alphabet here as I find it in Burnz's *Phonic Shorthand.* It is arranged on the basis of Isaac Pitman's *Phonography.* Isaac
Pitman was the originator and father of scientific phonography. It is
used throughout the globe. It was a memorable invention. He made it
public seventy-three years ago. The firm of Isaac Pitman & Sons, New
York, still exists, and they continue the master's work.

What should we gain?

First of all, we could spell *definitely*—and correctly—any word you
please, just by the *sound* of it. We can't do that with our present
alphabet. For instance, take the simple, every-day word *phthisis.* If
we tried to spell it by the sound of it, we should make it *tysis,* and be
laughed at by every educated person.

Secondly, we should gain in *reduction of labor* in writing.

Simplified Spelling makes valuable reductions in the case of several hundred words, but the new spelling must be *learned.* You can't
spell them by the sound; you must get them out of the book.

Alphabet of Phonic Shorthand.

CONSONANTS.

Letter.	Name.	Phonograph.	Sound as in
P	pee	\	p ole.
B	bee	\	b owl.
T	tee	|	t oe.
D	dee	|	d oe.
CH	chay	/	ch eer.
J	jay	/	j eer.
K	kay	—	c ame.
G	gay	—	g ame.
F	ef	\	f ear.
V	vee	\	v eer.
TH	ith	(	th igh.
Th	thee	(	th y.
S	es	)	s eal.
Z	zee	)	s eal.
SH	shee	/	vi ci ous
ZH	zhee	/	vi s ion.
L	lee.	(	l ay.
R	ur,ree	\	ai r. / r ay.
Y	yay	(	y ell.
W	way	(	w ell.
M	em	⌒	m et.
N	en	⌣	n et.
NG	ing	⌣	si ng.

Aspirate or Free Breath.

H	hay	⌒	h av.

VOWELS. Simple.

FIRST OR OPEN SOUNDS.
Long as in p a re. - p a r. P au l.

Short as in p a rry. Cub a. Po ll. ask.

SECOND, OR MEDIAL.
Long as in p a te. p u rl. po le.

Short as in p e t. c u t. wh o le. o mit.

THIRD, OR CLOSE.
p ee l. p oo l.

Short as in p i ll. p u ll.

VOWELS. Compound.
file. foil. fowl.

1st or open,

3d or close, few.

WORDS OF TWO SOUNDS.

aid. day. say. so. oath. they. tho'.

a.m. may. hoe. own. know. no.

us. up. ebb. etch. edge. ell.

But even if we knew the simplified form for every word in the language, the phonographic alphabet would still beat the Simplified Speller "hands down" in the important matter of economy of labor. I will illustrate:

Present form: through, laugh, highland.

Simplified form: thru, laff, hyland.

Phonograph form:

To write the word "through," the pen has to make twenty-one strokes.

To write the word "thru," the pen has to make twelve strokes—a good saving.

To write that same word with the phonographic alphabet, the pen has to make only *three* strokes.

To write the word "laugh," the pen has to make *fourteen* strokes.

To write "laff," the pen has to make the *same number* of strokes— no labor is saved to the penman.

To write the same word with the phonographic alphabet, the pen has to make only *three* strokes.

To write the word "highland," the pen has to make twenty-two strokes.

To write "hyland," the pen has to make eighteen strokes.

To write that word with the phonographic alphabet, the pen has to make only *five* strokes.

To write the words "phonographic alphabet," the pen has to make fifty-three strokes.

To write "fonografic alfabet," the pen has to make fifty strokes. To the penman, the saving in labor is insignificant.

To write that word (with vowels) with the phonographic alphabet, the pen has to make only *seventeen* strokes.

Without the vowels, only *thirteen* strokes. The vowels are hardly necessary, this time.

We make five pen-strokes in writing an *m*. Thus: a stroke down; a

stroke up; a second stroke down; a second stroke up; a final stroke
down. Total, five. The phonographic alphabet accomplishes the *m*
with a single stroke—a curve, like a parenthesis that has come home
drunk and has fallen down right at the front door where everybody
that goes along will see him and say, Alas!

When our written *m* is not the end of a word, but is otherwise located, it has to be connected with the next letter, and that requires
another pen-stroke, making six in all, before you get rid of that *m*.
But never mind about the connecting strokes—let them go. Without
counting them, the twenty-six letters of our alphabet consumed about
eighty pen-strokes for their construction—about three pen-strokes per
letter.

It is *three times the number* required by the phonographic alphabet.
It requires but *one* stroke for each letter.

My writing-gait is—well, I don't know what it is, but I will time myself and see. Result: it is twenty-four words per minute. I don't mean
composing; I mean *copying*. There isn't any definite composing-gait.

Very well, my copying-gait is 1,440 words per hour—say, 1,500. If I
could use the phonographic character with facility I could do the
1,500 in twenty minutes. I could do nine hours' copying in three hours;
I could do three years' copying in one year.

Also, if I had a typewriting machine with the phonographic alphabet
on it—oh, the miracles I could do!

I am not pretending to write that character well. I have never had a
lesson, and I am copying the letters from the book. But I can accomplish my desire, at any rate, which is, to make the reader get a good
and clear idea of the advantage it would be to us if we could discard
our present alphabet and put this better one in its place—using it in
books, newspapers, with the typewriter, and with the pen.

—*man dog horse*. I think it is graceful and would look comely in
print. And consider—once more, I beg—what a labor-saver it is! Ten
pen-strokes with the one system to convey those three words above,

and thirty-three by the other! I mean, in *some* ways, not in all. I suppose I might go so far as to say in most ways, and be within the facts, but never mind; let it go at *some*. One of the ways in which it exercises this birthright is—as I think—continuing to use our laughable alphabet these seventy-three years while there was a rational one at hand, to be had for the taking.

It has taken five hundred years to simplify some of Chaucer's rotten spelling—if I may be allowed to use so frank a term as that—and it will take five hundred more to get our exasperating new Simplified Corruptions accepted and running smoothly. And we sha'n't be any better off then than we are now; for in that day we shall still have the privilege the Simplifiers are exercising now: *anybody* can change the spelling that wants to.

But you can't change the phonographic spelling; there isn't any way. It will always follow the *sound*. If you want to change the spelling, you have to change the sound first.

Mind, I myself am a Simplified Speller; I belong to that unhappy guild that is patiently and hopefully trying to reform our drunken old alphabet by reducing his whisky. Well, it will improve him. When they get through and have reformed him all they can by their system he will be only *half* drunk. Above that condition their system can never lift him. There is no competent, and lasting, and real reform for him but to take away his whisky entirely, and fill up his jug with Pitman's wholesome and undiseased alphabet.

One great drawback to Simplified Spelling is, that in print a simplified word looks so like the very nation! and when you bunch a whole squadron of the Simplified together the spectacle is very nearly unendurable.

The da ma ov koars kum when the publik ma be expektd to get rekonsyled to the bezair asspekt of the Simplified Kombynashuns, but—if I may be allowed the expression—is it worth the wasted time?

To see our letters put together in ways to which we are not accustomed offends the eye, and also takes the *expression* out of the words.

La on, Makduf, and damd be he hoo furst krys hold, enuf!

It doesn't thrill you as it used to do. The simplifications have sucked the thrill all out of it.

But a written character with which we are *not acquainted* does not offend us—Greek, Hebrew, Russian, Arabic, and the others—they have an interesting look, and we see beauty in them, too. And this is true of hieroglyphics, as well. There is something pleasant and engaging about the mathematical signs when we do not understand them. The mystery hidden in these things has a fascination for us; we can't come across a printed page of shorthand without being impressed by it and wishing we could read it.

Very well, what I am offering for acceptance and adoption is not shorthand, but longhand, written with the *shorthand alphabet unreduced.* You can write three times as many words in a minute with it as you can write with our alphabet. And so, in a way, it *is* properly a shorthand. It has a pleasant look, too; a beguiling look, an inviting look. I will write something in it, in my rude and untaught way:

Even when *I* do it it comes out prettier than it does in Simplified Spelling. Yes, and in the Simplified it costs one hundred and twenty-three pen-strokes to write it, whereas in the phonographic it costs only twenty-nine.

is probably

Let us hope so anyway.

1917

Taming the Bicycle[1]

I

I thought the matter over, and concluded I could do it. So I went down and bought a barrel of Pond's Extract and a bicycle. The Expert came home with me to instruct me. We chose the back yard, for the sake of privacy, and went to work.

Mine was not a full-grown bicycle, but only a colt—a fifty-inch, with the pedals shortened up to forty-eight—and skittish, like any other colt. The Expert explained the thing's points briefly, then he got on its back and rode around a little, to show me how easy it was to do. He said that the dismounting was perhaps the hardest thing to learn, and so we would leave that to the last. But he was in error there. He found, to his surprise and joy, that all that he needed to do was to get me on to the machine and stand out of the way; I could get off, myself. Although I was wholly inexperienced, I dismounted in the best time on record. He was on that side, shoving up the machine; we all came down with a crash, he at the bottom, I next, and the machine on top.

We examined the machine, but it was not in the least injured. This was hardly believable. Yet the Expert assured me that it was true; in fact, the examination proved it. I was partly to realize, then, how admirably these things are constructed. We applied some Pond's Extract, and resumed. The Expert got on the *other* side to shove up this time, but I dismounted on that side; so the result was as before.

The machine was not hurt. We oiled ourselves up again, and resumed. This time the Expert took up a sheltered position behind, but somehow or other we landed on him again.

He was full of surprised admiration; said it was abnormal. She was all right, not a scratch on her, not a timber started anywhere. I said it was wonderful, while we were greasing up, but he said that when I came to know these steel spider-webs I would realize that nothing but

[1] Paine says this was written in the early eighties but not offered for publication. The bicycle of those days was a formidable antagonist.—C.N.

dynamite could cripple them. Then he limped out to position, and we resumed once more. This time the Expert took up the position of short-stop, and got a man to shove up behind. We got up a handsome speed, and presently traversed a brick, and I went out over the top of the tiller and landed, head down, on the instructor's back, and saw the machine fluttering in the air between me and the sun. It was well it came down on us, for that broke the fall, and it was not injured.

Five days later I got out and was carried down to the hospital, and found the Expert doing pretty fairly. In a few more days I was quite sound. I attribute this to my prudence in always dismounting on something soft. Some recommend a feather bed, but I think an Expert is better.

The Expert got out at last, brought four assistants with him. It was a good idea. These four held the graceful cobweb upright while I climbed into the saddle; then they formed in column and marched on either side of me while the Expert pushed behind; all hands assisted at the dismount.

The bicycle had what is called the "wabbles," and had them very badly. In order to keep my position, a good many things were required of me, and in every instance the thing required was against nature. Against nature, but not against the *laws* of nature. That is to say, that whatever the needed thing might be, my nature, habit, and breeding moved me to attempt it in one way, while some immutable and un-suspected law of physics required that it be done in just the other way. I perceived by this how radically and grotesquely wrong had been the lifelong education of my body and members. They were steeped in ignorance; they knew nothing—nothing which it could profit them to know. For instance, if I found myself falling to the right, I put the tiller hard down the other way, by a quite natural impulse, and so violated a law, and kept on going down. The law required the opposite thing—the big wheel must be turned in the direction in which you are falling. It is hard to believe this, when you are told it. And not merely hard to believe it, but impossible; it is opposed to all your notions. And it is just as hard to do it, after you do come to believe it. Believing it, and knowing by the most convincing proof that it is true, does not help it: you can't any more *do* it than you could before; you can neither force nor persuade yourself to do it at first. The intellect has to come to the front, now. It has to teach the limbs to discard their old education and adopt the new.

The steps of one's progress are distinctly marked. At the end of each lesson he knows he has acquired something, and he also knows what that something is, and likewise that it will stay with him. It is not like studying German, where you mull along, in a groping, uncertain way, for thirty years; and at last, just as you think you've got it, they spring the subjunctive on you, and there you are. No—and I see now, plainly enough, that the great pity about the German language is, that you can't fall off it and hurt yourself. There is nothing like that feature to make you attend strictly to business. But I also see, by what I have learned of bicycling, that the right and only sure way to learn German is by the bicycling method. That is to say, take a grip on one villainy of it at a time, and learn it—not ease up and shirk to the next, leaving that one half learned.

When you have reached the point in bicycling where you can balance the machine tolerably fairly and propel it and steer it, then comes your next task—how to mount it. You do it in this way: you hop along behind it on your right foot, resting the other on the mounting-peg, and grasping the tiller with your hands. At the word, you rise on the peg, stiffen your left leg, hang your other one around in the air in a general and indefinite way, lean your stomach against the rear of the saddle, and then fall off, maybe on one side, maybe on the other; but you fall off. You get up and do it again; and once more; and then several times.

By this time you have learned to keep your balance; and also to steer without wrenching the tiller out by the roots (I say tiller because it *is* a tiller; "handle-bar" is a lamely descriptive phrase). So you steer along, straight ahead, a little while, then you rise forward, with a steady strain, bringing your right leg, and then your body, into the saddle, catch your breath, fetch a violent hitch this way and then that, and down you go again.

But you have ceased to mind the going down by this time; you are getting to light on one foot or the other with considerable certainty. Six more attempts and six more falls make you perfect. You land in the saddle comfortably, next time, and stay there—that is, if you can be content to let your legs dangle, and leave the pedals alone a while; but if you grab at once for the pedals, you are gone again. You soon learn to wait a little and perfect your balance before reaching for the pedals; then the mounting-art is acquired, is complete, and a little practice will make it simple and easy to you, though spectators ought to keep off a rod or two to one side, along at first, if you have nothing against them.

And now you come to the voluntary dismount; you learned the other kind first of all. It is quite easy to tell one how to do the voluntary dismount; the words are few, the requirement simple, and apparently undifficult; let your left pedal go down till your left leg is nearly straight, turn your wheel to the left, and get off as you would from a horse. It certainly does sound exceedingly easy; but it isn't. I don't know why it isn't, but it isn't. Try as you may, you don't get down as you would from a horse, you get down as you would from a house afire. You make a spectacle of yourself every time.

II

During eight days I took a daily lesson of an hour and a half. At the end of this twelve working-hours' apprenticeship I was graduated—in the rough. I was pronounced competent to paddle my own bicycle without outside help. It seems incredible, this celerity of acquirement. It takes considerably longer than that to learn horseback-riding in the rough.

Now it is true that I could have learned without a teacher, but it would have been risky for me, because of my natural clumsiness. The self-taught man seldom knows anything accurately, and he does not know a tenth as much as he could have known if he had worked under teachers; and, besides, he brags, and is the means of fooling other thoughtless people into going and doing as he himself has done. There are those who imagine that the unlucky accidents of life—life's "experiences"—are in some way useful to us. I wish I could find out how. I never knew one of them to happen twice. They always change off and swamp around and catch you on your inexperienced side. If personal experience can be worth anything as an education, it wouldn't seem likely that you could trip Methuselah; and yet if that old person could come back here it is more than likely that one of the first things he would do would be to take hold of one of these electric wires and tie himself all up in a knot. Now the surer thing and the wiser thing would be for him to ask somebody whether it was a good thing to take hold of. But that would not suit him; he would be one of the self-taught kind that go by experience; he would want to examine for himself. And he would find, for his instruction, that the coiled patriarch shuns the electric wire; and it would be useful to him, too, and would leave his education in quite a complete and rounded-out condition, till he should come again, some day, and go to bouncing a dynamite-can around to find out what was in it.

But we wander from the point. However, get a teacher; it saves much time and Pond's Extract.

Before taking final leave of me, my instructor inquired concerning my physical strength, and I was able to inform him that I hadn't any. He said that that was a defect which would make up-hill wheeling pretty difficult for me at first; but he also said the bicycle would soon remove it. The contrast between his muscles and mine was quite marked. He wanted to test mine, so I offered my biceps—which was my best. It almost made him smile. He said, "It is pulpy, and soft, and yielding, and rounded; it evades pressure, and glides from under the fingers; in the dark a body might think it was an oyster in a rag." Perhaps this made me look grieved, for he added, briskly: "Oh, that's all right; you needn't worry about that; in a little while you can't tell it from a petrified kidney. Just go right along with your practice; you're all right."

Then he left me, and I started out alone to seek adventures. You don't really have to seek them—that is nothing but a phrase—they come to you.

I chose a reposeful Sabbath-day sort of a back street which was about thirty yards wide between the curbstones. I knew it was not wide enough; still, I thought that by keeping strict watch and wasting no space unnecessarily I could crowd through.

Of course I had trouble mounting the machine, entirely on my own responsibility, with no encouraging moral support from the outside, no sympathetic instructor to say, "Good! now you're doing well—good again—don't hurry—there, now, you're all right—brace up, go ahead." In place of this I had some other support. This was a boy, who was perched on a gate-post munching a hunk of maple sugar.

He was full of interest and comment. The first time I failed and went down he said that if he was me he would dress up in pillows, that's what he would do. The next time I went down he advised me to go and learn to ride a tricycle first. The third time I collapsed he said he didn't believe I could stay on a horse-car. But next time I succeeded, and got clumsily under way in a weaving, tottering, uncertain fashion, and occupying pretty much all of the street. My slow and lumbering gait filled the boy to the chin with scorn, and he sung out, "My, but don't he rip along!" Then he got down from his post and loafed along the sidewalk, still observing and occasionally commenting. Presently he dropped into my wake and followed along behind. A little girl passed by, balancing a wash-board on her head, and giggled, and seemed about to make a remark, but the boy said, rebukingly, "Let him alone, he's going to a funeral."

I had been familiar with that street for years, and had always sup-

posed it was a dead level; but it was not, as the bicycle now informed
me, to my surprise. The bicycle, in the hands of a novice, is as alert
and acute as a spirit-level in the detecting of delicate and vanishing
shades of difference in these matters. It notices a rise where your
untrained eye would not observe that one existed; it notices any decline which water will run down. I was toiling up a slight rise, but was
not aware of it. It made me tug and pant and perspire; and still, labor
as I might, the machine came almost to a standstill every little while.
At such times the boy would say: "That's it! take a rest—there ain't
no hurry. They can't hold the funeral without *you*."

Stones were a bother to me. Even the smallest ones gave me a panic
when I went over them. I could hit any kind of a stone, no matter how
small, if I tried to miss it; and of course at first I couldn't help trying
to do that. It is but natural. It is part of the ass that is put in us all,
for some inscrutable reason.

I was at the end of my course, at last, and it was necessary for me to
round to. This is not a pleasant thing, when you undertake it for the
first time on your own responsibility, and neither is it likely to succeed.
Your confidence oozes away, you fill steadily up with nameless apprehensions, every fiber of you is tense with a watchful strain, you start a
cautious and gradual curve, but your squirmy nerves are all full of
electric anxieties, so the curve is quickly demoralized into a jerky
and perilous zigzag; then suddenly the nickel-clad horse takes the bit
in its mouth and goes slanting for the curbstone, defying all prayers
and all your powers to change its mind—your heart stands still, your
breath hangs fire, your legs forget to work, straight on you go, and
there are but a couple of feet between you and the curb now. And
now is the desperate moment, the last chance to save yourself; of
course all your instructions fly out of your head, and you whirl your
wheel *away* from the curb instead of *toward* it, and so you go sprawling on that granite-bound inhospitable shore. That was my luck; that
was my experience. I dragged myself out from under the indestructible
bicycle and sat down on the curb to examine.

I started on the return trip. It was now that I saw a farmer's wagon
poking along down toward me, loaded with cabbages. If I needed
anything to perfect the precariousness of my steering, it was just that.
The farmer was occupying the middle of the road with his wagon,
leaving barely fourteen or fifteen yards of space on either side. I
couldn't shout at him—a beginner can't shout; if he opens his mouth he
is gone; he must keep all his attention on his business. But in this
grisly emergency, the boy came to the rescue, and for once I had to be

grateful to him. He kept a sharp lookout on the swiftly varying impulses and inspirations of my bicycle, and shouted to the man accordingly:

"To the left. Turn to the left, or this jackass'll run over you!" The man started to do it. "No, to the right, to the right! Hold on! *that* won't do!—to the left!—to the right!—to the *left!*—right! left—ri— Stay where you *are*, or you're a goner!"

And just then I caught the off horse in the starboard and went down in a pile. I said, "Hang it! Couldn't you *see* I was coming?"

"Yes, I see you was coming, but I couldn't tell which *way* you was coming. Nobody could—now, *could* they? You couldn't yourself—now, *could* you? So what could *I* do?"

There was something in that, and so I had the magnanimity to say so. I said I was no doubt as much to blame as he was.

Within the next five days I achieved so much progress that the boy couldn't keep up with me. He had to go back to his gate-post, and content himself with watching me fall at long range.

There was a row of low stepping-stones across one end of the street, a measured yard apart. Even after I got so I could steer pretty fairly I was so afraid of those stones that I always hit them. They gave me the worst falls I ever got in that street, except those which I got from dogs. I have seen it stated that no expert is quick enough to run over a dog; that a dog is always able to skip out of his way. I think that that may be true: but I think that the reason he couldn't run over the dog was because he was trying to. I did not try to run over any dog. But I ran over every dog that came along. I think it makes a great deal of difference. If you try to run over the dog he knows how to calculate, but if you are trying to miss him he does not know how to calculate, and is liable to jump the wrong way every time. It was always so in my experience. Even when I could not hit a wagon I could hit a dog that came to see me practise. They all liked to see me practise, and they all came, for there was very little going on in our neighborhood to entertain a dog. It took time to learn to miss a dog, but I achieved even that.

I can steer as well as I want to, now, and I will catch that boy out one of these days and run over *him* if he doesn't reform.

Get a bicycle. You will not regret it, if you live.

1917

Adam's Soliloquy

(The spirit of Adam is supposed to be visiting New York City inspecting the dinosaur at the Museum of Natural History)

I

It is strange . . . very strange. *I* do not remember this creature. (*After gazing long and admiringly.*) Well, it is wonderful! The mere *skeleton* fifty-seven feet long and sixteen feet high! Thus far, it seems, they've found only this sample—without doubt a merely medium-sized one; a person could not step out here into the Park and happen by luck upon the largest horse in America; no, he would happen upon one that would look small along-side of the biggest Normandy. It is quite likely that the biggest dinosaur was ninety feet long and twenty feet high. It would be five times as long as an elephant; an elephant would be to it what a calf is to an elephant. The bulk of the creature! The weight of him! As long as the longest whale, and twice the substance in him! And all good wholesome pork, most likely; meat enough to last a village a year. . . . Think of a hundred of them in line, draped in shining cloth of gold!—a majestic thing for a coronation procession. But expensive, for he would eat much, only kings and millionaires could afford him.

I have no recollection of him; neither Eve nor I had heard of him until yesterday. We spoke to Noah about him; he colored and changed the subject. Being brought back to it—and pressed a little—he confessed that in the matter of stocking the Ark the stipulations had not been carried out with absolute strictness—that is, in minor details, unessentials. There were some irregularities. He said the boys were to blame for this—the boys mainly, his own fatherly indulgence partly. They were in the giddy heyday of their youth at the time, the happy spring-time of life; their hundred years sat upon them lightly, and—well, he had once been a boy himself, and he had not the heart to be too exacting with them. And so—well, they did things they shouldn't have done, and he—to be candid, he winked. But on the whole they did pretty faithful work, considering their age. They collected and stowed a good share of the really useful animals; and also, when Noah was not watching, a multitude of useless ones, such as flies, mosquitoes, snakes, and so on, but they did certainly leave ashore a good many creatures which might possibly have had value some time or other, in the course of time. Mainly these were vast saurians a hundred feet long, and monstrous mammals, such as the megatherium and that sort, and there was really some excuse for leaving them behind, for two reasons: (1) it was manifest that some time or other they would be needed as fossils for museums and (2) there had been a miscalculation, the Ark was smaller than it should have been, and so there wasn't room for those creatures. There was actually fossil material enough all by itself to freight twenty-five Arks like that one. As for the dinosaur— But Noah's conscience was easy; it was not named in his cargo list and he and the boys were not aware that there was such a creature. He said he could not blame himself for not knowing about the dinosaur, because it was an American animal, and America had not then been discovered.

Noah went on to say, "I did reproach the boys for not making the most of the room we had, by discarding trashy animals and substituting beasts like the mastodon, which could be useful to man in doing heavy work such as the elephant performs, but they said those great creatures would have increased our labors beyond our strength, in the matter of feeding and watering them, we being short-handed. There was something in that. We had no pump; there was but one window; we had to let down a bucket from that and haul it up a good fifty feet, which was very tiresome; then we had to carry the water downstairs—fifty feet again, in cases where it was for the elephants and their kind, for we kept them in the hold to serve for ballast. As it was, we lost many animals—choice animals that would have been valuable in menageries —different breeds of lions, tigers, hyenas, wolves, and so on; for they wouldn't drink the water after the salt sea water got mixed with the fresh. But we never lost a locust, nor a grasshopper, nor a weevil, nor a rat, nor a cholera germ, nor any of that sort of beings. On the whole, I think we did very well, everything considered. We were shepherds and farmers; we had never been to sea before; we were ignorant of naval matters, and I know this for certain, that there is more difference between agriculture and navigation than a person would think. It is my opinion that the two trades do not belong together. Shem thinks the same; so does Japheth. As for what Ham thinks, it is not important.

Ham is biased. You find me a Presbyterian that isn't, if you think you can."

He said it aggressively; it had in it the spirit of a challenge. I avoided argument by changing the subject. With Noah, arguing is a passion, a disease, and it is growing upon him; has been growing upon him for thirty thousand years, and more. It makes him unpopular, unpleasant; many of his oldest friends dread to meet him. Even strangers soon get to avoiding him, although at first they are glad to meet him and gaze at him, on account of his celebrated adventure. For a time they are proud of his notice, because he is so distinguished; but he argues them to rags, and before long they begin to wish, like the rest, that something had happened to the Ark.

II

(*On the bench in the Park, midafternoon, dreamily noting the drift of the human species back and forth.*) To think—this multitude is but a wee little fraction of the earth's population! And all blood kin to me, every one! Eve ought to have come with me; this would excite her affectionate heart. She was never able to keep her composure when she came upon a relative; she would try to kiss every one of these people, black and white and all. (*A baby wagon passes.*) How little change one can notice—none at all, in fact. I remember the first child well—— Let me see . . . it is three hundred thousand years ago come Tuesday. This one is just like it. So between the first one and the last one there is really nothing to choose. The same insufficiency of hair, the same absence of teeth, the same feebleness of body and apparent vacancy of mind, the same general unattractiveness all around. Yet Eve worshiped that early one, and it was pretty to see her with it. This latest one's mother worships *it;* it shows in her eyes—it is the very look that used to shine in Eve's. To think that so subtle and intangible a thing as a *look* could flit and flash from face to face down a procession three hundred thousand years long and remain the same, without shade of change! Yet here it is, lighting this young creature's face just as it lighted Eve's in the long ago—the newest thing I have seen in the earth, and the oldest. Of course, the dinosaur—— But that is in another class.

She drew the baby wagon to the bench and sat down and began to shove it softly back and forth with one hand while she held up a newspaper with the other and absorbed herself in its contents. Presently, "My!" she exclaimed; which startled me, and I ventured to ask her, modestly and respectfully, what was the matter. She courteously passed the paper to me and said—pointing with her finger:

"There—it reads like fact, but I don't know."

It was very embarrassing. I tried to look at my ease, and nonchalantly turned the paper this and that and the other way, but her eye was upon me and I felt that I was not succeeding. Pretty soon she asked, hesitatingly:

"Can't—can't—you—read?"

I had to confess that I couldn't. It filled her with wonder. But it had one pleasant effect—it interested her in me, and I was thankful, for I was getting lonesome for some one to talk to and listen to. The young fellow who was showing me around—on his own motion, I did not invite him—had missed his appointment at the Museum, and I was feeling disappointed, for he was good company. When I told the young woman I could not read, she asked me another embarrassing question:

"Where are you from?"

I skirmished—to gain time and position. I said:

"Make a guess. See how near you can come."

She brightened, and exclaimed:

"I shall dearly like it, sir, if you don't mind. If I guess right will you tell me?"

"Yes."

"Honor bright?"

"Honor bright? What is that?"

She laughed delightedly and said:

"That's a good start! I was *sure* that that phrase would catch you. I know one thing, now, all right. I know——"

"What do you know?"

"That you are not an American. And you aren't, *are* you?"

"No. You are right. I'm not—honor bright, as you say."

She looked immensely pleased with herself, and said:

"I reckon I'm not always smart, but *that* was smart, anyway. But not so *very*, after all, because I already knew—believed I knew—that you were a foreigner, by another sign."

"What was that?"

"Your accent."

She was an accurate observer; I do speak English with a heavenly accent, and she had detected the foreign twang in it. She ran charmingly on, most naïvely and engagingly pleased with her triumph:

"The minute you said, 'See 'ow near you can come to it,' I said to myself, 'Two to one he is a foreigner, and ten to one he's English.' Now that *is* your nationality, *isn't* it?"

I was sorry to spoil her victory, but I had to do it: "Ah—you'll have to guess again."

"What—you are not an Englishman?"

"No—honor bright."

She looked me searchingly over, evidently communing with herself —adding up my points, then she said:

"Well, you don't *look* like an Englishman, and that is true." After a little she added, "The fact is, you don't look like *any* foreigner—not quite like . . . like *anybody* I've seen before. I will guess some more."

She guessed every country whose name she could think of and grew gradually discouraged. Finally she said:

"You must be the Man Without a Country—the one the story tells about. You don't seem to have any nationality at all. How did you come to come to America? Have you any kinfolks here?"

"Yes—several."

"Oh, then you came to see *them*."

"Partly—yes."

She sat awhile, thinking, then:

"Well, I'm not going to give up quite yet. Where do you live when you are at home—in a city, or in the country?"

"Which do you think?"

"Well, I don't quite know. You *do* look a little countrified, if you don't mind my saying it; but you look a little citified, too—not much, but a little, although you can't read, which is very curious, and you are not used to newspapers. Now *my* guess is that you live mainly in the country when you are at home, and not very much in the city. Is that right?"

"Yes, quite right."

"Oh, good! Now I'll take a fresh start."

Then she wore herself to the bone, naming cities. No success. Next she wanted me to help her a little with some "pointers," as she phrased it. Was my city large? Yes. Was it very large? Yes. Did they have mobiles there? No. Electric light? No. Railroads, hospitals, colleges, cops? No.

"Why, then, it's not civilized! Where *can* that place be? Be good and tell me just one peculiarity of it—then maybe I can guess."

"Well, then, just one; it has gates of pearl."

"Oh, go along! That's the New Jerusalem. It isn't fair to joke. Never mind. I'll guess it yet—it will come into my head pretty soon, just when I'm not expecting it. Oh, I've got an idea! Please talk a little in your own language—that'll be a good pointer." I accommodated her with a sentence or two. She shook her head despondently.

"No," she said, "it doesn't sound human. I mean, it doesn't sound like any of these other foreigners. It's pretty enough—it's quite pretty, I think—but I'm sure I've not heard it before. Maybe if you were to pronounce your name—— What *is* your name, if you'll be so good?"

"Adam."

"Adam?"

"Yes."

"But Adam *what?*"

"That is all—just Adam."

"Nothing at all but just that? Why, how curious! There's plenty of Adams; how can they tell you from the rest?"

"Oh, that is no trouble. I'm the only one there is, there where I'm from."

"Upon my word! Well, it beats the band! It reminds a person of the old original. That was his name, too, and he hadn't any but that—just like you." Then, archly, "You've heard of him, I suppose?"

"Oh yes! Do you know him? Have you ever seen him?"

"*Seen* him? Seen *Adam?* Thanks to goodness, no! It would scare me into fits."

"I don't see why."

"You don't?"

"No."

"*Why* don't you see why?"

"Because there is no sense in a person being scared of his kin."

"*Kin?*"

"Yes. Isn't he a distant relative of yours?"

She thought it was prodigiously funny, and said it was perfectly true, but *she* never would have been bright enough to think of it. I found it a new and most pleasant sensation to have my wit admired, and was about to try to do some more when that young fellow came. He planted himself on the other side of the young woman and began a vapid remark about the weather, but she gave him a look that withered him and got stiffly up and wheeled the baby away.

1923

Advice to Youth

Being told I would be expected to talk here, I inquired what sort of a talk I ought to make. They said it should be something suitable to youth—something didactic, instructive, or something in the nature of good advice. Very well. I have a few things in my mind which I have often longed to say for the instruction of the young; for it is in one's tender early years that such things will best take root and be most enduring and most valuable. First, then, I will say to you, my young friends—and I say it beseechingly, urgingly——

Always obey your parents, when they are present. This is the best policy in the long run, because if you don't they will make you. Most parents think they know better than you do, and you can generally make more by humoring that superstition than you can by acting on your own better judgment.

Be respectful to your superiors, if you have any, also to strangers, and sometimes to others. If a person offend you, and you are in doubt as to whether it was intentional or not, do not resort to extreme measures; simply watch your chance and hit him with a brick. That will be sufficient. If you shall find that he had not intended any offense, come out frankly and confess yourself in the wrong when you struck him; acknowledge it like a man and say you didn't mean to. Yes, always avoid violence; in this age of charity and kindliness, the time has gone by for such things. Leave dynamite to the low and unrefined.

Go to bed early, get up early—this is wise. Some authorities say get up with the sun; some others say get up with one thing, some with another. But a lark is really the best thing to get up with. It gives you a splendid reputation with everybody to know that you get up with the lark; and if you get the right kind of a lark, and work at him right, you can easily train him to get up at half past nine, every time—it is no trick at all.

Now as to the matter of lying. You want to be very careful about lying; otherwise you are nearly sure to get caught. Once caught, you can never again be, in the eyes of the good and the pure, what you were before. Many a young person has injured himself permanently through a single clumsy and ill-finished lie, the result of carelessness born of incomplete training. Some authorities hold that the young ought not to lie at all. That, of course, is putting it rather stronger than necessary; still, while I cannot go quite so far as that, I do maintain, and I believe I am right, that the young ought to be temperate in the use of this great art until practice and experience shall give them that confidence, elegance, and precision which alone can make the accomplishment graceful and profitable. Patience, diligence, painstaking attention to detail—these are the requirements; these, in time, will make the student perfect; upon these, and upon these only, may he rely as the sure foundation for future eminence. Think what tedious years of study, thought, practice, experience, went to the equipment of that peerless old master who was able to impose upon the whole world the lofty and sounding maxim that "truth is mighty and will prevail"—the most majestic compound fracture of fact which any of woman born has yet achieved. For the history of our race, and each individual's experience, are sown thick with evidence that a truth is not hard to kill and that a lie told well is immortal. There in Boston is a monument of the man who discovered anesthesia; many people are aware, in these latter days, that that man didn't discover it at all, but stole the discovery from another man. Is this truth mighty, and will it prevail? Ah no, my hearers, the monument is made of hardy material, but the lie it tells will outlast it a million years. An awkward, feeble, leaky lie is a thing which you ought to make it your unceasing study to avoid; such a lie as that has no more real permanence than an average truth. Why, you might as well tell the truth at once and be done with it. A feeble, stupid, preposterous lie will not live two years—except it be a slander upon somebody. It is indestructible, then, of course, but that is no merit of yours. A final word: begin your practice of this gracious and beautiful art early—begin now. If I had begun earlier, I could have learned how.

Never handle firearms carelessly. The sorrow and suffering that have been caused through the innocent but heedless handling of firearms by the young! Only four days ago, right in the next farmhouse to the one where I am spending the summer, a grandmother, old and gray and sweet, one of the loveliest spirits in the land, was sitting at her work, when her young grandson crept in and got down an old, battered, rusty gun which had not been touched for many years and was supposed not to be loaded, and pointed it at her, laughing and threatening to shoot. In her fright she ran screaming and pleading toward the door on the other side of the room; but as she passed him he placed the gun

almost against her very breast and pulled the trigger! He had supposed it was not loaded. And he was right—it wasn't. So there wasn't
any harm done. It is the only case of that kind I ever heard of. Therefore, just the same, don't you meddle with old unloaded firearms; they
are the most deadly and unerring things that have ever been created
by man. You don't have to take any pains at all with them; you don't
have to have a rest, you don't have to have any sights on the gun, you
don't have to take aim, even. No, you just pick out a relative and bang
away, and you are sure to get him. A youth who can't hit a cathedral
at thirty yards with a Gatling gun in three-quarters of an hour, can
take up an old empty musket and bag his grandmother every time,
at a hundred. Think what Waterloo would have been if one of the
armies had been boys armed with old muskets supposed not to be
loaded, and the other army had been composed of their female relations. The very thought of it makes one shudder.

There are many sorts of books; but good ones are the sort for the
young to read. Remember that. They are a great, an inestimable, an
unspeakable means of improvement. Therefore be careful in your
selection, my young friends; be very careful; confine yourselves exclusively to Robertson's Sermons, Baxter's *Saint's Rest, The Innocents
Abroad,* and works of that kind.

But I have said enough. I hope you will treasure up the instructions
which I have given you, and make them a guide to your feet and a
light to your understanding. Build your character thoughtfully and
painstaking upon these precepts, and by and by, when you have got
it built, you will be surprised and gratified to see how nicely and
sharply it resembles everybody else's.

1923

As Regards Patriotism[1]

It is agreed, in this country, that if a man can arrange his religion so
that it perfectly satisfies his conscience, it is not incumbent upon him
to care whether the arrangement is satisfactory to anyone else or not.

[1] Paine says this was written "about 1900."—C.N.

In Austria and some other countries this is not the case. There the state arranges a man's religion for him, he has no voice in it himself.

Patriotism is merely a religion—love of country, worship of country, devotion to the country's flag and honor and welfare.

In absolute monarchies it is furnished from the throne, cut and dried, to the subject; in England and America it is furnished, cut and dried, to the citizen by the politician and the newspaper.

The newspaper-and-politician-manufactured Patriot often gags in private over his dose; but he takes it, and keeps it on his stomach the best he can. Blessed are the meek.

Sometimes, in the beginning of an insane shabby political upheaval, he is strongly moved to revolt, but he doesn't do it—he knows better. He knows that his maker would find it out—the maker of his Patriotism, the windy and incoherent six-dollar subeditor of his village newspaper—and would bray out in print and call him a Traitor. And how dreadful that would be. It makes him tuck his tail between his legs and shiver. We all know—the reader knows it quite well—that two or three years ago nine tenths of the human tails in England and America performed just that act. Which is to say, nine tenths of the Patriots in England and America turned traitor to keep from being called traitor. Isn't it true? You know it to be true. Isn't it curious?

Yet it was not a thing to be very seriously ashamed of. A man can seldom—very, very seldom—fight a winning fight against his training; the odds are too heavy. For many a year—perhaps always—the training of the two nations had been dead against independence in political thought, persistently inhospitable toward patriotism manufactured on a man's own premises, Patriotism reasoned out in the man's own head and fire-assayed and tested and proved in his own conscience. The resulting Patriotism was a shop-worn product procured at second hand. The Patriot did not know just how or when or where he got his opinions, neither did he care, so long as he was with what seemed the majority—which was the main thing, the safe thing, the comfortable thing. Does the reader believe he knows three men who have actual reasons for their pattern of Patriotism—and can furnish them? Let him not examine, unless he wants to be disappointed. He will be likely to find that his men got their Patriotism at the public trough, and had no hand in its preparation themselves.

Training does wonderful things. It moved the people of this country to oppose the Mexican War; then moved them to fall in with what they supposed was the opinion of the majority—majority Patriotism is the customary Patriotism—and go down there and fight. Before the

Civil War it made the North indifferent to slavery and friendly to the slave interest; in that interest it made Massachusetts hostile to the American flag, and she would not allow it to be hoisted on her State House—in her eyes it was the flag of a faction. Then by and by, training swung Massachusetts the other way, and she went raging South to fight under that very flag and against that aforetime protected interest of hers.

There is nothing that training cannot do. Nothing is above its reach or below it. It can turn bad morals to good, good morals to bad; it can destroy principles, it can recreate them; it can debase angels to men and lift men to angelship. And it can do any one of these miracles in a year—even in six months.

Then men can be trained to manufacture their own Patriotism. They can be trained to labor it out in their own heads and hearts and in the privacy and independence of their own premises. It can train them to stop taking it by command, as the Austrian takes his religion.

1923

Bible Teaching and Religious Practice

Religion had its share in the changes of civilization and national character, of course. What share? The lion's. In the history of the human race this has always been the case, will always be the case, to the end of time, no doubt; or at least until man by the slow processes of evolution shall develop into something really fine and high—some billions of years hence, say.

The Christian's Bible is a drug store. Its contents remain the same; but the medical practice changes. For eighteen hundred years these changes were slight—scarcely noticeable. The practice was allopathic—allopathic in its rudest and crudest form. The dull and ignorant physician day and night, and all the days and all the nights, drenched his patient with vast and hideous doses of the most repulsive drugs to be found in the store's stock; he bled him, cupped him, purged him, puked him, salivated him, never gave his system a chance to rally, nor nature a chance to help. He kept him religion sick for eighteen centuries, and allowed him not a well day during all that time. The stock in the store was made up of about equal portions of baleful and debilitating poisons, and healing and comforting medicines; but the practice of the time confined the physician to the use of the former; by consequence, he could only damage his patient, and that is what he did.

Not until far within our century was any considerable change in the practice introduced; and then mainly, or in effect only, in Great Britain and the United States. In the other countries to-day, the patient either still takes the ancient treatment or does not call the physician at all. In the English-speaking countries the changes observable in our century were forced by that very thing just referred to—the revolt of the patient against the system; they were not projected by the physician. The patient fell to doctoring himself, and the physician's practice began to fall off. He modified his method to get back his trade. He did it gradually, reluctantly; and never yielded more at a time than the pressure compelled. At first he relinquished the daily dose of hell and damnation, and administered it every other day only; next he allowed another day to pass; then another and presently another; when he had restricted it at last to Sundays, and imagined that now there would surely be a truce, the homoeopath arrived on the field and made him abandon hell and damnation altogether, and administered Christ's love, and comfort, and charity and compassion in its stead. These had been in the drug store all the time, gold labeled and conspicuous among the long shelfloads of repulsive purges and vomits and poisons, and so the practice was to blame that they had remained unused, not the pharmacy. To the ecclesiastical physician of fifty years ago, his predecessor for eighteen centuries was a quack; to the ecclesiastical physician of to-day, his predecessor of fifty years ago was a quack. To the every-man-his-own-ecclesiastical-doctor of—when?— what will the ecclesiastical physician of to-day be? Unless evolution, which has been a truth ever since the globes, suns, and planets of the solar system were but wandering films of meteor dust, shall reach a limit and become a lie, there is but one fate in store for him.

The methods of the priest and the parson have been very curious, their history is very entertaining. In all the ages the Roman Church has owned slaves, bought and sold slaves, authorized and encouraged her children to trade in them. Long after some Christian peoples had freed their slaves the Church still held on to hers. If any could know, to absolute certainty, that all this was right, and according to God's will and desire, surely it was she, since she was God's specially appointed representative in the earth and sole authorized and infallible expounder of his Bible. There were the texts; there was no mistaking their meaning; she was right, she was doing in this thing what the Bible had mapped out for her to do. So unassailable was her position that in all the centuries she had no word to say against human slavery. Yet now at last, in our immediate day, we hear a Pope saying slave trading is wrong, and we see him sending an expedition to Africa to stop it. The texts remain: it is the practice that has changed. Why? Because the world has corrected the Bible. The Church never corrects it; and also never fails to drop in at the tail of the procession—and take the credit of the correction. As she will presently do in this instance.

Christian England supported slavery and encouraged it for two hundred and fifty years, and her Church's consecrated ministers looked on, sometimes taking an active hand, the rest of the time indifferent. England's interest in the business may be called a Christian interest, a Christian industry. She had her full share in its revival after a long period of inactivity, and this revival was a Christian monopoly; that is to say, it was in the hands of Christian countries exclusively. English parliaments aided the slave traffic and protected it; two English kings held stock in slave-catching companies. The first regular English slave hunter—John Hawkins, of still revered memory—made such successful havoc, on his second voyage, in the matter of surprising and burning villages, and maiming, slaughtering, capturing, and selling their unoffending inhabitants, that his delighted queen conferred the chivalric honor of knighthood on him—a rank which had acquired its chief esteem and distinction in other and earlier fields of Christian effort. The new knight, with characteristic English frankness and brusque simplicity, chose as his device the figure of a negro slave, kneeling and in chains. Sir John's work was the invention of Christians, was to remain a bloody and awful monopoly in the hands of Christians for a quarter of a millennium, was to destroy homes, separate families, enslave friendless men and women, and break a myriad of human hearts, to the end that Christian nations might be prosperous and comfortable, Christian churches be built, and the gospel of the meek and merciful Redeemer be spread abroad in the earth; and so in the name of his ship, unsuspected but eloquent and clear, lay hidden prophecy. She was called *The Jesus.*

But at last in England, an illegitimate Christian rose against slavery. It is curious that when a Christian rises against a rooted wrong at all, he is usually an illegitimate Christian, member of some despised and bastard sect. There was a bitter struggle, but in the end the slave trade had to go—and went. The Biblical authorization remained, but the practice changed.

Then—the usual thing happened; the visiting English critic among us began straightway to hold up his pious hands in horror at our slavery. His distress was unappeasable, his words full of bitterness and contempt. It is true we had not so many as fifteen hundred thousand slaves for him to worry about, while his England still owned twelve millions, in her foreign possessions; but that fact did not modify his wail any, or stay his tears, or soften his censure. The fact that every time we had tried to get rid of our slavery in previous generations, but had always been obstructed, balked, and defeated by England, was a matter of no consequence to him; it was ancient history, and not worth the telling.

Our own conversion came at last. We began to stir against slavery. Hearts grew soft, here, there, and yonder. There was no place in the land where the seeker could not find some small budding sign of pity for the slave. No place in all the land but one—the pulpit. It yielded at last; it always does. It fought a strong and stubborn fight, and then did what it always does, joined the procession—at the tail end. Slavery fell. The slavery text remained; the practice changed, that was all.

During many ages there were witches. The Bible said so. The Bible commanded that they should not be allowed to live. Therefore the Church, after doing its duty in but a lazy and indolent way for eight hundred years, gathered up its halters, thumbscrews, and firebrands, and set about its holy work in earnest. She worked hard at it night and day during nine centuries and imprisoned, tortured, hanged, and burned whole hordes and armies of witches, and washed the Christian world clean with their foul blood.

Then it was discovered that there was no such thing as witches, and never had been. One does not know whether to laugh or to cry. Who discovered that there was no such thing as a witch—the priest, the parson? No, these never discover anything. At Salem, the parson clung pathetically to his witch text after the laity had abandoned it in remorse and tears for the crimes and cruelties it has persuaded them to do. The parson wanted more blood, more shame, more brutalities; it was the unconsecrated laity that stayed his hand. In Scotland the parson killed the witch after the magistrate had pronounced her innocent; and when the merciful legislature proposed to sweep the hideous laws against witches from the statute book, it was the parson who came imploring, with tears and imprecations, that they be suffered to stand.

There are no witches. The witch text remains; only the practice has changed. Hell fire is gone, but the text remains. Infant damnation is gone, but the text remains. More than two hundred death penalties are gone from the law books, but the texts that authorized them remain.

Is it not well worthy of note that of all the multitude of texts through which man has driven his annihilating pen he has never once made the mistake of obliterating a good and useful one? It does certainly seem to suggest that if man continues in the direction of enlightenment, his religious practice may, in the end, attain some semblance of human decency.

1923

The Cholera Epidemic in Hamburg

I believe I have never been so badly situated before as I have been during these last four weeks. To begin with, the time-hallowed and businessworn thunderbolt out of the clear sky fell about the 18th of August—people in Hamburg dying like flies of something resembling cholera! A normal death rate of forty a day suddenly transformed into a terrific daily slaughter without notice to anybody to prepare for such a surprise! Certainly that was recognizable as that kind of a thunderbolt.

It was at this point that the oddity of the situation above referred to began. For you will grant that it is odd to live four weeks a twelve-hour journey from a devastating plague nest and remain baffled and defeated all that time in all your efforts to get at the state of the case there. Naturally one flies to the newspapers when a pestilence breaks out in his neighborhood. He feels sure of one thing, at any rate: that the paper will cast all other interests into the background and devote itself to the one supreme interest of the day; that it will throw wide its columns and cram them with information, valuable and otherwise, concerning that great event; and that it will even leave out the idle jaunts of little dukes and kinglets to make room for the latest plague item. I sought the newspapers, and was disappointed. I know now that nothing that can happen in this world can stir the German daily journal out of its eternal lethargy. When the Last Day comes it will note the destruction of the world in a three-line paragraph and turn over and go to sleep again.

This sort of journalism furnishes plenty of wonders. I have seen ostensible telegrams from Hamburg four days old, gravely put forth as news, and no apology offered. I have tracked a news item from one paper to another day after day until it died of old age and fatigue— and yet everybody treated it with respect, nobody laughed. Is it believable that these antiquities are forwarded by telegraph? It would be more rational to send them by slow freight, because less expensive and more speedy.

Then, the meagerness of the news meal is another marvel. That department of the paper is not headed "Poverty Column," nobody knows why. We know that multitudes of people are being swept away daily in Hamburg, yet the daily telegrams from there could be copied on a half page of note paper as a rule. If any newspaper has sent a special reporter thither he has not arrived yet.

The final miracle of all is the character of this daily dribble of so-called news. The wisest man in the world can get no information out of it. It is an Irish stew made up of unrelated odds and ends, a mere chaotic confusion and worthless. What can one make out of statistics like these:

Up to noon, 655 cases, 333 deaths. Of these 189 were previously reported.

The report that 650 bodies are lying unburied is not true. There are only 340, and the most of these will be buried to-night.

There are 2,062 cases in the hospitals, 215 deaths.

The figures are never given in such a way as to afford one an opportunity to compare the death list of one day with that of another; consequently there is no way of finding out whether the pest abates or increases. Sometimes a report uses the expression "to-day" and does not say when the day began or ended; sometimes the deaths for several days are bunched together in a divisionless lump; sometimes the figures make you think the deaths are five or six hundred a day, while other figures in the same paragraph seem to indicate that the rate is below two hundred.

A day or two ago the word cholera was not discoverable at all in that day's issue of one of our principal dailies; in to-day's issue of the same paper there is no cholera report from Hamburg. Yet a private letter from there says the raging pestilence is actually increasing.

One might imagine that the papers are forbidden to publish cholera news. I had that impression myself. It seemed the only explanation of the absence of special Hamburg correspondence. But it appears now, that the Hamburg papers are crammed with matter pertaining to the cholera, therefore that idea was an error. How does one find this out? In this amazing way: that a daily newspaper located ten or twelve hours from Hamburg describes with owl-eyed wonder the stirring contents of a Hamburg daily journal *six days old*, and yet gets from it the only informing matter, the only matter worth reading, which it has yet published from that smitten city concerning the pestilence.

You see, it did not even occur to that petrified editor to bail his columns dry of their customary chloroform and copy that Hamburg journal entire. He is so used to shoveling gravel that he doesn't know a diamond when he sees it. I would trust that man with untold bushels of precious news, and nobody to watch him. Among other things which he notes in the Hamburg paper is the fact that its supplements contained one hundred of the customary elaborate and formal German death notices. That means—what nobody has had reason to suppose before—that the slaughter is not confined to the poor and friendless. I think so, because that sort of death notice occupies a formidable amount of space in an advertising page, and must cost a good deal of money.

I wander from my proper subject to observe that one hundred of these notices in a single journal must make that journal a sorrow to the eye and a shock to the taste, even among the Germans themselves, who are bred to endure and perhaps enjoy a style of "display ads" which far surpasses even the vilest American attempts, for insane and outrageous ugliness. Sometimes a death notice is as large as a foolscap page, has big black display lines, and is bordered all around with a coarse mourning border as thick as your finger. The notices are of all sizes from foolscap down to a humble two-inch square, and they suggest lamentation of all degrees, from the hundred-dollar hurricane of grief to the two-shilling sigh of a composed and modest regret. A newspaper page blocked out with mourning compartments of fifty different sizes flung together without regard to order or system or size must be a spectacle to see.

The notice copied [on the following page] is modest and straightforward. The advertiser informs sympathizing friends and acquaintances that his dear friend and old and faithful fellow laborer has been suddenly smitten with death; then signs his name and adds "of the firm of Beck & Steingoetter," which is perhaps another way of saying that the business will be continued as usual at the old stand. The average notice is often refreshed with a whiff of business at the end.

The 100 formal notices in the Hamburg paper did not mean merely 100 deaths; each told of one death, but many of them told of more—in some cases they told of four and five. In the same issue there were 132 one-line death notices. If the dates of these deaths were all stated, the 232 notices together could be made the basis of a better guess at the current mortality in Hamburg than the "official" reports furnished, perhaps. You would know that a certain number died on a certain day who left behind them people able to publish the fact and pay for it. Then you could correctly assume that the vast bulk of that day's harvest were people who were penniless and left penniless friends behind. You could add your facts to your assumption and get *some* sort of idea of the death rate, and this would be strikingly better than the official reports, since they give you no idea at all.

To-day a physician was speaking of a private letter received here yesterday from a physician in Hamburg which stated that every day numbers of poor people are snatched from their homes to the pest houses, and that that is the last that is heard of a good many of them. No intelligible record is kept; they die unknown and are buried so. That no intelligible record is kept seems proven by the fact that the public cannot get hold of a burial list for one day that is not made impossible by the record of the day preceding and the one following it.

What I am trying to make the reader understand is, the strangeness of the situation here—a mighty tragedy being played upon a stage that is close to us, and yet we are as ignorant of its details as we should be if the stage were in China. We sit "in front," and the audience is in fact the world; but the curtain is down and from behind it we hear only an inarticulate murmur. The Hamburg disaster must go into history as the disaster without a history. And yet a well-trained newspaper staff would find a way to secure an accurate list of the new hospital cases and the burials daily, and would do it, and not take it out in complaining of the foolishness and futility of the official reports. Every day we know exactly what is going on in the two cholera-stricken ships in the harbor of New York. That is all the cholera news we get that is worth printing or believing.

All along we have heard rumors that the force of workers at Hamburg was too small to cope with the pestilence; that more help was impossible to get; and we have seen statements which confirmed these sorrowful facts; statements which furnished the pitiful spectacle of brave workers dying at their posts from exhaustion; of corpses lying in the halls of the hospitals, waiting there because there was no worker idle; and now comes another confirmatory item; it is in the physician's letter above referred to—an item which shows you how hard pressed the authorities are by their colossal burden—an item which gives you a sudden and terrific sense of the situation there; for in a line it flashes before you this ghastly picture, a thing seen by the physician: a wagon going along the street with five sick people in it, and with them four corpses!

1923

Consistency

A paper read at the Hartford Monday Evening Club, following the Blaine-Cleveland campaign, 1884.

We are continually warned to be consistent—by the pulpit, by the newspaper, by our associates. When we depart from consistency, we are reproached for it by these censors. When a man who has been born and brought up a Jew becomes a Christian, the Jews sorrow over it and reproach him for his inconstancy; all his life he has denied the divinity of Christ, but now he makes a lie of all his past; upon him rests the stigma of inconsistency; we can never be sure of him again. We put in the deadly parallel columns what he said formerly and what he says now, and his credit is gone. We say, Trust him not; we know him now; he will change again; and possibly again and yet again; he has no stability.

There are men called life-long Democrats, life-long Republicans. If one of these departs from his allegiance and votes the other ticket, the same thing happens as in the Jew's case. The man loses character. He is inconsistent. He is a traitor. His past utterances will be double columned with his present ones, and he is damned; also despised— even by his new political associates, for in theirs, as in all men's eyes, inconsistency is a treason and matter for scorn.

These are facts—common, every-day facts; and I have chosen them for that reason; facts known to everybody, facts which no one denies.

What is the most rigorous law of our being? Growth. No smallest atom of our moral, mental, or physical structure can stand still a year. It grows—it must grow; nothing can prevent it. It must grow downward or upward; it must grow smaller or larger, better or worse—it cannot stand still. In other words, we change—and must change, constantly, and keep on changing as long as we live. What, then, is the true Gospel of consistency? Change. Who is the really consistent man? The man who changes. Since change is the law of his being, he cannot be consistent if he stick in a rut.

Yet, as the quoted facts show, there are those who would misteach us that to stick in a rut is consistency—and a virtue; and that to climb out of the rut is inconsistency—and a vice. They will grant you certain things, without murmur or dissent—as things which go without saying; truisms. They will grant that in time the crawling baby walks and must not be required to go on crawling; that in time the youth has outgrown the child's jacket and must not be required to crowd himself into it; they grant you that a child's knowledge is becoming and proper to the child only so they grant him a school and teach him, so that he may change and grow; they grant you that he must keep on learning—through youth and manhood and straight on—he must not be allowed to suppose that the knowledge of thirty can be any proper equipment for his fiftieth year; they will grant you that a young man's opinions about mankind and the universe are crude, and sometimes foolish, and they would not dream of requiring him to stick to them

the rest of his life, lest by changing them he bring down upon himself
the reproach of inconsistency. They will grant you these, and everything else you can think of, in the line of progress and change, until
you get down to politics and religion; there they draw the line. These
must suffer no change. Once a Presbyterian, always a Presbyterian,
or you are inconsistent and a traitor; once a Democrat, always a
Democrat, or you are inconsistent and a traitor—a turncoat.

It is curious logic. Is there but one kind of treason? No man remains
the same sort of Presbyterian he was at first—the thing is impossible;
time and various influences modify his Presbyterianism; it narrows or
it broadens, grows deeper or shallower, but does not stand still. In
some cases it grows so far beyond itself, upward or downward, that
nothing is really left of it but the name, and perhaps an inconsequential rag of the original substance, the bulk being now Baptist or Bud-
dhist or something. Well, if he go over to the Buddhists, he is a traitor.
To whom? To what? No man can answer those questions rationally.
Now if he does not go over what is he? Plainly a traitor to himself, a
traitor to the best and the highest and the honestest that is in him.
Which of these reasons is the blackest one—and the shamefulest?
Which is the real and right consistency? To be consistent to a sham
and an empty name, or consistent to the law of one's being, which is
change, and in this case requires him to move forward and keep
abreast of his best mental and moral progress, his highest convictions
of the right and the true? Suppose this treason to the name of a
church should carry him clear outside of all churches? Is that a blacker
treason than to remain? So long as he is loyal to his best self, what
should he care for other loyalties? It seems to me that a man should
secure the Well done, faithful servant, of his own conscience first and
foremost, and let all other loyalties go.

I have referred to the fact that when a man retires from his political
party he is a traitor—that he is so pronounced in plain language. That
is bold; so bold as to deceive many into the fancy that it is true.
Desertion, treason—these are the terms applied. Their military form
reveals the thought in the man's mind who uses them; to him a political party is an army. Well, is it? Are the two things identical? Do they
even resemble each other? Necessarily a political party is not an army
of conscripts, for they are in the ranks by compulsion. Then it must be
a regular army, or an army of volunteers. Is it a regular army? No, for
these enlist for a specified and well-understood term and can retire
without reproach when the term is up. Is it an army of volunteers who
have enlisted for the war, and may righteously be shot if they leave

before the war is finished? No, it is not even an army in that sense.
Those fine military terms are high-sounding, empty lies—and are no
more rationally applicable to a political party than they would be to
an oyster bed. The volunteer soldier comes to the recruiting office
and strips himself, and proves that he is so many feet high, and has
sufficiently good teeth, and no fingers gone, and is sufficiently sound
in body generally; he is accepted, but not until he has sworn a deep
oath, or made other solemn form of promise, to march under that flag
until that war is done or his term of enlistment completed. What is the
process when a voter joins a party? Must he prove that he is sound
in any way, mind or body? Must he prove that he knows anything—
whatever—is capable of anything? Does he take an oath or make a
promise of any sort?—or doesn't he leave himself entirely free? If he
were informed by the political boss that if he join it must be forever;
that he must be that party's chattel and wear its brass collar the rest of
his days, would not that insult him? It goes without saying. He would
say some rude, unprintable thing and turn his back on that preposterous organization. But the political boss puts no conditions upon him
at all; and his volunteer makes no promises, enlists for no stated term.
He has in no sense become a part of an army, he is in no way re-
strained of his freedom. Yet he will presently find that his bosses and
his newspapers have assumed just the reverse of that; that they have
blandly arrogated to themselves an iron-clad military authority over
him; and within twelve months, if he is an average man, he will have
surrendered his liberty, and will actually be silly enough to believe
that he cannot leave that party, for any cause whatever, without being
a shameful traitor, a deserter, a legitimately dishonored man.

There you have the just measure of that freedom of conscience,
freedom of opinion, freedom of speech and action, which we hear so
much inflated foolishness about, as being the precious possession of the
Republic. Whereas, in truth, the surest way for a man to make of
himself a target for almost universal scorn, obloquy, slander, and
insult is to stop twaddling about these priceless independencies, and
attempt to exercise one of them. If he is a preacher, half his congregation will clamor for his expulsion, and will expel him, except they find
it will injure real estate in the neighborhood; if he is a mechanic, he
will be discharged, promptly; if he is a lawyer, his clients will take
their business elsewhere; if he is a doctor, his own dead will turn
against him.

I repeat that the new party member who supposed himself independent will presently find that the party has somehow got a mortgage

on his soul, and that within a year he will recognize the mortgage, deliver up his liberty, and actually believe he cannot retire from that party from any motive, howsoever high and right, in his own eyes, without shame and dishonor.

Is it possible for human wickedness to invent a doctrine more infernal and poisonous than this? Is there imaginable a baser servitude than it imposes? What slave is so degraded as the slave who is proud that he is a slave? What is the essential difference between a life-long Democrat and any other kind of life-long slave? Is it less humiliating to dance to the lash of one master than another?

This atrocious doctrine of allegiance to party plays directly into the hands of politicians of the baser sort—and doubtless for that it was borrowed—or stolen—from the monarchical system. It enables them to foist upon the country officials whom no self-respecting man would vote for, if he could but come to understand that loyalty to himself in his first and highest duty, not loyalty to any party name. The wire workers, convention packers, know they are not obliged to put up the fittest man for the office, for they know that the docile party will vote for any forked thing they put up, even though it do not even strictly resemble a man.

I am persuaded—convinced—that this idea of consistency—unchanging allegiance to party—has lowered the manhood of the whole nation —pulled it down and dragged it in the mud. When Mr. Blaine was nominated for the Presidency, I knew the man; no, I judged I knew him; I don't know him now, but at that time I judged I knew him; for my daily paper had been painting him black, and blacker, and blacker still, for a series of years, during which it had no call to speak anything but the truth about him, no call to be malicious toward him, no call to be otherwise than just simply and honestly candid about him, since he belonged to its own party and was not before the nation as a detectable candidate for anything. But within thirty days after the nomination that paper had him all painted up white again. That is not allegiance to one's best self, one's straitest convictions; it is allegiance to party. Nobody likes to eat a ton of black paint, and none but the master can make the slave do it. Was this paper alone at this singular feast? No; ten thousand other Republican newspapers sat down at the same table and worried down their ton apiece; and not any fewer than 100,000 more-or-less-prominent politicians sat down all over this country and worried down their ton apiece; and after long, long and bitter gagging, some millions of the common serfdom of the party sat down and worried down their ton apiece. Paint? It was dirt. Enough of it was eaten by the meek Republican party to build a railroad embankment from here to Japan; and it pains me to think that a year from now they will probably have to eat it all over again.

Well, there was a lot of queer feasting done in those days. One learned in the law pondered the Mulligan letters and other frightful literature, and rendered this impressive verdict: he said the evidence would not convict Mr. Blaine in a court of law, and so he would vote for him. He did not say whether the evidences would prove him innocent or not. That wasn't important.

Now, he knew that this verdict was absolutely inconclusive. He knew that it settled nothing, established nothing whatever, and was wholly valueless as a guide for his action, an answer to his questionings.

He knew that the merciful and righteous barriers raised up by the laws of our humane age for the shelter and protection of the possibly innocent, have often and over again protected and rescued the certainly guilty. He knew that in this way many and many a prisoner has gone unchastised from the court when judge and jury and the whole public believed with all their hearts that he was guilty. He knew— all credit not discredit to our age that it is so—that this result is so frequent, so almost commonplace, that the mere failure to satisfy the exacting forms of law and prove a man guilty in a court, is a hundred thousand miles from proving him innocent. You see a hiccoughing man wallowing in the gutter at two o'clock in the morning; you think the thing all over and weigh the details of it in your mind as you walk home, and with immeasurable wisdom arrive at the verdict that you don't know he wasn't a Prohibitionist. Of course you don't, and if you stop and think a minute you would realize that you don't know he was, either.

Well, a good clergyman who read the Mulligan and other published evidences was not able to make up his mind, but concluded to take refuge in the verdict rendered by the citizen learned in the law; take his intellectual and moral food at second-hand, though he doesn't rank as an intellectual infant, unable to chew his own moral and mental nourishment; he decided that an apparently colored person who couldn't be proven to be black in the baffling crosslights of a court of law was white enough for him, he being a little color blind, anyway, in matters where the party is concerned, and so he came reluctantly to the polls, with his redeeming blush on his countenance, and put in his vote.

I met a certain other clergyman on the corner the day after the nomination. He was very uncompromising. He said: "I know Blaine to

the core; I have known him from boyhood up; and I know him to be
utterly unprincipled and unscrupulous." Within six weeks after that,
this clergyman was at a Republican mass meeting in the Opera House,
and I think he presided. At any rate, he made a speech. If you did not
know that the character depicted in it meant Mr. Blaine, you would
suppose it meant—well, there isn't anybody down here on the earth
that you can use as a comparison. It is praise, praise, praise; laudation,
laudation, laudation; glorification, glorification, canonization. Conceive
of the general crash and upheaval and ripping and tearing and read-
justment of things that must have been going on in that man's moral
and mental chaos for six weeks! What is any combination of inflammatory rheumatism and St. Vitus's dance to this? When the doctrine
of allegiance to party can utterly up-end a man's moral constitution
and make a temporary fool of him besides, what excuse are you going
to offer for preaching it, teaching it, extending it, perpetuating it?
Shall you say, the best good of the country demands allegiance to
party? Shall you also say it demands that a man kick his truth and
his conscience into the gutter, and become a mouthing lunatic, besides?
Oh, no! you say; it does not demand that. But what if it produce that,
in spite of you? There is no obligation upon a man to do things which
he ought not to do, when drunk, but most men will do them, just the
same, and so we hear no arguments about obligations in the matter;
we only hear men warned to avoid the habit of drinking; get rid of the
thing that can betray men into such things.

This is a funny business, all round. The same men who enthusias-
tically preach loyal consistency to church and party are always ready
and willing and anxious to persuade a Chinaman or an Indian or a
Kanaka to desert his Church, or a fellow-American to desert his party.
The man who deserts to them is all that is high and pure and beautiful
—apparently; the man who deserts from them is all that is foul and
despicable. This is Consistency with a capital C.

With the daintiest and self-complacentest sarcasm the life-long loy-
alist scoffs at the Independent—or, as he calls him, with cutting irony,
the Mugwump; makes himself too killingly funny for anything in this
world about him. But—the Mugwump can stand it, for there is a great
history at his back, stretching down the centuries, and he comes of a
mighty ancestry. He knows that in the whole history of the race of men
no single great and high and beneficent thing was ever done for the
souls and bodies, the hearts and the brains, of the children of this
world, but a Mugwump started it and Mugwumps carried it to victory.
And their names are the stateliest in history: Washington, Garrison,

Galileo, Luther, Christ. Loyalty to petrified opinions never yet broke a chain or freed a human soul in this world—and never will.

To return to the starting point: I am persuaded that the world has been tricked into adopting some false and most pernicious notions about consistency—and to such a degree that the average man has turned the rights and wrongs of things entirely around, and is proud to be "consistent," unchanging, immovable, fossilized, where it should be his humiliation that he is so.

1923

Corn-pone Opinions

Fifty years ago, when I was a boy of fifteen and helping to inhabit a Missourian village on the banks of the Mississippi, I had a friend whose society was very dear to me because I was forbidden by my mother to partake of it. He was a gay and impudent and satirical and delightful young black man—a slave—who daily preached sermons from the top of his master's woodpile, with me for sole audience. He imitated the pulpit style of the several clergymen of the village, and did it well, and with fine passion and energy. To me he was a wonder. I believed he was the greatest orator in the United States and would some day be heard from. But it did not happen; in the distribution of rewards he was overlooked. It is the way, in this world.

He interrupted his preaching, now and then, to saw a stick of wood; but the sawing was a pretense—he did it with his mouth; exactly imitating the sound the bucksaw makes in shrieking its way through the wood. But it served its purpose; it kept his master from coming out to see how the work was getting along. I listened to the sermons from the open window of a lumber room at the back of the house. One of his texts was this:

"You tell me whar a man gits his corn pone, en I'll tell you what his 'pinions is."

I can never forget it. It was deeply impressed upon me. By my mother. Not upon my memory, but elsewhere. She had slipped in upon me while I was absorbed and not watching. The black philosopher's idea was that a man is not independent, and cannot afford views which might interfere with his bread and butter. If he would prosper, he must train with the majority; in matters of large moment, like politics and religion, he must think and feel with the bulk of his neighbors, or suffer damage in his social standing and in his business prosperities. He must restrict himself to corn-pone opinions—at least on the surface. He must get his opinions from other people; he must reason out none for himself; he must have no first-hand views.

I think Jerry was right, in the main, but I think he did not go far enough.

1. It was his idea that a man conforms to the majority view of his locality by calculation and intention.

This happens, but I think it is not the rule.

2. It was his idea that there is such a thing as a first-hand opinion; an original opinion; an opinion which is coldly reasoned out in a man's head, by a searching analysis of the facts involved, with the heart unconsulted, and the jury room closed against outside influences. It may be that such an opinion has been born somewhere, at some time or other, but I suppose it got away before they could catch it and stuff it and put it in the museum.

I am persuaded that a coldly-thought-out and independent verdict upon a fashion in clothes, or manners, or literature, or politics, or religion, or any other matter that is projected into the field of our notice and interest, is a most rare thing—if it has indeed ever existed.

A new thing in costume appears—the flaring hoopskirt, for example—and the passers-by are shocked, and the irreverent laugh. Six months later everybody is reconciled; the fashion has established itself; it is admired, now, and no one laughs. Public opinion resented it before, public opinion accepts it now, and is happy in it. Why? Was the resentment reasoned out? Was the acceptance reasoned out? No. The instinct that moves to conformity did the work. It is our nature to conform; it is a force which not many can successfully resist. What is its seat? The inborn requirement of self-approval. We all have to bow to that; there are no exceptions. Even the woman who refuses from first to last to wear the hoopskirt comes under that law and is its slave; she could not wear the skirt and have her own approval; and that she *must* have, she cannot help herself. But as a rule our self-approval has its source in but one place and not elsewhere—the approval of other people. A person of vast consequences can introduce any kind of novelty in dress and the general world will presently adopt it—moved to do it, in the first place, by the natural instinct to passively yield to that vague something recognized as authority, and in the second place by the human instinct to train with the multitude and have its approval. An empress introduced the hoopskirt, and we know the result. A nobody introduced the bloomer, and we know the result. If Eve should come again, in her ripe renown, and reintroduce her quaint styles—well, we know what would happen. And we should be cruelly embarrassed, along at first.

The hoopskirt runs its course and disappears. Nobody reasons about it. One woman abandons the fashion; her neighbor notices this and follows her lead; this influences the next woman; and so on and so on, and presently the skirt has vanished out of the world, no one knows how nor why, nor cares, for that matter. It will come again, by and by and in due course will go again.

Twenty-five years ago, in England, six or eight wine glasses stood grouped by each person's plate at a dinner party, and they were used, not left idle and empty; to-day there are but three or four in the group, and the average guest sparingly uses about two of them. We have not adopted this new fashion yet, but we shall do it presently. We shall not think it out; we shall merely conform, and let it go at that. We get our notions and habits and opinions from outside influences; we do not have to study them out.

Our table manners, and company manners, and street manners change from time to time, but the changes are not reasoned out; we merely notice and conform. We are creatures of outside influences; as a rule we do not think, we only imitate. We cannot invent standards that will stick; what we mistake for standards are only fashions, and perishable. We may continue to admire them, but we drop the use of them. We notice this in literature. Shakespeare is a standard, and fifty years ago we used to write tragedies which we couldn't tell from—from somebody else's; but we don't do it any more, now. Our prose standard, three quarters of a century ago, was ornate and diffuse; some authority or other changed it in the direction of compactness and simplicity, and conformity followed, without argument. The historical novel starts up suddenly, and sweeps the land. Everybody writes one, and the nation is glad. We had historical novels before; but nobody read them, and the rest of us conformed—without reasoning it out. We are conforming in the other way, now, because it is another case of everybody.

The outside influences are always pouring in upon us, and we are always obeying their orders and accepting their verdicts. The Smiths like the new play; the Joneses go to see it, and they copy the Smith verdict. Morals, religions, politics, get their following from surrounding influences and atmospheres, almost entirely; not from study, not from thinking. A man must and will have his own approval first of all, in each and every moment and circumstance of his life—even if he must repent of a self-approved act the moment after its commission, in order to get his self-approval *again*: but, speaking in general terms, a man's self-approval in the large concerns of life has its source in the approval of the peoples about him, and not in a searching personal examination of the matter. Mohammedans are Mohammedans because they are born and reared among that sect, not because they have thought it out and can furnish sound reasons for being Mohammedans; we know why Catholics are Catholics; why Presbyterians are Presbyterians; why Baptists are Baptists; why Mormons are Mormons; why thieves are thieves; why monarchists are monarchists; why Republicans are Republicans and Democrats, Democrats. We know it is a matter of association and sympathy, not reasoning and examination; that hardly a man in the world has an opinion upon morals, politics, or religion which he got otherwise than through his associations and sympathies. Broadly speaking, there are none but corn-pone opinions. And broadly speaking, corn-pone stands for self-approval. Self-approval is acquired mainly from the approval of other people. The result is conformity. Sometimes conformity has a sordid business interest—the bread-and-butter interest—but not in most cases, I think. I think that in the majority of cases it is unconscious and not calculated; that it is born of the human being's natural yearning to stand well with his fellows and have their inspiring approval and praise—a yearning which is commonly so strong and so insistent that it cannot be effectually resisted, and must have its way.

A political emergency brings out the corn-pone opinion in fine force in its two chief varieties—the pocketbook variety, which has its origin in self-interest, and the bigger variety, the sentimental variety—the one which can't bear to be outside the pale; can't bear to be in disfavor; can't endure the averted face and the cold shoulder; wants to stand well with his friends, wants to be smiled upon, wants to be welcome, wants to hear the precious words, "*He's* on the right track!" Uttered, perhaps by an ass, but still an ass of high degree, an ass whose approval is gold and diamonds to a smaller ass, and confers glory and honor and happiness, and membership in the herd. For these gauds many a man will dump his life-long principles into the street, and his conscience along with them. We have seen it happen. In some millions of instances.

Men think they think upon great political questions, and they do; but they think with their party, not independently; they read its literature, but not that of the other side; they arrive at convictions, but they are drawn from a partial view of the matter in hand and are of no particular value. They swarm with their party, they feel with their party, they are happy in their party's approval; and where the party leads they will follow, whether for right and honor, or through blood and dirt and a mush of mutilated morals.

In our late canvass half of the nation passionately believed that in silver lay salvation, the other half as passionately believed that that way lay destruction. Do you believe that a tenth part of the people, on either side, had any rational excuse for having an opinion about the matter at all? I studied that mighty question to the bottom—came out empty. Half of our people passionately believe in high tariff, the other half believe otherwise. Does this mean study and examination, or only feeling? The latter, I think. I have deeply studied that question, too— and didn't arrive. We all do no end of feeling, and we mistake it for thinking. And out of it we get an aggregation which we consider a boon. Its name is Public Opinion. It is held in reverence. It settles everything. Some think it the Voice of God.

1923

The Dervish and the Offensive Stranger

The Dervish: I will say again, and yet again, and still again, that a good deed——

The Offensive Stranger: Peace, and, O man of narrow vision! There is no such thing as a good *deed*——

The Dervish: O shameless blasphe——

The Offensive Stranger: And no such thing as an evil deed. There are good *impulses*, there are evil impulses, and that is all. Half of the results of a good intention are evil; half the results of an evil intention are good. No man can command the results, nor allot them.

The Dervish: And so——

The Offensive Stranger: And so you shall praise men for their good

intentions, and not blame them for the evils resulting; you shall blame
men for their evil intentions, and not praise them for the good resulting.

The Dervish: O maniac! will you say——

The Offensive Stranger: Listen to the law: From *every* impulse,
whether good or evil, flow two streams; the one carries health, the
other carries poison. From the beginning of time this law has not
changed, to the end of time it will not change.

The Dervish: If I should strike thee dead in anger——

The Offensive Stranger: Or kill me with a drug which you hoped
would give me new life and strength——

The Dervish: Very well. Go on.

The Offensive Stranger: In either case the results would be the
same. Age-long misery of mind for you—an evil result; peace, repose,
the end of sorrow for me—a good result. Three hearts that hold me
dear would break; three pauper cousins of the third removed would
get my riches and rejoice; you would go to prison and your friends
would grieve, but your humble apprentice-priest would step into your
shoes and your fat sleek life and be happy. And are these all the goods
and all the evils that would flow from the well-intended or ill-intended
act that cut short my life, O thoughtless one, O purblind creature? The
good and evil results that flow from *any* act, even the smallest, breed
on and on, century after century, forever and ever and ever, creeping
by inches around the globe, affecting all its coming and going populations until the end of time, until the final cataclysm!

The Dervish: Then, there being no such thing as a good deed——

The Offensive Stranger: Don't I tell you there are good *intentions,*
and evil ones, and there an end? The *results* are not foreseeable. They
are of both kinds, in all cases. It is the law. Listen: this is far-Western
history:

VOICES OUT OF UTAH

I

The White Chief (to his people): This wide plain was a desert. By
our Heaven-blest industry we have damned the river and utilized its
waters and turned the desert into smiling fields whose fruitage makes
prosperous and happy a thousand homes where poverty and hunger
dwelt before. How noble, how beneficent, is Civilization!

II

Indian Chief (to his people): This wide plain, which the Spanish priests taught our fathers to irrigate, was a smiling field, whose fruitage made our homes prosperous and happy. The white American has damned our river, taken away our water for his own valley, and turned our field into a desert; wherefore we starve.

The Dervish: I perceive that the good intention did really bring both good and evil results in equal measure. But a single case cannot prove the rule. Try again.

The Offensive Stranger: Pardon me, *all* cases prove it. Columbus discovered a new world and gave to the plodding poor and the landless of Europe farms and breathing space and plenty and happiness—

The Dervish: A good result.

The Offensive Stranger: And they hunted and harried the original owners of the soil, and robbed them, beggared them, drove them from their homes, and exterminated them, root and branch.

The Dervish: An evil result, yes.

The Offensive Stranger: The French Revolution brought desolation to the hearts and homes of five million families and drenched the country with blood and turned its wealth to poverty.

The Dervish: An evil result.

The Offensive Stranger: But every great and precious liberty enjoyed by the nations of continental Europe to-day is the gift of that Revolution.

The Dervish: A good result, I concede it.

The Offensive Stranger: In our well-meant effort to lift up the Filipino to our own moral altitude with a musket, we have slipped on the ice and fallen down to his.

The Dervish: A large evil result.

The Offensive Stranger: But as an offset we are a World Power.

The Dervish: Give me time. I must think this one over. Pass on.

The Offensive Stranger: By help of three hundred thousand soldiers and eight hundred million dollars England has succeeded in her good purpose of lifting up the unwilling Boers and making them better and purer and happier than they could ever have become by their own devices.

The Dervish: Certainly that is a good result.

The Offensive Stranger: But there are only eleven Boers left now.

The Dervish: It has the appearance of an evil result. But I will think it over before I decide.

The Offensive Stranger: Take yet one more instance. With the best intentions the missionary has been laboring in China for eighty years.

The Dervish: The evil result is——

The Offensive Stranger: That nearly a hundred thousand Chinamen have acquired our Civilization.

The Dervish: And the good result is——

The Offensive Stranger: That by the compassion of God four hundred millions have escaped it.

1923

Dr. Loeb's Incredible Discovery

Experts in biology will be apt to receive with some skepticism the announcement of Dr. Jacques Loeb of the University of California as to the creation of life by chemical agencies. . . . Doctor Loeb is a very bright and ingenious experimenter, but *a consensus of opinion among biologists* would show that he is voted rather as a man of lively imagination than an inerrant investigator of natural phenomena.—New York *Times,* March 2d.

I wish I could be as young as that again. Although I seem so old, now, I was once as young as that. I remember, as if it were but thirty or forty years ago, how a paralyzing Consensus of Opinion accumulated from Experts a-setting around, about brother experts who had patiently and laboriously cold-chiseled their way into one or another of nature's safe-deposit vaults and were reporting that they had found something valuable was a plenty for me. It settled it.

But it isn't so now—no. Because, in the drift of the years I by and by found out that a Consensus examines a new thing with its feelings rather oftener than with its mind. You know, yourself, that that is so. Do those people examine with feelings that are friendly to evidence? You know they don't. It is the other way about. They do the examining by the light of their prejudices—now isn't that true?

With curious results, yes. So curious that you wonder the Consensuses do not go out of the business. Do you know of a case where a Consensus won a game? You can go back as far as you want to and you will find history furnishing you this (until now) unwritten maxim for your guidance and profit: Whatever new thing a Consensus coppers (colloquial for "bets against"), bet your money on that very card and do not be afraid.

There was that primitive steam engine—ages back, in Greek times: a Consensus made fun of it. There was the Marquis of Worcester's steam engine, 250 years ago: a Consensus made fun of it. There was Fulton's steamboat of a century ago: a French Consensus, including the Great Napoleon, made fun of it. There was Priestly, with his oxygen: a Consensus scoffed at him, mobbed him, burned him out, banished him. While a Consensus was proving, by statistics and things, that a steamship could not cross the Atlantic, a steamship did it. A Consensus consisting of all the medical experts in Great Britain made fun of Jenner and inoculation. A Consensus consisting of all the medical experts in France made fun of the stethoscope. A Consensus of all the medical experts in Germany made fun of that young doctor (his name? forgotten by all but doctors, now, revered now by doctors alone) who discovered and abolished the cause of that awful disease, puerperal fever; made fun of him, reviled him, hunted him, persecuted him, broke his heart, killed him. Electric telegraph, Atlantic cable, telephone, all "toys," and of no practical value—verdict of the Consensuses. Geology, palaeontology, evolution—all brushed into space by a Consensus of theological experts, comprising all the preachers in Christendom, assisted by the Duke of Argyle and (at first) the other scientists. And do look at Pasteur and his majestic honor roll of prodigious benefactions! Damned—each and every one of them in its turn— by frenzied and ferocious Consensuses of medical and chemical Experts comprising, for years, every member of the tribe in Europe; damned without even a casual *look* at what he was doing—and he pathetically imploring them to come and take at least one little look before making the damnation eternal. They shortened his life by their malignities and persecutions; and thus robbed the world of the further and priceless services of a man who—along certain lines and within certain limits—had done more for the human race than any other one man in all its long history: a man whom it had taken the Expert brotherhood ten thousand years to produce, and whose mate and match the brotherhood may possibly not be able to bring forth and assassinate in another ten thousand. The preacher has an old and tough reputation for bullheaded and unreasoning hostility to new light; why, he is not "in it" with the doctor! Nor, perhaps, with some of the other breeds of Experts that sit around and get up the Consensuses and squelch the new things as fast as they come from the hands of the plodders, the searchers, the inspired dreamers, the Pasteurs that come bearing pearls to scatter in the Consensus sty.

This is warm work! It puts my temperature up to 106 and raises my pulse to the limit. It always works just so when the red rag of a Consensus jumps my fence and starts across my pasture. I have been a Consensus more than once myself, and I know the business—and its vicissitudes. I am a compositor-expert, of old and seasoned experience; nineteen years ago I delivered the final-and-for-good verdict that the linotype would never be able to earn its own living nor anyone else's: it takes fourteen acres of ground, now, to accommodate its factories in England. Thirty-five years ago I was an expert precious-metal quartz-miner. There was an outcrop in my neighborhood that assayed $600 a ton—gold. But every fleck of gold in it was shut up tight and fast in an intractable and impersuadable base-metal shell. Acting as a Consensus, I delivered the finality verdict that no human ingenuity would ever be able to set free two dollars' worth of gold out of a ton of that rock. The fact is, I did not foresee the cyanide process. Indeed, I have been a Consensus ever so many times since I reached maturity and approached the age of discretion, but I call to mind no instance in which I won out.

These sorrows have made me suspicious of Consensuses. Do you know, I tremble and the goose flesh rises on my skin every time I encounter one, now. I sheer warily off and get behind something, saying to myself, "It looks innocent and all right, but no matter, ten to one there's a cyanide process under that thing somewhere."

Now as concerns this "creation of life by chemical agencies." Reader, take my advice: don't you copper it. I don't say bet on it; no, I only say, don't you copper it. As you see, there is a Consensus out against it. If you find that you can't control your passions; if you feel that you have *got* to copper something and can't help it, copper the Consensus. It is the safest way—all history confirms it. If you are young, you will, of course, have to put up, on one side or the other, for you will not be able to restrain yourself; but as for me, I am old, and I am going to wait for a new deal.

P.S.—In the same number of the *Times* Doctor Funk says: "Man may be as badly fooled by believing too little as by believing too much; the hard-headed skeptic Thomas was the only disciple who was cheated." Is that the right and rational way to look at it? I will not be sure, for my memory is faulty, but it has always been my impression that Thomas was the only one who made an examination and proved a fact, while the others were accepting, or discounting, the fact on trust —like any other Consensus. If that is so, Doubting Thomas removed a doubt which must otherwise have confused and troubled the world until now. Including Doctor Funk. It seems to me that we owe that hard-headed—or sound-headed—witness something more than a slur. Why does Doctor Funk *examine* into spiritism, and then throw stones at Thomas. Why doesn't he take it on trust? Has inconsistency become a jewel in Lafayette Place?

OLD-MAN-AFRAID-OF-THE-CONSENSUS.

Extract from Adam's Diary.—Then there was a Consensus about it. It was the very first one. It sat six days and nights. It was then delivered of the verdict that a world could not be made out of nothing; that such small things as sun and moon and stars might, maybe, but it would take years and years, if there was considerable many of them. Then the Consensus got up and looked out of the window, and there was the whole outfit spinning and sparkling in space! You never saw such a disappointed lot.

his
Adam—i—
mark
1923

Down the Rhône

In old times a summer sail down the Rhône was a favorite trip with travelers. But that day is long gone by. The conveniences for the sail disappeared many years ago—driven out of existence by the railway.

In August, 1891, I made this long-neglected voyage with a boatman and a courier. The following account of it is part diary and part comment. The main idea of the voyage was, not to see sights, but to rest up from sight-seeing. There was little or nothing on the Rhône to examine or study or write didactically about; consequently, to glide down the stream in an open boat, moved by the current only, would afford many days of lazy repose, with opportunity to smoke, read, doze, talk, accumulate comfort, get fat and all the while be out of reach of the news and remote from the world and its concerns.

Our point of departure was to be the Castle of Châtillon on Lake Bourget, not very far from Aix-les-Bains. I went down from Geneva by rail on a Saturday afternoon, and reached the station nearest the castle during the evening. I found the courier waiting for me. He had been down in the lake region several days, hunting for a boat, engaging the boatman, etc.

From my log.—The luggage was given to the porters—a couple of peasant girls of seventeen or eighteen years, and a couple of younger ones—children, one might say, of twelve or thirteen. It consisted of heavy satchels and holdalls, but they gathered it up and trudged away, not seeming to mind the weight. The road was through woods and uphill—dark and steep and long. I tried to take the heavy valise from the smallest one, telling her I would carry it myself. She did not understand, of course, and resisted. I tried, then, to take the bag by gentle force. This alarmed her. The courier came and explained that she was afraid she was going to lose the trifle of money she was earning.

The courier told her this was not the case, but she looked doubtful and concluded to hang on to a sure thing.

"How much is it she's going to get?"

"She will charge about half a franc."

"Then pay her *now,* and she'll give up the bag."

But that scheme failed, too. The child hung to the bag and seemed distressed. No explanation could be got out of her, but one of the other girls said the child was afraid that if she gave it up, the fact would be used against her with tourists as proof that she was not strong enough to carry their luggage for them, and so she would lose chances to get work.

By and by the winding road carried us by an open space where we could see very well—see the ruins of a burned-out little hamlet of the humblest sort—stone walls with empty window holes, narrow alleys cluttered with wreckage and fallen thatch, etc. Our girls were eager to have us stop and view this wonder, the result of the only conflagration they had ever seen, the only large event that had ever accented their monotonous lives. It had happened a couple of months before, and the villagers had lost everything, even to their stockings of savings, and were too poor to rebuild their houses. A young woman, an old one, and all the horses had been burned to death; the young girls said they could take us among the ruins and show us the very spot.

We finally came out on the top of the hill, and there stood the castle, a rather picturesque old stack of masonry with a walled yard about it and an odd old stumpy tower in a corner of the yard handsomely clothed in vines. The castle is a private residence, whose owner leaves it in charge of his housekeeper and some menservants, and lives in Lyons except when he wants to fish or shoot.

The courier had engaged rooms, but the fact had probably been forgotten, for we had trouble in rousing the garrison. It was getting late and they were asleep. Eventually a man unlocked and unbarred the door and led us up a winding stair of heavy and very plain stonework. My bed was higher from the floor than necessary. This is apparently the rule in old French houses of the interior. But there is a stepladder.

In the morning I looked out of my window and saw the tops of trees below me, thick and beautiful foliage, and below the trees was the bright blue water of the lake shining in the sun. The window seemed to be about two hundred feet above the water. An airy and inspiring situation, indeed. A pope was born in that room a couple of centuries ago. I forget his name.

In that old day they built for utility, this was evident. Everything—floors, sashes, shutters, beams, joists—were cheap, coarse, ornamentless, but everlastingly solid and substantial. On the wall hung an indication of the politics of the present owner. This was a small photograph with "Philippe Comte de Paris" written under it.

The castle was ancient, in its way, but over the door of one of its rooms there was a picture set in a frame whose profound antiquity made all its surroundings seem modern and fresh. This frame was of good firm oak, as black as a coal, and had once been part of a lake-dweller's house. It was already a thing of antiquity when the Romans were planting colonies in France before the time of Christ. The remains of a number of lake villages have been dug out of the mud of Lake Bourget.

Breakfast was served in the open air on a precipice in a little arbor sheltered by vines, with glimpses through the tree tops of the blue water far below, and with also a wide prospect of mountain scenery. The coffee was the best I ever drank in Europe.

Presently there was a bugle blast from somewhere about the battlements—a fine Middle Age effect—and after a moment it was answered from the further shore of the lake, and we saw a boat put out from that shore. It was ours. We were soon on board and away.

It was a roomy, long flatboat, very light and easy to manage—easy to manage because it sides tapered a little toward both ends, and both ends curved up free from the water and made the steering prompt and easy. The rear half was sheltered from sun and rain by a temporary (and removable) canopy stretched over hoop-pole arches, after the fashion of the old-time wagon covers of the emigrants to California. We at once rolled the sides of the canopy high up, so that we might have the breeze and a free view on every hand.

On the other side of the lake we entered a narrow canal, and here we had our last glimpse of that picturesque Châtillon perched on its high promontory. The sides of the canal were walled with vines heavily laden with black grapes. The vine leaves were white with the stuff which is squirted on them from a thing like a fire extinguisher to kill the calamitous phylloxera. We saw only one living creature for the first lonely mile—a man with his extinguisher strapped on his back and hard at his deadly work. I asked our admiral, Joseph Rougier, of the village of Chanaz, if it would be a good idea to offer to sell this Sabbath breaker a few choice samples of foreign phylloxera, and he said yes, if one wanted to play the star part in an inquest.

At last two women and a man strolling churchward in their Sunday best gave us a courteous hail and walked briskly along abreast of us, plying the courier and the sailor with eager questions about our curious and unaccountable project, and by the time they had got their fill and dropped astern to digest the matter and finish wondering over it, we were serene again and busy discussing the scenery; for now there was really some scenery to look at, of a mild but pleasant type—low precipices, a country road shaded by large trees, a few cozy thatched cabins scattered along, and now and then an irruption of joyous children who flocked to inspect us and admire, followed by friendly dogs who stood and barked at us, but wagged their tails to say no offense was intended.

Soon the precipice grew bolder, and presently Chanaz came in sight and the canal bore us along its front—along its street, for it had only one. We stepped ashore. There was a roll of distant drums, and soon a company or two of French infantry came marching by. All the citizens were out, and every male took off his hat politely as the soldiers moved past him, and this salute was always returned by the officers.

I wanted envelopes, wine, grapes, and postage stamps, and was directed to a stone stairway and told to go up one flight. Up there I found a small well-smoked kitchen paved with worn-out bricks, with pots and pans hanging about the walls, and a bent and humped woman of seventy cooking a very frugal dinner. The tiredest dog I have seen this year lay asleep under the stove, in a roasting heat, an incredible heat, a heat that would have pulled a remark of the Hebrew children; but the dog slept along with perfect serenity and did not seem to know that there was anything the matter with the weather. The old woman set off her coffee pot. Next she removed her pork chop to the table; it seemed to me that this was premature—the dog was better done.

We asked for the envelopes and things; she motioned us to the left with her ladle. We passed through a door and found ourselves in the smallest wholesale and retail commercial house in the world, I suppose. The place was not more than nine feet square. The proprietor was polite and cheerful enough for a place five or six times as large. He was weighing out two ounces of parched coffee for a little girl, and when the balances came level at last he took off a light bean and put on a heavier one in the handsomest way and then tied up the purchase in a piece of paper and handed it to the child with as nice a bow as one would see anywhere. In that shop he had a couple of bushels of wooden shoes—a dollar's worth, altogether, perhaps—but he had no other articles in such lavish profusion. Yet he had a pound or so or a dipperful of any kind of thing a person might want. You couldn't buy two things of a kind there, but you could buy one of any and every kind. It was a useful shop, and a sufficient one, no doubt, yet its contents could not have cost more than ten dollars. Here was home on a small scale, but everything comfortable, no haggard looks visible, no financial distress apparent. I got all the things I came for except double-postage stamps for foreign service; I had to take domestic stamps instead. The merchant said he kept a double-stamp in stock a couple of years, but there was no market for it, so he sent it back to Paris, because it was eating up its insurance. A careful man and thrifty; and of such is the commonwealth of France.

We got some hot fried fish in Chanaz and took them aboard and cleared out. With grapes and claret and bread they made a satisfactory luncheon. We paddled a hundred yards, turned a rock corner, and here was the furious gray current of the Rhône just a-whistling by! We crept into it from the narrow canal, and laid in the oars. The floating was begun. One needs no oar-help in a current like that. The shore seemed to fairly spin past. Where the current assaults the heavy stone barriers thrown out from the shores to protect the banks, it makes a break like the break of a steamboat, and you can hear the roar a couple of hundred yards off.

The river where we entered it was about a hundred yards wide, and very deep. The water was at medium stage. The Rhône is not a very long river—six hundred miles—but it carries a bigger mass of water to the sea than any other French stream.

For the first few miles we had lonely shores—hardly ever a house. On the left bank we had high precipices and domed hills; right bank low and wooded.

At one point in the face of a precipice we saw a great cross (carved out of the living rock, the Admiral said) forty feet above the carriage road, where a doctor has had his tomb scooped in the rock and lies in there safe from his surviving patients—if any.

At 1.25 P.M. we passed the slumbrous village of Massigneux de Rive on the right and the ditto village of Huissier on the left (in Savoie). We had to take all names by sound from the Admiral; he said nobody could spell them. There was a ferry at the former village. A wire is stretched across the river high overhead; along this runs a wheel which has ropes leading down and made fast to the ferryboat in such a way that the boat's head is held farther upstream than its stern. This angle enables the current to drive the boat across, and no other motive force is needed. This would be a good thing on minor rivers in America.

2.10 P.M.—It is delightfully cool, breezy, shady (under the canopy), and still. Much smoking and lazy reflecting. There is no sound but the rippling of the current and the moaning of far-off breaks, except that now and then the Admiral dips a screechy oar to change the course half a point. In the distance one catches the faint singing and laughter of playing children on the softened note of a church bell or town clock. But the reposeful stillness—that is the charm—and the smooth swift gliding—and the fresh, clear, lively, gray-green water. There was such a rush, and boom, and life, and confusion, and activity in Geneva yesterday—how remote all that seems now, how wholly vanished away and gone out of this world!

2.15.—Village of Yenne. Iron suspension bridge. On the heights back of the town a chapel with a tower like a thimble, and a very tall white Virgin standing on it.

2.25.—Precipices on both sides now. River narrow—sixty yards.

2.30.—Immense precipice on right bank, with groups of buildings

(Pierre Châtel) planted on the very edge of it. In its near neighborhood a massive and picturesque fortification.

All this narrow gut from the bridge down to the next bridge—a mile
or two—is picturesque with its frowning high walls of rock.

In the face of the precipice above the second bridge sits a painted
house on a rock bench—a chapel, *we* think, but the Admiral says
it is for the storage of wine.

More fortifications at the corner where the river turns—no cannon,
but narrow slits for musketry commanding the river. Also narrow slits
in the solid (hollowed-out) precipice. Perhaps there is no need of
cannon here where you can throw a biscuit across from precipice to
precipice.

2.45.—Below that second bridge. On top of the bluffs more fortifications. Low banks on both sides here.

2.50.—Now both sets of fortifications show up, look huge and formidable, and are finely grouped. Through the glass they seem deserted
and falling to ruin. Out of date, perhaps.

One will observe, by these paragraphs, that the Rhône is swift
enough to keep one's view changing with a very pleasant alacrity.

At midafternoon we passed a steep and lofty bluff—right bank—
which was crowned with the moldering ruins of a castle overgrown
with trees. A relic of Roman times, the Admiral said. Name? No,
he didn't know any name for it. Had it a history? Perhaps; he didn't
know. Wasn't there even a legend connected with it? He didn't know
of any.

Not even a legend. One's first impulse was to be irritated; whereas
one should be merely thankful; for if there is one sort of invention in
this world that is flatter than another, it is the average folklore legend.
It could probably be proven that even the adventures of the saints
in the Roman calendar are not of a lower grade as works of the inventor's art.

The dreamy repose, the infinite peace of these tranquil shores, this
Sabbath stillness, this noiseless motion, this strange absence of the
sense of sin, and the stranger absence of the desire to commit it—this
was the perfectest day the year had brought! Now and then we
slipped past low shores with grassy banks. A solitary thatched cottage
close to the edge, one or two big trees with dense foliage sheltering
the cottage, and the family in their Sunday clothes grouped in the
deep shade, chatting, smoking, knitting, the dogs asleep about their
feet, the kittens helping with the knitting, and all hands content and
praising God without knowing it. We always got a friendly word of

greeting and returned it. One of these families contained eighteen sons, and all were present. The Admiral was acquainted with everybody along the banks, and with all the domestic histories, notwithstanding he was so ineffectual on old Roman matters.

4.20.—Bronze statue of the Virgin on a sterile hill slope.

4.45.—Ruined Roman tower on a bluff. Belongs to the no-name series.

5.—Some more Roman ruins in the distance.

At 6 o'clock we rounded to. We stepped ashore in a woodsy and lonely place and walked a short mile through a country lane to the sizable and rather modern-looking village of St.-Genix. Part of the way we followed another pleasure party—six or eight little children riding aloft on a mountain of fragrant hay. This is the earliest form of the human pleasure excursion, and for utter joy and perfect contentment it stands alone in a man's threescore years and ten; all that come after it have flaws, but this has none.

We put up at the Hôtel Labully, in the little square where the church stands. Satisfactory dinner. Later I took a twilight tramp along the high banks of a moist ditch called the Guires River. If it was my river I wouldn't leave it outdoors nights, in this careless way, where any dog can come along and lap it up. It is a tributary of the Rhône when it is in better health.

It became dark while we were on our way back, and then the bicyclers gave us many a sudden chill. They never furnished us an early warning, but delivered the paralyzing shock of their rubber-horn hoot right at our shoulder blades and then flashed spectrally by on their soundless wheels and floated into the depths of the darkness and vanished from sight before a body could collect his remark and get it out. Sometimes they get shot. This is right.

I went to my room, No. 16. The floor was bare, which is the rule down the Rhône. Its planks were light colored, and had been smoothed by use rather than art; they had conspicuous black knots in them. The usual high and narrow bed was there, with the usual little marble-topped commode by the head of it and the usual strip of foot carpet alongside, where you climb in. The wall paper was dark—which is usual on the Continent; even in the northern regions of Germany, where the daylight in winter is of such poor quality that they don't even tax it now.

When I woke in the morning it was eight o'clock and raining hard, so I stayed in bed and had my breakfast and a ripe old Paris paper of last week brought up. It was a good breakfast—one often gets that;

and a liberal one—one seldom gets that. There was a big bowl for the coffee instead of a stingy cup which has to be refilled just as you are getting interested in it; there was a quart of coffee in the pot instead of a scant half pint; instead of the usual hollow curl of brittle butter which evades you when you try to scoop it on to the knife and crumbles when you try to carve it, there was a solid cream-colored lump as big as a brick; there was abundance of hot milk, and there was also the usual ostensible cream of Europe. There *must* be cream in Europe. There *must* be cream in Europe somewhere, but it is not in the cows; they have been examined!

The rain continued to pour until noon, then the sun burst out and we were soon up and filing through the village. By the time we had tramped our mile and pushed out into the stream, the watches marked 1.10 and the day was brilliant and perfect.

Over on the right were ruins of two castles, one of them of some size.

We passed under a suspension bridge; alongside of it was an iron bridge of a later pattern. Near by was a little steamer lying at the bank with no signs of life about her—the first boat, except ferryboats, encountered since we had entered the Rhône. A lonely river, truly.

We drifted past lofty highlands, but there was nothing inspiring about them. In Switzerland the velvet heights are sprinkled with homes clear to the clouds, but these hills were sterile, desolate, gray, melancholy, and so thin was the skin on them that the rocky bones showed through in places.

1.30.—We seem lost in the intricate channels of an archipelago of flat islands covered with bushes.

1.50.—We whirl around a corner into open river again, and observe that a vast bank of leaden clouds is piling itself up on the horizon; the tint thrown upon the distant stretches of water is rich and fine.

The river is wide now—a hundred and fifty yards—and without islands. Suddenly it has become nearly currentless and is like a lake. The Admiral explains that from this point for nine miles it is called L'Eau Morte—Dead Water.

The region is not entirely barren of life, it seems—solitary woman paddling a punt across the wide still pool.

The boat moved, but that is about all one could say. It was indolent progress; still, it was comfortable. There were flaming sunshine behind and that rich thunder gloom ahead, and now and then the fitful fanning of a pleasant breeze.

A woman paddled across—a rather young woman with a face like the "Mona Lisa." I had seen the "Mona Lisa" only a little while before, and stood two hours in front of that painting, repeating to myself: "People come from around the globe to stand here and worship. What is it they find in it?" To me it was merely a serene and subdued face, and there an end. There might be more in it, but I could not find it. The complexion was bad; in fact, it was not even human; there are no people of that color. I finally concluded that maybe others still saw in the picture faded and vanished marvels which *had* been there once and were now forever vanished.

Then I remembered something told me once by Noel Flagg,[1] the artist. There was a time, he said, when he wasn't yet an artist but thought he was. His pictures sold, and gave satisfaction, and that seemed a good-enough verdict. One day he was daubing away in his studio and feeling good and inspired, when Dr. Horace Bushnell, that noble old Roman, straggled in there without an invitation and fastened that deep eye of his on the canvas. The youth was proud enough of such a call, and glad there was something on the easel that was worthy of it. After a long look the great divine said:

"You have talent, boy." (That sounded good.) "What you want is teaching."

Teaching—he, an accepted and competent artist! He didn't like that. After another long look:

"Do you know the higher mathematics?"

"I? No, sir."

"You must acquire them."

"As a proper part of an artist's training?" This with veiled irony.

"As an *essential* part of it. Do you know anatomy?"

"No, sir."

"You must learn how to dissect a body. What are you studying, now—principally?"

"Nothing, I believe."

"And the time flying, the time flying! Where are your books? What do you read?"

"There they are, on the shelves."

"I see. Poetry and romance. They must wait. Get to your mathematics and your anatomy right away. Another point: you must train your eye—you must teach yourself to see."

"Teach myself to see? I believe I was born with that ability."

"But nobody is born with a *trained* ability—nobody. A cow sees—

[1] Of Hartford, Connecticut.

she sees all the outsides of things, no doubt, but it is only the trained eye that sees deeper, sees the soul of them, the meaning of them, the spiritual essence. Are you sure that you see more than the cow sees? You must go to Paris. You will never learn to see here. There they'll teach you; there they'll train you; there they'll work you like a slave; there they'll bring out the talent that's in you. Be off! Don't twaddle here any longer!"

Flagg thought it over and resolved that the advice was worth taking. He and his brother cleared for Paris. They put in their first afternoon there scoffing at the works of the old masters in the Louvre. They laughed at themselves for crossing a wide ocean to learn what masterly painting might be by staring at these odious things. As for the "Mona Lisa," they exhausted their treasure of wit in making fun of it.

Next day they put themselves into the hands of the Beaux Arts people, and that was the end of play. They had to start at the very bottom of their trade and learn it over again, detail by detail, and learn it *right*, this time. They slaved away, night and day for three months, and wore themselves to shadows. Then they had a day off, and drifted into the Louvre. Neither said a word for some time; each disliked to begin; but at last, in front of the "Mona Lisa," after standing mute awhile one of them said:

"Speak out. Say it."

"Say it yourself."

"Well, then, we *were* cows before!"

"Yes—it's the right name for it. That is what we were. It is unbelievable, the change that has come over these pictures in three months. It is the difference between a landscape in the twilight and the same landscape in the daytime." Then they fell into each other's arms.

This all came back to me, now, as I saw this living "Mona Lisa" punting across L'Eau Morte.

2.40 P.M.—Made for a village on the right bank with all speed—Port de Groslee. Remains of Roman aqueduct on hilltop back of village. Rain!—Deluges of it. Took refuge in an inn on the bank—Hôtel des Voyageurs. The public room was full of voyageurs and tobacco smoke. The voyageurs may have been river folk in the old times when the inn was built, but this present crowd was made up of teamsters. They sat at bare tables, under their feet was the bare floor, about them were the four bare walls—a dreary place at any time, a heartbreaking place now in the dark of the downpour. However, it is manifestly not dreary to the teamsters. They were sipping red wine and smoking; they all talked at once, and with great energy and spirit, and every now and then they gave their thighs a sounding slap and burst into a general horse laugh. The courier said that this was in response to rude wit and coarse anecdotes. The brace of modest-looking girls who were waiting on the teamsters did not seem troubled. The courier said that they were used to all kinds of language and were not defiled by it: that they had probably seldom heard a spade called anything but a spade, therefore the foulest words came innocent to their ears.

This inn was built of stone—of course; everybody's house on the Continent, from palace to hovel, is built of that dismal material, and as a rule it is as square as a box and odiously plain and destitute of ornament; it is formal, forbidding, and breeds melancholy thoughts in people used to friendlier and more perishable materials of construction. The frame house and the log house molder and pass away, even in the builder's time, and this makes a proper bond of sympathy and fellowship between the man and his home; but the stone house remains always the same to the person born in it; in his old age it is still as hard, and indifferent, and unaffected by time as it was in the long-vanished days of his childhood. The other kind of house shows by many touching signs that it has noted his griefs and misfortunes and has felt for them, but the stone house doesn't—it is not of his evanescent race, it has no kinship with him, nor any interest in him.

A professional letter writer happened along presently, and one of the young girls got him to write a letter for her. It seemed strange that she could not write it herself. The courier said that the peasant women of the Rhône do not care for education, but only for religion; that they are all good Catholics, and that their main ambition in life is to see the Rhône's long procession of stone and bronze Virgins added to, until the river shall be staked out with them from end to end; and that their main pleasure in life is to contribute from their scant centimes to this gracious and elevating work. He says it is a quite new caprice; that ten years ago there was not a Virgin in this part of France at all, and never had been. This may be true, and, of course, that is nothing unreasonable about it, but I have already found out that the courier's statements are not always exact.

I had a hot fried fish and coffee in a garden shed roofed with a mat of vines, but the rain came through in streams and I got drenched in spite of our umbrellas, for one cannot manage table implements and umbrellas all at the same time with anything like good success.

Mem.—Last evening, for economy's sake, proposed to be a Frenchman because Americans and English are always overcharged. Courier said it wouldn't deceive unless I played myself for a deaf-and-dumb Frenchman—which I did, and so the rooms were only a franc and a half each. But the Admiral must have let it out that I was only deaf and dumb in French, for prices were raised in the bill this morning.

4.10 P.M.—Left Port de Groslee.

4.50 P.M.—Château of the Count Cassiloa—or something like that—the Admiral's pronunciation is elusive. Courier guesses the spelling at "Quintionat." I don't quite see the resemblance. This courier's confidence in himself is a valuable talent. He must be descended from the idiot who taught our forefathers to spell tizzik with a *ph* and a *th*.

The river here is as still and smooth and nearly as dead as a lake. The water is swirly, though, and consequently makes uneasy steering.

River seems to draw together and greatly narrow itself below the count's house. No doubt the current will smarten up there.

Three new quarries along here. Dear me! how little there is in the way of sight-seeing, when a quarry is an event! Remarked upon with contentment.

Swept through the narrow canallike place with a good current.

On the left-hand point below, bush-grown ruins of an ancient convent (St. Alban's), picturesquely situated on a low bluff. There is a higher and handsomer bluff a trifle lower down. How did they overlook it? Those people generally went for the best, not second best. Shapely hole in latter bluff one hundred feet above the water—anchorite's nest? Interesting-looking hole, and would have cost but little time and trouble to examine it, but it was not done. It is no matter; one can find other holes.

At last, below bluffs, we find some greensward—not extensive, but a pleasant novelty.

5.30.—Lovely sunset. Mottled clouds richly painted by sinking sun, and fleecy shreds of clouds drifting along the fronts of neighboring blue mountains. Harrow in a field. Apparently harrow, but was distant and could not tell; could have been a horse.

5.35—Very large gray broken-arched and unusually picturesque ruin crowning a hilltop on right. Name unknown. This is a liberal mile above village of Briord (my spelling—the Admiral's pronunciation), on same side. Passed the village swiftly, and left it behind. The villagers came out and made fun of our strange tub. The dogs chased us and were more noisy than necessary.

6 P.M.—Another suspension bridge—this is the sixth one. They have

ceased to interest. There was nothing exciting about them, from the
start. Presently landed on left bank and shored the boat for the night.
Hôtel du Rhône Moine. Isolated. Situated right on the bank. Sort of a
village—villagette, to be exact—a little back. Hôtel is two stories high
and not pretentious—family dwelling and cow stable all under one
roof.

I had been longing to have personal experience of peasant life—be
"on the inside" and see it for myself, instead of at second hand in
books. This was an opportunity and I was excited about it and glad.
The kitchen was not clean, but it was a sociable place, and the family
were kind and full of good will. There were three little children, a
young girl, father, mother, grandparents, some dogs, and a plurality
of cats. There was no discord; perfect harmony prevailed.

Our table was placed on the lawn on the river bank. One had no
right to expect any finer style here than he would find in the cheapest
and shabbiest little tavern in America, for the Hôtel du Rhône
Moine was for foot wanderers and laborers on the flatboats that convey
stone and sand and wood to Lyons, yet the style *was* superior—very
much so. The tablecloth was white, and it and the table furniture were
perfectly clean. We had a fish of a pretty coarse grain, but it was fresh
from the river and hot from the pan; the bread was good, there was
abundance of excellent butter, the milk was rich and pure, the sugar
was white, the coffee was considerably better than that which is
furnished by the choice hotels of the capitals of the Continent. Thus
far, peasant life was a disappointment, it was so much better than
anything we were used to at home in some respects. Two of the dogs
came out, presently, and sat down by the table and rested their chins
on it, and so remained. It was not to beg, for they showed no interest
in the supper; they were merely there to be friendly, it was the only
idea they had. A squadron of cats came out by and by and sat
down in the neighborhood and looked me over languidly, then wandered away without passion, in fact with what looked like studied indifference. Even the cats and the dogs are well and sufficiently fed
at the Hôtel du Rhône Moine—their dumb testimony was as good as
speech.

I went to bed early. It is inside the house, not outside, that one
really finds the peasant life. Our rooms were over the stable, and this
was not an advantage. The cows and horses were not very quiet, the
smell was extraordinary, the fleas were a disorderly lot, and these
things helped the coffee to keep one awake. The family went to bed
at nine and got up at two. The beds were very high; one could not

climb into them without help of a chair; and as they were narrow and arched, there was danger of rolling out in case one drifted into dreams of an imprudent sort. These lofty bedsteads were not high from caprice, but for a purpose—they contained chests of drawers, and the drawers were full of clothing and other family property. On the table in my room were some bright-colored, even gorgeous little waxen saints and a Virgin under bell-glasses; also the treasures of the house—jewelry and a silver watch. It was not costly jewelry, but it was jewelry, at any rate, and without doubt the family valued it. I judged that this household were accustomed to having honest guests and neighbors or they would have removed these things from the room when I entered it, for I do not look honester than others.

Not that I have always thought in this way about myself, for I haven't. I thought the reverse until the time I lost my overcoat, once, when I was going down to New York to see the Water Color exhibition, and had a sort of adventure in consequence. The house had been robbed in the night, and when I came downstairs to rush for the early train there was no overcoat. It was a raw day, and when I got to New York at noon I grew colder and colder as I walked along down the Avenue. When I reached East Thirty-fourth street I stopped on the corner and began to consider. It seemed to me that it must have been just about there that Smith,[2] the artist, took me one winter's night, with others, five years before, and caroused us with roasted oysters and Southern stories and hilarity in his fourth story until three or four in the morning; and now if I could only call to mind which of those houses over the way was his, I could borrow an overcoat. All the time that I was thinking and standing there and trying to recollect, I was dimly conscious of a figure near me, but only dimly, very dimly; but now as I came out of my reverie and found myself gazing, rapt but totally unconscious, at one of the houses over there, that figure solidified itself and became at once the most conspicuous thing in the landscape. It was a policeman. He was standing not six feet away, and was gazing as intently at my face as I had been gazing at the house. I was embarrassed—it is always embarrassing to come to yourself and find a stranger staring at you. You blush, even when you have not been doing any harm. So I blushed—a thing that does not commend a person to a policeman; also I tried to smile a placating smile, but it did not get any response, so then I tried to make it a kind of friendly smile, which was a mistake, because that only hardens a policeman, and I

[2] *Note, 1904.* Hopkinson Smith, now a distinguished man in literature, art, and architecture. S.L.C.

saw at once that this smile had hardened this one and made my situation more difficult than ever; and so, naturally, my judgment being greatly impaired by now, I spoke—which was an error, because in these circumstances one cannot arrange without reflection a remark which will not seem to have a kind of suspicious something about it to a policeman, and that was what happened this time; for I had fanned up that haggard smile again, which had been dying out when I wasn't noticing, and said:

"Could you tell me, please, if there's a Mr. Smith lies over there in—"

"*What* Smith?"

That rude abruptness drove his other name out of my mind; and as I saw I never should be able to think of it with the policeman standing there cowing me with his eye, that way, it seemed to me best to get out a name of some kind, so as to avert further suspicion, therefore I brought out the first one which came into my mind, which was John —another error. The policeman turned purple—apparently with a sense of injury and insult—and said there were a million John Smiths in New York, and *which* one was this? Also what did I want with Smith? I could not remember—the overcoat was gone out of my mind. So I told him he was a pupil of mine and that I was giving him lessons in morals; moral culture—a new system.

That was a lucky hit, anyway. I was merely despicable, now, to the policeman, but harmless—I could see it in his eye. He looked me over a moment then said:

"You give him lessons, do you?"

"Yes, sir."

"How long have you been giving him lessons?"

"Two years, next month." I was getting my wind again, and confidence.

"Which house does he live in?"

"That one—the middle one in the block."

"Then what did you ask *me* for, a minute ago?"

I did not see my way out. He waited for an answer, but got tired before I could think of one that would fit the case and said:

"How is it that you haven't an overcoat on, such a day as this?"

"I—well, I never wear them. It doesn't seem cold to me."

He thought awhile, with his eye on me, then said, with a sort of sigh:

"Well, maybe you are all right—I don't know—but you want to walk pretty straight while you are on my beat; for, morals or no morals, blamed if I take much stock in you. Move on, now."

Then he turned away, swinging his club by its string. But his eye was over his shoulder, my way; so I had to cross to that house, though I didn't want to any more. I did not expect it to be Smith's house, now that I was so out of luck, but I thought I would ring and ask, and if it proved to be some one else's house, then I would explain that I had come to examine the gas meter and thus get out the back way and be all right again. The door was opened by a middle-aged matron with a gentle and friendly face, and she had a sweet serenity about her that was a notable contrast to my nervous flurry. I asked after Smith and if he lived there, and to my surprise and gratitude she said that this was his home.

"Can I see him? Can I see him right away—immediately?"

No; he was gone downtown. My rising hopes fell to ruin.

"Then can I see Mrs. Smith?"

But alas and alas! she was gone downtown with him. In my distress I was suddenly smitten by one of those ghastly hysterical inspirations, you know, when you want to do an insane thing just to astonish and petrify somebody; so I said, with a rather overdone pretense of playful ease and assurance:

"Ah, this is a very handsome overcoat on the hat rack—be so good as to lend it to me for a day or two!"

"With pleasure," she said—and she had the coat on me before I knew what had happened. It had been my idea to astonish and petrify her, but I was the person astonished and petrified, myself. So astonished and so petrified, in fact, that I was out of the house and gone, without a thank-you or a question, before I came to my senses again. Then I drifted slowly along, reflecting—reflecting pleasantly. I said to myself, "She simply divined my character by my face—what a far clearer intuition she had than that policeman." The thought sent a glow of self-satisfaction through me.

Then a hand was laid on my shoulder and I shrank together with a crash. It was the policeman. He scanned me austerely and said:

"Where did you get that overcoat?"

Although I had not been doing any harm, I had all the sense of being caught—caught in something disreputable. The officer's accusing eye and unbelieving aspect heightened this effect. I told what had befallen me at the house in as straightforward a way as I could, but I was ashamed of the tale, and looked it, without doubt, for I knew and felt how improbable it must necessarily sound to anybody, particularly a policeman. Manifestly he did not believe me. He made me tell it all over again, then he questioned me:

"You don't know the woman?"

"No, I don't know her."

"Haven't the least idea who she is?"

"Not the least."

"You didn't tell her your name?"

"No."

"She didn't ask for it?"

"No."

"You just asked her to lend you the overcoat, and she let you take it?"

"She put it on me herself."

"And didn't look frightened?"

"Frightened? Of course not."

"Not even surprised?"

"Not in the slightest degree."

He paused. Presently he said:

"My friend, I don't believe a word of it. Don't you see, yourself, it's a tale that won't wash? Do *you* believe it?"

"Yes. I know it's true."

"Weren't you surprised?"

"Clear through to the marrow!"

He had been edging me along back to the house. He had a deep design; he sprung it on me now. Said he:

"Stop where you are. I'll mighty soon find out!"

He walked to the door and up the steps, keeping a furtive eye out toward me and ready to jump for me if I ran. Then he pretended to pull the bell, and instantly faced about to observe the effect on me. But there wasn't any; I walked toward him instead of running away. That unsettled him. He came down the steps, evidently perplexed, and said:

"Well, I can't make it out. It may be all right, but it's too many for me. I don't like your looks and I won't have such characters around. Go along, now, and look sharp. If I catch you prowling around here again I'll run you *in*."

I found Smith at the Water Color dinner that night, and asked him if it were merely my face that had enabled me to borrow the overcoat from a stranger, but he was surprised and said:

"No! What an idea—and what intolerable conceit! She is my housekeeper, and remembered your drawling voice from overhearing it a moment that night four or five years ago in my house; so she knew where to send the police if you didn't bring the coat back!"

After all those years I was sitting here, now, at midnight in the peasant hotel, in my night clothes, and honoring womankind in my thoughts; for here was another woman, with the noble and delicate intuitions of her sex, trusting me, a total stranger, with all her modest wealth. She entered the room, just then, and stood beaming upon me a moment with her sweet matronly eyes—then took away the jewelry.

Tuesday, September 22d.—Breakfast in open air. Extra canvas was now to be added to the boat's hood to keep the passengers and valises better protected during rainstorms. I passed through the villagette and started to walk over the wooded hill, the boat to find us on the river bank somewhere below, by and by. I soon got lost among the high bushes and turnip gardens. Plenty of paths, but none went to the river. Reflection. Decision—that the path most traveled was the one leading in the right direction. It was a poor conclusion. I got lost again; this time worse than before. But a peasant of above eighty (as she said, and certainly she was very old and wrinkled and gray and bent) found me presently and undertook to guide me safely. She was vigorous, physically, prompt and decided of movement, and altogether soldierlike; and she had a hawk's eye and beak, and a gypsy's complexion. She said that from her girlhood up to not so very many years ago she had done a man's work on a woman's pay on the big keel boats that carry stone down the river, and was as good a man as the best, in the matter of handling stone. Said she had seen the great Napoleon when she was a little child. Her face was so wrinkled and dark and so eaglelike that she reminded me of old Indians one sees out on the Great Plains—the outside signs of age, but in the eye an indestructible spirit. She had a couple of laden baskets with her which I had found heavy after three minutes' carrying, when she was finding the way for me, but they seemed nothing to her. She impressed one rather as a man than as a woman; and so, when she spoke of her child that was drowned, and her voice broke a little and her lip quivered, it surprised me; I was not expecting it. "Grandchild?" No—it was her own child. "Indeed? When?" So then it came out that it was sixty years ago. It seemed strange that she should mind it so long. But that was the woman of it, no doubt. She had a fragment of newspaper—religious—with rude holy woodcuts in it and doubtful episodes in the lives of mediaeval saints and anchorites—and she could read these instructive matters in fine print without glasses; also, her eyes were as

good at long distances. She led hither and thither among the paths
and finally brought me out overlooking the river. There was a steep
sandy frontage there, where there had recently been a small landslide,
and the faint new path ran straight across it for forty feet, like a slight
snow track along the slant of a very steep roof. I halted and declined. I
had no mind to try the crumbly path and creep and quake along it
with the boiling river—and maybe some rocks—under my elbow thirty
feet below. Such places turn my stomach. The old woman took note
of me, understood, and said what sounded like, "*Lass' ma allez au
premier*"—then she tramped briskly and confidently across with her
baskets, sending miniature avalanches of sand and gravel down into
the river with each step. One of her feet plowed from under her, about
midway, but she snatched it back and marched on, not seeming to
mind it. My pride urged me to move along, and put me to shame.
After a time the old woman came back and coaxed me to try, and did
at last get me started in her wake and I got as far as midway all
right; but then to hearten me still more and show me how easy and
safe it was, she began to prance and dance her way along, with her
knuckles in her hips, kicking a landslide loose with every skip. The
exhibition struck a cold panic through me and made my brain swim. I
leaned against the slope and said I would stay there until the boat
came and testified as to whether there were rocks under me or not.
For the third time in my life I was in that kind of a fix—in a place
where I could not go backward or forward, and mustn't stay where I
was. The boat was a good while coming, but it seemed longer than
that. Where I was, the slope was like a roof; where the slope ended
the wall was perpendicular thence to the water, and one could not see
over and tell what the state of things might be down there. When
the boat came along, the courier said there was nothing down there
but deep water—no rocks. I did not mind the water; so my fears disappeared, now, and I finished my march without discomfort. I gave
the old woman some money, which pleased her very much and she
tried her grateful best to give us a partridge, newly killed, which she
rummaged out of one of her baskets, and seemed disappointed when
I would not take it. But I couldn't; it would have been a shabby act.
Then she went her way with her heavy baskets and I got aboard
and afloat once more, feeling a great respect for her and very friendly
toward her. She waved a good-by every now and then till her figure
faded out in the plain, joining that interminable procession of friends
made and lost in an hour that drifts past a man's life from cradle to

grave and returns on its course no more. The courier said she was probably a poacher and stole the partridge.

The courier was not able to understand why I had not nerve enough to walk along a crumbling slope with a precipice only thirty feet high below me; but I had no difficulty in understanding it. It is constitutional with me to get nervous and incapable under the probability of getting myself dropped thirty feet on to a pile of rocks; it does not come from culture. Some people are made in one way, and some in another—and the above is my way. Some people who can skirt precipices without a tremor have a strong dread of the dentist's chair, whereas I was born without any prejudices against the dentist's chair; when in it I am interested, am not in a hurry, and do not greatly mind the pain. Taken by and large, my style of make has advantages over the other, I think. Few of us are obliged to circumnavigate precipices, but we all have to take a chance at the dental chair.

People who early learn the right way to choose a dentist have their reward. Professional superiority is not everything; it is only part. All dentists talk while they work. They have inherited this from their professional ancestors, the barbers. The dentist who talks well—other things being equal—is the one to choose. He tells anecdotes all the while and keeps his man so interested and entertained that he hardly notices the flight of time. For he not only tells anecdotes that are good in themselves, but he adds nice shadings to them with his instruments as he goes along, and now and then brings out effects which could not be produced with any other kind of tools at all. All the time that such a dentist as this is plowing down into a cavity with that spinning gouge which he works with a treadle, it is observable that he has found out where he has uncovered a nerve down in there, and that he only visits it at intervals, according to the needs of his anecdote, touching it lightly, very lightly and swiftly, now and then, to brighten up some happy conceit in his tale and call a delicate electric attention to it; and all the while he is working gradually and steadily up toward his climax with veiled and consummate art—then at last the spindle stops whirling and thundering in the cavity, and you know that the grand surprise is imminent, now—is hanging in the very air. You can hear your heart beat as the dentist bends over you with his grip on the spindle and his voice diminished to a murmur. The suspense grows bigger—bigger—bigger—your breath stops—then your heart. Then with lightning suddenness the "nub" is sprung and the spindle drives into the raw nerve! The most brilliant surprises of the stage are pale and artificial compared with this.

It is believed by people generally—or at least by many—that the exquisitely sharp sensation which results from plunging the steel point into the raw nerve is pain, but I think that this is doubtful. It is so vivid and sudden that one has no time to examine properly into its character. It is probably impossible, with our human limitations, to determine with certainty whether a sensation of so high and perfect an order as that is pain or whether it is pleasure. Its location brings it under the disadvantage of a common prejudice; and so men mistake it for pain when they might perceive that it is the opposite of that if it were anywhere but in a tooth. I may be in error, but I have experimented with it a great deal and I am satisfied in my own mind that it is not pain. It is true that it always feels like pain, but that proves nothing—ice against a naked back always passes for fire. I have every confidence that I can eventually prove to everyone's satisfaction that a nerve-stab produces pleasure; and not only that, but the most exquisite pleasure, the most perfect felicity which we are capable of feeling. I would not ask more than to be remembered hereafter as the man who conferred this priceless benefaction upon his race.

11.30.—Approaching the Falls of the Rhône. Canal to the left, walled with compact and beautiful masonry. It is a cut-off. We could pass through it and avoid the Falls—are advised by the Admiral to do it, but all decline, preferring to have a dangerous adventure to talk about.

However . . .

The truth is, the current began to grow ominously swift—and presently pretty lumpy and perturbed; soon we seemed to be simply flying past the shores. Then all of a sudden three hundred yards of boiling and tossing river burst upon our sight through the veiling tempest of rain! I did not see how our flimsy ark could live through such a place. If we were wrecked, swimming could not save us; the packed multitude of tall humps of water meant a bristling chaos of big rocks underneath, and the first rock we hit would break our bones. If I had been fortified with ignorance I might have wanted to stay in the boat and see the fun; but I have had much professional familiarity with water, and I doubted if there was going to be any fun there. So I said I would get out and walk, and I did. I need not tell anybody at home; I could leave out the Falls of the Rhône; they are not on the map, anyhow. If an adventure worth recording resulted, the Admiral and the courier would have it, and that would answer. I could see it from the bank—nothing could be better; it seemed even providential.

I ran along the bank in the driving rain, and enjoyed the sight to the full. I never saw a finer show than the passage of that boat was, through the fierce turmoil of water. Alternately she rose high and plunged deep, throwing up sheets of foaming spray and shaking them off like a mane. Several times she seemed to fairly bury herself, and I thought she was gone for good, but always she sprang high aloft the next moment, a gallant and stirring spectacle to see. The Admiral's steering was great. I have not seen the equal of it before.

The boat waited for me down at the Villebois bridge, and I presently caught up and went aboard. There was a stretch of a hundred yards of offensively rough water below the bridge, but it had no dangerous features about it. Still, I was obliged to claim that it had, and that these perils were much greater than the others.

Noon.—A mile of perpendicular precipices—very handsome. On the left, at the termination of this stately wall, a darling little old tree-grown ruin abreast a wooded islet with a large white mansion on it. Near that ruin nature has gotten up a clever counterfeit of one, tree-grown and all that, and, as its most telling feature, has furnished it a battered monolith that stands up out of the underbrush by itself and looks as if men had shaped it and put it there and time had gnawed it and worn it.

This is the prettiest piece of river we have found. All its aspects are dainty and gracious and alluring.

1 P.M.—Château de la Salette. This is the port of the Grotte de la Balme, "one of the seven wonders of Dauphiny." It is across a plain in the face of a bluff a mile from the river. A grotto is out of the common order, and I should have liked to see this one, but the rains have made the mud very deep and it did not seem well to venture so long a trip through it.

2.15 P.M.—St.-Etienne. On a distant ridge inland a tall openwork structure commandingly situated, with a statue of the Virgin standing on it.

Immense empty freight barges being towed upstream by teams of two and four big horses—not on the bank, but under it; not on the land, but always in the water—sometimes breast deep—and around the big flat bars.

We reached a not very promising-looking village about four o'clock, and concluded to land; munching fruit and filling the hood with pipe smoke had grown monotonous. We could not have the hood furled, because the floods of rain fell unceasingly. The tavern was on the river bank, as is the custom. It was dull there, and melancholy—nothing to do but look out of the window into the drenching rain and shiver; one could do that, for it was bleak and cold and windy, and there was no fire. Winter overcoats were not sufficient; they had to be supplemented with rugs. The raindrops were so large and struck the river with such force that they knocked up the water like pebble splashes.

With the exception of a very occasional woodenshod peasant, nobody was abroad in this bitter weather—I mean of our sex. But all weathers are alike to the women in these continental countries. To them and the other animals life is serious; nothing interrupts their slavery. Three of them were washing clothes in the river under the window when we arrived, and they continued at it as long as there was light to work by. One was apparently thirty; another—the mother? —above fifty; the third—grandmother?—so old and worn and gray she could have passed for eighty. They had no waterproofs or rubbers, of course; over their heads and shoulders they wore gunny sacks— simply conductors for rivers of water; some of the volume reached ground, the rest soaked in on the way.

At last a vigorous fellow of thirty-five arrived, dry and comfortable, smoking his pipe under his big umbrella in an open donkey cart—husband, son, and grandson of those women? He stood up in the cart, sheltering himself, and began to superintend, issuing his orders in a masterly tone of command, and showing temper when they were not obeyed swiftly enough. Without complaint or murmur the drowned women patiently carried out the orders, lifting the immense baskets of soaked clothing into the cart and stowing them to the man's satisfaction. The cart being full now, he descended, with his umbrella, entered the tavern, and the women went drooping homeward in the wake of the cart, and soon were blended with the deluge and lost to sight. We would tar and feather that fellow in America, and ride him on a rail.

When we came down into the public room he had his bottle of wine and plate of food on a bare table black with grease, and was chomping like a horse. He had the little religious paper which is in everybody's hands on the Rhône borders, and was enlightening himself with the histories of French saints who used to flee to the desert in the Middle Ages to escape the contamination of women.

Wednesday.—After breakfast, got under way. Still storming as hard as ever. The whole land looks defeated and discouraged. And very lonely; here and there a woman in the fields. They merely accent the loneliness.

1923

Dueling

This pastime is as common in Austria to-day as it is in France. But with this difference—that here in the Austrian states the duel is dangerous, while in France it is not. Here it is tragedy, in France it is comedy; here it is a solemnity, there it is monkeyshines; here the duelist risks his life, there he does not even risk his shirt. Here he fights with pistol or saber, in France with a hairpin—a blunt one. Here the desperately wounded man tries to walk to the hospital; there they paint the scratch so that they can find it again, lay the sufferer on a stretcher, and conduct him off the field with a band of music.

At the end of a French duel the pair hug and kiss and cry, and praise each other's valor; then the surgeons make an examination and pick out the scratched one, and the other one helps him on to the litter and pays his fare; and in return the scratched one treats to champagne and oysters in the evening, and then "the incident is closed," as the French say. It is all polite, and gracious, and pretty, and impressive. At the end of an Austrian duel the antagonist that is alive gravely offers his hand to the other man, utters some phrases of courteous regret, then bids him good-by and goes his way, and that incident also is closed. The French duelist is painstakingly protected from danger, by the rules of the game. His antagonist's weapon cannot reach so far as his body; if he gets a scratch it will not be above his elbow. But in Austria the rules of the game do not provide against danger, they carefully provide *for* it, usually. Commonly the combat must be kept up until one of the men is disabled; a non-disabling slash or stab does not retire him.

For a matter of three months I watched the Viennese journals, and whenever a duel was reported in their telegraphic columns I scrap-booked it. By this record I find that dueling in Austria is not confined to journalists and old maids, as in France, but is indulged in by military men, journalists, students, physicians, lawyers, members of the leg-islature, and even the Cabinet, the bench, and the police. Dueling is forbidden by law; and so it seems odd to see the makers and ad-ministrators of the laws dancing on their work in this way. Some

THE COMPLETE ESSAYS OF MARK TWAIN

months ago Count Badeni, at that time chief of the government, fought a pistol duel here in the capital city of the Empire with Representative Wolf, and both of those distinguished Christians came near getting turned out of the Church—for the Church as well as the state forbids dueling.

In one case, lately, in Hungary, the police interfered and stopped a duel after the first innings. This was a saber duel between the chief of police and the city attorney. Unkind things were said about it by the newspapers. They said the police remembered their duty uncommonly well when their own officials were the parties concerned in duels. But I think the underlings showed bread-and-butter judgment. If their superiors had carved each other well, the public would have asked, "Where were the police?" and their place would have been endangered; but custom does not require them to be around where mere unofficial citizens are explaining a thing with sabers.

There was another duel—a double duel—going on in the immediate neighborhood at the time, and in this case the police obeyed custom and did not disturb it. Their bread and butter was not at stake there. In this duel a physician fought a couple of surgeons, and wounded both—one of them lightly, the other seriously. An undertaker wanted to keep people from interfering, but that was quite natural again.

Selecting at random from my record, I next find a duel at Tranopol between military men. An officer of the Tenth Dragoons charged an officer of the Ninth Dragoons with an offense against the laws of the card table. There was a defect or a doubt somewhere in the matter, and this had to be examined and passed upon by a court of honor. So the case was sent up to Lemberg for this purpose. One would like to know what the defect was, but the newspaper does not say. A man here who has fought many duels and has a graveyard says that probably the matter in question was as to whether the accusation was true or not; that if the charge was a very grave one—cheating, for instance—proof of its truth would rule the guilty officer out of the field of honor; the court would not allow a gentleman to fight with such a person. You see what a solemn thing it is; you see how particular they are; any little careless speech can lose you your privilege of getting yourself shot, here. The court seems to have gone into the matter of a searching and careful fashion, for several months elapsed before it reached a decision. It then sanctioned a duel and the accused killed his accuser.

Next I find a duel between a prince and a major; first with pistols—

no result satisfactory to either party; then with sabers, and the major badly hurt.

Next, a saber duel between journalists—the one a strong man, the other feeble and in poor health. It was brief; the strong one drove his sword through the weak one, and death was immediate.

Next, a duel between a lieutenant and a student of medicine. According to the newspaper report, these are the details: The student was in a restaurant one evening; passing along, he halted at a table to speak with some friends; near by sat a dozen military men; the student conceived that one of these was "staring" at him; he asked the officer to step outside and explain. This officer and another one gathered up their capes and sabers and went out with the student. Outside—this is the student's account—the student introduced himself to the offending officer and said, "You seemed to stare at me"; for answer, the officer struck the student with his fist; the student parried the blow; both officers drew their sabers and attacked the young fellow, and one of them gave him a wound on the left arm; then they withdrew. This was Saturday night. The duel followed on Monday, in the military riding school—the customary dueling ground all over Austria, apparently. The weapons were pistols. The dueling terms were somewhat beyond custom in the matter of severity, if I may gather that from the statement that the combat was fought "unter sehr schweren Bedingungen"—to wit, "distance, 15 steps—with 3 steps advance." There was but one exchange of shots. The student was hit. "He put his hand on his breast, his body began to bend slowly forward, then collapsed in death and sank to the ground."

It is pathetic. There are other duels in my list, but I find in each and all of them one and the same ever-recurring defect—the *principals* are never present, but only by their sham representatives. The *real* principals in any duel are not the duelists themselves, but their *families*. They do the mourning, the suffering; theirs is the loss and theirs the misery. They stake all that, the duelist stakes nothing but his life, and that is a trivial thing compared with what his death must cost those whom he leaves behind him. Challenges should not mention the duelist; he has nothing much at stake, and the real vengeance cannot reach him. The challenge should summon the offender's old gray mother and his young wife and his little children—these, or any of whom he is a dear and worshiped possession—and should say, "You have done me no harm, but I am the meek slave of a custom which requires me to crush the happiness out of your hearts and condemn you to years of pain and grief, in order that I may wash clean with your tears a stain which has been put upon me by another person."

The logic of it is admirable; a person has robbed me of a penny; I must begger ten innocent persons to make good my loss. Surely nobody's "honor" is worth all that.

Since the duelist's family are the real principals in a duel, the state ought to compel them to be present at it. Custom, also, ought to be so amended as to require it; and without it no duel ought to be allowed to go on. If that student's unoffending mother had been present and watching the officer through her tears as he raised his pistol, he—why, he would have fired in the air! We know that. For we know how we are all made. Laws ought to be based upon the ascertained facts of our nature. It would be a simple thing to make a dueling law which would stop dueling.

As things are now, the mother is never invited. She submits to this; and without outward complaint, for she, too, is the vassal of custom, and custom requires her to conceal her pain when she learns the disastrous news that her son must go to the dueling field, and by the powerful force that is lodged in habit and custom she is enabled to obey this trying requirement—a requirement which exacts a miracle of her, and gets it. In January a neighbor of ours who has a young son in the army was awakened by this youth at three o'clock one morning, and she sat up in bed and listened to his message:

"I have come to tell you something, mother, which will distress you, but you must be good and brave and bear it. I have been affronted by a fellow officer and we fight at three this afternoon. Lie down and sleep, now, and think no more about it."

She kissed him good night and lay down paralyzed with grief and fear, but said nothing. But she did not sleep; she prayed and mourned till the first streak of dawn, then fled to the nearest church and implored the Virgin for help; and from that church she went to another and another; church after church, and still church after church, and so spent all the day until three o'clock on her knees in agony and tears; then dragged herself home and sat down, comfortless and desolate, to count the minutes, and wait, with an outward show of calm, for what had been ordained for her—happiness, or endless misery. Presently she heard the clank of a saber—she had not known before what music was in that sound—and her son put his head in and said:

"X was in the wrong and he apologized."

So that incident was closed; and for the rest of her life the mother will always find something pleasant about the clank of a saber, no doubt.

In one of my listed duels— However, let it go, there is nothing particularly striking about it except that the seconds interfered. And prematurely, too, for neither man was dead. This was certainly irregular. Neither of the men liked it. It was a duel with cavalry sabers, between an editor and a lieutenant. The editor walked to the hospital; the lieutenant was carried. In Austria an editor who can write well is valuable, but he is not likely to remain so unless he can handle a saber with charm.

The following very recent telegram shows that also in France duels are humanely stopped as soon as they approach the (French) danger point:

(Reuter's Telegram)

PARIS, *March 5th.*

The duel between Colonels Henry and Picquart took place this morning in the riding school of the École Militaire, the doors of which were strictly guarded in order to prevent intrusion. The combatants, who fought with swords, were in position at ten o'clock.

At the first re-engagement Lieut.-Col. Henry was slightly scratched in the forearm, and just at the same moment his own blade appeared to touch his adversary's neck. Senator Ranc, who was Colonel Picquart's second, stopped the fight, but as it was found that his principal had not been touched, the combat continued. A very sharp encounter ensued, in which Colonel Henry was wounded in the elbow, and the duel then terminated.

After which the stretcher and the band. In lurid contrast with this delicate flirtation, we have an account of a deadly duel of day before yesterday in Italy, where the earnest Austrian duel is in vogue. I knew one of the principals, Cavalotti, slightly, and this gives me a sort of personal interest in his duel. I first saw him in Rome several years ago. He was sitting on a block of stone in the Forum, and was writing something in his notebook—a poem or a challenge, or something like that—and the friend who pointed him out to me said, "That is Cavalotti—he has fought thirty duels; do not disturb him." I did not disturb him.

1923

Eve Speaks

They drove us from the Garden with their swords of flame, the fierce cherubim. And what had we done? We meant no harm. We were ignorant, and did as any other children might do. We could not know it was wrong to disobey the command, for the words were strange to us and we did not understand them. We did not know right from wrong—how should we know? We could not, without the Moral Sense; it was not possible. If we had been given the Moral Sense first—ah, that would have been fairer, that would have been kinder; then we should be to blame if we disobeyed. But to say to us poor ignorant children words which we could not understand, and then punish us because we did not do as we were told—ah, how can that be justified? We knew no more then than this littlest child of mine knows now, with its four years—oh, not so much, I think. Would I say to it, "If thou touchest this bread I will overwhelm thee with unimaginable disaster, even to the dissolution of thy corporeal elements," and when it took the bread and smiled up in my face, thinking no harm, as not understanding those strange words, would I take advantage of its innocence and strike it down with the mother hand it trusted? Whoso knoweth the mother heart, let him judge if it would do that thing. Adam says my brain is turned by my troubles and that I am become wicked. I am as I am; I did not make myself.

They drove us out. Drove us out into this harsh wilderness, and shut the gates against us. We that had meant no harm. It is three months. We were ignorant then; we are rich in learning, now—ah, how rich! We know hunger, thirst, and cold; we know pain, disease, and grief; we know hate, rebellion, and deceit; we know remorse, the conscience that prosecutes guilt and innocence alike, making no distinction; we know weariness of body and spirit, the unrefreshing sleep, the rest which rests not, the dreams which restore Eden, and banish it again with the waking; we know misery; we know torture and the heartbreak; we know humiliation and insult; we know indecency, immodesty, and the soiled mind; we know the scorn that attaches to the transmitted image of God exposed unclothed to the day; we know fear; we know vanity, folly, envy, hypocrisy; we know irreverence; we know blasphemy; we know right from wrong, and how to avoid the one and do the other; we know all the rich product of the Moral Sense, and it is our possession. Would we could sell it for one hour of Eden and white purity; would we could degrade the animals with it!

We have it all—that treasure. All but death. Death. . . . Death. What may that be?

Adam comes.

"Well?"

"He still sleeps."

That is our second-born—our Abel.

"He has slept enough for his good, and his garden suffers for his care. Wake him."

"I have tried and cannot."

"Then he is very tired. Let him sleep on."

"I think it is his hurt that makes him sleep so long."

I answer: "It may be so. Then we will let him rest; no doubt the sleep is healing it."

II

It is a day and a night, now, that he has slept. We found him by his altar in his field, that morning, his face and body drenched in blood. He said his eldest brother struck him down. Then he spoke no more and fell asleep. We laid him in his bed and washed the blood away, and were glad to know the hurt was light and that he had no pain; for if he had had pain he would not have slept.

It was in the early morning that we found him. All day he slept that sweet, reposeful sleep, lying always on his back, and never moving, never turning. It showed how tired he was, poor thing. He is so good and works so hard, rising with the dawn and laboring till the dark. And now he is overworked; it will be best that he tax himself less, after this, and I will ask him; he will do anything I wish.

All the day he slept. I know, for I was always near, and made dishes for him and kept them warm against his waking. Often I crept in and fed my eyes upon his gentle face, and was thankful for that blessed sleep. And still he slept on—slept with his eyes wide; a strange thing, and made me think he was awake at first, but it was not so, for

I spoke and he did not answer. He always answers when I speak. Cain has moods and will not answer, but not Abel.

I have sat by him all the night, being afraid he might wake and want his food. His face was very white; and it changed, and he came to look as he had looked when he was a little child in Eden long ago, so sweet and good and dear. It carried me back over the abyss of years, and I was lost in dreams and tears—oh, hours, I think. Then I came to myself; and thinking he stirred, I kissed his cheek to wake him, but he slumbered on and I was disappointed. His cheek was cold. I brought sacks of wool and the down of birds and covered him, but he was still cold, and I brought more. Adam has come again, and says he is not yet warm. I do not understand it.

III

We cannot wake him! With my arms clinging about him I have looked into his eyes, through the veil of my tears, and begged for one little word, and he will not answer. Oh, is it that long sleep—is it death? And will he wake no more?

FROM SATAN'S DIARY

Death has entered the world, the creatures are perishing; one of The Family is fallen; the product of the Moral Sense is complete. The Family think ill of death—they will change their minds.

1923

The Finished Book

(On Finishing *Joan of Arc*)

Do you know that shock? I mean, when you come, at your regular hour, into the sick room where you have watched for months, and find the medicine bottles all gone, the night table removed, the bed stripped, the furniture set stiffly to rights, the windows up, the room cold, stark, vacant—and you catch your breath. Do you know that shock?

The man who has written a long book has that experience the morning after he has revised it for the last time, seen the bearers convey it from the house, and sent it away to the printer. He steps into his study at the hour established by the habit of months—and he gets that little shock. All the litter and the confusion are gone. The piles of dusty reference books are gone from the chairs, the maps from the floor; the chaos of letters, manuscripts, notebooks, paper knives, pipes, matches, photographs, tobacco jars, and cigar boxes is gone from the writing table. The furniture is back where it used to be in the long ago. The housemaid, forbidden the place for five months, has been there, and tidied it up, and scoured it clean, and made it repellent and awful.

I stand here this morning, contemplating this desolation, and I realize that if I would bring back the spirit that made this hospital homelike and pleasant to me, I must restore the aids to lingering dissolution to their wonted places, and nurse another patient through and send it forth for the last rites, with many or few to assist there, as may happen; and that I will do.

1923

Foreign Critics

If I look harried and worn, it is not from an ill conscience. It is from sitting up nights to worry about the foreign critic. He won't concede that we have a civilization—a "real" civilization. Five years ago, he said we had never contributed anything to the betterment of the world. And now comes Sir Lepel Griffin, whom I had not suspected of being in the world at all, and says, "There is no country calling itself civilized where one would not rather live than in America, except Russia." That settles it. That is, it settles it for Europe; but it doesn't make me any more comfortable than I was before.

What is "real" civilization? Nobody can answer that conundrum. They have all tried. Then suppose we try to get at what it is not, and then subtract the what it is not from the general sum, and call the remainder "real" civilization—so as to have a place to stand on while we throw bricks at these people. Let us say, then, in broad terms, that any system which has in it any one of these things—to wit, human slavery, despotic government, inequality, numerous and brutal punishments for crime, superstition almost universal, ignorance almost universal, and dirt and poverty almost universal—is not a real civilization, and any system which has none of them is. If you grant these terms, one may then consider this conundrum: How old is real civilization? The answer is easy and unassailable. A century ago it had not appeared anywhere in the world during a single instant since the world was made. If you grant these terms—and I don't see why it shouldn't be fair, since civilization must surely be fair, since civilization must surely mean the humanizing of a people, not a class—there is to-day but one real civilization in the world, and it is not yet thirty years old. We made the trip and hoisted its flag when we disposed of our slavery.

However, there are some partial civilizations scattered around over Europe—pretty lofty civilizations they are, too—but who begot them? What is the seed from which they sprang? Liberty and intelligence. What planted that seed? There are dates and statistics which suggest that it was the American Revolution that planted it. When that revolution began, monarchy had been on trial some thousands of years, over there, and was a distinct and convicted failure, every time. It had never produced anything but a vast, a nearly universal savagery, with a thin skim of civilization on top, and the main part of that was nickel plate and tinsel. The French, imbruted and impoverished by centuries of oppression and official robbery, were a starving nation clothed in rags, slaves of an aristocracy and smirking dandies clad in unearned silks and velvet. It makes one's cheek burn to read of the laws of the time and realize that they were for human beings; realize that they originated in this world and not in hell. Germany was unspeakable. In the Scotch lowlands the people lived in sties and were human swine; in the highlands drunkenness was general and it hardly smirched a young girl to have a family of her own. In England there was a sham liberty, and not much of that; crime was general; ignorance the same; poverty and misery were widespread; London fed a tenth of her population by charity; the law awarded the death penalty to almost every conceivable offense; what was called medical science by courtesy stood where it had stood for two thousand years; Tom Jones and Squire Western were gentlemen.

The printer's art had been known in Germany and France three and a quarter centuries, and in England three. In all that time there had not been a newspaper in Europe that was worthy the name. Monarchies had no use for that sort of dynamite. When we hoisted the banner of revolution and raised the first genuine shout for human liberty that had ever been heard, this was a newspaperless globe. Eight years later there were six daily journals in London to proclaim to all the nations the greatest birth this world had ever seen. Who woke that printing press out of its trance of three hundred years? Let us be permitted to consider that we did it. Who summoned the French slaves to rise and set the nation free? We did it. What resulted in England and on the Continent? Crippled liberty took up its bed and walked. From that day to this its march has not halted, and please God it never will. We are called the nation of inventors. And we are. We could still claim that title and wear its loftiest honors if we had stopped with the first thing we ever invented—which was human liberty. Out of that invention has come the Christian world's great civilization. Without it it was impossible—as the history of all the centuries has proved. Well, then, who invented civilization? Even Sir Lepel Griffin ought to be able to answer that question. It looks easy enough. *We* have contributed *nothing!* Nothing hurts me like ingratitude.

1923

Instructing the Soldier

THIRTEENTH ANNUAL REUNION OF THE ARMY OF THE POTOMAC, HELD IN HARTFORD, CONNECTICUT, JUNE 8, 1881

(Reported by the Hartford *Courant*)

To the regular toast, "The Benefit of Judicious Training," Samuel L. Clemens (Mark Twain), responded as follows:
"*Let but the thoughtful civilian instruct the soldier in his duties, and the victory is sure.*"—*Martin Farquhar Tupper on the Art of War.*

Mr. Chairman,—I gladly join with my fellow-townsmen in extending a hearty welcome to these illustrious generals and war-scarred soldiers of the Republic. This is a proud day for us, and, if the sincere desire of our hearts has been fulfilled, it has not been an unpleasant day for them. I am in full accord, sir, with the sentiment of the toast—for I have always maintained, with enthusiasm, that the only wise and true way is for the soldier to fight the battle and the unprejudiced civilian to tell him how to do it; yet when I was invited to respond to this toast and furnish this advice and instruction, I was almost as embarrassed as I was gratified; for I could bring to this great service but the one virtue of absence of prejudice and set opinion.

Still, but one other qualification was needed, and it was of only minor importance—I mean, knowledge of the subject—therefore I was not disheartened, for I could acquire that, there being two weeks to spare. A general of high rank in this Army of the Potomac said two weeks was really more than I would need for the purpose—he had known people of my style who had learned enough in forty-eight hours to enable them to advise an army. Aside from the compliment, this was gratifying, because it confirmed the impression I had had before. He told me to go to the United States Military Academy at West Point—said in his flowery professional way that the cadets would "load me up." I went there and stayed two days, and his prediction proved correct. I make no boast on my own account—none; all I know about military matters I got from the gentlemen at West Point, and to them belongs the credit. They treated me with courtesy from the first; but when my mission was revealed, this mere courtesy blossomed into the warmest zeal. Everybody, officers and all, put down their work and turned their whole attention to giving me military information. Every question I asked was promptly and exhaustively answered. Therefore I feel proud to state that in the advice which I am about to give you, as soldiers, I am backed up by the highest military authority in the land, yes, in the world, if an American does say it— West Point!

To begin, gentlemen. When an engagement is meditated, it is best to feel the enemy first. That is, if it is night; for, as one of the cadets explained to me, you do not need to feel him in the daytime, because you can see him then. I never should have thought of that, but it is true—perfectly true. In the daytime the methods of procedure are various; but the best, it seems to me, is one which was introduced by General Grant. General Grant always sent an active young redoubt to reconnoitre and get the enemy's bearings. I got this from a high officer at the Point, who told me he used to be a redoubt on General Grant's staff and had done it often.

When the hour for the battle is come, move to the field with celerity —fool away no time. Under this head I was told of a favorite maxim of General Sheridan's. General Sheridan always said, "If the siege train isn't ready, don't wait; go by any train that is handy; to get there is the main thing." Now that is the correct idea. As you approach the field it is best to get out and walk. This gives you a better chance to dispose your forces judiciously for the assault. Get your artillery in position, and throw out stragglers to right and left to hold your lines of communication against surprise. See that every hodcarrier connected with the mortar battery is at his post. They told me at the Point that Napoleon despised mortar batteries and never would use them; he said that for real efficiency he wouldn't give a hatful of brickbats for a ton of mortar. However, that is all *he* knew about it.

Everything being ready for the assault, you want to enter the field with your baggage to the front. This idea was invented by our renowned guest, General Sherman. They told me General Sherman said the trunks and steamer chairs make a good protection for the soldiers, but that chiefly they attract the attention and rivet the interest of the enemy and this gives you an opportunity to whirl the other end of the column around and attack him in the rear. I have given a good deal of study to this tactic since I learned about it, and it appears to me it is a rattling-good idea. Never fetch on your reserves at the start. This was Napoleon's first mistake at Waterloo; next he assaulted with his bomb proofs and embrasures and ambulances, when he ought to have used a heavier artillery; thirdly, he retired his right by ricochet—which uncovered his pickets—when his only possibility of success lay in doubling up his center flank by flank and throwing out his chevaux-de-frise by the left oblique to relieve the skirmish line and confuse the enemy—and at West Point they said it would. It was about this time that the emperor had two horses shot under him. How often you see the remark that General So-and-So in such and such a battle had two or three horses shot under him. General Burnside and many great European military men—as I was informed by a high artillery officer at West Point, has justly characterized this as a wanton waste of projectiles, and he impressed upon me a conversation held in the tent of the Prussian chiefs at Gravelotte, in the course of which our honored guest just referred to—General Burnside—observed that if you can't aim a horse so as to hit the general with it, shoot it over him and you may bag somebody on the other side, whereas a horse shot under a general does no sort of damage. I agree cordially with General Burnside, and Heaven knows I shall rejoice to see the artillerists of this land and all lands cease from this wicked and idiotic custom.

At West Point they told me of another mistake at Waterloo, *viz.*, that the French were under fire from the beginning of the fight until the end of it, which was plainly a most effeminate and ill-timed attention to comfort, and a fatal and foolish division of military strength; for it probably took as many men to keep up the fires as it did to do the fighting. It would have been much better to have a small fire in the rear and let the men go there by detachments and get warm, and not try to warm up the whole army at once. All the cadets said that. An assault along the whole line was the one thing which could have restored Napoleon's advantages at this juncture; and he was actually rising in his stirrups to order it when a sutler burst at his side and covered him with dirt and debris; and before he could recover his lost opportunity Wellington opened a tremendous and devastating fire upon him from a monster battery of vivandières, and the star of the great captains' glory set, to rise no more. The cadet wept while he told me these mournful particulars.

When you leave a battlefield, always leave it in good order. Remove the wreck and rubbish and tidy up the place. However, in the case of a drawn battle, it is neither party's business to tidy up anything—you can leave the field looking as if the city government of New York had bossed the fight.

When you are traversing in the enemy's country in order to destroy his supplies and cripple his resources, you want to take along plenty of camp followers—the more the better. They are a tremendously effective arm of the service, and they inspire in the foe the liveliest dread. A West Point professor told me that the wisdom of this was recognized as far back as Scripture times. He quoted the verse. He said it was from the new revision and was a little different from the way it reads in the old one. I do not recollect the exact wording of it now, but I remember that it wound up with something about such-and-such a devastating agent being as "terrible as any army with bummers."

I believe I have nothing further to add but this: The West Pointer said a private should preserve a respectful attitude toward his superiors, and should seldom or never proceed so far as to offer suggestions to his general in the field. If the battle is not being conducted to suit him it is better for him to resign. By the etiquette of war, it is permitted to none below the rank of newspaper correspondent to dictate to the general in the field.

1923

Letters to Satan

If Your Grace would prepay your postage it would be a pleasant change. I am not meaning to speak harshly, but only sorrowfully. My remark applies to all my outland correspondents, and to everybody's. None of them puts on the full postage, and that is just the same as putting on none at all: the foreign governments ignore the half postage, and we who are abroad have to pay full postage on those half-paid letters. And as for writing on thin paper, none of my friends ever think of it; they all use pasteboard, or sole leather, or things like that. But enough of that subject; it is painful.

I believe you have set me a hard task; for if it is true that you have not been in the world for three hundred years, and have not received into your establishment an educated person in all that time, I shall be obliged to talk to you as if you had just been born and knew nothing at all about the things I speak of. However, I will do the best I can, and will faithfully try to put in all the particulars, trivial ones as well as the other sorts. If my report shall induce Your Grace to come out of your age-long seclusion and make a pleasure tour through the world in person, instead of doing it by proxy through me, I shall feel that I have labored to good purpose. You have many friends in the world; more than you think. You would have a vast welcome in Paris, London, New York, Chicago, Washington, and the other capitals of the world; if you would go on the lecture platform you could charge what you pleased. You would be the most formidable attraction on the planet. The curiosity to see you would be so great that no place of amusement would contain the multitude that would come. In London many devoted people who have seen the Prince of Wales only fifteen hundred or two thousand times would be willing to miss one chance of seeing him again for the sake of seeing you. In Paris, even with the Tsar on view, you could do a fairly good business; and in Chicago— Oh, but you ought to go to Chicago, you know. But further of this anon. I will to my report, now, and tell you about Lucerne, and how I journeyed hither; for doubtless you will travel by the same route when you come.

I kept house a few months in London, with my family, while I arranged the matters which you were good enough to intrust me with. There were no adventures, except that we saw the Jubilee. Afterward I was invited to one of the Queen's functions, which was a royal garden party. A garden is a green and bloomy countrified stretch of land which— But you remember the Garden of Eden; well, it is like that. The invitation prescribed the costume that must be worn: "Morning dress with trousers." I was intending to wear mine, for I always wear something at garden parties where ladies are to be present; but I was hurt by this arbitrary note of compulsion, and did not go. All the European courts are particular about dress, and you are not allowed to choose for yourself in any case; you are always told exactly what you must wear; and whether it is going to become you or not, you are not allowed to make any changes. Yet the court taste is often bad, and sometimes even indelicate. I was once invited to dine with an emperor when I was living awhile in Germany, and the invitation card named the dress I must wear: "Frock coat and black cravat." To put it in English, that meant swallow-tail and black cravat. It was cold weather, too, the middle of winter; and not only that, but ladies were to be present. That was five years ago. By this time the coat has gone out, I suppose, and you would feel at home there if you still remember the old Eden styles.

As soon as the Jubilee was fairly over we broke up housekeeping and went for a few days to what is called in England "an hotel." If we could have afforded an horse and an hackney cab we could have had an heavenly good time flitting around on our preparation errands, and could have finished them up briskly; but the buses are slow and they wasted many precious hours for us. A bus is a sort of great cage on four wheels, and is six times as strong and eleven times as heavy as the service required of it demands—but that is the English of it. The bus aptly symbolized the national character. The Englishman requires that everything about him shall be stable, strong, and permanent, except the house which he builds to rent. His own private house is as strong as a fort. The rod which holds up the lace curtains could hold up an hippopotamus. The three-foot flagstaff on his bus, which supports a Union Jack the size of a handkerchief, would still support it if it were one of the gates of Gaza. Everything he constructs is a deal heavier and stronger than it needs to be. He built ten miles of terraced benches to view the Jubilee procession from, and put timber enough in them to make them a permanent contribution to the solidities of the world—yet they were intended for only two days' service.

When they were being removed an American said, "Don't do it—save them for the Resurrection." If anything gets in the way of the Englishman's bus it must get out of it or be bowled down—and that is English. It is the serene self-sufficient spirit which has carried his flag so far. He ought to put his aggressive bus in his coat of arms, and take the gentle unicorn out.

We made our preparations for Switzerland as fast as we could; then bought the tickets. Bought them of Thomas Cook & Sons, of course—nowadays shortened to "Cook's," to save time and words. Things have changed in thirty years. I can remember when to be a "Cook's tourist" was a thing to be ashamed of, and when everybody felt privileged to make fun of Cook's "personally conducted" gangs of economical provincials. But that has all gone by, now. All sorts and conditions of men fly to Cook in our days. In the bygone times travel in Europe was made hateful and humiliating by the wanton difficulties, hindrances, annoyances, and vexations put upon it by ignorant, stupid, and disobliging transportation officals, and one had to travel with a courier or risk going mad. You could not buy a railway ticket on one day which you purposed to use next day—it was not permitted. You could not buy a ticket for *any* train until fifteen minutes before that train was due to leave. Though you had twenty trunks, you must manage somehow to get them weighed and the extra weight paid for within that fifteen minutes; if the time was not sufficient you would have to leave behind such trunks as failed to pass the scales. If you missed your train, your ticket was no longer good. As a rule, you could make neither head nor tail of the railway guide, and if your intended journey was a long one you would find that the officials could tell you little about which way to go; consequently you often brought the wrong ticket and got yourself lost. But Cook has remedied all these things and made travel simple, easy, and a pleasure. He will sell you a ticket to any place on the globe, or all the places, and give you all the time you need, and as much more besides; and it is good for all trains of its class, and its baggage is weighable at all hours. It provides hotels for you everywhere, if you so desire; and you cannot be overcharged, for the coupons show just how much you must pay. Cook's servants at the great stations will attend to your baggage, get you a cab, tell you how much to pay cabmen and porters, procure guides for you, or horses, donkeys, camels, bicycles, or anything else you want, and make life a comfort and a satisfaction to you. And if you get tired of traveling and want

to stop, Cook will take back the remains of your ticket, with 10 per
cent off. Cook is your banker everywhere, and his establishment your
shelter when you get caught out in the rain. His clerks will answer all
the questions you ask, and do it courteously. I recommend Your Grace
to travel on Cook's tickets when you come; and I do this without embarrassment, for I get no commission. I do not know Cook. (But if
you would rather travel with a courier, let me recommend Joseph
Very. I employed him twenty years ago, and spoke of him very highly
in a book, for he was an excellent courier—then. I employed him again,
six or seven years ago—for a while. Try him. And when you go home,
take him with you.)

That London hotel was a disappointment. It was up a back alley,
and we supposed it would be cheap. But, no, it was built for the
moneyed races. It was all costliness and show. It had a brass band for
dinner—and little else—and it even had a telephone and a lift. A
telephone is a wire stretched on poles or underground, and has a thing
at each end of it. These things are to speak into and to listen at. The
wire carries the words; it can carry them several hundred miles. It is a
time-saving, profanity-breeding, useful invention, and in America is
to be found in all houses except parsonages. It is dear in America, but
cheap in England; yet in England telephones are as rare as are icebergs
in your place. I know of no way to account for this; I only know that
it is extraordinary. The English take kindly to the other modern conveniences, but for some puzzling reason or other they will not use the telephone. There are 44,000,000 people there who have never even seen
one.

The lift is an elevator. Like the telephone, it also is an American
invention. Its office is to hoist people to the upper stories and save
them the fatigue and delay of climbing. That London hotel could
accommodate several hundred people, and it had just one lift—a lift
which would hold four persons. In America such a hotel would have
from two to six lifts. When I was last in Paris, three years ago, they
were using there what they thought was a lift. It held two persons,
and traveled at such a slow gait that a spectator could not tell which
way it was going. If the passengers were going to the sixth floor, they
took along something to eat; and at night, bedding. Old people did
not use it; except such as were on their way to the good place, anyhow.
Often people that had been lost for days were found in those lifts,
jogging along, jogging along, frequently still alive. The French took
great pride in their ostensible lift, and called it by a grand name—
ascenseur. An hotel that had a lift did not keep it secret, but advertised

it in immense letters, *Il y a une ascenseur,*" with three exclamation points after it.

In that London hotel— But never mind that hotel; it was a cruelly expensive and tawdry and ill-conditioned place, and I wish I could do it a damage. I will think up a way some time. We went to Queenboro by the railroad. A railroad is a—well, a railroad is a railroad. I will describe it more explicitly another time.

Then we went by steamer to Flushing—eight hours. If you sit at home you can make the trip in less time, because then you can travel by the steamer company's advertisement, and that will take you across the Channel five hours quicker than their boats can do it. Almost everywhere in Europe the advertisements can give the facts several hours' odd in the twenty-four and get in first.

II

We tarried overnight at a summer hotel on the seashore near Flushing—the Grand Hôtel des Bains. The word Grand means nothing in this connection; it has no descriptive value. On the Continent, all hotels, inns, taverns, hash houses and slop troughs employ it. It is tiresome. This one was a good-enough hotel, and comfortable, but there was nothing grand about it but the bill, and even that was not extravagant enough to make the title entirely justifiable. Except in the case of one item—Scotch whisky. I ordered a sup of that, for I always take it at night as a preventive of toothache. I have never had the toothache; and what is more, I never intend to have it. They charged me a dollar and a half for it. A dollar and a half for half a pint; a dollar and a half for that wee little mite—really hardly enough to break a pledge with. It will be a kindness to me if Your Grace will show the landlord some special attentions when he arrives. Not merely on account of that piece of extortion, but because he got us back to town and the station next day, more than an hour before train time.

There were no books or newspapers for sale there, and nothing to look at but a map. Fortunately it was an interesting one. It was a railway map of the Low Countries, and was of a new sort to me, for it was made of tiles—the ground white, the lines black. It could be washed if it got soiled, and if no accident happens to it it will last ten thousand years and still be as bright and fine and new and beautiful then as it is to-day. It occupied a great area of the wall, and one could study it in comfort halfway across the house. It would be a valuable thing if our own railway companies would adorn their waiting rooms with maps like that.

We left at five in the afternoon. The Dutch road was admirably rough; we went bumping and bouncing and swaying and sprawling along in a most vindictive and disorderly way; then passed the frontier into Germany, and straightway quieted down and went gliding as smoothly through the landscape as if we had been on runners. We reached Cologne after midnight.

But this letter is already too long. I will close it by saying that I was charmed with England and sorry to leave it. It is easy to do business there. I carried out all of Your Grace's instructions, and did it without difficulty. I doubted if it was needful to grease Mr. Cecil Rhodes's palm any further, for I think he would serve you just for the love of it; still, I obeyed your orders in the matter. I made him Permanent General Agent for South Africa, got him and his South Africa Company whitewashed by the Committee of Inquiry, and promised him a dukedom. I also continued the European Concert in office, without making any change in its material. In my opinion this is the best material for the purpose that exists outside of Your Grace's own personal Cabinet. It coddles the Sultan, it has defiled and degraded Greece, it has massacred a hundred thousand Christians in Armenia and a splendid multitude of them in Turkey, and has covered civilization and the Christian name with imperishable shame. If Your Grace would instruct me to add the Concert to the list of your publicly acknowledged servants, I think it would have a good effect. The Foreign Offices of the whole European world are now under your sovereignty, and little attentions like this would keep them so.

1923

The Lost Napoleon

The Lost Napoleon is a part of a mountain range. Several miles of it—say six. When you stand at the right viewpoint and look across the plain, there, miles away, stretched out on his back under the sky, you see the great Napoleon, sleeping, with his arm folded upon his breast. You recognize him at once and you catch your breath and a thrill goes through you from head to foot—a most natural thing to happen, for you have never been so superbly astonished in your life before, and you realize, if you live a century, it is not likely that you will ever encounter the like of that tremendous surprise again. You see, it is unique. You have seen mountain ridges before that looked like men lying down, but there was always some one to pilot you to the right viewpoint, and prepare you for the show, and then tell you which is the head and which the feet and which the stomach, and at last you get the idea and say, "Yes, now I see it, now I make it out—it *is* a man, and wonderful, too." But all this has damaged the surprise and there is not much thrill; moreover, the man is only a third-rate celebrity or no celebrity at all—he is no Napoleon the Great. But I discovered this stupendous Napoleon myself and was caught wholly by surprise, hence the splendid emotion, the uplifting astonishment.

We have all seen mountains that looked like whales, elephants, recumbent lions—correctly figured, too, and a pleasure to look upon—but we did not discover them, somebody pointed them out to us, and in the same circumstances we have seen and enjoyed stately crags and summits known to the people there abouts as "The Old Man's Head," "The Elephant's Head," "Anthony's Nose," "The Lady's Head," etc., and we have seen others that were named "Shakespeare's Head," and "Satan's Head," but still the fine element of surprise was in almost all cases wanting.

The Lost Napoleon is easily the most colossal and impressive statue in the world. It is several miles long; in form and proportions it is perfect. It represents Napoleon himself and not another; and there is something about the dignity and repose of the great figure that stirs the imagination and half persuades it that this is not an unsentient artifice of nature, but the master of the world sentient and dreaming—dreaming of battle, conquest, empire. I call it the Lost Napoleon because I cannot remember just where I was when I saw it. My hope, in writing this, is that I may move some wandering tourist or artist to go over my track and seek for it—seek for it, find it, locate it exactly, describe it, paint it, and so preserve it against loss again.

My track was down the Rhône; I made the excursion ten or eleven years ago in the pleasantest season of the year. I took a courier with me and went from Geneva a couple of hours by rail to the blue little Lake Bourget, and spent the night in a mediaeval castle on an island in that little lake. In the early morning our boat came for us. It was a roomy open boat fifteen or twenty feet long, with a single pair of long oars, and with it came its former owner, a sturdy big boatman. The boat was mine now; I think I paid five dollars for it. I was to pay the boatman a trifling daily wage and his keep, and he was to take us all the way down the Rhône to Marseilles. It was warm weather and very sunny, but we built a canvas arch, like a wagon cover, over the aftermost third of the boat, with a curtain at its rear which could be rolled up to let the breeze blow through, and I occupied that tent and was always comfortable. The sailor sat amidships and manned the oars, and the courier had the front third of the boat to himself. We crossed the lake and went winding down a narrow canal bordered by peasant houses and vineyards, and after about a league of this navigation we came in sight of the Rhône, a troubled gray stream which went tearing past the mouth of the peaceful canal at a racing gait. We emerged into it and laid in the oars. We could go fast enough in that current without artificial aid. During the first days we slipped along down the curving bends at a speed of about five miles an hour, but it slackened later.

Our days were all about alike. About four in the afternoon we tied up at a village and I dined on the greensward in front of the inn by the water's edge, on the choicest chickens, vegetables, fruit, butter, and bread, prepared in French perfection and served upon the whitest linen; and as a rule I had the friendly house cat and dog for guests and company and willing and able helpers. I slept in the inn; often in clean and satisfactory quarters, sometimes in the same room with the cows and the fleas. I breakfasted on the lawn in the morning with cat and dog again; then laid in a stock of grapes and other fruits gathered fresh from the garden and some bottles of red wine made on the premises, and at eight or nine we went floating down the river again. At noon we went ashore at a village, bought a freshly caught fish or two, had them broiled, got some bread and vegetables, and set sail again at once. We always lunched on board as we floated along. I spent my days reading books, making notes, smoking, and in other lazy and enchanting ways, and had the delightfulest ten-day voyage I have ever experienced.

It took us ten days to float to Arles. There the current gave out and I closed the excursion and returned to Geneva by rail. It was twenty-eight miles to Marseilles, and we should have been obliged to row. That would not have been pleasure; it would have meant work for the sailor, and I do not like work even when another person does it.

I think it was about the eighth day that I discovered Napoleon. My notes cover four or five days; there they stop; the charm of the trip had taken possession of me, and I had no energy left. It was getting toward four in the afternoon—time to tie up for the day. Down ahead on the right bank I saw a compact jumble of yellowy-browny cubes stacked together, some on top of the others, and no visible cracks in the mass, and knew it for a village—a village common to that region down there; a village jammed together without streets or alleys, substantially—where your progress is mainly *through* the houses, not *by* them, and where privacy is a thing practically unknown; a village which probably hadn't had a house added to the jumble for five hundred years. We were anywhere from half a mile to a mile above the village when I gave the order to proceed to that place and tie up. Just then I glanced to my left toward the distant mountain range, and got that soul-stirring shock which I have said so much about. I pointed out the grand figure to the courier, and said:

"Name it. Who is it?"

"Napoleon!"

"Yes, it is Napoleon. Show it to the sailor and ask him to name it."

The sailor said, "Napoleon." We watched the figure all the time then until we reached the village. We walked up the river bank in the morning to see how far one might have to go before the shape would materially change, but I do not now remember the result. We watched it afterward as we floated away from the village, but I cannot remember at what point the shape began to be marred. However, the mountains being some miles away, I think that the figure would be recognizable as Napoleon along a stretch of as much as a mile above and a mile below the village, though I think that the likeness would be strongest at the point where I first saw it—that is, half a mile or more above the village.

We talked the grand apparition over at great length and with a strong interest. I said I believed that if its presence were known to the world such shoals of tourists would come flocking there to see it that all the spare ground would soon be covered with hotels; and I think so yet. I think it would soon be the most celebrated natural curiosity on the planet, that it would be more visited than Niagara or the Alps, and that all the other famous natural curiosities of the globe would fall to a rank away below it. I think so still.

There is a line of lumbering and thundering great freight steamers on the Rhône, and I think that if some man will board one of them at Arles and make a trip of some hours upstream—say from three to six—and keep an eye out to the right and watch that mountain range he will be certain to find the Lost Napoleon and have no difficulty in re-discovering the mighty statue when he comes to the right point. It will cost nothing to make the experiment, and I hope it will be done.

NOTE.—Mark Twain's biographer rediscovered it in 1913. It is some miles below Valence, opposite the village of Beauchastel.—ALBERT BIGELOW PAINE.

1923

On Speech-making Reform[1]

Like many another well-intentioned man, I have made too many speeches. And like other transgressors of this sort, I have from time to time reformed, binding myself, by oath, on New Year's Days, to never make another speech. I found that a new oath holds pretty well; but that when it is become old and frayed out and damaged by a dozen annual retyings of its remains, it ceases to be serviceable; any little strain will snap it. So, last New Year's Day I strengthened my reform with a money penalty, and made that penalty so heavy that it has enabled me to remain pure from that day to this. Although I am falling once more, now, I think I can behave myself from this out, be-cause the penalty is going to be doubled ten days hence. I see before me and about me the familiar faces of many poor, sorrowing fellow sufferers, victims of the passion for speech making—poor, sad-eyed brothers in affliction, who, fast in the grip of this fell, degrading, de-moralizing vice, have grown weak with struggling, as the years drifted by, and at last have all but given up hope. To them I say, in this last final obituary of mine, don't give up—don't do it; there is still hope for you. I beseech you, swear one more oath, and back it up with cash. I do not say this to all, of course; for there are some among you who are past reform; some who, being long accustomed to success and to the delicious intoxication of the applause which follows it, are too wedded to their dissipation to be capable now or hereafter of abandon-ing it. They have thoroughly learned the deep art of speech making, and they suffer no longer from those misgivings and embarrassments

[1] Paine says this was an after-dinner speech delivered "about 1884."—C.N.

and apprehensions which are really the only things that ever make a speech maker want to reform. They have learned their art by long observation and slowly compacted experience; so now they know what they did not know at first, that the best and most telling speech is not the actual impromptu one, but the counterfeit of it; they know that that speech is most worth listening to which has been carefully prepared in private and tried on a plaster cast, or an empty chair, or any other appreciative object that will keep quiet until the speaker has got his matter and his delivery limbered up so that they will seem impromptu to an audience. The expert knows that. A touch of indifferent grammar flung in here and there, apparently at random, has a good effect—often restores the confidence of a suspicious audience. He arranges these errors in private; for a really random error wouldn't do any good; it would be sure to fall in the wrong place. He also leaves blanks here and there—leaves them where genuine impromptu remarks can be dropped in, of a sort that will add to the natural aspect of the speech without breaking its line of march. At the banquet he listens to the other speakers, invents happy turns upon remarks of theirs, and sticks these happy turns into his blanks for impromptu use by and by when he shall be called up. When this expert rises to his feet, he looks around over the house with the air of a man who had just been strongly impressed by something. The uninitiated cannot interpret his aspect; but the initiated can.

They know what is coming. When the noise of the clapping and stamping has subsided this veteran says, "Aware that the hour is late, Mr. Chairman, it was my intention to abide by a purpose which I framed in the beginning of the evening—to simply rise and return my duty and thanks, in case I should be called upon, and then make way for men more able and who have come with something to say. But, sir, I was so struck by General Smith's remark concerning the proneness of evil to fly upward, that"—etc., etc., etc., and before you know it he has slidden smoothly along on his compliment to the general, and out of it and into his set speech, and you can't tell, to save you, where it was nor when it was that he made the connection. And that man will soar along, in the most beautiful way, on the wings of a practiced memory, heaving in a little decayed grammar here, and a little wise tautology there, and a little neatly counterfeited embarrassment yonder, and a little finely acted stumbling and stammering for a word, rejecting this word and that, and finally getting the right one, and fetching it out with ripping effect, and with the glad look of a man who has got out of a bad hobble entirely by accident—and wouldn't take a hundred dollars down for that accident; and every now and then he will sprinkle you in one of those happy turns on something that has previously been said; and at last, with supreme art, he will catch himself, when in the very act of sitting down, and lean over the table and fire a parting rocket, in the way of an afterthought, which makes everybody stretch his mouth as it goes up, and dims the very stars in heaven when it explodes. And yet that man has been practicing that afterthought and that attitude for about a week.

Well, you can't reform that kind of a man. It's a case of Eli joined to his idols. Let him alone. But there is one sort that can be reformed. That is the genuine impromptu speaker. I mean the man who "didn't expect to be called upon and isn't prepared," and yet goes waddling and warbling along, just as if he thought it wasn't any harm to commit a crime so long as it wasn't premeditated. Now and then he says, "but I must not detain you longer"; every little while he says, "Just one word more and I am done"—but at these times he always happens to think of two or three more unnecessary things and so he stops to say them. Now that man has no way of finding out how long his windmill is going. He likes to hear it creak, and so he goes on creaking, and listening to it, and enjoying it, never thinking of the flight of time; and when he comes to sit down at last and look under his hopper, he is the most surprised person in the house to see what a little bit of a grist he has ground and how unconscionably long he has been grinding it. As a rule, he finds that he hasn't said anything—a discovery which the unprepared man ought always to make, and does usually make—and has the added grief of making it at second hand, too.

This is a man who can be reformed. And so can his near relative, who now rises out of my reconstructed past—the man who provisions himself with a single prepared bit of a sentence or so, and trusts to luck to catch quails and manna as he goes along. This person frequently gets left. You can easily tell when he has finished his prepared bit and begun on the impromptu part. Often the prepared portion has been built during the banquet; it may consist of ten sentences, but it oftener consists of two—oftenest of all, it is but a single sentence; and it has seemed so happy and pat and bright and good that the creator of it, the person that laid it, has been sitting there cackling privately over it and admiring it and petting it and shining it up and imagining how fine it is going to "go," when, of course, he ought to have been laying another one, and still another one, and maybe a basketful, if it's a fruitful day; yes, and he is thinking that when he comes to hurl that egg at the house there is going to be such electric explosion of applause that the inspiration of it will fill him instantly with ideas and clothe the ideas in brilliant language, and that an impromptu speech will result which will be infinitely finer than anything he could have deliberately prepared. But there are two damaging things which he is leaving out of the calculation: one is the historical fact that a man is never called up as soon as he thinks he is going to be called up, and that every speech that is injected into the proceedings ahead of him gives his fires an added chance to cool; and the other thing which he is forgetting is that he can't sit there and keep saying that fine sentence of his over and over to himself for three quarters of an hour without by and by getting a trifle tired of it and losing somewhat of confidence in it.

When at last his chance comes and he touches off his pet sentence, it makes him sick to see how shamefacedly and apologetically he has done it, and how compassionate the applause is, and how sorry everybody feels; and then he bitterly thinks what a lie it is to call this a free country, where none but the unworthy and the undeserving may swear. And at this point, naked and blind and empty, he swallows off into his *real* impromptu speech; stammers out three or four incredibly flat things, then collapses into his seat, murmuring, "I wish I was in——" He doesn't say where, because he doesn't. The stranger at his left, says, "Your opening was very good"; stranger at his right says, "I liked your opening"; man opposite says, "Opening very good indeed—*very* good"; two or three other people mumble something about his opening. People always feel obliged to pour some healing thing on a crippled man that way. They mean if for oil; they think it *is* oil; but the sufferer recognizes it for aquafortis.

1923

Samuel Erasmus Moffett

HIS CHARACTER AND HIS DEATH

August 16th[1]—Early in the evening of the first day of this month the telephone brought us a paralyzing shock: my nephew, Samuel E. Moffett, was drowned. It was while sea bathing. The seas were running high and he was urged not to venture out, but he was a strong swimmer and not afraid. He made the plunge with confidence, his frightened little son looking on. Instantly he was helpless. The great waves tossed him hither and thither, they buried him, they struck the life out of him. In a minute it was all over.

He was forty-eight years old, he was at his best, physically and mentally, and was well on his way toward earned distinction. He was large-minded and large-hearted, there was no blot nor fleck upon his character, his ideals were high and clean, and by native impulse and without effort he lived up to them.

He had been a working journalist, an editorial writer, for nearly thirty years, and yet in that exposed position had preserved his independence in full strength and his principles undecayed. Several years ago he accepted a high place on the staff of *Collier's Weekly* and was occupying it when he died.

In an early chapter of my *Autobiography*, written three years ago, I have told how he wrote from San Francisco, when he was a stripling and asked me to help him get a berth on a daily paper there; and how he submitted to the severe conditions I imposed, and got the berth and kept it sixteen years.

As child and lad his health was delicate, capricious, insecure, and his eyesight affected by a malady which debarred him from book study and from reading. This was a bitter hardship for him, for he had a wonderful memory and a sharp hunger for knowledge. School was not for him, yet while still a little boy he acquired an education, and a good one. He managed it after a method of his own devising: he got permission to listen while the classes of the normal school recited their abstruse lessons and blackboarded their mathematics. By ques-

[1] 1908.— C.N.

tioning the little chap it was found that he was keeping up with the star scholars of the school.

In those days he paid us a visit in Hartford. It was when he was about twelve years old. I was laboriously constructing an ancient-history game at the time, to be played by my wife and myself, and I was digging the dates and facts for it out of cyclopaedias, a dreary and troublesome business. I had sweated blood over that work and was pardonably proud of the result, as far as I had gone. I showed the child my mass of notes, and he was at once as excited as I should have been over a Sunday-school picnic at his age. He wanted to help, he was eager to help, and I was as willing to let him as I should have been to give away an interest in a surgical operation that I was tired of. I made him free of the cyclopaedias, but he never consulted them —he had their contents in his head. All alone he built and completed the game rapidly and without effort.

Away back in '80 or '81 when the grand eruption of Krakatoa, in the Straits of Sunda, occurred, the news reached San Francisco late in the night—too late for editors to hunt for information about that unknown volcano in cyclopaedias and write it up exhaustively and learnedly in time for the first edition. The managing editor said, "Send to Moffett's home; rout him out and fetch him; he will know all about it; he won't need the cyclopaedia." Which was true. He came to the office and swiftly wrote it all up without having to refer to books.

I will take a few paragraphs from the article about him in *Collier's Weekly:*

If you wanted to know any fact about any subject it was quicker to go to him than to books of reference. His good nature made him the martyr of interruptions. In the middle of a sentence, in a hurry hour, he would look up happily, and whether the thing you wanted was railroad statistics or international law, he would bring it out of one of the pigeonholes in his brain. A born dispenser of the light, he made the giving of information a privilege and a pleasure on all occasions.

This cyclopaedic faculty was marvelous because it was only a small part of his equipment which became invaluable in association with other gifts. A student and a humanist, he delighted equally in books and in watching all the workings of a political convention.

For any one of the learned professions he had conspicuous ability. He chose that which, in the cloister of the editorial rooms, makes fame for others. Any judge or Cabinet Minister of our time may well be proud of a career of such usefulness as his. Men with such a quality of mind as Moffett's are rare.

Anyone who discussed with him the things he advocated stood a little awed to discover that here was a man who had carefully thought out what would be best for all the people in the world two or three generations hence, and guided his work according to that standard. This was the one broad subject that covered all his interests; in detail they included the movement for universal peace about which he wrote repeatedly; so small a thing as a plan to place flowers on the window sills and fire escapes of New York tenement houses enlisted not only the advocacy of his pen, but his direct personal presence and co-operation; again and again, in his department in this paper, he gave indorsement and aid to similar movements, whether broad or narrow in their scope—the saving of the American forests, fighting tuberculosis, providing free meals for poor school children in New York, old-age pensions, safety appliances for protecting factory employees, the beautifying of American cities, the creation of inland waterways, industrial peace.

He leaves behind him wife, daughter, and son—inconsolable mourners. The son is thirteen, a beautiful human creature, with the broad and square face of his father and his grandfather, a face in which one reads high character and intelligence. This boy will be distinguished, by and by, I think.

In closing this slight sketch of Samuel E. Moffett I wish to dwell with lingering and especial emphasis upon the dignity of his character and ideals. In an age when we would rather have money than health, and would rather have another man's money than our own, he lived and died unsordid; in a day when the surest road to national greatness and admiration is by showy and rotten demagoguery in politics and by giant crimes in finance, he lived and died a gentleman.

1923

Skeleton Plan of a Proposed Casting Vote Party[1]

ITS MAIN OBJECT

To compel the two Great Parties to nominate their *best man* always.

FOUNDATION PRINCIPLES

With the offices all filled by the best men of either of the two Great Parties, we shall have good government. We hold that this is beyond dispute, and does not need to be argued.

DETAILS

1. The C. V. Party should be *organized.* This, in order to secure its continuance and permanency.

2. Any of the following acts must sever the connection of a member with the Casting Vote party:

The seeking of any office, appointive or elective.

The acceptance of a nomination to any such office.

The acceptance of such an office.

3. The organization should never vote for *any but a nominee of one or the other of the two Great Parties,* and should then cast their *entire vote* for that nominee.

4. They should have no dealings with minor parties.

5. There should be ward organizations, township, town, city, congressional district, state and national organizations. The party should work wherever there is an elective office, from the lowest up to the Presidency.

6. As a rule, none of the organizations will need to be large. In most cases they will be able to control the action of the two Great Parties without that. In the matter of membership, quality will be the main thing, rather than quantity.

[1] According to Paine, this was written in 1901.—C.N.

In small constituencies, where a town constable or a justice of the peace is to be elected it will often be the case that a Casting Vote lodge of fifty members can elect the nominee it prefers. In every such community the material for the fifty is present. It will be found among the men who are disgusted with the prevailing political methods, the low ambitions and ideals, of the politicians; dishonesty in office; corruption; the frank distribution of appointments among characterless and incompetent men as pay for party service; the evasion and sometimes straight-out violation of the civil-service laws. The fifty will be found among the men who are ashamed of this condition of things and who have despaired of seeing it bettered; *who stay away from the polls and do not vote;* who do not attend primaries, and would be insulted there if they did.

The fifty exist in every little community; they are not seen, not heard, not regarded—but they are there. There, and deeply and sincerely desirous of good and sound government, and ready to give the best help they can if any will place before them a competent way. They are reserved and quiet merchants and shopkeepers, middle-aged; they are young men making their way in the offices of doctors and lawyers and behind counters; they are journeyman high-class mechanics; they are organizers of, and workers for, the community's charities, art and other social-improvement clubs, university settlements, Young Men's Christian Association, circulating libraries; they are readers of books, frequenters of the library. They have never seen a primary, and they have an aversion for the polls.

7. Men proposing to create a Casting Vote lodge should not advertise their purpose; conspiracies for good, like conspiracies for evil, are best conducted privately until success is sure. The poll of the two Great Parties should be examined, and the winning party's majority noted. *It is this majority which the Casting Vote must overcome and nullify.* If the total vote cast was 1,000 and the majority vote fifty, the proposers of a lodge should canvass privately until they have secured 75 or 100 names; they can organize then, without solicitude; the balance of power is in their hands, and this fact by itself will add names to its membership. If the total vote is 10,000 and the majority-vote 1,000, the procedure should be as before: the thousand-and-upward should be secured by private canvass before public organization is instituted. Where a total vote is 1,000,000 the majority vote is not likely to exceed 30,000. Five or six canvassers can begin the listing; each man secured becomes a canvasser, ten know three apiece who will join; the thirty know three apiece who will join; the ninety know

three hundred, the three hundred know a thousand, the thousand know three thousand—and so on; the required thirty or forty thousand can be secured in ten days, the lodge organized, and its casting vote be ready and self-pledged and competent to elect the best of the nominees the two Great Parties may put up at that date or later.

8. In every ward of every city there is enough of this material to hold the balance of power over the two Great Parties in a ward election; in every city there is enough of it to determine which of the two nominees shall be mayor; in every congressional district there is enough of it to elect the Governor; also to elect the legislature and choose the U. S. Senators; and in the United States there is enough of it to throw the Casting Vote for its choice between the nominees of the two Great Parties and seat him in the presidential chair.

9. From constable up to President there is no office for which the two Great Parties cannot furnish able, clean, and acceptable men. Whenever the balance of power shall be lodged in a permanent third party with no candidates of its own and no function but to cast its *whole vote* for the best man put forward by the Republicans and Democrats, these two parties *will select the best men they have in their ranks.* Good and clean government will follow, let its party complexion be what it may; and the country will be quite content.

THE LODGES

The primal lodge—call it A—should consist of 10 men only. It is enough and can meet in a dwelling house or a shop, and get well acquainted at once. It has before it the names of the nominees of the two Great Parties—Jones (Republican), Smith (Democrat). It fails of unanimity—both candidates perchance being good men and about equally acceptable—and casts seven votes, say, for Jones and three for Smith.

It elects one of its ten to meet similar delegates from any number of local A lodges and hand in its vote. This body—call it a B lodge —examines the aggregate vote; this time the majority may be with Smith. The members carry the result to the A lodges; and these, by the conditions of their membership, must vote for Smith.

In the case of a state election, bodies each consisting of a number of B lodges would elect a delegate to a state council, and the state council would examine the aggregate vote and give its decision in favor of the Republican or Democratic candidate receiving the majority of the Casting Vote's suffrages.

In the case of a presidential contest, the state council would appoint delegates to a national convention, and these would examine the aggregate Casting Vote vote and determine and announce the choice of the Casting Vote organizations of the whole country. At the presidential election the A lodges throughout the land would vote for presidential electors of the Party indicated.

If the reader thinks well of the project, let him begin a private canvass among his friends and give it a practical test, without waiting for other people to begin. If in the hands of men who regard their citizenship as a high trust this scheme shall fail upon trial, a better must be sought, a better must be invented; for it cannot be well or safe to let the present political conditions continue indefinitely. They can be improved, and American citizenship should rouse up from its disheartenment and see that it is done.

1923

Sold to Satan

It was at this time that I concluded to sell my soul to Satan. Steel was away down, so was St. Paul; it was the same with all the desirable stocks, in fact, and so, if I did not turn out to be away down myself, now was my time to raise a stake and make my fortune. Without further consideration I sent word to the local agent, Mr. Blank, with description and present condition of the property, and an interview with Satan was promptly arranged, on a basis of 2½ per cent, this commission payable only in case a trade should be consummated.

I sat in the dark, waiting and thinking. How still it was! Then came the deep voice of a far-off bell proclaiming midnight— Boom-m-m! Boom-m-m! Boom-m-m!—and I rose to receive my guest, and braced myself for the thunder crash and the brimstone stench which should announce his arrival. But there was no crash, no stench. Through the closed door, and noiseless, came the modern Satan, just as we see him on the stage—tall, slender, graceful, in tights and trunks, a short cape mantling his shoulders, a rapier at his side, a single drooping feather in his jaunty cap, and on his intellectual face the well-known and high-bred Mephistophelian smile.

But he was not a fire coal; he was not red, no! On the contrary. He was a softly glowing, richly smoldering torch, column, statue of pallid light, faintly tinted with a spiritual green, and out from him a lunar splendor flowed such as one sees glinting from the crinkled waves of tropic seas when the moon rides high in cloudless skies.

He made his customary stage obeisance, resting his left hand upon his sword hilt and removing his cap with his right and making that handsome sweep with it which we know so well; then we sat down. Ah, he was an incandescent glory, a nebular dream, and so much improved by his change of color. He must have seen the admiration in my illuminated face, but he took no notice of it, being long ago used to it in faces of other Christians with whom he had had trade relations.

. . . A half hour of hot toddy and weather chat, mixed with occasional tentative feelers on my part and rejoinders of, "Well, I could hardly pay *that* for it, you know," on his, had much modified my shyness and put me so much at my ease that I was emboldened to feed my curiosity a little. So I chanced the remark that he was surprisingly different from the traditions, and I wished I knew what it was he was made of. He was no offended, but answered with frank simplicity:

"Radium!"

"That accounts for it!" I exclaimed. "It is the loveliest effulgence I have ever seen. The hard and heartless glare of the electric doesn't compare with it. I suppose Your Majesty weighs about—about——"

"I stand six feet one; fleshed and blooded I would weigh two hundred and fifteen; but radium, like other metals, is heavy. I weigh nine hundred-odd."

I gazed hungrily upon him, saying to myself:

"What riches! what a mine! Nine hundred pounds at, say, $3,500,000 a pound, would be—would be——" Then a treacherous thought burst into my mind!

He laughed a good hearty laugh, and said:

"I perceive your thought; and what a handsomely original idea it is!—to kidnap Satan, and stock him, and incorporate him, and water the stock up to ten billions—just three times its actual value—and blanket the world with it!" My blush had turned the moonlight to a crimson mist, such as veils and spectralizes the domes and towers of Florence at sunset and makes the spectator drunk with joy to see, and he pitied me, and dropped his tone of irony, and assumed a grave and reflective one which had a pleasanter sound for me, and under its kindly influence my pains were presently healed, and I thanked him for his courtesy. Then he said:

"One good turn deserves another, and I will pay you a compliment. Do you know I have been trading with your poor pathetic race for ages, and you are the first person who has ever been intelligent enough to divine the large commercial value of my make-up."

I purred to myself and looked as modest as I could.

"Yes, you are the first," he continued. "All through the Middle Ages I used to buy Christian souls at fancy rates, building bridges and cathedrals in a single night in return, and getting swindled out of my Christian nearly every time that I dealt with a priest—as history will concede—but making it up on the lay square-dealer now and then, as I admit; but none of those people ever guessed where the *real* big money lay. You are the first."

I refilled his glass and gave him another Cavour. But he was experienced, by this time. He inspected the cigar pensively awhile; then:

"What do you pay for these?" he asked.

"Two cents—but they come cheaper when you take a barrel."

He went on inspecting; also mumbling comments, apparently to himself:

"Black—rough-skinned—rumpled, irregular, wrinkled, barky, with crispy curled-up places on it—burnt-leather aspect, like the shoes of the damned that sit in pairs before the room doors at home of a Sunday morning." He sighed at thought of his home, and was silent a moment; then he said, gently, "Tell me about this projectile."

"It is the discovery of a great Italian statesman," I said, "Cavour. One day he lit his cigar, then laid it down and went on writing and forgot it. It lay in a pool of ink and got soaked. By and by he noticed it—and laid it on the stove to dry. When it was dry he lit it and at once noticed that it didn't taste the same as it did before. And so——"

"Did he say what it tasted like before?"

"No, I think not. But he called the government chemist and told him to find out the source of that new taste, and report. The chemist applied the tests, and reported that the source was the presence of sulphate of iron, touched up and spiritualized with vinegar—the combination out of which one makes ink. Cavour told him to introduce the brand in the interest of the finances. So, ever since then this brand passes through the ink factory, with the great result that both the ink and the cigar suffer a sea change into something new and strange. This is history, Sire, not a work of the imagination."

So then he took up his present again, and touched it to the forefinger of his other hand for an instant, which made it break into flame

and fragrance—but he changed his mind at that point and laid the
torpedo down, saying, courteously:

"With permission I will save it for Voltaire."

I was greatly pleased and flattered to be connected in even this
little way with that great man and be mentioned to him, as no
doubt would be the case, so I hastened to fetch a bundle of fifty for
distribution among others of the renowned and lamented—Goethe,
and Homer, and Socrates, and Confucius, and so on—but Satan said he
had nothing against those. Then he dropped back into reminiscences
of the old times once more, and presently said:

"They knew nothing about radium, and it would have had no value
for them if they had known about it. In twenty million years it has had
no value for your race until the revolutionizing steam-and-machinery
age was born—which was only a few years before you were born
yourself. It was a stunning little century, for sure, that nineteenth!
But it's a poor thing compared to what the twentieth is going to be."

By request, he explained why he thought so.

"Because power was so costly, then, and everything goes by power
—the steamship, the locomotive, and everything else. Coal, you see!
You have to have it; no steam and no electricity without it; and it's
such a waste—for you burn it up, and it's gone! But radium—that's another matter! With my nine hundred pounds you could light the
world, and heat it, and run all its ships and machines and railways a
hundred million years, and not use up five pounds of it in the whole
time! And then———"

"Quick—my soul is yours, dear Ancestor; take it—we'll start a company!"

But he asked my age, which is sixty-eight, then politely sidetracked
the proposition, probably not wishing to take advantage of himself.
Then he went on talking admiringly of radium, and how with its own
natural and inherent heat it could go on melting its own weight of
ice twenty-four times in twenty-four hours, and keep it up forever
without losing bulk or weight; and how a pound of it, if exposed in
this room, would blast the place like a breath from hell, and burn me
to a crisp in a quarter of a minute—and was going on like that, but I
interrupted and said:

"But *you* are here, Majesty—nine hundred pounds—and the temperature is balmy and pleasant. I don't understand."

"Well," he said, hesitatingly, "it is a secret, but I may as well reveal
it, for these prying and impertinent chemists are going to find it out
sometime or other, anyway. Perhaps you have read what Madame

Curie says about radium; how she goes searching among its splendid
secrets and seizes upon one after another of them and italicizes its
specialty; how she says 'the compounds of radium are *spontaneously luminous'*—require no coal in the production of light, you see;
how she says, 'a glass vessel containing radium *spontaneously charges
itself with electricity'*—no coal or water power required to generate it,
you see; how she says 'radium possesses the remarkable property of
liberating heat spontaneously and continuously'—no coal required to
fire-up on the world's machinery, you see. She ransacks the pitch-
blende for its radioactive substances, and captures three and labels
them; one, which is embodied with bismuth, she names polonium;
one, which is embodied with barium, she names radium; the name
given to the third was actinium. Now listen; she says '*the question
now was to separate the polonium from the bismuth . . .* this is the
task that has occupied us for years and has been a most difficult one.'
For years, you see—for *years*. That is their way, those plagues, those
scientists—peg, peg, peg—dig, dig, dig—plod, plod, plod. I wish I could
catch a cargo of them for my place; it would be an economy. Yes,
for years, you see. They never give up. Patience, hope, faith, per-
severance; it is the way of all the breed. Columbus and the rest. In
radium this lady has added a new world to the planet's possessions,
and matched—Columbus—and his peer. She has set herself the task
of divorcing polonium and bismuth; when she succeeds she will have
done—what, should you say?"

"Pray name it, Majesty."

"It's another new world added—a gigantic one. I will explain; for
you would never divine the size of it, and she herself does not suspect it."

"Do, Majesty, I beg of you."

"Polonium, freed from bismuth and made independent, is the one
and only power that can control radium, restrain its destructive forces,
tame them, reduce them to obedience, and make them do useful and
profitable work for your race. Examine my skin. What do you think
of it?"

"It is delicate, silky, transparent, thin as a gelatine film—exquisite,
beautiful, Majesty!"

"It is made of polonium. All the rest of me is radium. If I should strip
off my skin the world would vanish away in a flash of flame and a puff
of smoke, and the remnants of the extinguished moon would sift down
through space a mere snow-shower of gray ashes!"

I made no comment, I only trembled.

"You understand, now," he continued. "I burn, I suffer within, my pains are measureless and eternal, but my skin protects you and the globe from harm. Heat is power, energy, but is only useful to man when he can control it and graduate its application to his needs. You cannot do that with radium, now; it will not be prodigiously useful to you until polonium shall put the slave whip in your hand. I can release from my body the radium force in any measure I please, great or small; at my will I can set in motion the works of a lady's watch or destroy a world. You saw me light that unholy cigar with my finger?"

I remembered it.

"Try to imagine how minute was the fraction of energy released to do that small thing! You are aware that everything is made up of restless and revolving molecules?—everything—furniture, rocks, water, iron, horses, men—everything that exists."

"Yes."

"Molecules of scores of different sizes and weights, but none of them big enough to be seen by help of any microscope?"

"Yes."

"And that each molecule is made up of thousands of separate and never-resting little particles called atoms?"

"Yes."

"And that up to recent times the smallest atom known to science was the hydrogen atom, which was a thousand times smaller than the atom that went to the building of any other molecule?"

"Yes."

"Well, the radium atom from the positive pole is 5,000 times smaller than *that* atom! This unspeakably minute atom is called an *electron*. Now then, out of my long affection for you and for your lineage, I will reveal to you a secret—a secret known to no scientist as yet—the secret of the firefly's light and the glowworm's; it is produced by a single electron imprisoned in a polonium atom."

"Sire, it is a wonderful thing, and the scientific world would be grateful to know this secret, which has baffled and defeated all its searchings for more than two centuries. To think!—a single electron, 5,000 times smaller than the invisible hydrogen atom, to produce that explosion of vivid light which makes the summer night so beautiful!"

"And consider," said Satan; "it is the only instance in all nature where radium exists in a pure state unencumbered by fettering alliances; where polonium enjoys the like emancipation; and where the pair are enabled to labor together in a gracious and beneficent and effective partnership. Suppose the protecting polonium envelope were removed; the radium spark would flash but once and the firefly would be consumed to vapor! Do you value this old iron letterpress?"

"No, Majesty, for it is not mine."

"Then I will destroy it and let you see. I lit the ostensible cigar with the heat energy of a single electron, the equipment of a single lightning bug. I will turn on twenty thousand electrons now."

He touched the massive thing and it exploded with a cannon crash, leaving nothing but vacancy where it had stood. For three minutes the air was a dense pink fog of sparks, through which Satan loomed dim and vague, then the place cleared and his soft rich moonlight pervaded it again. He said:

"You see? The radium in 20,000 lightning bugs would run a racing-mobile forever. There's no waste, no diminution of it." Then he remarked in a quite casual way, "We use nothing but radium at home."

I was astonished. And interested, too, for I have friends there, and relatives. I had always believed—in accordance with my early teachings—that the fuel was soft coal and brimstone. He noticed the thought, and answered it.

"Soft coal and brimstone is the tradition, yes, but it is an error. We could use it; at least we could make out with it after a fashion, but it has several defects: it is not cleanly, it ordinarily makes but a temperate fire, and it would be exceedingly difficult, if even possible, to heat it up to standard, Sundays; and as for the supply, all the worlds and systems could not furnish enough to keep us going halfway through eternity. Without radium there could be no hell; certainly not a satisfactory one."

"Why?"

"Because if we hadn't radium we should have to dress the souls in some other material; then, of course, they would burn up and get out of trouble. They would not last an hour. You know that?"

"Why—yes, now that you mention it. But I supposed they were dressed in their natural flesh; they look so in the pictures—in the Sistine Chapel and in the illustrated books, you know."

"Yes, our damned look as they looked in the world, but it isn't flesh; flesh could not survive any longer than that copying press survived—it would explode and turn to a fog of sparks, and the result desired in sending it there would be defeated. Believe me, radium is the only wear."

"I see it now," I said, with prophetic discomfort, "I know that you are right, Majesty."

"I am. I speak from experience. You shall see, when you get there."

He said this as if he thought I was eaten up with curiosity, but it was because he did not know me. He sat reflecting a minute, then he said:

"I will make your fortune."

It cheered me up and I felt better. I thanked him and was all eagerness and attention.

"Do you know," he continued, "where they find the bones of the extinct moa, in New Zealand? All in a pile—thousands and thousands of them banked together in a mass twenty feet deep. And do you know where they find the tusks of the extinct mastodon of the Pleistocene? Banked together in acres off the mouth of the Lena—an ivory mine which has furnished freight for Chinese caravans for five hundred years. Do you know the phosphate beds of our South? They are miles in extent, a limitless mass and jumble of bones of vast animals whose like exists no longer in the earth—a cemetery, a mighty cemetery, that is what it is. All over the earth there are such cemeteries. Whence came the instinct that made those families of creatures go to a chosen and particular spot to die when sickness came upon them and they perceived that their end was near? It is a mystery; not even science has been able to uncover the secret of it. But there stands the fact. Listen, then. For a million years there has been a firefly cemetery."

Hopefully, appealingly, I opened my mouth—he motioned me to close it, and went on:

"It is in a scooped-out bowl half as big as this room on the top of a snow summit of the Cordileras. That bowl is level full—of what? Pure firefly radium and the glow and heat of hell! For countless ages myriads of fireflies have daily flown thither and died in that bowl and been burned to vapor in an instant, each fly leaving as its contribution its only indestructible particle, its single electron of pure radium. There is energy enough there to light the whole world, heat the whole world's machinery, supply the whole world's transportation power from now till the end of eternity. The massed riches of the planet could not furnish its value in money. You are mine, it is yours; when Madame Curie isolates polonium, clother yourself in a skin of it and go and take possession!"

Then he vanished and left me in the dark when I was just in the act of thanking him. I can find the bowl by the light it will cast upon the sky; I can get the polonium presently, when that illustrious lady in France isolates it from the bismuth. Stock is for sale. Apply to Mark Twain.

1923

Some National Stupidities[1]

The slowness of one section of the world about adopting the valuable ideas of another section of it is a curious thing and unaccountable. This form of stupidity is confined to no community, to no nation; it is universal. The fact is the human race is not only slow about borrowing valuable ideas—it sometimes persists in not borrowing them at all.

Take the German stove, for instance—the huge white porcelain monument that towers toward the ceiling in the corner of the room, solemn, unsympathetic, and suggestive of death and the grave—where can you find it outside of the German countries? I am sure I have never seen it where German was not the language of the region. Yet it is by long odds the best stove and the most convenient and economical that has yet been invented.

To the uninstructed stranger it promises nothing; but he will soon find that it is a masterly performer, for all that. It has a little bit of a door which you couldn't get your head into—a door which seems foolishly out of proportion to the rest of the edifice; yet the door is right, for it is not necessary that bulky fuel shall enter it. Small-sized fuel is used, and marvelously little of that. The door opens into a tiny cavern which would not hold more fuel than a baby could fetch in its arms. The process of firing is quick and simple. At half past seven on a cold morning the servant brings a small basketful of slender pine sticks—say a modified armful—and puts half of these in, lights them with a match, and closes the door. They burn out in ten or twelve minutes. He then puts in the rest and *locks* the door, and carries off the key. The work is done. He will not come again until next morning. All day long and until past midnight all parts of the room will be delightfully warm and comfortable, and there will be no headaches and no sense of closeness or oppression. In an American room, whether heated by steam, hot water, or open fires, the neighborhood of the register or the fireplace is warmest—the heat is not equally diffused through the room; but in a German room one is as comfortable in one part of it as in another. Nothing is gained or lost by being near the

[1] Written 1891–2, according to Paine.—C.N.

stove. Its surface is not hot; you can put your hand on it anywhere and not get burnt. Consider these things. One firing is enough for the day; the cost is next to nothing; the heat produced is the same all day, instead of too hot and too cold by turns; one may absorb himself in his business in peace; he does not need to feel any anxieties or solicitudes about his fire; his whole day is a realized dream of bodily comfort.

The German stove is not restricted to wood; peat is used in it, and coal bricks also. These coal bricks are made of waste coal dust pressed in a mold. In effect they are dirt and in fact are dirt cheap. The brick is about as big as your two fists; the stove will burn up twenty of them in half an hour, then it will need no more fuel for that day.

This noble stove is at its very best when its front has a big square opening in it for a *visible* wood fire. The real heating is done in the hidden regions of the great structure, of course—the open fire is merely to rejoice your eye and gladden your heart.

America could adopt this stove, but does America do it? No, she sticks placidly to her own fearful and wonderful inventions in the stove line. She has fifty kinds, and not a rational one in the lot. The American wood stove, of whatsoever breed, is a terror. There can be no tranquillity of mind where it is. It requires more attention than a baby. It has to be fed every little while, it has to be watched all the time; and for all reward you are roasted half your time and frozen the other half. It warms no part of the room but its own part; it breeds headaches and suffocation, and makes one's skin feel dry and feverish; and when your wood bill comes in you think you have been supporting a volcano.

We have in America many and many a breed of coal stoves, also—fiendish things, everyone of them. The base-burner sort are handy and require but little attention; but none of them, of whatsoever kind, distributes its heat uniformly through the room, or keeps it at an unvarying temperature, or fails to take the life out of the atmosphere and leave it stuffy and smothery and stupefying.

It seems to me that the ideal of comfort would be a German stove to heat one's room, and an open wood fire to make it cheerful; then have furnace-heat in the halls. We could easily find some way to make the German stove beautiful, and that is all it needs at present. Still, even as it is to-day, it is lovely, it is a darling, compared with any "radiator" that has yet been intruded upon the world. That odious gilded skeleton! It makes all places ugly that it inhabits—just by contagion.

It is certainly strange that useful customs and devices do not spread from country to country with more facility and promptness than they do. You step across the German border almost anywhere, and suddenly the German stove has disappeared. In Italy you find a foolish and ineffectual modification of it, in Paris you find an unprepossessing "adaptation" of our base-burner on a reduced pattern.

Fifteen years ago Paris had a cheap and cunning little fire kindler consisting of a pine shaving, curled as it came from the carpenter's plane, and gummed over with an inflammable substance which would burn several minutes and set fire to the most obdurate wood. It was cheap and handy, but no stranger carried the idea home with him. Paris has another swift and victorious kindler, now, in the form of a small black cake made of I don't know what; but you shove it under the wood and touch a match to it and your fire is made. No one will think to carry that device to America, or elsewhere. In America we prefer to kindle the fire with the kerosene can and chance the inquest. I have been in a multitude of places where pine cones were abundant, but only in the French Riviera and in one place in Italy have I seen them in the wood box to kindle the fires with.

For perfect adaptation to the service required, look at the American gum shoe and the American arctic. Their virtues ought to have carried them to all wet and snowy lands; but they haven't done anything of the kind. There are few places on the continent of Europe where one can buy them.

And observe how slowly our typewriting machine makes its way. In the great city of Florence I was able to find only one place where I could get typewriting done; and then it was not done by a native, but by an American girl. In the great city of Munich I found one typewriting establishment, but the operator was sick and that suspended the business. I was told that there was no opposition house. In the prodigious city of Berlin I was not able to find a typewriter at all. There was not even one in our Embassy or its branches. Our representative there sent to London for the best one to be had in that capital, and got an incapable, who would have been tarred and feathered in Mud Springs, Arizona. Four years ago a typewritten page was a seldom sight in Europe, and when you saw it it made you heartsick, it was so inartistic, and so blurred and shabby and slovenly. It was because the Europeans made the machines themselves, and the making of nice machinery is not one of their gifts. England imports ours, now. This is wise; she will have her reward.

In all these years the American fountain pen has hardly got a start in Europe. There is no market for it. It is too handy, too inspiring, too capable, too much of a time saver. The dismal steel pen and the compass-jawed quill are preferred. And semiliquid mud is preferred to ink, apparently, everywhere in Europe. This in face of the fact that there is ink to be had in America—and at club rates, too.

Then there is the elevator, lift, *ascenseur*. America has had the benefit of this invaluable contrivance for a generation and a half, and it is now used in all our cities and villages, in all hotels, in all lofty business buildings and factories, and in many private dwellings. But we can't spread it, we can't beguile Europe with it. In Europe an elevator is even to this day a rarity and a curiosity. Especially a curiosity. As a rule it seats but three or four persons—often only two—and it travels so slowly and cautiously and timorously and piously and solemnly that it makes a person feel creepy and crawly and scary and dismal and repentant. Anybody with sound legs can give the continental elevator two flights the start and beat it to the sixth floor. Every time these nations merely import an American idea, instead of importing the concreted thing itself, the result is a failure. They tried to make the sewing machine, and couldn't; they are trying to make fountain pens and typewriters and can't; they are making these dreary elevators, now—and patenting them! Satire can no further go.

I think that as a rule we develop a borrowed European idea forward, and that Europe develops a borrowed American idea backward. We borrowed gas lighting and the railroad from England, and the arc light from France, and these things have improved under our culture. We have lent Europe our tramway, telegraph, sewing machine, phonograph, telephone, and kodak, and while we may not claim that in these particular instances she has developed them backward, we are justified in claiming that she has added no notable improvements to them. We have added the improvements ourselves and she has accepted them. Why she has not accepted and universally adopted the improved elevator is a surprising and puzzling thing. Its rightful place is among the great ideas of our great age. It is an epoch maker. It is a concentrator of population, and economizer of room. It is going to build our cities skyward instead of out toward the horizons. It is going to enable five millions of people to live comfortably on the same ground space that one million uncomfortably lives on now. It is going to make cheap quarters for Tom, Dick, and Harry near their work, in place of three miles from it, as is the rule to-day. It is going to save them the necessity of adding a six-flight climb to the already sufficient fatigue of their day's labor.

We imitate some of the good things which we find in Europe, and
we ought to imitate more of them. At the same time Europe ought to
imitate us somewhat more than she does. The crusty, ill-mannered
and in every way detestable Parisian cabman ought to imitate our
courteous and friendly Boston cabman—and stop there. He can't learn
anything from the guild in New York. And it would morally help the
Parisian shopkeeper if he would imitate the fair dealing of his American cousin. With us it is not necessary to ask the price of small
articles before we buy them, but in Paris the person who fails to take
that precaution will get scorched. In business we are prompt, fair, and
trustworthy in all our small trade matters. It is the rule. In the friend-
liest spirit I would recommend France to imitate these humble virtues.
Particularly in the kodak business. Pray get no kodak pictures developed in France—and especially in Nice. They will send you your bill
to Rome or Jericho, or whithersoever you have gone, but that is all
you will get. You will never see your negatives again, or the developed pictures, either. And by and by the head house in Paris will demand payment once more, and constructively threaten you with
"proceedings." If you inquire if they mailed your package across the
frontier without registering it, they are coldly silent. If you inquire
how they expected to trace and recover a lost package without a
post-office receipt, they are dumb again. A little intelligence inserted
into the kodak business in those regions would be helpful, if it could
be done without shock.

But the worst of all is, that Europe cannot be persuaded to imitate
our railway methods. Two or three years ago I liked the European
methods, but experience has dislodged that superstition. All over the
Continent the system—to call it by an extravagant term—is sufficiently
poor and slow and clumsy, or unintelligent; but in these regards
Italy and France are entitled to the chromo. In Italy it takes more
than half an hour to buy a through ticket to Paris at Cook & Sons'
offices, there is such a formidable amount of red tape and recording
connected with the vast transaction. Every little detail of the matter
must be written down in a set of books—your name, condition, nationality, religion, date, hour, number of the train, and all that; and at
last you get your ticket and think you are done, but you are not; it
must be carried to the station and stamped; and even that is not the
end, for if you stop over at any point it must be stamped again or it is
forfeited. And yet you save time and trouble by going to Cook instead of to the station. Buying your ticket does not finish your job.
Your trunks must be weighed, and paid for at about human-being

rates. This takes another quarter of an hour of your time—perhaps half an hour if you are at the tail of the procession. You get paper checks, which are twice as easy to lose as brass ones. You cannot secure a seat beforehand, but must take your chances with the general rush to the train. If you have your family with you, you may have to distribute them among several cars. There is one annoying feature which is common all over the Continent, and that is, that if you want to make a short journey you cannot buy your ticket whenever you find the ticket office open, but must wait until it is doing business for your particular train; and that only begins, as a rule, a quarter of an hour before the train's time of starting. The cars are most ingeniously inconvenient, cramped, and uncomfortable, and in Italy they are phenomenally dirty. The European "system" was devised either by a maniac or by a person whose idea was to hamper, bother, and exasperate the traveler in all conceivable ways and sedulously and painstakingly discourage custom. In Italy, as far as my experience goes, it is the custom to use the sleeping cars on the day trains and take them off when the sun goes down. One thing is sure, anyway: if that is not the case, it will be, presently, when they think of it. They can be depended upon to snap up as darling an idea as that with joy.

No, we are bad enough about not importing valuable European ideas, but Europe is still slower about introducing ours. Europe has always—from away back—been neglectful in this regard. Take our admirable postal and express system, for instance. We had it perfectly developed and running smoothly and beautifully more than three hundred years ago; and Europe came over and admired it and eloquently praised it—but didn't adopt it. We Americans . . . But let Prescott tell about it. I quote from the *Conquest of Peru*, chapter 2, vol. 1:

As the distance each courier had to perform was small, they ran over the ground with great swiftness, and messages were carried through the whole extent of the long routes at the rate of a hundred and fifty miles a day. Their office was not limited to carrying dispatches. They brought various articles. Fish from the distant ocean, fruits, game, and different commodities from the hot regions of the coast were taken to the capital in good condition. It is remarkable that this important institution should have been found among two barbarian nations of the New World long before it was introduced among the civilized nations of Europe. By these wise contrivances of the Incas, the most distant parts of the long-extended empire of Peru were brought into intimate relations with each other. And while the capitals of Christendom, but a few hundred miles apart, remained as far asunder as if seas had rolled between them, the great capitals Cuzco and Quito were placed in immediate correspondence. Intelligence from the numerous provinces was transmitted on the wings of the wind to the Peruvian metropolis, the great focus to which all the lines of communication converged.

There—that is what we had, three hundred and twenty-five years before Europe had anything that could be called a businesslike and effective postal and express service. We are a great people. We have always been a great people, from the start: always alive, alert, up early in the morning, and ready to teach. But Europe has been a slow and discouraging pupil from the start; always, from the very start. It seems to me that something ought to be done about this.

1923

The Temperance Crusade and Woman's Rights[1]

The women's crusade against the rum sellers continues. It began in an Ohio village early in the new year, and has now extended itself eastwardly to the Atlantic seaboard, 600 miles, and westwardly (at a bound, without stopping by the way,) to San Francisco, about 2,500 miles. It has also scattered itself along down the Ohio and Mississippi rivers southwardly some ten or twelve hundred miles. Indeed, it promises to sweep, eventually, the whole United States, with the exception of the little cluster of commonwealths which we call New England. Puritan New England is sedate, reflective, conservative, and very hard to inflame.

The method of the crusaders is singular. They contemn the use of force in the breaking up of the whisky traffic. They only assemble before a drinking shop, or within it, and sing hymns and pray, hour after hour—and day after day, if necessary—until the publican's business is broken up and he surrenders. This is not force, at least they do not consider it so. After the surrender the crusaders march back to headquarters and proclaim the victory, and ascribe it to the powers

---

[1] Paine says this was composed in 1873.—C.N.

above. They rejoice together awhile, and then go forth again in their strength and conquer another whisky shop with their prayers and hymns and their staying capacity (pardon the rudeness), and spread *that* victory upon the battle flag of the powers above. In this generous way the crusaders have parted with the credit of not less than three thousand splendid triumphs, which some carping people say they gained their own selves, without assistance from any quarter. If I am one of these, I am the humblest. If I seem to doubt that prayer is the agent that conquers these rum sellers, I do it honestly, and not in a flippant spirit. If the crusaders were to stay at home and pray for the rum seller and for his adoption of a better way of life, or if the crusaders even assembled together in a church and offered up such a prayer with a united voice, and it accomplished a victory, I would then feel that it was the praying that moved Heaven to do the miracle; for I believe that if the prayer is the agent that brings about the desired result, it cannot be necessary to pray the prayer in any particular place in order to get the ear, or move the grace, of the Deity. When the crusaders go and invest a whisky shop and fall to praying, one suspects that they are praying rather less to the Deity than *at* the rum man. So I cannot help feeling (after carefully reading the details of the rum sieges) that as much as nine tenths of the credit of each of the 3,000 victories achieved thus far belongs of right to the crusaders themselves, and it grieves me to see them give it away with such spendthrift generosity.

I will not afflict you with statistics, but I desire to say just a word or two about the character of this crusade. The crusaders are young girls and women—not the inferior sort, but the very best in the village communities. The telegraph keeps the newspapers supplied with the progress of the war, and thus the praying infection spreads from town to town, day after day, week after week. When it attacks a community it seems to seize upon almost everybody in it at once. There is a meeting in a church, speeches are made, resolutions are passed, a purse for expenses is made up, a "praying band" is appointed; if it be a large town, half a dozen praying bands, each numbering as many as a hundred women, are appointed, and the working district of each band marked out. Then comes a grand assault in force, all along the line. Every stronghold of rum is invested; first one and then another champion ranges up before the proprietor and offers up a special petition for him; he has to stand meekly there behind his bar, under the eyes of a great concourse of ladies who are better than he is and are aware of it, and hear all the secret iniquities of his business divulged to the angels above, accompanied by the sharp sting of wishes for his regeneration, which imply an amount of need for it which is in the last degree uncomfortable to him. If he holds out bravely, the crusaders hold out more bravely still—or at least more persistently; though I doubt if the grandeur of the performance would not be considerably heightened if one solitary crusader were to try praying at a hundred rum sellers in a body for a while, and see how it felt to have everybody against her instead of for her. If the man holds out the crusaders camp before his place and keep up the siege till they wear him out. In one case they besieged a rum shop two whole weeks. They built a shed before it and kept up the praying all night and all day long every day of the fortnight, and this in the bitterest winter weather, too. They conquered.

You may ask if such an investment and such interference with a man's business (in cases where he is "protected" by a license) is lawful? By no means. But the whole community being with the crusaders, the authorities have usually been overawed and afraid to execute the laws, the authorities being, in too many cases, mere little politicians, and more given to looking to chances of re-election than fearlessly discharging their duty according to the terms of their official oaths.

Would you consider the conduct of these crusaders justifiable? I do —thoroughly justifiable. They find themselves voiceless in the making of laws and the election of officers to execute them. Born with brains, born in the country, educated, having large interests at stake, they find their tongues tied and their hands fettered, while every ignorant whisky-drinking foreign-born savage in the land may hold office, help to make the laws, degrade the dignity of the former and break the latter at his own sweet will. They see their fathers, husbands, and brothers sit inanely at home and allow the scum of the country to assemble at the "primaries," name the candidates for office from their own vile ranks, and, unrebuked, elect them. They live in the midst of a country where there is no end to the laws and no beginning to the execution of them. And when the laws intended to protect their sons from destruction by intemperance lie torpid and without sign of life year after year, they recognize that here is a matter which interests them personally—a matter which comes straight home to them. And since they are allowed to lift no legal voice against the outrageous state of things they suffer under this regard, I think it is no wonder that their patience has broken down at last, and they have contrived to persuade themselves that they are justifiable in breaking the law of trespass when the laws that should make the trespass needless are allowed by the voters to lie dead and inoperative.

I cannot help glorying in the pluck of these women, sad as it is to see them displaying themselves in these unwomanly ways; sad as it is to see them carrying their grace and their purity into places which should never know their presence; and sadder still as it is to see them trying to save a set of men who, it seems to me, there can be no reasonable object in saving. It does not become us to scoff at the crusaders, remembering what it is they have borne all these years, but it does become us to admire their heroism that boldly faces jeers, curses, ribald language, obloquy of every kind and degree—in a word, every manner of thing that pure-hearted, pure-minded women such as these are naturally dread and shrink from, and remains steadfast through it all, undismayed, patient, hopeful, giving no quarter, asking none, determined to conquer and succeeding. It is the same old superb spirit that animated that other devoted, magnificent, mistaken crusade of six hundred years ago. The sons of such women as these must surely be worth saving from the destroying power of rum.

The present crusade will doubtless do but little work against intemperance that will be really permanent, but it will do what is as much, or even more, to the purpose, I think. I think it will suggest to more than one man that if women could vote they would vote on the side of morality, even if they did vote and speak rather frantically and furiously; and it will also suggest that when the women once made up their minds that it was not good to leave the all-powerful "primaries" in the hands of loafers, thieves, and pernicious little politicians, they would not sit indolently at home as their husbands and brothers do now, but would hoist their praying banners, take the field in force, pray the assembled political scum back to the holes and slums where they belong, and set up some candidates fit for decent human beings to vote for.

I dearly want the women to be raised to the political altitude of the negro, the imported savage, and the pardoned thief, and allowed to vote. It is our last chance, I think. The women will be voting before long, and then if a B. F. Butler can still continue to lord it in Congress; if the highest offices in the land can still continue to be occupied by perjurers and robbers; if another Congress (like the forty-second) consisting of 15 honest men and 296 of the other kind can once more be created, it will at last be time, I fear, to give over trying to save the country by human means, and appeal to Providence. Both the great parties have failed. I wish we might have a woman's party now, and see how that would work. I feel persuaded that in extending the suffrage to women this country could lose absolutely nothing and might gain a great deal. For thirty centuries history has been iterating and reiterating that in a moral fight woman is simply dauntless, and we all know, even with our eyes shut upon Congress and our voters, that from the day that Adam ate of the apple and told on Eve down to the present day, man, in a moral fight, has pretty uniformly shown himself to be an arrant coward.

I will mention casually that while I cannot bring myself to find fault with the women whom we call the crusaders, since I feel that they, being politically fettered, have the natural right of the oppressed to rebel, I have a very different opinion about the clergymen who have in a multitude of instances attached themselves to the movement, and by voice and act have countenanced and upheld the women in unlawfully trespassing upon whisky mills and interrupting the rum sellers' business. It seems to me that it would better become clergymen to teach their flocks to respect the laws of the land, and urge them to refrain from breaking them. But it is not a new thing for a thoroughly good and well-meaning preacher's soft heart to run away with his soft head.

1923

That Day in Eden

(Passage from Satan's Diary)

Long ago I was in the bushes near the Tree of Knowledge when the Man and the Woman came there and had a conversation. I was present, now, when they came again after all these years. They were as before—mere boy and girl—trim, rounded, slender, flexible, snow images lightly flushed with the pink of the skies, innocently unconscious of their nakedness, lovely to look upon, beautiful beyond words.

I listened again. Again as in that former time they puzzled over those words, Good, Evil, Death, and tried to reason out their meaning; but, of course, they were not able to do it. Adam said:

"Come, maybe we can find Satan. He might know these things."

Then I came forth, still gazing upon Eve and admiring, and said to her:

"You have not seen me before, sweet creature, but I have seen you. I have seen all the animals, but in beauty none of them equals you. Your hair, your eyes, your face, your flesh tints, your form, the tapering grace of your white limbs—all are beautiful, adorable, perfect."

It gave her pleasure, and she looked herself over, putting out a foot and a hand and admiring them; then she naïvely said:

"It is a joy to be so beautiful. And Adam—he is the same."

She turned him about, this way and that, to show him off, with such guileless pride in her blue eyes, and he—he took it all as just matter of course, and was innocently happy in it, and said, "When I have flowers on my head it is better still."

Eve said, "It is true—you shall see," and she flitted hither and thither like a butterfly and plucked flowers, and in a moment laced their stems together in a glowing wreath and set it upon his head; then tiptoed and gave it a pat here and there with her nimble fingers, with each pat enhancing its grace and shape, none knows how, nor why it should so result, but in it there is a law somewhere, though the delicate art and mystery of it is her secret alone, and not learnable by another; and when at last it was to her mind she clapped her hands for pleasure, then reached up and kissed him—as pretty a sight, taken altogether, as in my experience I have seen.

Presently, to the matter in hand. The meaning of those words—would I tell her?

Certainly none could be more willing, but how was I to do it? I could think of no way to make her understand, and I said so. I said:

"I will try, but it is hardly of use. For instance—what is pain?"

"Pain? I do not know."

"Certainly. How should you? Pain is not of your world; pain is impossible to you; you have never experienced a physical pain. Reduce that to a formula, a principle, and what have we?"

"What have we?"

"This: Things which are outside of our orbit—our own particular world—things which by our constitution and equipment we are unable to see, or feel, or otherwise experience—*cannot be made comprehensible to us in words*. There you have the whole thing in a nutshell. It is a principle, it is axiomatic, it is a law. Now do you understand?"

The gentle creature looked dazed, and for all result she was delivered of this vacant remark:

"What is axiomatic?"

She had missed the point. Necessarily she would. Yet her effort was success for me, for it was a vivid confirmation of the truth of what I had been saying. Axiomatic was for the present a thing outside of the world of her experience, therefore it had no meaning for her. I ignored her question and continued:

"What is fear?"

"Fear? I do not know."

"Naturally. Why should you? You have not felt it, you cannot feel it, it does not belong in your world. With a hundred thousand words I should not be able to make you understand what fear is. How then am I to explain death to you? You have never seen it, it is foreign to your world, it is impossible to make the word mean anything to you, so far as I can see. In a way, it is a sleep——"

"Oh, I know what that is!"

"But it is a sleep only in a way, as I said. It is more than a sleep."

"Sleep is pleasant, sleep is lovely!"

"But death is a long sleep—very long."

"Oh, all the lovelier! Therefore I think nothing could be better than death."

I said to myself, "Poor child, some day you may know what a pathetic truth you have spoken; some day you may say, out of a broken heart, 'Come to me, O Death the compassionate! steep me in the merciful oblivion, O refuge of the sorrowful, friend of the forsaken and the desolate!'" Then I said aloud, "But this sleep is enternal."

The word went over her head. Necessarily it would.

"Eternal. What is eternal?"

"Ah, that also is outside of your world, as yet. There is no way to make you understand it."

It was a hopeless case. Words referring to things outside of her experience were a foreign language to her, and meaningless. She was like a little baby whose mother says to it, "Don't put your finger in the candle flame; it will burn you." Burn—it is a foreign word to the baby, and will have no terrors for it until experience shall have revealed its meaning. It is not worth while for mamma to make the remark, the baby will goo-goo cheerfully, and put its finger in the pretty flame—once. After these private reflections I said again that I did not think there was any way to make her understand the meaning of the word eternal. She was silent awhile, turning these deep matters over in the unworn machinery of her mind; then she gave up the puzzle and shifted her ground saying:

"Well, there are those other words. What is good, and what is evil?"

"It is another difficulty. They, again, are outside of your world; they have place in the moral kingdom only. You have no morals."

"What are morals?"

"A system of law which distinguishes between right and wrong, good morals and bad. These things do not exist for you. I cannot make it clear; you would not understand."

"But try."

"Well, obedience to constituted authority is a moral law. Suppose Adam should forbid you to put your child in the river and leave it there overnight—would you put the child there?"

She answered with a darling simplicity and guilelessness:

"Why, yes, if I wanted to."

"There, it is just as I said—you would not know any better; you have no idea of duty, command, obedience; they have no meaning for you. In your present estate you are in no possible way responsible for anything you do or say or think. It is impossible for you to do wrong, for you have no more notion of right and wrong than the other animals have. You and they can do only right; whatever you and they do is right and innocent. It is a divine estate, the loftiest and purest attainable in heaven and in earth. It is the angel gift. The angels are wholly pure and sinless, for they do not know right from wrong, and all the acts of such are blameless. No one can do wrong without knowing how to distinguish between right and wrong."

"Is it an advantage to know?"

"Most certainly not! That knowledge would remove all that is divine, all that is angelic, from the angels, and immeasurably degrade them."

"Are there any persons that know right from wrong?"

"Not in—well, not in heaven."

"What gives that knowledge?"

"The Moral Sense."

"What is that?"

"Well—no matter. Be thankful that you lack it."

"Why?"

"Because it is a degradation, a disaster. Without it one cannot do wrong; with it, one can. Therefore it has but one office, only one— to teach how to do wrong. It can teach no other thing—no other thing whatever. It is the *creator* of wrong; wrong cannot exist until the Moral Sense brings it into being."

"How can one acquire the Moral Sense?"

"By eating of the fruit of the Tree, here. But why do you wish to know? Would you like to have the Moral Sense?"

She turned wistfully to Adam:

"Would you like to have it?"

He showed no particular interest, and only said:

"I am indifferent. I have not understood any of this talk, but if you like we will eat it, for I cannot see that there is any objection to it."

Poor ignorant things, the command of refrain had meant nothing to them, they were but children, and could not understand untried things and verbal abstractions which stood for matters outside of their little world and their narrow experience. Eve reached for an apple!—oh, farewell, Eden and your sinless joys, come poverty and pain, hunger and cold and hearbreak, bereavement, tears and shame, envy, strife, malice and dishonor, age, weariness, remorse; then desperation and the prayer for the release of death, indifferent that the gates of hell yawn beyond it!

She tasted—the fruit fell from her hand.

It was pitiful. She was like one who wakens slow and confusedly out of a sleep. She gazed half vacantly at me, then at Adam, holding her curtaining fleece of golden hair back with her hand; then her wandering glance fell upon her naked person. The red blood mounted to her cheek, and she sprang behind a bush and stood there crying, and saying:

"Oh, my modesty is lost to me—my unoffending form is become a shame to me!" She moaned and muttered in her pain, and dropped her head, saying, "I am degraded—I have fallen, oh, so low, and I shall never rise again."

Adam's eyes were fixed upon her in a dreamy amazement, for he could not understand what had happened, it being outside his world as yet, and her words having no meaning for one void of the Moral Sense. And now his wonder grew: for, unknown to Eve, her hundred years rose upon her, and faded the heaven of her eyes and the tints of her young flesh, and touched her hair with gray, and traced faint sprays of wrinkles about her mouth and eyes, and shrunk her form, and dulled the satin luster of her skin.

All this the fair boy saw: then loyally and bravely he took the apple and tasted it, saying nothing.

The change came upon him also. Then he gathered boughs for both and clothed their nakedness, and they turned and went their way, hand in hand and bent with age, and so passed from sight.

1923

The United States of Lyncherdom[1]

I

And so Missouri has fallen, that great state! Certain of her children have joined the lynchers, and the smirch is upon the rest of us. That handful of her children have given us a character and labeled us with a name, and to the dwellers in the four quarters of the earth we are "lynchers," now, and ever shall be. For the world will not stop and think—it never does, it is not its way, its way is to generalize from a single sample. It will not say, "Those Missourians have been busy eighty years in building an honorable good name for themselves; these hundred lynchers down in the corner of the state are not real Missourians, they are renegades." No, that truth will not enter its mind; it will generalize from the one or two misleading samples and say, "The Missourians are lynchers." It has no reflection, no logic, no sense of proportion. With it, figures go for nothing; to it, figures reveal nothing, it cannot reason upon them rationally; it would say, for instance, that China is being swiftly and surely Christianized, since nine Chinese Christians are being made every day; and it would fail, with him, to notice that the fact that 33,000 pagans are *born* there every day, damages the argument. It would say, "There are a hundred lynchers there, therefore the Missourians are lynchers"; the considerable fact that there are two and a half million Missourians who are *not* lynchers would not affect their verdict.

II

Oh, Missouri!

The tragedy occurred near Pierce City, down in the southwestern corner of the state. On a Sunday afternoon a young white woman who had started alone from church was found murdered. For there are churches there; in my time religion was more general, more pervasive, in the South than it was in the North, and more virile and earnest, too, I think; I have some reason to believe that this is still the case. The

[1] Written in 1901, according to Paine.—C.N.

young woman was found murdered. Although it was a region of churches and schools the people rose, lynched three negroes—two of them very aged ones—burned out five negro households, and drove thirty negro families into the woods.

I do not dwell upon the provocation which moved the people to these crimes, for that has nothing to do with the matter; the only question is, does the assassin *take the law into his own hands?* It is very simple, and very just. If the assassin be proved to have usurped the law's prerogative in righting his wrongs, that ends the matter; a thousand provocations are no defense. The Pierce City people had bitter provocation—indeed, as revealed by certain of the particulars, the bitterest of all provocations—but no matter, they took the law into their own hands, when by the terms of their statutes their victim would certainly hang if the law had been allowed to take its course, for there are but few negroes in that region and they are without authority and without influence in overawing juries.

Why has lynching, with various barbaric accompaniments, become a favorite regulator in cases of "the usual crime" in several parts of the country? Is it because men think a lurid and terrible punishment a more forcible object lesson and a more effective deterrent than a sober and colorless hanging done privately in a jail would be? Surely sane men do not think that. Even the average child should know better. It should know that any strange and much-talked-of event is always followed by imitations, the world being so well supplied with excitable people who only need a little stirring up to make them lose what is left of their heads and do mad things which they would not have thought of ordinarily. It should know that if a man jump off Brooklyn Bridge another will imitate him; that if a person venture down Niagara Whirlpool in a barrel another will imitate him; that if a Jack the Ripper make notoriety by slaughtering women in dark alleys he will be imitated; that if a man attempt a king's life and the newspapers carry the noise of it around the globe, regicides will crop up all around. The child should know that one much-talked-of outrage and murder committed by a negro will upset the disturbed intellects of several other negroes and produce a series of the very tragedies the community would so strenuously wish to prevent; that each of these crimes will produce another series, and year by year steadily increase the tale of these disasters instead of diminishing it; that, in a word, the lynchers are themselves the worst enemies of their women. The child should also know that by a law of our make, communities, as well as individuals, are imitators; and that a much-talked-of lynching will infallibly produce other lynchings here and there and yonder, and that in time these will breed a mania, a fashion; a fashion which will spread wide and wider, year by year, covering state after state, as with an advancing disease. Lynching has reached Colorado, it has reached California, it has reached Indiana—and now Missouri! I may live to see a negro burned in Union Square, New York, with fifty thousand people present, and not a sheriff visible, not a governor, not a constable, not a colonel, not a clergyman, not a law-and-order representative of any sort.

Increase in Lynching.—In 1900 there were eight more cases than in 1899, and probably this year there will be more than there were last year. The year is little more than half gone, and yet there are eighty-eight cases as compared with one hundred and fifteen for all of last year. The four Southern states, Alabama, Georgia, Louisiana, and Mississippi are the worst offenders. Last year there were eight cases in Alabama, sixteen in Georgia, twenty in Louisiana, and twenty in Mississippi—over one-half the total. This year to date there have been nine in Alabama, twelve in Georgia, eleven in Louisiana, and thirteen in Mississippi—again more than one-half the total number in the whole United States.—Chicago *Tribune.*

It must be that the increase comes of the inborn human instinct to imitate—that and man's commonest weakness, his aversion to being unpleasantly conspicuous, pointed at, shunned, as being on the unpopular side. Its other name is Moral Cowardice, and is the commanding feature of the make-up of 9,999 men to the 10,000. I am not offering this as a discovery; privately the dullest of us knows it to be true. History will not allow us to forget or ignore this supreme trait of our character. It persistently and sardonically reminds us that from the beginning of the world no revolt against a public infamy or oppression has ever been begun but by the one daring man in the 10,000, the rest timidly waiting, and slowly and reluctantly joining, under the influence of that man and his fellows from the other ten thousands. The abolitionists remember. Privately the public feeling was with them early, but each man was afraid to speak out until he got some hint that his neighbor was privately feeling as he privately felt himself. Then the boom followed. It always does. It will occur in New York, some day; and even in Pennsylvania.

It has been supposed—and said—that the people at a lynching enjoy the spectacle and are glad of a chance to see it. It cannot be true; all experience is against it. The people in the South are made like the people in the North—the vast majority of whom are right-hearted and compassionate, and would be cruelly pained by such a spectacle—and *would attend it,* and let on to be pleased with it, if the public approval seemed to require it. We are made like that, and we cannot help it. The other animals are not so, but we cannot help that, either. They lack the Moral Sense; we have no way of trading ours off, for a nickel or some other thing above its value. The Moral Sense teaches us what is right, and how to avoid it—when unpopular.

It is thought, as I have said, that a lynching crowd enjoys a lynching. It certainly is not true; it is impossible of belief. It is freely asserted—you have seen it in print many times of late—that the lynching impulse has been misinterpreted; that it is *not* the outcome of a spirit of revenge, but of a "mere atrocious hunger *to look upon human suffering.*" If that were so, the crowds that saw the Windsor Hotel burn down would have enjoyed the horrors that fell under their eyes. Did they? No one will think that of them, no one will make that charge. Many risked their lives to save the men and women who were in peril. Why did they do that? Because *none would disapprove.* There was no restraint; they could follow their natural impulse. Why does a crowd of the same kind of people in Texas, Colorado, Indiana, stand by, smitten to the heart and miserable, and by ostentatious outward signs pretend to enjoy a lynching? Why does it lift no hand or voice in protest? Only because it would be unpopular to do it, I think; each man is afraid of his neighbor's disapproval—a thing which, to the general run of the race, is more dreaded than wounds and death. When there is to be a lynching the people hitch up and come miles to see it, bringing their wives and children. Really to see it? No—they come only because they are afraid to stay at home, lest it be noticed and offensively commented upon. We may believe this, for we all know how *we* feel about such spectacles—also, how we would act under the like pressure. We are not any better nor any braver than anybody else, and we must not try to creep out of it.

A Savonarola can quell and scatter a mob of lynchers with a mere glance of his eye: so can a Merrill[2] or a Beloat.[3] For no mob has any sand in the presence of a man known to be splendidly brave. Besides, a lynching mob would *like* to be scattered, for of a certainty there are never ten men in it who would not prefer to be somewhere else—

[2] Sheriff of Carroll County, Georgia.—M.T.
[3] Sheriff, Princeton, Indiana. By that formidable power which lies in an established reputation for cold pluck they faced lynching mobs and securely held the field against them.—M.T.

and would be, if they but had the courage to go. When I was a boy I saw a brave gentleman deride and insult a mob and drive it away; and afterward, in Nevada, I saw a noted desperado make two hundred men sit still, with the house burning under them, until he gave them permission to retire. A plucky man can rob a whole passenger train by himself; and the half of a brave man can hold up a stage-coach and strip its occupants.

Then perhaps the remedy for lynchings comes to this: station a brave man in each affected community to encourage, support, and bring to light the deep disapproval of lynching hidden in the secret places of its heart—for it is there, beyond question. Then those communities will find something better to imitate—of course, being human, they must imitate something. Where shall these brave men be found? That is indeed a difficulty; there are not three hundred of them in the earth. If merely *physically* brave men would do, then it were easy; they could be furnished by the cargo. When Hobson called for seven volunteers to go with him to what promised to be certain death, four thousand men responded—the whole fleet, in fact. Because *all the world would approve.* They knew that; but if Hobson's project had been charged with the scoffs and jeers of the friends and associates, whose good opinion and approval the sailors valued, he could not have got his seven.

No, upon reflection, the scheme will not work. There are not enough morally brave men in stock. We are out of moral-courage material; we are in a condition of profound poverty. We have those two sheriffs down South who—but never mind, it is not enough to go around; they have to stay and take care of their own communities.

But if we only *could* have three or four more sheriffs of that great breed! Would it help? I think so. For we are all imitators: other brave sheriffs would follow; to be a dauntless sheriff would come to be recognized as the correct and only thing, and the dreaded disapproval would fall to the share of the other kind; courage in this office would become custom, the absence of it a dishonor, just as courage presently replaces the timidity of the new soldier; then the mobs and the lynchings would disappear, and——

However. It can never be done without some starters, and where are we to get the starters? Advertise? Very well, then, let us advertise.

In the meantime, there is another plan. Let us import American missionaries from China, and send them into the lynching field. With 1,511 of them out there converting two Chinamen apiece per annum against an uphill birth rate of 33,000 pagans per day,[4] it will take upward of a million years to make the conversions balance the output and bring the Christianizing of the country in sight to the naked eye; therefore, if we can offer our missionaries as rich a field at home at lighter expense and quite satisfactory in the matter of danger, why shouldn't they find it fair and right to come back and give us a trial? The Chinese are universally conceded to be excellent people, honest, honorable, industrious, trustworthy, kind-hearted, and all that—leave them alone, they are plenty good enough just as they are; and besides, almost every convert runs a risk of catching our civilization. We ought to be careful. We ought to think twice before we encourage a risk like that; for, *once civilized, China can never be uncivilized again*. We have not been thinking of that. Very well, we ought to think of it now. Our missionaries will find that we have a field for them—and not only for the 1511, but for 15,011. Let them look at the following telegram and see if they have anything in China that is more appetizing. It is from Texas:

The negro was taken to a tree and swung in the air. Wood and fodder were piled beneath his body and a hot fire was made. *Then it was suggested that the man ought not to die too quickly, and he was let down to the ground while a party went to Dexter, about two miles distant, to procure coal oil.* This was thrown on the flames and the work completed.

We implore them to come back and help us in our need. Patriotism imposes this duty on them. Our country is worse off than China; they are our countrymen, their motherland supplicates their aid in this her hour of deep distress. They are competent; our people are not. They are used to scoffs, sneers, revilings, danger; our people are not. They have the martyr spirit; nothing but the martyr spirit can brave a lynching mob, and cow it and scatter it. They can save their country, we beseech them to come home and do it. We ask them to read that telegram again, and yet again, and picture the scene in their minds, and soberly ponder it; then multiply it by 115, add 88; place the 203 in a row, allowing 600 feet of space for each human torch, so that there may be viewing room around it for 5000 Christian American men, women, and children, youths and maidens; make it night, for grim

[4] These figures are not fanciful; all of them are genuine and authentic. They are from official missionary records in China. See Doctor Morrison's book on his pedestrian journey across China; he quotes them and gives his authorities. For several years he has been the London *Times's* representative in Peking, and was there through the siege.—M.T.

effect; have the show in a gradually rising plain, and let the course of the stakes be uphill; the eye can then take in the whole line of twenty-four miles of blood-and-flesh bonfires unbroken, whereas if it occupied level ground the ends of the line would bend down and be hidden from view by the curvature of the earth. All being ready, now, and the darkness opaque, the stillness impressive—for there should be no sound but the soft moaning of the night wind and the muffled sobbing of the sacrifices—let all the far stretch of kerosened pyres be touched off simultaneously and the glare and the shrieks and the agonies burst heavenward to the Throne.

There are more than a million persons present; the light from the fires flushes into vague outline against the night the spires of five thousand churches. O kind missionary, O compassionate missionary, leave China! come home and convert these Christians!

I believe that if anything can stop this epidemic of bloody insanities it is martial personalities that can face mobs without flinching; and as such personalities are developed only by familiarity with danger and by the training and seasoning which come of resisting it, the likeliest place to find them must be among the missionaries who have been under tuition in China during the past year or two. We have abundance of work for them, and for hundreds and thousands more, and the field is daily growing and spreading. Shall we find them? We can try. In 75,000,000 there must be other Merrills and Beloats; and it is the law of our make that each example shall wake up drowsing chevaliers of the same great knighthood and bring them to the front.

1923

The War Prayer[1]

It was a time of great and exalting excitement. The country was up in arms, the war was on, in every breast burned the holy fire of patriotism; the drums were beating, the bands playing, the toy pistols popping, the bunched firecrackers hissing and spluttering; on every hand and far down the receding and fading spread of roofs and balconies a fluttering wilderness of flags flashed in the sun; daily the young volunteers marched down the wide avenue gay and fine in

[1] Paine says that this was dictated 1904–05.—C.N.

their new uniforms, the proud fathers and mothers and sisters and
sweethearts cheering them with voices choked with happy emotion
as they swung by; nightly the packed mass meetings listened, panting,
to patriot oratory which stirred the deepest deeps of their hearts, and
which they interrupted at briefest intervals with cyclones of applause,
the tears running down their cheeks the while; in the churches the
pastors preached devotion to flag and country, and invoked the God
of Battles, beseeching His aid in our good cause in outpouring of
fervid eloquence which moved every listener. It was indeed a glad
and gracious time, and the half dozen rash spirits that ventured to
disapprove of the war and cast a doubt upon its righteousness straightway got such a stern and angry warning that for their personal safety's
sake they quickly shrank out of sight and offended no more in that way.

Sunday morning came—next day the battalions would leave for the
front; the church was filled; the volunteers were there, their young
faces alight with martial dreams—visions of the stern advance, the
gathering momentum, the rushing charge, the flashing sabers, the
flight of the foe, the tumult, the enveloping smoke, the fierce pursuit,
the surrender!—then home from the war, bronzed heroes, welcomed,
adored, submerged in golden seas of glory! With the volunteers sat
their dear ones, proud, happy, and envied by the neighbors and
friends who had no sons and brothers to send forth to the field of honor,
there to win for the flag, or, failing, die the noblest of noble deaths.
The service proceeded; a war chapter from the Old Testament was
read; the first prayer was said; it was followed by an organ burst that
shook the building, and with one impulse the house rose, with glowing
eyes and beating hearts, and poured out that tremendous invocation—

> "God the all-terrible! Thou who ordainest,
> Thunder thy clarion and lightning thy sword!"

Then came the "long" prayer. None could remember the like of it
for passionate pleading and moving and beautiful language. The burden of its supplication was, that an ever-merciful and benignant
Father of us all would watch over our noble young soldiers, and aid,
comfort, and encourage them in their patriotic work; bless them, shield
them in the day of battle and the hour of peril, bear them in His
mighty hand, make them strong and confident, invincible in the bloody
onset; help them to crush the foe, grant to them and to their flag and
country imperishable honor and glory—

An aged stranger entered and moved with slow and noiseless step
up the main aisle, his eyes fixed upon the minister, his long body

clothed in a robe that reached to his feet, his head bare, his white hair descending in a frothy cataract to his shoulders, his seamy face unnaturally pale, pale even to ghastliness. With all eyes following him and wondering, he made his silent way; without pausing, he ascended to the preacher's side and stood there, waiting. With shut lids the preacher, unconscious of his presence, continued his moving prayer, and at last finished it with the words, uttered in fervent appeal, "Bless our arms, grant us the victory, O Lord our God, Father and Protector of our land and flag!"

The stranger touched his arm, motioned him to step aside—which the startled minister did—and took his place. During some moments he surveyed the spellbound audience with solemn eyes, in which burned an uncanny light; then in a deep voice he said:

"I come from the Throne—bearing a message from Almighty God!" The words smote the house with a shock; if the stranger perceived it he gave no attention. "He has heard the prayer of His servant your shepherd, and will grant it if such shall be your desire after I, His messenger, shall have explained to you its import—that is to say, its full import. For it is like unto many of the prayers of men, in that it asks for more than he who utters it is aware of—except he pause and think.

"God's servant and yours has prayed his prayer. Has he paused and taken thought? Is it one prayer? No, it is two—one uttered, the other not. Both have reached the ear of Him Who heareth all supplications, the spoken and the unspoken. Ponder this—keep it in mind. If you would beseech a blessing upon yourself, beware! lest without intent you invoke a curse upon a neighbor at the same time. If you pray for the blessing of rain upon your crop which needs it, by that act you are possibly praying for a curse upon some neighbor's crop which may not need rain and can be injured by it.

"You have heard your servant's prayer—the uttered part of it. I am commissioned of God to put into words the other part of it—that part which the pastor—and also you in your hearts—fervently prayed silently. And ignorantly and unthinkingly? God grant that it was so! You heard these words: 'Grant us the victory, O Lord our God!' That is sufficient. The *whole* of the uttered prayer is compact into those pregnant words. Elaborations were not necessary. When you have prayed for victory you have prayed for many unmentioned results which follow victory—*must* follow it, cannot help but follow it. Upon the listening spirit of God the Father fell also the unspoken part of the prayer. He commandeth me to put it into words. Listen!

"O Lord our Father, our young patriots, idols of our hearts, go
forth to battle—be Thou near them! With them—in spirit—we also go
forth from the sweet peace of our beloved firesides to smite the foe.
O Lord our God, help us to tear their soldiers to bloody shreds with
our shells; help us to cover their smiling fields with the pale forms of
their patriot dead; help us to drown the thunder of the guns with
the shrieks of their wounded, writhing in pain; help us to lay waste
their humble homes with a hurricane of fire; help us to wring the
hearts of their unoffending widows with unavailing grief; help us to
turn them out roofless with their little children to wander unfriended
the wastes of their desolated land in rags and hunger and thirst, sports
of the sun flames of summer and the icy winds of winter, broken in
spirit, worn with travail, imploring Thee for the refuge of the grave
and denied it—for our sakes who adore Thee, Lord, blast their hopes,
blight their lives, protract their bitter pilgrimage, make heavy their
steps, water their way with their tears, stain the white snow with the
blood of their wounded feet! We ask it, in the spirit of love, of Him
Who is the Source of Love, and Who is the ever-faithful refuge and
friend of all that are sore beset and seek His aid with humble and
contrite hearts. Amen."

(*After a pause.*) "Ye have prayed it; if ye still desire it, speak! The
messenger of the Most High waits."

It was believed afterward that the man was a lunatic, because there
was no sense in what he said.

1923

A Word of Encouragement for Our
Blushing Exiles[1]

. . . Well, what do you think of our country *now*? And what do you
think of the figure she is cutting before the eyes of the world? For one, I
am ashamed—(Extract from a long and heated letter from a Voluntary
Exile, Member of the American Colony, Paris.)

[1] Composed in 1898, according to Paine.—C.N.

And so you are ashamed. I am trying to think out what it can have been that has produced this large attitude of mind and this fine flow of sarcasm. Apparently you are ashamed to look Europe in the face; ashamed of the American name; temporarily ashamed of your nationality. By the light of remarks made to me by an American here in Vienna, I judge that you are ashamed because:

1. We are meddling where we have no business and no right; meddling with the private family matters of a sister nation; intruding upon her sacred right to do as she pleases with her own, unquestioned by anybody.

2. We are doing this under a sham humanitarian pretext.

3. Doing it in order to filch Cuba, the formal and distinct disclaimer in the ultimatum being very, very thin humbug, and easily detectable as such by you and virtuous Europe.

4. And finally you are ashamed of all this because it is new, and base, and brutal, and dishonest; and because Europe, having had no previous experience of such things, is horrified by it and can never respect us nor associate with us any more.

Brutal, base, dishonest? We? Land thieves? Shedders of innocent blood? We? Traitors to our official word? We? Are we going to lose Europe's respect because of this new and dreadful conduct? Russia's, for instance? Is she lying stretched out on her back in Manchuria, with her head among her Siberian prisons and her feet in Port Arthur, trying to read over the fairy tales she told Lord Salisbury, and not able to do it for crying because we are maneuvering to treacherously smouch Cuba from feeble Spain, and because we are ungently shedding innocent Spanish blood?

Is it France's respect that we are going to lose? Is our unchivalric conduct troubling a nation which exists to-day because a brave young girl saved it when its poltroons had lost it—a nation which deserted her as one man when her day of peril came? Is our treacherous assault upon a weak people distressing a nation which contributed Bartholomew's Day to human history? Is our ruthless spirit offending the sensibilities of the nation which gave us the Reign of Terror to read about? Is our unmanly intrusion into the private affairs of a sister nation shocking the feelings of the people who sent Maximilian to Mexico? Are our shabby and pusillanimous ways outraging the fastidious people who have sent an innocent man (Dreyfus) to a living hell, taken to their embraces the slimy guilty one, and submitted to a thousand indignities Emile Zola—the manliest man in France?

Is it Spain's respect that we are going to lose? Is she sitting sadly conning her great history and contrasting it with our meddling, cruel, perfidious one—our shameful history of foreign robberies, humanitarian shams, and annihilations of weak and unoffending nations? Is she remembering with pride how she sent Columbus home in chains; how she sent half of the harmless West Indians into slavery and the rest to the grave, leaving not one alive; how she robbed and slaughtered the Inca's gentle race, then beguiled the Inca into her power with fair promises and burned him at the stake; how she drenched the New World in blood, and earned and got the name of The Nation with the Bloody Footprint; how she drove all the Jews out of Spain in a day, allowing them to sell their property, but forbidding them to carry any money out of the country; how she roasted heretics by the thousands and thousands in her public squares, generation after generation, her kings and her priests looking on as at a holiday show; how her Holy Inquisition imported hell into the earth; how she was the first to institute it and the last to give it up—and then only under compulsion; how, with a spirit unmodified by time, she still tortures her prisoners to-day; how, with her ancient passion for pain and blood unchanged, she still crowds the arena with ladies and gentlemen and priests to see with delight a bull harried and persecuted and a gored horse dragging his entrails on the ground; and how, with this incredible character surviving all attempts to civilize it, her Duke of Alva rises again in the person of General Weyler—to-day the most idolized personage in Spain—and we see a hundred thousand women and children shut up in pens and pitilessly starved to death?

Are we indeed going to lose Spain's respect? Is there no way to avoid this calamity—or this compliment? Are we going to lose her respect because we have made a promise in our ultimatum which she thinks we shall break? And meantime is she trying to recall some promise of her own which she has kept?

Is the Professional Official Fibber of Europe really troubled with our morals? Dear Parisian friend, are you taking seriously the daily remark of the newspaper and the orator about "this noble nation with an illustrious history"? That is mere kindness, mere charity for a people in temporary hard luck. The newspaper and the orator do not mean it. They wink when they say it.

And so you are ashamed. Do not be ashamed; there is no occasion for it.

1923

Letter from the Recording Angel

OFFICE OF THE RECORDING ANGEL
Department of Petitions, Jan. 20

Andrew Langdon
Coal Dealer
Buffalo, New York

I have the honor, as per command, to inform you that your recent act of benevolence and self-sacrifice has been recorded upon a page of the Book called *Golden Deeds of Men:* a distinction, I am permitted to remark, which is not merely extraordinary, it is unique.

As regards your prayers, for the week ending the 19th, I have the honor to report as follows:

1. For weather to advance hard coal 15 cents a ton. Granted.

2. For influx of laborers to reduce wages 10 per cent. Granted.

3. For a break in rival soft-coal prices. Granted.

4. For a visitation upon the man, or upon the family of the man, who has set up a competing retail coal-yard in Rochester. Granted, as follows: diphtheria, 2, 1 fatal; scarlet fever, 1, to result in deafness and imbecility. N O T E . This prayer should have been directed against this subordinate's principals, The N. Y. Central R. R. Co.

5. For deportation to Sheol of annoying swarms of persons who apply daily for work, or for favors of one sort or another. Taken under advisement for later decision and compromise, this petition appearing to conflict with another one of the same date, which will be cited further along.

6. For application of some form of violent death to neighbor who threw brick at family cat, whilst the same was serenading. Reserved for consideration and compromise because of conflict with a prayer of even date to be cited further along.

7. To "damn the missionary cause." Reserved also—as above.

8. To increase December profits of $22,230 to $45,000 for January, and perpetuate a proportionate monthly increase thereafter—"which will satisfy you." The prayer granted; the added remark accepted with reservations.

9. For cyclone, to destroy the works and fill up the mine of the North Pennsylvania Co. N o t e : Cyclones are not kept in stock in the winter season. A reliable article of fire-damp can be furnished upon application.

Especial note is made of the above list, they being of particular moment. The 298 remaining supplications classifiable under the head of Special Providences, Schedule A, for the week ending 19th, are granted in a body, except that 3 of the 32 cases requiring immediate death have been modified to incurable disease.

This completes the week's invoice of petitions known to this office under the technical designation of Secret Supplications of the Heart, and which for a reason which may suggest itself, always receive our first and especial attention.

The remainder of the week's invoice falls under the head of what we term Public Prayers, in which classification we place prayers uttered in Prayer Meeting, Sunday School, Class Meeting, Family Worship, etc. These kinds of prayers have value according to classification of Christian uttering them. By rule of this office, Christians are divided into two grand classes, to wit: 1, Professing Christians; 2, Professional Christians. These, in turn, are minutely subdivided and classified by size, species, and family; and finally, standing is determined by carats, the minimum being 1, the maximum 1000.

As per balance-sheet for quarter ending Dec. 31, 1847, you stood classified as follows:

Grand Classification, Professing Christian.

Size, one-fourth of maximum.

Species, Human-Spiritual.

Family, A of the Elect, Division 16.

Standing, 322 carats fine.

As per balance-sheet for quarter just ended—that is to say, forty years later—you stand classified as follows:

Grand Classification, Professional Christian.

Size, six one-hundredths of maximum.

Species, Human-Animal.

Family, W of the Elect, Division 1547.

Standing, 3 carats fine.

I have the honor to call your attention to the fact that you seem to have deteriorated.

To resume report upon your Public Prayers—with the side remark that in order to encourage Christians of your grade and of approximate grades, it is the custom of this office to grant many things to them which would not be granted to Christians of a higher grade—partly because they would not be asked for:

Prayer for weather mercifully tempered to the needs of the poor and the naked. Denied. This was a Prayer-Meeting Prayer. It conflicts with Item 1 of this report, which was a Secret Supplication of the Heart. By a rigid rule of this office, certain sorts of Public Prayers of Professional Christians are forbidden to take precedence of Secret Supplications of the Heart.

Prayer for better times and plentier food "for the hard-handed son of toil whose patient and exhausting labors make comfortable the homes, and pleasant the ways, of the more fortunate, and entitle him to our vigilant and effective protection from the wrongs and injustices which grasping avarice would do him, and to the tenderest offices of our grateful hearts." Prayer-Meeting Prayer. Refused. Conflicts with Secret Supplication of the Heart No. 2.

Prayer "that such as in any way obstruct our preferences may be generously blessed, both themselves and their families, we here calling our hearts to witness that in their wordly prosperity we are spiritually blessed, and our joys made perfect." Prayer-Meeting Prayer. Refused. Conflicts with Secret Supplications of the Heart Nos. 3 and 4.

"Oh, let none fall heir to the pains of perdition through words or acts of ours." Family Worship. Received fifteen minutes in advance of Secret Supplications of the Heart No. 5, with which it distinctly conflicts. It is suggested that one or the other of these prayers be withdrawn, or both of them modified.

"Be mercifully inclined toward all who would do us offense in our persons or our property." Includes man who threw brick at cat. Family Prayer. Received some minutes in advance of No. 6, Secret Supplications of the Heart. Modification suggested, to reconcile discrepancy.

"Grant that the noble missionary cause, the most precious labor entrusted to the hands of man, may spread and prosper without let or limit in all heathen lands that do as yet reproach us with their spiritual darkness." Uninvited prayer shoved in at meeting of American Board. Received nearly half a day in advance of No. 7, Secret Supplications of the Heart. This office takes no stock in missionaries, and is not connected in any way with the American Board. We should like to grant one of these prayers but cannot grant both. It is suggested that the American Board one be withdrawn.

This office desires for the twentieth time to call urgent attention to your remark appended to No. 8. It is a chestnut.

Of the 464 specifications contained in your Public Prayers for the week, and not previously noted in this report, we grant 2, and deny the rest. To wit: Granted, (1), "that the clouds may continue to perform their office; (2), and the sun his." It was the divine purpose anyhow; it will gratify you to know that you have not disturbed it. Of the 462 details refused, 61 were uttered in Sunday School. In this connection I must once more remind you that we grant no Sunday School Prayers of Professional Christians of the classification technically known in this office as the John Wanamaker grade. We merely enter them as "words," and they count to his credit according to number uttered within certain limits of time; 3000 per quarter-minute required, or no score; 4200 in a possible 5000 is a quite common Sunday School score among experts, and counts the same as two hymns and a bouquet furnished by young ladies in the assassin's cell, execution-morning. Your remaining 401 details count for wind only. We bunch them and use them for head-winds in retarding the ships of improper people, but it takes so many of them to make an impression that we cannot allow anything for their use.

I desire to add a word of my own to this report. When certain sorts of people do a sizable good deed, we credit them up a thousand-fold more for it than we would in the case of a better man—on account of the strain. You stand far away above your classification-record here, because of certain self-sacrifices of yours which greatly exceed what could have been expected of you. Years ago, when you were worth only $100,000, and sent $2 to your impoverished cousin the widow when she appealed to you for help, there were many in heaven who were not able to believe it, and many more who believed that the money was counterfeit. Your character went up many degrees when it was shown that these suspicions were unfounded. A year or two later, when you sent the poor girl $4 in answer to another appeal, everybody believed it, and you were the talk here for days together. Two years later you sent $6, upon supplication, when the widow's youngest child died, and that act made perfect your good fame. Everybody in heaven said, "Have you heard about Andrew?"—for you are now affectionately called Andrew here. Your increasing donation, every two or three years, has kept your name on all lips, and warm in all hearts. All heaven watches you Sundays, as you drive to church in your handsome carriage; and when your hand retires from the contribution plate, the glad shout is heard even to the ruddy walls of remote Sheol, "Another nickel from Andrew!"

But the climax came a few days ago, when the widow wrote and said she could get a school in a far village to teach if she had $50 to get herself and her two surviving children over the long journey; and you counted up last month's clear profit from your three coal mines— $22,230—and added to it the certain profit for the current month— $45,000 and a possible fifty—and then got down your pen and your check-book and mailed her *fifteen whole dollars!* Ah, Heaven bless and keep you forever and ever, generous heart! There was not a dry eye in the realms of bliss; and amidst the hand-shakings, and em-bracings, and praisings, the decree was thundered forth from the shining mount, that this deed should out-honor all the historic self-sacrifices of men and angels, and be recorded by itself upon a page of its own, for that the strain of it upon you had been heavier and bitterer than the strain it costs ten thousand martyrs to yield up their lives at the fiery stake; and all said, "What is the giving up of life, to a noble soul, or to ten thousand noble souls, compared with the giving up of fifteen dollars out of the greedy grip of the meanest white man that ever lived on the face of the earth?"

And it was a true word. And Abraham, weeping, shook out the contents of his bosom and pasted the eloquent label there, "RESERVED"; and Peter, weeping, said, "He shall be received with a torchlight procession when he comes"; and then all heaven boomed, and was glad you were going there. And so was hell.

[Signed]

THE RECORDING ANGEL [Seal]

By command.

1946

Index

Index of Titles

for

THE COMPLETE ESSAYS OF MARK TWAIN
THE COMPLETE HUMOROUS SKETCHES AND
TALES OF MARK TWAIN
THE COMPLETE SHORT STORIES OF MARK TWAIN